JavaScript

The Definitive Guide

FOURTH EDITION

JavaScript

The Definitive Guide

David Flanagan

O'REILLY®

Beijing • Cambridge • Farnham • Köln • Paris • Sebastopol • Taipei • Tokyo

JavaScript: The Definitive Guide, Fourth Edition
by David Flanagan

Published by O'Reilly & Associates, Inc., 1005 Gravenstein Highway North, Sebastopol, CA 95472.

O'Reilly & Associates books may be purchased for educational, business, or sales promotional use. Online editions are also available for most titles (*safari.oreilly.com*). For more information contact our corporate/institutional sales department: (800) 998-9938 or *corporate@oreilly.com*.

Editor: Paula Ferguson

Production Editor: Rachel Wheeler

Cover Designer: Edie Freedman

Interior Designer: David Futato

Printing History:

August 1996:	Beta Edition.
January 1997:	Second Edition.
June 1998:	Third Edition.
January 2002:	Fourth Edition.

ISBN: 0-596-00048-0

[M] [6/03]

This book is dedicated to all
who teach peace and resist violence.

Table of Contents

Part II. Client-Side JavaScript

Preface

There have been many changes in the world of web programming with JavaScript™ since the third edition of this book was published, including:

- Second and third editions of the ECMA-262 standard have been published, updating the core JavaScript language. Conformant versions of Netscape's JavaScript interpreter and Microsoft's JScript interpreter have been released.
- The source code for Netscape's JavaScript interpreters (one written in C and one written in Java™) has been released as open source and is available to anyone who wants to embed a scripting language in his application.
- The World Wide Web Consortium (W3C) has published two versions (or levels) of a Document Object Model (DOM) standard. Recent browsers support this standard (to varying degrees) and allow client-side JavaScript to interact with document content to produce sophisticated Dynamic HTML (DHTML) effects. Support for other W3C standards, such as HTML 4, CSS1, and CSS2, has also become widespread.
- The Mozilla organization, using source code originally contributed by Netscape, has produced a good fifth-generation browser. At the time of this writing, the Mozilla browser is not yet at the 1.0 release level, but the browser is mature enough that Netscape has based its 6.0 and 6.1 browsers upon the Mozilla code base.
- Microsoft's Internet Explorer has become the overwhelmingly dominant browser on desktop systems. However, the Netscape/Mozilla browser remains relevant to web developers, especially because of its superior support for web standards. In addition, minor browsers such as Opera (*http://www.opera.com*) and Konquerer (*http://www.konqueror.org*) should be seen as equally relevant.
- Web browsers (and JavaScript interpreters) are no longer confined to the desktop but have migrated to PDAs and even cell phones.

In summary, the core JavaScript language has matured. It has been standardized and is used in a wider variety of environments than it was previously. The collapse of

Netscape's market share has allowed the universe of desktop web browsers to expand, and JavaScript-enabled web browsers have also become available on non-desktop platforms. There has been a distinct, if not complete, move toward web standards. The (partial) implementation of the DOM standard in recent browsers gives web developers a long-awaited vendor-independent API to which they can code.

What's New in the Fourth Edition

This edition of *JavaScript: The Definitive Guide* has been thoroughly updated in light of the changes I just described. Major new features include complete coverage of JavaScript 1.5 and the third edition of the ECMA-262 standard on which it is based, and complete coverage of the Level 2 DOM standard.

Throughout the book, the focus has shifted from documenting particular JavaScript and browser implementations (JavaScript 1.2, Netscape 4, Internet Explorer 5, etc.) to documenting the standards upon which those implementations are (or ought to be) based. Because of the proliferation of implementations, it is no longer practical for any one book to attempt to document—or for any one developer to attempt to understand—every feature, proprietary extension, quirk, and bug of every implementation. Focusing on the specifications instead of the implementations makes this book easier to use and, if you take the same approach, will make your JavaScript code more portable and maintainable. You'll particularly notice the increased emphasis on standards in the new material on core JavaScript and the DOM.

Another major change in this edition is that the reference section has been split into three distinct parts. First, the core JavaScript material has been separated from the client-side JavaScript material (Part IV) and placed in a section of its own (Part III). This division is for the convenience of JavaScript programmers who are working with the language in an environment other than a web browser and who are not interested in client-side JavaScript.

Second, the new material documenting the W3C DOM has been placed in a section of its own (Part V), separate from the existing client-side JavaScript material. The DOM standard defines an API that is quite distinct from the "legacy" API of traditional client-side JavaScript. Depending on the browser platforms they are targeting, developers typically use one API or the other and usually do not need to switch back and forth. Keeping these two APIs distinct also preserves the organization of the existing client-side reference material, which is convenient for readers of the third edition who upgrade to this edition.

In order to accommodate all the new material without making the book much, much larger, I've gotten rid of reference pages for the trivial properties of objects. These properties are already described once on the reference page for the object, and putting another description in a reference page of its own was redundant and wasteful.

Properties that require substantial description, as well as all methods, still have reference pages of their own. Furthermore, the design wizards at O'Reilly have created a new interior design for the book that remains easy and pleasant to read but takes up less space.

Conventions Used in This Book

I use the following formatting conventions in this book:

Bold
: Is occasionally used to refer to particular keys on a computer keyboard or to portions of a user interface, such as the **Back** button or the **Options** menu.

Italic
: Is used for emphasis and to signify the first use of a term. *Italic* is also used for email addresses, web sites, FTP sites, file and directory names, and newsgroups. Finally, *italic* is used in this book for the names of Java classes, to help keep Java class names distinct from JavaScript names.

`Constant width`
: Is used in all JavaScript code and HTML text listings, and generally for anything that you would type literally when programming.

`Constant width italic`
: Is used for the names of function arguments, and generally as a placeholder to indicate an item that should be replaced with an actual value in your program.

Errata

Please help us at O'Reilly & Associates, Inc. improve future editions and future printings of this book by reporting any errors, inaccuracies, bugs, misleading or confusing statements, and plain old typos that you find anywhere in this book. O'Reilly maintains a web site for this book that includes a listing of all known errors. You can find the errata list by following a link from the book's catalog page:

http://www.oreilly.com/catalog/jscript4/

The errata page includes a link to a form that allows you to report any bugs you find. You can also report bugs or ask questions about this book by sending email to:

bookquestions@oreilly.com

Finding the Examples Online

The examples printed in this book are available for download from the book's web site. Follow the Examples link from the book's catalog page:

http://www.oreilly.com/catalog/jscript4/

Comments and Questions

Please address comments and questions concerning this book to the publisher:

O'Reilly & Associates, Inc.
1005 Gravenstein Highway North
Sebastopol, CA 95472
(800) 998-9938 (in the United States or Canada)
(707) 829-0515 (international/local)
(707) 829-0104 (fax)

To comment or ask technical questions about this and other O'Reilly books, you can also send email to:

bookquestions@oreilly.com

For more information about books, conferences, Resource Centers, and the O'Reilly Network, see the O'Reilly web site at:

http://www.oreilly.com

Acknowledgments

Brendan Eich of the Mozilla organization is the originator and chief innovator of JavaScript. I, and many JavaScript developers, owe Brendan a tremendous debt of gratitude for developing JavaScript and for taking the time out of his crazy schedule to answer our questions and even solicit our input. Besides patiently answering my many questions, Brendan also read and provided very helpful comments on the first and third editions of this book.

This book has been blessed with top-notch technical reviewers, whose comments have gone a long way toward making it a stronger, more accurate book. Waldemar Horwat at Netscape reviewed the new material on JavaScript 1.5 in this fourth edition. The new material on the W3C DOM was reviewed by Philippe Le Hegaret of the W3C; by Peter-Paul Koch, Head of Client-Side Programming at the Dutch Internet consultancy and creation company Netlinq Framfab (*http://www.netlinqframfab.nl*); by Dylan Schiemann of SitePen (*http://www.sitepen.com*); and by independent web developer Jeff Yates. Two of these reviewers maintain useful web sites about web design with the DOM. Peter-Paul's site is at *http://www.xs4all.nl/~ppk/js/*. Jeff's site is *http://www.pbwizard.com*. Although he was not a reviewer, Joseph Kesselman of IBM Research was very helpful in answering my questions about the W3C DOM.

The third edition of the book was reviewed by Brendan Eich, Waldemar Horwat, and Vidur Apparao at Netscape; Herman Venter at Microsoft; and two independent JavaScript developers, Jay Hodges and Angelo Sirigos. Dan Shafer of CNET's Builder.Com did some preliminary work on the third edition. Although his material was not used in this edition, his ideas and general outline were quite helpful. Norris

Boyd and Scott Furman at Netscape also provided useful information for this edition, and Vidur Apparao of Netscape and Scott Issacs of Microsoft each took the time to talk to me about the forthcoming Document Object Model standard. Finally, Dr. Tankred Hirschmann provided challenging insights into the intricacies of JavaScript 1.2.

The second edition benefited greatly from the help and comments of Nick Thompson and Richard Yaker of Netscape; Dr. Shon Katzenberger, Larry Sullivan, and Dave C. Mitchell at Microsoft; and Lynn Rollins of R&B Communications. The first edition was reviewed by Neil Berkman of Bay Networks, and by Andrew Schulman and Terry Allen of O'Reilly & Associates.

This book also gains strength from the diversity of editors it has had. Paula Ferguson is the editor of this edition and of the third edition. She's given the book a thorough and much-needed going over, making it easier to read and easier to understand. Frank Willison edited the second edition, and Andrew Schulman edited the first.

Finally, my thanks, as always and for so many reasons, to Christie.

—David Flanagan
September 2001

CHAPTER 1

Introduction to JavaScript

JavaScript is a lightweight, interpreted programming language with object-oriented capabilities. The general-purpose core of the language has been embedded in Netscape, Internet Explorer, and other web browsers and embellished for web programming with the addition of objects that represent the web browser window and its contents. This client-side version of JavaScript allows executable content to be included in web pages—it means that a web page need no longer be static HTML, but can include programs that interact with the user, control the browser, and dynamically create HTML content.

Syntactically, the core JavaScript language resembles C, C++, and Java, with programming constructs such as the `if` statement, the `while` loop, and the `&&` operator. The similarity ends with this syntactic resemblance, however. JavaScript is an untyped language, which means that variables do not need to have a type specified. Objects in JavaScript are more like Perl's associative arrays than they are like structures in C or objects in C++ or Java. The object-oriented inheritance mechanism of JavaScript is like those of the little-known languages Self and NewtonScript; it is quite different from inheritance in C++ and Java. Like Perl, JavaScript is an interpreted language, and it draws inspiration from Perl in a number of places, such as its regular expression and array-handling features.

This chapter provides a quick overview of JavaScript; it explains what JavaScript can and cannot do and exposes some myths about the language. It distinguishes the core JavaScript language from embedded and extended versions of the language, such as the client-side JavaScript that is embedded in web browsers and the server-side JavaScript that is embedded in Netscape's web servers. (This book documents core and client-side JavaScript.) This chapter also demonstrates real-world web programming with some client-side JavaScript examples.

1.1 JavaScript Myths

JavaScript is the subject of a fair bit of misinformation and confusion. Before proceeding any further with our exploration of JavaScript, it is important that we debunk some common and persistent myths about the language.

1.1.1 JavaScript Is Not Java

One of the most common misconceptions about JavaScript is that it is a simplified version of Java, the programming language from Sun Microsystems. Other than an incomplete syntactic resemblance and the fact that both Java and JavaScript can provide executable content in web browsers, the two languages are entirely unrelated. The similarity of names is purely a marketing ploy (the language was originally called LiveScript; its name was changed to JavaScript at the last minute).

JavaScript and Java do, however, make a good team. The two languages have different sets of capabilities. JavaScript can control browser behavior and content but cannot draw graphics or perform networking. Java has no control over the browser as a whole but can do graphics, networking, and multithreading. Client-side JavaScript can interact with and control Java applets embedded in a web page, and, in this sense, JavaScript really can script Java (see Chapter 22 for details).

1.1.2 JavaScript Is Not Simple

JavaScript is touted as a scripting language instead of a programming language, the implication being that scripting languages are simpler, that they are programming languages for non-programmers. Indeed, JavaScript appears at first glance to be a fairly simple language, perhaps of the same complexity as BASIC. JavaScript does have a number of features designed to make it more forgiving and easier to use for new and unsophisticated programmers. Non-programmers can use JavaScript for limited, cookbook-style programming tasks.

Beneath its thin veneer of simplicity, however, JavaScript is a full-featured programming language, as complex as any and more complex than some. Programmers who attempt to use JavaScript for nontrivial tasks often find the process frustrating if they do not have a solid understanding of the language. This book documents JavaScript comprehensively, so you can develop a sophisticated understanding of the language.

1.2 Versions of JavaScript

JavaScript has evolved over the years, and Netscape has released several versions of the language. Microsoft has released similar versions of the JavaScript language under the name "JScript." And ECMA (*http://www.ecma.ch*) has published three versions of the ECMA-262 standard that standardize the JavaScript language under the awkward name "ECMAScript."

Table 1-1 lists these various versions and explains their key features and how they are related to one another. In this book, I often use the name "JavaScript" to refer to any implementation of the language, including Microsoft's JScript. When I'm specifically referring to ECMAScript, I often use the terms "ECMA-262" or "ECMA."

Table 1-1. Versions of JavaScript

Version	Description
JavaScript 1.0	The original version of the language. It was buggy and is now essentially obsolete. Implemented by Netscape 2.
JavaScript 1.1	Introduced a true Array object; most serious bugs resolved. Implemented by Netscape 3.
JavaScript 1.2	Introduced the `switch` statement, regular expressions, and a number of other features. Almost compliant with ECMA v1, but has some incompatibilities. Implemented by Netscape 4.
JavaScript 1.3	Fixed incompatibilities of JavaScript 1.2. Compliant with ECMA v1. Implemented by Netscape 4.5.
JavaScript 1.4	Implemented only in Netscape server products.
JavaScript 1.5	Introduced exception handling. Compliant with ECMA v3. Implemented by Mozilla and Netscape 6.
JScript 1.0	Roughly equivalent to JavaScript 1.0. Implemented by early releases of IE 3.
JScript 2.0	Roughly equivalent to JavaScript 1.1. Implemented by later releases of IE 3.
JScript 3.0	Roughly equivalent to JavaScript 1.3. Compliant with ECMA v1. Implemented by IE 4.
JScript 4.0	Not implemented by any web browser.
JScript 5.0	Supported exception handling. Partially compliant with ECMA v3. Implemented by IE 5.
JScript 5.5	Roughly equivalent to JavaScript 1.5. Fully compliant with ECMA v3. Implemented by IE 5.5 and IE 6. (IE 6 actually implements JScript 5.6, but 5.6 is not different from 5.5 in any way that is relevant to client-side JavaScript programmers.)
ECMA v1	The first standard version of the language. Standardized the basic features of JavaScript 1.1 and added a few new features. Did not standardize the `switch` statement or regular expression support. Conformant implementations are JavaScript 1.3 and JScript 3.0.
ECMA v2	A maintenance release of the standard that included clarifications but defined no new features.
ECMA v3	Standardized the `switch` statement, regular expressions, and exception handling. Conformant implementations are JavaScript 1.5 and JScript 5.5.

1.3 Client-Side JavaScript

When a JavaScript interpreter is embedded in a web browser, the result is client-side JavaScript. This is by far the most common variant of JavaScript; when most people refer to JavaScript, they usually mean client-side JavaScript. This book documents client-side JavaScript, along with the core JavaScript language that client-side JavaScript incorporates.

We'll discuss client-side JavaScript and its capabilities in much more detail later in this chapter. In brief, though, client-side JavaScript combines the scripting ability of a JavaScript interpreter with the document object model (DOM) defined by a web browser. These two distinct technologies combine in a synergistic way, so the result is greater than the sum of its parts: client-side JavaScript enables executable content to be distributed over the Web and is at the heart of a new generation of Dynamic HTML (DHTML) documents.

Just as the ECMA-262 specification defined a standard version of the core JavaScript language, the World Wide Web Consortium (W3C) has published a DOM specification (or recommendation) that standardizes the features a browser must support in its DOM. We'll learn much more about this standard in Chapters 17, 18, and 19. Although the W3C DOM standard is not yet as well supported as it could be, it is supported well enough that web developers can start writing JavaScript code that relies on it.

Table 1-2 shows the core language version and DOM capabilities supported by various browser versions from Netscape and Microsoft. Note that the versions of Internet Explorer listed in the table refer to the Windows version of that browser. The capabilities of Macintosh versions of IE often vary (sometimes significantly) from the same-numbered versions for Windows. Also, bear in mind that IE allows the JScript interpreter to be upgraded independently of the browser itself, so it is possible to encounter an installation of IE that supports a version of the language greater than that shown here.

Table 1-2. Client-side JavaScript features by browser

Browser	Language	DOM capabilities
Netscape 2	JavaScript 1.0	Form manipulation
Netscape 3	JavaScript 1.1	Image rollovers
Netscape 4	JavaScript 1.2	DHTML with Layers
Netscape 4.5	JavaScript 1.3	DHTML with Layers
Netscape 6 / Mozilla	JavaScript 1.5	Substantial support for W3C DOM standard; support for Layers discontinued
IE 3	JScript 1.0/2.0	Form manipulation
IE 4	JScript 3.0	Image rollovers; DHTML with `document.all[]`
IE 5	JScript 5.0	DHTML with `document.all[]`
IE 5.5	JScript 5.5	Partial support for W3C DOM standard
IE 6	JScript 5.5	Partial support for W3C DOM standard; lacks support for W3C DOM event model

The differences and incompatibilities between Netscape's and Microsoft's client-side versions of JavaScript are much greater than the differences between their respective implementations of the core language. However, both browsers do agree upon a large subset of client-side JavaScript features. For lack of better names, versions of client-side JavaScript are sometimes referred to by the version of the core language on which they are based. Thus, in client-side contexts the term "JavaScript 1.2" refers to the version of client-side JavaScript supported by Netscape 4 and Internet Explorer 4. When I use core-language version numbers to refer to client-side versions of JavaScript, I am referring to the compatible subset of features supported by both Netscape and Internet Explorer. When I discuss client-side features specific to one browser or the other, I refer to the browser by name and version number.

Note that Netscape and Internet Explorer are not the only browsers that support client-side JavaScript. For example, Opera (*http://www.opera.com*) supports client-side JavaScript as well. However, since Netscape and Internet Explorer have the vast majority of market share, they are the only browsers discussed explicitly in this book. Client-side JavaScript implementations in other browsers should conform fairly closely to the implementations in these two browsers.

Similarly, JavaScript is not the only programming language that can be embedded within a web browser. For example, Internet Explorer supports a language known as VBScript, a variant of Microsoft's Visual Basic language that provides many of the same features as JavaScript but can be used only with Microsoft browsers. Also, the HTML 4.0 specification uses the Tcl programming language as an example of an embedded scripting language in its discussion of the HTML `<script>` tag. While there are no mainstream browsers that support Tcl for this purpose, there is no reason that a browser could not easily support this language.

Previous editions of this book have covered Netscape browsers more thoroughly than Microsoft browsers. The reason for this bias was that Netscape was the inventor of JavaScript and (for a time, at least) held the dominant position in the web-browser market. This bias toward Netscape has declined in each subsequent edition of the book, and the current edition is heavily focused on standards, such as ECMAScript and the W3C DOM, rather than on particular browsers. Nevertheless, readers may find that some of the original bias toward Netscape comes through in the material that remains from older editions.

1.4 JavaScript in Other Contexts

JavaScript is a general-purpose programming language; its use is not restricted to web browsers. JavaScript was designed to be embedded within, and provide scripting capabilities for, any application. From the earliest days, in fact, Netscape's web servers included a JavaScript interpreter, so that server-side scripts could be written in JavaScript. Similarly, Microsoft uses its JScript interpreter in its IIS web server and in its Windows Scripting Host product, in addition to using it in Internet Explorer.

Both Netscape and Microsoft have made their JavaScript interpreters available to companies and programmers who want to embed them in their applications. Netscape's interpreter was released as open source and is now available through the Mozilla organization (see *http://www.mozilla.org/js/*). Mozilla actually provides two different versions of the JavaScript 1.5 interpreter. One is written in C and is called "SpiderMonkey." The other is written in Java and, in a flattering reference to this book, is called "Rhino."

We can expect to see more and more applications that use JavaScript as an embedded scripting language.* If you are writing scripts for such an application, you'll find the first half of this book, documenting the core language, to be useful. The web-browser specific chapters, however, will probably not be applicable to your scripts.

1.5 Client-Side JavaScript: Executable Content in Web Pages

When a web browser is augmented with a JavaScript interpreter, it allows executable content to be distributed over the Internet in the form of JavaScript scripts. Example 1-1 shows a simple JavaScript program, or script, embedded in a web page.

Example 1-1. A simple JavaScript program

```
<html>
<body>
<head><title>Factorials</title></head>
<script language="JavaScript">
document.write("<h2>Table of Factorials</h2>");
for(i = 1, fact = 1; i < 10; i++, fact *= i) {
    document.write(i + "! = " + fact);
    document.write("<br>");
}
</script>
</body>
</html>
```

When loaded into a JavaScript-enabled browser, this script produces the output shown in Figure 1-1.

As you can see in this example, the `<script>` and `</script>` tags are used to embed JavaScript code within an HTML file. We'll learn more about the `<script>` tag in Chapter 12. The main feature of JavaScript demonstrated by this example is the use of the `document.write()` method.† This method is used to dynamically output HTML text that is parsed and displayed by the web browser; we'll encounter it many more times in this book.

Besides allowing control over the content of web pages, JavaScript allows control over the browser and over the content of the HTML forms that appear in the browser. We'll learn about these capabilities of JavaScript in more detail later in this chapter and in much more detail later in this book.

JavaScript can control not only the content of HTML documents, but also the behavior of those documents. That is, a JavaScript program might respond in some way

* ActionScript, the scripting language available in Macromedia's Flash 5, is modeled after the ECMAScript standard, but it is not actually JavaScript.

† "Method" is the object-oriented term for function or procedure; you'll see it used throughout this book.

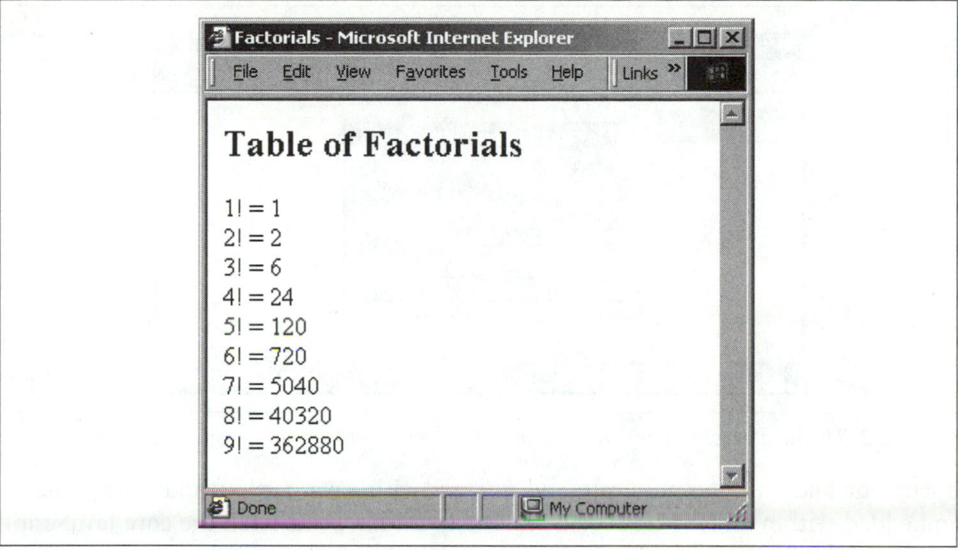

Figure 1-1. A web page generated with JavaScript

when you enter a value in an input field or click on an image in a document. JavaScript does this by defining *event handlers* for the document—pieces of JavaScript code that are executed when a particular event occurs, such as when the user clicks on a button. Example 1-2 shows the definition of a simple HTML form that includes an event handler that is executed in response to a button click.

Example 1-2. An HTML form with a JavaScript event handler defined

```
<form>
<input type="button"
       value="Click here"
       onclick="alert('You clicked the button');">
</form>
```

Figure 1-2 illustrates the result of clicking the button.

The `onclick` attribute shown in Example 1-2 was originally a Netscape extension added to HTML specifically for client-side JavaScript. Now, however, this and other event handler attributes have been standardized in HTML Version 4.0. All JavaScript event handlers are defined with HTML attributes like this one. The value of the `onclick` attribute is a string of JavaScript code to be executed when the user clicks the button. In this case, the `onclick` event handler calls the `alert( )` function. As you can see in Figure 1-2, `alert( )` pops up a dialog box to display the specified message.

Examples 1-1 and 1-2 highlight only the simplest features of client-side JavaScript. The real power of JavaScript on the client side is that scripts have access to a hierarchy of objects that are based on the content of the web page. For example, client-side JavaScript programs can access and manipulate each of the images that appear in a

Figure 1-2. The JavaScript response to an event

document and can communicate and interact with Java applets and other objects embedded within an HTML document. Once you have mastered the core JavaScript language, the key to using JavaScript effectively in web pages is learning to use the features of the DOM exposed by the browser.

1.6 Client-Side JavaScript Features

Another possible use of JavaScript is for writing programs to perform arbitrary computations. You can write simple scripts, for example, that compute Fibonacci numbers, or search for primes. In the context of the Web and web browsers, however, a more interesting application of the language might be a program that computed the sales tax on an online order, based on information supplied by the user in an HTML form. As mentioned earlier, the real power of JavaScript lies in the browser and document-based objects that the language supports. To give you an idea of JavaScript's potential, the following sections list and explain the important capabilities of client-side JavaScript and the objects it supports.

1.6.1 Control Document Appearance and Content

The JavaScript Document object, through its `write()` method, which we have already seen, allows you to write arbitrary HTML into a document as the document is being parsed by the browser. For example, you can include the current date and time in a document or display different content on different platforms.

You can also use the Document object to generate documents entirely from scratch. Properties of the Document object allow you to specify colors for the document background, the text, and the hypertext links within it. This amounts to the ability to generate dynamic and conditional HTML documents, a technique that works particularly well in multiframe documents. Indeed, in some cases dynamic generation of frame content allows a JavaScript program to replace a traditional server-side script entirely.

Internet Explorer 4 and Netscape 4 support proprietary techniques for producing Dynamic HTML effects that allow document content to be dynamically generated, moved, and altered. IE 4 also supports a complete DOM that gives JavaScript access to every single HTML element within a document. And IE 5.5 and Netscape 6 support the W3C DOM standard (or at least key portions of it), which defines a standard, portable way to access all of the elements and text within an HTML document and to position them and modify their appearance by manipulating their Cascading Style Sheets (CSS) style attributes. In these browsers, client-side JavaScript has complete power over document content, which opens an unlimited world of scripting possibilities.

1.6.2 Control the Browser

Several JavaScript objects allow control over the behavior of the browser. The Window object supports methods to pop up dialog boxes to display simple messages to the user and get simple input from the user. This object also defines a method to create and open (and close) entirely new browser windows, which can have any specified size and any combination of user controls. This allows you, for example, to open up multiple windows to give the user multiple views of your web site. New browser windows are also useful for temporary display of generated HTML, and, when created without the menu bar and other user controls, these windows can serve as dialog boxes for more complex messages or user input.

JavaScript does not define methods that allow you to create and manipulate frames directly within a browser window. However, the ability to generate HTML dynamically allows you to programmatically write the HTML tags that create any desired frame layout.

JavaScript also allows control over which web pages are displayed in the browser. The Location object allows you to download and display the contents of any URL in any window or frame of the browser. The History object allows you to move forward and back within the user's browsing history, simulating the action of the browser's **Forward** and **Back** buttons.

Yet another method of the Window object allows JavaScript to display arbitrary messages to the user in the status line of any browser window.

1.6.3 Interact with HTML Forms

Another important aspect of client-side JavaScript is its ability to interact with HTML forms. This capability is provided by the Form object and the form element objects it can contain: Button, Checkbox, Hidden, Password, Radio, Reset, Select, Submit, Text, and Textarea objects. These element objects allow you to read and write the values of the input elements in the forms in a document. For example, an online catalog might use an HTML form to allow the user to enter his order and could use JavaScript to read the input from that form in order to compute the cost of the order, the sales tax, and the shipping charge. JavaScript programs like this are, in fact, very common on the Web. We'll see a program shortly that uses an HTML form and JavaScript to allow the user to compute monthly payments on a home mortgage or other loan. JavaScript has an obvious advantage over server-based scripts for applications like these: JavaScript code is executed on the client, so the form's contents don't have to be sent to the server in order for relatively simple computations to be performed.

Another common use of client-side JavaScript with forms is for validating form data before it is submitted. If client-side JavaScript is able to perform all necessary error checking of a user's input, no round trip to the server is required to detect and inform the user of trivial input errors. Client-side JavaScript can also perform preprocessing of input data, which can reduce the amount of data that must be transmitted to the server. In some cases, client-side JavaScript can eliminate the need for scripts on the server altogether! (On the other hand, JavaScript and server-side scripting do work well together. For example, a server-side program can dynamically create JavaScript code on the fly, just as it dynamically creates HTML.)

1.6.4 Interact with the User

An important feature of JavaScript is the ability to define event handlers—arbitrary pieces of code to be executed when a particular event occurs. Usually, these events are initiated by the user, when, for example, she moves the mouse over a hypertext link, enters a value in a form, or clicks the **Submit** button in a form. This event-handling capability is a crucial one, because programming with graphical interfaces, such as HTML forms, inherently requires an event-driven model. JavaScript can trigger any kind of action in response to user events. Typical examples might be to display a special message in the status line when the user positions the mouse over a hypertext link or to pop up a confirmation dialog box when the user submits an important form.

1.6.5 Read and Write Client State with Cookies

A *cookie* is a small amount of state data stored permanently or temporarily by the client. Cookies may be transmitted along with a web page by the server to the client, which stores them locally. When the client later requests the same or a related web page, it passes the relevant cookies back to the server, which can use their values to alter the content it sends back to the client. Cookies allow a web page or web site to remember things about the client—for example, that the user has previously visited the site, has already registered and obtained a password, or has expressed a preference about the color and layout of web pages. Cookies help you provide the state information that is missing from the stateless HTTP protocol of the Web.

When cookies were invented, they were intended for use exclusively by server-side scripts; although stored on the client, they could be read or written only by the server. JavaScript changed this, because JavaScript programs can read and write cookie values and can dynamically generate document content based on the value of cookies.

1.6.6 Still More Features

In addition to the features I have already discussed, JavaScript has many other capabilities, including the following:

- JavaScript can change the image displayed by an `<img>` tag to produce image rollover and animation effects.
- JavaScript can interact with Java applets and other embedded objects that appear in the browser. JavaScript code can read and write the properties of these applets and objects and can also invoke any methods they define. This feature truly allows JavaScript to script Java.
- As mentioned at the start of this section, JavaScript can perform arbitrary computation. JavaScript has a floating-point data type, arithmetic operators that work with it, and a full complement of standard floating-point mathematical functions.
- The JavaScript Date object simplifies the process of computing and working with dates and times.
- The Document object supports a property that specifies the last-modified date for the current document. You can use it to automatically display a timestamp on any document.
- JavaScript has a `window.setTimeout()` method that allows a block of arbitrary JavaScript code to be executed some number of milliseconds in the future. This is useful for building delays or repetitive actions into a JavaScript program. In JavaScript 1.2, `setTimeout()` is augmented by another useful method called `setInterval()`.
- The Navigator object (named after the Netscape web browser, of course) has variables that specify the name and version of the browser that is running, as well as variables that identify the platform on which it is running. These variables allow scripts to customize their behavior based on browser or platform, so that they can take advantage of extra capabilities supported by some versions or work around bugs that exist on some platforms.
- In client-side JavaScript 1.2, the Screen object provides information about the size and color-depth of the monitor on which the web browser is being displayed.
- As of JavaScript 1.1, the `scroll()` method of the Window object allows JavaScript programs to scroll windows in the X and Y dimensions. In JavaScript 1.2, this method is augmented by a host of others that allow browser windows to be moved and resized.

1.6.7 What JavaScript Can't Do

Client-side JavaScript has an impressive list of capabilities. Note, however, that they are confined to browser- and document-related tasks. Since client-side JavaScript is used in a limited context, it does not have features that would be required for standalone languages:

- JavaScript does not have any graphics capabilities, except for the powerful ability to dynamically generate HTML (including images, tables, frames, forms, fonts, etc.) for the browser to display.
- For security reasons, client-side JavaScript does not allow the reading or writing of files. Obviously, you wouldn't want to allow an untrusted program from any random web site to run on your computer and rearrange your files!
- JavaScript does not support networking of any kind, except that it can cause the browser to download arbitrary URLs and it can send the contents of HTML forms across the network to server-side scripts and email addresses.

1.7 JavaScript Security

Any time that programs (such as JavaScript scripts, Visual Basic programs, or Microsoft Word macros) are included within shared documents, particularly documents that are transmitted over the Internet or by email, there is a potential for viruses or other malicious programs. The designers of JavaScript were aware of these security issues and took care not to give JavaScript programs the power to perform damaging acts. As described previously, for example, client-side JavaScript programs cannot read local files or perform networking operations.

Because of the complexity of the web-browser environment, however, a number of security problems did arise in early browser versions. In Netscape 2, for example, it was possible to write JavaScript code that could automatically steal the email address of any visitor to a page containing the code and then automatically send email in the visitor's name, without the visitor's knowledge or approval. This, and a number of other security holes, has been fixed. Although there is no guarantee that other security holes will not be found, most knowledgeable users are comfortable letting modern browsers run the JavaScript code found in web pages. Chapter 21 contains a complete discussion of security in client-side JavaScript.

1.8 Example: Computing Loan Payments with JavaScript

Example 1-3 is a listing of a complete, nontrivial JavaScript program. The program computes the monthly payment on a home mortgage or other loan, given the amount of the loan, the interest rate, and the repayment period. As you can see, the program consists of an HTML form made interactive with JavaScript code. Figure 1-3 shows what the HTML form looks like when displayed in a web browser. But the figure can only capture a static snapshot of the program. The addition of JavaScript code makes it dynamic: whenever the user changes the amount of the loan, the interest rate, or the number of payments, the JavaScript code recomputes the monthly payment, the total of all payments, and the total interest paid over the lifetime of the loan.

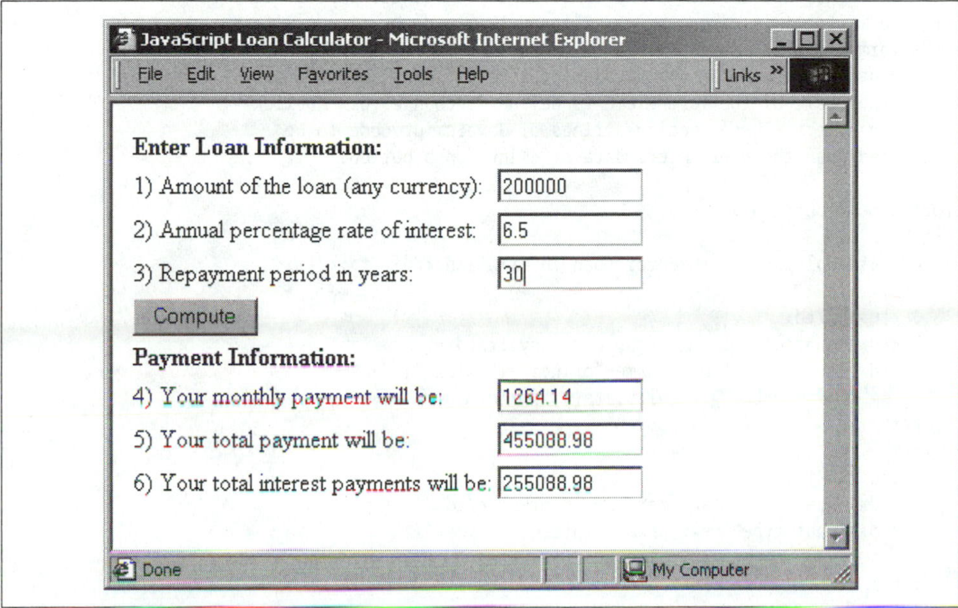

Figure 1-3. A JavaScript loan payment calculator

The first half of the example is an HTML form, nicely formatted using an HTML table. Note that several of the form elements define `onchange` or `onclick` event handlers. The web browser triggers these event handlers when the user changes the input or clicks on the **Compute** button displayed in the form. Note that in each case, the value of the event handler attribute is a string of JavaScript code: `calculate()`. When the event handler is triggered, it executes this code, which causes it to call the function `calculate()`.

The `calculate()` function is defined in the second half of the example, inside `<script>` tags. The function reads the user's input from the form, does the math required to compute the loan payments, and displays the results of these calculations using the bottom three form elements.

Example 1-3 is simple, but it is worth taking the time to look at it carefully. You shouldn't expect to understand all the JavaScript code at this point, but studying this example should give you a good idea of what JavaScript programs look like, how event handlers work, and how JavaScript code can be integrated with HTML forms. Note that comments (in English) are included within HTML between `<!--` and `-->` markers and within JavaScript code in lines that begin with the characters `//`.

Example 1-3. Computing loan payments with JavaScript

```
<head><title>JavaScript Loan Calculator</title></head>
<body bgcolor="white">
<!--
  This is an HTML form that allows the user to enter data and allows
  JavaScript to display the results it computes back to the user. The
  form elements are embedded in a table to improve their appearance.
  The form itself is given the name "loandata", and the fields within
  the form are given names such as "interest" and "years". These
  field names are used in the JavaScript code that follows the form.
  Note that some of the form elements define "onchange" or "onclick"
  event handlers. These specify strings of JavaScript code to be
  executed when the user enters data or clicks on a button.
-->
<form name="loandata">
  <table>
    <tr><td colspan="3"><b>Enter Loan Information:</b></td></tr>
    <tr>
      <td>1)</td>
      <td>Amount of the loan (any currency):</td>
      <td><input type="text" name="principal" size="12"
                 onchange="calculate();"></td>
    </tr>
    <tr>
      <td>2)</td>
      <td>Annual percentage rate of interest:</td>
      <td><input type="text" name="interest" size="12"
                 onchange="calculate();"></td>
    </tr>
    <tr>
      <td>3)</td>
      <td>Repayment period in years:</td>
      <td><input type="text" name="years" size="12"
                 onchange="calculate();"></td>
    </tr>
    <tr><td colspan="3">
      <input type="button" value="Compute" onclick="calculate();">
    </td></tr>
    <tr><td colspan="3">
      <b>Payment Information:</b>
    </td></tr>
    <tr>
      <td>4)</td>
      <td>Your monthly payment will be:</td>
      <td><input type="text" name="payment" size="12"></td>
    </tr>
    <tr>
      <td>5)</td>
      <td>Your total payment will be:</td>
      <td><input type="text" name="total" size="12"></td>
    </tr>
    <tr>
      <td>6)</td>
```

Example 1-3. Computing loan payments with JavaScript (continued)

```
      <td>Your total interest payments will be:</td>
      <td><input type="text" name="totalinterest" size="12"></td>
    </tr>
  </table>
</form>

<!--
  This is the JavaScript program that makes the example work. Note that
  this script defines the calculate() function called by the event
  handlers in the form. The function refers to values in the form
  fields using the names defined in the HTML code above.
-->
<script language="JavaScript">
function calculate() {
    // Get the user's input from the form. Assume it is all valid.
    // Convert interest from a percentage to a decimal, and convert from
    // an annual rate to a monthly rate. Convert payment period in years
    // to the number of monthly payments.
    var principal = document.loandata.principal.value;
    var interest = document.loandata.interest.value / 100 / 12;
    var payments = document.loandata.years.value * 12;

    // Now compute the monthly payment figure, using esoteric math.
    var x = Math.pow(1 + interest, payments);
    var monthly = (principal*x*interest)/(x-1);

    // Check that the result is a finite number. If so, display the results.
    if (!isNaN(monthly) &&
        (monthly != Number.POSITIVE_INFINITY) &&
        (monthly != Number.NEGATIVE_INFINITY)) {

        document.loandata.payment.value = round(monthly);
        document.loandata.total.value = round(monthly * payments);
        document.loandata.totalinterest.value =
            round((monthly * payments) - principal);
    }
    // Otherwise, the user's input was probably invalid, so don't
    // display anything.
    else {
        document.loandata.payment.value = "";
        document.loandata.total.value = "";
        document.loandata.totalinterest.value = "";
    }
}

// This simple method rounds a number to two decimal places.
function round(x) {
  return Math.round(x*100)/100;
}
</script>
</body>
</html>
```

1.9 Using the Rest of This Book

The rest of this book is in five parts. Part I, which immediately follows this chapter, documents the core JavaScript language. Chapters 2 through 6 begin this section with some bland but necessary reading—these chapters cover the basic information you need to understand when learning a new programming language:

- Chapter 2, *Lexical Structure*, explains the basic structure of the language.
- Chapter 3, *Data Types and Values*, documents the data types supported by JavaScript.
- Chapter 4, *Variables*, covers variables, variable scope, and related topics.
- Chapter 5, *Expressions and Operators*, explains expressions in JavaScript and documents each of the operators supported by JavaScript. Because JavaScript syntax is modeled on Java, which is, in turn, modeled on C and C++, experienced C, C++, or Java programmers can skim much of this chapter.
- Chapter 6, *Statements*, describes the syntax and usage of each of the JavaScript statements. Again, experienced C, C++, and Java programmers can skim some, but not all, of this chapter.

The next five chapters of this first section become more interesting. They still cover the core of the JavaScript language, but they document parts of the language that will not already be familiar to you even if you already know C or Java. These chapters must be studied carefully if you want to really understand JavaScript:

- Chapter 7, *Functions*, documents how functions are defined, invoked, and manipulated in JavaScript.
- Chapter 8, *Objects*, explains objects, the most important JavaScript data type. This chapter discusses object-oriented programming in JavaScript and explains how you can define your own classes of objects in JavaScript.
- Chapter 9, *Arrays*, describes the creation and use of arrays in JavaScript.
- Chapter 10, *Pattern Matching with Regular Expressions*, explains how to use regular expressions in JavaScript to perform pattern-matching and search-and-replace operations.
- Chapter 11, *Further Topics in JavaScript*, covers advanced topics that have not been covered elsewhere. You can skip this chapter the first time through the book, but the material it contains is important to understand if you want to become a JavaScript expert.

Part II explains client-side JavaScript. The chapters in this part document the web-browser objects that are at the heart of client-side JavaScript and provide detailed examples of their use. Any interesting JavaScript program running in a web browser will rely heavily on features specific to the client side.

Here's what you'll find in Part III:

- Chapter 12, *JavaScript in Web Browsers*, explains the integration of JavaScript with web browsers. It discusses the web browser as a programming environment and explains the various ways in which JavaScript is integrated into web pages for execution on the client side.
- Chapter 13, *Windows and Frames*, documents the most central and important object of client-side JavaScript, the Window object, as well as several important window-related objects.
- Chapter 14, *The Document Object*, explains the Document object and related objects that expose the contents of an HTML document to JavaScript code.
- Chapter 15, *Forms and Form Elements*, documents the Form object, which represents HTML forms. It also documents the various form element objects that appear within HTML forms and shows examples of JavaScript programming using forms.
- Chapter 16, *Scripting Cookies*, illustrates the use of cookies to save state in web programming.
- Chapter 17, *The Document Object Model*, explains the core pieces of the W3C DOM standard and shows how a JavaScript script can access any element of an HTML document.
- Chapter 18, *Cascading Style Sheets and Dynamic HTML*, explains the portions of the W3C DOM standard that allow a JavaScript program to manipulate the style, appearance, and position of the elements within an HTML document. This chapter shows how you can create many DHTML effects with CSS properties.
- Chapter 19, *Events and Event Handling*, covers JavaScript events and event handlers, which are central to all JavaScript programs that interact with the user. This chapter covers the traditional event model, the W3C DOM standard event model, and the Internet Explorer proprietary event model.
- Chapter 20, *Compatibility Techniques*, explores the important issue of compatibility in JavaScript programming and discusses techniques you can use to write JavaScript programs that run correctly (or fail gracefully) on a wide variety of web browsers.
- Chapter 21, *JavaScript Security*, enumerates the security restrictions built into client-side JavaScript and explains the rationale for them.
- Chapter 22, *Using Java with JavaScript*, explains how you can use JavaScript to communicate with and control Java applets. It also covers how you can do the reverse—invoke JavaScript code from Java applets.

Parts III, IV, and V are reference sections that document the objects defined by the core JavaScript language, the objects defined in traditional client-side JavaScript programming, and the objects defined by the new W3C DOM standard, respectively.

1.10 Exploring JavaScript

The way to really learn a new programming language is to write programs with it. As you read through this book, I encourage you to try out JavaScript features as you learn about them. There are a number of techniques that make it easy to experiment with JavaScript.

The most obvious way to explore JavaScript is to write simple scripts. One of the nice things about client-side JavaScript is that anyone with a web browser and a simple text editor has a complete development environment; there is no need to buy or download special-purpose software in order to begin writing JavaScript scripts. We saw an example that computed factorials at the beginning of this chapter. Suppose you wanted to modify it as follows to display Fibonacci numbers instead:

```
<script>
document.write("<h2>Table of Fibonacci Numbers</h2>");
for (i=0, j=1, k=0, fib =0; i<50; i++, fib=j+k, j=k, k=fib){
    document.write("Fibonacci ("  + i +  ") = " + fib);
    document.write("<br>");
}
</script>
```

This code may be convoluted (and don't worry if you don't yet understand it), but the point is that when you want to experiment with short programs like this, you can simply type them up and try them out in your web browser using a local `file:` URL. Note that the code uses the `document.write()` method to display its HTML output, so that you can see the results of its computations. This is an important technique for experimenting with JavaScript. As an alternative, you can also use the `alert()` method to display plain-text output in a dialog box:

```
alert("Fibonacci ("  + i +  ") = " + fib);
```

Note also that for simple JavaScript experiments like this, you can usually omit the `<html>`, `<head>`, and `<body>` tags in your HTML file.

For even simpler experiments with JavaScript, you can sometimes use the `javascript:` URL pseudoprotocol to evaluate a JavaScript expression and return the result. A JavaScript URL consists of the `javascript:` protocol specifier followed by arbitrary JavaScript code (with statements separated from one another by semicolons). When the browser loads such a URL, it executes the JavaScript code. The value of the last expression in such a URL is converted to a string, and this string is displayed by the web browser as its new document. For example, you might type the following JavaScript URLs into the **Location** field of your web browser to test your understanding of some of JavaScript's operators and statements:

```
javascript:5%2
javascript:x = 3; (x < 5)? "x is less": "x is greater"
javascript:d = new Date(); typeof d;
javascript:for(i=0,j=1,k=0,fib=1; i<10; i++,fib=j+k,k=j,j=fib) alert(fib);
javascript:s=""; for(i in document) s+=i+":"+document[i]+"\n"; alert(s);
```

While exploring JavaScript, you'll probably write code that doesn't work as you expect it to and want to debug it. The basic debugging technique for JavaScript is like that in many other languages: insert statements into your code to print out the values of relevant variables so that you can try to figure out what is actually happening. As we've seen, you can sometimes use the `document.write()` method to do this. This method doesn't work from within event handlers, however, and has some other shortcomings as well, so it's often easier to use the `alert()` function to display debugging messages in a separate dialog box.

The `for/in` loop (described in Chapter 6) is also useful for debugging. You can use it, along with the `alert()` method, to write a function that displays a list of the names and values of all properties of an object, for example. This kind of function can be handy when exploring the language or trying to debug code.

Good luck with JavaScript, and have fun exploring!

PART I
Core JavaScript

This part of the book, Chapters 2 through 11, documents the core JavaScript language as it is used in web browsers, web servers, and other embedded JavaScript implementations. This part is meant to be a JavaScript language reference. After you read through it once to learn the language, you may find yourself referring back to it to refresh your memory about some of the trickier points of JavaScript.

CHAPTER 2

Lexical Structure

The lexical structure of a programming language is the set of elementary rules that specifies how you write programs in that language. It is the lowest-level syntax of a language; it specifies such things as what variable names look like, what characters are used for comments, and how one program statement is separated from the next. This short chapter documents the lexical structure of JavaScript.

2.1 Character Set

JavaScript programs are written using the Unicode character set. Unlike the 7-bit ASCII encoding, which is useful only for English, and the 8-bit ISO Latin-1 encoding, which is useful only for English and major Western European languages, the 16-bit Unicode encoding can represent virtually every written language in common use on the planet. This is an important feature for internationalization and is particularly important for programmers who do not speak English.

American and other English-speaking programmers typically write programs using a text editor that supports only the ASCII or Latin-1 character encodings, and thus they don't have easy access to the full Unicode character set. This is not a problem, however, because both the ASCII and Latin-1 encodings are subsets of Unicode, so any JavaScript program written using those character sets is perfectly valid. Programmers who are used to thinking of characters as 8-bit quantities may be disconcerted to know that JavaScript represents each character using 2 bytes, but this fact is actually transparent to the programmer and can simply be ignored.

Although the ECMAScript v3 standard allows Unicode characters anywhere in a JavaScript program, Versions 1 and 2 of the standard allow Unicode characters only in comments and quoted string literals—all other parts of an ECMAScript v1 program are restricted to the ASCII character set. Versions of JavaScript that predate ECMAScript standardization typically do not support Unicode at all.

2.2 Case Sensitivity

JavaScript is a case-sensitive language. This means that language keywords, variables, function names, and any other identifiers must always be typed with a consistent capitalization of letters. The `while` keyword, for example, must be typed "while", not "While" or "WHILE". Similarly, `online`, `Online`, `OnLine`, and `ONLINE` are four distinct variable names.

Note, however, that HTML is not case-sensitive. Because of its close association with client-side JavaScript, this difference can be confusing. Many JavaScript objects and properties have the same names as the HTML tags and attributes they represent. While these tags and attribute names can be typed in any case in HTML, in JavaScript they typically must be all lowercase. For example, the HTML `onclick` event handler attribute is commonly specified as `onClick` in HTML, but it must be referred to as `onclick` in JavaScript code.

While core JavaScript is entirely and exclusively case-sensitive, exceptions to this rule are allowed in client-side JavaScript. In Internet Explorer 3, for example, all client-side objects and properties were case-insensitive. This caused problematic incompatibilities with Netscape, however, so in Internet Explorer 4 and later, client-side objects and properties are case-sensitive.

2.3 Whitespace and Line Breaks

JavaScript ignores spaces, tabs, and newlines that appear between tokens in programs, except those that are part of string or regular expression literals. A *token* is a keyword, variable name, number, function name, or some other entity in which you would obviously not want to insert a space or a line break. If you place a space, tab, or newline within a token, you break it up into two tokens—thus, `123` is a single numeric token, but `12 3` is two separate tokens (and constitutes a syntax error, incidentally).

Because you can use spaces, tabs, and newlines freely in your programs (except in strings, regular expressions, and tokens), you are free to format and indent your programs in a neat and consistent way that makes the code easy to read and understand. Note, however, that there is one minor restriction on the placement of line breaks; it is described in the following section.

2.4 Optional Semicolons

Simple statements in JavaScript are generally followed by semicolons (`;`), just as they are in C, C++, and Java. The semicolon serves to separate statements from each other. In JavaScript, however, you may omit the semicolon if each of your statements is placed on a separate line. For example, the following code could be written without semicolons:

```
a = 3;
b = 4;
```

But when formatted as follows, the first semicolon is required:

```
a = 3; b = 4;
```

Omitting semicolons is not a good programming practice; you should get in the habit of using them.

Although JavaScript theoretically allows line breaks between any two tokens, the fact that JavaScript automatically inserts semicolons for you causes some exceptions to this rule. Loosely, if you break a line of code in such a way that the line before the break appears to be a complete statement, JavaScript may think you omitted the semicolon and insert one for you, altering your meaning. Some places you should look out for this are with the `return`, `break`, and `continue` statements (which are described in Chapter 6). For example, consider the following:

```
return
true;
```

JavaScript assumes you meant:

```
return;
true;
```

However, you probably meant:

```
return true;
```

This is something to watch out for—this code does not cause a syntax error and will fail in a nonobvious way. A similar problem occurs if you write:

```
break
outerloop;
```

JavaScript inserts a semicolon after the `break` keyword, causing a syntax error when it tries to interpret the next line. For similar reasons, the ++ and -- postfix operators (see Chapter 5) must always appear on the same line as the expressions to which they are applied.

2.5 Comments

JavaScript, like Java, supports both C++ and C-style comments. Any text between a // and the end of a line is treated as a comment and is ignored by JavaScript. Any text between the characters /* and */ is also treated as a comment. These C-style comments may span multiple lines but may not be nested. The following lines of code are all legal JavaScript comments:

```
// This is a single-line comment.
/* This is also a comment */  // and here is another comment.
/*
 * This is yet another comment.
 * It has multiple lines.
 */
```

2.6 Literals

A *literal* is a data value that appears directly in a program. The following are all literals:

```
12               // The number twelve
1.2              // The number one point two
"hello world"    // A string of text
'Hi'             // Another string
true             // A boolean value
false            // The other boolean value
/javascript/gi   // A "regular expression" literal (for pattern matching)
null             // Absence of an object
```

In ECMAScript v3, expressions that serve as array and object literals are also supported. For example:

```
{ x:1, y:2 }    // An object initializer
[1,2,3,4,5]     // An array initializer
```

Note that these array and object literals have been supported since JavaScript 1.2 but were not standardized until ECMAScript v3.

Literals are an important part of any programming language, as it is impossible to write a program without them. The various JavaScript literals are described in detail in Chapter 3.

2.7 Identifiers

An *identifier* is simply a name. In JavaScript, identifiers are used to name variables and functions and to provide labels for certain loops in JavaScript code. The rules for legal identifier names are the same in JavaScript as they are in Java and many other languages. The first character must be a letter, an underscore (_), or a dollar sign ($).* Subsequent characters may be any letter or digit or an underscore or dollar sign. (Numbers are not allowed as the first character so that JavaScript can easily distinguish identifiers from numbers.) These are all legal identifiers:

```
i
my_variable_name
v13
_dummy
$str
```

In ECMAScript v3, identifiers can contain letters and digits from the complete Unicode character set. Prior to this version of the standard, JavaScript identifiers are restricted to the ASCII character set. ECMAScript v3 also allows Unicode escape sequences to appear in identifiers. A Unicode escape is the characters `\u` followed by 4 hexadecimal digits that specify a 16-bit character encoding. For example, the

* Note that dollar signs are not legal in identifiers prior to JavaScript 1.1. They are intended for use only by code-generation tools, so you should avoid using dollar signs in identifiers in the code you write yourself.

identifier π could also be written as `\u03c0`. Although this is an awkward syntax, it makes it possible to translate JavaScript programs that contain Unicode characters into a form that allows them to be manipulated with text editors and other tools that do not support the full Unicode character set.

Finally, identifiers cannot be the same as any of the keywords used for other purposes in JavaScript. The next section lists the special names that are reserved in JavaScript.

2.8 Reserved Words

There are a number of reserved words in JavaScript. These are words that you cannot use as identifiers (variable names, function names, and loop labels) in your JavaScript programs. Table 2-1 lists the keywords standardized by ECMAScript v3. These words have special meaning to JavaScript—they are part of the language syntax itself.

Table 2-1. Reserved JavaScript keywords

`break`	`do`	`if`	`switch`	`typeof`
`case`	`else`	`in`	`this`	`var`
`catch`	`false`	`instanceof`	`throw`	`void`
`continue`	`finally`	`new`	`true`	`while`
`default`	`for`	`null`	`try`	`with`
`delete`	`function`	`return`		

Table 2-2 lists other reserved keywords. These words are not currently used in JavaScript, but they are reserved by ECMAScript v3 as possible future extensions to the language.

Table 2-2. Words reserved for ECMA extensions

`abstract`	`double`	`goto`	`native`	`static`
`boolean`	`enum`	`implements`	`package`	`super`
`byte`	`export`	`import`	`private`	`synchronized`
`char`	`extends`	`int`	`protected`	`throws`
`class`	`final`	`interface`	`public`	`transient`
`const`	`float`	`long`	`short`	`volatile`
`debugger`				

In addition to some of the formally reserved words just listed, current drafts of the ECMAScript v4 standard are contemplating the use of the keywords `as`, `is`, `namespace`, and `use`. Current JavaScript interpreters will not prevent you from using these four words as identifiers, but you should avoid them anyway.

You should also avoid using as identifiers the names of global variables and functions that are predefined by JavaScript. If you create variables or functions with these names, either you will get an error (if the property is read-only) or you will redefine the existing variable or function—something you should not do unless you know exactly what you're doing. Table 2-3 lists global variables and functions defined by the ECMAScript v3 standard. Specific implementations may define other global properties, and each specific JavaScript embedding (client-side, server-side, etc.) will have its own extensive list of global properties.*

Table 2-3. Other identifiers to avoid

arguments	encodeURI	Infinity	Object	String
Array	Error	isFinite	parseFloat	SyntaxError
Boolean	escape	isNaN	parseInt	TypeError
Date	eval	Math	RangeError	undefined
decodeURI	EvalError	NaN	ReferenceError	unescape
decodeURIComponent	Function	Number	RegExp	URIError

* See the Window object in the client-side reference section of this book for a list of the additional global variables and functions defined by client-side JavaScript.

CHAPTER 3

Data Types and Values

Computer programs work by manipulating *values*, such as the number 3.14 or the text "Hello World". The types of values that can be represented and manipulated in a programming language are known as *data types*, and one of the most fundamental characteristics of a programming language is the set of data types it supports. JavaScript allows you to work with three primitive data types: numbers, strings of text (known as "strings"), and boolean truth values (known as "booleans"). JavaScript also defines two trivial data types, null and undefined, each of which defines only a single value.

In addition to these primitive data types, JavaScript supports a composite data type known as object. An object (that is, a member of the data type object) represents a collection of values (either primitive values, like numbers and strings, or composite values, like other objects). Objects in JavaScript have a dual nature: an object can represent an unordered collection of named values or an ordered collection of numbered values. In the latter case, the object is called an *array*. Although objects and arrays are fundamentally the same data type in JavaScript, they behave quite differently and will usually be considered distinct types throughout this book.

JavaScript defines another special kind of object, known as a *function*. A function is an object that has executable code associated with it. A function may be *invoked* to perform some kind of operation. Like arrays, functions behave differently from other kinds of objects, and JavaScript defines special language syntax for working with them. Thus, we'll treat the function data type independently of the object and array types.

In addition to functions and arrays, core JavaScript defines a few other specialized kinds of objects. These objects do not represent new data types, just new *classes* of objects. The Date class defines objects that represent dates, the RegExp class defines objects that represent regular expressions (a powerful pattern-matching tool described in Chapter 10), and the Error class defines objects that represent syntax and runtime errors that can occur in a JavaScript program.

The remainder of this chapter documents each of the primitive data types in detail. It also introduces the object, array, and function data types, which are fully documented in Chapters 7, 8, and 9. Finally, it provides an overview of the Date, RegExp, and Error classes, which are documented in full detail in the core reference section of this book.

3.1 Numbers

Numbers are the most basic data type; they require very little explanation. JavaScript differs from programming languages such as C and Java in that it does not make a distinction between integer values and floating-point values. All numbers in JavaScript are represented as floating-point values. JavaScript represents numbers using the 64-bit floating-point format defined by the IEEE 754 standard,* which means it can represent numbers as large as $\pm 1.7976931348623157 \times 10^{308}$ and as small as $\pm 5 \times 10^{-324}$.

When a number appears directly in a JavaScript program, we call it a numeric literal. JavaScript supports numeric literals in several formats, as described in the following sections. Note that any numeric literal can be preceded by a minus sign (–) to make the number negative. Technically, however, – is the unary negation operator (see Chapter 5), not part of the numeric literal syntax.

3.1.1 Integer Literals

In a JavaScript program, a base-10 integer is written as a sequence of digits. For example:

```
0
3
10000000
```

The JavaScript number format allows you to exactly represent all integers between –9007199254740992 (-2^{53}) and 9007199254740992 (2^{53}), inclusive. If you use integer values larger than this, you may lose precision in the trailing digits. Note, however, that certain integer operations in JavaScript (in particular the bitwise operators described in Chapter 5) are performed on 32-bit integers, which range from –2147483648 (-2^{31}) to 2147483647 ($2^{31}-1$).

3.1.2 Hexadecimal and Octal Literals

In addition to base-10 integer literals, JavaScript recognizes hexadecimal (base-16) values. A hexadecimal literal begins with "0x" or "0X", followed by a string of hexadecimal digits. A hexadecimal digit is one of the digits 0 through 9 or the letters a (or

* This format should be familiar to Java programmers as the format of the `double` type. It is also the `double` format used in almost all modern implementations of C and C++.

A) through f (or F), which are used to represent values 10 through 15. Examples of hexadecimal integer literals are:

```
0xff  // 15*16 + 15 = 255 (base 10)
0xCAFE911
```

Although the ECMAScript standard does not support them, some implementations of JavaScript allow you to specify integer literals in octal (base-8) format. An octal literal begins with the digit 0 and is followed by a sequence of digits, each between 0 and 7. For example:

```
0377  // 3*64 + 7*8 + 7 = 255 (base 10)
```

Since some implementations support octal literals and some do not, you should never write an integer literal with a leading zero—you cannot know whether an implementation will interpret it as an octal or decimal value.

3.1.3 Floating-Point Literals

Floating-point literals can have a decimal point; they use the traditional syntax for real numbers. A real value is represented as the integral part of the number, followed by a decimal point and the fractional part of the number.

Floating-point literals may also be represented using exponential notation: a real number followed by the letter e (or E), followed by an optional plus or minus sign, followed by an integer exponent. This notation represents the real number multiplied by 10 to the power of the exponent.

More succinctly, the syntax is:

```
[digits][.digits][(E|e)[(+|-)]digits]
```

For example:

```
3.14
2345.789
.333333333333333333
6.02e23         // 6.02×10^23
1.4738223E-32   // 1.4738223×10^-32
```

Note that there are infinitely many real numbers, but only a finite number of them (18437736874454810627, to be exact) can be represented exactly by the JavaScript floating-point format. This means that when you're working with real numbers in JavaScript, the representation of the number will often be an approximation of the actual number. The approximation is usually good enough, however, and this is rarely a practical problem.

3.1.4 Working with Numbers

JavaScript programs work with numbers using the arithmetic operators that the language provides. These include + for addition, - for subtraction, * for multiplication, and / for division. Full details on these and other arithmetic operators can be found in Chapter 5.

In addition to these basic arithmetic operations, JavaScript supports more complex mathematical operations through a large number of mathematical functions that are a core part of the language. For convenience, these functions are all stored as properties of a single Math object, so we always use the literal name `Math` to access them. For example, here's how to compute the sine of the numeric value `x`:

```
sine_of_x = Math.sin(x);
```

And to compute the square root of a numeric expression:

```
hypot = Math.sqrt(x*x + y*y);
```

See the Math object and subsequent listings in the core reference section of this book for full details on all the mathematical functions supported by JavaScript.

There is also one interesting method that you can use with numbers. The `toString()` method converts an integer to a string, using the radix, or base, specified by its argument (the base must be between 2 and 36). For example, to convert a number to binary, use `toString()` like this:

```
var x = 33;
var y = x.toString(2);  // y is "100001"
```

To invoke the `toString()` method on a number literal, you can use parentheses to prevent the `.` from being interpreted as a decimal point:

```
var y = (257).toString(0x10);  // y is "101"
```

3.1.5 Special Numeric Values

JavaScript uses several special numeric values. When a floating-point value becomes larger than the largest representable finite number, the result is a special infinity value, which JavaScript prints as `Infinity`. Similarly, when a negative value becomes lower than the last representable negative number, the result is negative infinity, printed as `-Infinity`.

Another special JavaScript numeric value is returned when a mathematical operation (such as division of zero by zero) yields an undefined result or an error. In this case, the result is the special not-a-number value, printed as `NaN`. The not-a-number value behaves unusually: it does not compare equal to any number, including itself! For this reason, a special function, `isNaN()`, is required to test for this value. A related function, `isFinite()`, tests whether a number is not NaN and is not positive or negative infinity.

Table 3-1 lists several constants that JavaScript defines to represent these special numeric values.

Table 3-1. Special numeric constants

Constant	Meaning
`Infinity`	Special value to represent infinity
`NaN`	Special not-a-number value
`Number.MAX_VALUE`	Largest representable number
`Number.MIN_VALUE`	Smallest (closest to zero) representable number
`Number.NaN`	Special not-a-number value
`Number.POSITIVE_INFINITY`	Special value to represent infinity
`Number.NEGATIVE_INFINITY`	Special value to represent negative infinity

The `Infinity` and `NaN` constants are defined by the ECMAScript v1 standard and are not implemented prior to JavaScript 1.3. The various `Number` constants, however, have been implemented since JavaScript 1.1.

3.2 Strings

A *string* is a sequence of Unicode letters, digits, punctuation characters, and so on—it is the JavaScript data type for representing text. As you'll see shortly, you can include string literals in your programs by enclosing them in matching pairs of single or double quotation marks. Note that JavaScript does not have a character data type such as `char`, like C, C++, and Java do. To represent a single character, you simply use a string that has a length of 1.

3.2.1 String Literals

A string is a sequence of zero or more Unicode characters enclosed within single or double quotes (`'` or `"`). Double-quote characters may be contained within strings delimited by single-quote characters, and single-quote characters may be contained within strings delimited by double quotes. String literals must be written on a single line; they may not be broken across two lines. If you need to include a newline character in a string literal, use the character sequence `\n`, which is documented in the next section. Examples of string literals are:

```
"" // The empty string: it has zero characters
'testing'
"3.14"
'name="myform"'
"Wouldn't you prefer O'Reilly's book?"
"This string\nhas two lines"
"π is the ratio of a circle's circumference to its diameter"
```

As illustrated in the last example string shown, the ECMAScript v1 standard allows Unicode characters within string literals. Implementations prior to JavaScript 1.3, however, typically support only ASCII or Latin-1 characters in strings. As we'll see in the next section, you can also include Unicode characters in your string literals using special "escape sequences." This is useful if your text editor does not provide complete Unicode support.

Note that when you use single quotes to delimit your strings, you must be careful with English contractions and possessives like can't and O'Reilly's. Since the apostrophe is the same as the single-quote character, you must use the backslash character (\) to escape any apostrophes that appear in single-quoted strings (this is explained in the next section).

In client-side JavaScript programming, JavaScript code often contains strings of HTML code, and HTML code often contains strings of JavaScript code. Like JavaScript, HTML uses either single or double quotes to delimit its strings. Thus, when combining JavaScript and HTML, it is a good idea to use one style of quotes for JavaScript and the other style for HTML. In the following example, the string "Thank you" is single-quoted within a JavaScript expression, which is double-quoted within an HTML event handler attribute:

```
<a href="" onclick="alert('Thank you')">Click Me</a>
```

3.2.2 Escape Sequences in String Literals

The backslash character (\) has a special purpose in JavaScript strings. Combined with the character that follows it, it represents a character that is not otherwise representable within the string. For example, `\n` is an *escape sequence* that represents a newline character.*

Another example, mentioned in the previous section, is the `\'` escape, which represents the single quote (or apostrophe) character. This escape sequence is useful when you need to include an apostrophe in a string literal that is contained within single quotes. You can see why we call these escape sequences—here, the backslash allows us to escape from the usual interpretation of the single-quote character. Instead of using it to mark the end of the string, we use it as an apostrophe:

```
'You\'re right, it can\'t be a quote'
```

Table 3-2 lists the JavaScript escape sequences and the characters they represent. Two of the escape sequences are generic ones that can be used to represent any character by specifying its Latin-1 or Unicode character code as a hexadecimal number. For example, the sequence `\xA9` represents the copyright symbol, which has the Latin-1 encoding given by the hexadecimal number A9. Similarly, the `\u` escape represents an arbitrary Unicode character specified by four hexadecimal digits. `\u03c0` represents the character π, for example. Note that Unicode escapes are required by the ECMAScript v1 standard but are not typically supported in implementations prior to JavaScript 1.3. Some implementations of JavaScript also allow a Latin-1 character to be

* C, C++, and Java programmers will already be familiar with this and other JavaScript escape sequences.

specified by three octal digits following a backslash, but this escape sequence is not supported in the ECMAScript v3 standard and should no longer be used.

Table 3-2. JavaScript escape sequences

Sequence	Character represented
`\0`	The NUL character (`\u0000`).
`\b`	Backspace (`\u0008`).
`\t`	Horizontal tab (`\u0009`).
`\n`	Newline (`\u000A`).
`\v`	Vertical tab (`\u000B`).
`\f`	Form feed (`\u000C`).
`\r`	Carriage return (`\u000D`).
`\"`	Double quote (`\u0022`).
`\'`	Apostrophe or single quote (`\u0027`).
`\\`	Backslash (`\u005C`).
`\x`*XX*	The Latin-1 character specified by the two hexadecimal digits *XX*.
`\u`*XXXX*	The Unicode character specified by the four hexadecimal digits *XXXX*.
`\`*XXX*	The Latin-1 character specified by the octal digits *XXX*, between 1 and 377. Not supported by ECMAScript v3; do not use this escape sequence.

Finally, note that the backslash escape cannot be used before a line break to continue a string (or other JavaScript) token across two lines or to include a literal line break in a string. If the `\` character precedes any character other than those shown in Table 3-2, the backslash is simply ignored (although future versions of the language may, of course, define new escape sequences). For example, `\#` is the same thing as `#`.

3.2.3 Working with Strings

One of the built-in features of JavaScript is the ability to *concatenate* strings. If you use the `+` operator with numbers, it adds them. But if you use this operator on strings, it joins them by appending the second to the first. For example:

```
msg = "Hello, " + "world";   // Produces the string "Hello, world"
greeting = "Welcome to my home page," + " " + name;
```

To determine the length of a string—the number of characters it contains—use the `length` property of the string. If the variable `s` contains a string, you access its length like this:

```
s.length
```

You can use a number of methods to operate on strings. For example, to get the last character of a string `s`:

```
last_char = s.charAt(s.length - 1)
```

To extract the second, third, and fourth characters from a string s:

```
sub = s.substring(1,4);
```

To find the position of the first letter a in a string s:

```
i = s.indexOf('a');
```

There are quite a few other methods that you can use to manipulate strings. You'll find full documentation of these methods in the core reference section of this book, under the String object and subsequent listings.

As you can tell from the previous examples, JavaScript strings (and JavaScript arrays, as we'll see later) are indexed starting with zero. That is, the first character in a string is character 0. C, C++, and Java programmers should be perfectly comfortable with this convention, but programmers used to languages with 1-based strings and arrays may find that it takes some getting used to.

In some implementations of JavaScript, individual characters can be read from strings (but not written into strings) using array notation, so the earlier call to `charAt( )` could also be written like this:

```
last_char = s[s.length - 1];
```

Note, however, that this syntax is not part of the ECMAScript v3 standard, is not portable, and should be avoided.

When we discuss the object data type, you'll see that object properties and methods are used in the same way that string properties and methods are used in the previous examples. This does not mean that strings are a type of object. In fact, strings are a distinct JavaScript data type. They use object syntax for accessing properties and methods, but they are not themselves objects. We'll see just why this is at the end of this chapter.

3.3 Boolean Values

The number and string data types have a large or infinite number of possible values. The boolean data type, on the other hand, has only two. The two legal boolean values are represented by the literals `true` and `false`. A boolean value represents a truth value—it says whether something is true or not.

Boolean values are generally the result of comparisons you make in your JavaScript programs. For example:

```
a == 4
```

This code tests to see if the value of the variable a is equal to the number `4`. If it is, the result of this comparison is the boolean value `true`. If `a` is not equal to `4`, the result of the comparison is `false`.

Boolean values are typically used in JavaScript control structures. For example, the `if/else` statement in JavaScript performs one action if a boolean value is `true` and another action if the value is `false`. You usually combine a comparison that creates a boolean value directly with a statement that uses it. The result looks like this:

```
if (a == 4)
  b = b + 1;
else
  a = a + 1;
```

This code checks if `a` equals `4`. If so, it adds `1` to `b`; otherwise, it adds `1` to `a`.

Instead of thinking of the two possible boolean values as `true` and `false`, it is sometimes convenient to think of them as `on` (`true`) and `off` (`false`) or `yes` (`true`) and `no` (`false`). Sometimes it is even useful to consider them equivalent to `1` (`true`) and `0` (`false`). (In fact, JavaScript does just this and converts `true` and `false` to `1` and `0` when necessary.)*

3.4 Functions

A *function* is a piece of executable code that is defined by a JavaScript program or predefined by the JavaScript implementation. Although a function is defined only once, a JavaScript program can execute or invoke it any number of times. A function may be passed arguments, or parameters, specifying the value or values upon which it is to perform its computation, and it may also return a value that represents the results of that computation. JavaScript implementations provide many predefined functions, such as the `Math.sin()` function that computes the sine of an angle.

JavaScript programs may also define their own functions with code that looks like this:

```
function square(x)  // The function is named square. It expects one argument, x.
{                   // The body of the function begins here.
  return x*x;       // The function squares its argument and returns that value.
}                   // The function ends here.
```

Once a function is defined, you can invoke it by following the function's name with an optional comma-separated list of arguments within parentheses. The following lines are function invocations:

```
y = Math.sin(x);
y = square(x);
d = compute_distance(x1, y1, z1, x2, y2, z2);
move();
```

An important feature of JavaScript is that functions are values that can be manipulated by JavaScript code. In many languages, including Java, functions are only a

* C programmers should note that JavaScript has a distinct boolean data type, unlike C, which simply uses integer values to simulate boolean values. Java programmers should note that although JavaScript has a boolean type, it is not nearly as pure as the Java `boolean` data type—JavaScript boolean values are easily converted to and from other data types, and so in practice, the use of boolean values in JavaScript is much more like their use in C than in Java.

syntactic feature of the language—they can be defined and invoked, but they are not data types. The fact that functions are true values in JavaScript gives a lot of flexibility to the language. It means that functions can be stored in variables, arrays, and objects, and it means that functions can be passed as arguments to other functions. This can quite often be useful. We'll learn more about defining and invoking functions, and also about using them as data values, in Chapter 7.

Since functions are values just like numbers and strings, they can be assigned to object properties just like other values can. When a function is assigned to a property of an object (the object data type and object properties are described in Section 3.5, "Objects"), it is often referred to as a *method* of that object. Methods are an important part of object-oriented programming. We'll see more about them in Chapter 8.

3.4.1 Function Literals

In the preceding section, we saw the definition of a function `square()`. The syntax shown there is used to define most functions in most JavaScript programs. However, ECMAScript v3 provides a syntax (implemented in JavaScript 1.2 and later) for defining function literals. A function literal is defined with the `function` keyword, followed by an optional function name, followed by a parenthesized list of function arguments and the body of the function within curly braces. In other words, a function literal looks just like a function definition, except that it does not have to have a name. The big difference is that function literals can appear within other JavaScript expressions. Thus, instead of defining the function `square()` with a function definition:

```
function square(x) { return x*x; }
```

We can define it with a function literal:

```
var square = function(x) { return x*x; }
```

Functions defined in this way are sometimes called *lambda functions* in homage to the LISP programming language, which was one of the first to allow unnamed functions to be embedded as literal data values within a program. Although it is not immediately obvious why one might choose to use function literals in a program, we'll see later that in advanced scripts they can be quite convenient and useful.

There is one other way to define a function: you can pass the argument list and the body of the function as strings to the `Function()` constructor. For example:

```
var square = new Function("x", "return x*x;");
```

Defining a function in this way is not often useful. It is usually awkward to express the function body as a string, and in many JavaScript implementations, functions defined in this way will be less efficient than functions defined in either of the other two ways.

3.5 Objects

An *object* is a collection of named values. These named values are usually referred to as *properties* of the object. (Sometimes they are called fields of the object, but this usage can be confusing.) To refer to a property of an object, you refer to the object, followed by a period and the name of the property. For example, if an object named `image` has properties named `width` and `height`, we can refer to those properties like this:

```
image.width
image.height
```

Properties of objects are, in many ways, just like JavaScript variables; they can contain any type of data, including arrays, functions, and other objects. Thus, you might see JavaScript code like this:

```
document.myform.button
```

This code refers to the `button` property of an object that is itself stored in the `myform` property of an object named `document`.

As mentioned earlier, when a function value is stored in a property of an object, that function is often called a method, and the property name becomes the method name. To invoke a method of an object, use the `.` syntax to extract the function value from the object, and then use the `()` syntax to invoke that function. For example, to invoke the `write()` method of the Document object, you can use code like this:

```
document.write("this is a test");
```

Objects in JavaScript have the ability to serve as associative arrays—that is, they can associate arbitrary data values with arbitrary strings. When an object is used in this way, a different syntax is generally required to access the object's properties: a string containing the name of the desired property is enclosed within square brackets. Using this syntax, we could access the properties of the `image` object mentioned previously with code like this:

```
image["width"]
image["height"]
```

Associative arrays are a powerful data type; they are useful for a number of programming techniques. We'll learn more about objects in their traditional and associative array usages in Chapter 8.

3.5.1 Creating Objects

As we'll see in Chapter 8, objects are created by invoking special *constructor* functions. For example, the following lines all create new objects:

```
var o = new Object();
var now = new Date();
var pattern = new RegExp("\\sjava\\s", "i");
```

Once you have created an object of your own, you can use and set its properties however you desire:

```
var point = new Object();
point.x = 2.3;
point.y = -1.2;
```

3.5.2 Object Literals

ECMAScript v3 defines (and JavaScript 1.2 implements) an object literal syntax that allows you to create an object and specify its properties. An object literal (also called an object initializer) consists of a comma-separated list of colon-separated property/value pairs, all enclosed within curly braces. Thus, the object `point` in the previous code could also be created and initialized with this line:

```
var point = { x:2.3, y:-1.2 };
```

Object literals can also be nested. For example:

```
var rectangle = { upperLeft: { x: 2, y: 2 },
                  lowerRight: { x: 4, y: 4}
                };
```

Finally, the property values used in object literals need not be constant—they can be arbitrary JavaScript expressions:

```
var square = { upperLeft: { x:point.x, y:point.y },
               lowerRight: { x:(point.x + side), y:(point.y+side) }};
```

3.6 Arrays

An *array* is a collection of data values, just as an object is. While each data value contained in an object has a name, each data value in an array has a number, or *index*. In JavaScript, you retrieve a value from an array by enclosing an index within square brackets after the array name. For example, if an array is named `a`, and `i` is a non-negative integer, `a[i]` is an element of the array. Array indexes begin with zero. Thus, `a[2]` refers to the *third* element of the array `a`.

Arrays may contain any type of JavaScript data, including references to other arrays or to objects or functions. For example:

```
document.images[1].width
```

This code refers to the `width` property of an object stored in the second element of an array stored in the `images` property of the `document` object.

Note that the arrays described here differ from the associative arrays described in Section 3.5, "Objects." The regular arrays we are discussing here are indexed by non-negative integers. Associative arrays are indexed by strings. Also note that JavaScript does not support multidimensional arrays, except as arrays of arrays. Finally, because JavaScript is an untyped language, the elements of an array do not all need to be of the same type, as they do in typed languages like Java. We'll learn more about arrays in Chapter 9.

3.6.1 Creating Arrays

Arrays can be created with the `Array()` constructor function. Once created, any number of indexed elements can easily be assigned to the array:

```
var a = new Array();
a[0] = 1.2;
a[1] = "JavaScript";
a[2] = true;
a[3] = { x:1, y:3 };
```

Arrays can also be initialized by passing array elements to the `Array()` constructor. Thus, the previous array-creation and -initialization code could also be written:

```
var a = new Array(1.2, "JavaScript", true, { x:1, y:3 });
```

If you pass only a single number to the `Array()` constructor, it specifies the length of the array. Thus:

```
var a = new Array(10);
```

creates a new array with 10 undefined elements.

3.6.2 Array Literals

ECMAScript v3 defines (and JavaScript 1.2 implements) a literal syntax for creating and initializing arrays. An array literal (or array initializer) is a comma-separated list of values contained within square brackets. The values within the brackets are assigned sequentially to array indexes starting with zero.* For example, in JavaScript 1.2 the array creation and initialization code in the previous section could also be written as:

```
var a = [1.2, "JavaScript", true, { x:1, y:3 }];
```

Like object literals, array literals can be nested:

```
var matrix = [[1,2,3], [4,5,6], [7,8,9]];
```

Also, as with object literals, the elements in array literals can be arbitrary expressions and need not be restricted to constants:

```
var base = 1024;
var table = [base, base+1, base+2, base+3];
```

* Netscape's JavaScript 1.2 implementation has a bug: when an array literal is specified with a number as its single element, that number specifies the length of the array rather than the value of the first element. While this behavior mirrors that of the `Array()` constructor, it is clearly inappropriate in this context.

Undefined elements can be included in an array literal by simply omitting a value between commas. For example, the following array contains five elements, including three undefined elements:

```
var sparseArray = [1,,,,5];
```

3.7 null

The JavaScript keyword `null` is a special value that indicates no value. `null` is usually considered to be a special value of object type—a value that represents no object. `null` is a unique value, distinct from all other values. When a variable holds the value `null`, you know that it does not contain a valid object, array, number, string, or boolean value.*

3.8 undefined

Another special value used occasionally by JavaScript is the `undefined` value returned when you use either a variable that has been declared but never had a value assigned to it, or an object property that does not exist. Note that this special `undefined` value is not the same as `null`.

Although `null` and the `undefined` value are distinct, the `==` equality operator considers them to be equal to one another. Consider the following:

```
my.prop == null
```

This comparison is `true` either if the `my.prop` property does not exist or if it does exist but contains the value `null`. Since both `null` and the `undefined` value indicate an absence of value, this equality is often what we want. However, if you truly must distinguish between a `null` value and an `undefined` value, use the `===` identity operator or the `typeof` operator (see Chapter 5 for details).

Unlike `null`, `undefined` is not a reserved word in JavaScript. The ECMAScript v3 standard specifies that there is always a global variable named `undefined` whose initial value is the `undefined` value. Thus, in a conforming implementation, you can treat `undefined` as a keyword, as long as you don't assign a value to the variable.

If you are not sure that your implementation has the `undefined` variable, you can simply declare your own:

```
var undefined;
```

By declaring but not initializing the variable, you assure that it has the `undefined` value. The `void` operator (see Chapter 5) provides another way to obtain the `undefined` value.

* C and C++ programmers should note that `null` in JavaScript is not the same as `0`, as it is in those languages. In certain circumstances `null` is converted to `0`, but the two are not equivalent.

3.9 The Date Object

The previous sections have described all of the fundamental data types supported by JavaScript. Date and time values are not one of these fundamental types, but JavaScript does provide a class of object that represents dates and times and can be used to manipulate this type of data. A Date object in JavaScript is created with the `new` operator and the `Date( )` constructor (the `new` operator will be introduced in Chapter 5, and we'll learn more about object creation in Chapter 8):

```
var now = new Date( );  // Create an object holding the current date and time.
// Create a Date object representing Christmas.
// Note that months are zero-based, so December is month 11!
var xmas = new Date(2000, 11, 25);
```

Methods of the Date object allow you to get and set the various date and time values and to convert the Date to a string, using either local time or GMT time. For example:

```
xmas.setFullYear(xmas.getFullYear( ) + 1);  // Change the date to next Christmas.
var weekday = xmas.getDay( );  // Christmas falls on a Tuesday in 2001.
document.write("Today is: " + now.toLocaleString( ));  // Current date/time.
```

The Date object also defines functions (not methods; they are not invoked through a Date object) to convert a date specified in string or numeric form to an internal millisecond representation that is useful for some kinds of date arithmetic.

You can find full documentation on the Date object and its methods in the core reference section of this book.

3.10 Regular Expressions

Regular expressions provide a rich and powerful syntax for describing textual patterns; they are used for pattern matching and for implementing search and replace operations. JavaScript has adopted the Perl programming language syntax for expressing regular expressions. Regular expression support was first added to the language in JavaScript 1.2 and was standardized and extended by ECMAScript v3.

Regular expressions are represented in JavaScript by the RegExp object and may be created using the `RegExp( )` constructor. Like the Date object, the RegExp object is not one of the fundamental data types of JavaScript; it is simply a specialized kind of object provided by all conforming JavaScript implementations.

Unlike the Date object, however, RegExp objects have a literal syntax and can be encoded directly into JavaScript 1.2 programs. Text between a pair of slashes constitutes a regular expression literal. The second slash in the pair can also be followed by one or more letters, which modify the meaning of the pattern. For example:

```
/^HTML/
/[1-9][0-9]*/
/\bjavascript\b/i
```

The regular expression grammar is complex and is documented in detail in Chapter 10. At this point, you need only know what a regular expression literal looks like in JavaScript code.

3.11 Error Objects

ECMAScript v3 defines a number of classes that represent errors. The JavaScript interpreter "throws" an object of one of these types when a runtime error occurs. (See the `throw` and `try` statements in Chapter 6 for a discussion of throwing and catching errors.) Each error object has a `message` property that contains an implementation-specific error message. The types of predefined error objects are Error, EvalError, RangeError, ReferenceError, SyntaxError, TypeError, and URIError. You can find out more about these classes in the core reference section of this book.

3.12 Primitive Data Type Wrapper Objects

When we discussed strings earlier in this chapter, I pointed out a strange feature of that data type: to operate on strings, you use object notation. For example, a typical operation involving strings might look like the following:

```
var s = "These are the times that try people's souls.";
var last_word = s.substring(s.lastIndexOf(" ")+1, s.length);
```

If you didn't know better, it would appear that s was an object and that you were invoking methods and reading property values of that object.

What's going on? Are strings objects, or are they primitive data types? The `typeof` operator (see Chapter 5) assures us that strings have the data type "string", which is distinct from the data type "object". Why, then, are strings manipulated using object notation?

The truth is that a corresponding object class is defined for each of the three key primitive data types. That is, besides supporting the number, string, and boolean data types, JavaScript also supports Number, String, and Boolean classes. These classes are wrappers around the primitive data types. A *wrapper* contains the same primitive data value, but it also defines properties and methods that can be used to manipulate that data.

JavaScript can flexibly convert values from one type to another. When we use a string in an object context—i.e., when we try to access a property or method of the string—JavaScript internally creates a String wrapper object for the string value. This String object is used in place of the primitive string value; the object has properties and methods defined, so the use of the primitive value in an object context succeeds. The same is true, of course, for the other primitive types and their corresponding wrapper objects; we just don't use the other types in an object context nearly as often as we use strings in that context.

Note that the String object created when we use a string in an object context is a transient one—it is used to allow us to access a property or method and then is no longer needed, so it is reclaimed by the system. Suppose s is a string and we determine the length of the string with a line like this:

```
var len = s.length;
```

In this case, s remains a string; the original string value itself is not changed. A new transient String object is created, which allows us to access the length property, and then the transient object is discarded, with no change to the original value s. If you think this scheme sounds elegant and bizarrely complex at the same time, you are right. Typically, however, JavaScript implementations perform this internal conversion very efficiently, and it is not something you should worry about.

If we want to use a String object explicitly in our program, we have to create a non-transient one that is not automatically discarded by the system. String objects are created just like other objects, with the new operator. For example:

```
var s = "hello world";                // A primitive string value
var S = new String("Hello World");  // A String object
```

Once we've created a String object S, what can we do with it? Nothing that we cannot do with the corresponding primitive string value. If we use the typeof operator, it tells us that S is indeed an object, and not a string value, but except for that case, we'll find that we can't normally distinguish between a primitive string and the String object.* As we've already seen, strings are automatically converted to String objects whenever necessary. It turns out that the reverse is also true. Whenever we use a String object where a primitive string value is expected, JavaScript automatically converts the String to a string. So if we use our String object with the + operator, a transient primitive string value is created so that the string concatenation operation can be performed:

```
msg = S + '!';
```

Bear in mind that everything we've discussed in this section about string values and String objects applies also to number and boolean values and their corresponding Number and Boolean objects. You can learn more about these classes from their respective entries in the core reference section of this book. In Chapter 11, we'll see more about this primitive type/object duality and about automatic data conversion in JavaScript.

* Note, however, that the eval() method treats string values and String objects differently, and it will not behave as you expect it to if you inadvertently pass it a String object instead of a primitive string value.

CHAPTER 4

Variables

A *variable* is a name associated with a value; we say that the variable stores or contains the value. Variables allow you to store and manipulate data in your programs. For example, the following line of JavaScript assigns the value 2 to a variable named i:

```
i = 2;
```

And the following line adds 3 to i and assigns the result to a new variable, sum:

```
var sum = i + 3;
```

These two lines of code demonstrate just about everything you need to know about variables. However, to fully understand how variables work in JavaScript, you need to master a few more concepts. Unfortunately, these concepts require more than a couple of lines of code to explain! The rest of this chapter explains the typing, declaration, scope, contents, and resolution of variables. It also explores garbage collection and the variable/property duality.*

4.1 Variable Typing

An important difference between JavaScript and languages such as Java and C is that JavaScript is *untyped*. This means, in part, that a JavaScript variable can hold a value of any data type, unlike a Java or C variable, which can hold only the one particular type of data for which it is declared. For example, it is perfectly legal in JavaScript to assign a number to a variable and then later assign a string to that variable:

```
i = 10;
i = "ten";
```

In C, C++, Java, or any other strongly typed language, code like this is illegal.

* These are tricky concepts, and a complete understanding of this chapter requires an understanding of concepts introduced in later chapters of the book. If you are relatively new to programming, you may want to read only the first two sections of this chapter and then move on to Chapters 5, 6, and 7 before returning to finish up the remainder of this chapter.

A feature related to JavaScript's lack of typing is that the language conveniently and automatically converts values from one type to another, as necessary. If you attempt to append a number to a string, for example, JavaScript automatically converts the number to the corresponding string so that it can be appended. We'll see more about data type conversion in Chapter 11.

JavaScript is obviously a simpler language for being untyped. The advantage of strongly typed languages such as C++ and Java is that they enforce rigorous programming practices, which makes it easier to write, maintain, and reuse long, complex programs. Since many JavaScript programs are shorter scripts, this rigor is not necessary and we benefit from the simpler syntax.

4.2 Variable Declaration

Before you use a variable in a JavaScript program, you must *declare* it.* Variables are declared with the `var` keyword, like this:

```
var i;
var sum;
```

You can also declare multiple variables with the same `var` keyword:

```
var i, sum;
```

And you can combine variable declaration with variable initialization:

```
var message = "hello";
var i = 0, j = 0, k = 0;
```

If you don't specify an initial value for a variable with the `var` statement, the variable is declared, but its initial value is `undefined` until your code stores a value into it.

Note that the `var` statement can also appear as part of the `for` and `for/in` loops (introduced in Chapter 6), allowing you to succinctly declare the loop variable as part of the loop syntax itself. For example:

```
for(var i = 0; i < 10; i++) document.write(i, "<br>");
for(var i = 0, j=10; i < 10; i++,j--) document.write(i*j, "<br>");
for(var i in o) document.write(i, "<br>");
```

Variables declared with `var` are *permanent*: attempting to delete them with the `delete` operator causes an error. (The `delete` operator is introduced in Chapter 5.)

4.2.1 Repeated and Omitted Declarations

It is legal and harmless to declare a variable more than once with the `var` statement. If the repeated declaration has an initializer, it acts as if it were simply an assignment statement.

* If you don't declare a variable explicitly, JavaScript will declare it implicitly for you.

If you attempt to read the value of an undeclared variable, JavaScript will generate an error. If you assign a value to a variable that you have not declared with var, JavaScript will implicitly declare that variable for you. Note, however, that implicitly declared variables are always created as global variables, even if they are used within the body of a function. To prevent the creation of a global variable (or the use of an existing global variable) when you meant to create a local variable for use within a single function, you must always use the var statement within function bodies. It's best to use var for all variables, whether global or local. (The distinction between local and global variables is explored in more detail in the next section.)

4.3 Variable Scope

The *scope* of a variable is the region of your program in which it is defined. A *global* variable has global scope—it is defined everywhere in your JavaScript code. On the other hand, variables declared within a function are defined only within the body of the function. They are *local* variables and have local scope. Function parameters also count as local variables and are defined only within the body of the function.

Within the body of a function, a local variable takes precedence over a global variable with the same name. If you declare a local variable or function parameter with the same name as a global variable, you effectively hide the global variable. For example, the following code prints the word "local":

```
var scope = "global";         // Declare a global variable
function checkscope( ) {
    var scope = "local";      // Declare a local variable with the same name
    document.write(scope);    // Use the local variable, not the global one
}
checkscope( );                // Prints "local"
```

Although you can get away with not using the var statement when you write code in the global scope, you must always use var to declare local variables. Consider what happens if you don't:

```
scope = "global";               // Declare a global variable, even without var
function checkscope( ) {
    scope = "local";            // Oops! We just changed the global variable
    document.write(scope);      // Uses the global variable
    myscope = "local";          // This implicitly declares a new global variable
    document.write(myscope);    // Uses the new global variable
}
checkscope( );                  // Prints "locallocal"
document.write(scope);          // This prints "local"
document.write(myscope);        // This prints "local"
```

In general, functions do not know what variables are defined in the global scope or what they are being used for. Thus, if a function uses a global variable instead of a local one, it runs the risk of changing a value upon which some other part of the program relies. Fortunately, avoiding this problem is simple: declare all variables with var.

In JavaScript 1.2 (and ECMAScript v3), function definitions can be nested. Each function has its own local scope, so it is possible to have several nested layers of local scope. For example:

```
var scope = "global scope";          // A global variable
function checkscope() {
    var scope = "local scope";       // A local variable
    function nested() {
        var scope = "nested scope";  // A nested scope of local variables
        document.write(scope);       // Prints "nested scope"
    }
    nested();
}
checkscope();
```

4.3.1 No Block Scope

Note that unlike C, C++, and Java, JavaScript does not have block-level scope. All variables declared in a function, no matter where they are declared, are defined *throughout* the function. In the following code, the variables i, j, and k all have the same scope: all three are defined throughout the body of the function. This would not be the case if the code were written in C, C++, or Java:

```
function test(o) {
    var i = 0;                        // i is defined throughout function
    if (typeof o == "object") {
        var j = 0;                    // j is defined everywhere, not just block
        for(var k = 0; k < 10; k++) { // k is defined everywhere, not just loop
            document.write(k);
        }
        document.write(k);            // k is still defined: prints 10
    }
    document.write(j);                // j is defined, but may not be initialized
}
```

The rule that all variables declared in a function are defined throughout the function can cause surprising results. The following code illustrates this:

```
var scope = "global";
function f() {
    alert(scope);          // Displays "undefined", not "global"
    var scope = "local";   // Variable initialized here, but defined everywhere
    alert(scope);          // Displays "local"
}
f();
```

You might think that the first call to alert() would display "global", since the var statement declaring the local variable has not yet been executed. Because of the scope rules, however, this is not what happens. The local variable is defined throughout the body of the function, which means the global variable by the same name is hidden throughout the function. Although the local variable is defined throughout, it is not actually initialized until the var statement is executed. Thus, the function f in the previous example is equivalent to the following:

```
function f( ) {
    var scope;          // Local variable is declared at the start of the function
    alert(scope);       // It exists here, but still has "undefined" value
    scope = "local";  // Now we initialize it and give it a value
    alert(scope);       // And here it has a value
}
```

This example illustrates why it is good programming practice to place all of your variable declarations together at the start of any function.

4.3.2 Undefined Versus Unassigned

The examples in the previous section demonstrate a subtle point in JavaScript programming: there are two different kinds of undefined variables. The first kind of undefined variable is one that has never been declared. An attempt to read the value of such an undeclared variable causes a runtime error. *Undeclared variables* are undefined because they simply do not exist. As described earlier, assigning a value to an undeclared variable does not cause an error; instead, it implicitly declares the variable in the global scope.

The second kind of undefined variable is one that has been declared but has never had a value assigned to it. If you read the value of one of these variables, you obtain its default value, undefined. This type of undefined variable might more usefully be called *unassigned*, to distinguish it from the more serious kind of undefined variable that has not even been declared and does not exist.

The following code fragment illustrates some of the differences between truly undefined and merely unassigned variables:

```
var x;     // Declare an unassigned variable. Its value is undefined.
alert(u);  // Using an undeclared variable causes an error.
u = 3;     // Assigning a value to an undeclared variable creates the variable.
```

4.4 Primitive Types and Reference Types

The next topic we need to consider is the content of variables. We often say that variables have or contain values. But just what is it that they contain? To answer this seemingly simple question, we must look again at the data types supported by JavaScript. The types can be divided into two groups: primitive types and reference types. Numbers, boolean values, and the null and undefined types are primitive. Objects, arrays, and functions are reference types.

A primitive type has a fixed size in memory. For example, a number occupies eight bytes of memory, and a boolean value can be represented with only one bit. The number type is the largest of the primitive types. If each JavaScript variable reserves eight bytes of memory, the variable can directly hold any primitive value.*

Reference types are another matter, however. Objects, for example, can be of any length—they do not have a fixed size. The same is true of arrays: an array can have any number of elements. Similarly, a function can contain any amount of JavaScript code. Since these types do not have a fixed size, their values cannot be stored directly in the eight bytes of memory associated with each variable. Instead, the variable stores a *reference* to the value. Typically, this reference is some form of pointer or memory address. It is not the data value itself, but it tells the variable where to look to find the value.

The distinction between primitive and reference types is an important one, as they behave differently. Consider the following code that uses numbers (a primitive type):

```
var a = 3.14;  // Declare and initialize a variable
var b = a;     // Copy the variable's value to a new variable
a = 4;         // Modify the value of the original variable
alert(b)       // Displays 3.14; the copy has not changed
```

There is nothing surprising about this code. Now consider what happens if we change the code slightly so that it uses arrays (a reference type) instead of numbers:

```
var a = [1,2,3];  // Initialize a variable to refer to an array
var b = a;        // Copy that reference into a new variable
a[0] = 99;        // Modify the array using the original reference
alert(b);         // Display the changed array [99,2,3] using the new reference
```

If this result does not seem surprising to you, you're already well familiar with the distinction between primitive and reference types. If it does seem surprising, take a closer look at the second line. Note that it is the reference to the array value, not the array itself, that is being assigned in this statement. After that second line of code, we still have only one array object; we just happen to have two references to it.

If the primitive versus reference type distinction is new to you, just try to keep the variable contents in mind. Variables hold the actual values of primitive types, but they hold only references to the values of reference types. The differing behavior of primitive and reference types is explored in more detail in Section 11.2, "By Value Versus by Reference."

You may have noticed that I did not specify whether strings are primitive or reference types in JavaScript. Strings are an unusual case. They have variable size, so obviously they cannot be stored directly in fixed-size variables. For efficiency, we would expect JavaScript to copy references to strings, not the actual contents of strings. On the other hand, strings behave like a primitive type in many ways. The question of whether strings are a primitive or reference type is actually moot, because strings are

* This is an oversimplification and is not intended as a description of an actual JavaScript implementation.

immutable: there is no way to change the contents of a string value. This means that we cannot construct an example like the previous one that demonstrates that arrays are copied by reference. In the end, it doesn't matter much whether you think of strings as an immutable reference type that behaves like a primitive type or as a primitive type implemented with the internal efficiency of a reference type.

4.5 Garbage Collection

Reference types do not have a fixed size; indeed, some of them can become quite large. As we've already discussed, variables do not directly hold reference values. The value is stored at some other location, and the variables merely hold a reference to that location. Now we need to focus briefly on the actual storage of the value.

Since strings, objects, and arrays do not have a fixed size, storage for them must be allocated dynamically, when the size is known. Every time a JavaScript program creates a string, array, or object, the interpreter must allocate memory to store that entity. Whenever memory is dynamically allocated like this, it must eventually be freed up for reuse, or the JavaScript interpreter will use up all the available memory on the system and crash.

In languages like C and C++, memory must be freed manually. It is the programmer's responsibility to keep track of all the objects that are created and to destroy them (freeing their memory) when they are no longer needed. This can be an onerous task and is often the source of bugs.

Instead of requiring manual deallocation, JavaScript relies on a technique called *garbage collection*. The JavaScript interpreter is able to detect when an object will never again be used by the program. When it determines that an object is unreachable (i.e., there is no longer any way to refer to it using the variables in the program), it knows that the object is no longer needed and its memory can be reclaimed. Consider the following lines of code, for example:

```
var s = "hello";           // Allocate memory for a string
var u = s.toUpperCase( );  // Create a new string
s = u;                     // Overwrite reference to original string
```

After this code runs, the original string "hello" is no longer reachable—there are no references to it in any variables in the program. The system detects this fact and frees up its storage space for reuse.

Garbage collection is automatic and is invisible to the programmer. You can create all the garbage objects you want, and the system will clean up after you! You need to know only enough about garbage collection to trust that it works; you don't have to wonder about where all the old objects go. For those who aren't satisfied, however, Section 11.3, "Garbage Collection," contains further details on the JavaScript garbage-collection process.

4.6 Variables as Properties

You may have noticed by now that there are a lot of similarities in JavaScript between variables and the properties of objects. They are both assigned the same way, they are used the same way in JavaScript expressions, and so on. Is there really any fundamental difference between the variable `i` and the property `i` of an object `o`? The answer is no. Variables in JavaScript are fundamentally the same as object properties.

4.6.1 The Global Object

When the JavaScript interpreter starts up, one of the first things it does, before executing any JavaScript code, is create a *global object*. The properties of this object are the global variables of JavaScript programs. When you declare a global JavaScript variable, what you are actually doing is defining a property of the global object.

The JavaScript interpreter initializes the global object with a number of properties that refer to predefined values and functions. For example, the `Infinity`, `parseInt`, and `Math` properties refer to the number infinity, the predefined `parseInt()` function, and the predefined Math object. You can read about these global values in the core reference section of this book.

In top-level code (i.e., JavaScript code that is not part of a function), you can use the JavaScript keyword `this` to refer to the global object. Within functions, `this` has a different use, which is described in Chapter 7.

In client-side JavaScript, the Window object serves as the global object for all JavaScript code contained in the browser window it represents. This global Window object has a self-referential `window` property that can be used instead of `this` to refer to the global object. The Window object defines the core global properties, such as `parseInt` and `Math`, and also global client-side properties, such as `navigator` and `screen`.

4.6.2 Local Variables: The Call Object

If global variables are properties of the special global object, then what are local variables? They too are properties of an object. This object is known as the *call object*. The call object has a shorter life span than the global object, but it serves the same purpose. While the body of a function is executing, the function arguments and local variables are stored as properties of this call object. The use of an entirely separate object for local variables is what allows JavaScript to keep local variables from overwriting the value of global variables with the same name.

4.6.3 JavaScript Execution Contexts

Each time the JavaScript interpreter begins to execute a function, it creates a new *execution context* for that function. An execution context is, obviously, the context in which any piece of JavaScript code executes. An important part of the context is the object in which variables are defined. Thus, JavaScript code that is not part of any function runs in an execution context that uses the global object for variable definitions. And every JavaScript function runs in its own unique execution context with its own call object in which local variables are defined.

An interesting point to note is that JavaScript implementations may allow multiple global execution contexts, each with a *different* global object. (Although, in this case, each global object is not entirely global.)* The obvious example is client-side JavaScript, in which each separate browser window, or each frame within a window, defines a separate global execution context. Client-side JavaScript code in each frame or window runs in its own execution context and has its own global object. However, these separate client-side global objects have properties that link them to one another. Thus, JavaScript code in one frame might refer to another frame with the expression `parent.frames[1]`, and the global variable `x` in the first frame might be referenced by the expression `parent.frames[0].x` in the second frame.

You don't need to fully understand how separate window and frame execution contexts are linked together in client-side JavaScript right now. We'll cover that topic in detail when we discuss the integration of JavaScript with web browsers in Chapter 12. What you should understand now is that JavaScript is flexible enough that a single JavaScript interpreter can run scripts in different global execution contexts and that those contexts need not be entirely separate—they can refer back and forth to each other.

This last point requires additional consideration. When JavaScript code in one execution context can read and write property values and execute functions that are defined in another execution context, we've reached a level of complexity that requires consideration of security issues. Take client-side JavaScript as an example. Suppose browser window A is running a script or contains information from your local intranet, and window B is running a script from some random site out on the Internet. In general, we do not want to allow the code in window B to be able to access the properties of window A. If we allow it to do this, it might be able to read sensitive company information and steal it, for example. Thus, in order to safely run JavaScript code, there must be a security mechanism that prevents access from one execution context to another when such access should not be permitted. We'll return to this topic in Chapter 21.

4.7 Variable Scope Revisited

When we first discussed the notion of variable scope, I based the definition solely on the lexical structure of JavaScript code: global variables have global scope and

* This is merely an aside; if it does not interest you, feel free to move on to the next section.

variables declared in functions have local scope. If one function definition is nested within another, variables declared within that nested function have a nested local scope. Now that we know that global variables are properties of a global object and that local variables are properties of a special call object, we can return to the notion of variable scope and reconceptualize it. This new description of scope offers a useful way to think about variables in many contexts; it provides a powerful new understanding of how JavaScript works.

Every JavaScript execution context has a *scope chain* associated with it. This scope chain is a list or chain of objects. When JavaScript code needs to look up the value of a variable `x` (a process called *variable name resolution*), it starts by looking at the first object in the chain. If that object has a property named `x`, the value of that property is used. If the first object does not have a property named `x`, JavaScript continues the search with the next object in the chain. If the second object does not have a property named `x`, the search moves on to the next object, and so on.

In top-level JavaScript code (i.e., code not contained within any function definitions), the scope chain consists of a single object, the global object. All variables are looked up in this object. If a variable does not exist, the variable value is undefined. In a (non-nested) function, however, the scope chain consists of two objects. The first is the function's call object, and the second is the global object. When the function refers to a variable, the call object (the local scope) is checked first, and the global object (the global scope) is checked second. A nested function would have three or more objects in its scope chain. Figure 4-1 illustrates the process of looking up a variable name in the scope chain of a function.

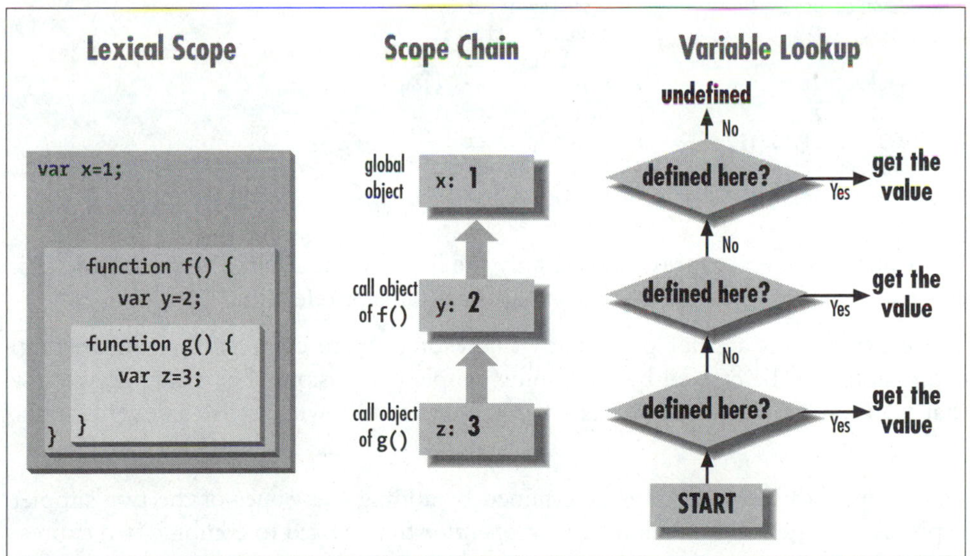

Figure 4-1. The scope chain and variable resolution

CHAPTER 5

Expressions and Operators

This chapter explains how expressions and operators work in JavaScript. If you are familiar with C, C++, or Java, you'll notice that the expressions and operators in JavaScript are very similar, and you'll be able to skim this chapter quickly. If you are not a C, C++, or Java programmer, this chapter tells you everything you need to know about expressions and operators in JavaScript.

5.1 Expressions

An *expression* is a phrase of JavaScript that a JavaScript interpreter can *evaluate* to produce a value. The simplest expressions are literals or variable names, like these:

```
1.7                          // A numeric literal
"JavaScript is fun!"         // A string literal
true                         // A boolean literal
null                         // The literal null value
/java/                       // A regular expression literal
{ x:2, y:2 }                 // An object literal
[2,3,5,7,11,13,17,19]        // An array literal
function(x){return x*x;}     // A function literal
i                            // The variable i
sum                          // The variable sum
```

The value of a literal expression is simply the literal value itself. The value of a variable expression is the value that the variable contains or refers to.

These expressions are not particularly interesting. More complex (and interesting) expressions can be created by combining simple expressions. For example, we saw that `1.7` is an expression and `i` is an expression. The following is also an expression:

```
i + 1.7
```

The value of this expression is determined by adding the values of the two simpler expressions. The + in this example is an *operator* that is used to combine two expressions into a more complex expression. Another operator is -, which is used to combine expressions by subtraction. For example:

```
(i + 1.7) - sum
```

This expression uses the - operator to subtract the value of the sum variable from the value of our previous expression, i + 1.7. JavaScript supports a number of other operators besides + and -, as you'll see in the next section.

5.2 Operator Overview

If you are a C, C++, or Java programmer, most of the JavaScript operators should already be familiar to you. Table 5-1 summarizes the operators; you can refer to this table for reference. Note that most operators are represented by punctuation characters such as + and =. Some, however, are represented by keywords such as delete and instanceof. Keyword operators are regular operators, just like those expressed with punctuation; they are simply expressed using a more readable and less succinct syntax.

In this table, the column labeled "P" gives the operator precedence and the column labeled "A" gives the operator associativity, which can be L (left-to-right) or R (right-to-left). If you do not already understand precedence and associativity, the subsections that follow the table explain these concepts. The operators themselves are documented following that discussion.

Table 5-1. JavaScript operators

P	A	Operator	Operand type(s)	Operation performed
15	L	.	object, identifier	Property access
	L	[]	array, integer	Array index
	L	( )	function, arguments	Function call
	R	new	constructor call	Create new object
14	R	++	lvalue	Pre- or post-increment (unary)
	R	--	lvalue	Pre- or post-decrement (unary)
	R	-	number	Unary minus (negation)
	R	+	number	Unary plus (no-op)
	R	~	integer	Bitwise complement (unary)
	R	!	boolean	Logical complement (unary)
	R	delete	lvalue	Undefine a property (unary)
	R	typeof	any	Return data type (unary)
	R	void	any	Return undefined value (unary)
13	L	*, /, %	numbers	Multiplication, division, remainder
12	L	+, -	numbers	Addition, subtraction
	L	+	strings	String concatenation
11	L	<<	integers	Left shift
	L	>>	integers	Right shift with sign-extension
	L	>>>	integers	Right shift with zero extension
10	L	<, <=	numbers or strings	Less than, less than or equal
	L	>, >=	numbers or strings	Greater than, greater than or equal

Table 5-1. JavaScript operators (continued)

P	A	Operator	Operand type(s)	Operation performed
	L	`instanceof`	object, constructor	Check object type
	L	`in`	string, object	Check whether property exists
9	L	`==`	any	Test for equality
	L	`!=`	any	Test for inequality
	L	`===`	any	Test for identity
	L	`!==`	any	Test for non-identity
8	L	`&`	integers	Bitwise AND
7	L	`^`	integers	Bitwise XOR
6	L	`|`	integers	Bitwise OR
5	L	`&&`	booleans	Logical AND
4	L	`||`	booleans	Logical OR
3	R	`?:`	boolean, any, any	Conditional operator (3 operands)
2	R	`=`	lvalue, any	Assignment
	R	`*=, /=, %=, +=, -=, <<=, >>=, >>>=, &=, ^=, |=`	lvalue, any	Assignment with operation
1	L	`,`	any	Multiple evaluation

5.2.1 Number of Operands

Operators can be categorized based on the number of operands they expect. Most JavaScript operators, like the `+` operator we saw earlier, are *binary operators* that combine two expressions into a single, more complex expression. That is, they operate on two operands. JavaScript also supports a number of *unary operators*, which convert a single expression into a single, more complex expression. The `-` operator in the expression `-3` is a unary operator that performs the operation of negation on the operand `3`. Finally, JavaScript supports one *ternary operator*, the conditional operator `?:`, which combines the value of three expressions into a single expression.

5.2.2 Type of Operands

When constructing JavaScript expressions, you must pay attention to the data types that are being passed to operators and to the data types that are returned. Different operators expect their operands' expressions to evaluate to values of a certain data type. For example, it is not possible to multiply strings, so the expression `"a" * "b"` is not legal in JavaScript. Note, however, that JavaScript tries to convert expressions to the appropriate type whenever possible, so the expression `"3" * "5"` is legal. Its value is the number `15`, not the string `"15"`. We'll consider JavaScript type conversions in detail in Section 11.1, "Data Type Conversion."

Furthermore, some operators behave differently depending on the type of the operands. Most notably, the + operator adds numeric operands but concatenates string operands. Also, if passed one string and one number, it converts the number to a string and concatenates the two resulting strings. For example, `"1" + 0` yields the string `"10"`.

Notice that the assignment operators, as well as a few other operators, expect their lefthand expressions to be lvalues. *lvalue* is a historical term that means "an expression that can legally appear on the lefthand side of an assignment expression." In JavaScript, variables, properties of objects, and elements of arrays are lvalues. The ECMAScript specification allows built-in functions to return lvalues but does not define any built-in functions that behave that way.

Finally, note that operators do not always return the same type as their operands. The comparison operators (less than, equal to, greater than, etc.) take operands of various types, but when comparison expressions are evaluated, they always return a boolean result that indicates whether the comparison is true or not. For example, the expression `a < 3` returns `true` if the value of variable `a` is in fact less than `3`. As we'll see, the boolean values returned by comparison operators are used in `if` statements, `while` loops, and `for` loops—JavaScript statements that control the execution of a program based on the results of evaluating expressions that contain comparison operators.

5.2.3 Operator Precedence

In Table 5-1, the column labeled "P" specifies the *precedence* of each operator. Operator precedence controls the order in which operations are performed. Operators with higher numbers in the "P" column are performed before those with lower numbers.

Consider the following expression:

```
w = x + y*z;
```

The multiplication operator `*` has a higher precedence than the addition operator `+`, so the multiplication is performed before the addition. Furthermore, the assignment operator `=` has the lowest precedence, so the assignment is performed after all the operations on the righthand side are completed.

Operator precedence can be overridden with the explicit use of parentheses. To force the addition in the previous example to be performed first, we would write:

```
w = (x + y)*z;
```

In practice, if you are at all unsure about the precedence of your operators, the simplest thing is to use parentheses to make the evaluation order explicit. The only rules that are important to know are these: multiplication and division are performed before addition and subtraction, and assignment has very low precedence and is almost always performed last.

5.2.4 Operator Associativity

In Table 5-1, the column labeled "A" specifies the *associativity* of the operator. A value of L specifies left-to-right associativity, and a value of R specifies right-to-left associativity. The associativity of an operator specifies the order in which operations of the same precedence are performed. Left-to-right associativity means that operations are performed from left to right. For example, the addition operator has left-to-right associativity, so:

```
w = x + y + z;
```

is the same as:

```
w = ((x + y) + z);
```

On the other hand, the following (almost nonsensical) expressions:

```
x = ~-~y;
w = x = y = z;
q = a?b:c?d:e?f:g;
```

are equivalent to:

```
x = ~(-(~y));
w = (x = (y = z));
q = a?b:(c?d:(e?f:g));
```

because the unary, assignment, and ternary conditional operators have right-to-left associativity.

5.3 Arithmetic Operators

Having explained operator precedence, associativity, and other background material, we can start to discuss the operators themselves. This section details the arithmetic operators:

Addition (+)
: The + operator adds numeric operands or concatenates string operands. If one operand is a string, the other is converted to a string and the two strings are then concatenated. Object operands are converted to numbers or strings that can be added or concatenated. The conversion is performed by the `valueOf()` method and/or the `toString()` method of the object.

Subtraction (-)
: When - is used as a binary operator, it subtracts its second operand from its first operand. If used with non-numeric operands, it attempts to convert them to numbers.

Multiplication (*)
: The * operator multiplies its two operands. If used with non-numeric operands, it attempts to convert them to numbers.

Division (/)

The / operator divides its first operand by its second. If used with non-numeric operands, it attempts to convert them to numbers. If you are used to programming languages that distinguish between integer and floating-point numbers, you might expect to get an integer result when you divide one integer by another. In JavaScript, however, all numbers are floating-point, so all divisions have floating-point results: `5/2` evaluates to `2.5`, not `2`. Division by zero yields positive or negative infinity, while `0/0` evaluates to `NaN`.

Modulo (%)

The % operator computes the first operand modulo the second operand. That is, it returns the remainder when the first operand is divided by the second operand an integral number of times. If used with non-numeric operands, the modulo operator attempts to convert them to numbers. The sign of the result is the same as the sign of the first operand. For example, `5 % 2` evaluates to `1`.

While the modulo operator is typically used with integer operands, it also works for floating-point values. For example, `-4.3 % 2.1` evaluates to `-0.1`.

Unary minus (-)

When - is used as a unary operator, before a single operand, it performs unary negation. In other words, it converts a positive value to an equivalently negative value, and vice versa. If the operand is not a number, this operator attempts to convert it to one.

Unary plus (+)

For symmetry with the unary minus operator, JavaScript also has a unary plus operator. This operator allows you to explicitly specify the sign of numeric literals, if you feel that this will make your code clearer:

```
var profit = +1000000;
```

In code like this, the + operator does nothing; it simply evaluates to the value of its argument. Note, however, that for non-numeric arguments, the + operator has the effect of converting the argument to a number. It returns `NaN` if the argument cannot be converted.

Increment (++)

The ++ operator increments (i.e., adds 1 to) its single operand, which must be a variable, an element of an array, or a property of an object. If the value of this variable, element, or property is not a number, the operator first attempts to convert it to one. The precise behavior of this operator depends on its position relative to the operand. When used before the operand, where it is known as the pre-increment operator, it increments the operand and evaluates to the incremented value of that operand. When used after the operand, where it is known as the post-increment operator, it increments its operand but evaluates to the *unincremented* value of that operand. If the value to be incremented is not a number, it is converted to one by this process.

For example, the following code sets both i and j to 2:

```
i = 1;
j = ++i;
```

But these lines set i to 2 and j to 1:

```
i = 1;
j = i++;
```

This operator, in both of its forms, is most commonly used to increment a counter that controls a loop. Note that, because of JavaScript's automatic semicolon insertion, you may not insert a line break between the post-increment or post-decrement operator and the operand that precedes it. If you do so, JavaScript will treat the operand as a complete statement by itself and will insert a semicolon before it.

Decrement (--)

The -- operator decrements (i.e., subtracts 1 from) its single numeric operand, which must be a variable, an element of an array, or a property of an object. If the value of this variable, element, or property is not a number, the operator first attempts to convert it to one. Like the ++ operator, the precise behavior of -- depends on its position relative to the operand. When used before the operand, it decrements and returns the decremented value. When used after the operand, it decrements the operand but returns the *undecremented* value.

5.4 Equality Operators

This section describes the JavaScript equality and inequality operators. These are operators that compare two values to determine whether they are the same or different and return a boolean value (true or false) depending on the result of the comparison. As we'll see in Chapter 6, they are most commonly used in things like if statements and for loops, to control the flow of program execution.

5.4.1 Equality (==) and Identity (===)

The == and === operators check whether two values are the same, using two different definitions of sameness. Both operators accept operands of any type, and both return true if their operands are the same and false if they are different. The === operator is known as the identity operator, and it checks whether its two operands are "identical" using a strict definition of sameness. The == operator is known as the equality operator; it checks whether its two operands are "equal" using a more relaxed definition of sameness that allows type conversions.

The identity operator is standardized by ECMAScript v3 and implemented in JavaScript 1.3 and later. With the introduction of the identity operator, JavaScript supports =, ==, and === operators. Be sure you understand the differences between the assignment, equality, and identity operators, and be careful to use the right one when coding! Although it is tempting to call all three operators "equals," it may help to reduce confusion if you read "gets or is assigned" for =, "is equal to" for ==, and "is identical to" for ===.

In JavaScript, numbers, strings, and boolean values are compared *by value*. In this case, two separate values are involved, and the == and === operators check that these two values are identical. This means that two variables are equal or identical only if they contain the same value. For example, two strings are equal only if they each contain exactly the same characters.

On the other hand, objects, arrays, and functions are compared *by reference*. This means that two variables are equal only if they *refer to* the same object. Two separate arrays are never equal or identical, even if they contain equal or identical elements. Two variables that contain references to objects, arrays, or functions are equal only if they refer to the same object, array, or function. If you want to test that two distinct objects contain the same properties or that two distinct arrays contain the same elements, you'll have to check the properties or elements individually for equality or identity. (And, if any of the properties or elements are themselves objects or arrays, you'll have to decide how deep you want the comparison to go.)

The following rules are used to determine whether two values are identical according to the === operator:

- If the two values have different types, they are not identical.
- If both values are numbers and have the same value, they are identical, unless either or both values are `NaN`, in which case they are not identical. The `NaN` value is never identical to any other value, including itself! To check whether a value is `NaN`, use the global `isNaN( )` function.
- If both values are strings and contain exactly the same characters in the same positions, they are identical. If the strings differ in length or content, they are not identical. Note that in some cases, the Unicode standard allows more than one way to encode the same string. For efficiency, however, JavaScript string comparison compares strictly on a character-by-character basis, and it assumes that all strings have been converted to a "normalized form" before they are compared. See the "String.localeCompare( )" reference page in the core reference section of this book for another way to compare strings.
- If both values are the boolean value `true` or both are the boolean value `false`, they are identical.
- If both values refer to the same object, array, or function, they are identical. If they refer to different objects (or arrays or functions) they are not identical, even if both objects have identical properties or both arrays have identical elements.
- If both values are `null` or both values are `undefined`, they are identical.

The following rules are used to determine whether two values are equal according to the == operator:

- If the two values have the same type, test them for identity. If the values are identical, they are equal; if they are not identical, they are not equal.
- If the two values do not have the same type, they may still be equal. Use the following rules and type conversions to check for equality:
  - If one value is `null` and the other is `undefined`, they are equal.
  - If one value is a number and the other is a string, convert the string to a number and try the comparison again, using the converted value.
  - If either value is `true`, convert it to 1 and try the comparison again. If either value is `false`, convert it to 0 and try the comparison again.
  - If one value is an object and the other is a number or string, convert the object to a primitive and try the comparison again. An object is converted to a primitive value by either its `toString()` method or its `valueOf()` method. The built-in classes of core JavaScript attempt `valueOf()` conversion before `toString()` conversion, except for the Date class, which performs `toString()` conversion. Objects that are not part of core JavaScript may convert themselves to primitive values in an implementation-defined way.
  - Any other combinations of values are not equal.

As an example of testing for equality, consider the comparison:

```
"1" == true
```

This expression evaluates to `true`, indicating that these very different-looking values are in fact equal. The boolean value `true` is first converted to the number 1, and the comparison is done again. Next, the string `"1"` is converted to the number 1. Since both numbers are now the same, the comparison returns `true`.

When the equality operator in JavaScript 1.1 attempted to convert a string to a number and failed, it displayed an error message noting that the string could not be converted, instead of converting the string to `NaN` and returning `false` as the result of the comparison. This bug has been fixed in JavaScript 1.2.

5.4.1.1 Equality and inequality in Netscape

The == operator always behaves as described previously, and the != operator always behaves as described in the next section, with one exception. In client-side JavaScript in Netscape 4 and later, when embedded in a `<script>` tag that explicitly specifies JavaScript 1.2 as its `language` attribute, the equality operator behaves like the identity operator, and the inequality operator behaves like the non-identity operator. To avoid this incompatibility, never use the `language="JavaScript1.2"` attribute to embed your client-side JavaScript code. See Section 11.6, "Netscape's JavaScript 1.2 Incompatibilities," for a complete list of similar JavaScript 1.2 incompatibilities.

5.4.2 Inequality (!=) and Non-Identity (!==)

The `!=` and `!==` operators test for the exact opposite of the `==` and `===` operators. The `!=` inequality operator returns `false` if two values are equal to each other and returns `true` otherwise. The `!==` non-identity operator returns `false` if two values are identical to each other and returns `true` otherwise. Note that this operator is standardized by ECMAScript v3 and implemented in JavaScript 1.3 and later.

As we'll see, the `!` operator computes the Boolean NOT operation. This makes it easy to remember that `!=` stands for "not equal to" and `!==` stands for "not identical to." See the previous section for details on how equality and identity are defined for different data types.

5.5 Relational Operators

This section describes the JavaScript relational operators. These are operators that test for a relationship (such as "less-than" or "property-of") between two values and return `true` or `false` depending on whether that relationship exists. As we'll see in Chapter 6, they are most commonly used in things like `if` statements and `while` loops, to control the flow of program execution.

5.5.1 Comparison Operators

The most commonly used types of relational operators are the comparison operators, which are used to determine the relative order of two values. The comparison operators are:

Less than (<)
: The < operator evaluates to `true` if its first operand is less than its second operand; otherwise it evaluates to `false`.

Greater than (>)
: The > operator evaluates to `true` if its first operand is greater than its second operand; otherwise it evaluates to `false`.

Less than or equal (<=)
: The <= operator evaluates to `true` if its first operand is less than or equal to its second operand; otherwise it evaluates to `false`.

Greater than or equal (>=)
: The >= operator evaluates to `true` if its first operand is greater than or equal to its second operand; otherwise it evaluates to `false`.

The operands of these comparison operators may be of any type. Comparison can be performed only on numbers and strings, however, so operands that are not numbers or strings are converted. Comparison and conversion occur as follows:

- If both operands are numbers, or if both convert to numbers, they are compared numerically.
- If both operands are strings or convert to strings, they are compared as strings.
- If one operand is or converts to a string and one is or converts to a number, the operator attempts to convert the string to a number and perform a numerical comparison. If the string does not represent a number, it converts to `NaN`, and the comparison is `false`. (In JavaScript 1.1, the string-to-number conversion causes an error instead of yielding `NaN`.)
- If an object can be converted to either a number or a string, JavaScript performs the numerical conversion. This means, for example, that Date objects are compared numerically, and it is meaningful to compare two dates to see whether one is earlier than the other.
- If the operands of the comparison operators cannot both be successfully converted to numbers or to strings, these operators always return `false`.
- If either operand is or converts to `NaN`, the comparison operator always yields `false`.

Keep in mind that string comparison is done on a strict character-by-character basis, using the numerical value of each character from the Unicode encoding. Although in some cases the Unicode standard allows equivalent strings to be encoded using different sequences of characters, the JavaScript comparison operators do not detect these encoding differences; they assume that all strings are expressed in normalized form. Note in particular that string comparison is case-sensitive, and in the Unicode encoding (at least for the ASCII subset), all capital letters are "less than" all lowercase letters. This rule can cause confusing results if you do not expect it. For example, according to the `<` operator, the string "Zoo" is less than the string "aardvark".

For a more robust string comparison algorithm, see the `String.localeCompare()` method, which also takes locale-specific definitions of "alphabetical order" into account. For case-insensitive comparisons, you must first convert the strings to all lowercase or all uppercase using `String.toLowerCase()` or `String.toUpperCase()`.

The `<=` (less-than-or-equal) and `>=` (greater-than-or-equal) operators do not rely on the equality or identity operators for determining whether two values are "equal." Instead, the less-than-or-equal operator is simply defined as "not greater than," and the greater-than-or-equal operator is defined as "not less than." The one exception is when either operand is (or converts to) `NaN`, in which case all four comparison operators return `false`.

5.5.2 The in Operator

The in operator expects a lefthand operand that is or can be converted to a string. It expects a righthand operand that is an object (or array). It evaluates to true if the lefthand value is the name of a property of the righthand object. For example:

```
var point = { x:1, y:1 };         // Define an object
var has_x_coord = "x" in point;  // Evaluates to true
var has_y_coord = "y" in point;  // Evaluates to true
var has_z_coord = "z" in point;  // Evaluates to false; not a 3-D point
var ts = "toString" in point;    // Inherited property; evaluates to true
```

5.5.3 The instanceof Operator

The instanceof operator expects a lefthand operand that is an object and a righthand operand that is the name of a class of objects. The operator evaluates to true if the lefthand object is an instance of the righthand class and evaluates to false otherwise. We'll see in Chapter 8 that, in JavaScript, classes of objects are defined by the constructor function that is used to initialize them. Thus, the righthand operand of instanceof should be the name of a constructor function. Note that all objects are instances of Object. For example:

```
var d = new Date();   // Create a new object with the Date( ) constructor
d instanceof Date;    // Evaluates to true; d was created with Date( )
d instanceof Object;  // Evaluates to true; all objects are instances of Object
d instanceof Number;  // Evaluates to false; d is not a Number object
var a = [1, 2, 3];    // Create an array with array literal syntax
a instanceof Array;   // Evaluates to true; a is an array
a instanceof Object;  // Evaluates to true; all arrays are objects
a instanceof RegExp;  // Evaluates to false; arrays are not regular expressions
```

If the lefthand operand of instanceof is not an object, or if the righthand operand is an object that is not a constructor function, instanceof returns false. On the other hand, it returns a runtime error if the righthand operand is not an object at all.

5.6 String Operators

As we've discussed in the previous sections, there are several operators that have special effects when their operands are strings.

The + operator concatenates two string operands. That is, it creates a new string that consists of the first string followed by the second. For example, the following expression evaluates to the string "hello there":

```
"hello" + " " + "there"
```

And the following lines produce the string "22":

```
a = "2"; b = "2";
c = a + b;
```

The <, <=, >, and >= operators compare two strings to determine what order they fall in. The comparison uses alphabetical order. As noted above, however, this alphabetical order is based on the Unicode character encoding used by JavaScript. In this encoding, all capital letters in the Latin alphabet come before (are less than) all lowercase letters, which can cause unexpected results.

The == and != operators work on strings, but, as we've seen, these operators work for all data types, and they do not have any special behavior when used with strings.

The + operator is a special one—it gives priority to string operands over numeric operands. As noted earlier, if either operand to + is a string (or an object), the other operand is converted to a string (or both operands are converted to strings) and concatenated, rather than added. On the other hand, the comparison operators perform string comparison only if *both* operands are strings. If only one operand is a string, JavaScript attempts to convert it to a number. The following lines illustrate:

```
1 + 2         // Addition. Result is 3.
"1" + "2"     // Concatenation. Result is "12".
"1" + 2       // Concatenation; 2 is converted to "2". Result is "12".
11 < 3        // Numeric comparison. Result is false.
"11" < "3"    // String comparison. Result is true.
"11" < 3      // Numeric comparison; "11" converted to 11. Result is false.
"one" < 3     // Numeric comparison; "one" converted to NaN. Result is false.
              // In JavaScript 1.1, this causes an error instead of NaN.
```

Finally, it is important to note that when the + operator is used with strings and numbers, it may not be associative. That is, the result may depend on the order in which operations are performed. This can be seen with examples like these:

```
s = 1 + 2 + " blind mice";    // Yields "3 blind mice"
t = "blind mice: " + 1 + 2;   // Yields "blind mice: 12"
```

The reason for this surprising difference in behavior is that the + operator works from left to right, unless parentheses change this order. Thus, the last two examples are equivalent to these:

```
s = (1 + 2) + "blind mice";     // 1st + yields number; 2nd yields string
t = ("blind mice: " + 1) + 2;   // Both operations yield strings
```

5.7 Logical Operators

The logical operators are typically used to perform Boolean algebra. They are often used in conjunction with comparison operators to express complex comparisons that involve more than one variable and are frequently used with the `if`, `while`, and `for` statements.

5.7.1 Logical AND (&&)

When used with boolean operands, the && operator performs the Boolean AND operation on the two values: it returns `true` if and only if both its first operand *and* its second operand are `true`. If one or both of these operands is `false`, it returns `false`.

The actual behavior of this operator is somewhat more complicated. It starts by evaluating its first operand, the expression on its left. If the value of this expression can be converted to `false` (for example, if the left operand evaluates to `null`, `0`, `""`, or `undefined`), the operator returns the value of the lefthand expression. Otherwise, it evaluates its second operand, the expression on its right, and returns the value of that expression.*

Note that, depending on the value of the lefthand expression, this operator may or may not evaluate the righthand expression. You may occasionally see code that purposely exploits this feature of the && operator. For example, the following two lines of JavaScript code have equivalent effects:

```
if (a == b) stop();
(a == b) && stop();
```

While some programmers (particularly Perl programmers) find this a natural and useful programming idiom, I recommend against using it. The fact that the righthand side is not guaranteed to be evaluated is a frequent source of bugs. Consider the following code, for example:

```
if ((a == null) && (b++ > 10)) stop();
```

This statement probably does not do what the programmer intended, since the increment operator on the righthand side is not evaluated whenever the comparison on the lefthand side is `false`. To avoid this problem, do not use expressions with side effects (assignments, increments, decrements, and function calls) on the righthand side of && unless you are quite sure you know exactly what you are doing.

Despite the fairly confusing way that this operator actually works, it is easiest, and perfectly safe, to think of it as merely a Boolean algebra operator. Although it does not actually return a boolean value, the value it returns can always be converted to a boolean value.

5.7.2 Logical OR (||)

When used with boolean operands, the `||` operator performs the Boolean OR operation on the two values: it returns `true` if either the first operand *or* the second operand is `true`, or if both are `true`. If both operands are `false`, it returns `false`.

Although the `||` operator is most often used simply as a Boolean OR operator, it, like the && operator, has more complex behavior. It starts by evaluating its first operand, the expression on its left. If the value of this expression can be converted to `true`, it

* In JavaScript 1.0 and JavaScript 1.1, if the lefthand expression evaluates to `false`, the && operator returns `false`, rather than returning the unconverted value of the lefthand expression.

returns the value of the lefthand expression. Otherwise, it evaluates its second operand, the expression on its right, and returns the value of that expression.*

As with the `&&` operator, you should avoid righthand operands that include side effects, unless you purposely want to make use of the fact that the righthand expression may not be evaluated.

Even when the `||` operator is used with operands that are not boolean values, it can still be considered a Boolean OR operator, since its return value, whatever the type, can be converted to a boolean value.

5.7.3 Logical NOT (!)

The `!` operator is a unary operator; it is placed before a single operand. Its purpose is to invert the boolean value of its operand. For example, if the variable `a` has the value `true` (or is a value that converts to `true`), `!a` has the value `false`. And if the expression `p && q` evaluates to `false` (or to a value that converts to `false`), `!(p && q)` evaluates to `true`. Note that you can convert any value `x` to a boolean value by applying this operator twice: `!!x`.

5.8 Bitwise Operators

Despite the fact that all numbers in JavaScript are floating-point, the bitwise operators require numeric operands that have integer values. They operate on these integer operands using a 32-bit integer representation instead of the equivalent floating-point representation. Four of these operators perform Boolean algebra on the individual bits of the operands, behaving as if each bit in each operand were a boolean value and performing similar operations to those performed by the logical operators we saw earlier. The other three bitwise operators are used to shift bits left and right.

In JavaScript 1.0 and JavaScript 1.1, the bitwise operators return `NaN` if used with operands that are not integers or that are too large to fit in a 32-bit integer representation. JavaScript 1.2 and ECMAScript, however, simply coerce the operands to 32-bit integers by dropping any fractional part of the operand or any bits beyond the 32nd. The shift operators require a righthand operand between 0 and 31. After converting this operand to a 32-bit integer as described earlier, they drop any bits beyond the 5th, which yields a number in the appropriate range.

If you are not familiar with binary numbers and the binary representation of decimal integers, you can skip the operators described in this section. The purpose of these operators is not described here; they are needed for low-level manipulation of binary numbers and are not commonly used in JavaScript programming. The bitwise operators are:

* In JavaScript 1.0 and JavaScript 1.1, if the lefthand expression could be converted to true, the operator returns true rather than returning the unconverted value of the lefthand expression.

Bitwise AND (&)

The `&` operator performs a Boolean AND operation on each bit of its integer arguments. A bit is set in the result only if the corresponding bit is set in both operands. For example, `0x1234 & 0x00FF` evaluates to `0x0034`.

Bitwise OR (|)

The | operator performs a Boolean OR operation on each bit of its integer arguments. A bit is set in the result if the corresponding bit is set in one or both of the operands. For example, `9 | 10` evaluates to `11`.

Bitwise XOR (^)

The ^ operator performs a Boolean exclusive OR operation on each bit of its integer arguments. Exclusive OR means that either operand one is true or operand two is true, but not both. A bit is set in this operation's result if a corresponding bit is set in one (but not both) of the two operands. For example, `9 ^ 10` evaluates to 3.

Bitwise NOT (~)

The ~ operator is a unary operator that appears before its single integer argument. It operates by reversing all bits in the operand. Because of the way signed integers are represented in JavaScript, applying the ~ operator to a value is equivalent to changing its sign and subtracting 1. For example `~0x0f` evaluates to `0xfffffff0`, or –16.

Shift left (<<)

The << operator moves all bits in its first operand to the left by the number of places specified in the second operand, which should be an integer between 0 and 31. For example, in the operation `a << 1`, the first bit (the ones bit) of a becomes the second bit (the twos bit), the second bit of a becomes the third, etc. A zero is used for the new first bit, and the value of the 32nd bit is lost. Shifting a value left by one position is equivalent to multiplying by 2, shifting two positions is equivalent to multiplying by 4, etc. For example, `7 << 1` evaluates to 14.

Shift right with sign (>>)

The >> operator moves all bits in its first operand to the right by the number of places specified in the second operand (an integer between 0 and 31). Bits that are shifted off the right are lost. The bits filled in on the left depend on the sign bit of the original operand, in order to preserve the sign of the result. If the first operand is positive, the result has zeros placed in the high bits; if the first operand is negative, the result has ones placed in the high bits. Shifting a value right one place is equivalent to dividing by 2 (discarding the remainder), shifting right two places is equivalent to integer division by 4, and so on. For example, `7 >> 1` evaluates to 3 and `-7 >> 1` evaluates to –4.

Shift right with zero fill (>>>)

The >>> operator is just like the >> operator, except that the bits shifted in on the left are always zero, regardless of the sign of the first operand. For example, `-1 >> 4` evaluates to –1, but `-1 >>> 4` evaluates to `268435455` (`0x0fffffff`).

5.9 Assignment Operators

As we saw in the discussion of variables in Chapter 4, = is used in JavaScript to assign a value to a variable. For example:

```
i = 0
```

While you might not normally think of such a line of JavaScript as an expression that can be evaluated, it is in fact an expression and, technically speaking, = is an operator.

The = operator expects its lefthand operand to be either a variable, the element of an array, or a property of an object. It expects its righthand operand to be an arbitrary value of any type. The value of an assignment expression is the value of the righthand operand. As a side effect, the = operator assigns the value on the right to the variable, element, or property on the left, so that future uses of the variable, element, or property refer to the value.

Because = is defined as an operator, you can include it in more complex expressions. For example, you can assign and test a value in the same expression with code like this:

```
(a = b) == 0
```

If you do this, be sure you are clear on the difference between the = and == operators!

The assignment operator has right-to-left associativity, which means that when multiple assignment operators appear in an expression, they are evaluated from right to left. Thus, you can write code like this to assign a single value to multiple variables:

```
i = j = k = 0;
```

Remember that each assignment expression has a value that is the value of the righthand side. So in the above code, the value of the first assignment (the rightmost one) becomes the righthand side for the second assignment (the middle one), and this value becomes the righthand side for the last (leftmost) assignment.

5.9.1 Assignment with Operation

Besides the normal = assignment operator, JavaScript supports a number of other assignment operators that provide shortcuts by combining assignment with some other operation. For example, the += operator performs addition and assignment. The following expression:

```
total += sales_tax
```

is equivalent to this one:

```
total = total + sales_tax
```

As you might expect, the += operator works for numbers or strings. For numeric operands, it performs addition and assignment; for string operands, it performs concatenation and assignment.

Similar operators include -=, *=, &=, and so on. Table 5-2 lists them all. In most cases, the expression:

```
a op= b
```

where *op* is an operator, is equivalent to the expression:

```
a = a op b
```

These expressions differ only if a contains side effects such as a function call or an increment operator.

Table 5-2. Assignment operators

Operator	Example	Equivalent
+=	a += b	a = a + b
-=	a -= b	a = a - b
*=	a *= b	a = a * b
/=	a /= b	a = a / b
%=	a %= b	a = a % b
<<=	a <<= b	a = a << b
>>=	a >>= b	a = a >> b
>>>=	a >>>= b	a = a >>> b
&=	a &= b	a = a & b
|=	a |= b	a = a | b
^=	a ^= b	a = a ^ b

5.10 Miscellaneous Operators

JavaScript supports a number of other miscellaneous operators, described in the following sections.

5.10.1 The Conditional Operator (?:)

The conditional operator is the only ternary operator (three operands) in JavaScript and is sometimes actually called the ternary operator. This operator is sometimes written ?:, although it does not appear quite that way in code. Because this operator has three operands, the first goes before the ?, the second goes between the ? and the :, and the third goes after the :. It is used like this:

```
x > 0 ? x*y : -x*y
```

The first operand of the conditional operator must be (or be convertable to) a boolean value—usually this is the result of a comparison expression. The second and third operands may have any value. The value returned by the conditional operator depends on the boolean value of the first operand. If that operand is true, the value of the conditional expression is the value of the second operand. If the first operand is false, the value of the conditional expression is the value of the third operand.

While you can achieve similar results using the if statement, the ?: operator often provides a handy shortcut. Here is a typical usage, which checks to be sure that a variable is defined, uses it if so, and provides a default value if not:

```
greeting = "hello " + (username != null ? username : "there");
```

This is equivalent to, but more compact than, the following if statement:

```
greeting = "hello ";
if (username != null)
    greeting += username;
else
    greeting += "there";
```

5.10.2 The typeof Operator

typeof is a unary operator that is placed before its single operand, which can be of any type. Its value is a string indicating the data type of the operand.

The typeof operator evaluates to "number", "string", or "boolean" if its operand is a number, string, or boolean value. It evaluates to "object" for objects, arrays, and (surprisingly) null. It evaluates to "function" for function operands and to "undefined" if the operand is undefined.

typeof evaluates to "object" when its operand is a Number, String, or Boolean wrapper object. It also evaluates to "object" for Date and RegExp objects. typeof evaluates to an implementation-dependent value for objects that are not part of core JavaScript but are provided by the context in which JavaScript is embedded. In client-side JavaScript, however, typeof typically evaluates to "object" for all client-side objects, just as it does for all core objects.

You might use the typeof operator in expressions like these:

```
typeof i
(typeof value == "string") ? "'" + value + "'" : value
```

Note that you can place parentheses around the operand to typeof, which makes typeof look like the name of a function rather than an operator keyword:

```
typeof(i)
```

Because typeof evaluates to "object" for all object and array types, it is useful only to distinguish objects from other, primitive types. In order to distinguish one object type from another, you must use other techniques, such as the instanceof operator or the constructor property (see the "Object.constructor" entry in the core reference section).

The typeof operator is defined by the ECMAScript v1 specification and is implemented in JavaScript 1.1 and later.

Core JavaScript

5.10.3 The Object Creation Operator (new)

The new operator creates a new object and invokes a constructor function to initialize it. new is a unary operator that appears before a constructor invocation. It has the following syntax:

```
new constructor(arguments)
```

constructor must be an expression that evaluates to a constructor function, and it should be followed by zero or more comma-separated arguments enclosed in parentheses. As a special case, for the new operator only, JavaScript simplifies the grammar by allowing the parentheses to be omitted if there are no arguments in the function call. Here are some examples using the new operator:

```
o = new Object;  // Optional parentheses omitted here
d = new Date();  // Returns a Date object representing the current time
c = new Rectangle(3.0, 4.0, 1.5, 2.75);  // Create an object of class Rectangle
obj[i] = new constructors[i]();
```

The new operator first creates a new object with no properties defined; next, it invokes the specified constructor function, passing the specified arguments and also passing the newly created object as the value of the this keyword. The constructor function can then use the this keyword to initialize the new object in any way desired. We'll learn more about the new operator, the this keyword, and constructor functions in Chapter 8.

The new operator can also be used to create arrays, using the new Array() syntax. We'll see more about creating and working with objects and arrays in Chapter 8 and Chapter 9.

5.10.4 The delete Operator

delete is a unary operator that attempts to delete the object property, array element, or variable specified as its operand.* It returns true if the deletion was successful, and false if the operand could not be deleted. Not all variables and properties can be deleted: some built-in core and client-side properties are immune from deletion, and user-defined variables declared with the var statement cannot be deleted. If delete is invoked on a nonexistent property, it returns true. (Surprisingly, the ECMAScript standard specifies that delete also evaluates to true if the operand is not a property, array element, or variable.) Here are some examples of the use of this operator:

```
var o = {x:1, y:2};  // Define a variable; initialize it to an object
delete o.x;          // Delete one of the object properties; returns true
```

* If you are a C++ programmer, note that the delete operator in JavaScript is nothing like the delete operator in C++. In JavaScript, memory deallocation is handled automatically by garbage collection, and you never have to worry about explicitly freeing up memory. Thus, there is no need for a C++-style delete to delete entire objects.

```
typeof o.x;          // Property does not exist; returns "undefined"
delete o.x;          // Delete a nonexistent property; returns true
delete o;            // Can't delete a declared variable; returns false
delete 1;            // Can't delete an integer; returns true
x = 1;               // Implicitly declare a variable without var keyword
delete x;            // Can delete this kind of variable; returns true
x;                   // Runtime error: x is not defined
```

Note that a deleted property, variable, or array element is not merely set to the `undefined` value. When a property is deleted, the property ceases to exist. See the related discussion in Section 4.3.2, "Undefined Versus Unassigned."

`delete` is standardized by the ECMAScript v1 specification and implemented in JavaScript 1.2 and later. Note that the `delete` operator exists in JavaScript 1.0 and 1.1 but does not actually perform deletion in those versions of the language. Instead, it merely sets the specified property, variable, or array element to `null`.

It is important to understand that `delete` affects only properties, not objects referred to by those properties. Consider the following code:

```
var my = new Object( );     // Create an object named "my"
my.hire = new Date( );      // my.hire refers to a Date object
my.fire = my.hire;          // my.fire refers to the same object
delete my.hire;             // hire property is deleted; returns true
document.write(my.fire);    // But my.fire still refers to the Date object
```

5.10.5 The void Operator

`void` is a unary operator that appears before its single operand, which may be of any type. The purpose of this operator is an unusual one: it discards its operand value and returns `undefined`. The most common use for this operator is in a client-side `javascript:` URL, where it allows you to evaluate an expression for its side effects without the browser displaying the value of the evaluated expression.

For example, you might use the `void` operator in an HTML tag as follows:

```
<a href="javascript:void window.open( );">Open New Window</a>
```

Another use for `void` is to purposely generate the `undefined` value. `void` is specified by ECMAScript v1 and implemented in JavaScript 1.1. The global `undefined` property, however, is specified by ECMAScript v3 and implemented in JavaScript 1.5. Thus, for backward compatibility, you may find it useful to use an expression like `void 0` instead of relying on the `undefined` property.

5.10.6 The Comma Operator (,)

The comma operator is a simple one. It evaluates its left argument, evaluates its right argument, and then returns the value of its right argument. Thus, the following line:

```
i=0, j=1, k=2;
```

evaluates to 2, and is basically equivalent to:

```
i = 0;
j = 1;
k = 2;
```

This strange operator is useful only in a few limited circumstances, primarily when you need to evaluate several independent expressions with side effects in a situation where only a single expression is allowed. In practice, the comma operator is really used only in conjunction with the for loop statement, which we'll see in Chapter 6.

5.10.7 Array and Object Access Operators

As noted briefly in Chapter 3, you can access elements of an array using square brackets ([]), and you can access elements of an object using a dot (.). Both [] and . are treated as operators in JavaScript.

The . operator expects an object as its left operand and an identifier (a property name) as its right operand. The right operand should not be a string or a variable that contains a string; it should be the literal name of the property or method, without quotes of any kind. Here are some examples:

```
document.lastModified
navigator.appName
frames[0].length
document.write("hello world")
```

If the specified property does not exist in the object, JavaScript does not issue an error, but instead simply returns undefined as the value of the expression.

Most operators allow arbitrary expressions for either operand, as long as the type of the operand is suitable. The . operator is an exception: the righthand operand must be an identifier. Nothing else is allowed.

The [] operator allows access to array elements. It also allows access to object properties without the restrictions that the . operator places on the righthand operand. If the first operand (which goes before the left bracket) refers to an array, the second operand (which goes between the brackets) should be an expression that evaluates to an integer. For example:

```
frames[1]
document.forms[i + j]
document.forms[i].elements[j++]
```

If the first operand to the [] operator is a reference to an object, the second operand should be an expression that evaluates to a string that names a property of the object. Note that in this case, the second operand is a string, not an identifier. It should be a constant in quotes or a variable or expression that refers to a string. For example:

```
document["lastModified"]
frames[0]['length']
data["val" + i]
```

The [] operator is typically used to access the elements of an array. It is less convenient than the . operator for accessing properties of an object because of the need to quote the name of the property. When an object is used as an associative array, however, and the property names are dynamically generated, the . operator cannot be used; only the [] operator will do. This is commonly the case when you use the for/in loop, which is introduced in Chapter 6. For example, the following JavaScript code uses a for/in loop and the [] operator to print out the names and values of all of the properties in an object o:

```
for (f in o) {
    document.write('o.' + f + ' = ' + o[f]);
    document.write('<br>');
}
```

5.10.8 The Function Call Operator

The ( ) operator is used to invoke functions in JavaScript. This is an unusual operator in that it does not have a fixed number of operands. The first operand is always the name of a function or an expression that refers to a function. It is followed by the left parenthesis and any number of additional operands, which may be arbitrary expressions, each separated from the next with a comma. The right parenthesis follows the final operand. The ( ) operator evaluates each of its operands and then invokes the function specified by the first operand, with the values of the remaining operands passed as arguments. For example:

```
document.close( )
Math.sin(x)
alert("Welcome " + name)
Date.UTC(2000, 11, 31, 23, 59, 59)
funcs[i].f(funcs[i].args[0], funcs[i].args[1])
```

CHAPTER 6

Statements

As we saw in the last chapter, expressions are JavaScript phrases that can be evaluated to yield a value. Operators within an expression may have side effects, but in general, expressions don't do anything. To make something happen, you use a JavaScript *statement*, which is akin to a complete sentence or command. This chapter describes the various statements in JavaScript and explains their syntax. A JavaScript program is simply a collection of statements, so once you are familiar with the statements of JavaScript, you can begin writing JavaScript programs.

Before we examine JavaScript statements, recall from Section 2.4, "Optional Semicolons," that statements in JavaScript are separated from each other with semicolons. If you place each statement on a separate line, however, JavaScript allows you to leave out the semicolons. Nevertheless, it is a good idea to get in the habit of using semicolons everywhere.

6.1 Expression Statements

The simplest kinds of statements in JavaScript are expressions that have side effects. We've seen this sort of statement in Chapter 5. Assignment statements are one major category of expression statements. For example:

```
s = "Hello " + name;
i *= 3;
```

The increment and decrement operators, ++ and --, are related to assignment statements. These have the side effect of changing a variable value, just as if an assignment had been performed:

```
counter++;
```

The delete operator has the important side effect of deleting an object property. Thus, it is almost always used as a statement, rather than as part of a larger expression:

```
delete o.x;
```

Function calls are another major category of expression statements. For example:

```
alert("Welcome, " + name);
window.close( );
```

These client-side function calls are expressions, but they also affect the web browser, so they are statements, too. If a function does not have any side effects, there is no sense in calling it, unless it is part of an assignment statement. For example, you wouldn't just compute a cosine and discard the result:

```
Math.cos(x);
```

Instead, you'd compute the value and assign it to a variable for future use:

```
cx = Math.cos(x);
```

Again, please note that each line of code in each of these examples is terminated with a semicolon.

6.2 Compound Statements

In Chapter 5, we saw that the comma operator can be used to combine a number of expressions into a single expression. JavaScript also has a way to combine a number of statements into a single statement, or *statement block*. This is done simply by enclosing any number of statements within curly braces. Thus, the following lines act as a single statement and can be used anywhere that JavaScript expects a single statement:

```
{
    x = Math.PI;
    cx = Math.cos(x);
    alert("cos(" + x + ") = " + cx);
}
```

Note that although this statement block acts as a single statement, it does *not* end with a semicolon. The primitive statements within the block end in semicolons, but the block itself does not.

Although combining expressions with the comma operator is an infrequently used technique, combining statements into larger statement blocks is extremely common. As we'll see in the following sections, a number of JavaScript statements themselves contain statements (just as expressions can contain other expressions); these statements are *compound statements*. Formal JavaScript syntax specifies that each of these compound statements contains a single substatement. Using statement blocks, you can place any number of statements within this single allowed substatement.

To execute a compound statement, the JavaScript interpreter simply executes the statements that comprise it one after another, in the order in which they are written. Normally, the JavaScript interpreter executes all of the statements. In some circumstances, however, a compound statement may terminate abruptly. This termination occurs if the compound statement contains a `break`, `continue`, `return`, or `throw` statement, if it causes an error, or if it calls a function that causes an uncaught error or throws an uncaught exception. We'll learn more about these abrupt terminations in later sections.

6.3 if

The `if` statement is the fundamental control statement that allows JavaScript to make decisions, or, more precisely, to execute statements conditionally. This statement has two forms. The first is:

```
if (expression)
    statement
```

In this form, *`expression`* is evaluated. If the resulting value is `true` or can be converted to true, *`statement`* is executed. If *`expression`* is `false` or converts to `false`, *`statement`* is not executed. For example:

```
if (username == null)       // If username is null or undefined,
    username = "John Doe";  // define it
```

Or similarly:

```
// If username is null, undefined, 0, "", or NaN, it converts to false,
// and this statement will assign a new value to it.
if (!username) username = "John Doe";
```

Although they look extraneous, the parentheses around the expression are a required part of the syntax for the `if` statement.

As mentioned in the previous section, we can always replace a single statement with a statement block. So the `if` statement might also look like this:

```
if ((address == null) || (address == "")) {
    address = "undefined";
    alert("Please specify a mailing address.");
}
```

The indentation used in these examples is not mandatory. Extra spaces and tabs are ignored in JavaScript, and since we used semicolons after all the primitive statements, these examples could have been written all on one line. Using line breaks and indentation as shown here, however, makes the code easier to read and understand.

The second form of the `if` statement introduces an else clause that is executed when *`expression`* is `false`. Its syntax is:

```
if (expression)
    statement1
else
    statement2
```

In this form of the statement, *`expression`* is evaluated, and if it is `true`, *`statement1`* is executed; otherwise, *`statement2`* is executed. For example:

```
if (username != null)
    alert("Hello " + username + "\nWelcome to my home page.");
```

```
else {
    username = prompt("Welcome!\n What is your name?");
    alert("Hello " + username);
}
```

When you have nested if statements with else clauses, some caution is required to ensure that the else clause goes with the appropriate if statement. Consider the following lines:

```
i = j = 1;
k = 2;
if (i == j)
    if (j == k)
        document.write("i equals k");
else
    document.write("i doesn't equal j");     // WRONG!!
```

In this example, the inner if statement forms the single statement allowed by the syntax of the outer if statement. Unfortunately, it is not clear (except from the hint given by the indentation) which if the else goes with. And in this example, the indenting hint is wrong, because a JavaScript interpreter actually interprets the previous example as:

```
if (i == j) {
    if (j == k)
        document.write("i equals k");
else
    document.write("i doesn't equal j");     // OOPS!
}
```

The rule in JavaScript (as in most programming languages) is that an else clause is part of the nearest if statement. To make this example less ambiguous and easier to read, understand, maintain, and debug, you should use curly braces:

```
if (i == j) {
    if (j == k) {
        document.write("i equals k");
    }
}
else {  // What a difference the location of a curly brace makes!
    document.write("i doesn't equal j");
}
```

Although it is not the style used in this book, many programmers make a habit of enclosing the bodies of if and else statements (as well as other compound statements, such as while loops) within curly braces, even when the body consists of only a single statement. Doing so consistently can prevent the sort of problem just shown.

6.4 else if

We've seen that the if/else statement is useful for testing a condition and executing one of two pieces of code, depending on the outcome. But what about when we need to execute one of many pieces of code? One way to do this is with an else if statement. else if is not really a JavaScript statement, but simply a frequently used programming idiom that results when repeated if/else statements are used:

```
if (n == 1) {
    // Execute code block #1
}
else if (n == 2) {
    // Execute code block #2
}
else if (n == 3) {
    // Execute code block #3
}
else {
    // If all else fails, execute block #4
}
```

There is nothing special about this code. It is just a series of if statements, where each if is part of the else clause of the previous statement. Using the else if idiom is preferable to, and more legible than, writing these statements out in their syntactically equivalent fully nested form:

```
if (n == 1) {
    // Execute code block #1
}
else {
    if (n == 2) {
        // Execute code block #2
    }
    else {
        if (n == 3) {
            // Execute code block #3
        }
        else {
            // If all else fails, execute block #4
        }
    }
}
```

6.5 switch

An if statement causes a branch in the flow of a program's execution. You can use multiple if statements, as in the previous section, to perform a multiway branch. However, this is not always the best solution, especially when all of the branches depend on the value of a single variable. In this case, it is wasteful to repeatedly check the value of the same variable in multiple if statements.

The switch statement (implemented in JavaScript 1.2 and standardized by ECMAScript v3) handles exactly this situation, and it does so more efficiently than repeated if statements. The JavaScript switch statement is quite similar to the switch statement in Java or C. The switch keyword is followed by an expression and a block of code, much like the if statement:

```
switch(expression) {
    statements
}
```

However, the full syntax of a switch statement is more complex than this. Various locations in the block of code are labeled with the case keyword followed by a value and a colon. When a switch executes, it computes the value of *expression* and then looks for a case label that matches that value. If it finds one, it starts executing the block of code at the first statement following the case label. If it does not find a case label with a matching value, it starts execution at the first statement following a special-case default: label. Or, if there is no default: label, it skips the block of code altogether.

switch is a confusing statement to explain; its operation becomes much clearer with an example. The following switch statement is equivalent to the repeated if/else statements shown in the previous section:

```
switch(n) {
  case 1:                      // Start here if n == 1
    // Execute code block #1.
    break;                     // Stop here
  case 2:                      // Start here if n == 2
    // Execute code block #2.
    break;                     // Stop here
  case 3:                      // Start here if n == 3
    // Execute code block #3.
    break;                     // Stop here
  default:                     // If all else fails...
    // Execute code block #4.
    break;                     // stop here
}
```

Note the break keyword used at the end of each case in the code above. The break statement, described later in this chapter, causes execution to jump to the end of a switch statement or loop. The case clauses in a switch statement specify only the *starting point* of the desired code; they do not specify any ending point. In the absence of break statements, a switch statement begins executing its block of code at the case label that matches the value of its *expression* and continues executing statements until it reaches the end of the block. On rare occasions, it is useful to write code like this that falls through from one case label to the next, but 99% of the time you should be careful to end every case within a switch with a break statement. (When using switch inside a function, however, you may use a return statement instead of a break statement. Both serve to terminate the switch statement and prevent execution from falling through to the next case.)

Here is a more realistic example of the switch statement; it converts a value to a string in a way that depends on the type of the value:

```
function convert(x) {
    switch(typeof x) {
      case 'number':            // Convert the number to a hexadecimal integer
        return x.toString(16);
      case 'string':            // Return the string enclosed in quotes
        return '"' + x + '"';
      case 'boolean':           // Convert to TRUE or FALSE, in uppercase
        return x.toString().toUpperCase();
      default:                  // Convert any other type in the usual way
        return x.toString()
    }
}
```

Note that in the two previous examples, the case keywords are followed by number and string literals. This is how the switch statement is most often used in practice, but note that the ECMAScript v3 standard allows each case to be followed by an arbitrary expression.* For example:

```
case 60*60*24:
case Math.PI:
case n+1:
case a[0]:
```

The switch statement first evaluates the expression that follows the switch keyword, then evaluates the case expressions, in the order in which they appear, until it finds a value that matches.† The matching case is determined using the === identity operator, not the == equality operator, so the expressions must match without any type conversion.

Note that it is not good programming practice to use case expressions that contain side effects such as function calls or assignments, because not all of the case expressions are evaluated each time the switch statement is executed. When side effects occur only sometimes, it can be difficult to understand and predict the correct behavior of your program. The safest course is simply to limit your case expressions to constant expressions.

As explained earlier, if none of the case expressions match the switch expression, the switch statement begins executing its body at the statement labeled default:. If there is no default: label, the switch statement skips its body altogether. Note that in the earlier examples, the default: label appears at the end of the switch body, following all the case labels. This is a logical and common place for it, but it can actually appear anywhere within the body of the statement.

* This makes the JavaScript switch statement much different from the switch statement of C, C++, and Java. In those languages, the case expressions must be compile-time constants, they must evaluate to integers or other integral types, and they must all evaluate to the same type.

† This means that the JavaScript switch statement is not nearly as efficient as the switch statement in C, C++, and Java. Since the case expressions in those languages are compile-time constants, they never need to be evaluated at runtime as they are in JavaScript. Furthermore, since the case expressions are integral values in C, C++, and Java, the switch statement can often be implemented using a highly efficient "jump table."

The `switch` statement is implemented in JavaScript 1.2, but it does not fully conform to the ECMAScript specification. In JavaScript 1.2, `case` expressions must be literals or compile-time constants that do not involve any variables or method calls. Furthermore, although ECMAScript allows the `switch` and `case` expressions to be of any type, JavaScript 1.2 and JavaScript 1.3 require that the expressions evaluate to primitive numbers, strings, or boolean values.

6.6 while

Just as the `if` statement is the basic control statement that allows JavaScript to make decisions, the `while` statement is the basic statement that allows JavaScript to perform repetitive actions. It has the following syntax:

```
while (expression)
    statement
```

The `while` statement works by first evaluating *`expression`*. If it is `false`, JavaScript moves on to the next statement in the program. If it is `true`, the *`statement`* that forms the body of the loop is executed and *`expression`* is evaluated again. Again, if the value of *`expression`* is `false`, JavaScript moves on to the next statement in the program; otherwise, it executes *`statement`* again. This cycle continues until *`expression`* evaluates to `false`, at which point the `while` statement ends and JavaScript moves on. Note that you can create an infinite loop with the syntax `while(true)`.

Usually, you do not want JavaScript to perform exactly the same operation over and over again. In almost every loop, one or more variables change with each *iteration* of the loop. Since the variables change, the actions performed by executing *`statement`* may differ each time through the loop. Furthermore, if the changing variable or variables are involved in *`expression`*, the value of the expression may be different each time through the loop. This is important—otherwise, an expression that starts off `true` would never change and the loop would never end! Here is an example `while` loop:

```
var count = 0;
while (count < 10) {
    document.write(count + "<br>");
    count++;
}
```

As you can see, the variable `count` starts off at 0 in this example and is incremented each time the body of the loop runs. Once the loop has executed 10 times, the expression becomes `false` (i.e., the variable `count` is no longer less than 10), the `while` statement finishes, and JavaScript can move on to the next statement in the program. Most loops have a counter variable like `count`. The variable names `i`, `j`, and `k` are commonly used as a loop counters, though you should use more descriptive names if it makes your code easier to understand.

6.7 do/while

The `do/while` loop is much like a `while` loop, except that the loop expression is tested at the bottom of the loop rather than at the top. This means that the body of the loop is always executed at least once. The syntax is:

```
do
    statement
while (expression);
```

The `do/while` statement is implemented in JavaScript 1.2 and later and standardized by ECMAScript v3.

The `do/while` loop is less commonly used than its `while` cousin. This is because, in practice, it is somewhat uncommon to encounter a situation in which you are always sure that you want a loop to execute at least once. For example:

```
function printArray(a) {
    if (a.length == 0)
        document.write("Empty Array");
    else {
        var i = 0;
        do {
          document.write(a[i] + "<br>");
        } while (++i < a.length);
    }
}
```

There are a couple of differences between the `do/while` loop and the ordinary `while` loop. First, the `do` loop requires both the `do` keyword (to mark the beginning of the loop) and the `while` keyword (to mark the end and introduce the loop condition). Also, unlike the `while` loop, the `do` loop is terminated with a semicolon. This is because the `do` loop ends with the loop condition, rather than simply with a curly brace that marks the end of the loop body.

In JavaScript 1.2, there is a bug in the behavior of the `continue` statement (see Section 6.12, "continue") when it is used inside a `do/while` loop. For this reason, you should avoid the use of `continue` within `do/while` statements in JavaScript 1.2.

6.8 for

The `for` statement provides a looping construct that is often more convenient than the `while` statement. The `for` statement takes advantage of a pattern common to most loops (including the earlier `while` loop example). Most loops have a counter variable of some kind. This variable is initialized before the loop starts and is tested as part of the *expression* evaluated before each iteration of the loop. Finally, the counter variable is incremented or otherwise updated at the end of the loop body, just before *expression* is evaluated again.

The initialization, the test, and the update are the three crucial manipulations of a loop variable; the `for` statement makes these three steps an explicit part of the loop syntax. This makes it especially easy to understand what a `for` loop is doing and prevents mistakes such as forgetting to initialize or increment the loop variable. The syntax of the `for` statement is:

```
for(initialize ; test ; increment)
    statement
```

The simplest way to explain what this `for` loop does is to show the equivalent `while` loop:*

```
initialize;
while(test) {
    statement
    increment;
}
```

In other words, the *`initialize`* expression is evaluated once, before the loop begins. To be useful, this is an expression with side effects (usually an assignment). JavaScript also allows *`initialize`* to be a `var` variable declaration statement, so that you can declare and initialize a loop counter at the same time. The *`test`* expression is evaluated before each iteration and controls whether the body of the loop is executed. If the *`test`* expression is `true`, the *`statement`* that is the body of the loop is executed. Finally, the *`increment`* expression is evaluated. Again, this must be an expression with side effects in order to be useful. Generally, either it is an assignment expression or it uses the `++` or `--` operators.

The example `while` loop of the previous section can be rewritten as the following `for` loop, which counts from 0 to 9:

```
for(var count = 0 ; count < 10 ; count++)
    document.write(count + "<br>");
```

Notice that this syntax places all the important information about the loop variable on a single line, which makes it clear how the loop executes. Also note that placing the *`increment`* expression in the `for` statement itself simplifies the body of the loop to a single statement; we don't even need to use curly braces to produce a statement block.

Loops can become a lot more complex than these simple examples, of course, and sometimes multiple variables change with each iteration of the loop. This situation is the only place that the comma operator is commonly used in JavaScript—it provides a way to combine multiple initialization and increment expressions into a single expression suitable for use in a `for` loop. For example:

```
for(i = 0, j = 10 ; i < 10 ; i++, j--)
    sum += i * j;
```

* As we will see when we consider the `continue` statement, this `while` loop is not an exact equivalent to the `for` loop.

6.9 for/in

The for keyword is used in two ways in JavaScript. We've just seen how it is used in the for loop. It is also used in the for/in statement. This statement is a somewhat different kind of loop with the following syntax:

```
for (variable in object)
    statement
```

variable should be either the name of a variable, a var statement declaring a variable, an element of an array, or a property of an object (i.e., it should be something suitable as the leftthand side of an assignment expression). *object* is the name of an object or an expression that evaluates to an object. As usual, *statement* is the statement or statement block that forms the body of the loop.

You can loop through the elements of an array by simply incrementing an index variable each time through a while or for loop. The for/in statement provides a way to loop through the properties of an object. The body of the for/in loop is executed once for each property of *object*. Before the body of the loop is executed, the name of one of the object's properties is assigned to *variable*, as a string. Within the body of the loop, you can use this variable to look up the value of the object's property with the [] operator. For example, the following for/in loop prints the name and value of each property of an object:

```
for (var prop in my_object) {
    document.write("name: " + prop + "; value: " + my_object[prop], "<br>");
}
```

Note that the *variable* in the for/in loop may be an arbitrary expression, as long as it evaluates to something suitable for the lefthand side of an assignment. This expression is evaluated each time through the loop, which means that it may evaluate differently each time. For example, you could use code like the following to copy the names of all object properties into an array:

```
var o = {x:1, y:2, z:3};
var a = new Array( );
var i = 0;
for(a[i++] in o) /* empty loop body */;
```

JavaScript arrays are simply a specialized kind of object. Therefore, the for/in loop enumerates array indexes as well as object properties. For example, following the previous code block with this line enumerates the array "properties" 0, 1, and 2:

```
for(i in a) alert(i);
```

The for/in loop does not specify the order in which the properties of an object are assigned to the variable. There is no way to tell what the order will be in advance, and the behavior may differ between implementations or versions of JavaScript. If the body of a for/in loop deletes a property that has not yet been enumerated, that property will not be enumerated. If the body of the loop defines new properties, whether or not those properties will be enumerated by the loop is implementation-dependent.

The for/in loop does not actually loop through all possible properties of all objects. In the same way that some object properties are flagged to be read-only or permanent (nondeletable), certain properties are flagged to be nonenumerable. These properties are not enumerated by the for/in loop. While all user-defined properties are enumerated, many built-in properties, including all built-in methods, are not enumerated. As we'll see in Chapter 8, objects can inherit properties from other objects. Inherited properties that are user-defined are also enumerated by the for/in loop.

6.10 Labels

The case and default: labels used in conjunction with the switch statement are a special case of a more general label statement. In JavaScript 1.2, any statement may be labeled by preceding it with an identifier name and a colon:

```
identifier: statement
```

The *identifier* can be any legal JavaScript identifier that is not a reserved word. Label names are distinct from variable and function names, so you do not need to worry about name collisions if you give a label the same name as a variable or function. Here is an example of a labeled while statement:

```
parser:
  while(token != null) {
      // Code omitted here
}
```

By labeling a statement, you give it a name that you can use to refer to it elsewhere in your program. You can label any statement, although the only statements that are commonly labeled are loops: while, do/while, for, and for/in. By giving a loop a name, you can use break and continue to exit the loop or to exit a single iteration of the loop.

6.11 break

The break statement causes the innermost enclosing loop or a switch statement to exit immediately. Its syntax is simple:

```
break;
```

Because it causes a loop or switch to exit, this form of the break statement is legal only if it appears within one of these statements.

ECMAScript v3 and JavaScript 1.2 allow the break keyword to be followed by the name of a label:

```
break labelname;
```

Note that *labelname* is simply an identifier; it is not followed by a colon, as it would be when defining a labeled statement.

When break is used with a label, it jumps to the end of, or terminates, the named statement, which may be any enclosing statement. The named statement need not be a loop or switch; a break statement used with a label need not even be contained within a loop or switch. The only restriction on the label of the break statement is that it name an *enclosing* statement. The label can name an if statement, for example, or even a block of statements grouped within curly braces, for the sole purpose of naming the block with a label.

As discussed in Chapter 2, a newline is not allowed between the break keyword and the *labelname*. This is an oddity of JavaScript syntax caused by its automatic insertion of omitted semicolons. If you break a line of code between the break keyword and the following label, JavaScript assumes you meant to use the simple, unlabeled form of the statement and adds a semicolon for you.

We've already seen examples of the break statement within a switch statement. In loops, it is typically used to exit prematurely when, for whatever reason, there is no longer any need to complete the loop. When a loop has complex termination conditions, it is often easier to implement some of these conditions with break statements, rather than trying to express them all in a single loop expression.

The following code searches the elements of an array for a particular value. The loop terminates naturally when it reaches the end of the array; it terminates with a break statement if it finds what it is looking for in the array:

```
for(i = 0; i < a.length; i++) {
    if (a[i] == target)
        break;
}
```

You need the labeled form of the break statement only when you are using nested loops or switch statements and need to break out of a statement that is not the innermost one.

The following example shows labeled for loops and labeled break statements. See if you can figure out what its output will be:

```
outerloop:
  for(var i = 0; i < 10; i++) {
    innerloop:
      for(var j = 0; j < 10; j++) {
          if (j > 3) break;             // Quit the innermost loop
          if (i == 2) break innerloop;  // Do the same thing
          if (i == 4) break outerloop;  // Quit the outer loop
          document.write("i = " + i + " j = " + j + "<br>");
      }
  }
  document.write("FINAL i = " + i + " j = " + j + "<br>");
```

6.12 continue

The `continue` statement is similar to the `break` statement. Instead of exiting a loop, however, `continue` restarts a loop in a new iteration. The `continue` statement's syntax is just as simple as the `break` statement's:

```
continue;
```

In ECMAScript v3 and JavaScript 1.2, the `continue` statement can also be used with a label:

```
continue labelname;
```

The `continue` statement, in both its labeled and unlabeled forms, can be used only within the body of a `while`, `do/while`, `for`, or `for/in` loop. Using it anywhere else causes a syntax error.

When the `continue` statement is executed, the current iteration of the enclosing loop is terminated and the next iteration begins. This means different things for different types of loops:

- In a `while` loop, the specified *`expression`* at the beginning of the loop is tested again, and if it's `true`, the loop body is executed starting from the top.
- In a `do/while` loop, execution skips to the bottom of the loop, where the loop condition is tested again before restarting the loop at the top. Note, however, that JavaScript 1.2 contains a bug that causes the `continue` statement to jump directly to the top of a `do/while` loop without testing the loop condition. Therefore, if you plan to use a `continue` statement in a loop, you should avoid the `do/while` loop. This is not a serious problem, however, because you can always replace a `do/while` loop with an equivalent `while` loop.
- In a `for` loop, the *`increment`* expression is evaluated and the *`test`* expression is tested again to determine if another iteration should be done.
- In a `for/in` loop, the loop starts over with the next property name being assigned to the specified variable.

Note the difference in behavior of the `continue` statement in the `while` and `for` loops—a `while` loop returns directly to its condition, but a `for` loop first evaluates its *`increment`* expression and then returns to its condition. Previously, in the discussion of the `for` loop, I explained the behavior of the `for` loop in terms of an equivalent `while` loop. Because the `continue` statement behaves differently for these two loops, it is not possible to perfectly simulate a `for` loop with a `while` loop.

The following example shows an unlabeled `continue` statement being used to exit the current iteration of a loop when an error occurs:

```
for(i = 0; i < data.length; i++) {
    if (data[i] == null)
        continue;  // Can't proceed with undefined data
    total += data[i];
}
```

Like the break statement, the continue statement can be used in its labeled form within nested loops, when the loop to be restarted is not the immediately enclosing loop. Also, like the break statement, line breaks are not allowed between the continue statement and its *labelname*.

6.13 var

The var statement allows you to explicitly declare a variable or variables. The syntax of this statement is:

```
var name_1 [ = value_1] [ ,..., name_n [= value_n]]
```

The var keyword is followed by a comma-separated list of variables to declare; each variable in the list may optionally have an initializer expression that specifies its initial value. For example:

```
var i;
var j = 0;
var p, q;
var greeting = "hello" + name;
var x = 2.34, y = Math.cos(0.75), r, theta;
```

The var statement defines each named variable by creating a property with that name either in the call object of the enclosing function or, if the declaration does not appear within a function body, in the global object. The property or properties created by a var statement cannot be deleted with the delete operator. Note that enclosing a var statement in a with statement (see Section 6.18, "with") does not change its behavior.

If no initial value is specified for a variable with the var statement, the variable is defined but its initial value is undefined.

Note that the var statement can also appear as part of the for and for/in loops. For example:

```
for(var i = 0; i < 10; i++) document.write(i, "<br>");
for(var i = 0, j=10; i < 10; i++,j--) document.write(i*j, "<br>");
for(var i in o) document.write(i, "<br>");
```

Chapter 4 contains much more information on JavaScript variables and variable declarations.

6.14 function

The function statement defines a JavaScript function. It has the following syntax:

```
function funcname([arg1 [,arg2 [..., argn]]]) {
    statements
}
```

funcname is the name of the function being defined. This must be an identifier, not a string or an expression. The function name is followed by a comma-separated list of argument names in parentheses. These identifiers can be used within the body of the function to refer to the argument values passed when the function is invoked.

The body of the function is composed of any number of JavaScript statements, contained within curly braces. These statements are not executed when the function is defined. Instead, they are compiled and associated with the new function object for execution when the function is invoked with the `()` function call operator. Note that the curly braces are a required part of the `function` statement. Unlike statement blocks used with `while` loops and other statements, a function body requires curly braces, even if the body consists of only a single statement.

A function definition creates a new function object and stores that object in a newly created property named *funcname*. Here are some example function definitions:

```
function welcome( ) { alert("Welcome to my home page!"); }

function print(msg) {
    document.write(msg, "<br>");
}

function hypotenuse(x, y) {
    return Math.sqrt(x*x + y*y);  // return is documented below
}

function factorial(n) {            // A recursive function
    if (n <= 1) return 1;
    return n * factorial(n - 1);
}
```

Function definitions usually appear in top-level JavaScript code. They may also be nested within other function definitions, but only at the "top level" of those functions; that is, function definitions may not appear within `if` statements, `while` loops, or any other statements.

Technically speaking, the `function` statement is not a statement. Statements cause dynamic behavior in a JavaScript program, while function definitions describe the static structure of a program. Statements are executed at runtime, but functions are defined when JavaScript code is parsed, or compiled, before it is actually run. When the JavaScript parser encounters a function definition, it parses and stores (without executing) the statements that comprise the body of the function. Then it defines a property (in the call object if the function definition is nested in another function; otherwise, in the global object) with the same name as the function to hold the function.

The fact that function definitions occur at parse time rather than at runtime causes some surprising effects. Consider the following code:

```
alert(f(4));       // Displays 16. f( ) can be called before it is defined.
var f = 0;         // This statement overwrites the property f.
function f(x) {  // This "statement" defines the function f before either
```

```
    return x*x;  // of the lines above are executed.
}
alert(f);        // Displays 0. f() has been overwritten by the variable f.
```

These unusual results occur because function definition occurs at a different time than variable definition. Fortunately, these situations do not arise very often.

We'll learn more about functions in Chapter 7.

6.15 return

As you'll recall, invoking a function with the ( ) operator is an expression. All expressions have values; the `return` statement is used to specify the value returned by a function. This value is the value of the function invocation expression. The syntax of the `return` statement is:

```
return expression;
```

A `return` statement may appear only within the body of a function. It is a syntax error for it to appear anywhere else. When the `return` statement is executed, *`expression`* is evaluated and returned as the value of the function. Execution of the function stops when the `return` statement is executed, even if there are other statements remaining in the function body. The `return` statement can be used to return a value like this:

```
function square(x) { return x*x; }
```

The `return` statement may also be used without an *`expression`* to simply terminate execution of the function without returning a value. For example:

```
function display_object(obj) {
    // First make sure our argument is valid
    // Skip the rest of the function if it is not
    if (obj == null) return;
    // Rest of function goes here...
}
```

If a function executes a `return` statement with no *`expression`*, or if it returns because it reaches the end of the function body, the value of the function call expression is `undefined`.

Because of JavaScript's automatic semicolon insertion, you may not include a line break between the `return` keyword and the expression that follows it.

6.16 throw

An *exception* is a signal that indicates that some sort of exceptional condition or error has occurred. To *throw* an exception is to signal such an error or exceptional condition. To *catch* an exception is to handle it—to take whatever actions are necessary or appropriate to recover from the exception. In JavaScript, exceptions are thrown whenever a runtime error occurs and whenever the program explicitly throws one using the throw statement. Exceptions are caught with the try/catch/finally statement, which is described in the next section.*

The throw statement has the following syntax:

```
throw expression;
```

expression may evaluate to a value of any type. Commonly, however, it is an Error object or an instance of one of the subclasses of Error. It can also be useful to throw a string that contains an error message, or a numeric value that represents some sort of error code. Here is some example code that uses the throw statement to throw an exception:

```
function factorial(x) {
    // If the input argument is invalid, thrown an exception!
    if (x < 0) throw new Error("x must not be negative");
    // Otherwise, compute a value and return normally
    for(var f = 1; x > 1; f *= x, x--) /* empty */ ;
    return f;
}
```

When an exception is thrown, the JavaScript interpreter immediately stops normal program execution and jumps to the nearest exception handler. Exception handlers are written using the catch clause of the try/catch/finally statement, which is described in the next section. If the block of code in which the exception was thrown does not have an associated catch clause, the interpreter checks the next highest enclosing block of code to see if it has an exception handler associated with it. This continues until a handler is found. If an exception is thrown in a function that does not contain a try/catch/finally statement to handle it, the exception propagates up to the code that invoked the function. In this way, exceptions propagate up through the lexical structure of JavaScript methods and up the call stack. If no exception handler is ever found, the exception is treated as an error and is reported to the user.

The throw statement is standardized by ECMAScript v3 and implemented in JavaScript 1.4. The Error class and its subclasses are also part of ECMAScript v3, but they are not implemented until JavaScript 1.5.

6.17 try/catch/finally

The try/catch/finally statement is JavaScript's exception-handling mechanism. The try clause of this statement simply defines the block of code whose exceptions are to be handled. The try block is followed by a catch clause, which is a block of statements that are invoked when an exception occurs anywhere within the try block. The catch clause is followed by a finally block containing cleanup code that is guaranteed to be executed, regardless of what happens in the try block. Both the catch and

* The JavaScript throw and try/catch/finally statements are similar to but not exactly the same as the corresponding statements in C++ and Java.

finally blocks are optional, but a try block must be accompanied by at least one of these blocks. The try, catch, and finally blocks all begin and end with curly braces. These are a required part of the syntax and cannot be omitted, even if the clause contains only a single statement. Like the throw statement, the try/catch/finally statement is standardized by ECMAScript v3 and implemented in JavaScript 1.4.

The following code illustrates the syntax and purpose of the try/catch/finally statement. In particular, note that the catch keyword is followed by an identifier in parentheses. This identifier is like a function argument. It names a local variable that exists only within the body of the catch block. JavaScript assigns whatever exception object or value was thrown to this variable:

```
try {
  // Normally, this code runs from the top of the block to the bottom
  // without problems. But it can sometimes throw an exception,
  // either directly, with a throw statement, or indirectly, by calling
  // a method that throws an exception.
}
catch (e) {
  // The statements in this block are executed if, and only if, the try
  // block throws an exception. These statements can use the local variable
  // e to refer to the Error object or other value that was thrown.
  // This block may handle the exception somehow, or it may ignore the
  // exception by doing nothing, or it may rethrow the exception with throw.
}
finally {
  // This block contains statements that are always executed, regardless of
  // what happens in the try block. They are executed whether the try
  // block terminates:
  //   1) normally, after reaching the bottom of the block
  //   2) because of a break, continue, or return statement
  //   3) with an exception that is handled by a catch clause above
  //   4) with an uncaught exception that is still propagating
}
```

Here is a more realistic example of the try/catch statement. It uses the factorial() method defined in the previous section and the client-side JavaScript methods prompt() and alert() for input and output:

```
try {
    // Ask the user to enter a number
    var n = prompt("Please enter a positive integer", "");
    // Compute the factorial of the number, assuming that the user's
    // input is valid
    var f = factorial(n);
    // Display the result
    alert(n + "! = " + f);
}
catch (ex) {  // If the user's input was not valid, we end up here
    // Tell the user what the error is
    alert(ex);
}
```

This example is a try/catch statement with no finally clause. Although finally is not used as often as catch, it can often be useful. However, its behavior requires additional explanation. The finally clause is guaranteed to be executed if any portion of the try block is executed, regardless of how the code in the try block completes. It is generally used to clean up after the code in the try clause.

In the normal case, control reaches the end of the try block and then proceeds to the finally block, which performs any necessary cleanup. If control leaves the try block because of a return, continue, or break statement, the finally block is executed before control transfers to its new destination.

If an exception occurs in the try block and there is an associated catch block to handle the exception, control transfers first to the catch block and then to the finally block. If there is no local catch block to handle the exception, control transfers first to the finally block and then propagates up to the nearest containing catch clause that can handle the exception.

If a finally block itself transfers control with a return, continue, break, or throw statement, or by calling a method that throws an exception, the pending control transfer is abandoned and this new transfer is processed. For example, if a finally clause throws an exception, that exception replaces any exception that was in the process of being thrown. If a finally clause issues a return statement, the method returns normally, even if an exception has been thrown and has not yet been handled.

try and finally can be used together without a catch clause. In this case, the finally block is simply cleanup code that is guaranteed to be executed, regardless of any break, continue, or return statements within the try clause. For example, the following code uses a try/finally statement to ensure that a loop counter variable is incremented at the end of each iteration, even when an iteration terminates abruptly because of a continue statement:

```
var i = 0, total = 0;
while(i < a.length) {
    try {
        if ((typeof a[i] != "number") || isNaN(a[i])) // If it is not a number,
            continue;   // go on to the next iteration of the loop.
        total += a[i];  // Otherwise, add the number to the total.
    }
    finally {
        i++;  // Always increment i, even if we used continue above.
    }
}
```

6.18 with

In Chapter 4, we discussed variable scope and the scope chain—a list of objects that are searched in order, to perform variable name resolution. The with statement is used to temporarily modify the scope chain. It has the following syntax:

```
with (object)
    statement
```

This statement effectively adds *object* to the front of the scope chain, executes *statement*, and then restores the scope chain to its original state.

In practice, you can use the `with` statement to save yourself a lot of typing. In client-side JavaScript, for example, it is common to work with deeply nested object hierarchies. For instance, you may have to type expressions like this one to access elements of an HTML form:

```
frames[1].document.forms[0].address.value
```

If you need to access this form a number of times, you can use the `with` statement to add the form to the scope chain:

```
with(frames[1].document.forms[0]) {
    // Access form elements directly here. For example:
    name.value = "";
    address.value = "";
    email.value = "";
}
```

This reduces the amount of typing you have to do—you no longer need to prefix each form property name with `frames[1].document.forms[0]`. That object is temporarily part of the scope chain and is automatically searched when JavaScript needs to resolve an identifier like `address`.

Despite its occasional convenience, the use of the `with` statement is frowned upon. JavaScript code that uses `with` is difficult to optimize and may therefore run more slowly than the equivalent code written without the `with` statement. Furthermore, function definitions and variable initializations within the body of a `with` statement can have surprising and counterintuitive behavior.* For these reasons, it is recommended that you avoid the `with` statement.

Note that there are other, perfectly legitimate ways to save yourself typing. For instance, we could rewrite the previous example as follows:

```
var form = frames[1].document.forms[0];
form.name.value = "";
form.address.value = "";
form.email.value = "";
```

6.19 The Empty Statement

One final legal statement in JavaScript is the empty statement. It looks like this:

```
;
```

* This behavior, and the reasons behind it, are too complicated to explain here.

Executing the empty statement obviously has no effect and performs no action. You might think there would be little reason to ever use such a statement, but the empty statement is occasionally useful when you want to create a loop that has an empty body. For example:

```
// Initialize an array a
for(i=0; i < a.length; a[i++] = 0) ;
```

Note that the accidental inclusion of a semicolon after the right parenthesis of a `for` loop, `while` loop, or `if` statement can cause frustrating bugs that are difficult to detect. For example, the following code probably does not do what the author intended:

```
if ((a == 0) || (b == 0));   // Oops! This line does nothing...
    o = null;                // and this line is always executed.
```

When you intentionally use the empty statement, it is a good idea to comment your code in a way that makes it clear that you are doing it on purpose. For example:

```
for(i=0; i < a.length; a[i++] = 0) /* Empty */ ;
```

6.20 Summary of JavaScript Statements

This chapter introduced each of the statements of the JavaScript language. Table 6-1 summarizes these statements, listing the syntax and purpose of each.

Table 6-1. JavaScript statement syntax

Statement	Syntax	Purpose
`break`	`break;` `break` *`labelname`*`;`	Exit from the innermost loop or `switch` statement or from the statement named by *`label`*.
`case`	`case` *`expression`*`:`	Label a statement within a `switch` statement.
`continue`	`continue;` `continue` *`labelname`*`;`	Restart the innermost loop or the loop named by *`label`*.
`default`	`default:`	Label the default statement within a `switch` statement.

`do/while`	`do`
	    `statement`
	`while (`*`expression`*`);`
		An alternative to the `while` loop.

`empty`	`;`	Do nothing.
`for`	`for (`*`initialize`* `;` *`test`* `;` *`increment`*`)` *`statement`*	An easy-to-use loop.
`for/in`	`for (`*`variable`* `in` *`object`*`)` *`statement`*	Loop through the properties of an object.

`function`	`function` *`funcname`*`([`*`arg1`*`[...,` *`argn`*`]])`
	`{`
	    `statements`
	`}`
		Declare a function.

Table 6-1. JavaScript statement syntax (continued)

Statement	Syntax	Purpose

`if/else`	`if (expression)`
	`    statement1`
	`[else statement2]`
		Conditionally execute code.

`label`	`identifier: statement`	Give *statement* the name *identifier*.
`return`	`return [expression];`	Return from a function or return the value of *expression* from a function.

`switch`	`switch (expression) {`
	`    statements`
	`}`
		Multiway branch to statements labeled with `case` or `default:`.

`throw`	`throw expression;`	Throw an exception.

`try`	`try {`
	`    statements`
	`}`
	`catch (identifier) {`
	`    statements`
	`}`
	`finally {`
	`    statements`
	`}`
		Catch an exception.

`var`	`var name_1 [ = value_1]` `[ ..., name_n [ = value_n]];`	Declare and initialize variables.
`while`	`while (expression)` `    statement`	A basic loop construct.
`with`	`with (object)` `    statement`	Extend the scope chain. (Deprecated.)

CHAPTER 7

Functions

Functions are an important and complex part of the JavaScript language. This chapter examines functions from several points of view. First, we discuss functions from the syntactic standpoint, explaining how they are defined and invoked. Second, we cover functions as a data type, with examples of the useful programming techniques that are made possible by treating functions as data. Finally, we consider the topic of variable scope within the body of a function and examine some of the useful function-related properties that are available to an executing function. This includes a discussion of how to write JavaScript functions that accept an arbitrary number of arguments.

This chapter focuses on defining and invoking user-defined JavaScript functions. It is also important to remember that JavaScript supports quite a few built-in functions, such as `eval()`, `parseInt()`, and the `sort()` method of the Array class. Client-side JavaScript defines others, such as `document.write()` and `alert()`. Built-in functions in JavaScript can be used in exactly the same ways as user-defined functions. You can find more information about the built-in functions mentioned here in the core and client-side reference sections of this book.

Functions and objects are intertwined in JavaScript. For this reason, I'll defer discussion of some features of functions until Chapter 8.

7.1 Defining and Invoking Functions

As we saw in Chapter 6, the most common way to define a function is with the `function` statement. This statement consists of the `function` keyword, followed by:

- The name of the function
- An optional comma-separated list of parameter names in parentheses
- The JavaScript statements that comprise the body of the function, contained within curly braces

Example 7-1 shows the definitions of several functions. Although these functions are short and simple, they all contain each of the elements I just listed. Note that functions may be defined to expect varying numbers of arguments and that they may or may not contain a `return` statement. The `return` statement was introduced in Chapter 6; it causes the function to stop executing and to return the value of its expression (if any) to the caller. If a function does not contain a `return` statement, it simply executes each statement in the function body and returns the `undefined` value to the caller.

Example 7-1. Defining JavaScript functions

```
// A shortcut function, sometimes useful instead of document.write()
// This function has no return statement, so it returns no value
function print(msg)
{
    document.write(msg, "<br>");
}
// A function that computes and returns the distance between two points
function distance(x1, y1, x2, y2)
{
    var dx = x2 - x1;
    var dy = y2 - y1;
    return Math.sqrt(dx*dx + dy*dy);
}
// A recursive function (one that calls itself) that computes factorials
// Recall that x! is the product of x and all positive integers less than it
function factorial(x)
{
    if (x <= 1)
        return 1;
    return x * factorial(x-1);
}
```

Once a function has been defined, it may be invoked with the `()` operator, introduced in Chapter 5. Recall that the parentheses appear after the name of the function and that an optional comma-separated list of argument values (or expressions) appears within the parentheses. The functions defined in Example 7-1 could be invoked with code like the following:

```
print("Hello, " + name);
print("Welcome to my home page!");
total_dist = distance(0,0,2,1) + distance(2,1,3,5);
print("The probability of that is: " + factorial(39)/factorial(52));
```

When you invoke a function, each of the expressions you specify between the parentheses is evaluated and the resulting value is used as an argument of the function. These values are assigned to the parameters named when the function was defined, and the function operates on its parameters by referring to them by name. Note that these parameter variables are defined only while the function is being executed; they do not persist once the function returns.

Since JavaScript is an untyped language, you are not expected to specify a data type for function parameters, and JavaScript does not check whether you have passed the type of data that the function expects. If the data type of an argument is important, you can test it yourself with the `typeof` operator. JavaScript does not check whether you have passed the correct number of arguments, either. If you pass more arguments than the function expects, the extra values are simply ignored. If you pass fewer than expected, some of the parameters are given the `undefined` value—which, in many circumstances, causes your function to behave incorrectly. Later in this chapter, we'll see a technique you can use to test whether the correct number of arguments have been passed to a function.

Note that the `print()` function does not contain a `return` statement, so it always returns the `undefined` value and cannot meaningfully be used as part of a larger expression. The `distance()` and `factorial()` functions, on the other hand, can be invoked as parts of larger expressions, as was shown in the previous examples.

7.1.1 Nested Functions

ECMAScript v1 and implementations prior to JavaScript 1.2 allow functions to be defined only in top-level global code. JavaScript 1.2 and ECMAScript v3, however, allow function definitions to be nested within other functions. For example:

```
function hypotenuse(a, b) {
    function square(x) { return x*x; }
    return Math.sqrt(square(a) + square(b));
}
```

Note that ECMAScript v3 does not allow function definitions to appear anywhere; they are still restricted to top-level global code and top-level function code. This means that function definitions may not appear within loops or conditionals, for example.* These restrictions on function definitions apply only to function declarations with the `function` statement. As we'll discuss later in this chapter, function literals (another feature introduced in JavaScript 1.2 and standardized by ECMAScript v3) may appear within any JavaScript expression, which means that they can appear within `if` and other statements.

7.1.2 The Function( ) Constructor

The `function` statement is not the only way to define a new function. ECMAScript v1 and JavaScript 1.1 allow you to define a function dynamically with the `Function()` constructor and the `new` operator. (We saw the `new` operator in Chapter 5, and we'll

* Different implementations of JavaScript may be more relaxed about function definitions than the standard requires. For example, Netscape's implementation of JavaScript 1.5 allows "conditional function definitions" that appear within `if` statements.

learn more about constructors in Chapter 8.) Here is an example of creating a function in this way:

```
var f = new Function("x", "y", "return x*y;");
```

This line of code creates a new function that is more or less equivalent to a function defined with the familiar syntax:

```
function f(x, y) { return x*y; }
```

The `Function()` constructor expects any number of string arguments. The last argument is the body of the function—it can contain arbitrary JavaScript statements, separated from each other by semicolons. All other arguments to the constructor are strings that specify the names of the parameters to the function being defined. If you are defining a function that takes no arguments, you simply pass a single string—the function body—to the constructor.

Notice that the `Function()` constructor is not passed any argument that specifies a name for the function it creates. The unnamed functions created with the `Function()` constructor are sometimes called *anonymous functions*.

You might well wonder what the point of the `Function()` constructor is. Why not simply define all functions with the `function` statement? One reason is that `Function()` allows us to dynamically build and compile functions; it does not restrict us to the precompiled function bodies of the `function` statement. The flip side of this benefit is that the `Function()` constructor has to compile a function each time it is called. Therefore, you probably do not want to call this constructor within the body of a loop or within a frequently used function.

Another reason to use the `Function()` constructor is that it is sometimes convenient, and even elegant, to be able to define a function as part of a JavaScript expression, rather than as a statement. We'll see examples of this usage later in this chapter. In JavaScript 1.2, when you want to define a function in an expression rather than a statement, a function literal is an even more elegant choice than the `Function()` constructor. We'll consider function literals next.

7.1.3 Function Literals

ECMAScript v3 defines and JavaScript 1.2 implements function literals, which are a third way to create functions. As discussed in Chapter 3, a function literal is an expression that defines an unnamed function. The syntax for a function literal is much like that of the `function` statement, except that it is used as an expression rather than as a statement and no function name is required. The following three lines of code define three more or less identical functions using the `function` statement, the `Function()` constructor, and a function literal:

```
function f(x) { return x*x; }                 // function statement
var f = new Function("x", "return x*x;"); // Function() constructor
var f = function(x) { return x*x; };          // function literal
```

Although function literals create unnamed functions, the syntax allows a function name to be optionally specified, which is useful when writing recursive functions that call themselves. For example:

```
var f = function fact(x) { if (x <= 1) return 1; else return x*fact(x-1); };
```

This line of code defines an unnamed function and stores a reference to it in the variable `f`. It does not actually create a function named `fact()`, but it does allow the body of the function to refer to itself using that name. Note, however, that this type of named function literal is not properly implemented before JavaScript 1.5.

Keep in mind that the `function` statement is available in all versions of JavaScript, the `Function()` constructor is available only in JavaScript 1.1 and later, and function literals are available only in JavaScript 1.2 and later. Recall that we said the three functions defined earlier are "more or less" equivalent—there are some differences between these three techniques for function definition, which we'll consider in Section 11.5, "The Function() Constructor and Function Literals."

Function literals are useful in much the same way as functions created with the `Function()` constructor. Because they are created by JavaScript expressions rather than statements, they can be used in more flexible ways and are particularly suited for functions that are used only once and need not be named. For example, the function specified by a function literal expression can be stored into a variable, passed to another function, or even invoked directly:

```
a[0] = function(x) { return x*x; };  // Define a function and store it
a.sort(function(a,b){return a-b;});  // Define a function; pass it to another
var tensquared = (function(x) {return x*x;})(10);  // Define and invoke
```

Like the `Function()` constructor, function literals create unnamed functions and do not automatically store those functions into properties. Function literals have an important advantage over the `Function()` constructor, however. The body of a function created by `Function()` must be specified in a string, and it can be awkward to express long, complex function bodies in this way. The body of a function literal, however, uses standard JavaScript syntax. Also, a function literal is parsed and compiled only once, while the JavaScript code passed as a string to the `Function()` constructor must be parsed and compiled each time the constructor is invoked.

7.2 Functions as Data

The most important features of functions are that they can be defined and invoked, as shown in the previous section. Function definition and invocation are syntactic features of JavaScript and of most other programming languages. In JavaScript, however, functions are not only syntax but also data, which means that they can be assigned to variables, stored in the properties of objects or the elements of arrays, passed as arguments to functions, and so on.*

To understand how functions can be JavaScript data as well as JavaScript syntax, consider this function definition:

```
function square(x) { return x*x; }
```

This definition creates a new function object and assigns it to the variable square. The name of a function is really immaterial—it is simply the name of a variable that holds the function. The function can be assigned to another variable and still work the same way:

```
var a = square(4);  // a contains the number 16
var b = square;     // Now b refers to the same function that square does
var c = b(5);       // c contains the number 25
```

Functions can also be assigned to object properties rather than global variables. When we do this, we call them methods:

```
var o = new Object;
o.square = new Function("x", "return x*x");  // Note Function() constructor
y = o.square(16);                            // y equals 256
```

Functions don't even require names at all, as when we assign them to array elements:

```
var a = new Array(3);
a[0] = function(x) { return x*x; }  // Note function literal
a[1] = 20;
a[2] = a[0](a[1]);                  // a[2] contains 400
```

The function invocation syntax in this last example looks strange, but it is still a legal use of the JavaScript ( ) operator!

Example 7-2 is a detailed example of the things that can be done when functions are used as data. It demonstrates how functions can be passed as arguments to other functions and also how they can be stored in associative arrays (which were introduced in Chapter 3 and are explained in detail in Chapter 8.) This example may be a little tricky, but the comments explain what is going on; it is worth studying carefully.

Example 7-2. Using functions as data

```
// We define some simple functions here
function add(x,y) { return x + y; }
function subtract(x,y) { return x - y; }
function multiply(x,y) { return x * y; }
function divide(x,y) { return x / y; }
```

* This may not seem like a particularly interesting point to you unless you are familiar with languages like Java, in which functions are part of a program but cannot be manipulated by the program.

Example 7-2. Using functions as data (continued)

```
// Here's a function that takes one of the above functions
// as an argument and invokes it on two operands
function operate(operator, operand1, operand2)
{
    return operator(operand1, operand2);
}

// We could invoke this function like this to compute the value (2+3) + (4*5):
var i = operate(add, operate(add, 2, 3), operate(multiply, 4, 5));

// For the sake of example, we implement the functions again, this time
// using function literals. We store the functions in an associative array.
var operators = new Object( );
operators["add"] = function(x,y) { return x+y; };
operators["subtract"] = function(x,y) { return x-y; };
operators["multiply"] = function(x,y) { return x*y; };
operators["divide"] = function(x,y) { return x/y; };
operators["pow"] = Math.pow;  // Works for predefined functions too

// This function takes the name of an operator, looks up that operator
// in the array, and then invokes it on the supplied operands. Note
// the syntax used to invoke the operator function.
function operate2(op_name, operand1, operand2)
{
    if (operators[op_name] == null) return "unknown operator";
    else return operators[op_name](operand1, operand2);
}

// We could invoke this function as follows to compute
// the value ("hello" + " " + "world"):
var j = operate2("add", "hello", operate2("add", " ", "world"))
// Using the predefined Math.pow( ) function:
var k = operate2("pow", 10, 2)
```

If the preceding example does not convince you of the utility of being able to pass functions as arguments to other functions and otherwise treat functions as data values, consider the `Array.sort( )` function. This function sorts the elements of an array. Because there are many possible orders to sort by (numerical order, alphabetical order, date order, ascending, descending, and so on), the `sort( )` function optionally takes another function as an argument to tell it how to perform the sort. This function has a simple job—it takes two elements of the array, compares them, and then returns a value that specifies which element comes first. This function argument makes the `Array.sort( )` method perfectly general and infinitely flexible—it can sort any type of data into any conceivable order!

7.3 Function Scope: The Call Object

As described in Chapter 4, the body of a JavaScript function executes in a local scope that differs from the global scope. This new scope is created by adding the call object to the front of the scope chain. Since the call object is part of the scope chain, any properties of this object are accessible as variables within the body of the function. Local variables declared with the `var` statement are created as properties of this object; the parameters of the function are also made available as properties of the object.

In addition to local variables and parameters, the call object defines one special property named `arguments`. This property refers to another special object known as the Arguments object, which is discussed in the next section. Because the `arguments` property is a property of the call object, it has exactly the same status as local variables and function parameters. For this reason, the identifier `arguments` should be considered a reserved word and should not be used as a variable or parameter name.

7.4 Function Arguments: The Arguments Object

Within the body of a function, the identifier `arguments` always has special meaning. `arguments` is a special property of the call object that refers to an object known as the *Arguments object*. The Arguments object is like an array that allows the argument values passed to the function to be retrieved by number, but it is not actually an Array object. The Arguments object also defines an additional `callee` property, described later.

Although a JavaScript function is defined with a fixed number of named arguments, it can be passed any number of arguments when it is invoked. The `arguments[]` array allows full access to these argument values, even when some are unnamed. Suppose you define a function `f` that expects to be passed one argument, `x`. If you invoke this function with two arguments, the first argument is accessible within the function by the parameter name `x` or as `arguments[0]`. The second argument is accessible only as `arguments[1]`. Furthermore, like all arrays, `arguments` has a `length` property that specifies the number of elements it contains. Thus, within the body of our function `f`, invoked with two arguments, `arguments.length` has the value 2.

The `arguments[]` array is useful in a number of ways. The following example shows how you can use it to check that a function is invoked with the correct number of arguments, since JavaScript doesn't do this for you:

```
function f(x, y, z)
{
    // First, check that the right number of arguments were passed
    if (arguments.length != 3) {
        throw new Error("function f called with " + arguments.length +
                        "arguments, but it expects 3 arguments.");
    }
    // Now do the actual function...
}
```

The `arguments[]` array also opens up an important possibility for JavaScript functions: they can be written so that they work with any number of arguments. Here's an example that shows how you can write a simple `max()` function that accepts any number of arguments and returns the value of the largest argument it is passed (see also the built-in function `Math.max()`, which in ECMAScript v3 also accepts any number of arguments):

```
function max( )
{
    var m = Number.NEGATIVE_INFINITY;

    // Loop through all the arguments, looking for, and
    // remembering, the biggest
    for(var i = 0; i < arguments.length; i++)
        if (arguments[i] > m) m = arguments[i];
    // Return the biggest
    return m;
}

var largest = max(1, 10, 100, 2, 3, 1000, 4, 5, 10000, 6);
```

You can also use the `arguments[]` array to write functions that expect a fixed number of named arguments followed by an arbitrary number of unnamed arguments.

Throughout this section we've been referring to the "`arguments` array." Keep in mind, however, that `arguments` is not really an array; it is an Arguments object. Each Arguments object defines numbered array elements and a `length` property, but it is not technically an array—it is better to think of it as an object that happens to have some numbered properties. The ECMAScript specification does not require the Arguments object to implement any of the special behavior that arrays do. Although you can assign a value to the `arguments.length` property, for example, ECMAScript does not require you to do so to actually alter the number of array elements defined in the object. (See Chapter 9 for an explanation of the special behavior of the `length` property of true Array objects.)

The Arguments object has one *very* unusual feature. When a function has named arguments, the array elements of the Arguments object are synonyms for the local variables that hold the function arguments. The `arguments[]` array and the argument named `arguments` are two different ways of referring to the same variable. Changing the value of an argument with an argument name changes the value that is retrieved through the `arguments[]` array. Changing the value of an argument through the `arguments[]` array changes the value that is retrieved by the argument name. For example:

```
function f(x) {
    alert(x);             // Displays the initial value of the argument
    arguments[0] = null;  // Changing the array element also changes x
    alert(x);             // Now displays "null"
}
```

7.4.1 The callee Property

In addition to its array elements, the Arguments object defines a `callee` property that refers to the function that is currently being executed. This is useful, for example, to allow unnamed functions to invoke themselves recursively. For instance, here is an unnamed function literal that computes factorials:

```
function(x) {
    if (x <= 1) return 1;
    return x * arguments.callee(x-1);
}
```

The `callee` property is defined by ECMAScript v1 and implemented in JavaScript 1.2.

7.5 Function Properties and Methods

We've seen that functions can be used as data values in JavaScript programs and that they can be created with the `Function()` constructor. These are sure signs that functions are actually represented by a type of JavaScript object, the Function object. Since functions are objects, they have properties and methods, just like the String and Date objects, for example. Now that we've discussed the call and Arguments objects that are used in the context of function invocation, let's turn to the Function object itself.

7.5.1 The length Property

As we've seen, within the body of a function, the `length` property of the `arguments` array specifies the number of arguments that were passed to the function. The `length` property of a function itself, however, has a different meaning. This read-only property returns the number of arguments that the function *expects* to be passed—that is, the number of parameters it declares in its parameter list. Recall that a function can be invoked with any number of arguments, which it can retrieve through the `arguments` array, regardless of the number of parameters it declares. The `length` property of the Function object specifies exactly how many declared parameters a function has. Note that unlike `arguments.length`, this `length` property is available both inside and outside of the function body.

The following code defines a function named `check()` that is passed the `arguments` array from another function. It compares the `arguments.length` property to the `Function.length` property (which it accesses as `arguments.callee.length`) to see if the function was passed the number of arguments it expected. If not, it throws an exception. The `check()` function is followed by a test function `f()` that demonstrates how `check()` can be used:

```
function check(args) {
    var actual = args.length;           // The actual number of arguments
    var expected = args.callee.length;  // The expected number of arguments
```

```
    if (actual != expected) {  // Throw an exception if they don't match
        throw new Error("Wrong number of arguments: expected: " +
                        expected + "; actually passed " + actual);
    }
}

function f(x, y, z) {
    // Check that the actual # of args matches the expected # of args
    // Throw an exception if they don't match
    check(arguments);
    // Now do the rest of the function normally
    return x + y + z;
}
```

The `length` property of the Function object is standardized by ECMAScript v1 and implemented in JavaScript 1.1 and later.*

7.5.2 The prototype Property

Every function has a `prototype` property that refers to a predefined *prototype object*. This prototype object comes into play when the function is used as a constructor with the `new` operator; it plays an important role in the process of defining new object types. We'll explore this property in detail in Chapter 8.

7.5.3 Defining Your Own Function Properties

When a function needs to use a variable whose value persists across invocations, it is often convenient to use a property of the Function object, instead of cluttering up the namespace by defining a global variable. For example, suppose we want to write a function that returns a unique identifier whenever it is invoked. The function must never return the same value twice. In order to manage this, the function needs to keep track of the values it has already returned, and this information must persist across function invocations. We could store this information in a global variable, but that is unnecessary because the information is used only by the function itself. It is better to store the information in a property of the Function object. Here is an example that returns a unique integer whenever it is called:

```
// Create and initialize the "static" variable.
// Function declarations are processed before code is executed, so
// we really can do this assignment before the function declaration.
uniqueInteger.counter = 0;

// Here's the function. It returns a different value each time
// it is called and uses a "static" property of itself to keep track
// of the last value it returned.
```

* In Netscape 4.0, a bug prevents this property from working correctly unless the `language` attribute of the `<script>` tag is explicitly set to "JavaScript1.2".

```
function uniqueInteger() {
    // Increment and return our "static" variable
    return uniqueInteger.counter++;
}
```

7.5.4 The apply() and call() Methods

ECMAScript v3 defines two methods that are defined for all functions, `call()` and `apply()`. These methods allow you to invoke a function as if it were a method of some other object. (Note that we have not discussed methods yet; you may find this section more understandable once you have read Chapter 8.) The first argument to both `call()` and `apply()` is the object on which the function is to be invoked; this argument becomes the value of the `this` keyword within the body of the function. Any remaining arguments to `call()` are the values that are passed to the function that is invoked. For example, to pass two numbers to the function `f()` and invoke it as if it were a method of the object `o`, you could use code like this:

```
f.call(o, 1, 2);
```

This is similar to the following lines of code:

```
o.m = f;
o.m(1,2);
delete o.m;
```

The `apply()` method is like the `call()` method, except that the arguments to be passed to the function are specified as an array:

```
f.apply(o, [1,2]);
```

For example, to find the largest number in an array of numbers, you could use the `apply()` method to pass the elements of the array to the `Math.max()` function:*

```
var biggest = Math.max.apply(null, array_of_numbers);
```

The `apply()` method is implemented in JavaScript 1.2, but the `call()` method is not implemented until JavaScript 1.5.

* This example assumes we are using the ECMAScript v3 `Math.max()` function, which accepts an arbitrary number of arguments; the ECMAScript v1 version of the function accepts only two arguments.

CHAPTER 8

Objects

Chapter 3 explained that objects are one of the fundamental data types in JavaScript. They are also one of the most important. This chapter describes JavaScript objects in detail. Basic usage of objects, described in the next section, is straightforward, but as we'll see in later sections, objects have more complex uses and behaviors.

8.1 Objects and Properties

Objects are composite data types: they aggregate multiple values into a single unit and allow us to store and retrieve those values by name. Another way to explain this is to say that an object is an unordered collection of *properties*, each of which has a name and a value. The named values held by an object may be primitive values like numbers and strings, or they may themselves be objects.

8.1.1 Creating Objects

Objects are created with the `new` operator. This operator must be followed by the name of a constructor function that serves to initialize the object. For example, we can create an empty object (an object with no properties) like this:

```
var o = new Object( );
```

JavaScript supports other built-in constructor functions that initialize newly created objects in other, less trivial, ways. For example, the `Date( )` constructor initializes an object that represents a date and time:

```
var now = new Date( );                      // The current date and time
var new_years_eve = new Date(2000, 11, 31);  // Represents December 31, 2000
```

Later in this chapter, we'll see that it is possible to define custom constructor methods to initialize newly created objects in any way you desire.

Object literals provide another way to create and initialize new objects. As we saw in Chapter 3, an object literal allows us to embed an object description literally in JavaScript code in much the same way that we embed textual data into JavaScript code as quoted strings. An object literal consists of a comma-separated list of property specifications enclosed within curly braces. Each property specification in an object literal consists of the property name followed by a colon and the property value. For example:

```
var circle = { x:0, y:0, radius:2 }
var homer = {
                name: "Homer Simpson",
                age: 34,
                married: true,
                occupation: "plant operator",
                email: "homer@simpsons.com"
};
```

The object literal syntax is defined by the ECMAScript v3 specification and implemented in JavaScript 1.2 and later.

8.1.2 Setting and Querying Properties

You normally use the `.` operator to access the value of an object's properties. The value on the left of the `.` should be a reference to an object (usually just the name of the variable that contains the object reference). The value on the right of the `.` should be the name of the property. This must be an identifier, not a string or an expression. For example, you would refer to the property `p` in object `o` with `o.p` or to the property `radius` in the object `circle` with `circle.radius`. Object properties work like variables: you can store values in them and read values from them. For example:

```
// Create an object. Store a reference to it in a variable.
var book = new Object( );

// Set a property in the object.
book.title = "JavaScript: The Definitive Guide"

// Set some more properties. Note the nested objects.
book.chapter1 = new Object( );
book.chapter1.title = "Introduction to JavaScript";
book.chapter1.pages = 19;
book.chapter2 = { title: "Lexical Structure", pages: 6 };

// Read some property values from the object.
alert("Outline: " + book.title + "\n\t" +
      "Chapter 1 " + book.chapter1.title + "\n\t" +
      "Chapter 2 " + book.chapter2.title);
```

An important point to notice about this example is that you can create a new property of an object simply by assigning a value to it. Although we declare variables with the `var` keyword, there is no need (and no way) to do so with object properties. Furthermore, once you have created an object property by assigning a value to it, you can change the value of the property at any time simply by assigning a new value:

```
book.title = "JavaScript: The Rhino Book"
```

8.1.3 Enumerating Properties

The for/in loop discussed in Chapter 6 provides a way to loop through, or enumerate, the properties of an object. This can be useful when debugging scripts or when working with objects that may have arbitrary properties whose names you do not know in advance. The following code shows a function you can use to list the property names of an object:

```
function DisplayPropertyNames(obj) {
    var names = "";
    for(var name in obj) names += name + "\n";
    alert(names);
}
```

Note that the for/in loop does not enumerate properties in any specific order, and although it enumerates all user-defined properties, it does not enumerate certain predefined properties or methods.

8.1.4 Undefined Properties

If you attempt to read the value of a property that does not exist (in other words, a property that has never had a value assigned to it), you end up retrieving the undefined value (introduced in Chapter 3).

You can use the delete operator to delete a property of an object:

```
delete book.chapter2;
```

Note that deleting a property does not merely set the property to undefined; it actually removes the property from the object. The for/in loop demonstrates this difference: it enumerates properties that have been set to the undefined value, but it does not enumerate deleted properties.

8.2 Constructors

We saw previously that you can create and initialize a new object in JavaScript by using the new operator in conjunction with a predefined constructor function such as Object( ), Date( ), or Function( ). These predefined constructors and the built-in object types they create are useful in many instances. However, in object-oriented programming, it is also common to work with custom object types defined by your program. For example, if you are writing a program that manipulates rectangles, you might want to represent rectangles with a special type, or *class*, of object. Each object of this Rectangle class would have a width property and a height property, since those are the essential defining characteristics of rectangles.

To create objects with properties such as width and height already defined, we need to write a constructor to create and initialize these properties in a new object. A constructor is a JavaScript function with two special features:

- It is invoked through the new operator.
- It is passed a reference to a newly created, empty object as the value of the this keyword, and it is responsible for performing appropriate initialization for that new object.

Example 8-1 shows how the constructor function for a Rectangle object might be defined and invoked.

Example 8-1. A Rectangle object constructor function

```
// Define the constructor.
// Note how it initializes the object referred to by "this".
function Rectangle(w, h)
{
    this.width = w;
    this.height = h;
}

// Invoke the constructor to create two Rectangle objects.
// We pass the width and height to the constructor,
// so it can initialize each new object appropriately.
var rect1 = new Rectangle(2, 4);
var rect2 = new Rectangle(8.5, 11);
```

Notice how the constructor uses its arguments to initialize properties of the object referred to by the this keyword. Keep in mind that a constructor function simply initializes the specified object; it does not have to return that object.

We have defined a class of objects simply by defining an appropriate constructor function—all objects created with the Rectangle( ) constructor are now guaranteed to have initialized width and height properties. This means that we can write programs that rely on this fact and treat all Rectangle objects uniformly. Because every constructor defines a class of objects, it is stylistically important to give a constructor function a name that indicates the class of objects it creates. Creating a rectangle with new Rectangle(1,2) is a lot more intuitive than with new init_rect(1,2), for example.

Constructor functions typically do not have return values. They initialize the object passed as the value of this and return nothing. However, a constructor is allowed to return an object value, and, if it does so, that returned object becomes the value of the new expression. In this case, the object that was the value of this is simply discarded.

8.3 Methods

A *method* is nothing more than a JavaScript function that is invoked through an object. Recall that functions are data values and that there is nothing special about the names with which they are defined—a function can be assigned to any variable, or even to any property of an object. If we have a function f and an object o, we can define a method named m with the following line:

```
o.m = f;
```

Having defined the method m( ) of the object o, we invoke it like this:

```
o.m( );
```

Or, if m( ) expects two arguments, we might invoke it like this:

```
o.m(x, x+2);
```

Methods have one very important property: the object through which a method is invoked becomes the value of the this keyword within the body of the method. For example, when we invoke o.m( ), the body of the method can refer to the object o with the this keyword.

The discussion of the this keyword should begin to clarify why we use methods at all. Any function that is used as a method is effectively passed an extra argument—the object through which it is invoked. Typically, a method performs some sort of operation on that object, so the method invocation syntax is a particularly elegant way to express the fact that a function is operating on an object. Compare the following two lines of code:

```
rect.setSize(width, height);
setRectSize(rect, width, height);
```

These two lines may perform exactly the same operation on the object rect, but the method invocation syntax in the first line more clearly indicates the idea that it is the object rect that is the primary focus, or *target*, of the operation. (If the first line does not seem a more natural syntax to you, you are probably new to object-oriented programming. With a little experience, you will learn to love it!)

While it is useful to think of functions and methods differently, there is not actually as much difference between them as there initially appears to be. Recall that functions are values stored in variables and that variables are nothing more than properties of a global object. Thus, when you invoke a function, you are actually invoking a method of the global object. Within such a function, the this keyword refers to the global object. Thus, there is no technical difference between functions and methods. The real difference lies in design and intent: methods are written to operate somehow on the this object, while functions usually stand alone and do not use the this object.

The typical usage of methods is more clearly illustrated through an example. Example 8-2 returns to the Rectangle objects of Example 8-1 and shows how a method that operates on Rectangle objects can be defined and invoked.

Example 8-2. Defining and invoking a method

```
// This function uses the this keyword, so it doesn't make sense to
// invoke it by itself; it needs instead to be made a method of some
// object that has "width" and "height" properties defined.
```

Example 8-2. Defining and invoking a method (continued)

```
function compute_area( )
{
    return this.width * this.height;
}

// Create a new Rectangle object, using the constructor defined earlier.
var page = new Rectangle(8.5, 11);

// Define a method by assigning the function to a property of the object.
page.area = compute_area;

// Invoke the new method like this:
var a = page.area( );    // a = 8.5*11 = 93.5
```

One shortcoming is evident in Example 8-2: before you can invoke the area( ) method for the rect object, you must assign that method to a property of the object. While we can invoke the area( ) method on the particular object named page, we can't invoke it on any other Rectangle objects without first assigning the method to them. This quickly becomes tedious. Example 8-3 defines some additional Rectangle methods and shows how they can automatically be assigned to all Rectangle objects with a constructor function.

Example 8-3. Defining methods in a constructor

```
// First, define some functions that will be used as methods.
function Rectangle_area( ) { return this.width * this.height; }
function Rectangle_perimeter( ) { return 2*this.width + 2*this.height; }
function Rectangle_set_size(w,h) { this.width = w; this.height = h; }
function Rectangle_enlarge( ) { this.width *= 2; this.height *= 2; }
function Rectangle_shrink( ) { this.width /= 2; this.height /= 2; }

// Then define a constructor method for our Rectangle objects.
// The constructor initializes properties and also assigns methods.
function Rectangle(w, h)
{
    // Initialize object properties.
    this.width = w;
    this.height = h;

    // Define methods for the object.
    this.area = Rectangle_area;
    this.perimeter = Rectangle_perimeter;
    this.set_size = Rectangle_set_size;
    this.enlarge = Rectangle_enlarge;
    this.shrink = Rectangle_shrink;
}
// Now, when we create a rectangle, we can immediately invoke methods on it:
var r = new Rectangle(2,2);
var a = r.area( );
r.enlarge( );
var p = r.perimeter( );
```

The technique shown in Example 8-3 also has a shortcoming. In this example, the `Rectangle()` constructor sets seven properties of each and every Rectangle object it initializes, even though five of those properties have constant values that are the same for every rectangle. Each property takes up memory space; by adding methods to our Rectangle class, we've more than tripled the memory requirements of each Rectangle object. Fortunately, JavaScript has a solution to this problem: it allows an object to inherit properties from a prototype object. The next section describes this technique in detail.

8.4 Prototypes and Inheritance

We've seen how inefficient it can be to use a constructor to assign methods to the objects it initializes. When we do this, each and every object created by the constructor has identical copies of the same method properties. There is a much more efficient way to specify methods, constants, and other properties that are shared by all objects in a class.

JavaScript objects "inherit" properties from a *prototype object*.* Every object has a prototype; all of the properties of the prototype object appear to be properties of any objects for which it is a prototype. That is, each object *inherits* properties from its prototype.

The prototype of an object is defined by the constructor function that was used to create and initialize the object. All functions in JavaScript have a `prototype` property that refers to an object. This prototype object is initially empty, but any properties you define in it will be inherited by all objects created by the constructor.

A constructor defines a class of objects and initializes properties, such as `width` and `height`, that are the state variables for the class. The prototype object is associated with the constructor, so each member of the class inherits exactly the same set of properties from the prototype. This means that the prototype object is an ideal place for methods and other constant properties.

Note that inheritance occurs automatically, as part of the process of looking up a property value. Properties are *not* copied from the prototype object into new objects; they merely appear as if they were properties of those objects. This has two important implications. First, the use of prototype objects can dramatically decrease the amount of memory required by each object, since the object can inherit many of its properties. The second implication is that an object inherits properties even if they are added to its prototype *after* the object is created.

Each class has one prototype object, with one set of properties. But there are potentially many instances of a class, each of which inherits those prototype properties. Because one prototype property can be inherited by many objects, JavaScript must

* Prototypes were introduced in JavaScript 1.1; they are not supported in the now obsolete JavaScript 1.0.

enforce a fundamental asymmetry between reading and writing property values. When you read property p of an object o, JavaScript first checks to see if o has a property named p. If it does not, it next checks to see if the prototype object of o has a property named p. This is what makes prototype-based inheritance work.

When you write the value of a property, on the other hand, JavaScript does not use the prototype object. To see why, consider what would happen if it did: suppose you try to set the value of the property o.p when the object o does not have a property named p. Further suppose that JavaScript goes ahead and looks up the property p in the prototype object of o and allows you to set the property of the prototype. Now you have changed the value of p for a whole class of objects—not at all what you intended.

Therefore, property inheritance occurs only when you read property values, not when you write them. If you set the property p in an object o that inherits that property from its prototype, what happens is that you create a new property p directly in o. Now that o has its own property named p, it no longer inherits the value of p from its prototype. When you read the value of p, JavaScript first looks at the properties of o. Since it finds p defined in o, it doesn't need to search the prototype object and never finds the value of p defined there. We sometimes say that the property p in o "shadows" or "hides" the property p in the prototype object. Prototype inheritance can be a confusing topic. Figure 8-1 illustrates the concepts we've discussed here.

Because prototype properties are shared by all objects of a class, it generally makes sense to use them only to define properties that are the same for all objects within the class. This makes prototypes ideal for defining methods. Other properties with constant values (such as mathematical constants) are also suitable for definition with prototype properties. If your class defines a property with a very commonly used default value, you might define this property and its default value in a prototype object. Then, the few objects that want to deviate from the default value can create their own private, unshared copies of the property and define their own nondefault values.

Let's move from an abstract discussion of prototype inheritance to a concrete example. Suppose we define a Circle() constructor function to create objects that represent circles. The prototype object for this class is Circle.prototype,* so we can define a constant available to all Circle objects like this:

```
Circle.prototype.pi = 3.14159;
```

* The prototype object of a constructor is created automatically by JavaScript. In most versions of JavaScript, every function is automatically given an empty prototype object, just in case it is used as a constructor. In JavaScript 1.1, however, the prototype object is not created until the function is used as a constructor for the first time. This means that if you require compatibility with JavaScript 1.1, you should create at least one object of a class before you use the prototype object to assign methods and constants to objects of that class. So, if we have defined a Circle() constructor but have not yet used it to create any Circle objects, we'd define the constant property pi like this:

```
// First create and discard a dummy object; forces prototype object creation.
new Circle();
// Now we can set properties in the prototype.
Circle.prototype.pi = 3.14159;
```

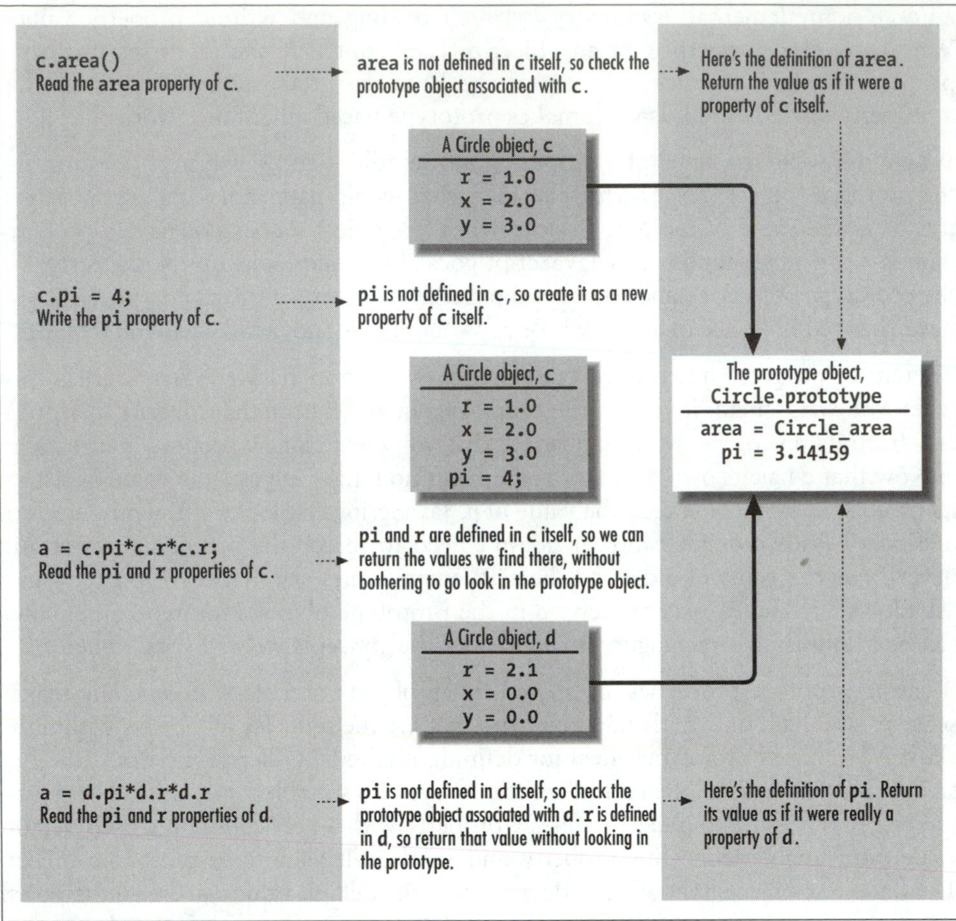

Figure 8-1. Objects and prototypes

Example 8-4 shows our Circle example fully fleshed out. The code defines a `Circle` class by first defining a `Circle( )` constructor to initialize each individual object and then setting properties of `Circle.prototype` to define methods and constants shared by all instances of the class.

Example 8-4. Defining a Circle class with a prototype object

```
// Define a constructor method for our class.
// Use it to initialize properties that will be different for
// each individual Circle object.
function Circle(x, y, r)
{
    this.x = x;  // The X-coordinate of the center of the circle
    this.y = y;  // The Y-coordinate of the center of the circle
    this.r = r;  // The radius of the circle
}
```

Example 8-4. Defining a Circle class with a prototype object (continued)

```
// Create and discard an initial Circle object.
// This forces the prototype object to be created in JavaScript 1.1.
new Circle(0,0,0);

// Define a constant: a property that will be shared by
// all circle objects. Actually, we could just use Math.PI,
// but we do it this way for the sake of instruction.
Circle.prototype.pi = 3.14159;

// Define a method to compute the circumference of the circle.
// First declare a function, then assign it to a prototype property.
// Note the use of the constant defined above.
function Circle_circumference( ) { return 2 * this.pi * this.r; }
Circle.prototype.circumference = Circle_circumference;

// Define another method. This time we use a function literal to define
// the function and assign it to a prototype property all in one step.
Circle.prototype.area = function( ) { return this.pi * this.r * this.r; }

// The Circle class is defined.
// Now we can create an instance and invoke its methods.
var c = new Circle(0.0, 0.0, 1.0);
var a = c.area( );
var p = c.circumference( );
```

8.4.1 Prototypes and Built-in Classes

It is not only user-defined classes that have prototype objects. Built-in classes, such as String and Date, have prototype objects too, and you can assign values to them.* For example, the following code defines a new method that is available for all String objects:

```
// Returns true if the last character is c
String.prototype.endsWith = function(c) {
    return (c == this.charAt(this.length-1))
}
```

Having defined the new `endsWith( )` method in the String prototype object, we can use it like this:

```
var message = "hello world";
message.endsWith('h')  // Returns false
message.endsWith('d')  // Returns true
```

8.5 Object-Oriented JavaScript

Although JavaScript supports a data type we call an object, it does not have a formal notion of a class. This makes it quite different from classic object-oriented languages

* In JavaScript 1.1 and later.

such as C++ and Java. The common conception about object-oriented programming languages is that they are strongly typed and support class-based inheritance. By these criteria, it is easy to dismiss JavaScript as not being a true object-oriented language. On the other hand, we've seen that JavaScript makes heavy use of objects and that it has its own type of prototype-based inheritance. JavaScript is a true object-oriented language. It draws inspiration from a number of other (relatively obscure) object-oriented languages that use prototype-based inheritance instead of class-based inheritance.

Although JavaScript is not a class-based object-oriented language, it does a good job of simulating the features of class-based languages such as Java and C++. I've been using the term class informally throughout this chapter. This section more formally explores the parallels between JavaScript and true class-based inheritance languages such as Java and C++.*

Let's start by defining some basic terminology. An *object*, as we've already seen, is a data structure that contains various pieces of named data and may also contain various methods to operate on those pieces of data. An object groups related values and methods into a single convenient package, which generally makes programming easier by increasing the modularity and reusability of code. Objects in JavaScript may have any number of properties, and properties may be dynamically added to an object. This is not the case in strictly typed languages such as Java and C++. In those languages, each object has a predefined set of properties,† where each property is of a predefined type. When we are using JavaScript objects to simulate object-oriented programming techniques, we generally define in advance the set of properties for each object and the type of data that each property holds.

In Java and C++, a *class* defines the structure of an object. The class specifies exactly what fields an object contains and what types of data each holds. It also defines the methods that operate on an object. JavaScript does not have a formal notion of a class, but, as we've seen, it approximates classes with its constructors and their prototype objects.

In both JavaScript and class-based object-oriented languages, there may be multiple objects of the same class. We often say that an object is an *instance* of its class. Thus, there may be many instances of any class. Sometimes we use the term *instantiate* to describe the process of creating an object (i.e., an instance of a class).

In Java, it is a common programming convention to name classes with an initial capital letter and to name objects with lowercase letters. This convention helps keep classes and objects distinct from each other in code; it is a useful convention to follow in JavaScript programming as well. In previous sections, for example, we've

* You should read this section even if you are not familiar with those languages and that style of object-oriented programming.

† They are usually called "fields" in Java and C++, but we'll refer to them as properties here, since that is the JavaScript terminology.

defined the Circle and Rectangle classes and have created instances of those classes named c and rect.

The members of a Java class may be of four basic types: instance properties, instance methods, class properties, and class methods. In the following sections, we'll explore the differences between these types and show how they are simulated in JavaScript.

8.5.1 Instance Properties

Every object has its own separate copies of its *instance properties*. In other words, if there are 10 objects of a given class, there are 10 copies of each instance property. In our Circle class, for example, every Circle object has a property r that specifies the radius of the circle. In this case, r is an instance property. Since each object has its own copy of the instance properties, these properties are accessed through individual objects. If c is an object that is an instance of the Circle class, for example, we refer to its radius as:

```
c.r
```

By default, any object property in JavaScript is an instance property. To truly simulate object-oriented programming, however, we will say that instance properties in JavaScript are those properties that are created and/or initialized in an object by the constructor function.

8.5.2 Instance Methods

An *instance method* is much like an instance property, except that it is a method rather than a data value. (In Java, functions and methods are not data, as they are in JavaScript, so this distinction is more clear.) Instance methods are invoked on a particular object, or instance. The area() method of our Circle class is an instance method. It is invoked on a Circle object c like this:

```
a = c.area();
```

Instance methods use the this keyword to refer to the object or instance on which they are operating. An instance method can be invoked for any instance of a class, but this does not mean that each object contains its own private copy of the method, as it does with instance properties. Instead, each instance method is shared by all instances of a class. In JavaScript, we define an instance method for a class by setting a property in the constructor's prototype object to a function value. This way, all objects created by that constructor share an inherited reference to the function and can invoke it using the method invocation syntax shown earlier.

8.5.3 Class Properties

A *class property* in Java is a property that is associated with a class itself, rather than with each instance of a class. No matter how many instances of the class are created, there is only one copy of each class property. Just as instance properties are accessed through an instance of a class, class properties are accessed through the class itself. `Number.MAX_VALUE` is an example of a class property in JavaScript: the `MAX_VALUE` property is accessed through the Number class. Because there is only one copy of each class property, class properties are essentially global. What is nice about them, however, is that they are associated with a class and they have a logical niche, a position in the JavaScript namespace, where they are not likely to be overwritten by other properties with the same name. As is probably clear, we simulate a class property in JavaScript simply by defining a property of the constructor function itself. For example, to create a class property `Circle.PI` to store the mathematical constant *pi*, we can do the following:

```
Circle.PI = 3.14;
```

`Circle` is a constructor function, but because JavaScript functions are objects, we can create properties of a function just as we can create properties of any other object.

8.5.4 Class Methods

Finally, we come to class methods. A *class method* is a method associated with a class rather than with an instance of a class; they are invoked through the class itself, not through a particular instance of the class. The `Date.parse( )` method (which you can look up in the core reference section of this book) is a class method. You always invoke it through the Date constructor object, rather than through a particular instance of the Date class.

Because class methods are not invoked through a particular object, they cannot meaningfully use the `this` keyword—`this` refers to the object for which an instance method is invoked. Like class properties, class methods are global. Because they do not operate on a particular object, class methods are generally more easily thought of as functions that happen to be invoked through a class. Again, associating these functions with a class gives them a convenient niche in the JavaScript namespace and prevents namespace collisions. To define a class method in JavaScript, we simply make the appropriate function a property of the constructor.

8.5.5 Example: The Circle Class

Example 8-5 is a reimplementation of our Circle class that contains examples of each of these four basic types of members.

Example 8-5. Defining instance and class properties and methods

```
function Circle(radius) {   // The constructor defines the class itself.
    // r is an instance property, defined and initialized in the constructor.
    this.r = radius;
}
```

Example 8-5. Defining instance and class properties and methods (continued)

```
// Circle.PI is a class property--it is a property of the constructor function.
Circle.PI = 3.14159;

// Here is a function that computes a circle's area.
function Circle_area( ) { return Circle.PI * this.r * this.r; }

// Here we make the function into an instance method by assigning it
// to the prototype object of the constructor.
// Note: with JavaScript 1.2, we can use a function literal to
// define the function without naming it Circle_area.
Circle.prototype.area = Circle_area;

// Here's another function. It takes two Circle objects as arguments and
// returns the one that is larger (i.e., has the larger radius).
function Circle_max(a,b) {
    if (a.r > b.r) return a;
    else return b;
}

// Since this function compares two Circle objects, it doesn't make sense as
// an instance method operating on a single Circle object. But we don't want
// it to be a standalone function either, so we make it into a class method
// by assigning it to the constructor function:
Circle.max = Circle_max;

// Here is some code that uses each of these fields:
var c = new Circle(1.0);      // Create an instance of the Circle class
c.r = 2.2;                    // Set the r instance property
var a = c.area();             // Invoke the area( ) instance method
var x = Math.exp(Circle.PI);  // Use the PI class property in our own computation
var d = new Circle(1.2);      // Create another Circle instance
var bigger = Circle.max(c,d); // Use the max( ) class method
```

8.5.6 Example: Complex Numbers

Example 8-6 is another example, somewhat more formal than the last, of defining a class of objects in JavaScript. The code and the comments are worth careful study. Note that this example uses the function literal syntax of JavaScript 1.2. Because it requires this version of the language (or later), it does not bother with the JavaScript 1.1 compatibility technique of invoking the constructor once before assigning to its prototype object.

Example 8-6. A complex number class

```
/*
 * Complex.js:
 * This file defines a Complex class to represent complex numbers.
 * Recall that a complex number is the sum of a real number and an
 * imaginary number and that the imaginary number i is the
 * square root of -1.
 */
```

Example 8-6. A complex number class (continued)

```
/*
 * The first step in defining a class is defining the constructor
 * function of the class. This constructor should initialize any
 * instance properties of the object. These are the essential
 * "state variables" that make each instance of the class different.
 */
function Complex(real, imaginary) {
    this.x = real;       // The real part of the number
    this.y = imaginary;  // The imaginary part of the number
}

/*
 * The second step in defining a class is defining its instance
 * methods (and possibly other properties) in the prototype object
 * of the constructor. Any properties defined in this object will
 * be inherited by all instances of the class. Note that instance
 * methods operate implicitly on the this keyword. For many methods,
 * no other arguments are needed.
 */

// Return the magnitude of a complex number. This is defined
// as its distance from the origin (0,0) of the complex plane.
Complex.prototype.magnitude = function( ) {
    return Math.sqrt(this.x*this.x + this.y*this.y);
};

// Return a complex number that is the negative of this one.
Complex.prototype.negative = function( ) {
    return new Complex(-this.x, -this.y);
};

//  Convert a Complex object to a string in a useful way.
//  This is invoked when a Complex object is used as a string.
Complex.prototype.toString = function( ) {
    return "{" + this.x + "," + this.y + "}";
};

// Return the real portion of a complex number. This function
// is invoked when a Complex object is treated as a primitive value.
Complex.prototype.valueOf = function( ) { return this.x; }

/*
 * The third step in defining a class is to define class methods,
 * constants, and any needed class properties as properties of the
 * constructor function itself (instead of as properties of the
 * prototype object of the constructor). Note that class methods
 * do not use the this keyword: they operate only on their arguments.
 */

// Add two complex numbers and return the result.
Complex.add = function (a, b) {
    return new Complex(a.x + b.x, a.y + b.y);
};
```

Example 8-6. A complex number class (continued)

```
// Subtract one complex number from another.
Complex.subtract = function (a, b) {
    return new Complex(a.x - b.x, a.y - b.y);
};

// Multiply two complex numbers and return the product.
Complex.multiply = function(a, b) {
    return new Complex(a.x * b.x - a.y * b.y,
                       a.x * b.y + a.y * b.x);
};

// Here are some useful predefined complex numbers.
// They are defined as class properties, where they can be used as
// "constants." (Note, though, that they are not actually read-only.)
Complex.zero = new Complex(0,0);
Complex.one = new Complex(1,0);
Complex.i = new Complex(0,1);
```

8.5.7 Superclasses and Subclasses

In Java, C++, and other class-based object-oriented languages, there is an explicit concept of the *class hierarchy*. Every class can have a *superclass* from which it inherits its properties and methods. Any class can be extended, or subclassed, so that the resulting *subclass* inherits its behavior. As we've seen, JavaScript supports prototype inheritance instead of class-based inheritance. Still, JavaScript analogies to the class hierarchy can be drawn. In JavaScript, the Object class is the most generic, and all other classes are specialized versions, or subclasses, of it. Another way to say this is that Object is the superclass of all the built-in classes. All classes inherit a few basic methods (described later in this chapter) from Object.

We've learned that objects inherit properties from the prototype object of their constructor. How do they also inherit properties from the Object class? Remember that the prototype object is itself an object; it is created with the `Object()` constructor. This means the prototype object itself inherits properties from `Object.prototype`! So, an object of class Complex inherits properties from the `Complex.prototype` object, which itself inherits properties from `Object.prototype`. Thus, the Complex object inherits properties of both objects. When you look up a property in a Complex object, the object itself is searched first. If the property is not found, the `Complex.prototype` object is searched next. Finally, if the property is not found in that object, the `Object.prototype` object is searched.

Note that because the Complex prototype object is searched before the Object prototype object, properties of `Complex.prototype` hide any properties with the same name in `Object.prototype`. For example, in the class definition shown in Example 8-6, we defined a `toString()` method in the `Complex.prototype` object. `Object.prototype` also defines a method with this name, but Complex objects never see it because the definition of `toString()` in `Complex.prototype` is found first.

The classes we've shown in this chapter are all direct subclasses of Object. This is typical of JavaScript programming; there is not usually any need to produce a more complex class hierarchy. When necessary, however, it is possible to subclass any other class. For example, suppose we want to produce a subclass of Complex in order to add some more methods. To do this, we simply have to make sure that the prototype object of the new class is itself an instance of Complex, so that it inherits all the properties of `Complex.prototype`:

```
// This is the constructor for the subclass.
function MoreComplex(real, imaginary) {
    this.x = real;
    this.y = imaginary;
}

// We force its prototype to be a Complex object. This means that
// instances of our new class inherit from MoreComplex.prototype,
// which inherits from Complex.prototype, which inherits from
// Object.prototype.
MoreComplex.prototype = new Complex(0,0);

// Now add a new method or other new features to this subclass.
MoreComplex.prototype.swap = function( ) {
    var tmp = this.x;
    this.x = this.y;
    this.y = tmp;
}
```

There is one subtle shortcoming to the subclassing technique shown here. Since we explicitly set `MoreComplex.prototype` to an object of our own creation, we overwrite the prototype object provided by JavaScript and discard the `constructor` property we are given. This `constructor` property, described later in this chapter, is supposed to refer to the constructor function that created the object. A `MoreComplex` object, however, inherits the `constructor` property of its superclass, rather than having one of its own. One solution is to set this property explicitly:

```
MoreComplex.prototype.constructor = MoreComplex;
```

Note, however, that in JavaScript 1.1, the `constructor` property is read-only and cannot be set in this way.

8.6 Objects as Associative Arrays

We've seen the `.` operator used to access the properties of an object. It is also possible to use the `[]` operator, which is more commonly used with arrays, to access these properties. Thus, the following two JavaScript expressions have the same value:

```
object.property
object["property"]
```

The important difference to note between these two syntaxes is that in the first, the property name is an identifier, and in the second, the property name is a string. We'll see why this is so important shortly.

In C, C++, Java, and similar strongly typed languages, an object can have only a fixed number of properties, and the names of these properties must be defined in advance. Since JavaScript is a loosely typed language, this rule does not apply—a program can create any number of properties in any object. When you use the `.` operator to access a property of an object, however, the name of the property is expressed as an identifier. Identifiers must be typed literally into your JavaScript program—they are not a data type, so they cannot be manipulated by the program.

On the other hand, when you access a property of an object with the `[]` array notation, the name of the property is expressed as a string. Strings are JavaScript data types, so they can be manipulated and created while a program is running. So, for example, you could write the following code in JavaScript:

```
var addr = "";
for(i = 0; i < 4; i++) {
    addr += customer["address" + i] + '\n';
}
```

This code reads and concatenates the `address0`, `address1`, `address2`, and `address3` properties of the `customer` object.

This brief example demonstrates the flexibility of using array notation to access properties of an object with string expressions. We could have written this example using the `.` notation, but there are cases where only the array notation will do. Suppose, for example, that you are writing a program that uses network resources to compute the current value of the user's stock market investments. The program allows the user to type in the name of each stock she owns, as well as the number of shares of each stock. You might use an object named `portfolio` to hold this information. The object has one property for each stock. The name of the property is the name of the stock and the property value is the number of shares of that stock. So, for example, if a user holds 50 shares of stock in IBM, the `portfolio.ibm` property has the value `50`.

Part of this program needs to have a loop that prompts the user to enter the name of a stock she owns and then asks her to enter the number of shares she owns of that stock. Inside the loop, you'd have code something like this:

```
var stock_name = get_stock_name_from_user();
var shares = get_number_of_shares();
portfolio[stock_name] = shares;
```

Since the user enters stock names at runtime, there is no way that you can know the property names ahead of time. Since you can't know the property names when you write the program, there is no way you can use the `.` operator to access the properties of the portfolio object. You can use the [] operator, however, because it uses a string value (which is dynamic and can change at runtime), rather than an identifier (which is static and must be hardcoded in the program), to name the property.

When an object is used this fashion, it is often called an *associative array*—a data structure that allows you to dynamically associate arbitrary values with arbitrary strings. JavaScript objects are actually implemented internally as associative arrays. The . notation for accessing properties makes them seem like the static objects of C++ and Java, and they work perfectly well in that capacity. But they also have the powerful ability to associate values with arbitrary strings. In this respect, JavaScript objects are much more like Perl arrays than C++ or Java objects.

Chapter 6 introduced the for/in loop. The real power of this JavaScript statement becomes clear when we consider its use with associative arrays. To return to the stock portfolio example, we might use the following code after the user has entered her portfolio and we are computing its current total value:

```
var value = 0;
for (stock in portfolio) {
    // For each stock in the portfolio, get the per share value
    // and multiply it by the number of shares.
    value += get_share_value(stock) * portfolio[stock];
}
```

We cannot write this code without the for/in loop because the names of the stocks aren't known in advance. This is the only way to extract those property names from the associative array (or JavaScript object) named portfolio.

8.7 Object Properties and Methods

As we discussed earlier, all objects in JavaScript inherit from the Object class. While more specialized classes, such as the built-in String class or a user-defined Complex class, define properties and methods of their own, all objects, whatever their class, also support the properties and methods defined by the Object class. Because of their universality, these properties and methods are of particular interest.

8.7.1 The constructor Property

Starting with JavaScript 1.1, every object has a constructor property that refers to the constructor function used to initialize the object. For example, if I create an object o with the Complex( ) constructor, the property o.constructor refers to Complex:

```
var o = new Complex(1,2);
o.constructor == Complex;  // Evaluates to true
```

Each Complex object (or object of whatever type) does not have its own unique constructor property, of course; instead, this property is inherited from the prototype object. As discussed earlier in this chapter, JavaScript creates a prototype object for each constructor function you define and assigns that object to the prototype property of the constructor. What I did not reveal earlier, however, is that the prototype object is not initially empty. When created, it includes a constructor property that refers to the constructor function. That is, for any function f, f.prototype.constructor is always equal to f (unless we set it to something else).

Since the constructor function defines the class of an object, the constructor property can be a powerful tool for determining the type of any given object. For example, you might use code like the following to determine the type of an unknown object:

```
if ((typeof o == "object") && (o.constructor == Date))
    // Then do something with the Date object...
```

The existence of the constructor property is not always guaranteed, however. The author of a class might replace the prototype object of a constructor with an entirely new object, for example, and the new object might not have a valid constructor property.

8.7.2 The toString( ) Method

The toString( ) method takes no arguments; it returns a string that somehow represents the type and/or value of the object on which it is invoked. JavaScript invokes this method of an object whenever it needs to convert the object to a string. This occurs, for example, when you use the + operator to concatenate a string with an object or when you pass an object to a method such as alert( ) or document.write( ).

The default toString( ) method is not very informative. For example, the following lines of code simply cause the browser to display the string "[object Object]":*

```
c = new Circle(1, 0, 0);
document.write(c);
```

Because this default method does not display much useful information, many classes define their own versions of toString( ). For example, when an array is converted to a string, we obtain a list of the array elements, themselves each converted to a string, and when a function is converted to a string, we obtain the source code for the function.

The idea behind toString( ) is that each class of objects has its own particular string representation, so it should define an appropriate toString( ) method to convert objects to that string form. Thus, when you define a class, you should define a custom toString( ) method for it so that instances of the class can be converted to

* In client-side JavaScript in Netscape, if the language attribute of the <script> tag is explicitly set to "JavaScript1.2", the toString( ) method behaves differently: it displays the names and values of all the fields of the object, using object literal notation. This violates the ECMAScript specification.

meaningful strings. The string should contain information about the object being converted, as this is useful for debugging purposes. If the string conversion is chosen carefully, it can also be useful in programs themselves.

The following code shows a `toString()` method we might define for the Circle class of Example 8-5:

```
Circle.prototype.toString = function () {
    return "[Circle of radius " + this.r + ", centered at ("
        + this.x + ", " + this.y + ").]";
}
```

With this `toString()` method defined, a typical Circle object might be converted to the string "[Circle of radius 1, centered at (0,0).]".

If you look back at Example 8-6, you'll see that it defines a `toString()` method for our Complex class of complex numbers.

One interesting feature of the default `toString()` method defined by the Object class is that it reveals some internal type information about built-in objects. This default `toString()` method always returns a string of the form:

```
[object class]
```

`class` is the internal type of the object and usually corresponds to the name of the constructor function for the object. For example, Array objects have a *`class`* of "Array", Function objects have a *`class`* of "Function", and Date objects have a *`class`* of "Date". The built-in Math object has a *`class`* of "Math", and all Error objects (including instances of the various Error subclasses) have a *`class`* of "Error". Client-side JavaScript objects and any other objects defined by the JavaScript implementation have an implementation-defined *`class`* (such as "Window", "Document", or "Form"). User-defined objects, such as the Circle and Complex classes defined earlier in this chapter, always have a *`class`* of "Object".

Note that this *`class`* value provides useful information that is not supplied by the `typeof` operator (which returns either "Object" or "Function" for all objects). The *`class`* value provides information like that provided by the `constructor` property described earlier, but the *`class`* value provides it in the form of a string, instead of in the form of a constructor function. The only way to obtain this *`class`* value, however, is through the default `toString()` method defined by Object. Because classes often define their own versions of this method, we cannot simply invoke the `toString()` method of an object:

```
o.toString()  // May invoke a customized toString() method for the object
```

Instead, we have to refer explicitly to the default `toString()` function as the `Object.prototype.toString` object and use the `apply()` method of the function to invoke it on the desired object:

```
Object.prototype.toString.apply(o); // Always invokes the default toString()
```

We can use this technique to define a function that provides enhanced "type of" functionality:

```
// An enhanced "type of" function. Returns a string that describes the
// type of x. Note that it returns "Object" for any user-defined object types.
function Typeof(x) {
    // Start with the typeof operator
    var t = typeof x;
    // If the result is not vague, return it
    if (t != "object")  return t;
    // Otherwise, x is an object. Get its class value to try to
    // find out what kind of object it is.
    var c = Object.prototype.toString.apply(x);  // Returns "[object class]"
    c = c.substring(8, c.length-1);              // Strip off "[object" and "]"
    return c;
}
```

8.7.3 The toLocaleString( ) Method

In ECMAScript v3 and JavaScript 1.5, the Object class defines a `toLocaleString( )` method in addition to its `toString( )` method. The purpose of this method is to return a localized string representation of the object. The default `toLocaleString( )` method defined by Object doesn't do any localization itself; it always return exactly the same thing as `toString( )`. Subclasses, however, may define their own versions of `toLocaleString( )`. In ECMAScript v3, the Array, Date, and Number classes do define `toLocaleString( )` methods that return localized values.

8.7.4 The valueOf( ) Method

The `valueOf( )` method is much like the `toString( )` method, but it is called when JavaScript needs to convert an object to some primitive type other than a string—typically, a number. Where possible, the function should return a primitive value that somehow represents the value of the object referred to by the `this` keyword.

By definition, objects are not primitive values, so most objects do not have a primitive equivalent. Thus, the default `valueOf( )` method defined by the Object class performs no conversion and simply returns the object on which it is invoked. Classes such as Number and Boolean have obvious primitive equivalents, so they override the `valueOf( )` method to return appropriate primitive values. This is why Number and Boolean objects can behave so much like their equivalent primitive values.

Occasionally, you may define a class that has some reasonable primitive equivalent. In this case, you may want to define a custom `valueOf( )` method for the class. If you refer back to Example 8-6, you'll see that we defined a `valueOf( )` method for the Complex class. This method simply returned the real part of the complex number.

Thus, when a Complex object is used in a numeric context, it behaves as if it were a real number without its imaginary component. For example, consider the following code:

```
var a = new Complex(5,4);
var b = new Complex(2,1);
var c = Complex.subtract(a,b);  // c is the complex number {3,3}
var d = a - b;                  // d is the number 3
```

One note of caution about defining a `valueOf( )` method: the `valueOf( )` method can, in some circumstances, take priority over the `toString( )` method when converting an object to a string. Thus, when you define a `valueOf( )` method for a class, you may need to be more explicit about calling the `toString( )` method when you want to force an object of that class to be converted to a string. To continue with the Complex example:

```
alert("c = " + c);             // Uses valueOf( ); displays "c = 3"
alert("c = " + c.toString( )); // Displays "c = {3,3}"
```

8.7.5 The hasOwnProperty( ) Method

The `hasOwnProperty( )` method returns `true` if the object locally defines a noninherited property with the name specified by the single string argument. Otherwise, it returns `false`. For example:

```
var o = new Object( );
o.hasOwnProperty("undef");     // false: the property is not defined
o.hasOwnProperty("toString");  // false: toString is an inherited property
Math.hasOwnProperty("cos");    // true: the Math object has a cos property
```

8.7.6 The propertyIsEnumerable( ) Method

The `propertyIsEnumerable( )` method returns `true` if the object defines a property with the name specified by the single string argument to the method and if that property would be enumerated by a `for/in` loop. Otherwise, it returns `false`. For example:

```
var o = { x:1 };
o.propertyIsEnumerable("x");        // true: property exists and is enumerable
o.propertyIsEnumerable("y");        // false: property doesn't exist
o.propertyIsEnumerable("valueOf");  // false: property isn't enumerable
```

Note that the ECMAScript specification states that `propertyIsEnumerable( )` considers only properties defined directly by the object, not inherited properties. This unfortunate restriction makes the function less useful, because a return value of `false` may mean either that the property is not enumerable or that it is enumerable but is an inherited property.

8.7.7 The isPrototypeOf( ) Method

The isPrototypeOf( ) method returns true if the object is the prototype object of the argument. Otherwise, it returns false. Using this method is similar to using the constructor property of an object. For example:

```
var o = new Object( );
Object.prototype.isPrototypeOf(o);          // true: o.constructor == Object
Object.isPrototypeOf(o);                    // false
o.isPrototypeOf(Object.prototype);          // false
Function.prototype.isPrototypeOf(Object);   // true: Object.constructor == Function
```

CHAPTER 9

Arrays

Chapter 8 documented the JavaScript object type—a composite data type that holds named values. This chapter documents arrays—a composite data type that holds numbered values. Note that the arrays we'll discuss in this chapter are different from the associative arrays described in the previous chapter. Associative arrays associate values with strings. The arrays described in this chapter are just regular numeric arrays; they associate values with non-negative integers.

Throughout this book, we often treat objects and arrays as distinct data types. This is a useful and reasonable simplification; you can treat objects and arrays as separate types for most of your JavaScript programming. To fully understand the behavior of objects and arrays, however, you have to know the truth: an array is nothing more than an object with a thin layer of extra functionality. We see this when we use the `typeof` operator: applied to an array value, it returns the string "object". Note that the extra functionality of arrays was introduced in JavaScript 1.1. Arrays are not supported in JavaScript 1.0.

This chapter documents basic array syntax, array programming techniques, and methods that operate on arrays.

9.1 Arrays and Array Elements

An *array* is a data type that contains or stores numbered values. Each numbered value is called an *element* of the array, and the number assigned to an element is called its *index*. Because JavaScript is an untyped language, an element of an array may be of any type, and different elements of the same array may be of different types. Array elements may even contain other arrays, which allows you to create data structures that are arrays of arrays.

9.1.1 Creating Arrays

In JavaScript 1.1 and later, arrays are created with the `Array( )` constructor and the `new` operator. You can invoke the `Array( )` constructor in three distinct ways.

The first way is to call it with no arguments:

```
var a = new Array( );
```

This method creates an empty array with no elements.

The second method of invoking the `Array( )` constructor allows you to explicitly specify values for the first *n* elements of an array:

```
var a = new Array(5, 4, 3, 2, 1, "testing, testing");
```

In this form, the constructor takes a list of arguments. Each argument specifies an element value and may be of any type. Elements are assigned to the array starting with element 0. The `length` property of the array is set to the number of arguments passed to the constructor.

The third way to invoke the `Array( )` constructor is to call it with a single numeric argument, which specifies a length:

```
var a = new Array(10);
```

This technique creates an array with the specified number of elements (each of which has the `undefined` value) and sets the array's `length` property to the value specified.*

Finally, array literals provide another way to create arrays. An array literal allows us to embed an array value directly into a JavaScript program in the same way that we define a string literal by placing the string text between quotation marks. To create an array literal, simply place a comma-separated list of values between square brackets. For example:

```
var primes = [2, 3, 5, 7, 11];
var a = ['a', true, 4.78];
```

Array literals can contain object literals or other array literals:

```
var b = [[1,{x:1, y:2}], [2, {x:3, y:4}]];
```

Chapter 3 provides complete details on array literals.

9.1.2 Reading and Writing Array Elements

You access an element of an array using the `[]` operator. A reference to the array should appear to the left of the brackets. An arbitrary expression that has a non-negative integer value should be inside the brackets. You can use this syntax to both read and write the value of an element of an array. Thus, the following are all legal JavaScript statements:

```
value = a[0];
a[1] = 3.14;
```

* In client-side JavaScript in Netscape, if the `language` attribute of the `<script>` tag is explicitly set to "JavaScript1.2", this third form of the `Array( )` constructor behaves like the second form: it creates an array of length one and initializes that array element to the constructor argument. This does not conform to the ECMAScript standard.

```
i = 2;
a[i] = 3;
a[i + 1] = "hello";
a[a[i]] = a[0];
```

In some languages, the first element of an array is at index 1. In JavaScript (as in C, C++, and Java), however, the first element of an array is at index 0.

As we saw in Chapter 8, the [] operator can also be used to access named object properties:

```
my['salary'] *= 2;
```

This is a clue that tells us that objects and arrays are fundamentally the same thing.

Note that array indexes must be integers greater than or equal to 0 and less than $2^{32}-1$. If you use a number that is too large, a negative number, or a floating-point number (or a boolean, an object, or other value), JavaScript converts it to a string and uses the resulting string as the name of an object property, not as an array index. Thus, the following line creates a new property named "–1.23"; it does not define a new array element:

```
a[-1.23] = true;
```

9.1.3 Adding New Elements to an Array

In languages such as C and Java, an array has a fixed number of elements that must be specified when you create the array. This is not the case in JavaScript—an array can have any number of elements, and you can change the number of elements at any time.

To add a new element to an array, simply assign a value to it:

```
a[10] = 10;
```

Arrays in JavaScript may be *sparse*. This means that array indexes need not fall into a contiguous range of numbers; a JavaScript implementation may allocate memory only for those array elements that are actually stored in the array. Thus, when you execute the following lines of code, the JavaScript interpreter will typically allocate memory only for array indexes 0 and 10,000, not for the 9,999 indexes between:

```
a[0] = 1;
a[10000] = "this is element 10,000";
```

Note that array elements can also be added to objects:

```
var c = new Circle(1,2,3);
c[0] = "this is an array element of an object!"
```

This example merely defines a new object property named "0", however. Adding array elements to an object does not make it an array. Arrays created with the `Array()` constructor or an array literal have some special features, explained below, that objects do not share.

9.1.4 Array Length

All arrays, whether created with the `Array()` constructor or defined with an array literal, have a special `length` property that specifies how many elements the array contains. More precisely, since arrays can have undefined elements, the `length` property is *always* one larger than the largest element number in the array. Unlike regular object properties, the `length` property of an array is automatically updated to maintain this invariant when new elements are added to the array. The following code illustrates:

```
var a = new Array();    // a.length == 0  (no elements defined)
a = new Array(10);      // a.length == 10 (empty elements 0-9 defined)
a = new Array(1,2,3);   // a.length == 3  (elements 0-2 defined)
a = [4, 5];             // a.length == 2  (elements 0 and 1 defined)
a[5] = -1;              // a.length == 6  (elements 0, 1, and 5 defined)
a[49] = 0;              // a.length == 50 (elements 0, 1, 5, and 49 defined)
```

Remember that array indexes must be less than $2^{32}-1$, which means that the largest possible value for the `length` property is $2^{32}-1$.

Probably the most common use of the `length` property of an array is to allow us to loop through the elements of an array:

```
var fruits = ["mango", "banana", "cherry", "pear"];
for(var i = 0; i < fruits.length; i++)
    alert(fruits[i]);
```

This example assumes, of course, that elements of the array are contiguous and begin at element 0. If this were not the case, we would want to test that each array element was defined before using it:

```
for(var i = 0; i < fruits.length; i++)
    if (fruits[i] != undefined) alert(fruits[i]);
```

The `length` property of an array is a read/write value. If you set `length` to a value smaller than its current value, the array is truncated to the new length; any elements that no longer fit are discarded and their values are lost. If you make `length` larger than its current value, new, undefined elements are added at the end of the array to increase it to the newly specified size.

Truncating an array by setting its `length` property is the only way that you can actually shorten an array. If you use the `delete` operator to delete an array element, that element becomes undefined, but the `length` property does not change.

Note that although objects can be assigned array elements, they do not have a `length` property. The `length` property, with its special behavior, is the most important feature of arrays. The other features that make arrays different from objects are the various methods defined by the Array class, which are described in Section 9.2, "Array Methods."

9.1.5 Multidimensional Arrays

JavaScript does not support true multidimensional arrays, but it does allow you to approximate them quite nicely with arrays of arrays. To access a data element in an array of arrays, simply use the [] operator twice. For example, suppose the variable matrix is an array of arrays of numbers. Every element matrix[x] is an array of numbers. To access a particular number within this array, you would write matrix[x][y].

9.2 Array Methods

In addition to the [] operator, arrays can be manipulated through various methods provided by the Array class. The following sections introduce these methods. Many of the methods were inspired in part by the Perl programming language; Perl programmers may find them comfortingly familiar. As usual, this is an overview only; complete details can be found in the core reference section of this book.

9.2.1 join( )

The Array.join( ) method converts all the elements of an array to strings and concatenates them. You can specify an optional string that is used to separate the elements in the resulting string. If no separator string is specified, a comma is used. For example, the following lines of code produce the string "1,2,3":

```
var a = [1, 2, 3];  // Create a new array with these three elements
var s = a.join( );  // s == "1,2,3"
```

The following invocation specifies the optional separator to produce a slightly different result:

```
s = a.join(", ");   // s == "1, 2, 3"
```

Notice the space after the comma. The Array.join( ) method is the inverse of the String.split( ) method, which creates an array by breaking up a string into pieces.

9.2.2 reverse( )

The Array.reverse( ) method reverses the order of the elements of an array and returns the reversed array. It does this in place—in other words, it doesn't create a new array with the elements rearranged, but instead rearranges them in the already existing array. For example, the following code, which uses the reverse( ) and join( ) methods, produces the string "3,2,1":

```
var a = new Array(1,2,3);  // a[0] = 1, a[1] = 2, a[2] = 3
a.reverse( );              // now a[0] = 3, a[1] = 2, a[2] = 1
var s = a.join( );         // s == "3,2,1"
```

9.2.3 sort( )

`Array.sort()` sorts the elements of an array in place and returns the sorted array. When `sort()` is called with no arguments, it sorts the array elements in alphabetical order (temporarily converting them to strings to perform the comparison, if necessary):

```
var a = new Array("banana", "cherry", "apple");
a.sort();
var s = a.join(", ");  // s == "apple, banana, cherry"
```

If an array contains undefined elements, they are sorted to the end of the array.

To sort an array into some order other than alphabetical, you must pass a comparison function as an argument to `sort()`. This function decides which of its two arguments should appear first in the sorted array. If the first argument should appear before the second, the comparison function should return a number less than zero. If the first argument should appear after the second in the sorted array, the function should return a number greater than zero. And if the two values are equivalent (i.e., if their order is irrelevant), the comparison function should return 0. So, for example, to sort array elements into numerical rather than alphabetical order, you might do this:

```
var a = [33, 4, 1111, 222];
a.sort();                 // Alphabetical order:  1111, 222, 33, 4
a.sort(function(a,b) {   // Numerical order: 4, 33, 222, 1111
           return a-b;    // Returns < 0, 0, or > 0, depending on order
       });
```

Note the convenient use of a function literal in this code. Since the comparison function is used only once, there is no need to give it a name.

As another example of sorting array items, you might perform a case-insensitive alphabetical sort on an array of strings by passing a comparison function that converts both of its arguments to lowercase (with the `toLowerCase()` method) before comparing them. You can probably think of other comparison functions that sort numbers into various esoteric orders: reverse numerical order, odd numbers before even numbers, etc. The possibilities become more interesting, of course, when the array elements you are comparing are objects, rather than simple types like numbers or strings.

9.2.4 concat( )

The `Array.concat()` method creates and returns a new array that contains the elements of the original array on which `concat()` was invoked, followed by each of the arguments to `concat()`. If any of these arguments is itself an array, it is flattened and its elements are added to the returned array. Note, however, that `concat()` does not recursively flatten arrays of arrays. Here are some examples:

```
var a = [1,2,3];
a.concat(4, 5)          // Returns [1,2,3,4,5]
```

```
a.concat([4,5]);          // Returns [1,2,3,4,5]
a.concat([4,5],[6,7])     // Returns [1,2,3,4,5,6,7]
a.concat(4, [5,[6,7]])    // Returns [1,2,3,4,5,[6,7]]
```

9.2.5 slice( )

The `Array.slice( )` method returns a *slice*, or subarray, of the specified array. Its two arguments specify the start and end of the slice to be returned. The returned array contains the element specified by the first argument and all subsequent elements up to, but not including, the element specified by the second argument. If only one argument is specified, the returned array contains all elements from the start position to the end of the array. If either argument is negative, it specifies an array element relative to the last element in the array. An argument of –1, for example, specifies the last element in the array, and an argument of –3 specifies the third from last element of the array. Here are some examples:

```
var a = [1,2,3,4,5];
a.slice(0,3);    // Returns [1,2,3]
a.slice(3);      // Returns [4,5]
a.slice(1,-1);   // Returns [2,3,4]
a.slice(-3,-2);  // Returns [3]
```

9.2.6 splice( )

The `Array.splice( )` method is a general-purpose method for inserting or removing elements from an array. `splice( )` modifies the array in place; it does not return a new array, as `slice( )` and `concat( )` do. Note that `splice( )` and `slice( )` have very similar names but perform substantially different operations.

`splice( )` can delete elements from an array, insert new elements into an array, or perform both operations at the same time. Array elements that appear after the insertion or deletion are moved as necessary so that they remain contiguous with the rest of the array. The first argument to `splice( )` specifies the array position at which the insertion and/or deletion is to begin. The second argument specifies the number of elements that should be deleted from (spliced out of) the array. If this second argument is omitted, all array elements from the start element to the end of the array are removed. `splice( )` returns an array of the deleted elements, or an empty array if no elements were deleted. For example:

```
var a = [1,2,3,4,5,6,7,8];
a.splice(4);    // Returns [5,6,7,8]; a is [1,2,3,4]
a.splice(1,2);  // Returns [2,3]; a is [1,4]
a.splice(1,1);  // Returns [4]; a is [1]
```

The first two arguments to `splice( )` specify which array elements are to be deleted. These arguments may be followed by any number of additional arguments that specify elements to be inserted into the array, starting at the position specified by the first argument. For example:

```
var a = [1,2,3,4,5];
a.splice(2,0,'a','b');  // Returns []; a is [1,2,'a','b',3,4,5]
a.splice(2,2,[1,2],3);  // Returns ['a','b']; a is [1,2,[1,2],3,3,4,5]
```

Note that, unlike concat( ), splice( ) does not flatten array arguments that it inserts. That is, if it is passed an array to insert, it inserts the array itself, not the elements of that array.

9.2.7 push( ) and pop( )

The push( ) and pop( ) methods allow us to work with arrays as if they were stacks. The push( ) method appends one or more new elements to the end of an array and returns the new length of the array.* The pop( ) method does the reverse: it deletes the last element of an array, decrements the array length, and returns the value that it removed. Note that both of these methods modify the array in place rather than producing a modified copy of the array. The combination of push( ) and pop( ) allows us to use a JavaScript array to implement a first in, last out stack. For example:

```
var stack = [];       // stack: []
stack.push(1,2);      // stack: [1,2]     Returns 2
stack.pop( );         // stack: [1]       Returns 2
stack.push(3);        // stack: [1,3]     Returns 2
stack.pop( );         // stack: [1]       Returns 3
stack.push([4,5]);    // stack: [1,[4,5]] Returns 2
stack.pop( )          // stack: [1]       Returns [4,5]
stack.pop( );         // stack: []        Returns 1
```

9.2.8 unshift( ) and shift( )

The unshift( ) and shift( ) methods behave much like push( ) and pop( ), except that they insert and remove elements from the beginning of an array, rather than from the end. unshift( ) adds an element or elements to the beginning of the array, shifts the existing array elements up to higher indexes to make room, and returns the new length of the array. shift( ) removes and returns the first element of the array, shifting all subsequent elements down one place to occupy the newly vacant space at the start of the array. For example:

```
var a = [];              // a:[]
a.unshift(1);            // a:[1]           Returns: 1
a.unshift(22);           // a:[22,1]        Returns: 2
a.shift( );              // a:[1]           Returns: 22
a.unshift(3,[4,5]);      // a:[3,[4,5],1]   Returns: 3
a.shift( );              // a:[[4,5],1]     Returns: 3
a.shift( );              // a:[1]           Returns: [4,5]
a.shift( );              // a:[]            Returns: 1
```

* In Netscape, when the language attribute of the <script> tag is explicitly set to "JavaScript1.2", push( ) returns the last value it appends to the array, rather than the new length of the array.

Note the possibly surprising behavior of unshift( ) when it's invoked with multiple arguments. Instead of being inserted into the array one at a time, arguments are inserted all at once (as with the splice( ) method). This means that they appear in the resulting array in the same order in which they appeared in the argument list. Had the elements been inserted one at a time, their order would have been reversed.

9.2.9 toString( ) and toLocaleString( )

An array, like any JavaScript object, has a toString( ) method. For an array, this method converts each of its elements to a string (calling the toString( ) methods of its elements, if necessary) and outputs a comma-separated list of those strings. Note that the output does not include square brackets or any other sort of delimiter around the array value. For example:

```
[1,2,3].toString( )          // Yields '1,2,3'
["a", "b", "c"].toString( )  // Yields 'a,b,c'
[1, [2,'c']].toString( )     // Yields '1,2,c'
```

Note that toString( ) returns the same string the join( ) method does when it is invoked with no arguments.*

toLocaleString( ) is the localized version of toString( ). It converts each array element to a string by calling the toLocaleString( ) method of the element, and then it concatenates the resulting strings using a locale-specific (and implementation-defined) separator string.

* In Netscape, when the language attribute of the <script> tag is set to "JavaScript1.2", toString( ) behaves in a more complex way. In this case, it converts arrays to strings that include square brackets, and includes quotation marks around array elements that are strings, so that the resulting strings are valid array literal expressions.

CHAPTER 10

Pattern Matching with Regular Expressions

A *regular expression* is an object that describes a pattern of characters. The JavaScript RegExp class represents regular expressions, and both String and RegExp define methods that use regular expressions to perform powerful pattern-matching and search-and-replace functions on text.*

JavaScript regular expressions were standardized in ECMAScript v3. JavaScript 1.2 implements a subset of the regular expression features required by ECMAScript v3, and JavaScript 1.5 implements the full standard. JavaScript regular expressions are strongly based on the regular expression facilities of the Perl programming language. Roughly speaking, we can say that JavaScript 1.2 implements Perl 4 regular expressions, and JavaScript 1.5 implements a large subset of Perl 5 regular expressions.

This chapter begins by defining the syntax that regular expressions use to describe textual patterns. Then it moves on to describe the String and RegExp methods that use regular expressions.

10.1 Defining Regular Expressions

In JavaScript, regular expressions are represented by RegExp objects. RegExp objects may be created with the `RegExp()` constructor, of course, but they are more often created using a special literal syntax. Just as string literals are specified as characters within quotation marks, regular expression literals are specified as characters within a pair of slash (/) characters. Thus, your JavaScript code may contain lines like this:

```
var pattern = /s$/;
```

This line creates a new RegExp object and assigns it to the variable `pattern`. This particular RegExp object matches any string that ends with the letter "s". (We'll talk

* The term "regular expression" is an obscure one that dates back many years. The syntax used to describe a textual pattern is indeed a type of expression. However, as we'll see, that syntax is far from regular! A regular expression is sometimes called a "regexp" or even an "RE."

about the grammar for defining patterns shortly.) This regular expression could have equivalently been defined with the `RegExp()` constructor like this:

```
var pattern = new RegExp("s$");
```

Creating a RegExp object, either literally or with the `RegExp()` constructor, is the easy part. The more difficult task is describing the desired pattern of characters using regular expression syntax. JavaScript adopts a fairly complete subset of the regular expression syntax used by Perl, so if you are an experienced Perl programmer, you already know how to describe patterns in JavaScript.

Regular expression pattern specifications consist of a series of characters. Most characters, including all alphanumeric characters, simply describe characters to be matched literally. Thus, the regular expression `/java/` matches any string that contains the substring "java". Other characters in regular expressions are not matched literally, but have special significance. For example, the regular expression `/s$/` contains two characters. The first, "s", matches itself literally. The second, "$", is a special metacharacter that matches the end of a string. Thus, this regular expression matches any string that contains the letter "s" as its last character.

The following sections describe the various characters and metacharacters used in JavaScript regular expressions. Note, however, that a complete tutorial on regular expression grammar is beyond the scope of this book. For complete details of the syntax, consult a book on Perl, such as *Programming Perl*, by Larry Wall, Tom Christiansen, and Jon Orwant (O'Reilly). *Mastering Regular Expressions*, by Jeffrey E.F. Friedl (O'Reilly), is another excellent source of information on regular expressions.

10.1.1 Literal Characters

As we've seen, all alphabetic characters and digits match themselves literally in regular expressions. JavaScript regular expression syntax also supports certain nonalphabetic characters through escape sequences that begin with a backslash (\). For example, the sequence `\n` matches a literal newline character in a string. Table 10-1 lists these characters.

Table 10-1. Regular expression literal characters

Character	Matches
Alphanumeric character	Itself
`\0`	The NUL character (`\u0000`)
`\t`	Tab (`\u0009`)
`\n`	Newline (`\u000A`)
`\v`	Vertical tab (`\u000B`)
`\f`	Form feed (`\u000C`)
`\r`	Carriage return (`\u000D`)
`\x`*nn*	The Latin character specified by the hexadecimal number *nn*; for example, `\x0A` is the same as `\n`

Table 10-1. Regular expression literal characters (continued)

Character	Matches
\u*xxxx*	The Unicode character specified by the hexadecimal number *xxxx*; for example, \u0009 is the same as \t
\c*X*	The control character ^*X*; for example, \cJ is equivalent to the newline character \n

A number of punctuation characters have special meanings in regular expressions. They are:

```
^ $ . * + ? = ! : | \ / ( ) [ ] { }
```

We'll learn the meanings of these characters in the sections that follow. Some of these characters have special meaning only within certain contexts of a regular expression and are treated literally in other contexts. As a general rule, however, if you want to include any of these punctuation characters literally in a regular expression, you must precede them with a \. Other punctuation characters, such as quotation marks and @, do not have special meaning and simply match themselves literally in a regular expression.

If you can't remember exactly which punctuation characters need to be escaped with a backslash, you may safely place a backslash before any punctuation character. On the other hand, note that many letters and numbers have special meaning when preceded by a backslash, so any letters or numbers that you want to match literally should not be escaped with a backslash. To include a backslash character literally in a regular expression, you must escape it with a backslash, of course. For example, the following regular expression matches any string that includes a backslash: `/\\/`.

10.1.2 Character Classes

Individual literal characters can be combined into *character classes* by placing them within square brackets. A character class matches any one character that is contained within it. Thus, the regular expression `/[abc]/` matches any one of the letters a, b, or c. Negated character classes can also be defined—these match any character except those contained within the brackets. A negated character class is specified by placing a caret (^) as the first character inside the left bracket. The regexp `/[^abc]/` matches any one character other than a, b, or c. Character classes can use a hyphen to indicate a range of characters. To match any one lowercase character from the Latin alphabet, use `/[a-z]/`, and to match any letter or digit from the Latin alphabet, use `/[a-zA-Z0-9]/`.

Because certain character classes are commonly used, the JavaScript regular expression syntax includes special characters and escape sequences to represent these common classes. For example, \s matches the space character, the tab character, and any other Unicode whitespace character, and \S matches any character that is *not* Unicode whitespace. Table 10-2 lists these characters and summarizes character class syntax. (Note that several of these character class escape sequences match only

ASCII characters and have not been extended to work with Unicode characters. You can explicitly define your own Unicode character classes; for example, /[\u0400-04FF]/ matches any one Cyrillic character.)

Table 10-2. Regular expression character classes

Character	Matches
[...]	Any one character between the brackets.
[^...]	Any one character not between the brackets.
.	Any character except newline or another Unicode line terminator.
\w	Any ASCII word character. Equivalent to [a-zA-Z0-9_].
\W	Any character that is not an ASCII word character. Equivalent to [^a-zA-Z0-9_].
\s	Any Unicode whitespace character.
\S	Any character that is not Unicode whitespace. Note that \w and \S are not the same thing.
\d	Any ASCII digit. Equivalent to [0-9].
\D	Any character other than an ASCII digit. Equivalent to [^0-9].
[\b]	A literal backspace (special case).

Note that the special character class escapes can be used within square brackets. \s matches any whitespace character and \d matches any digit, so /[\s\d]/ matches any one whitespace character or digit. Note that there is one special case. As we'll see later, the \b escape has a special meaning. When used within a character class, however, it represents the backspace character. Thus, to represent a backspace character literally in a regular expression, use the character class with one element: /[\b]/.

10.1.3 Repetition

With the regular expression syntax we have learned so far, we can describe a two-digit number as /\d\d/ and a four-digit number as /\d\d\d\d/. But we don't have any way to describe, for example, a number that can have any number of digits or a string of three letters followed by an optional digit. These more complex patterns use regular expression syntax that specifies how many times an element of a regular expression may be repeated.

The characters that specify repetition always follow the pattern to which they are being applied. Because certain types of repetition are quite commonly used, there are special characters to represent these cases. For example, + matches one or more occurrences of the previous pattern. Table 10-3 summarizes the repetition syntax. The following lines show some examples:

```
/\d{2,4}/     // Match between two and four digits
/\w{3}\d?/    // Match exactly three word characters and an optional digit
/\s+java\s+/  // Match "java" with one or more spaces before and after
/[^"]*/       // Match zero or more non-quote characters
```

Table 10-3. Regular expression repetition characters

Character	Meaning
`{n,m}`	Match the previous item at least *n* times but no more than *m* times.
`{n,}`	Match the previous item *n* or more times.
`{n}`	Match exactly *n* occurrences of the previous item.
`?`	Match zero or one occurrences of the previous item. That is, the previous item is optional. Equivalent to `{0,1}`.
`+`	Match one or more occurrences of the previous item. Equivalent to `{1,}`.
`*`	Match zero or more occurrences of the previous item. Equivalent to `{0,}`.

Be careful when using the * and ? repetition characters. Since these characters may match zero instances of whatever precedes them, they are allowed to match nothing. For example, the regular expression `/a*/` actually matches the string "bbbb", because the string contains zero occurrences of the letter a!

10.1.3.1 Non-greedy repetition

The repetition characters listed in Table 10-3 match as many times as possible while still allowing any following parts of the regular expression to match. We say that the repetition is "greedy." It is also possible (in JavaScript 1.5 and later—this is one of the Perl 5 features not implemented in JavaScript 1.2) to specify that repetition should be done in a non-greedy way. Simply follow the repetition character or characters with a question mark: `??`, `+?`, `*?`, or even `{1,5}?`. For example, the regular expression `/a+/` matches one or more occurrences of the letter a. When applied to the string "aaa", it matches all three letters. But `/a+?/` matches one or more occurrences of the letter a, matching as few characters as necessary. When applied to the same string, this pattern matches only the first letter a.

Using non-greedy repetition may not always produce the results you expect. Consider the pattern `/a*b/`, which matches zero or more letters a followed by the letter b. When applied to the string "aaab", it matches the entire string. Now let's use the non-greedy version: `/a*?b/`. This should match the letter b preceded by the fewest number of a's possible. When applied to the same string "aaab", you might expect it to match only the last letter b. In fact, however, this pattern matches the entire string as well, just like the greedy version of the pattern. This is because regular expression pattern matching is done by finding the first position in the string at which a match is possible. The non-greedy version of our pattern does match at the first character of the string, so this match is returned; matches at subsequent characters are never even considered.

10.1.4 Alternation, Grouping, and References

The regular expression grammar includes special characters for specifying alternatives, grouping subexpressions, and referring to previous subexpressions. The `|` character separates alternatives. For example, `/ab|cd|ef/` matches the string "ab" or the string "cd" or the string "ef". And `/\d{3}|[a-z]{4}/` matches either three digits or four lowercase letters.

Note that alternatives are considered left to right until a match is found. If the left alternative matches, the right alternative is ignored, even if it would have produced a "better" match. Thus, when the pattern `/a|ab/` is applied to the string "ab", it matches only the first letter.

Parentheses have several purposes in regular expressions. One purpose is to group separate items into a single subexpression, so that the items can be treated as a single unit by `|`, `*`, `+`, `?`, and so on. For example, `/java(script)?/` matches "java" followed by the optional "script". And `/(ab|cd)+|ef)/` matches either the string "ef" or one or more repetitions of either of the strings "ab" or "cd".

Another purpose of parentheses in regular expressions is to define subpatterns within the complete pattern. When a regular expression is successfully matched against a target string, it is possible to extract the portions of the target string that matched any particular parenthesized subpattern. (We'll see how these matching substrings are obtained later in the chapter.) For example, suppose we are looking for one or more lowercase letters followed by one or more digits. We might use the pattern `/[a-z]+\d+/`. But suppose we only really care about the digits at the end of each match. If we put that part of the pattern in parentheses (`/[a-z]+(\d+)/`), we can extract the digits from any matches we find, as explained later.

A related use of parenthesized subexpressions is to allow us to refer back to a subexpression later in the same regular expression. This is done by following a `\` character by a digit or digits. The digits refer to the position of the parenthesized subexpression within the regular expression. For example, `\1` refers back to the first subexpression and `\3` refers to the third. Note that, because subexpressions can be nested within others, it is the position of the left parenthesis that is counted. In the following regular expression, for example, the nested subexpression `([Ss]cript)` is referred to as `\2`:

```
/([Jj]ava([Ss]cript)?)\sis\s(fun\w*)/
```

A reference to a previous subexpression of a regular expression does *not* refer to the pattern for that subexpression, but rather to the text that matched the pattern. Thus, references can be used to enforce a constraint that separate portions of a string contain exactly the same characters. For example, the following regular expression matches zero or more characters within single or double quotes. However, it does not require the opening and closing quotes to match (i.e., both single quotes or both double quotes):

```
/['"][^'"]*['"]/
```

To require the quotes to match, we can use a reference:

```
/(['"])[^'"]*\1/
```

The `\1` matches whatever the first parenthesized subexpression matched. In this example, it enforces the constraint that the closing quote match the opening quote. This regular expression does not allow single quotes within double-quoted strings or vice versa. It is not legal to use a reference within a character class, so we cannot write:

```
/(['"])[^\1]*\1/
```

Later in this chapter, we'll see that this kind of reference to a parenthesized subexpression is a powerful feature of regular expression search-and-replace operations.

In JavaScript 1.5 (but not JavaScript 1.2), it is possible to group items in a regular expression without creating a numbered reference to those items. Instead of simply grouping the items within `(` and `)`, begin the group with `(?:` and end it with `)`. Consider the following pattern, for example:

```
/([Jj]ava(?:[Ss]cript)?)\sis\s(fun\w*)/
```

Here, the subexpression `(?:[Ss]cript)` is used simply for grouping, so the `?` repetition character can be applied to the group. These modified parentheses do not produce a reference, so in this regular expression, `\2` refers to the text matched by `(fun\w*)`.

Table 10-4 summarizes the regular expression alternation, grouping, and referencing operators.

Table 10-4. Regular expression alternation, grouping, and reference characters

Character	Meaning
`|`	Alternation. Match either the subexpressions to the left or the subexpression to the right.
`(...)`	Grouping. Group items into a single unit that can be used with `*`, `+`, `?`, `|`, and so on. Also remember the characters that match this group for use with later references.
`(?:...)`	Grouping only. Group items into a single unit, but do not remember the characters that match this group.
`\n`	Match the same characters that were matched when group number *n* was first matched. Groups are subexpressions within (possibly nested) parentheses. Group numbers are assigned by counting left parentheses from left to right. Groups formed with `(?:` are not numbered.

10.1.5 Specifying Match Position

We've seen that many elements of a regular expression match a single character in a string. For example, `\s` matches a single character of whitespace. Other regular expression elements match the positions between characters, instead of actual characters. `\b`, for example, matches a word boundary—the boundary between a `\w` (ASCII word character) and a `\W` (non-word character), or the boundary between an ASCII word character and the beginning or end of a string.* Elements like `\b` do not specify any characters to be used in a matched string; what they do specify, however, is legal positions at which a match can occur. Sometimes these elements are called regular expression anchors, because they anchor the pattern to a specific position in the search

* Except within a character class (square brackets), where `\b` matches the backspace character.

string. The most commonly used anchor elements are ^, which ties the pattern to the beginning of the string, and $, which anchors the pattern to the end of the string.

For example, to match the word "JavaScript" on a line by itself, we could use the regular expression `/^JavaScript$/`. If we wanted to search for "Java" used as a word by itself (not as a prefix, as it is in "JavaScript"), we might try the pattern `/\sJava\s/`, which requires a space before and after the word. But there are two problems with this solution. First, it does not match "Java" if that word appears at the beginning or the end of a string, but only if it appears with space on either side. Second, when this pattern does find a match, the matched string it returns has leading and trailing spaces, which is not quite what we want. So instead of matching actual space characters with `\s`, we instead match (or anchor to) word boundaries with `\b`. The resulting expression is `/\bJava\b/`. The element `\B` anchors the match to a location that is not a word boundary. Thus, the pattern `/\B[Ss]cript/` matches "JavaScript" and "postscript", but not "script" or "Scripting".

In JavaScript 1.5 (but not JavaScript 1.2), you can also use arbitrary regular expressions as anchor conditions. If you include an expression within `(?=` and `)` characters, it is a look-ahead assertion, and it specifies that the following characters must match, without actually matching them. For example, to match the name of a common programming language, but only if it is followed by a colon, you could use `/[Jj]ava([Ss]cript)?(?=\:)/`. This pattern matches the word "JavaScript" in "JavaScript: The Definitive Guide", but it does not match "Java" in "Java in a Nutshell" because it is not followed by a colon.

If you instead introduce an assertion with `(?!`, it is a negative look-ahead assertion, which specifies that the following characters must not match. For example, `/Java(?!Script)([A-Z]\w*)/` matches "Java" followed by a capital letter and any number of additional ASCII word characters, as long as "Java" is not followed by "Script". It matches "JavaBeans" but not "Javanese", and it matches "JavaScrip" but not "JavaScript" or "JavaScripter".

Table 10-5 summarizes regular expression anchors.

Table 10-5. Regular expression anchor characters

Character	Meaning
`^`	Match the beginning of the string and, in multiline searches, the beginning of a line.
`$`	Match the end of the string and, in multiline searches, the end of a line.
`\b`	Match a word boundary. That is, match the position between a `\w` character and a `\W` character or between a `\w` character and the beginning or end of a string. (Note, however, that `[\b]` matches backspace.)
`\B`	Match a position that is not a word boundary.
`(?=`*p*`)`	A positive look-ahead assertion. Require that the following characters match the pattern *p*, but do not include those characters in the match.
`(?!`*p*`)`	A negative look-ahead assertion. Require that the following characters do not match the pattern *p*.

10.1.6 Flags

There is one final element of regular expression grammar. Regular expression flags specify high-level pattern-matching rules. Unlike the rest of regular expression syntax, flags are specified outside of the / characters; instead of appearing within the slashes, they appear following the second slash. JavaScript 1.2 supports two flags. The `i` flag specifies that pattern matching should be case-insensitive. The `g` flag specifies that pattern matching should be global—that is, all matches within the searched string should be found. Both flags may be combined to perform a global case-insensitive match.

For example, to do a case-insensitive search for the first occurrence of the word "java" (or "Java", "JAVA", etc.), we could use the case-insensitive regular expression `/\bjava\b/i`. And to find all occurrences of the word in a string, we would add the `g` flag: `/\bjava\b/gi`.

JavaScript 1.5 supports an additional flag: `m`. The `m` flag performs pattern matching in multiline mode. In this mode, if the string to be searched contains newlines, the `^` and `$` anchors match the beginning and end of a line in addition to matching the beginning and end of a string. For example, the pattern `/Java$/im` matches "java" as well as "Java\nis fun".

Table 10-6 summarizes these regular expression flags. Note that we'll see more about the `g` flag later in this chapter, when we consider the String and RegExp methods used to actually perform matches.

Table 10-6. Regular expression flags

Character	Meaning
`i`	Perform case-insensitive matching.
`g`	Perform a global match. That is, find all matches rather than stopping after the first match.
`m`	Multiline mode. `^` matches beginning of line or beginning of string, and `$` matches end of line or end of string.

10.1.7 Perl RegExp Features Not Supported in JavaScript

We've said that ECMAScript v3 specifies a relatively complete subset of the regular expression facilities from Perl 5. Advanced Perl features that are not supported by ECMAScript include the following:

- The `s` (single-line mode) and `x` (extended syntax) flags
- The `\a`, `\e`, `\l`, `\u`, `\L`, `\U`, `\E`, `\Q`, `\A`, `\Z`, `\z`, and `\G` escape sequences
- The `(?<=` positive look-behind anchor and the `(?<!` negative look-behind anchor
- The `(?#` comment and the other extended `(?` syntaxes

10.2 String Methods for Pattern Matching

Until now, we've been discussing the grammar used to create regular expressions, but we haven't examined how those regular expressions can actually be used in JavaScript code. In this section, we discuss methods of the String object that use regular expressions to perform pattern matching and search-and-replace operations. In the sections that follow this one, we'll continue the discussion of pattern matching with JavaScript regular expressions by discussing the RegExp object and its methods and properties. Note that the discussion that follows is merely an overview of the various methods and properties related to regular expressions. As usual, complete details can be found in the core reference section of this book.

Strings support four methods that make use of regular expressions. The simplest is `search()`. This method takes a regular expression argument and returns either the character position of the start of the first matching substring, or –1 if there is no match. For example, the following call returns 4:

```
"JavaScript".search(/script/i);
```

If the argument to `search()` is not a regular expression, it is first converted to one by passing it to the `RegExp` constructor. `search()` does not support global searches—it ignores the g flag of its regular expression argument.

The `replace()` method performs a search-and-replace operation. It takes a regular expression as its first argument and a replacement string as its second argument. It searches the string on which it is called for matches with the specified pattern. If the regular expression has the g flag set, the `replace()` method replaces all matches in the string with the replacement string; otherwise, it replaces only the first match it finds. If the first argument to `replace()` is a string rather than a regular expression, the method searches for that string literally rather than converting it to a regular expression with the `RegExp()` constructor, as `search()` does. As an example, we could use `replace()` as follows to provide uniform capitalization of the word "JavaScript" throughout a string of text:

```
// No matter how it is capitalized, replace it with the correct capitalization
text.replace(/javascript/gi, "JavaScript");
```

`replace()` is more powerful than this, however. Recall that parenthesized subexpressions of a regular expression are numbered from left to right and that the regular expression remembers the text that each subexpression matches. If a `$` followed by a digit appears in the replacement string, `replace()` replaces those two characters with the text that matched the specified subexpression. This is a very useful feature. We can use it, for example, to replace straight quotes in a string with curly quotes, simulated with ASCII characters:

```
// A quote is a quotation mark, followed by any number of
// non-quotation-mark characters (which we remember), followed
// by another quotation mark.
var quote = /"([^"]*)"/g;
```

```
// Replace the straight quotation marks with "curly quotes,"
// and leave the contents of the quote (stored in $1) unchanged.
text.replace(quote, "``$1''");
```

The replace() method has other important features as well, which are described in the "String.replace()" reference page in the core reference section. Most notably, the second argument to replace() can be a function that dynamically computes the replacement string.

The match() method is the most general of the String regular expression methods. It takes a regular expression as its only argument (or converts its argument to a regular expression by passing it to the RegExp() constructor) and returns an array that contains the results of the match. If the regular expression has the g flag set, the method returns an array of all matches that appear in the string. For example:

```
"1 plus 2 equals 3".match(/\d+/g)  // returns ["1", "2", "3"]
```

If the regular expression does not have the g flag set, match() does not do a global search; it simply searches for the first match. However, match() returns an array even when it does not perform a global search. In this case, the first element of the array is the matching string, and any remaining elements are the parenthesized subexpressions of the regular expression. Thus, if match() returns an array a, a[0] contains the complete match, a[1] contains the substring that matched the first parenthesized expression, and so on. To draw a parallel with the replace() method, a[*n*] holds the contents of $*n*.

For example, consider parsing a URL with the following code:

```
var url = /(\w+):\/\/([\w.]+)\/(\S*)/;
var text = "Visit my home page at http://www.isp.com/~david";
var result = text.match(url);
if (result != null) {
    var fullurl = result[0];   // Contains "http://www.isp.com/~david"
    var protocol = result[1];  // Contains "http"
    var host = result[2];      // Contains "www.isp.com"
    var path = result[3];      // Contains "~david"
}
```

Finally, there is one more feature of the match() method that you should know about. The array it returns has a length property, as all arrays do. When match() is invoked on a nonglobal regular expression, however, the returned array also has two other properties: the index property, which contains the character position within the string at which the match begins; and the input property, which is a copy of the target string. So in the previous code, the value of the result.index property would be 21, since the matched URL begins at character position 21 in the text. The result.input property would hold the same string as the text variable. For a regular expression r that does not have the g flag set, calling s.match(r) returns the same value as r.exec(s). We'll discuss the RegExp.exec() method a little later in this chapter.

The last of the regular expression methods of the String object is split( ). This method breaks the string on which it is called into an array of substrings, using the argument as a separator. For example:

```
"123,456,789".split(","); // Returns ["123","456","789"]
```

The split( ) method can also take a regular expression as its argument. This ability makes the method more powerful. For example, we can now specify a separator character that allows an arbitrary amount of whitespace on either side:

```
"1,2, 3 , 4 ,5".split(/\s*,\s*/); // Returns ["1","2","3","4","5"]
```

The split( ) method has other features as well. See the "String.split()" entry in the core reference section for complete details.

10.3 The RegExp Object

As mentioned at the beginning of this chapter, regular expressions are represented as RegExp objects. In addition to the RegExp( ) constructor, RegExp objects support three methods and a number of properties. An unusual feature of the RegExp class is that it defines both class (or static) properties and instance properties. That is, it defines global properties that belong to the RegExp( ) constructor as well as other properties that belong to individual RegExp objects. RegExp pattern-matching methods and properties are described in the next two sections.

The RegExp( ) constructor takes one or two string arguments and creates a new RegExp object. The first argument to this constructor is a string that contains the body of the regular expression—the text that would appear within slashes in a regular expression literal. Note that both string literals and regular expressions use the \ character for escape sequences, so when you pass a regular expression to RegExp( ) as a string literal, you must replace each \ character with \\. The second argument to RegExp( ) is optional. If supplied, it indicates the regular expression flags. It should be g, i, m, or a combination of those letters. For example:

```
// Find all five digit numbers in a string. Note the double \\ in this case.
var zipcode = new RegExp("\\d{5}", "g");
```

The RegExp( ) constructor is useful when a regular expression is being dynamically created and thus cannot be represented with the regular expression literal syntax. For example, to search for a string entered by the user, a regular expression must be created at runtime with RegExp( ).

10.3.1 RegExp Methods for Pattern Matching

RegExp objects define two methods that perform pattern-matching operations; they behave similarly to the String methods described earlier. The main RegExp pattern-matching method is exec( ). It is similar to the String match( ) method described above, except that it is a RegExp method that takes a string, rather than a String method that takes a RegExp. The exec() method executes a regular expression on the specified string. That is, it searches the string for a match. If it finds none, it returns null. If it does find one, however, it returns an array just like the array returned by the match() method for nonglobal searches. Element 0 of the array contains the string that matched the regular expression, and any subsequent array elements contain the substrings that matched any parenthesized subexpressions. Furthermore, the index property contains the character position at which the match occurred, and the input property refers to the string that was searched.

Unlike the match() method, exec() returns the same kind of array whether or not the regular expression has the global g flag. Recall that match() returns an array of matches when passed a global regular expression. exec(), by contrast, always returns a single match and provides complete information about that match. When exec() is called for a regular expression that has the g flag, it sets the lastIndex property of the regular expression object to the character position immediately following the matched substring. When exec() is invoked a second time for the same regular expression, it begins its search at the character position indicated by the lastIndex property. If exec() does not find a match, it resets lastIndex to 0. (You can also set lastIndex to 0 at any time, which you should do whenever you quit a search before you find the last match in one string and begin searching another string with the same RegExp object.) This special behavior allows us to call exec() repeatedly in order to loop through all the regular expression matches in a string. For example:

```
var pattern = /Java/g;
var text = "JavaScript is more fun than Java!";
var result;
while((result = pattern.exec(text)) != null) {
    alert("Matched `" + result[0] + "'" +
          " at position " + result.index +
          "; next search begins at " + pattern.lastIndex);
}
```

The other RegExp method is test(). test() is a much simpler method than exec(). It takes a string and returns true if the string matches the regular expression:

```
var pattern = /java/i;
pattern.test("JavaScript");  // Returns true
```

Calling test() is equivalent to calling exec() and returning true if the return value of exec() is not null. Because of this equivalence, the test() method behaves the same way as the exec() method when invoked for a global regular expression: it begins searching the specified string at the position specified by lastIndex, and if it finds a match, it sets lastIndex to the position of the character immediately following the match. Thus, we can loop through a string using the test() method just as we can with the exec() method.

The String methods search(), replace(), and match() do not use the lastIndex property as exec() and test() do. In fact, the String methods simply reset lastIndex( ) to 0. If you use exec( ) or test( ) on a pattern that has the g flag set and you are searching multiple strings, you must either find all the matches in each string, so that lastIndex is automatically reset to zero (this happens when the last search fails), or you must explicitly set the lastIndex property to 0 yourself. If you forget to do this, you may start searching a new string at some arbitrary position within the string rather than from the beginning. Finally, remember that this special lastIndex behavior occurs only for regular expressions with the g flag. exec( ) and test( ) ignore the lastIndex property of RegExp objects that do not have the g flag.

10.3.2 RegExp Instance Properties

Each RegExp object has five properties. The source property is a read-only string that contains the text of the regular expression. The global property is a read-only boolean value that specifies whether the regular expression has the g flag. The ignoreCase property is a read-only boolean value that specifies whether the regular expression has the i flag. The multiline property is a read-only boolean value that specifies whether the regular expression has the m flag. The final property is lastIndex, a read-write integer. For patterns with the g flag, this property stores the position in the string at which the next search is to begin. It is used by the exec( ) and test( ) methods, as described in the previous section.

CHAPTER 11

Further Topics in JavaScript

This chapter covers miscellaneous JavaScript topics that would have bogged down previous chapters had they been covered earlier. Now that you have read through the preceding chapters and are experienced with the core JavaScript language, you are prepared to tackle the more advanced and detailed concepts presented here. You may prefer, however, to move on to other chapters and learn about the specifics of client-side JavaScript before returning to this chapter.

11.1 Data Type Conversion

We've seen that JavaScript is an untyped language (or, perhaps more accurately, a loosely typed or dynamically typed language). This means, for example, that we don't have to specify the data type of a variable when we declare it. Being untyped gives JavaScript the flexibility and simplicity that are desirable for a scripting language (although those features come at the expense of rigor, which is important for the longer, more complex programs often written in stricter languages such as C and Java). An important feature of JavaScript's flexible treatment of data types is the automatic type conversions it performs. For example, if you pass a number to the `document.write()` method, JavaScript automatically converts that value into its equivalent string representation. Similarly, if you test a string value in the condition of an `if` statement, JavaScript automatically converts that string to a boolean value—to `false` if the string is empty and to `true` otherwise.

The basic rule is that when a value of one type is used in a context that requires a value of some other type, JavaScript automatically attempts to convert the value as needed. So, for example, if a number is used in a boolean context, it is converted to a boolean. If an object is used in a string context, it is converted to a string. If a string is used in a numeric context, JavaScript attempts to convert it to a number. Table 11-1 summarizes each of these conversions—it shows the conversion that is performed when a particular type of value is used in a particular context. The sections that follow the table provide more detail about type conversions in JavaScript.

Table 11-1. Automatic data type conversions

Value	Context in which value is used			
	String	Number	Boolean	Object
Undefined value	"undefined"	NaN	false	Error
null	"null"	0	false	Error
Nonempty string	As is	Numeric value of string or NaN	true	String object
Empty string	As is	0	false	String object
0	"0"	As is	false	Number object
NaN	"NaN"	As is	false	Number object
Infinity	"Infinity"	As is	true	Number object
Negative infinity	"-Infinity"	As is	true	Number object
Any other number	String value of number	As is	true	Number object
true	"true"	1	As is	Boolean object
false	"false"	0	As is	Boolean object
Object	toString( )	valueOf( ) or toString( ) or NaN	true	As is

11.1.1 Object-to-Primitive Conversion

Table 11-1 specifies how JavaScript objects are converted to primitive values. Several details of this conversion require additional discussion, however. First, note that whenever a non-null object is used in a boolean context, it converts to true. This is true for all objects (including all arrays and functions), even wrapper objects that represent primitive values that convert to false. For example, all of the following objects convert to true when used in a boolean context:*

```
new Boolean(false)  // Internal value is false, but object converts to true
new Number(0)
new String("")
new Array( )
```

Table 11-1 shows that objects are converted to numbers by first calling the valueOf( ) method of the object. Most objects inherit the default valueOf( ) method of Object, which simply returns the object itself. Since the default valueOf( ) method does not return a primitive value, JavaScript next tries to convert the object to a number by calling its toString( ) method and converting the resulting string to a number.

This leads to interesting results for arrays. Recall that the toString( ) method of arrays converts the array elements to strings, then returns the result of concatenating these strings, with commas in between. Therefore, an array with no elements converts to the empty string, which (as you can see in the table) converts to the number zero!

* Note, though, that in JavaScript 1.1 and 1.2 these objects all convert to false, which is ECMAScript compliant.

Also, if an array has a single element that is a number *n*, the array converts to a string representation of *n*, which is then converted back to *n* itself. If an array contains more than one element, or if its one element is not a number, the array converts to `NaN`.*

Table 11-1 specifies how an object is converted when used in a string context and how it is converted when used in a numeric context. However, there are a couple of places in JavaScript where the context is ambiguous! The + operator and the comparison operators (<, <=, >, and >=) operate on both numbers and strings, so when an object is used with one of these operators, it is not clear whether it should be converted to a number or a string. In most cases, JavaScript first attempts to convert the object by calling its `valueOf( )` method. If this method returns a primitive value (usually a number), that value is used. Often, however, `valueOf( )` simply returns the unconverted object; in this case, JavaScript then tries to convert the object to a string by calling its `toString( )` method.

There is only one exception to this conversion rule: when a Date object is used with the + operator, conversion is performed with the `toString( )` method. This exception exists because Date has both `toString( )` and `valueOf( )` methods. When a Date is used with +, you almost always want to perform a string concatenation. But when using a Date with the comparison operators, you almost always want to perform a numeric comparison to determine which of two times is earlier than the other.

Most objects either don't have `valueOf( )` methods or don't have `valueOf( )` methods that return useful results. When you use an object with the + operator, you usually get string concatenation rather than addition. When you use an object with a comparison operator, you usually get string comparison rather than numeric comparison.

An object that defines a custom `valueOf( )` method may behave differently. If you define a `valueOf( )` method that returns a number, you can use arithmetic and other operators with your object, but adding your object to a string may not behave as you expect: the `toString( )` method is no longer called, and a string representation of the number returned by `valueOf( )` is concatenated to the string.

Finally, remember that `valueOf( )` is not called `toNumber( )`: strictly speaking, its job is to convert an object to a reasonable primitive value, so some objects may have `valueOf( )` methods that return strings.

11.1.2 Explicit Type Conversions

Table 11-1 listed the automatic data type conversions that JavaScript performs. It is also possible to explicitly convert values from one type to another. JavaScript does not define a cast operator as C, C++, and Java do, but it does provide similar facilities for converting data values.

* Note, however, that in JavaScript 1.1 and 1.2, when an array is used in a numeric context it is converted to its length.

As of JavaScript 1.1 (and the ECMA-262 standard), `Number()`, `Boolean()`, `String()`, and `Object()` may be called as functions as well as being invoked as constructors. When invoked in this way, these functions attempt to convert their arguments to the appropriate type. For example, you could convert any value `x` to a string with `String(x)` and convert any value y to an object with `Object(y)`.

There are a few other tricks that can be useful for performing explicit conversions. To convert a value to a string, concatenate it with the empty string:

```
var x_as_string = x + "";
```

To force a value to a number, subtract zero from it:

```
var x_as_number = x - 0;
```

And to force a value to boolean, use the ! operator twice:

```
var x_as_boolean = !!x;
```

Because of JavaScript's tendency to automatically convert data to whatever type is required, explicit conversions are usually unnecessary. They are occasionally helpful, however, and can also be used to make your code clearer and more precise.

11.1.3 Converting Numbers to Strings

The number-to-string conversion is probably the one most often performed in JavaScript. Although it usually happens automatically, there are a couple of useful ways to explicitly perform this conversion. We saw two of them above:

```
var string_value = String(number);  // Use the String() constructor as a function
var string_value = number + "";     // Concatenate with the empty string
```

Another technique for converting numbers to strings is with the `toString()` method:

```
string_value = number.toString();
```

The `toString()` method of the Number object (primitive numbers are converted to Number objects so that this method can be called) takes an optional argument that specifies a radix, or base, for the conversion. If you do not specify the argument, the conversion is done in base 10. But you can also convert numbers in other bases (between 2 and 36).* For example:

```
var n = 17;
binary_string = n.toString(2);        // Evaluates to "10001"
octal_string = "0" + n.toString(8);   // Evaluates to "021"
hex_string = "0x" + n.toString(16);   // Evaluates to "0x11"
```

A shortcoming of JavaScript prior to JavaScript 1.5 is that there is no built-in way to convert a number to a string and specify the number of decimal places to be

* Note that the ECMAScript specification supports the radix argument to the `toString()` method, but it allows the method to return an implementation-defined string for any radix other than 10. Thus, conforming implementations may simply ignore the argument and always return a base-10 result. In practice, implementations from Netscape and Microsoft do honor the requested radix.

included, or to specify whether exponential notation should be used. This can make it difficult to display numbers that have traditional formats, such as numbers that represent monetary values.

ECMAScript v3 and JavaScript 1.5 solve this problem by adding three new number-to-string methods to the Number class. `toFixed()` converts a number to a string and displays a specified number of digits after the decimal point. It does not use exponential notation. `toExponential()` converts a number to a string using exponential notation, with one digit before the decimal point and a specified number of digits after the decimal point. `toPrecision()` displays a number using the specified number of significant digits. It uses exponential notation if the number of significant digits is not large enough to display the entire integer portion of the number. Note that all three of these methods round the trailing digits of the resulting string as appropriate. Consider the following examples:

```
var n = 123456.789;
n.toFixed(0);          // "123457"
n.toFixed(2);          // "123456.79"
n.toExponential(1);    // "1.2e+5"
n.toExponential(3);    // "1.235e+5"
n.toPrecision(4);      // "1.235e+5"
n.toPrecision(7);      // "123456.8"
```

11.1.4 Converting Strings to Numbers

We've seen that strings that represent numbers are automatically converted to actual numbers when used in a numeric context. As shown earlier, we can make this conversion explicit:

```
var number = Number(string_value);
var number = string_value - 0;
```

The trouble with this sort of string-to-number conversion is that it is overly strict. It works only with base-10 numbers, and although it does allow leading and trailing spaces, it does not allow any non-space characters to appear in the string following the number.

To allow more flexible conversions, you can use `parseInt()` and `parseFloat()`. These functions convert and return any number at the beginning of a string, ignoring any trailing non-numbers. `parseInt()` parses only integers, while `parseFloat()` parses both integers and floating-point numbers. If a string begins with "0x" or "0X", `parseInt()` interprets it as a hexadecimal number.* For example:

```
parseInt("3 blind mice");    // Returns 3
parseFloat("3.14 meters");   // Returns 3.14
```

* The ECMAScript specification says that if a string begins with "0" (but not "0x" or "0X"), `parseInt()` may parse it as an octal number or as a decimal number. Because the behavior is unspecified, you should never use `parseInt()` to parse numbers with leading zeros, unless you explicitly specify the radix to be used!

```
parseInt("12.34");              // Returns 12
parseInt("0xFF");               // Returns 255
```

parseInt( ) can even take a second argument specifying the radix (base) of the number to be parsed. Legal values are between 2 and 36. For example:

```
parseInt("11", 2);              // Returns 3 (1*2 + 1)
parseInt("ff", 16);             // Returns 255 (15*16 + 15)
parseInt("zz", 36);             // Returns 1295 (35*36 + 35)
parseInt("077", 8);             // Returns 63 (7*8 + 7)
parseInt("077", 10);            // Returns 77 (7*10 + 7)
```

If parseInt( ) or parseFloat( ) cannot convert the specified string to a number, it returns NaN:

```
parseInt("eleven");             // Returns NaN
parseFloat("$72.47");           // Returns NaN
```

11.2 By Value Versus by Reference

In JavaScript, as in all programming languages, there are three important ways that you can manipulate a data value. First, you can copy it; for example, by assigning it to a new variable. Second, you can pass it as an argument to a function or method. Third, you can compare it with another value to see if the two values are equal. To understand any programming language, you must understand how these three operations are performed in that language.

There are two fundamentally distinct ways to manipulate data values. These techniques are called "by value" and "by reference." When a value is manipulated by value, it is the *value* of the datum that matters. In an assignment, a copy of the actual value is made and that copy is stored in a variable, object property, or array element; the copy and the original are two totally independent values that are stored separately. When a datum is passed by value to a function, a copy of the datum is passed to the function; if the function modifies the value, the change affects only the function's copy of the datum—it does not affect the original datum. Finally, when a datum is compared by value to another datum, the two distinct pieces of data must represent exactly the same value (which usually means that a byte-by-byte comparison finds them to be equal).

The other way of manipulating a value is by reference. With this technique, there is only one actual copy of the value; references to that value are manipulated.* If a value is manipulated by reference, variables do not hold that value directly; they hold only references to it. It is these references that are copied, passed, and compared. So, in an assignment made by reference, it is the reference to the value that is assigned, not a copy of the value and not the value itself. After the assignment, the new variable refers to the same value that the original variable refers to. Both references are

* C programmers and anyone else familiar with the concept of pointers should understand the idea of a reference in this context. Note, however, that JavaScript does not support pointers.

equally valid and both can be used to manipulate the value—if the value is changed through one reference, that change also appears through the original reference. The situation is similar when a value is passed to a function by reference. A reference to the value is passed to the function, and the function can use that reference to modify the value itself; any such modifications are visible outside the function. Finally, when a value is compared to another by reference, the two references are compared to see if they refer to the same unique copy of a value; references to two distinct values that happen to be equivalent (i.e., consist of the same bytes) are not treated as equal.

These are two very different ways of manipulating values, and they have important implications that you should understand. Table 11-2 summarizes these implications. This discussion of manipulating data by value and by reference has been a general one, but the distinctions apply to all programming languages. The sections that follow explain how these distinctions apply specifically to JavaScript; they discuss which data types are manipulated by value and which are manipulated by reference.

Table 11-2. By value versus by reference

	By value	By reference
Copy	The value is actually copied; there are two distinct, independent copies.	Only a reference to the value is copied. If the value is modified through the new reference, that change is also visible through the original reference.
Pass	A distinct copy of the value is passed to the function; changes to it have no effect outside the function.	A reference to the value is passed to the function. If the function modifies the value through the passed reference, the modification is visible outside the function.
Compare	Two distinct values are compared (often byte by byte) to see if they are the same value.	Two references are compared to see if they refer to the same value. Two references to distinct values are not equal, even if the two values consist of the same bytes.

11.2.1 Primitive Types and Reference Types

The basic rule in JavaScript is this: primitive types are manipulated by value, and reference types, as the name suggests, are manipulated by reference. Numbers and booleans are primitive types in JavaScript—primitive because they consist of nothing more than a small, fixed number of bytes that are easily manipulated at the low (primitive) levels of the JavaScript interpreter. Objects, on the other hand, are reference types. Arrays and functions, which are specialized types of objects, are therefore also reference types. These data types can contain arbitrary numbers of properties or elements, so they cannot be manipulated as easily as fixed-size primitive values can. Since object and array values can become quite large, it doesn't make sense to manipulate these types by value, as this could involve the inefficient copying and comparing of large amounts of memory.

What about strings? A string can have an arbitrary length, so it would seem that strings should be reference types. In fact, though, they are usually considered to be primitive types in JavaScript simply because they are not objects. Strings don't actually fit into the primitive versus reference type dichotomy. We'll have more to say about strings and their behavior a little later.

The best way to explore the differences between data manipulation by value and by reference is through example. Study the following examples carefully, paying attention to the comments. Example 11-1 copies, passes, and compares numbers. Since numbers are primitive types, this example illustrates data manipulation by value.

Example 11-1. Copying, passing, and comparing by value

```
// First we illustrate copying by value
var n = 1;  // Variable n holds the value 1
var m = n;  // Copy by value: variable m holds a distinct value 1

// Here's a function we'll use to illustrate passing by value
// As we'll see, the function doesn't work the way we'd like it to
function add_to_total(total, x)
{
    total = total + x;  // This line changes only the internal copy of total
}

// Now call the function, passing the numbers contained in n and m by value.
// The value of n is copied, and that copied value is named total within the
// function. The function adds a copy of m to that copy of n. But adding
// something to a copy of n doesn't affect the original value of n outside
// of the function. So calling this function doesn't accomplish anything.
add_to_total(n, m);

// Now, we'll look at comparison by value.
// In the following line of code, the literal 1 is clearly a distinct numeric
// value encoded in the program. We compare it to the value held in variable
// n. In comparison by value, the bytes of the two numbers are checked to
// see if they are the same.
if (n == 1) m = 2;  // n contains the same value as the literal 1; m is now 2
```

Now, consider Example 11-2. This example copies, passes, and compares an object. Since objects are reference types, these manipulations are performed by reference. This example uses Date objects, which you can read more about in the core reference section of this book.

Example 11-2. Copying, passing, and comparing by reference

```
// Here we create an object representing the date of Christmas, 2001
// The variable xmas contains a reference to the object, not the object itself
var xmas = new Date(2001, 11, 25);

// When we copy by reference, we get a new reference to the original object
var solstice = xmas;  // Both variables now refer to the same object value

// Here we change the object through our new reference to it
solstice.setDate(21);

// The change is visible through the original reference, as well
```

Example 11-2. Copying, passing, and comparing by reference (continued)

```
xmas.getDate( );  // Returns 21, not the original value of 25

// The same is true when objects and arrays are passed to functions.
// The following function adds a value to each element of an array.
// A reference to the array is passed to the function, not a copy of the array.
// Therefore, the function can change the contents of the array through
// the reference, and those changes will be visible when the function returns.
function add_to_totals(totals, x)
{
    totals[0] = totals[0] + x;
    totals[1] = totals[1] + x;
    totals[2] = totals[2] + x;
}

// Finally, we'll examine comparison by reference.
// When we compare the two variables defined above, we find they are
// equal, because they refer to the same object, even though we were trying
// to make them refer to different dates:
(xmas == solstice)  // Evaluates to true

// The two variables defined next refer to two distinct objects, both
// of which represent exactly the same date.
var xmas = new Date(2001, 11, 25);
var solstice_plus_4 = new Date(2001, 11, 25);

// But, by the rules of "compare by reference," distinct objects are not equal!
(xmas != solstice_plus_4)  // Evaluates to true
```

Before we leave the topic of manipulating objects and arrays by reference, we need to clear up a point of nomenclature. The phrase "pass by reference" can have several meanings. To some readers, the phrase refers to a function invocation technique that allows a function to assign new values to its arguments and to have those modified values visible outside the function. This is not the way the term is used in this book. Here, we mean simply that a reference to an object or array—not the object itself—is passed to a function. A function can use the reference to modify properties of the object or elements of the array. But if the function overwrites the reference with a reference to a new object or array, that modification is not visible outside of the function. Readers familiar with the other meaning of this term may prefer to say that objects and arrays are passed by value, but the value that is passed is actually a reference rather than the object itself. Example 11-3 illustrates this issue.

Example 11-3. References themselves are passed by value

```
// This is another version of the add_to_totals( ) function. It doesn't
// work, though, because instead of changing the array itself, it tries to
// change the reference to the array.
function add_to_totals2(totals, x)
{
    newtotals = new Array(3);
    newtotals[0] = totals[0] + x;
```

Example 11-3. References themselves are passed by value (continued)

```
    newtotals[1] = totals[1] + x;
    newtotals[2] = totals[2] + x;
    totals = newtotals;  // This line has no effect outside of the function
}
```

11.2.2 Copying and Passing Strings

As mentioned earlier, JavaScript strings don't fit neatly into the primitive type versus reference type dichotomy. Since strings are not objects, it is natural to assume that they are primitive. If they are primitive types, then by the rules given above, they should be manipulated by value. But since strings can be arbitrarily long, it would seem inefficient to copy, pass, and compare them byte by byte. Therefore, it would also be natural to assume that strings are implemented as reference types.

Instead of making assumptions about strings, suppose we write some JavaScript code to experiment with string manipulation. If strings are copied and passed by reference, we should be able to modify the contents of a string through the reference stored in another variable or passed to a function.

When we set out to write the code to perform this experiment, however, we run into a major stumbling block: there is no way to modify the contents of a string. The `charAt()` method returns the character at a given position in a string, but there is no corresponding `setCharAt()` method. This is not an oversight. JavaScript strings are intentionally *immutable*—that is, there is no JavaScript syntax, method, or property that allows you to change the characters in a string.

Since strings are immutable, our original question is moot: there is no way to tell if strings are passed by value or by reference. We can assume that, for efficiency, JavaScript is implemented so that strings are passed by reference, but in actuality it doesn't matter, since it has no practical bearing on the code we write.

11.2.3 Comparing Strings

Despite the fact that we cannot determine whether strings are copied and passed by value or by reference, we can write JavaScript code to determine whether they are compared by value or by reference. Example 11-4 shows the code we might use to make this determination.

Example 11-4. Are strings compared by value or by reference?

```
// Determining whether strings are compared by value or reference is easy.
// We compare two clearly distinct strings that happen to contain the same
// characters. If they are compared by value they will be equal, but if they
// are compared by reference, they will not be equal:
var s1 = "hello";
var s2 = "hell" + "o";
if (s1 == s2) document.write("Strings compared by value");
```

This experiment demonstrates that strings are compared by value. This may be surprising to some programmers. In C, C++, and Java, strings are reference types and are compared by reference. If you want to compare the actual contents of two strings, you must use a special method or function. JavaScript, however, is a higher-level language and recognizes that when you compare strings, you most often want to compare them by value. Thus, despite the fact that, for efficiency, JavaScript strings are (presumably) copied and passed by reference, they are compared by value.

11.2.4 By Value Versus by Reference: Summary

Table 11-3 summarizes the way that the various JavaScript types are manipulated.

Table 11-3. Data type manipulation in JavaScript

Type	Copied by	Passed by	Compared by
Number	Value	Value	Value
Boolean	Value	Value	Value
String	Immutable	Immutable	Value
Object	Reference	Reference	Reference

11.3 Garbage Collection

As explained in Chapter 4, JavaScript uses garbage collection to reclaim the memory occupied by strings, objects, arrays, and functions that are no longer in use. This frees you, the programmer, from having to explicitly deallocate memory yourself and is an important part of what makes JavaScript programming easier than, say, C programming.

A key feature of garbage collection is that the garbage collector must be able to determine when it is safe to reclaim memory. Obviously, it must never reclaim values that are still in use and should collect only values that are no longer reachable; that is, values that cannot be referred to through any of the variables, object properties, or array elements in the program. If you are the curious type, you may be wondering just how a garbage collector distinguishes between garbage to be collected and values that are still being used or that could potentially be used. The following sections explain some of the gory details.

11.3.1 Mark-and-Sweep Garbage Collection

The computer science literature on garbage collection is large and technical; the actual operation of the garbage collector is really an implementation-specific detail that may vary in different implementations of the language. Still, almost all serious garbage collectors use some variation on a basic garbage-collection algorithm known as "mark and sweep."

A mark-and-sweep garbage collector periodically traverses the list of all variables in the JavaScript environment and marks any values referred to by these variables. If any referenced values are objects or arrays, it recursively marks the object properties and array elements. By recursively traversing this tree or graph of values, the garbage collector is able to find (and mark) every single value that is still reachable. It follows, then, that any unmarked values are unreachable and are therefore garbage.

Once a mark-and-sweep garbage collector has finished marking all reachable values, it begins its sweep phase. During this phase, it looks through the list of all values in the environment and deallocates any that are not marked. Classic mark-and-sweep garbage collectors do a complete mark and a complete sweep all at once, which causes a noticeable slowdown in the system during garbage collection. More sophisticated variations on the algorithm make the process relatively efficient and perform collection in the background, without disrupting system performance.

The details of garbage collection are implementation-specific, and you should not need to know anything about the garbage collector to write JavaScript programs. All modern JavaScript implementations use some kind of mark-and-sweep garbage collection. However, JavaScript 1.1, as implemented in Netscape 3, used a somewhat simpler garbage-collection scheme that has some shortcomings. If you are writing JavaScript code to be compatible with Netscape 3, the following section explains the shortcomings of the garbage collector in that browser. Netscape 2 used an even simpler garbage-collection technique with serious flaws. Since that browser is now entirely obsolete, the details are not described here.

11.3.2 Garbage Collection by Reference Counting

In JavaScript 1.1, as implemented in Netscape 3, garbage collection is performed by reference counting. This means that every object (whether a user object created by JavaScript code or a built-in HTML object created by the browser) keeps track of the number of references to it. Recall that objects are assigned by reference in JavaScript, rather than having their complete values copied.

When an object is created and a reference to it is stored in a variable, the object's reference count is one. When the reference to the object is copied and stored in another variable, the reference count is incremented to two. When one of the two variables that holds these references is overwritten with some new value, the object's reference count is decremented back to one. If the reference count reaches zero, there are no more references to the object. Since there are no references to copy, there can never again be a reference to the object in the program. Therefore, JavaScript knows that it is safe to destroy the object and garbage collect the memory associated with it.

Unfortunately, there are shortcomings to using reference counting as a garbage-collection scheme. In fact, some people don't even consider reference counting to be true garbage collection and reserve that term for better algorithms, such as mark-and-sweep garbage collection. Reference counting is a simple form of garbage collection that is easy to implement and works fine in many situations. There is an important situation, however, in which reference counting cannot correctly detect and collect all garbage, and you need to be aware of it.

The basic flaw with reference counting has to do with *cyclical references*. If object A contains a reference to object B and object B contains a reference to object A, a cycle of references exists. A cycle would also exist, for example, if A referred to B, B referred to C, and C referred back to A. In cycles such as these, there is always a reference from within the cycle to every element in the cycle. Thus, even if none of the elements of the cycle has any remaining outside references, their reference counts will never drop below one and they can never be garbage collected. The entire cycle may be garbage if there is no way to refer to any of these objects from a program, but because they all refer to each other, a reference-counting garbage collector cannot detect and free this unused memory.

This problem with cycles is the price that must be paid for a simple garbage-collection scheme. The only way to prevent this problem is by manual intervention. If you create a cycle of objects, you must recognize this fact and take steps to ensure that the objects are garbage collected when they are no longer needed. To allow a cycle of objects to be garbage collected, you must break the cycle. You can do this by picking one of the objects in the cycle and setting the property of it that refers to the next object to `null`. For example, suppose that A, B, and C are objects that each have a `next` property, and the value of this property is set so that these objects refer to each other and form a cycle. When these objects are no longer in use, you can break the cycle by setting `A.next` to `null`. This means that object B no longer has a reference from A, so its reference count can drop to zero and it can be garbage collected. Once it has been garbage collected, it will no longer refer to C, so C's reference count can drop to zero and it can be garbage collected. Once C is garbage collected, A can finally be garbage collected.

Note, of course, that none of this can happen if A, B, and C are stored in global variables in a window that is still open, because those variables A, B, and C still refer to the objects. If these were local variables in a function and you broke their cycle before the function returned, they could be garbage collected. But if they are stored in global variables, they remain referenced until the window that contains them closes. In this case, if you want to force them to be garbage collected, you must break the cycle and set all the variables to `null`:

```
A.next = null;     // Break the cycle
A = B = C = null;  // Remove the last remaining external references
```

11.4 Lexical Scoping and Nested Functions

Functions in JavaScript are lexically rather than dynamically scoped. This means that they run in the scope in which they are defined, not the scope from which they are executed. Prior to JavaScript 1.2, functions could be defined only in the global scope, and lexical scoping was not much of an issue: all functions were executed in the same global scope (with the call object of the function chained to that global scope).

In JavaScript 1.2 and later, however, functions can be defined anywhere, and tricky issues of scope arise. For example, consider a function `g` defined within a function `f`. `g` is always executed in the scope of `f`. Its scope chain includes three objects: its own call object, the call object of `f()`, and the global object. Nested functions are perfectly understandable when they are invoked in the same lexical scope in which they are defined. For example, the following code does not do anything particularly surprising:

```
var x = "global";
function f() {
    var x = "local";
    function g() { alert(x); }
    g();
}
f(); // Calling this function displays "local"
```

In JavaScript, however, functions are data just like any other value, so they can be returned from functions, assigned to object properties, stored in arrays, and so on. This does not cause anything particularly surprising either, except when nested functions are involved. Consider the following code, which includes a function that returns a nested function. Each time it is called, it returns a function. The JavaScript code of the returned function is always the same, but the scope in which it is created differs slightly on each invocation, because the values of the arguments to the outer function differ on each invocation. If we save the returned functions in an array and then invoke each one, we'll see that each returns a different value. Since each function consists of identical JavaScript code and each is invoked from exactly the same scope, the only factor that could be causing the differing return values is the scope in which the functions were defined:

```
// This function returns a function each time it is called
// The scope in which the function is defined differs for each call
function makefunc(x) {
    return function() { return x; }
}

// Call makefunc() several times, and save the results in an array:
var a = [makefunc(0), makefunc(1), makefunc(2)];

// Now call these functions and display their values.
// Although the body of each function is the same, the scope is
// different, and each call returns a different value:
alert(a[0]()); // Displays 0
alert(a[1]()); // Displays 1
alert(a[2]()); // Displays 2
```

The results of this code may be surprising. Still, they are the results expected from a strict application of the lexical scoping rule: a function is executed in the scope in which it was defined. That scope includes the state of local variables and arguments.

Even though local variables and function arguments are transient, their state is frozen and becomes part of the lexical scope of any functions defined while they are in effect. In order to make lexical scoping work with nested functions, a JavaScript implementation must use a *closure*, which can be thought of as a combination of a function definition and the scope chain that was in effect when the function was defined.

11.5 The Function( ) Constructor and Function Literals

As we saw in Chapter 7, there are two ways to define functions other than the basic `function` statement. As of JavaScript 1.1, functions can be defined using the `Function( )` constructor, and in JavaScript 1.2 and later, they can be defined with function literals. You should be aware of some important differences between these two techniques.

First, the `Function( )` constructor allows JavaScript code to be dynamically created and compiled at runtime. Function literals, however, are a static part of program structure, just as `function` statements are.

Second, as a corollary of the first difference, the `Function( )` constructor parses the function body and creates a new function object each time it is called. If the call to the constructor appears within a loop or within a frequently called function, this process can be inefficient. On the other hand, a function literal or nested function that appears within a loop or function is not recompiled each time it is encountered. Nor is a different function object created each time a function literal is encountered. (Although, as noted earlier, a new closure may be required to capture differences in the lexical scope in which the function is defined.)

The third difference between the `Function( )` constructor and function literals is that functions created with the `Function( )` constructor do not use lexical scoping; instead, they are always compiled as if they were top-level functions, as the following code demonstrates:

```
var y = "global";
function constructFunction( ) {
    var y = "local";
    return new Function("return y");  // Does not capture the local scope!
}
// This line displays "global", because the function returned by the
// Function( ) constructor does not use the local scope. Had a function
// literal been used instead, this line would have displayed "local".
alert(constructFunction()( ));  // Displays "global"
```

11.6 Netscape's JavaScript 1.2 Incompatibilities

Netscape's implementation of JavaScript 1.2 was released (as part of the Netscape 4.0 browser) while the ECMAScript v1 specification was still being finalized. The engineers at Netscape made some guesses about what would be in the specification, and based on those guesses, they made some changes to the way JavaScript behaved. Because these changes were not compatible with previous versions of JavaScript, the changes were implemented only when JavaScript 1.2 was explicitly requested. (In web browsers, this is done by setting the `language` attribute of the HTML `<script>` tag to "JavaScript1.2".) This was an excellent way to introduce new behavior without breaking old scripts. Unfortunately, when work on ECMAScript v1 was completed, the new behavior that Netscape engineers had guessed at was not part of the standard. What this means is that Netscape's implementation of JavaScript 1.2 has special-case behavior that is not compatible with JavaScript 1.1 and does not conform to the ECMAScript specification.

For compatibility with scripts that rely on the nonconforming behavior of JavaScript 1.2, all future implementations of JavaScript from Netscape have retained this special behavior when Version 1.2 is explicitly requested. Note, however, that if you request a version greater than 1.2 (with a `language` attribute of "JavaScript1.3", for example) you will get ECMAScript-compliant behavior. Because this special behavior is present only in JavaScript implementations from Netscape, you should not rely on it in your scripts, and the best practice is to never explicitly specify Version 1.2. Nevertheless, for those cases when you must use JavaScript 1.2, the special behaviors of that version are listed here:

- The equality and inequality operators behave like the identity and non-identity operators. That is, `==` works like `===` and `!=` works like `!==`.
- The default `Object.toString()` method displays the values of all properties defined by the object, returning a string formatted using object literal syntax.
- The `Array.toString()` method separates array elements with a comma and a space, instead of just a comma, and returns the list of elements within square brackets. In addition, string elements of the array are quoted, so that the result is a string in legal array literal syntax.
- When a single numeric argument *n* is passed to the `Array()` constructor, it returns an array with *n* as its single element, rather than an array of length *n*.
- When an array object is used in a numeric context, it evaluates to its length. When used in a boolean context, it evaluates to `false` if its length is 0 and otherwise evaluates to `true`.
- The `Array.push()` method returns the last value pushed rather than the new array length.
- When the `Array.splice()` method splices out a single element *x*, it returns *x* itself, rather than an array containing *x* as its only element. When `splice()` does not remove any elements from the array, it returns nothing instead of returning an empty array.

- When `String.substring()` is called with a starting position greater than its ending position, it returns the empty string rather than correctly swapping the arguments and returning the substring between them.
- The `String.split()` method displays special behavior inherited from Perl: if the specified separator character is a single space, it discards any leading and trailing whitespace in the string before splitting the remainder of the string.

PART II

Client-Side JavaScript

This part of the book, Chapters 12 through 22, documents JavaScript as it is implemented in web browsers. These chapters introduce a host of new JavaScript objects that represent the web browser and the contents of HTML documents. Many examples show typical uses of these client-side objects. You will find it helpful to study these examples carefully.

- Chapter 12, *JavaScript in Web Browsers*
- Chapter 13, *Windows and Frames*
- Chapter 14, *The Document Object*
- Chapter 15, *Forms and Form Elements*
- Chapter 16, *Scripting Cookies*
- Chapter 17, *The Document Object Model*
- Chapter 18, *Cascading Style Sheets and Dynamic HTML*
- Chapter 19, *Events and Event Handling*
- Chapter 20, *Compatibility Techniques*
- Chapter 21, *JavaScript Security*
- Chapter 22, *Using Java with JavaScript*

CHAPTER 12

JavaScript in Web Browsers

The first part of this book described the core JavaScript language. Now we move on to JavaScript as used within web browsers, commonly called client-side JavaScript.* Most of the examples we've seen so far, while legal JavaScript code, had no particular context; they were JavaScript fragments that ran in no specified environment. This chapter provides that context. It begins with a conceptual introduction to the web browser programming environment and basic client-side JavaScript concepts. Next, it discusses how we actually embed JavaScript code within HTML documents so it can run in a web browser. Finally, the chapter goes into detail about how JavaScript programs are executed in a web browser.

12.1 The Web Browser Environment

To understand client-side JavaScript, you must understand the conceptual framework of the programming environment provided by a web browser. The following sections introduce three important features of that programming environment:

- The Window object that serves as the global object and global execution context for client-side JavaScript code
- The client-side object hierarchy and the document object model that forms a part of it
- The event-driven programming model

12.1.1 The Window as Global Execution Context

The primary task of a web browser is to display HTML documents in a window. In client-side JavaScript, the Document object represents an HTML document, and the

* The term "client-side JavaScript" is left over from the days when JavaScript was used in only two places: web browsers (clients) and web servers. As JavaScript is adopted as a scripting language in more and more environments, the term client-side makes less and less sense because it doesn't specify the client side of *what*. Nevertheless, we'll continue to use the term in this book.

Window object represents the window (or frame) that displays the document. While the Document and Window objects are both important to client-side JavaScript, the Window object is more important, for one substantial reason: the Window object is the global object in client-side programming.

Recall from Chapter 4 that in every implementation of JavaScript there is always a global object at the head of the scope chain; the properties of this global object are global variables. In client-side JavaScript, the Window object is the global object. The Window object defines a number of properties and methods that allow us to manipulate the web browser window. It also defines properties that refer to other important objects, such as the `document` property for the Document object. Finally, the Window object has two self-referential properties, `window` and `self`. You can use either of these global variables to refer directly to the Window object.

Since the Window object is the global object in client-side JavaScript, all global variables are defined as properties of the window. For example, the following two lines of code perform essentially the same function:

```
var answer = 42;     // Declare and initialize a global variable
window.answer = 42;  // Create a new property of the Window object
```

The Window object represents a web browser window or a frame within a window. To client-side JavaScript, top-level windows and frames are essentially equivalent. It is common to write JavaScript applications that use multiple frames, and it is possible, if less common, to write applications that use multiple windows. Each window or frame involved in an application has a unique Window object and defines a unique execution context for client-side JavaScript code. In other words, a global variable declared by JavaScript code in one frame is not a global variable within a second frame. However, the second frame *can* access a global variable of the first frame; we'll see how when we consider these issues in more detail in Chapter 13.

12.1.2 The Client-Side Object Hierarchy and the Document Object Model

We've seen that the Window object is the key object in client-side JavaScript. All other client-side objects are connected to this object. For example, every Window object contains a `document` property that refers to the Document object associated with the window and a `location` property that refers to the Location object associated with the window. A Window object also contains a `frames[]` array that refers to the Window objects that represent the frames of the original window. Thus, `document` represents the Document object of the current window, and `frames[1].document` refers to the Document object of the second child frame of the current window.

An object referenced through the current window or through some other Window object may itself refer to other objects. For example, every Document object has a `forms[]` array containing Form objects that represent any HTML forms appearing in the document. To refer to one of these forms, you might write:

```
window.document.forms[0]
```

To continue with the same example, each Form object has an `elements[]` array containing objects that represent the various HTML form elements (input fields, buttons, etc.) that appear within the form. In extreme cases, you can write code that refers to an object at the end of a whole chain of objects, ending up with expressions as complex as this one:

```
parent.frames[0].document.forms[0].elements[3].options[2].text
```

We've seen that the Window object is the global object at the head of the scope chain and that all client-side objects in JavaScript are accessible as properties of other objects. This means that there is a hierarchy of JavaScript objects, with the Window object at its root. Figure 12-1 shows this hierarchy. Study this figure carefully; understanding the hierarchy and the objects it contains is crucial to successful client-side JavaScript programming. Most of the remaining chapters of this book are devoted to fleshing out the details of the objects shown in this figure.

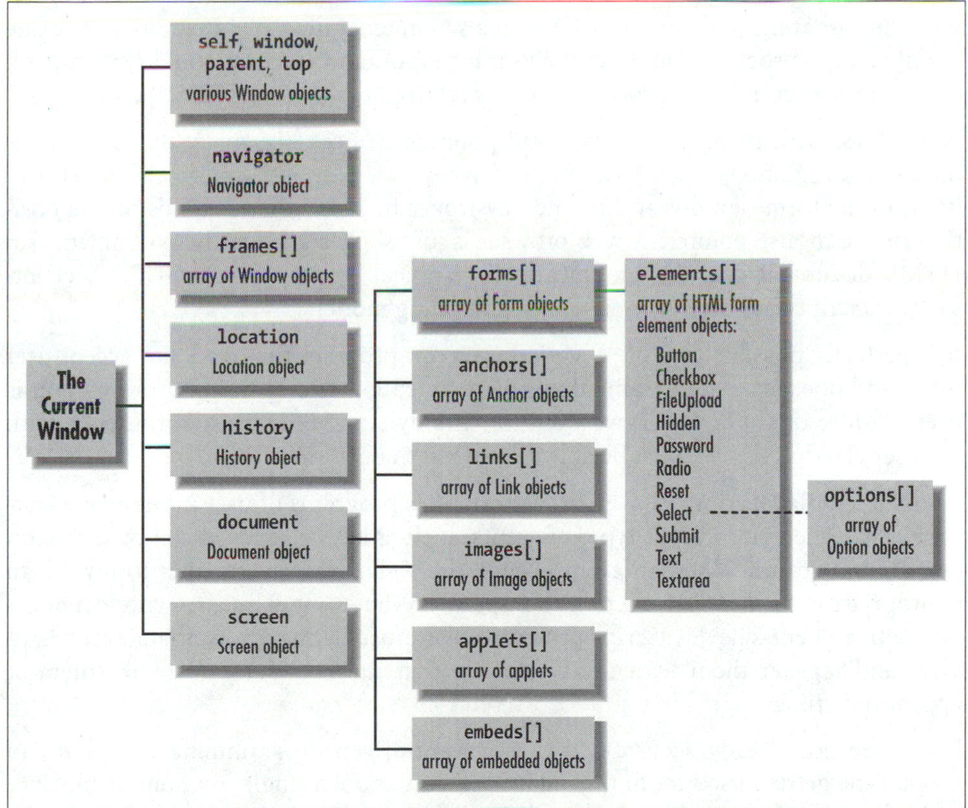

Figure 12-1. The client-side object hierarchy and Level 0 DOM

Note that Figure 12-1 shows just the object properties that refer to other objects. Most of the objects shown in the diagram have quite a few more properties than those shown.

Many of the objects pictured in Figure 12-1 descend from the Document object. This subtree of the larger client-side object hierarchy is known as the document object model (DOM), which is interesting because it has been the focus of a standardization effort. Figure 12-1 illustrates the Document objects that have become de facto standards because they are consistently implemented by all major browsers. Collectively, they are known as the Level 0 DOM, because they form a base level of document functionality that JavaScript programmers can rely on in all browsers. These basic Document objects are the subject of Chapters 14 and 15. A more advanced document object model that has been standardized by the W3C is the subject of Chapters 17 and 18.

12.1.3 The Event-Driven Programming Model

In the old days, computer programs often ran in batch mode—they read in a batch of data, did some computation on that data, and then wrote out the results. Later, with time-sharing and text-based terminals, limited kinds of interactivity became possible—the program could ask the user for input, and the user could type in data. The computer could then process the data and display the results on screen.

Nowadays, with graphical displays and pointing devices like mice, the situation is different. Programs are generally event driven; they respond to asynchronous user input in the form of mouse-clicks and keystrokes in a way that depends on the position of the mouse pointer. A web browser is just such a graphical environment. An HTML document contains an embedded graphical user interface (GUI), so client-side JavaScript uses the event-driven programming model.

It is perfectly possible to write a static JavaScript program that does not accept user input and does exactly the same thing every time. Sometimes this sort of program is useful. More often, however, we want to write dynamic programs that interact with the user. To do this, we must be able to respond to user input.

In client-side JavaScript, the web browser notifies programs of user input by generating *events*. There are various types of events, such as keystroke events, mouse motion events, and so on. When an event occurs, the web browser attempts to invoke an appropriate *event handler* function to respond to the event. Thus, to write dynamic, interactive client-side JavaScript programs, we must define appropriate event handlers and register them with the system, so that the browser can invoke them at appropriate times.

If you are not already accustomed to the event-driven programming model, it can take a little getting used to. In the old model, you wrote a single, monolithic block of code that followed some well-defined flow of control and ran to completion from beginning to end. Event-driven programming stands this model on its head. In event-driven programming, you write a number of independent (but mutually interacting) event handlers. You do not invoke these handlers directly, but allow the system to invoke them at the appropriate times. Since they are triggered by the user's input, the handlers will be invoked at unpredictable, asynchronous times. Much of the time, your program is not running at all but merely sitting waiting for the system to invoke one of its event handlers.

Client-Side JavaScript

The next section explains how JavaScript code is embedded within HTML files. It shows how we can define both static blocks of code that run synchronously from start to finish and event handlers that are invoked asynchronously by the system. We'll also discuss events and event handling in much greater detail in Chapter 19.

12.2 Embedding JavaScript in HTML

Client-side JavaScript code is embedded within HTML documents in a number of ways:

- Between a pair of `<script>` and `</script>` tags
- From an external file specified by the `src` attribute of a `<script>` tag
- In an event handler, specified as the value of an HTML attribute such as `onclick` or `onmouseover`
- As the body of a URL that uses the special `javascript:` protocol

The following sections document each of these JavaScript embedding techniques in more detail. Together, they explain all the ways to include JavaScript in web pages—that is, they explain the allowed structure of JavaScript programs on the client side.

12.2.1 The <script> Tag

Client-side JavaScript scripts are part of an HTML file and are coded within `<script>` and `</script>` tags. You may place any number of JavaScript statements between these tags; they are executed in order of appearance, as part of the document loading process. `<script>` tags may appear in either the `<head>` or `<body>` of an HTML document.

A single HTML document may contain any number of nonoverlapping pairs of `<script>` and `</script>` tags. These multiple, separate scripts are executed in the order in which they appear within the document. While separate scripts within a single file are executed at different times during the loading and parsing of the HTML file, they constitute part of the same JavaScript program: functions and variables defined in one script are available to all scripts that follow in the same file. For example, you can have the following script somewhere in an HTML page:

```
<script>var x = 1;</script>
```

Later on in the same HTML page, you can refer to x, even though it's in a different script block. The context that matters is the HTML page, not the script block:

```
<script>document.write(x);</script>
```

The document.write() method is an important and commonly used one. When used as shown here, it inserts its output into the document at the location of the script. When the script finishes executing, the HTML parser resumes parsing the document and starts by parsing any text produced with document.write().

Example 12-1 shows a sample HTML file that includes a simple JavaScript program. Note the difference between this example and many of the code fragments shown earlier in this book: this one is integrated with an HTML file and has a clear context in which it runs. Note also the use of a language attribute in the <script> tag. This is explained in the next section.

Example 12-1. A simple JavaScript program in an HTML file

```
<html>
<head>
<title>Today's Date</title>
    <script language="JavaScript">
    // Define a function for later use
    function print_todays_date() {
        var d = new Date();                    // Get today's date and time
        document.write(d.toLocaleString());   // Insert it into the document
    }
    </script>
</head>
<body>
The date and time are:<br>
<script language="JavaScript">
  // Now call the function we defined above
  print_todays_date();
</script>
</body>
</html>
```

12.2.1.1 The language and type attributes

Although JavaScript is by far the most commonly used client-side scripting language, it is not the only one. In order to tell a web browser what language a script is written in, the <script> tag has an optional language attribute. Browsers that understand the specified scripting language run the script; browsers that do not know the language ignore it.

If you are writing JavaScript code, use the language attribute as follows:

```
<script language="JavaScript">
    // JavaScript code goes here
</script>
```

If, for example, you are writing a script in Microsoft's Visual Basic Scripting Edition language,* you would use the attribute like this:

```
<script language="VBScript">
    ' VBScript code goes here (' is a comment character like // in JavaScript)
</script>
```

JavaScript is the default scripting language for the Web, and if you omit the `language` attribute, both Netscape and Internet Explorer will assume that your scripts are written in JavaScript.

The HTML 4 specification standardizes the `<script>` tag, but it deprecates the `language` attribute because there is no standard set of names for scripting languages. Instead, the specification prefers the use of a `type` attribute that specifies the scripting language as a MIME type. Thus, in theory, the preferred way to embed a JavaScript script is with a tag that looks like this:

```
<script type="text/javascript">
```

In practice, the `language` attribute is still better supported than this new `type` attribute.

The HTML 4 specification also defines a standard (and useful) way to specify the default scripting language for an entire HTML file. If you plan to use JavaScript as the only scripting language in a file, simply include the following line in the `<head>` of the document:

```
<meta http-equiv="Content-Script-Type" content="text/javascript">
```

If you do this, you can safely use JavaScript scripts without specifying the `language` or `type` attributes.

Since JavaScript is the default scripting language, those of us who program with it never really need to use the `language` attribute to specify the language in which a script is written. However, there is an important secondary purpose for this attribute: it can also be used to specify what version of JavaScript is required to interpret a script. When you specify the `language="JavaScript"` attribute for a script, any JavaScript-enabled browser will run the script. Suppose, however, that you have written a script that uses the exception-handling features of JavaScript 1.5. To avoid syntax errors in browsers that do not support this version of the language, you could embed your script with this tag:

```
<script language="JavaScript1.5">
```

If you do this, only browsers that support JavaScript 1.5 (and its exception-handling features) will run the script; any others will ignore it.

* Also known as VBScript. The only browser that supports VBScript is Internet Explorer, so scripts written in this language are not portable. VBScript interfaces with HTML objects in the same way that JavaScript does, but the core language itself has a different syntax than JavaScript. VBScript is not documented in this book.

The use of the string "JavaScript1.2" in the language attribute deserves special mention. When Netscape 4 was being prepared for release, it appeared that the emerging ECMA-262 standard would require some incompatible changes to certain features of the language. To prevent these incompatible changes from breaking existing scripts, the designers of JavaScript at Netscape took the sensible precaution of implementing the changes only when "JavaScript1.2" was explicitly specified in the language attribute. Unfortunately, the ECMA standard was not finalized before Netscape 4 was released, and after the release, the proposed incompatible changes to the language were removed from the standard. Thus, specifying language="JavaScript1.2" makes Netscape 4 behave in ways that are not compatible with previous browsers or with the ECMA specification. (See Section 11.6, "Netscape's JavaScript 1.2 Incompatibilities," for complete details on these incompatibilities.) For this reason, you may want to avoid specifying "JavaScript1.2" as a value for the language attribute.

12.2.1.2 The </script> tag

You may at some point find yourself writing a script that uses the document.write() method to output a script into some other browser window or frame. If you do this, you'll need to write out a </script> tag to terminate the script you are writing. You must be careful, though—the HTML parser makes no attempt to understand your JavaScript code, and if it sees the string "</script>" in your code, even if it appears within quotes, it assumes that it has found the closing tag of the currently running script. To avoid this problem, simply break up the tag into pieces and write it out using an expression like "</" + "script>":

```
<script>
f1.document.write("<script>");
f1.document.write("document.write('<h2>This is the quoted script</h2>')");
f1.document.write("</" + "script>");
</script>
```

Alternatively, you can escape the / in </script> with a backslash:

```
f1.document.write("<\/script>");
```

12.2.1.3 The defer attribute

The HTML 4 standard defines an attribute of the <script> tag that is not yet in common use but is nonetheless important. As I mentioned briefly earlier, a script may call the document.write() method to dynamically add content to a document. Because of this, when the HTML parser encounters a script, it must stop parsing the document and wait for the script to execute.

If you write a script that does not produce any document output—for example, a script that defines a function but never calls document.write()—you may use the defer attribute in the <script> tag as a hint to the browser that it is safe for it to continue parsing the HTML document and defer execution of the script until it encounters a script that cannot be deferred. Doing this may result in improved performance in browsers that take advantage of the defer attribute. Note that defer does not have a value; it simply must be present in the tag:

```
<script defer>
    // Any JavaScript code that does not call document.write()
</script>
```


12.2.2 Including JavaScript Files

As of JavaScript 1.1, the <script> tag supports a src attribute. The value of this attribute specifies the URL of a file containing JavaScript code. It is used like this:

```
<script src="../../javascript/util.js"></script>
```

A JavaScript file typically has a *.js* extension and contains pure JavaScript, without <script> tags or any other HTML.

A <script> tag with the src attribute specified behaves exactly as if the contents of the specified JavaScript file appeared directly between the <script> and </script> tags. Any code that does appear between these tags is ignored by browsers that support the src attribute (although it is still executed by browsers such as Netscape 2 that do not recognize the attribute). Note that the closing </script> tag is required even when the src attribute is specified and there is no JavaScript between the <script> and </script> tags.

There are a number of advantages to using the src tag:

- It simplifies your HTML files by allowing you to remove large blocks of JavaScript code from them.
- When you have a function or other JavaScript code used by several different HTML files, you can keep it in a single file and read it into each HTML file that needs it. This reduces disk usage and makes code maintenance much easier.
- When JavaScript functions are used by more than one page, placing them in a separate JavaScript file allows them to be cached by the browser, making them load more quickly. When JavaScript code is shared by multiple pages, the time savings of caching more than outweigh the small delay required for the browser to open a separate network connection to download the JavaScript file the first time it is requested.
- Because the src attribute takes an arbitrary URL as its value, a JavaScript program or web page from one web server can employ code (such as subroutine libraries) exported by other web servers.

12.2.3 Event Handlers

JavaScript code in a script is executed once, when the HTML file that contains it is read into the web browser. A program that uses only this sort of static script cannot dynamically respond to the user. More dynamic programs define event handlers that are automatically invoked by the web browser when certain events occur—for example, when the user clicks on a button within a form. Because events in client-side JavaScript originate from HTML objects (such as buttons), event handlers are defined as attributes of those objects. For example, to define an event handler that is invoked when the user clicks on a checkbox in a form, you specify the handler code as an attribute of the HTML tag that defines the checkbox:

```
<input type="checkbox" name="opts" value="ignore-case"
       onclick="ignore-case = this.checked;"
>
```

What's of interest to us here is the `onclick` attribute.* The string value of the `onclick` attribute may contain one or more JavaScript statements. If there is more than one statement, the statements must be separated from each other with semicolons. When the specified event—in this case, a click—occurs on the checkbox, the JavaScript code within the string is executed.

While you can include any number of JavaScript statements within an event handler definition, a common technique when more than one or two simple statements are required is to define the body of an event handler as a function between `<script>` and `</script>` tags. Then you can simply invoke this function from the event handler. This keeps most of your actual JavaScript code within scripts and reduces the need to mingle JavaScript and HTML.

We'll cover events and event handlers in much more detail in Chapter 19, but you'll see them used in a variety of examples before then. Chapter 19 includes a comprehensive list of event handlers, but these are the most common:

`onclick`
: This handler is supported by all button-like form elements, as well as `<a>` and `<area>` tags. It is triggered when the user clicks on the element. If an `onclick` handler returns `false`, the browser does not perform any default action associated with the button or link; for example, it doesn't follow a hyperlink (for an `<a>` tag) or submit a form (for a **Submit** button).

`onmousedown`, `onmouseup`
: These two event handlers are a lot like `onclick`, but they are triggered separately when the user presses and releases a mouse button. Document elements that support `onclick` also support these handlers. In IE 4 and Netscape 6, these handlers are actually supported by just about all document elements.

`onmouseover`, `onmouseout`
: These two event handlers are triggered when the mouse pointer moves over or out of a document element, respectively. They are used most frequently with `<a>`

* All HTML event handler attribute names begin with "on".

tags. If the onmouseover handler of an <a> tag returns true, it prevents the browser from displaying the URL of the link in the status line.

onchange
: This event handler is supported by the <input>, <select>, and <textarea> elements. It is triggered when the user changes the value displayed by the element and then tabs or otherwise moves focus out of the element.

onsubmit, onreset
: These event handlers are supported by the <form> tag and are triggered when the form is about to be submitted or reset. They can return false to cancel the submission or reset. The onsubmit handler is commonly used to perform client-side form validation.

For a realistic example of the use of event handlers, take another look at the interactive loan-payment script in Example 1-3. The HTML form in this example contains a number of event handler attributes. The body of these handlers is simple: they simply call the calculate() function defined elsewhere within a <script>.

12.2.4 JavaScript in URLs

Another way that JavaScript code can be included on the client side is in a URL following the javascript: pseudoprotocol specifier. This special protocol type specifies that the body of the URL is arbitrary JavaScript code to be run by the JavaScript interpreter. If the JavaScript code in a javascript: URL contains multiple statements, the statements must be separated from one another by semicolons. Such a URL might look like this:

```
javascript:var now = new Date(); "<h1>The time is:</h1>" + now;
```

When the browser loads one of these JavaScript URLs, it executes the JavaScript code contained in the URL and uses the string value of the last JavaScript statement as the contents of the new document to display. This string value may contain HTML tags and is formatted and displayed just like any other document loaded into the browser.

JavaScript URLs may also contain JavaScript statements that perform actions but return no value. For example:

```
javascript:alert("Hello World!")
```

When this sort of URL is loaded, the browser executes the JavaScript code, but because there is no value to display as the new document, it does not modify the currently displayed document.

Often, we want to use a javascript: URL to execute some JavaScript code without altering the currently displayed document. To do this, you must be sure that the last statement in the URL has no return value. One way to ensure this is to use the void operator to explicitly specify an undefined return value. Simply use the statement void 0; at the end of your javascript: URL. For example, here is a URL that opens a new, blank browser window without altering the contents of the current window:

```
javascript:window.open("about:blank"); void 0;
```

Without the void operator in this URL, the return value of the Window.open( ) method call would be converted to a string and displayed, and the current document would be overwritten by a document that appears something like this:

```
[object Window]
```

You can use a javascript: URL anywhere you'd use a regular URL. One important way to use this syntax is to type it directly into the **Location** field of your browser, where you can test arbitrary JavaScript code without having to open your editor and create an HTML file containing the code.

javascript: URLs can be used in bookmarks, where they form useful mini-JavaScript programs, or "bookmarklets," that can be easily launched from a menu or toolbar of bookmarks.

javascript: URLs can also be used as the href value of a hyperlink. When the user clicks on such a link, the specified JavaScript code is executed. Or, if you specify a javascript: URL as the value of the action attribute of a <form> tag, the JavaScript code in the URL is executed when the user submits the form. In these contexts, the javascript: URL is essentially a substitute for an event handler.

There are a few circumstances where a javascript: URL can be used with objects that do not support event handlers. For example, the <area> tag does not support an onclick event handler on Windows platforms in Netscape 3 (though it does in Netscape 4). So, if you want to execute JavaScript code when the user clicks on a client-side image map in Netscape 3, you must use a javascript: URL.

12.2.5 JavaScript in Nonstandard Contexts

Both Netscape and Microsoft have implemented proprietary extensions in their browsers, and you may occasionally see JavaScript code in a context other than those described here. For example, Internet Explorer allows you to define event handlers in a <script> tag that uses special for and event attributes. Netscape 4 allows you to use JavaScript as an alternative syntax for defining CSS style sheets within a <style> tag. Netscape 4 also extends the HTML entity syntax and allows JavaScript to appear within entities (but only within the values of HTML attributes). This can result in HTML that looks like this:

```
<table border="&{getBorderWidth( )};">
```

Finally, Netscape 4 also supports a form of conditional comment based on this JavaScript entity syntax. Note that Netscape 6 and the Mozilla browser on which it is based no longer support these nonstandard uses of JavaScript.

12.3 Execution of JavaScript Programs

The previous section discussed the mechanics of integrating JavaScript code into an HTML file. Now we move on to discuss exactly how that integrated JavaScript code is executed by the JavaScript interpreter. The following sections explain how different forms of JavaScript code are executed. While some of this material is fairly obvious, there are a number of important details that are not so obvious.

12.3.1 Scripts

JavaScript statements that appear between `<script>` and `</script>` tags are executed in order of appearance; when more than one script appears in a file, the scripts are executed in the order in which they appear. If a script calls `document.write()`, any text passed to that method is inserted into the document immediately after the closing `</script>` tag and is parsed by the HTML parser when the script finishes running. The same rules apply to scripts included from separate files with the `src` attribute.

The detail that is not so obvious, but is nevertheless important to remember, is that execution of scripts occurs as part of the web browser's HTML parsing process. Thus, if a script appears in the `<head>` section of an HTML document, none of the `<body>` section of the document has been defined yet. This means that the JavaScript objects that represent the contents of the document body, such as Form and Link, have not been created yet and cannot be manipulated by that code.

Your scripts should not attempt to manipulate objects that have not yet been created. For example, you can't write a script that manipulates the contents of an HTML form if the script appears before the form in the HTML file. Some other, similar rules apply on a case-by-case basis. For example, there are properties of the Document object that may be set only from a script in the `<head>` section of an HTML document, before the browser has begun to parse the document content in the `<body>` section. Any special rules of this sort are documented in the reference page for the affected object or property in the client-side reference.

Since scripts are executed while the HTML document that contains them is being parsed and displayed, they should not take too long to run. Because scripts can create dynamic document content with `document.write()`, the HTML parser must stop parsing the document whenever the JavaScript interpreter is running a script. An HTML document cannot be fully displayed until all the scripts it contains have finished executing. If a script performs some computationally intensive task that takes a long time to run, the user may become frustrated waiting for the document to be displayed. Thus, if you need to perform a lot of computation with JavaScript, you should define a function to do the computation and invoke that function from an event handler when the user requests it, rather than doing the computation when the document is first loaded.

As I noted earlier, scripts that use the `src` attribute to read in external JavaScript files are executed just like scripts that include their code directly in the file. What this means is that the HTML parser and the JavaScript interpreter must both stop and wait for the external JavaScript file to be downloaded. (Unlike embedded images, scripts cannot be downloaded in the background while the HTML parser continues to run.) Downloading an external file of JavaScript code, even over a relatively fast modem connection, can cause noticeable delays in the loading and execution of a web page. Of course, once the JavaScript code is cached locally, this problem effectively disappears.

12.3.2 Functions

Remember that defining a function is not the same as executing it. It is perfectly safe to define a function that manipulates objects that have not yet been created. Just take care that the function is not executed or invoked until the necessary variables, objects, and so on all exist. I said earlier that you can't write a script to manipulate an HTML form if the script appears before the form in the HTML file. You can, however, write a script that defines a function to manipulate the form, regardless of the relative locations of the script and form. In fact, this is a common practice. Many JavaScript programs start off with a script in the `<head>` of the document that does nothing more than define functions that are used in the `<body>` of the HTML file.

It is also common to write JavaScript programs that use scripts simply to define functions that are later invoked through event handlers. As we'll see in the next section, you must take care in this case to ensure two things: that all functions are defined before any event handler attempts to invoke them, and that event handlers and the functions they invoke do not attempt to use objects that have not yet been defined.

12.3.3 Event Handlers

Defining an event handler as the value of an `onclick` or another HTML attribute is much like defining a JavaScript function: the code is not immediately executed. Event-handler execution is asynchronous. Since events generally occur when the user interacts with HTML objects, there is no way to predict when an event handler will be invoked.

Event handlers share an important restriction with scripts: they should not take a long time to execute. As we've seen, scripts should run quickly because the HTML parser cannot continue parsing until the script finishes executing. Event handlers, on the other hand, should not take long to run because the user cannot interact with your program until the program has finished handling the event. If an event handler performs some time-consuming operation, it may appear to the user that the program has hung, frozen, or crashed.

If for some reason you must perform a long operation in an event handler, be sure that the user has explicitly requested that operation, and then notify him that there will be a wait. As we'll see in Chapter 13, you can notify the user by posting an `alert()` dialog box or displaying text in the browser's status line. Also, if your program requires a lot of background processing, you can schedule a function to be called repeatedly during idle time with the `setTimeout()` method.

It is important to understand that event handlers may be invoked before a web page is fully loaded and parsed. This is easier to understand if you imagine a slow network connection—even a half-loaded document may display hypertext links and form elements that the user can interact with, thereby causing event handlers to be invoked before the second half of the document is loaded.

The fact that event handlers can be invoked before a document is fully loaded has two important implications. First, if your event handler invokes a function, you must be sure that the function is already defined before the handler calls it. One way to guarantee this is to define all your functions in the `<head>` section of an HTML document. This section of a document is always completely parsed (and any functions in it defined) before the `<body>` section of the document is parsed. Since all objects that define event handlers must themselves be defined in the `<body>` section, functions in the `<head>` section are guaranteed to be defined before any event handlers are invoked.

The second implication is that you must be sure that your event handler does not attempt to manipulate HTML objects that have not yet been parsed and created. An event handler can always safely manipulate its own object, of course, and also any objects that are defined before it in the HTML file. One strategy is simply to define your web page's user interface in such a way that event handlers refer only to previously defined objects. For example, if you define a form that uses event handlers only on the **Submit** and **Reset** buttons, you just need to place these buttons at the bottom of the form (which is where good user-interface style says they should go anyway).

In more complex programs, you may not be able to ensure that event handlers manipulate only objects defined before them, so you need to take extra care with these programs. If an event handler manipulates only objects defined within the same form, it is pretty unlikely that you'll ever have problems. When you manipulate objects in other forms or other frames, however, this starts to be a real concern. One technique is to test for the existence of the object you want to manipulate before you manipulate it. You can do this simply by comparing it (and any parent objects) to `null`. For example:

```
<script>
function set_name_other_frame(name)
{
    if (parent.frames[1] == null) return;    // Other frame not yet defined
    if (!parent.frames[1].document) return;  // Document not yet loaded in it
    if (!parent.frames[1].document.myform) return;      // Form not yet defined
    if (!parent.frames[1].document.myform.name) return;  // Field not yet defined
```

```
    parent.frames[1].document.myform.name.value = name;
}
</script>

<input type="text" name="lastname"
       onchange="set_name_other_frame(this.value)";
>
```

In JavaScript 1.5 and later, you can omit the existence tests in the previous code if you instead use the `try/catch` statement to catch the exception that will be thrown if the function is invoked before the document is fully loaded.

Another technique that an event handler can use to ensure that all required objects are defined involves the `onload` event handler. This event handler is defined in the `<body>` or `<frameset>` tag of an HTML file and is invoked when the document or frameset is fully loaded. If you set a flag within the `onload` event handler, other event handlers can test this flag to see if they can safely run, with the knowledge that the document is fully loaded and all objects it contains are defined. For example:

```
<body onload="window.fullyLoaded = true;">
  <form>
    <input type="button" value="Do It!"
           onclick="if (window.fullyLoaded) doit();">
  </form>
</body>
```

12.3.3.1 onload and onunload event handlers

The `onload` event handler and its partner `onunload` are worth a special mention in the context of the execution order of JavaScript programs. Both of these event handlers are defined in the `<body>` or `<frameset>` tag of an HTML file. (No HTML file can legally contain both of these tags.) The `onload` handler is executed when the document or frameset is fully loaded, which means that all images have been downloaded and displayed, all subframes have loaded, any Java applets have started running, and so on. Be aware that when you are working with multiple frames, there is no guarantee of the order in which the `onload` event handler is invoked for the various frames, except that the handler for the parent frame is invoked after the handlers of all its child frames.

The `onunload` handler is executed just before the page is unloaded, which occurs when the browser is about to move on to a new page. You can use it to undo the effects of your `onload` handler or other scripts in your web page. For example, if your web page opens up a secondary browser window, the `onunload` handler provides an opportunity to close that window when the user moves on to some other web page. The `onunload` handler should not run any kind of time-consuming operation, nor should it pop up a dialog box. It exists simply to perform a quick cleanup operation; running it should not slow down or impede the user's transition to a new page.

12.3.4 JavaScript URLs

JavaScript code in a `javascript:` URL is not executed when the document containing the URL is loaded. It is not interpreted until the browser tries to load the document to which the URL refers. This may be when a user types in a JavaScript URL or, more likely, when a user follows a link, clicks on a client-side image map, or submits a form. `javascript:` URLs are often used as an alternative to event handlers, and as with event handlers, the code in those URLs can be executed before a document is fully loaded. Thus, you must take the same precautions with `javascript:` URLs that you take with event handlers to ensure that they do not attempt to reference objects (or functions) that are not yet defined.

12.3.5 Window and Variable Lifetime

A final topic in our investigation of how client-side JavaScript programs run is the issue of variable lifetime. We've seen that the Window object is the global object for client-side JavaScript and that all global variables are properties of the Window object. What happens to Window objects and the variables they contain when the web browser moves from one web page to another?

Whenever a new document is loaded into a window or a frame, the Window object for that window or frame is restored to its default state: any properties and functions defined by a script in the previous document are deleted, and any of the standard system properties that may have been altered or overwritten are restored. Every document begins with a "clean slate." Your scripts can rely on this—they will not inherit a corrupted environment from the previous document. Any variables and functions your scripts define persist only until the document is replaced with a new one.

The clean slate we're discussing here is the Window object that represents the window or frame into which the document is loaded. As we've discussed, this Window object is the global object for JavaScript code in that window or frame. However, if you're working with multiple frames or multiple windows, a script in one window may refer to the Window objects that represent other windows or frames. So in addition to considering the persistence of variables and functions defined in Window objects, we must also consider the persistence of the Window object itself.

A Window object that represents a top-level browser window exists as long as that window exists. A reference to the Window object remains valid regardless of how many web pages the window loads and unloads. The Window object is valid as long as the top-level window is open.*

* A Window object may not actually be destroyed when its window is closed. If there are still references to the Window object from other windows, the object is not garbage collected. However, a reference to a window that has been closed is of very little practical use.

A Window object that represents a frame remains valid as long as that frame remains within the frame or window that contains it. For example, if frame A contains a script that has a reference to the Window object for frame B, and a new document is loaded into frame B, frame A's reference to the Window object remains valid. Any variables or functions defined in frame B's Window object will be deleted when the new document is loaded, but the Window object itself remains valid (until the containing frame or window loads a new document and overwrites both frame A and frame B).

This means that Window objects, whether they represent top-level windows or frames, are quite persistent. The lifetime of a Window object may be longer than that of the web pages it contains and displays and longer than the lifetime of the scripts contained in the web pages it displays.

CHAPTER 13

Windows and Frames

Chapter 12 described the Window object and the central role it plays in client-side JavaScript. We've seen that the Window object serves as the global object for client-side JavaScript programs, and, as illustrated in Figure 12-1, it is also the root of the client-side object hierarchy.

Besides these special roles, the Window object is an important object in its own right. Every web browser window and every frame within every window is represented by a Window object. The Window object defines quite a few properties and methods that are important in client-side JavaScript programming. This chapter explores those properties and methods and demonstrates some important techniques for programming with windows and frames. Note that because the Window object is so central to client-side programming, this chapter is quite long. Don't feel you have to master all this material at once—you may find it easier to study this chapter in several shorter chunks!

13.1 Window Overview

We begin this chapter with an overview of some of the most commonly used properties and methods of the Window object. Later sections of the chapter explain this material in more detail. As usual, the client-side reference section contains complete coverage of Window object properties and methods.

The most important properties of the Window object are the following:

`closed`
: A boolean value that is `true` only if the window has been closed.

`defaultStatus, status`
: The text that appears in the status line of the browser.

`document`
: A reference to the Document object that represents the HTML document displayed in the window. The Document object is covered in detail in Chapter 14.

`frames[]`
: An array of Window objects that represent the frames (if any) within the window.

`history`
: A reference to the History object that represents the user's browsing history for the window.

`location`
: A reference to the Location object that represents the URL of the document displayed in the window. Setting this property causes the browser to load a new document.

`name`
: The name of the window. Can be used with the `target` attribute of the HTML `<a>` tag, for example.

`opener`
: A reference to the Window object that opened this one, or `null` if this window was opened by the user.

`parent`
: If the current window is a frame, a reference to the frame of the window that contains it.

`self`
: A self-referential property; a reference to the current Window object. A synonym for `window`.

`top`
: If the current window is a frame, a reference to the Window object of the top-level window that contains the frame. Note that `top` is different from `parent` for frames nested within other frames.

`window`
: A self-referential property; a reference to the current Window object. A synonym for `self`.

The Window object also supports a number of important methods:

`alert()`, `confirm()`, `prompt()`
: Display simple dialog boxes to the user and, for `confirm()` and `prompt()`, get the user's response.

`close()`
: Close the window.

`focus()`, `blur()`
: Request or relinquish keyboard focus for the window. The `focus()` method also ensures that the window is visible by bringing it to the front of the stacking order.

`moveBy()`, `moveTo()`
: Move the window.

`open()`
: Open a new top-level window to display a specified URL with a specified set of features.

`print()`
: Print the window or frame—same as if the user had selected the **Print** button from the window's toolbar (Netscape 4 and later and IE 5 and later only).

`resizeBy()`, `resizeTo()`
: Resize the window.

`scrollBy()`, `scrollTo()`
: Scroll the document displayed within the window.

`setInterval()`, `clearInterval()`
: Schedule or cancel a function to be repeatedly invoked with a specified delay between invocations.

`setTimeout()`, `clearTimeout()`
: Schedule or cancel a function to be invoked once after a specified number of milliseconds.

Client-Side JavaScript

As you can see from these lists, the Window object provides quite a bit of functionality. The remainder of this chapter explores much of that functionality in more detail.

13.2 Simple Dialog Boxes

Three commonly used Window methods are `alert()`, `confirm()`, and `prompt()`. These methods pop up simple dialog boxes. `alert()` displays a message to the user, `confirm()` asks the user to click an **Ok** or **Cancel** button to confirm or cancel an operation, and `prompt()` asks the user to enter a string. Sample dialog boxes produced by these three methods are shown in Figure 13-1.

Note that the text displayed by these dialog boxes is plain text, not HTML-formatted text. You can format these dialog boxes only with spaces, newlines, and various punctuation characters. Adjusting the layout generally requires trial and error. Bear in mind, though, that the dialog boxes look different on different platforms and in different browsers, so you can't always count on your formatting to look right on all possible browsers.

Some browsers (such as Netscape 3 and 4) display the word "JavaScript" in the titlebar or upper-left corner of all dialog boxes produced by `alert()`, `confirm()`, and `prompt()`. Although designers find this annoying, it should be considered a feature instead of a bug: it is there to make the origin of the dialog box clear to users and to prevent you from writing Trojan-horse code that spoofs system dialog boxes and tricks users into entering their passwords or doing other things that they shouldn't do.

The `confirm()` and `prompt()` methods *block*—that is, those methods do not return until the user dismisses the dialog boxes they display. This means that when you pop

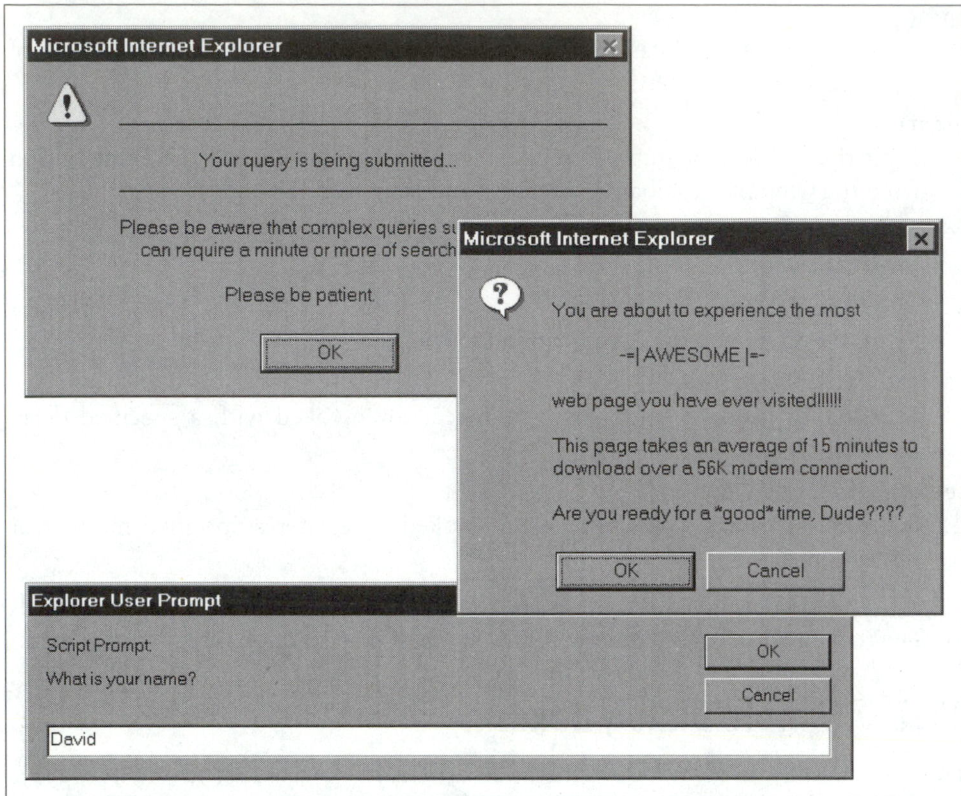

Figure 13-1. alert(), confirm(), and prompt() dialog boxes

up one of these boxes, your code stops running and the currently loading document, if any, stops loading until the user responds with the requested input. There is no alternative to blocking for these methods—their return value is the user's input, so they must wait for the user before they can return. In most browsers, the `alert( )` method also blocks and waits for the user to dismiss the dialog box. In some browsers, however (notably Netscape 3 and 4 on Unix platforms), `alert( )` does not block. In practice, this minor incompatibility rarely causes problems.

Example 13-1 shows some typical uses of these methods.

Example 13-1. Using the alert(), confirm(), and prompt() methods

```
// Here's a function that uses the alert( ) method to tell the user
// that form submission will take some time and that the user should
// be patient. It would be suitable for use in the onsubmit event handler
// of an HTML form.
// Note that all formatting is done with spaces, newlines, and underscores.
function warn_on_submit( )
{
    alert("\n_________________________________________________\n\n" +
          "                  Your query is being submitted...\n"    +
```

Example 13-1. Using the alert(), confirm(), and prompt() methods (continued)

```
        "________________________________________________\n\n"   +
        "Please be aware that complex queries such as yours\n"     +
        "     can require a minute or more of search time.\n\n"    +
        "                         Please be patient.");
}

// Here is a use of the confirm() method to ask if the user really
// wants to visit a web page that takes a long time to download. Note that
// the return value of the method indicates the user response. Based
// on this response, we reroute the browser to an appropriate page.
var msg = "\nYou are about to experience the most\n\n" +
          "                 -=| AWESOME |=-\n\n" +
          "web page you have ever visited!!!!!!\n\n" +
          "This page takes an average of 15 minutes to\n" +
          "download over a 56K modem connection.\n\n" +
          "Are you ready for a *good* time, Dude????";

if (confirm(msg))
    location.replace("awesome_page.html");
else
    location.replace("lame_page.html");

// Here's some very simple code that uses the prompt() method to get
// a user's name and then uses that name in dynamically generated HTML.
n = prompt("What is your name?", "");
document.write("<hr><h1>Welcome to my home page, " + n + "</h1><hr>");
```

13.3 The Status Line

Web browsers typically display a *status line* at the bottom of every window (except for those explicitly created without one), where the browser can display messages to the user. When the user moves the mouse over a hypertext link, for example, the browser usually displays the URL to which the link points. And when the user moves the mouse over a browser control button, the browser may display a simple context help message that explains the purpose of the button. You can also make use of this status line in your own programs. Its contents are controlled by two properties of the Window object: `status` and `defaultStatus`.

Although web browsers usually display the URL of a hypertext link when the user passes the mouse pointer over the link, you may have encountered some links that don't behave this way—links that display some text other than the link's URL. This effect is achieved with the `status` property of the Window object and the `onmouseover` event handler of hypertext links:

```
<!-- Here's how you set the status line in a hyperlink.
  -- Note that the event handler *must* return true for this to work. -->
Lost? Dazed and confused? Visit the
<a href="sitemap.html" onmouseover="status='Go to Site Map'; return true;">
  Site Map
</a>
```

```
<!-- You can do the same thing for client-side image maps -->
<img src="images/imgmap1.gif" usemap="#map1">
<map name="map1">
  <area coords="0,0,50,20" href="info.html"
    onmouseover="status='Visit our Information Center'; return true;">
  <area coords="0,20,50,40" href="order.html"
    onmouseover="status='Place an order'; return true;">
  <area coords="0,40,50,60" href="help.html"
    onmouseover="status='Get help fast!'; return true;">
</map>
```

The `onmouseover` event handler in this example must return `true`. This tells the browser that it should not perform its own default action for the event—that is, it should not display the URL of the link in the status line. If you forget to return `true`, the browser overwrites whatever message the handler displays in the status line with its own URL. Don't worry if you do not fully understand the event handler in this example. We'll explain events in Chapter 19.

When the user moves the mouse pointer over a hyperlink, the browser displays the URL for the link, then erases the URL when the mouse moves off the hyperlink. The same is true when you use an `onmouseover` event handler to set the Window `status` property—your custom message is displayed while the mouse is over the hyperlink and is erased when the mouse moves off the link.

The `status` property is intended for exactly the sort of transient message we saw in the previous example. Sometimes, though, you want to display a message that is not so transient in the status line—for example, you might display a welcome message to users visiting your web page or a simple line of help text for novice visitors. To do this, you set the `defaultStatus` property of the Window object; this property specifies the default text displayed in the status line. That text is temporarily replaced with URLs, context help messages, or other transient text when the mouse pointer is over hyperlinks or browser control buttons, but once the mouse moves off those areas, the default text is restored.

You might use the `defaultStatus` property like this to provide a friendly and helpful message to real beginners:

```
<script>
defaultStatus = "Welcome!  Click on underlined blue text to navigate.";
</script>
```

13.4 Timeouts and Intervals

The `setTimeout()` method of the Window object schedules a piece of JavaScript code to be run at some specified time in the future. The `clearTimeout()` method can be used to cancel the execution of that code. `setTimeout()` is commonly used to perform animations or other kinds of repetitive actions. If a function runs and then uses `setTimeout()` to schedule itself to be called again, we get a process that repeats without any user intervention. JavaScript 1.2 has added the `setInterval()` and clearInterval() methods, which are like setTimeout() and clearTimeout(), except that they automatically reschedule the code to run repeatedly; there is no need for the code to reschedule itself.

The setTimeout() method is commonly used in conjunction with the status or defaultStatus properties to animate some kind of message in the status bar of the browser. In general, animations involving the status bar are gaudy, and you should shun them! There are, however, a few status-bar animation techniques that can be useful and in good taste. Example 13-2 shows such a tasteful status-bar animation. It displays the current time in the status bar and updates that time once a minute. Because the update occurs only once a minute, this animation does not produce a constant flickering distraction at the bottom of the browser window, like so many others do.

Note the use of the onload event handler of the <body> tag to perform the first call to the display_time_in_status_line() method. This event handler is invoked once when the HTML document is fully loaded into the browser. After this first call, the method uses setTimeout() to schedule itself to be called every 60 seconds so that it can update the displayed time.

Example 13-2. A digital clock in the status line

```
<html>
<head>
<script>
// This function displays the time in the status line
// Invoke it once to activate the clock; it will call itself from then on
function display_time_in_status_line()
{
    var d = new Date();                 // Get the current time
    var h = d.getHours();               // Extract hours: 0 to 23
    var m = d.getMinutes();             // Extract minutes: 0 to 59
    var ampm = (h >= 12)?"PM":"AM";     // Is it a.m. or p.m.?
    if (h > 12) h -= 12;                // Convert 24-hour format to 12-hour
    if (h == 0) h = 12;                 // Convert 0 o'clock to midnight
    if (m < 10) m = "0" + m;            // Convert 0 minutes to 00 minutes, etc.
    var t = h + ':' + m + ' ' + ampm;   // Put it all together

    defaultStatus = t;                  // Display it in the status line

    // Arrange to do it all again in one minute
    setTimeout("display_time_in_status_line()", 60000);  // 60000 ms is one minute
}
</script>
</head>
<!-- Don't bother starting the clock till everything is loaded. The
  -- status line will be busy with other messages during loading, anyway. -->
<body onload="display_time_in_status_line();">
<!-- The HTML document contents go here -->
</body>
</html>
```

In JavaScript 1.2, Example 13-2 could be written using `setInterval()` instead of `setTimeout()`. In this case, the `setTimeout()` call would be removed from the `display_time_in_status_line()` method, and we'd remove the `onload` event handler. Instead, after defining `display_time_in_status_line()`, our script would call `setInterval()` to schedule an invocation of the function that automatically repeats once every 60,000 milliseconds.

13.5 Error Handling

The `onerror` property of a Window object is special. If you assign a function to this property, the function will be invoked whenever a JavaScript error occurs in that window: the function you assign becomes an error handler for the window.

Three arguments are passed to an error handler. The first is a message describing the error that occurred. This may be something like "missing operator in expression", "self is read-only", or "myname is not defined". The second argument is a string that contains the URL of the document containing the JavaScript code that caused the error. The third argument is the line number within the document where the error occurred. An error handler can use these arguments for any purpose it desires. A typical error handler might display the error message to the user, log it somewhere, or force the error to be ignored.

In addition to those three arguments, the return value of the `onerror` handler is significant. Browsers typically display an error message in a dialog box or in the status line when an error occurs. If the `onerror` handler returns `true`, it tells the system that the handler has handled the error and that no further action is necessary—in other words, the system should not display its own error message. For example, if you do not want your users to be pestered by error messages, no matter how buggy the code you write is, you could use a line of code like this at the start of all your JavaScript programs:

```
self.onerror = function() { return true; }
```

Of course, doing this will make it very difficult for users to give you feedback when your programs fail silently without producing error messages.

We'll see a sample use of an `onerror` handler in Example 14-1. That example uses the `onerror` handler to display the error details to the user and allow the user to submit a bug report containing those details.

Note that the `onerror` error handler is buggy in Netscape 6. Although the function you specify is triggered when an error occurs, the three arguments that are passed are incorrect and unusable. Netscape 6 and other browsers that support JavaScript 1.5 have an alternative means of catching and handling errors, however: they can use the `try/catch` statement. (See Chapter 6 for details.)

13.6 The Navigator Object

The `Window.navigator` property refers to a Navigator object that contains information about the web browser as a whole, such as the version and a list of the data formats it can display. The Navigator object is named after Netscape Navigator, but it is also supported by Internet Explorer. IE also supports `clientInformation` as a vendor-neutral synonym for `navigator`. Unfortunately, Netscape and Mozilla do not support this property.

The Navigator object has five main properties that provide version information about the browser that is running:

`appName`
: The simple name of the web browser.

`appVersion`
: The version number and/or other version information for the browser. Note that this should be considered an "internal" version number, since it does not always correspond to the version number displayed to the user. For example, Netscape 6 reports a version number of 5.0, since there never was a Netscape 5 release. Also, IE Versions 4 through 6 all report a version number of 4.0, to indicate compatibility with the baseline functionality of fourth-generation browsers.

`userAgent`
: The string that the browser sends in its `USER-AGENT` HTTP header. This property typically contains all the information in both `appName` and `appVersion`.

`appCodeName`
: The code name of the browser. Netscape uses the code name "Mozilla" as the value of this property. For compatibility, IE does the same thing.

`platform`
: The hardware platform on which the browser is running. This property was added in JavaScript 1.2.

The following lines of JavaScript code display each of these Navigator object properties in a dialog box:

```
var browser = "BROWSER INFORMATION:\n";
for(var propname in navigator) {
    browser += propname + ": " + navigator[propname] + "\n"
}
alert(browser);
```

Figure 13-2 shows the dialog box displayed when the code is run on IE 6.

As you can see from Figure 13-2, the properties of the Navigator object have values that are sometimes more complex than we are interested in. We are often interested in only the first digit of the `appVersion` property, for example. When using the

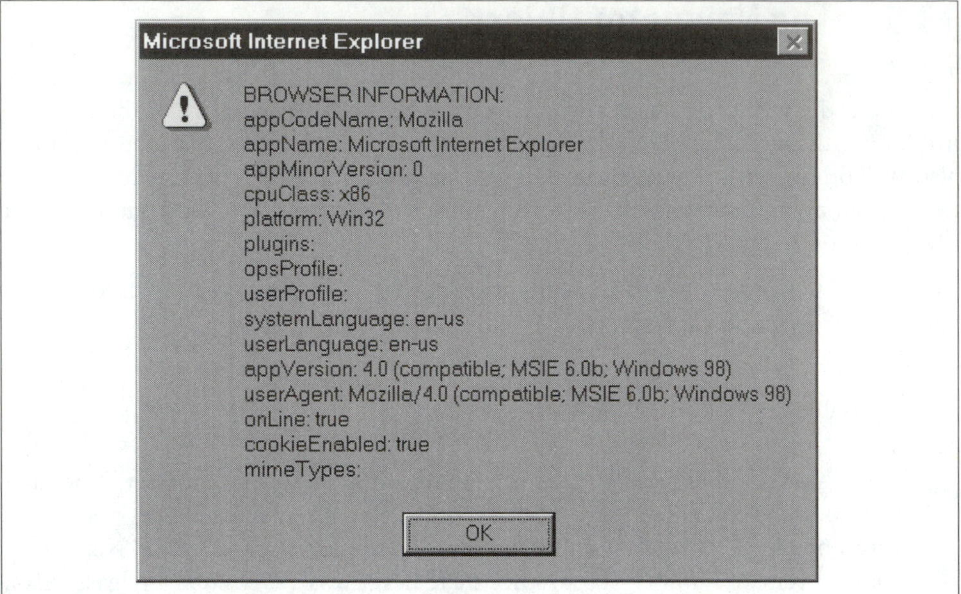

Figure 13-2. Navigator object properties

Navigator object to test browser information, we often use methods such as `parseInt()` and `String.indexOf()` to extract only the information we want. Example 13-3 shows some code that does this: it processes the properties of the Navigator object and stores them in an object named `browser`. These properties, in their processed form, are easier to use than the raw `navigator` properties. The general term for code like this is a "client sniffer," and you can find more complex and general-purpose sniffer code on the Internet.* For many purposes, however, something as simple as that shown in Example 13-3 works just fine.

Example 13-3. Determining browser vendor and version

```
/*
 * File: browser.js
 * Include with: <script SRC="browser.js"></script>
 *
 * A simple "sniffer" that determines browser version and vendor.
 * It creates an object named "browser" that is easier to use than
 * the "navigator" object.
 */
// Create the browser object
var browser = new Object();

// Figure out the browser's major version
browser.version = parseInt(navigator.appVersion);
```

* See, for example, *http://www.mozilla.org/docs/web-developer/sniffer/browser_type.html*.

Example 13-3. Determining browser vendor and version (continued)

```
// Now figure out if the browser is from one of the two
// major browser vendors. Start by assuming it is not.
browser.isNetscape = false;
browser.isMicrosoft = false;
if (navigator.appName.indexOf("Netscape") != -1)
    browser.isNetscape = true;
else if (navigator.appName.indexOf("Microsoft") != -1)
    browser.isMicrosoft = true;
```


13.7 The Screen Object

In JavaScript 1.2, the `screen` property of a Window object refers to a Screen object that provides information about the size of the user's display and the number of colors available on it. The `width` and `height` properties specify the size of the display in pixels. The `availWidth` and `availHeight` properties specify the display size that is actually available; they exclude the space required by features such as the Windows taskbar. You can use these properties to help you decide what size images to include in a document, for example, or what size windows to create in a program that creates multiple browser windows.

The `colorDepth` property specifies the base-2 logarithm of the number of colors that can be displayed. Often, this value is the same as the number of bits per pixel used by the display. For example, an 8-bit display can display 256 colors, and if all of these colors were available for use by the browser, the `screen.colorDepth` property would be 8. In some circumstances, however, the browser may restrict itself to a subset of the available colors, and you might find a `screen.colorDepth` value that is lower than the bits-per-pixel value of the screen. If you have several versions of an image that were defined using different numbers of colors, you can test this `colorDepth` property to decide which version to include in a document.

Example 13-4, later in this chapter, shows how the Screen object can be used.

13.8 Window Control Methods

The Window object defines several methods that allow high-level control of the window itself. The following sections explore how these methods allow us to open and close windows, control window position and size, request and relinquish keyboard focus, and scroll the contents of a window. We conclude with an example that demonstrates several of these features.

13.8.1 Opening Windows

You can open a new web browser window with the `open()` method of the Window object. This method takes four optional arguments and returns a Window object that represents the newly opened window. The first argument to `open()` is the URL of the document to display in the new window. If this argument is omitted (or is null or the empty string), the window will be empty.

The second argument to open() is the name of the window. As we'll discuss later in the chapter, this name can be useful as the value of the target attribute of a <form> or <a> tag. If you specify the name of a window that already exists, open() simply returns a reference to that existing window, rather than opening a new one.

The third optional argument to open() is a list of features that specify the window size and GUI decorations. If you omit this argument, the new window is given a default size and has a full set of standard features: a menu bar, status line, toolbar, and so on. On the other hand, if you specify this argument, you can explicitly specify the size of the window and the set of features it includes. For example, to open a small, resizeable browser window with a status bar but no menu bar, toolbar, or location bar, you could use the following line of JavaScript:

```
var w = window.open("smallwin.html", "smallwin",
                    "width=400,height=350,status=yes,resizable=yes");
```

Note that when you specify this third argument, any features you do not explicitly specify are omitted. See Window.open() in the client-side reference section for the full set of available features and their names.

The fourth argument to open() is useful only when the second argument names an already existing window. This fourth argument is a boolean value that specifies whether the URL specified as the first argument should replace the current entry in the window's browsing history (true) or create a new entry in the window's browsing history (false), which is the default behavior.

The return value of the open() method is the Window object that represents the newly created window. You can use this Window object in your JavaScript code to refer to the new window, just as you use the implicit Window object window to refer to the window within which your code is running. But what about the reverse situation? What if JavaScript code in the new window wants to refer back to the window that opened it? In JavaScript 1.1 and later, the opener property of a window refers to the window from which it was opened. If the window was created by the user instead of by JavaScript code, the opener property is null.

An important point about the open() method is that it is almost always invoked as window.open(), even though window refers to the global object and should therefore be entirely optional. window is explicitly specified because the Document object also has an open() method, so specifying window.open() helps to make it very clear what we are trying to do. This is not just a helpful habit; it is required in some circumstances, because, as we'll learn in Chapter 19, event handlers execute in the scope of the object that defines them. When the event handler of an HTML button executes, for example, the scope chain includes the Button object, the Form object that contains the button, the Document object that contains the form, and, finally, the Window object that contains the document. Thus, if such an event handler refers merely to the open() method, this identifier ends up being resolved in the Document object, and the event handler opens a new document rather than opening a new window!

We'll see the open() method in use in Example 13-4.

13.8.2 Closing Windows

Just as the open() method opens a new window, the close() method closes one. If we've created a Window object w, we can close it with:

```
w.close();
```

JavaScript code running within that window itself could close it with:

```
window.close();
```

Again, note the explicit use of the window identifier to disambiguate the close() method of the Window object from the close() method of the Document object.

Most browsers allow you to automatically close only those windows that your own JavaScript code has created. If you attempt to close any other window, the user is presented with a dialog box that asks him to confirm (or cancel) that request to close the window. This precaution prevents inconsiderate scripters from writing code to close a user's main browsing window.

In JavaScript 1.1 and later, a Window object continues to exist after the window it represents has been closed. You should not attempt to use any of its properties or methods, however, except to test the closed property. This property is true if the window has been closed. Remember that the user can close any window at any time, so to avoid errors, it is a good idea to check periodically that the window you are trying to use is still open. We'll see this done in Example 13-4.

13.8.3 Window Geometry

In JavaScript 1.2, moveTo() moves the upper-left corner of the window to the specified coordinates. Similarly, moveBy() moves the window a specified number of pixels left or right and up or down. resizeTo() and resizeBy() resize the window by an absolute or relative amount; they are also new in JavaScript 1.2. Note that in order to prevent security attacks that rely on code running in small or offscreen windows that the user does not notice, browsers may restrict your ability to move windows offscreen or to make them too small.

13.8.4 Keyboard Focus and Visibility

The focus() and blur() methods also provide high-level control over a window. Calling focus() requests that the system give keyboard focus to the window, and blur() relinquishes keyboard focus. In addition, the focus() method ensures that the window is visible by moving it to the top of the stacking order. When you use the

Window.open( ) method to open a new window, the browser automatically creates that window on top. But if the second argument specifies the name of a window that already exists, the open( ) method does not automatically make that window visible. Thus, it is common practice to follow calls to open( ) with a call to focus( ).

focus( ) and blur( ) are defined in JavaScript 1.1 and later.

13.8.5 Scrolling

The Window object also contains methods that scroll the document within the window or frame. scrollBy( ) scrolls the document displayed in the window by a specified number of pixels left or right and up or down. scrollTo( ) scrolls the document to an absolute position. It moves the document so that the specified document coordinates are displayed in the upper-left corner of the document area within the window. These two methods are defined in JavaScript 1.2. In JavaScript 1.1, the scroll( ) method performs the same function as the JavaScript 1.2 scrollTo( ) method. scrollTo( ) is the preferred method, but the scroll( ) method remains for backward compatibility.

In JavaScript 1.2, the elements of the anchors[] array of the Document object are Anchor objects. Each Anchor object has x and y properties that specify the location of the anchor within the document. Thus, you can use these values in conjunction with the scrollTo( ) method to scroll to known locations within the document. Alternatively, in IE 4 and later and Netscape 6 and later, document elements all define a focus( ) method. Invoking this method on an element causes the document to scroll as needed to ensure that the element is visible.

13.8.6 Window Methods Example

Example 13-4 demonstrates the Window open(), close( ), and moveTo( ) methods and several other window-programming techniques that we've discussed. It creates a new window and then uses setInterval( ) to repeatedly call a function that moves it around the screen. It determines the size of the screen with the Screen object and then uses this information to make the window bounce when it reaches any edge of the screen.

Example 13-4. Moving a window

```
<script>
// Here are the initial values for our animation
var x = 0, y = 0, w=200, h=200;  // Window position and size
var dx = 5, dy = 5;              // Window velocity
var interval = 100;              // Milliseconds between updates

// Create the window that we're going to move around
// The javascript: URL is simply a way to display a short document
```

Example 13-4. Moving a window (continued)

```
// The final argument specifies the window size
var win = window.open('javascript:"<h1>BOUNCE!</h1>"', "",
                      "width=" + w + ",height=" + h);

// Set the initial position of the window
win.moveTo(x,y);

// Use setInterval( ) to call the bounce( ) method every interval
// milliseconds. Store the return value so that we can stop the
// animation by passing it to clearInterval( ).
var intervalID  = window.setInterval("bounce( )", interval);

// This function moves the window by (dx, dy) every interval ms
// It bounces whenever the window reaches the edge of the screen
function bounce( ) {
    // If the user closed the window, stop the animation
    if (win.closed) {
        clearInterval(intervalID);
        return;
    }

    // Bounce if we have reached the right or left edge
    if ((x+dx > (screen.availWidth - w)) || (x+dx < 0)) dx = -dx;

    // Bounce if we have reached the bottom or top edge
    if ((y+dy > (screen.availHeight - h)) || (y+dy < 0)) dy = -dy;

    // Update the current position of the window
    x += dx;
    y += dy;

    // Finally, move the window to the new position
    win.moveTo(x,y);
}
</script>

<!-- Clicking this button stops the animation! -->
<form>
<input type="button" value="Stop"
       onclick="clearInterval(intervalID); win.close( );">
</form>
```

13.9 The Location Object

The location property of a window is a reference to a Location object—a representation of the URL of the document currently being displayed in that window. The href property of the Location object is a string that contains the complete text of the URL. Other properties of this object, such as protocol, host, pathname, and search, specify the various individual parts of the URL.

The search property of the Location object is an interesting one. It contains any portion of a URL following (and including) a question mark. This is often some sort of query string. In general, the question-mark syntax in a URL is a technique for embedding arguments in the URL. While these arguments are usually intended for CGI scripts run on a server, there is no reason why they cannot also be used in JavaScript-enabled pages. Example 13-5 shows the definition of a general-purpose getArgs( ) function that you can use to extract arguments from the search property of a URL. It also shows how this getArgs( ) method could have been used to set initial values of the bouncing window animation parameters in Example 13-4.

Example 13-5. Extracting arguments from a URL

```
/*
 * This function parses comma-separated name=value argument pairs from
 * the query string of the URL. It stores the name=value pairs in
 * properties of an object and returns that object.
 */
function getArgs( ) {
    var args = new Object( );
    var query = location.search.substring(1);      // Get query string
    var pairs = query.split(",");                  // Break at comma
    for(var i = 0; i < pairs.length; i++) {
        var pos = pairs[i].indexOf('=');           // Look for "name=value"
        if (pos == -1) continue;                   // If not found, skip
        var argname = pairs[i].substring(0,pos);   // Extract the name
        var value = pairs[i].substring(pos+1);     // Extract the value
        args[argname] = unescape(value);           // Store as a property
        // In JavaScript 1.5, use decodeURIComponent( ) instead of escape( )
    }
    return args;                                   // Return the object
}

/*
 * We could have used getArgs( ) in the previous bouncing window example
 * to parse optional animation parameters from the URL
 */
var args = getArgs( );                   // Get arguments
if (args.x) x = parseInt(args.x);        // If arguments are defined...
if (args.y) y = parseInt(args.y);        // override default values
if (args.w) w = parseInt(args.w);
if (args.h) h = parseInt(args.h);
if (args.dx) dx = parseInt(args.dx);
if (args.dy) dy = parseInt(args.dy);
if (args.interval) interval = parseInt(args.interval);
```

In addition to its properties, the Location object can be used as if it were itself a primitive string value. If you read the value of a Location object, you get the same string as you would if you read the href property of the object (because the Location object has a suitable toString( ) method). What is far more interesting, though, is that you can assign a new URL string to the location property of a window. Assigning a URL to the Location object this way has an important side effect: it causes the browser to load and display the contents of the URL you assign. For example, you might assign a URL to the location property like this:

```
// If the user is using an old browser that can't display DHTML content,
// redirect to a page that contains only static HTML
if (parseInt(navigator.appVersion) < 4)
    location = "staticpage.html";
```

As you can imagine, making the browser load specified web pages into windows is a very important programming technique. While you might expect there to be a method you can call to make the browser display a new web page, assigning a URL to the location property of a window is the supported technique for accomplishing this end. Example 13-6, later in this chapter, includes an example of setting the location property.

Although the Location object does not have a method that serves the same function as assigning a URL directly to the location property of a window, this object does support two methods (added in JavaScript 1.1). The reload( ) method reloads the currently displayed page from the web server. The replace( ) method loads and displays a URL that you specify. But invoking this method for a given URL is different than assigning that URL to the location property of a window. When you call replace( ), the specified URL replaces the current one in the browser's history list, rather than creating a new entry in that history list. Therefore, if you use replace( ) to overwrite one document with a new one, the **Back** button does not take the user back to the original document, as it does if you load the new document by assigning a URL to the location property. For web sites that use frames and display a lot of temporary pages (perhaps generated by a CGI script), using replace( ) is often useful. Since temporary pages are not stored in the history list, the **Back** button is more useful to the user.

Finally, don't confuse the location property of the Window object, which refers to a Location object, with the location property of the Document object, which is simply a read-only string with none of the special features of the Location object. document.location is a synonym for document.URL, which in JavaScript 1.1 is the preferred name for this property (because it avoids the potential confusion). In most cases, document.location is the same as location.href. When there is a server redirect, however, document.location contains the URL as loaded, and location.href contains the URL as originally requested.

13.10 The History Object

The history property of the Window object refers to a History object for the window. The History object was originally designed to model the browsing history of a window as an array of recently visited URLs. This turned out to be a poor design choice, however; for important security and privacy reasons, it is almost never appropriate to give a script access to the list of web sites that the user has previously visited. Thus, the array elements of the History object are never actually accessible to scripts (except when the user has granted permission to a signed script in Netscape 4 and later). The `length` property of the History object is accessible, but it does not provide any useful information.

Although its array elements are inaccessible, the History object supports three methods (which can be used by normal, unsigned scripts in all browser versions). The `back()` and `forward()` methods move backward or forward in a window's (or frame's) browsing history, replacing the currently displayed document with a previously viewed one. This is similar to what happens when the user clicks on the **Back** and **Forward** browser buttons. The third method, `go()`, takes an integer argument and can skip forward or backward in the history list by multiple pages. Unfortunately, `go()` suffers from bugs in Netscape 2 and 3 and has incompatible behavior in Internet Explorer 3; it is best avoided prior to fourth-generation browsers.

Example 13-6 shows how you might use the `back()` and `forward()` methods of the History and Location objects to add a navigation bar to a framed web site. Figure 13-3 shows what a navigation bar looks like. Note that the example uses JavaScript with multiple frames, which is something we will discuss shortly. It also contains a simple HTML form and uses JavaScript to read and write values from the form. This behavior is covered in detail in Chapter 15.

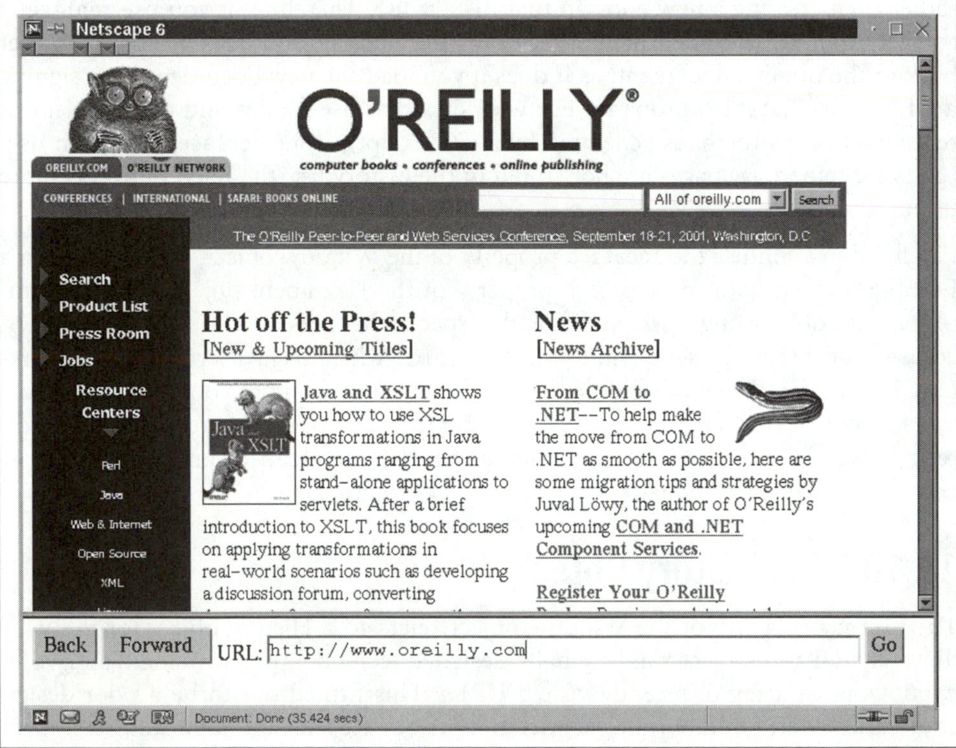

Figure 13-3. A navigation bar

Example 13-6. A navigation bar using the History and Location objects

```
<!-- This file implements a navigation bar, designed to go in a frame at
     the bottom of a window. Include it in a frameset like the following:
       <frameset rows="*,75">
       <frame src="about:blank">
       <frame src="navigation.html">
       </frameset>
-->

<script>
// The function is invoked by the Back button in our navigation bar
function go_back()
{
    // First, clear the URL entry field in our form
    document.navbar.url.value = "";

    // Then use the History object of the main frame to go back
    parent.frames[0].history.back();

    // Wait a second, and then update the URL entry field in the form
    // from the location.href property of the main frame. The wait seems
    // to be necessary to allow the location.href property to get in sync.
    setTimeout("document.navbar.url.value = parent.frames[0].location.href;",
               1000);
}

// This function is invoked by the Forward button in the navigation bar;
// it works just like the previous one
function go_forward()
{
    document.navbar.url.value = "";
    parent.frames[0].history.forward();
    setTimeout("document.navbar.url.value = parent.frames[0].location.href;",
               1000);
}

// This function is invoked by the Go button in the navigation bar and also
// when the form is submitted (when the user hits the Return key)
function go_to()
{
    // Just set the location property of the main frame to the URL
    // the user typed in
    parent.frames[0].location = document.navbar.url.value;
}
</script>

<!-- Here's the form, with event handlers that invoke the functions above -->
<form name="navbar" onsubmit="go_to(); return false;">
  <input type="button" value="Back" onclick="go_back();">
  <input type="button" value="Forward" onclick="go_forward();">
  URL:
  <input type="text" name="url" size="50">
  <input type="button" value="Go" onclick="go_to();">
</form>
```

13.11 Multiple Windows and Frames

Most of the client-side JavaScript examples we've seen so far have involved only a single window or frame. In the real world, JavaScript applications often involve multiple windows or frames. Recall that frames within a window are represented by Window objects; JavaScript makes little distinction between windows and frames. In the most interesting applications, there is JavaScript code that runs independently in each of several windows. The next section explains how the JavaScript code in each window can interact and cooperate with each of the other windows and with the scripts running in each of those windows.

13.11.1 Relationships Between Frames

We've already seen that the `open()` method of the Window object returns a new Window object representing the newly created window. We've also seen that this new window has an `opener` property that refers back to the original window. In this way, the two windows can refer to each other, and each can read properties and invoke methods of the other. The same thing is possible with frames. Any frame in a window can refer to any other frame through the use of the `frames`, `parent`, and `top` properties of the Window object.

Every window has a `frames` property. This property refers to an array of Window objects, each of which represents a frame contained within the window. (If a window does not have any frames, the `frames[]` array is empty and `frames.length` is zero.) Thus, a window (or frame) can refer to its first subframe as `frames[0]`, its second subframe as `frames[1]`, and so on. Similarly, JavaScript code running in a window can refer to the third subframe of its second frame like this:

```
frames[1].frames[2]
```

Every window also has a `parent` property, which refers to the Window object in which it is contained. Thus, the first frame within a window might refer to its sibling frame (the second frame within the window) like this:

```
parent.frames[1]
```

If a window is a top-level window and not a frame, `parent` simply refers to the window itself:

```
parent == self;  // For any top-level window
```

If a frame is contained within another frame that is contained within a top-level window, that frame can refer to the top-level window as `parent.parent`. The `top` property is a general-case shortcut, however: no matter how deeply a frame is nested, its `top` property refers to the top-level containing window. If a Window object represents a top-level window, `top` simply refers to that window itself. For frames that are direct children of a top-level window, the `top` property is the same as the `parent` property.

Frames are typically created with <frameset> and <frame> tags. In HTML 4, however, as implemented in IE 4 and later and Netscape 6 and later, the <iframe> tag can also be used to create an "inline frame" within a document. As far as JavaScript is concerned, frames created with <iframe> are the same as frames created with <frameset> and <frame>. Everything discussed here applies to both kinds of frames.

Figure 13-4 illustrates these relationships between frames and shows how code running in any one frame can refer to any other frame through the use of the `frames`, `parent`, and `top` properties. The figure shows a browser window that contains two frames, one on top of the other. The second frame (the larger one on the bottom) itself contains three subframes, side by side.

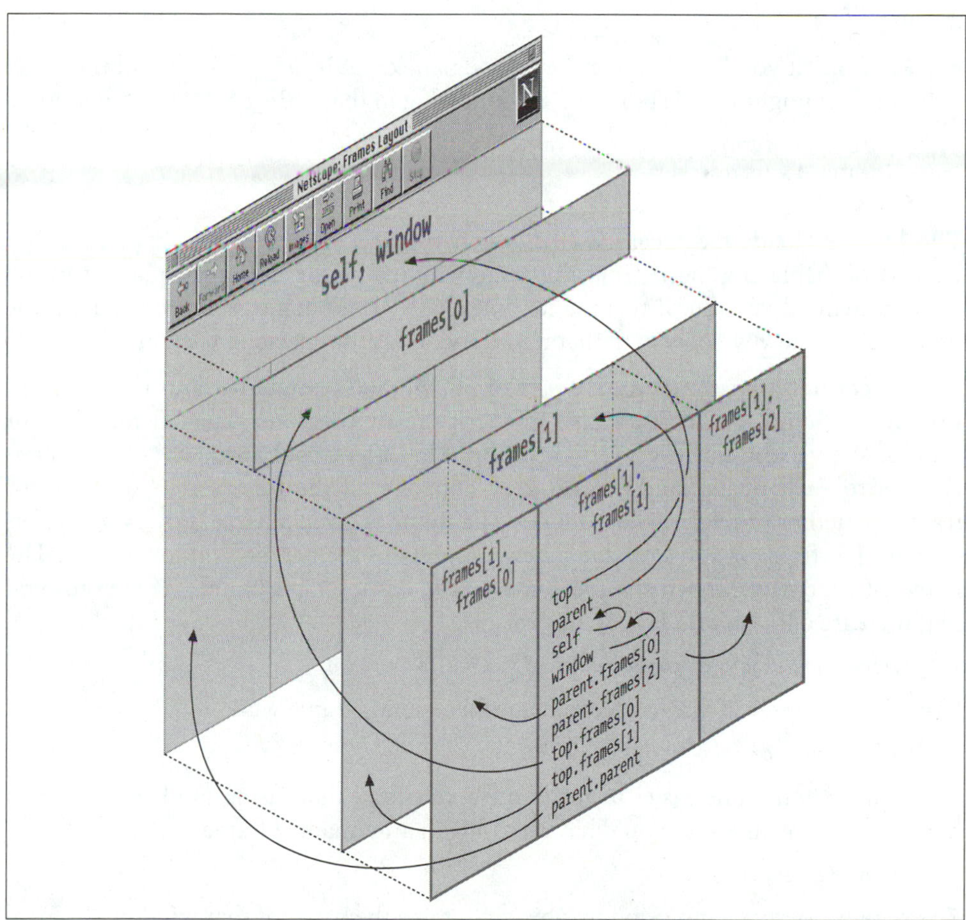

Figure 13-4. Relationships between frames

With this understanding of the relationships between frames, you may want to revisit Example 13-6, paying particular attention this time to the way the code (which is written to run in a second frame) refers to the history and location properties of the first frame.

13.11.2 Window and Frame Names

The second, optional argument to the open() method discussed earlier is a name for the newly created window. When you create a frame with the HTML <frame> tag, you can specify a name with the name attribute. An important reason to specify names for windows and frames is that those names can be used as the value of the target attribute of the <a>, <map>, and <form> tags. This value tells the browser where you want to display the results of activating a link, clicking on an image map, or submitting a form.

For example, if you have two windows, one named table_of_contents and the other mainwin, you might have HTML like the following in the table_of_contents window:

```
<a href="chapter01.html" target="mainwin">
  Chapter 1, Introduction
</a>
```

The browser loads the specified URL when the user clicks on this hyperlink, but instead of displaying the URL in the same window as the link, it displays it in the window named mainwin. If there is no window with the name mainwin, clicking the link creates a new window with that name and loads the specified URL into it.

The target and name attributes are part of HTML and operate without the intervention of JavaScript, but there are also JavaScript-related reasons to give names to your frames. We've seen that every Window object has a frames[] array that contains references to each of its frames. This array contains all the frames in a window (or frame), whether or not they have names. If a frame is given a name, however, a reference to that frame is also stored in a new property of the parent Window object. The name of that new property is the same as the name of the frame. Therefore, you might create a frame with HTML like this:

```
<frame name="table_of_contents" src="toc.html">
```

Now you can refer to that frame from another, sibling frame with:

```
parent.table_of_contents
```

This makes your code easier to read and understand than using (and relying on) a hardcoded array index, as you'd have to do with an unnamed frame:

```
parent.frames[1]
```

The name property of any Window object contains the name of that window. In JavaScript 1.0, this property is read-only. In JavaScript 1.1 and later, however, you can set this property, thereby changing the name of a window or a frame. One common reason to do this is to set the name of the initial browser window. When a browser starts up, the initial window has no name, so it cannot be used with the target attribute. If you set the name property of the window, however, you can then use that name in target attributes.

13.11.3 JavaScript in Interacting Windows

Client-Side JavaScript

Recall what we learned in Chapter 12: the Window object serves as the global object for client-side JavaScript code, and the window serves as the execution context for all JavaScript code it contains. This holds true for frames as well: every frame is an independent JavaScript execution context. Because every Window object is its own global object, each window defines its own namespace and its own set of global variables. When viewed from the perspective of multiple frames or windows, global variables do not seem all that global, after all!

Although each window and frame defines an independent JavaScript execution context, this does not mean that JavaScript code running in one window is isolated from code running in other windows. Code running in one frame has a different Window object at the top of its scope chain than code running in another frame. However, the code from both frames is executed by the same JavaScript interpreter, in the same JavaScript environment. As we've seen, one frame can refer to any other frame using the frames, parent, and top properties. So, although JavaScript code in different frames is executed with different scope chains, the code in one frame can still refer to and use the variables and functions defined by code in another frame.

For example, suppose code in frame A defines a variable i:

```
var i = 3;
```

That variable is nothing more than a property of the global object—a property of the Window object. Code in frame A could refer to the variable explicitly as such a property with either of these two expressions:

```
window.i
self.i
```

Now suppose that frame A has a sibling frame B that wants to set the value of the variable i defined by the code in frame A. If frame B just sets a variable i, it merely succeeds in creating a new property of its own Window object. So instead, it must explicitly refer to the property i in its sibling frame with code like this:

```
parent.frames[0].i = 4;
```

Recall that the function keyword that defines functions declares a variable just like the var keyword does. If JavaScript code in frame A declares a function f, that function is defined only within frame A. Code in frame A can invoke f like this:

```
f();
```

Code in frame B, however, must refer to f as a property of the Window object of frame A:

```
parent.frames[0].f();
```

If the code in frame B needs to use this function frequently, it might assign the function to a variable of frame B so that it can more conveniently refer to the function:

```
var f = parent.frames[0].f;
```

Now code in frame B can invoke the function as `f()`, just as code in frame A does.

When you share functions between frames or windows like this, it is very important to keep the rules of lexical scoping in mind. A function is executed in the scope in which it was defined, not in the scope from which it is invoked. Thus, to continue with the previous example, if the function `f` refers to global variables, these variables are looked up as properties of frame A, even when the function is invoked from frame B.

If you don't pay careful attention to this, you can end up with programs that behave in unexpected and confusing ways. For example, suppose you define the following function in the `<head>` section of a multiframe document, with the idea that it will help with debugging:

```
function debug(msg) {
    alert("Debugging message from frame: " + name + "\n" + msg);
}
```

The JavaScript code in each of your frames can refer to this function as `top.debug()`. Whenever this function is invoked, however, it looks up the variable `name` in the context of the top-level window in which the function is defined, rather than the context of the frame from which it is invoked. Thus, the debugging messages always carry the name of the top-level window, rather than the name of the frame that sent the message, as was intended.

Remember that constructors are also functions, so when you define a class of objects with a constructor function and an associated prototype object, that class is defined only for a single window. Recall the Complex class we defined in Chapter 8, and consider the following multiframed HTML document:

```
<head>
<script src="Complex.js"></script>
</head>
<frameset rows="50%,50%">
  <frame name="frame1" src="frame1.html">
  <frame name="frame2" src="frame2.html">
</frameset>
```

JavaScript code in the files *frame1.html* and *frame2.html* cannot create a Complex object with an expression like this:

```
var c = new Complex(1,2);  // Won't work from either frame
```

Instead, code in these files must explicitly refer to the constructor function:

```
var c = new top.Complex(3,4);
```

Alternatively, code in either frame can define its own variable to refer more conveniently to the constructor function:

```
var Complex = top.Complex;
var c = new Complex(1,2);
```

Unlike user-defined constructors, predefined constructors are automatically predefined in all windows. Note, however, that each window has an independent copy of the constructor and an independent copy of the constructor's prototype object. For example, each window has its own copy of the `String( )` constructor and the `String.prototype` object. So, if you write a new method for manipulating JavaScript strings and then make it a method of the String class by assigning it to the `String.prototype` object in the current window, all strings in that window can use the new method. However, the new method is not accessible to strings defined in other windows. Note that it does not matter which window holds a reference to the string; only the window in which the string was actually created matters.

Client-Side JavaScript

13.11.4 Example: Colored Frames

Example 13-7, a frame set that defines a grid of nine frames, demonstrates some of the techniques we've discussed in this chapter. The `<head>` section of the frame set includes a `<script>` that defines a JavaScript function named `setcolor( )`. The `onload` event handler of the `<frameset>` tag invokes `setcolor( )` once for each of the nine frames.

`setcolor( )` is passed a Window object as its argument. It generates a random color and uses it with the `Document.write( )` method to create a new document that is empty except for a background color. Finally, `setcolor( )` uses the `setTimeout( )` method to schedule itself to be called again in one second. This call to `setTimeout( )` is the most interesting part of the example. Notice especially how it uses the `parent` and `name` properties of Window objects.

Example 13-7. A frame color animation

```
<head>
<title>Colored Frames</title>
<script>
function setcolor(w) {
    // Generate a random color
    var r = Math.floor((Math.random( ) * 256)).toString(16);
    var g = Math.floor((Math.random( ) * 256)).toString(16);
    var b = Math.floor((Math.random( ) * 256)).toString(16);
    var colorString = "#" + r + g + b;

    // Set the frame background to the random color
    w.document.write("<body bgcolor='" + colorString + "'></body>");
    w.document.close( );

    // Schedule another call to this method in one second.
    // Since we call the setTimeout( ) method of the frame, the string
    // will be executed in that context, so we must prefix properties
    // of the top-level window with "parent.".
```

Example 13-7. A frame color animation (continued)

```
    w.setTimeout('parent.setcolor(parent.' + w.name + ')', 1000);

    // We could also have done the same thing more simply like this:
    // setTimeout('setcolor(' + w.name + ')', 1000);
}
</script>
</head>
<frameset rows="33%,33%,34%" cols="33%,33%,34%"
  onload="for(var i = 0; i < 9; i++) setcolor(frames[i]);">
<frame name="f1" src="javascript:''"><frame name="f2" src="javascript:''">
<frame name="f3" src="javascript:''"><frame name="f4" src="javascript:''">
<frame name="f5" src="javascript:''"><frame name="f6" src="javascript:''">
<frame name="f7" src="javascript:''"><frame name="f8" src="javascript:''">
<frame name="f9" src="javascript:''">
</frameset>
```

CHAPTER 14

The Document Object

Every Window object has a `document` property. This property refers to a Document object that represents the HTML document displayed in the window. The Document object is probably the most commonly used object in client-side JavaScript. We've already seen several examples in this book that use the `write()` method of the Document object to insert dynamic content into a document while it is being parsed. In addition to the frequently used `write()` method, the Document object defines properties that provide information about the document as a whole: its URL, its last-modified date, the URL of the document that linked to it, the colors in which it is displayed, and so on.

Client-side JavaScript exists to turn static HTML documents into interactive programs—it is the Document object that gives JavaScript interactive access to the content of otherwise static documents. In addition to the properties that provide information about a document as a whole, the Document object has a number of very important properties that provide information about document content. The `forms[]` array, for instance, contains Form objects that represent all the HTML forms in the document. And the `images[]` and `applets[]` arrays contain objects that represent the images and applets in the document. These arrays and the objects they contain open up a world of possibilities for client-side JavaScript programs, and the bulk of this chapter is devoted to documenting them.

This chapter covers the core features of the Document object that are implemented by virtually every JavaScript-enabled browser. Newer browsers, such as IE 4 and later and Netscape 6 and later, implement a full document object model, or DOM, that gives JavaScript complete access to and control over all document content. These advanced DOM features are covered in Chapter 17.

14.1 Document Overview

To illustrate the scope and importance of the Document object, this chapter begins with a quick summary of the methods and properties of the object. The following sections also explain other important material that is important to understand before reading the rest of the chapter.

14.1.1 Document Methods

The Document object defines four key methods. One is the `write()` method, which we've already seen several times, and the other three are related:

`close()`
: Close or end a document that was begun with `open()`.

`open()`
: Begin a new document, erasing any existing document content.

`write()`
: Append text to the currently open document.

`writeln()`
: Output text into the currently open document, and append a newline character.

14.1.2 Document Properties

The Document object defines the following properties:

`alinkColor`, `linkColor`, `vlinkColor`
: These properties describe the colors of hyperlinks. `linkColor` is the normal color of an unvisited link. `vlinkColor` is the normal color of a visited link. `alinkColor` is the color of a link while it is activated (i.e., while the user is clicking on it). These properties correspond to the `alink`, `link`, and `vlink` attributes of the `<body>` tag.

`anchors[]`
: An array of Anchor objects that represent the anchors in the document.

`applets[]`
: An array of Applet objects that represent the Java applets in the document.

`bgColor`, `fgColor`
: The background and foreground (i.e., text) colors of the document. These properties correspond to the `bgcolor` and `text` attributes of the `<body>` tag.

`cookie`
: A special property that allows JavaScript programs to read and write HTTP cookies. See Chapter 16 for details.

`domain`
: A property that allows mutually trusted web servers within the same Internet domain to collaboratively relax certain security restrictions on interactions between their web pages. See Chapter 21.

`forms[]`
: An array of Form objects that represent the `<form>` elements in the document.

`images[]`
: An array of Image objects that represent the `<img>` elements in the document.

`lastModified`
: A string that contains the modification date of the document.

`links[]`
: An array of Link objects that represent the hypertext links in the document.

`location`
: A deprecated synonym for the `URL` property.

`referrer`
: The URL of the document containing the link that brought the browser to the current document, if any.

`title`
: The text between the `<title>` and `</title>` tags for this document.

`URL`
: A string specifying the URL from which the document was loaded. The value of this property is the same as the `location.href` property of the Window object, except when a server redirect has occurred.

14.1.3 The Document Object and Standards

The Document object and the set of elements (such as forms, images, and links) that it exposes to JavaScript programs form a document object model. Historically, different browser vendors have implemented different DOMs, which has made it difficult for JavaScript programmers to portably use the advanced features of the vendor-specific DOMs. Fortunately, the World Wide Web Consortium (or W3C; see *http://www.w3.org*) has standardized a DOM and issued two versions of this standard, known as Level 1 and Level 2. Recent browsers, such as Netscape 6 and later and IE 5 and later, implement some or most of these standards. See Chapter 17 for all the details.

The DOM described in this chapter predates the W3C standards. By virtue of its nearly universal implementation, however, it is a de facto standard and is often referred to as the Level 0 DOM. You can use the techniques described in this chapter in any JavaScript-enabled web browser, with the exception of very old ones such as Netscape 2. Furthermore, the Document object methods and properties listed previously have been formalized as part of the Level 1 DOM, so they are guaranteed to remain supported by future browsers.

One important thing to understand about the W3C DOM standard is that it is a document object model for both XML and HTML documents. In this standard, the Document object provides generic functionality of use for both types of documents. HTML-specific functionality is provided by the HTMLDocument subclass. All the

Document properties and methods described in this chapter are HTML-specific, and you can find more details about them under the "Document" entry in the client-side reference section of this book. You'll also find related information in the DOM reference section, under "Document" and "HTMLDocument."

14.1.4 Naming Document Objects

Before we begin our discussion of the Document object and the various objects it exposes, there is one general principle that you'll find it helpful to keep in mind. As you'll see, every `<form>` element in an HTML document creates a numbered element in the `forms[]` array of the Document object. Similarly, every `<img>` element creates an element in the `images[]` array. The same applies for `<a>` and `<applet>` tags, which define elements in the `links[]` and `applets[]` arrays.

In addition to these arrays, however, a Form, Image, or Applet object may be referred to by name if its corresponding HTML tag is given a `name` attribute. When this attribute is present, its value is used to expose the corresponding object as a property of the Document object. So, for example, suppose an HTML document contains the following form:

```
<form name="f1">
<input type="button" value="Push Me">
</form>
```

Assuming that the `<form>` is the first one in the document, your JavaScript code can refer to the resulting Form object with either of the following two expressions:

```
document.forms[0]  // Refer to the form by position within the document
document.f1        // Refer to the form by name
```

In fact, setting the `name` attribute of a `<form>` also makes the Form object accessible as a named property of the `forms[]` array, so you could also refer to the form with either of these two expressions:

```
document.forms.f1       // Use property syntax
document.forms["f1"]    // Use array syntax
```

The same applies for images and applets: using the `name` attribute in your HTML allows you to refer to these objects by name in your JavaScript code.

As you might imagine, it is convenient to give names to frequently used Document objects so that you can refer to them more easily in your scripts. We'll see this technique used a number of times in this and later chapters.

14.1.5 Document Objects and Event Handlers

To be interactive, an HTML document and the elements within it must respond to user events. We discussed events and event handlers briefly in Chapter 12, and we've seen several examples that use simple event handlers. We'll see many more examples of event handlers in this chapter, because they are key to working with Document objects.

Unfortunately, we must defer a complete discussion of events and event handlers until Chapter 19. For now, remember that event handlers are defined by attributes of HTML elements, such as `onclick` and `onmouseover`. The values of these attributes should be strings of JavaScript code. This code is executed whenever the specified event occurs on the HTML element.

In addition, there is one other way to define event handlers that we'll occasionally see used in this and later chapters. We'll see in this chapter that Document objects such as Form and Image objects have JavaScript properties that match the HTML attributes of the `<form>` and `<img>` tags. For example, the HTML `<img>` tag has `src` and `width` attributes, and the JavaScript Image object has corresponding `src` and `width` properties. The same is true for event handlers. The HTML `<a>` tag supports an `onclick` event handler, for example, and the JavaScript Link object that represents a hyperlink has a corresponding `onclick` property. As another example, consider the `onsubmit` attribute of the `<form>` element. In JavaScript, the Form object has a corresponding `onsubmit` property. Remember that HTML is not case-sensitive, and attributes can be written in uppercase, lowercase, or mixed-case. In JavaScript, all event handler properties must be written in lowercase.

In HTML, event handlers are defined by assigning a string of JavaScript code to an event handler attribute. In JavaScript, however, they are defined by assigning a function to an event handler property. Consider the following `<form>` and its `onsubmit` event handler:

```
<form name="myform" onsubmit="return validateform();">...</form>
```

In JavaScript, instead of using a string of JavaScript code that invokes a function and returns its result, we could simply assign the function directly to the event handler property like this:

```
document.myform.onsubmit = validateform;
```

Note that there are no parentheses after the function name. That is because we don't want to invoke the function here; we just want to assign a reference to it. As another example, consider the following `<a>` tag and its `onmouseover` event handler:

```
<a href="help.html" onmouseover="status='Get Help Now!';">Help</a>
```

If we happen to know that this `<a>` tag is the first one in the document, we can refer to the corresponding Link object as `document.links[0]` and set the event handler this way instead:

```
document.links[0].onmouseover = function() { status = 'Get Help Now!'; }
```

See Chapter 19 for a complete discussion of assigning event handlers in this way.

14.2 Dynamically Generated Documents

One of the most important features of the Document object (and perhaps of client-side JavaScript in general) is the `write()` method, which allows you to dynamically generate web-page content from your JavaScript programs. This method can be used in two ways. The first and simplest way to use it is within a script, to output dynamically generated HTML into the document that is currently being parsed. This was discussed in Chapter 12. Consider the following code, which uses `write()` to add the current date and the document's last-modified date to an otherwise static HTML document:

```
<script>
var today = new Date();
document.write("<p>Document accessed on: " + today.toString());
document.write("<br>Document modified on: " + document.lastModified);
</script>
```

Using the `write()` method in this way is an extremely common JavaScript programming technique, and you'll see it in many scripts.

Be aware, however, that you can use the `write()` method to output HTML to the current document only while that document is being parsed. That is, you can call `document.write()` from within `<script>` tags only because these scripts are executed as part of the document parsing process. In particular, if you call `document.write()` from within an event handler and that handler is invoked once the document has already been parsed, you will end up overwriting the entire document (including its event handlers), instead of appending text to it. The reason for this will become clear as we examine the second way to use the `write()` method.

In addition to adding dynamic content to the current document as it is being parsed, `write()` can be used in conjunction with the `open()` and `close()` Document methods to create entirely new documents within a window or frame. Although you cannot usefully write to the current document from an event handler, there is no reason why you can't write to a document in another window or frame; doing so can be a useful technique with multiwindow or multiframe web sites. For example, JavaScript code in one frame of a multiframe site might display a message in another frame with code like this:

```
<script>
// Start a new document, erasing any content that was already in frames[0]
parent.frames[0].document.open();
// Add some content to the document
parent.frames[0].document.write("<hr>Hello from your sibling frame!<hr>");
// And close the document when we're done
parent.frames[0].document.close();
</script>
```

To create a new document, we first call the `open()` method of the Document object, then call `write()` any number of times to output the contents of the document, and finally call the close( ) method of the Document object to indicate that we have finished. This last step is important; if you forget to close the document, the browser does not stop the document loading animation it displays. Also, the browser may buffer the HTML you have written; it is not required to display the buffered output until you explicitly end the document by calling close( ).

In contrast to the close( ) call, which is required, the open( ) call is optional. If you call the write( ) method on a document that has already been closed, JavaScript implicitly opens a new HTML document, as if you had called the open( ) method. This explains what happens when you call document.write( ) from an event handler within the same document—JavaScript opens a new document. In the process, however, the current document (and its contents, including scripts and event handlers) is discarded. This is never what you want to do, and it can even cause some early browsers (such as Netscape 2) to crash. As a general rule of thumb, a document should never call write( ) on itself from within an event handler.

A couple of final notes about the write( ) method. First, many people do not realize that the write( ) method can take more than one argument. When you pass multiple arguments, they are output one after another, just as if they had been concatenated. So instead of writing:

```
document.write("Hello, "  + username + " Welcome to my home page!");
```

you might equivalently write:

```
var greeting = "Hello, ";
var welcome = " Welcome to my home page!";
document.write(greeting, username, welcome);
```

The second point to note about the write( ) method is that the Document object also supports a writeln( ) method, which is identical to the write( ) method in every way except that it appends a newline after outputting its arguments. Since HTML ignores line breaks, this newline character usually doesn't make a difference, but as we'll see in a bit, the writeln( ) method can be convenient when you're working with non-HTML documents.

Example 14-1 shows how you might create a complex dialog box with the Window open( ) method and the methods of the Document object. This example registers an onerror event handler function for the window; the function is invoked when a JavaScript error occurs. The error handler function creates a new window and uses the Document object methods to create an HTML form within the window. The form allows the user to see details about the error that occurred and email a bug report to the author of the JavaScript code.

Figure 14-1 shows a sample window. Recall from the discussion of the onerror error handler in Chapter 13 that Netscape 6 does not pass the correct arguments to the error handler function. For this reason, the output on Netscape 6 does not match what is illustrated here.

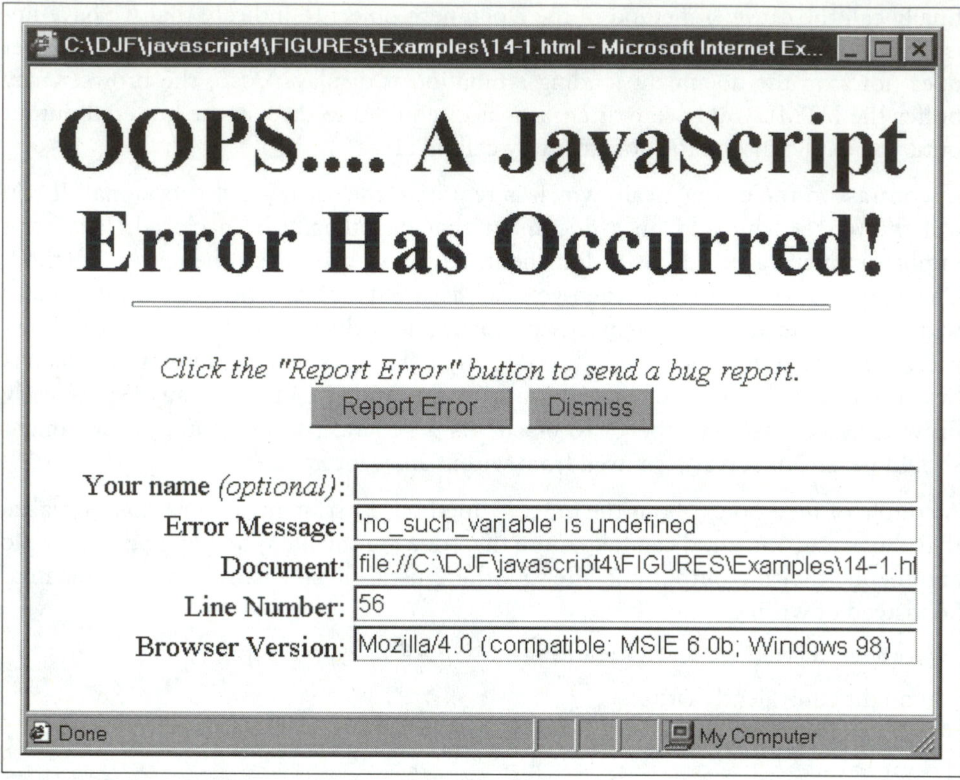

Figure 14-1. Using a browser window as a dialog box

Example 14-1. Dynamically creating a dialog window

```
<script>
// A variable we use to ensure that each error window we create is unique
var error_count = 0;

// Set this variable to your email address
var email = "myname@mydomain.com";

// Define the error handler. It generates an HTML form so the user
// can report the error to the author.
function report_error(msg, url, line)
{
    var w = window.open("",                          // URL (none specified)
                        "error"+error_count++,  // Name (force it to be unique)
                        "resizable,status,width=625,height=400"); // Features
    // Get the Document object of the new window
    var d = w.document;

    // Output an HTML document, including a form, into the new window
    // Note that we omit the optional call to document.open()
    d.write('<div align="center">');
    d.write('<font size="7" face="helvetica"><b>');
```

Example 14-1. Dynamically creating a dialog window (continued)

```
    d.write('OOPS.... A JavaScript Error Has Occurred!');
    d.write('</b></font><br><hr size="4" width="80%">');
    d.write('<form action="mailto:' + email + '" method=post');
    d.write(' enctype="text/plain">');
    d.write('<font size="3">');
    d.write('<i>Click the "Report Error" button to send a bug report.</i><br>');
    d.write('<input type="submit" value="Report Error">  ');
    d.write('<input type="button" value="Dismiss" onclick="self.close( );">');
    d.write('</div><div align="right">');
    d.write('<br>Your name <i>(optional)</i>: ');
    d.write('<input size="42" name="name" value="">');
    d.write('<br>Error Message: ');
    d.write('<input size="42" name="message" value="' + msg + '">');
    d.write('<br>Document: <input size="42" name="url" value="' + url + '">');
    d.write('<br>Line Number: <input size="42" name="line" value="'+line +'">');
    d.write('<br>Browser Version: ');
    d.write('<input size="42" name="version" value="'+navigator.userAgent+'">');
    d.write('</div></font>');
    d.write('</form>');
    // Remember to close the document when we're done
    d.close( );

    // Return true from this error handler, so that JavaScript does not
    // display its own error dialog box
    return true;
}

// Before the event handler can take effect, we have to register it
// for a particular window
self.onerror = report_error;
</script>

<script>
// The following line of code purposely causes an error as a test
alert(no_such_variable);
</script>
```

14.2.1 Non-HTML Documents

When you call the Document open( ) method with no arguments, it opens a new HTML document. Remember, though, that web browsers can display a number of other data formats besides HTML text. When you want to dynamically create and display a document using some other data format, you call the open( ) method with a single argument, which is the MIME type you desire.*

* This argument to the open( ) method has not been standardized by the W3C DOM. It works in IE 4 and later, and in Netscape 3 and 4. Surprisingly, it does not work in Netscape 6: only HTML documents are supported by that browser.

The MIME type for HTML is `text/html`. The most common format besides HTML is plain text, with a MIME type of `text/plain`. If you want to use the `write()` method to output text that uses newlines, spaces, and Tab characters for formatting, you should open the document by passing the string "text/plain" to the `open()` method. Example 14-2 shows one way you might do this. It implements a `debug()` function that you can use to output plain-text debugging messages from your scripts into a separate window that appears when needed. Figure 14-2 shows what the resulting window looks like.

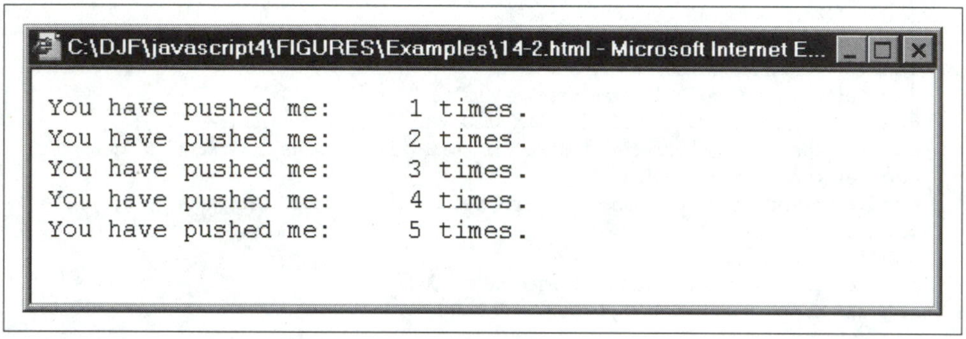

```
C:\DJF\javascript4\FIGURES\Examples\14-2.html - Microsoft Internet E...

You have pushed me:     1 times.
You have pushed me:     2 times.
You have pushed me:     3 times.
You have pushed me:     4 times.
You have pushed me:     5 times.
```

Figure 14-2. A window for plain-text debugging output

Example 14-2. Creating a plain-text document

```
<script>
var _console = null;

function debug(msg)
{
    // Open a window the first time we are called, or after an existing
    // console window has been closed
    if ((_console == null) || (_console.closed)) {
    _console = window.open("","console","width=600,height=300,resizable");
    // Open a document in the window to display plain text
    _console.document.open("text/plain");
}

    _console.focus( );                  // Make the window visible
    _console.document.writeln(msg);     // Output the message to it
    // Note that we purposely do not call close( ). Leaving the
    // document open allows us to append to it later.
}
</script>

<!-- Here's an example of using this script -->
<script>var n = 0;</script>
<form>
<input type="button" value="Push Me"
      onclick="debug('You have pushed me:\t' + ++n + ' times.');">
</form>
```

14.3 Document Color Properties

The bgColor, fgColor, linkColor, alinkColor, and vlinkColor properties of the Document object specify foreground, background, and link colors for the document. They are read/write properties, but they can be set only before the <body> tag is parsed. You can set them dynamically with JavaScript code in the <head> section of a document, or you can set them statically as attributes of the <body> tag, but you cannot set them elsewhere. The exception to this rule is the bgColor property. In many browsers, you can set this property at any time; doing so causes the background color of the browser window to change.* Other than bgColor, the color properties of the Document object merely expose attributes of the <body> tag and are basically uninteresting.

Each of these color properties has a string value. To set a color, you can use one of the predefined HTML color names, or you can specify the color as red, green, and blue color values, expressed as a string of six hexadecimal digits in the form *#RRGGBB*. You may recall that Example 13-7 set the bgcolor attribute of the <body> tag to a color string expressed in this fashion.

In the W3C DOM standard, the color properties of the Document object are deprecated in favor of properties of the Element object that represents the <body> tag. Furthermore, the HTML 4 standard deprecates the color attributes of the <body> tag in favor of CSS style sheets. What this means is that you probably should not write scripts that rely heavily on these doubly deprecated color properties!

14.4 Document Information Properties

Several properties of the Document object provide information about the document as a whole. For example, the following code shows how you can use the lastModified, title, and URL properties to include an automatic timestamp within a document. This feature allows users to judge how up-to-date (or out-of-date) a document is, and it can also be useful information when a document is printed.

```
<hr><font size="1">
Document: <i><script>document.write(document.title);</script></i><br>
URL: <i><script>document.write(document.URL);</script></i><br>
Last Update: <i><script>document.write(document.lastModified);</script></i>
</font>
```

referrer is another interesting property: it contains the URL of the document from which the user linked to the current document. One possible use is to save this value in a hidden field of a form on your web page. When the user submits the form (for whatever reason your page contains the form in the first place), you can save the referrer

* There is a bug in Netscape 3 on Unix platforms such that changing the background color can make the contents of the page disappear (usually until the window is scrolled or otherwise redrawn). In Netscape 6, you can set the bgColor only once; any additional settings are ignored.

data on the server so you can analyze the links that refer to your page and track the percentage of hits that come through various links. Another use of this property is a trick to prevent unauthorized links to your page from working correctly. For example, suppose you want to allow other sites to link only to the top-level page on your site. You can use the `referrer` property in conjunction with the `location` property of the Window object to redirect any links from outside the site to the top-level home page:

```
<script>
// If linked from somewhere offsite, go to home page first
if (document.referrer == "" || document.referrer.indexOf("mysite.com") == -1)
    window.location = "http://home.mysite.com";
</script>
```

Don't consider this trick to be any kind of serious security measure, of course. One obvious flaw is that it doesn't work for browsers that don't support JavaScript or for users who have disabled JavaScript.

14.5 Forms

The `forms[]` array of the Document object contains Form objects that represent any `<form>` elements in the document. Because HTML forms contain push buttons, text input fields, and the other input elements that usually comprise the GUI of a web application, the Form object is very important in client-side JavaScript. The Form object has an `elements[]` property that contains objects that represent the HTML input elements contained within the form. These Element objects allow JavaScript programs to set default values in the form and to read the user's input from the form. They are also important sites for the event handlers that add interactivity to a program.

Because forms and their elements are such a large and important part of client-side JavaScript programming, they deserve a chapter of their own. We will return to the `forms[]` array and the Form object in Chapter 15.

14.6 Images

The `images[]` property of the Document object is an array of Image elements, each representing one of the inline images, created with an `<img>` tag, that is contained in the document. The `images[]` array and the Image object were added in JavaScript 1.1. While web browsers have always been able to display images with the `<img>` tag, the addition of the Image object was a major step forward—it allowed programs to dynamically manipulate those images.

14.6.1 Image Replacement with the src Property

The main feature of the Image object is that its `src` property is read/write. You can read this property to obtain the URL from which an image was loaded, and, more importantly, you can set the src property to make the browser load and display a new image in the same space. For this to work, the new image must have the same width and height as the original one.

In practice, the most common use for image replacement is to implement image rollovers, in which an image changes when the mouse pointer moves over it. When you make images clickable by placing them inside your hyperlinks, rollover effects are a powerful way to invite the user to click on the image. Here is a simple HTML fragment that displays an image within an <a> tag and uses JavaScript code in the onmouseover and onmouseout event handlers to create a rollover effect:

```
<a href="help.html"
   onmouseover="document.helpimage.src='images/help_rollover.gif';"
   onmouseout="document.helpimage.src='images/help.gif';">
<img name="helpimage" src="images/help.gif" width="80" height="20" border="0">
</a>
```

Note that in this code fragment we gave the <img> tag a name attribute, to make it easy to refer to the corresponding Image object in the event handlers of the <a> tag. We used the border attribute to prevent the browser from displaying a blue hyperlink border around the image. The event handlers of the <a> tag do all the work: they change the image that is displayed simply by setting the src property of the image to the URLs of the desired images.

The ability to dynamically replace one image in a static HTML document with another image opens the door to any number of special effects, from animation to digital clocks that update themselves in real time. With a bit of thought, you can probably imagine many more potential uses for this technique.

14.6.2 Offscreen Images and Caching

To make image-replacement techniques viable, the animations or other special effects need to be responsive. This means that we need some way to ensure that the necessary images are "pre-fetched" into the browser's cache. To force an image to be cached, we first create an offscreen image using the Image( ) constructor. Next, we load an image into it by setting its src property to the desired URL (exactly as we would do for an onscreen image). Later, when the same URL is used for an onscreen image, we know it can be quickly loaded from the browser's cache, rather than slowly loaded over the network. Note that we never actually do anything with the offscreen image we create. In particular, we do *not* assign the offscreen Image object into the images[] array of the document.

The image-rollover code fragment shown in the previous section did not pre-fetch the rollover image it used, so the user will probably notice a delay in the rollover effect the first time she moves the mouse over the image. To fix this problem, we could modify the code as follows.

```
<script>
// Create an offscreen image and pre-fetch the rollover image.
// Note that we don't bother saving a reference to the offscreen image,
// since there is nothing we can do with it later.
(new Image(80,20)).src = "images/help_rollover.gif";
</script>
<a href="help.html"
    onmouseover="document.helpimage.src='images/help_rollover.gif';"
    onmouseout="document.helpimage.src='images/help.gif';">
<img name="helpimage" src="images/help.gif" width="80" height="20" border="0">
</a>
```

Example 14-3 shows code that performs a simple animation using image replacement and uses offscreen images to pre-fetch the frames of the animation. Note that in this example we retain the offscreen image objects we create, because they are a convenient way to hold the URLs of the images that make up the animation. To perform the animation, we assign the `src` property of one of the offscreen images to the `src` property of the onscreen image that is the subject of the animation.

Example 14-3. An animation using image replacement

```
<!-- The image that will be animated. Give it a name for convenience. -->
<img name="animation" src="images/0.gif">

<script>
// Create a bunch of offscreen images, and pre-fetch the "frames"
// of the animation into them so that they're cached when we need them
var aniframes = new Array(10);
for(var i = 0; i < 10; i++) {
    aniframes[i] = new Image();                  // Create an offscreen image
    aniframes[i].src = "images/" + i + ".gif";  // Tell it what URL to load
}

var frame = 0;          // The frame counter: keeps track of current frame
var timeout_id = null;  // Allows us to stop the animation with clearTimeout()

// This function performs the animation. Call it once to start.
// Note that we refer to the onscreen image using its name attribute.
function animate() {
    document.animation.src = aniframes[frame].src;  // Display the current frame
    frame = (frame + 1)%10;                         // Update the frame counter
    timeout_id = setTimeout("animate()", 250);      // Display the next frame later
}
</script>

<form>  <!-- This form contains buttons to control the animation -->
  <input type="button" value="Start"
         onclick="if (timeout_id == null) animate();">
  <input type="button" value="Stop"
         onclick="if (timeout_id) clearTimeout(timeout_id); timeout_id=null;">
</form>
```

14.6.3 Image Event Handlers

In Example 14-3, our animation does not begin until the user clicks the **Start** button, which allows plenty of time for our images to be loaded into the cache. But what about the more common case in which we want to automatically begin an animation as soon as all the necessary images are loaded? It turns out that images, whether created onscreen with an `<img>` tag or offscreen with the `Image()` constructor, have an `onload` event handler that is invoked when the image is fully loaded.

The following code fragment shows how we could modify Example 14-3 to use this event handler to count the number of images that have loaded and automatically start the animation when all the images have loaded. Since offscreen images are not part of the HTML document, the event handler cannot be assigned as an HTML attribute. Instead, we simply assign a function to the `onload` property of each Image object we create. When each image is loaded, the browser calls the function.

```
var aniframes = new Array(10);  // Hold the offscreen animation frames.
var num_loaded_images = 0;      // How many have been loaded so far?

// This function is used as an event handler. It counts how many images
// have been loaded and, when all have been loaded, it starts the animation.
function countImages() {
    if (++num_loaded_images == aniframes.length) animate();
}

// Create the offscreen images and assign the image URLs.
// Also assign an event handler to each image so we can track how many images
// have been loaded. Note that we assign the handler before the URL, because
// otherwise the image might finish loading (e.g., if it is already cached)
// before we assign the handler, and then the handler would never be triggered.
for(var i = 0; i < 10; i++) {
    aniframes[i] = new Image();                    // Create an offscreen image
    aniframes[i].onload = countImages;             // Assign the event handler
    aniframes[i].src = "images/" + i + ".gif";    // Tell it what URL to load
}
```

In addition to the `onload` event handler, the Image object supports two others. The `onerror` event handler is invoked when an error occurs during image loading, such as when the specified URL refers to corrupt image data. The `onabort` handler is invoked if the user cancels the image load (for example, by clicking the **Stop** button in the browser) before it has finished. For any image, one (and only one) of these handlers is called.

In addition to these handlers, each Image object also has a `complete` property. This property is `false` while the image is loading; it is changed to `true` once the image has loaded or once the browser has stopped trying to load it. In other words, the `complete` property becomes `true` after one of the three possible event handlers is invoked.

14.6.4 Other Image Properties

The Image object has a few other properties as well. Most of them are simply mirror attributes of the `<img>` tag that created the image. The `width`, `height`, `border`, `hspace`, and `vspace` properties are integers that specify the size of the image, the width of its border, and the size of its horizontal and vertical margins. These properties are set by the attributes of the `<img>` tag that share their names. In Netscape 3 and 4, the properties are read-only, but in IE 4 and later and Netscape 6 and later, you can also assign values to these properties to dynamically change the size, border, or margins of the image.

The `lowsrc` property of the Image object mirrors the `lowsrc` attribute of the `<img>` tag. It specifies the URL of an optional image to display when the page is viewed on a low-resolution device. The `lowsrc` property is a read/write string, like `src`, but unlike the `src` property, setting `lowsrc` does not cause the browser to load and display the newly specified, low-resolution image. If you want to perform an animation or some other special effect that works with low-resolution images as well as high-resolution ones, always remember to update the `lowsrc` property before you set the `src` property. If the browser is running on a low-resolution device when you set the `src` literal, it loads the new `lowsrc` image instead.

14.6.5 Image-Replacement Example

Because image replacement is such a versatile technique, we'll end our discussion of the Image object with an extended example. Example 14-4 defines a ToggleButton class that uses image replacement to simulate a graphical checkbox. Because this class uses images that we provide, we can use bolder graphics than those plain old graphics used by the standard HTML Checkbox object. Figure 14-3 shows how these toggle-button graphics could appear on a web page. This is a complex, real-world example and is worth studying carefully.

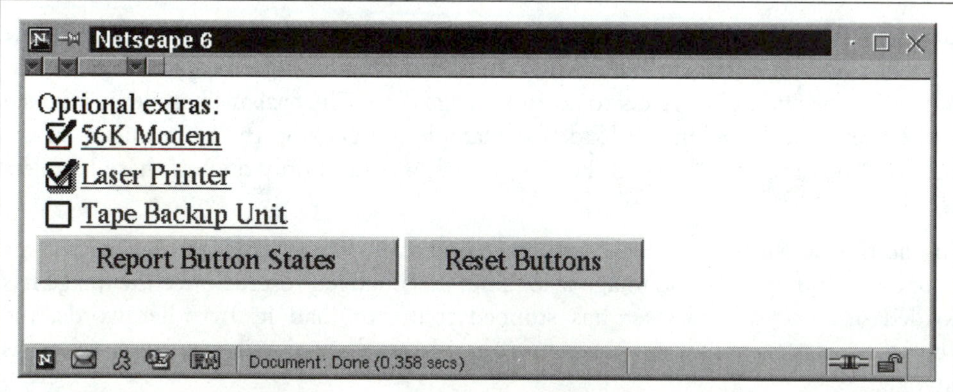

Figure 14-3. ToggleButtons implemented with image replacement

Example 14-4. Implementing a ToggleButton with image replacement

```
<script language="JavaScript1.1">
// This is the constructor function for our new ToggleButton class.
// Calling it creates a ToggleButton object and outputs the required
// <a> and <img> tags into the specified document at the current location.
// Therefore, don't call it for the current document from an event handler.
// Arguments:
//    document: The Document object in which the buttons are to be created.
//    checked:  A boolean that says whether the button is initially checked.
//    label:    An optional string that specifies text to appear after the button.
//    onclick:  An optional function to be called when the toggle button is
//              clicked. It is passed a boolean indicating the new state of
//              the button. You can also pass a string, which is converted
//              to a function that is passed a boolean argument named "state".
function ToggleButton(document, checked, label, onclick)
{
    // The first time we are called (and only the first time), we have
    // to do some special stuff. First, now that the prototype object
    // is created, we can set up our methods.
    // Second, we need to load the images we'll be using.
    // Doing this gets the images in the cache for when we need them.
    if (!ToggleButton.prototype.over) {
        // Initialize the prototype object to create our methods
        ToggleButton.prototype.over = _ToggleButton_over;
        ToggleButton.prototype.out = _ToggleButton_out;
        ToggleButton.prototype.click = _ToggleButton_click;

        // Now create an array of Image objects and assign URLs to them.
        // The URLs of the images are configurable and are stored in an
        // array property of the constructor function itself. They are
        // initialized below. Because of a bug in Netscape, we have
        // to maintain references to these images, so we store the array
        // in a property of the constructor rather than using a local variable.
        ToggleButton.images = new Array(4);
        for(var i = 0; i < 4; i++) {
            ToggleButton.images[i] = new Image(ToggleButton.width,
                                               ToggleButton.height);
            ToggleButton.images[i].src = ToggleButton.imagenames[i];
        }
    }

    // Save some of the arguments we were passed
    this.document = document;
    this.checked = checked;

    // Remember that the mouse is not currently on top of us
    this.highlighted = false;

    // Save the onclick argument to be called when the button is clicked.
    // If it is not already a function, attempt to convert it
    // to a function that is passed a single argument, named "state".
    this.onclick = onclick;
    if (typeof this.onclick == "string")
```

Example 14-4. Implementing a ToggleButton with image replacement (continued)

```
        this.onclick = new Function("state", this.onclick);

    // Figure out what entry in the document.images[] array the images
    // for this checkbox will be stored in
    var index = document.images.length;

    // Now output the HTML code for this checkbox. Use <a> and <img> tags.
    // The event handlers we output here are confusing but crucial to the
    // operation of this class. The "_tb" property is defined below, as
    // are the over(), out(), and click( ) methods.
    document.write(' <a href="about:blank" ' +
      'onmouseover="document.images[' + index + ']._tb.over( );return true;" '+
      'onmouseout="document.images[' + index + ']._tb.out( )" '+
      'onclick="document.images[' + index + ']._tb.click( ); return false;">');
    document.write('<img src="' + ToggleButton.imagenames[this.checked+0] +'"'+
                   ' width=' + ToggleButton.width +
                   ' height=' + ToggleButton.height +
                   ' border="0" hspace="0" vspace="0" align="absmiddle">');
    if (label) document.write(label);
    document.write('</a></br>');

    // Now that we've output the <img> tag, save a reference to the
    // Image object that it created in the ToggleButton object
    this.image = document.images[index];

    // Also make a link in the other direction, from the Image object
    // to this ToggleButton object. Do this by defining a "_tb" property
    // in the Image object.
    this.image._tb = this;
}

// This becomes the over( ) method
function _ToggleButton_over( )
{
    // Change the image, and remember that we're highlighted
    this.image.src = ToggleButton.imagenames[this.checked + 2];
    this.highlighted = true;
}

// This becomes the out( ) method
function _ToggleButton_out( )
{
    // Change the image, and remember that we're not highlighted
    this.image.src = ToggleButton.imagenames[this.checked + 0];
    this.highlighted = false;
}

// This becomes the click( ) method
function _ToggleButton_click( )
{
    // Toggle the state of the button, change the image, and call the
    // onclick method, if it was specified for this ToggleButton
```

Example 14-4. Implementing a ToggleButton with image replacement (continued)

```
    this.checked = !this.checked;
    this.image.src = ToggleButton.imagenames[this.checked+this.highlighted*2];
    if (this.onclick) this.onclick(this.checked);
}

// Initialize static class properties that describe the checkbox images. These
// are just defaults. Programs can override them by assigning new values.
// But they should be overridden *before* any ToggleButtons are created.
ToggleButton.imagenames = new Array(4);            // Create an array
ToggleButton.imagenames[0] = "images/button0.gif";  // The unchecked box
ToggleButton.imagenames[1] = "images/button1.gif";  // The box with a checkmark
ToggleButton.imagenames[2] = "images/button2.gif";  // Unchecked but highlighted
ToggleButton.imagenames[3] = "images/button3.gif";  // Checked and highlighted
ToggleButton.width = ToggleButton.height = 25;      // Size of all images
</script>

<!-- Here's how we might use the ToggleButton class -->
Optional extras:<br>
<script language="JavaScript1.1">
// Create ToggleButton objects and output the HTML that implements them
// One button has no click handler, one has a function, and one has a string
var tb1 = new ToggleButton(document, true, "56K Modem");
var tb2 = new ToggleButton(document, false, "Laser Printer",
                           function(clicked) {alert("printer: " + clicked);});
var tb3 = new ToggleButton(document, false, "Tape Backup Unit",
                            "alert('Tape backup: ' + state)");
</script>

<!-- Here's how we can use the ToggleButton objects from event handlers -->
<form>
<input type="button" value="Report Button States"
       onclick="alert(tb1.checked + '\n' + tb2.checked + '\n' + tb3.checked)">
<input type="button" value="Reset Buttons"
       onclick="if (tb1.checked) tb1.click();
                if (tb2.checked) tb2.click();
                if (tb3.checked) tb3.click();">
</form>
```

14.7 Links

The `links[]` array of the Document object contains Link objects that represent each of the hypertext links in a document. Recall that HTML hypertext links are coded with the `href` attribute of the `<a>` tag. In JavaScript 1.1 and later, the `<area>` tag in a client-side image map also creates a Link object in the Document `links[]` array.

The Link object represents the URL of the hypertext link and contains all the properties that the Location object (introduced in Chapter 13) does. For example, the `href` property of a Link object contains the complete text of the URL to which it is linked, while the `hostname` property contains only the hostname portion of that URL. See the client-side reference section for a complete list of these URL-related properties.

Example 14-5 shows a function that generates a list of all the links in a document. Note the use of the Document write( ) and close( ) methods to dynamically generate a document, as discussed earlier in this chapter.

Example 14-5. Listing the links in a document

```
/*
 * FILE: listlinks.js
 * List all links in the specified document in a new window
 */
function listlinks(d) {
    var newwin = window.open("", "linklist",
                             "menubar,scrollbars,resizable,width=600,height=300");

    for (var i = 0; i < d.links.length; i++) {
        newwin.document.write('<a href="' + d.links[i].href + '">')
        newwin.document.write(d.links[i].href);
        newwin.document.writeln("</a><br>");
    }
    newwin.document.close( );
}
```

14.7.1 Links, Web Crawlers, and JavaScript Security

One obvious use of the Link object and the links[] array is to write a web-crawler program. This program runs in one browser window or frame and reads web pages into another window or frame (by setting the location property of the Window object). For each page it reads in, it looks through the links[] array and recursively follows them. If carefully written (so it doesn't get caught in infinite recursion or start going in circles), such a program can be used, for example, to generate a list of all web pages that are accessible from a given starting page. This list can be quite useful in web-site maintenance.

Don't expect to crawl the entire Internet using these techniques, however. For security reasons, JavaScript does not allow an unsigned script in one window or frame to read the properties (such as document.links) of another window or frame unless both windows are displaying documents that came from the same web server. This restriction prevents important security breaches. Imagine that an employee at a large, security-conscious company is browsing the Internet through a corporate firewall and is also using another browser window to browse proprietary company information on the corporate intranet. Without the security restriction we've described, an untrusted script from some random Internet site could snoop on what was going on in the other window. The authors of the snooping script might not be able to glean much useful information from the links[] array of the proprietary documents, but this would nevertheless be a serious breach of security.

The web-crawler program we have described is not a threat to Internet security or privacy, but unfortunately, it is still subject to the general security restrictions of

JavaScript, which prevent it from crawling very far beyond the site from which it was loaded. (When the crawler loads a page from a different site, it appears as if that page simply has no links on it.) See Chapter 21 for a complete discussion of JavaScript security, including a description of how to avoid this security restriction with signed scripts.

14.7.2 Link Event Handlers

The Link object supports a number of interesting event handlers. We already saw the `onmouseover` event handler in Section 13.3, "The Status Line," where it was used with both `<a>` and `<area>` tags to change the message in the browser's status line when the mouse moved over the link. The `onclick` event handler is invoked when the user clicks on a hypertext link. In JavaScript 1.1 and later, if this event handler returns `false`, the browser doesn't follow the link as it would otherwise. As of JavaScript 1.1, both the `<a>` and `<area>` tags support an `onmouseout` event handler. This is simply the opposite of the `onmouseover` handler—it is run when the mouse pointer moves off a hypertext link.

The event-handling model has become much more general in JavaScript 1.2, and links support quite a few other event handlers. See Chapter 19 for details.

Finally, it is worth mentioning that `href` and the other URL properties of the Link object are read/write. Thus, you can write a JavaScript program that dynamically modifies the destinations of hypertext links! Here is a frivolous piece of JavaScript-enhanced HTML that uses a Link event handler to write to the `href` property and create a link whose destination is randomly chosen from the set of other links in the document:

```
<a href="about:"
   onmouseover="status = 'Take a chance... Click me.'; return true;"
   onclick="this.href =
           document.links[Math.floor(Math.random( )*document.links.length)];"
>
Random Link
</a>
```

This example demonstrates all the features of the Link object that we've considered: the `links[]` array, the use of Link event handlers, and the dynamic setting of the destination of a link. Note that the example sets the `href` property of the link but doesn't bother to read the `href` property of the link it randomly chooses. Instead, it relies on the `toString()` method of the Link object to return the URL.

14.8 Anchors

The `anchors[]` array of the Document object contains Anchor objects representing named locations in the HTML document that are marked with the `<a>` tag and its `name` attribute. The `anchors[]` array has existed since JavaScript 1.0, but the Anchor object is new in JavaScript 1.2. In previous versions, the elements of the anchors[] array were all undefined, and only the length property was useful.

The Anchor object is a simple one. The only standard property it defines is name, which is the value of the HTML name attribute. As with the Link object, the text that appears between the <a> and </a> tags of the anchor is specified by the text property in Netscape 4 and by the innerText property in Internet Explorer 4. Neither of these properties is supported by the W3C DOM standard, but we'll see other ways to obtain the text content of an element in Chapter 17.

Example 14-6 shows a function that creates a navigation window for a specified document. It displays the text, innerText, or name of all the anchors in the document. The anchor text or name is displayed within hypertext links—clicking on any anchor causes the original window to scroll to display that anchor. The code in this example is particularly useful if you write your HTML documents so that all section headings are enclosed in anchors. For example:

```
<a name="sect14.6"><h2>The Anchor Object</h2></a>
```

Example 14-6. Listing all anchors

```
/*
 * FILE: listanchors.js
 * The function listanchors() is passed a document as its argument and opens
 * a new window to serve as a "navigation window" for that document. The new
 * window displays a list of all anchors in the document. Clicking on any
 * anchor in the list causes the document to scroll to the position of that
 * anchor. A document should not call this function on itself until it is
 * fully parsed, or at least until all the anchors in it are parsed.
 */
function listanchors(d) {
    // Open the new window
    var newwin = window.open("", "navwin",
                             "menubar=yes,scrollbars=yes,resizable=yes," +
                             "width=600,height=300");

    // Give it a title
    newwin.document.writeln("<h1>Navigation Window:<br>" +
                            document.title + "</h1>");
    // List all anchors
    for(var i = 0; i < d.anchors.length; i++) {
        // For each anchor object, determine the text to display.
        // First, try to get the text between <a> and </a> using a
        // browser-dependent property. If none, use the name instead.
        var a = d.anchors[i];
        var text = null;
        if (a.text) text = a.text;                          // Netscape 4
        else if (a.innerText) text = a.innerText;           // IE 4+
        if ((text == null) || (text == '')) text = a.name;  // Default

        // Now output that text as a link. Note the use of the location
        // property of the original window.
```

Example 14-6. Listing all anchors (continued)

```
        newwin.document.write('<a href="#' + a.name + '"' +
                              ' onclick="opener.location.hash="' + a.name +
                              '"; return false;">');
        newwin.document.write(text);
        newwin.document.writeln('</a><br>');
    }
    newwin.document.close();  // Never forget to close the document!
}
```

Client-Side JavaScript

14.9 Applets

The applets[] array of the Document object contains objects that represent the applets embedded in the document with the <applet> or <object> tag. An applet is a portable, secure Java program that is loaded over the Internet and executed by the web browser; both Netscape and Internet Explorer support Java (although IE 6 no longer includes Java support by default).

As of Netscape 3 and Internet Explorer 3, both browsers allow JavaScript to invoke public methods and read and write the public properties of Java applets. (As we'll see in Chapter 22, Netscape also supports much richer bidirectional interactions between JavaScript and Java.) All applets have a few standard public methods that they inherit from their superclasses, but the most interesting methods and properties vary on a case-by-case basis. If you are the author of the applet that you want to control from JavaScript, you already know what public methods and properties it defines. If you are not the author, you should consult the applet's documentation to determine what you can do with it.

Here's how you might embed a Java applet in a web page with the <applet> tag and then invoke the start() and stop() methods of that applet from JavaScript event handlers:

```
<applet name="animation" code="Animation.class" width="500" height="200">
</applet>
<form>
<input type="button" value="Start" onclick="document.animation.start();">
<input type="button" value="Stop" onclick="document.animation.stop();">
</form>
```

All applets define start() and stop() methods. In this hypothetical example, the methods cause an animation to start and stop; by defining the HTML form, we've given the user control over starting and stopping the applet. Note that we've used the name attribute of the <applet> tag, so we can refer to the applet by name, rather than as a numbered element of the applets[] array.

This example does not fully demonstrate the power of JavaScript to script Java applets: the Java methods invoked from the JavaScript event handlers are passed no arguments and return no values. In fact, JavaScript can pass numbers, strings, and boolean values as arguments to Java methods and can accept numbers, strings, and boolean return values from those functions. (As we'll see in Chapter 22, Netscape can also pass and return JavaScript and Java objects to and from Java methods.) The automatic conversion of data between JavaScript and Java allows for rich interactions between the two programming environments. For example, an applet might implement a method that returns a string of JavaScript code. JavaScript could then use the `eval()` method to evaluate that code.

Applets can also implement methods that don't operate on the applet itself, but instead simply serve as conduits between JavaScript and the Java environment. For instance, an applet might define a method that invokes the `System.getProperty()` method for a given string argument. This applet would allow JavaScript to look up the value of Java system properties and determine, for example, the version of Java that is supported by the browser.

14.10 Embedded Data

The `embeds[]` array contains objects that represent data (other than applets) embedded in the document with the `<embed>` or `<object>` tag. Embedded data can take many forms (audio, video, spreadsheets, etc.). The browser must have an appropriate viewer installed or available so that it can display the data to the user. In Netscape, special modules known as plugins are responsible for displaying embedded data. In Internet Explorer, embedded data is displayed by ActiveX controls. Both plugins and ActiveX controls can be automatically downloaded from the network and installed as needed.

While the elements of the `applets[]` array all represent Java applets, the elements of the `embeds[]` array tend to be more diverse, and few generalizations can be made about them. The properties and methods of these objects depend upon the particular plugin or ActiveX control that is used to display the embedded data. You should consult the vendor-specific documentation for the plugin or ActiveX control you are using. If it supports any kind of scripting from JavaScript, the documentation should say so, and it should describe the properties and methods that you can use from JavaScript. For example, the documentation for the LiveVideo plugin from Netscape says that the LiveVideo object in the `embeds[]` array supports four methods: `play()`, `stop()`, `rewind()`, and `seek()`. With this information, you can write simple scripts that control how the plugin displays a movie you have embedded on a web page. Note that while some vendors may produce plugins (for Netscape) and ActiveX controls (for IE) that define the same public API, this is not always the case, and scripting embedded objects usually involves platform-specific JavaScript code.

CHAPTER 15

Forms and Form Elements

As we've seen in examples throughout this book, the use of HTML forms is basic to almost all JavaScript programs. This chapter explains the details of programming with forms in JavaScript. It is assumed that you are already somewhat familiar with the creation of HTML forms and with the input elements that they contain. If not, you may want to refer to a good book on HTML.* The client-side reference section of this book lists the HTML syntax along with the JavaScript syntax for forms and form elements; you may find these useful for quick reference.

If you are already familiar with server-side programming using HTML forms, you may find that things are done differently when forms are used with JavaScript. In the server-side model, a form with the input data it contains is submitted to the web server all at once. The emphasis is on processing a complete batch of input data and dynamically producing a new web page in response. With JavaScript, the programming model is quite different. In JavaScript programs, the emphasis is not on form submission and processing but instead on event handling. A form and all input elements in it have event handlers that JavaScript can use to respond to user interactions within the form. If the user clicks on a checkbox, for example, a JavaScript program can receive notification through an event handler and might respond by changing the value displayed in some other element of the form.

With server-side programs, an HTML form isn't useful unless it has a **Submit** button (or unless it has only a single text input field and allows the user to press the **Return** key as a shortcut for submission). With JavaScript, on the other hand, a **Submit** button is never necessary (unless the JavaScript program is working with a cooperating server-side program, of course). With JavaScript, a form can have any number of push buttons with event handlers that perform any number of actions when clicked. In previous chapters, we've seen some of the possible actions that such buttons can trigger: replacing one image with another, using the `location` property to load and display a new web page, opening a new browser window, and dynamically

* Such as *HTML: The Definitive Guide*, by Chuck Musciano and Bill Kennedy (O'Reilly).

generating a new HTML document in another window or frame. As we'll see later in this chapter, a JavaScript event handler can even trigger a form to be submitted.

As we've seen in examples throughout this book, event handlers are almost always the central element of any interesting JavaScript program. And the most commonly used event handlers (excluding the event handlers of the Link object) are those used with forms or form elements. This chapter introduces the JavaScript Form object and the various JavaScript objects that represent form elements. It concludes with an example that illustrates how you can use JavaScript to validate user input on the client before submitting it to a server-side program running on the web server.

15.1 The Form Object

The JavaScript Form object represents an HTML form. Forms are always found as elements of the `forms[]` array, which is a property of the Document object. Forms appear in this array in the order in which they appear within the document. Thus, `document.forms[0]` refers to the first form in a document. You can refer to the last form in a document with the following:

```
document.forms[document.forms.length-1]
```

The most interesting property of the Form object is the `elements[]` array, which contains JavaScript objects (of various types) that represent the various input elements of the form. Again, elements appear in this array in the same order they appear in the document. So you can refer to the third element of the second form in the document of the current window like this:

```
document.forms[1].elements[2]
```

The remaining properties of the Form object are of less importance. The `action`, `encoding`, `method`, and `target` properties correspond directly to the `action`, `encoding`, `method`, and `target` attributes of the `<form>` tag. These properties and attributes are all used to control how form data is submitted to the web server and where the results are displayed; they are therefore useful only when the form is actually submitted to a server-side program. See the client-side reference section for an explanation of the properties, or see a book on HTML or CGI programming* for a thorough discussion of the attributes. What is worth noting here is that these Form properties are all read/write strings, so a JavaScript program can dynamically set their values in order to change the way the form is submitted.

In the days before JavaScript, a form was submitted with a special-purpose **Submit** button, and form elements had their values reset with a special-purpose **Reset** button. The JavaScript Form object supports two methods, `submit()` and (as of JavaScript 1.1) `reset()`, that serve the same purpose. Invoking the `submit()` method of a Form submits the form, and invoking `reset()` resets the form elements.

* Such as *CGI Programming on the World Wide Web*, by Shishir Gundavaram (O'Reilly).

To accompany the `submit()` and `reset()` methods, the Form object provides the `onsubmit` event handler to detect form submission and (as of JavaScript 1.1) the `onreset` event handler to detect form resets. The `onsubmit` handler is invoked just before the form is submitted; it can cancel the submission by returning `false`. This provides an opportunity for a JavaScript program to check the user's input for errors in order to avoid submitting incomplete or invalid data over the network to a server-side program. We'll see an example of such error checking at the end of this chapter. Note that the `onsubmit` handler is triggered only by a genuine click on a **Submit** button. Calling the `submit()` method of a form does not trigger the `onsubmit` handler.

The `onreset` event handler is similar to the `onsubmit` handler. It is invoked just before the form is reset, and it can prevent the form elements from being reset by returning `false`. This allows a JavaScript program to ask for confirmation of the reset, which can be a good idea when the form is long or detailed. You might request this sort of confirmation with an event handler like the following:

```
<form...
    onreset="return confirm('Really erase ALL data and start over?')"
>
```

Like the `onsubmit` handler, `onreset` is triggered only by a genuine **Reset** button. Calling the `reset()` method of a form does not trigger `onreset`.

15.2 Defining Form Elements

HTML form elements are the primitive objects with which we create graphical user interfaces for our JavaScript programs. Figure 15-1 shows a complex form that contains at least one of each of the basic form elements. In case you are not already familiar with HTML form elements, the figure includes a numbered key identifying each type of element. We'll conclude this section with an example (Example 15-1) that shows the HTML and JavaScript code used to create the form pictured in Figure 15-1 and to hook up event handlers to each of the form elements.

Table 15-1 lists the types of form elements that are available to HTML designers and JavaScript programmers. The first column of the table names the type of form element, the second column shows the HTML tags that are used to define elements of that type, and the third column lists the value of the type property for each type of element. As we've seen, each Form object has an `elements[]` array that contains the objects that represent the form's elements. Each of these elements has a type property that can be used to distinguish one type of element from another. By examining the type property of an unknown form element, JavaScript code can determine the type of the element and figure out what it can do with that element. (We'll see this done in Example 15-2, at the end of the chapter.) Finally, the fourth column of the table provides a short description of each element and also lists the most important or most commonly used event handler for that element type.

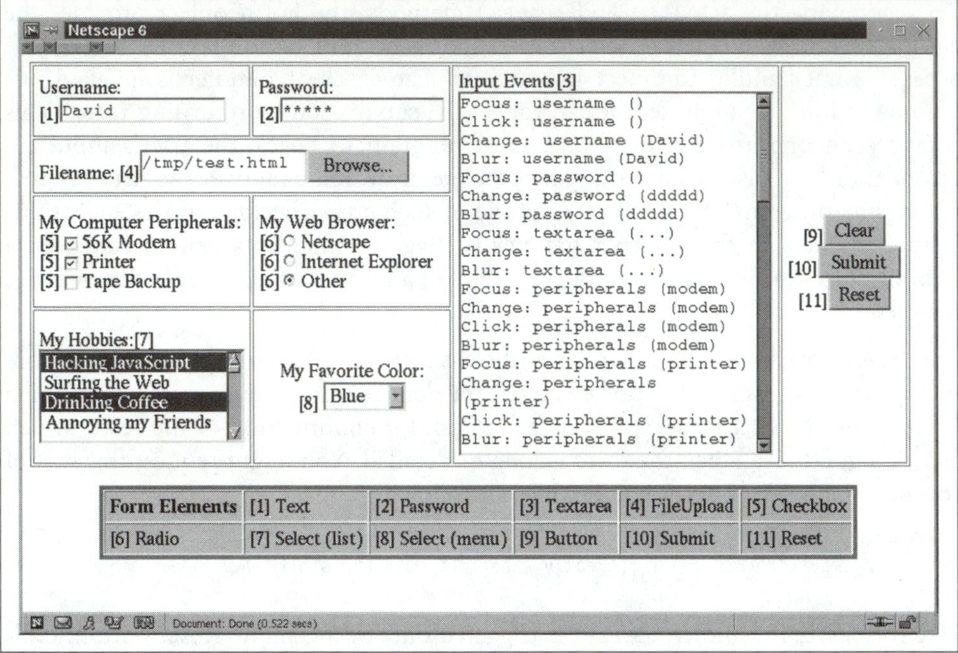

Figure 15-1. HTML form elements

We'll talk more about form elements later in this chapter. Complete details about the various types of elements are available in the client-side reference section, under the name listed in the first column of Table 15-1. Although each type of form element has a separate reference page, note that most of the elements are created with HTML `<input>` tags and are, in fact, all Input objects. The client-side reference page named "Input" lists the features that all these elements have in common, and the type-specific pages provide specific details about working with a particular type of form element. Note that the names Button, Checkbox, and so on from the first column of the table may not correspond to any actual object in a client-side JavaScript implementation, and note also that the DOM standard does not define any interfaces with these names. Still, each type of form element has a distinct appearance and distinct behavior, and it is useful to treat them as separate types, at least for the purposes of the client-side reference section. In the DOM reference section you can find material about forms and their elements under the names "HTMLFormElement," "HTMLInputElement," "HTMLTextAreaElement," "HTMLSelectElement," and "HTMLOptionElement."

Table 15-1. HTML form elements

Object	HTML tag	type property	Description and events
Button	`<input type="button">` or `<button type="button">`	"button"	A push button; `onclick`.
Checkbox	`<input type="checkbox">`	"checkbox"	A toggle button without radio-button behavior; `onclick`.

Table 15-1. HTML form elements (continued)

Object	HTML tag	type property	Description and events
FileUpload	`<input type="file">`	"file"	An input field for entering the name of a file to upload to the web server; onchange.
Hidden	`<input type="hidden">`	"hidden"	Data submitted with the form but not visible to the user; no event handlers.
Option	`<option>`	none	A single item within a Select object; event handlers are on the Select object, not on individual Option objects.
Password	`<input type="password">`	"password"	An input field for password entry—typed characters are not visible; onchange.
Radio	`<input type="radio">`	"radio"	A toggle button with radio-button behavior—only one selected at a time; onclick.
Reset	`<input type="reset">` or `<button type="reset">`	"reset"	A push button that resets a form; onclick.
Select	`<select>`	"select-one"	A list or drop-down menu from which one item may be selected; onchange. (See also Option object.)
Select	`<select multiple>`	"select-multiple"	A list from which multiple items may be selected; onchange. (See also Option object.)
Submit	`<input type="submit">` or `<button type="submit">`	"submit"	A push button that submits a form; onclick.
Text	`<input type="text">`	"text"	A single-line text entry field; onchange.
Textarea	`<textarea>`	"textarea"	A multiline text entry field; onchange.

Now that we've taken a look at the various types of form element and the HTML tags used to create them, Example 15-1 shows the HTML code used to create the form shown in Figure 15-1. Although the example consists primarily of HTML, it also contains JavaScript code used to define event handlers for each of the form elements. You'll notice that the event handlers are not defined as HTML attributes. Instead, they are JavaScript functions assigned to the properties of the objects in the form's `elements[]` array. The event handlers all call the function `report()`, which contains code that works with the various form elements. The next section of this chapter explains everything you need to know to understand what the `report()` function is doing.

Example 15-1. An HTML form containing all form elements

```
<form name="everything">                     <!-- A one-of-everything HTML form... -->
 <table border="border" cellpadding="5">    <!-- in a big HTML table -->
   <tr>
     <td>Username:<br>[1]<input type="text" name="username" size="15"></td>
     <td>Password:<br>[2]<input type="password" name="password" size="15"></td>
     <td rowspan="4">Input Events[3]<br>
       <textarea name="textarea" rows="20" cols="28"></textarea></td>
```

Example 15-1. An HTML form containing all form elements (continued)

```
    <td rowspan="4" align="center" valign="center">
      [9]<input type="button" value="Clear" name="clearbutton"><br>
      [10]<input type="submit" name="submitbutton" value="Submit"><br>
      [11]<input type="reset" name="resetbutton" value="Reset"></td></tr>
  <tr>
    <td colspan="2">
      Filename: [4]<input type="file" name="file" size="15"></td></tr>
  <tr>
    <td>My Computer Peripherals:<br>
      [5]<input type="checkbox" name="peripherals" value="modem">56K Modem<br>
      [5]<input type="checkbox" name="peripherals" value="printer">Printer<br>
      [5]<input type="checkbox" name="peripherals" value="tape">Tape Backup</td>
    <td>My Web Browser:<br>
      [6]<input type="radio" name="browser" value="nn">Netscape<br>
      [6]<input type="radio" name="browser" value="ie">Internet Explorer<br>
      [6]<input type="radio" name="browser" value="other">Other</td></tr>
  <tr>
    <td>My Hobbies:[7]<br>
      <select multiple="multiple" name="hobbies" size="4">
        <option value="programming">Hacking JavaScript
        <option value="surfing">Surfing the Web
        <option value="caffeine">Drinking Coffee
        <option value="annoying">Annoying my Friends
      </select></td>
    <td align="center" valign="center">My Favorite Color:<br>[8]
      <select name="color">
        <option value="red">Red        <option value="green">Green
        <option value="blue">Blue      <option value="white">White
        <option value="violet">Violet  <option value="peach">Peach
      </select></td></tr>
 </table>
</form>

<div align="center">        <!-- Another table--the key to the one above -->
  <table border="4" bgcolor="pink" cellspacing="1" cellpadding="4">
    <tr>
      <td align="center"><b>Form Elements</b></td>
      <td>[1] Text</td>  <td>[2] Password</td>  <td>[3] Textarea</td>
      <td>[4] FileUpload</td> <td>[5] Checkbox</td></tr>
    <tr>
      <td>[6] Radio</td>  <td>[7] Select (list)</td>
      <td>[8] Select (menu)</td>  <td>[9] Button</td>
      <td>[10] Submit</td>  <td>[11] Reset</td></tr>
  </table>
</div>

<script>
// This generic function appends details of an event to the big Textarea
// element in the form above. It is called from various event handlers.
function report(element, event) {
    var elmtname = element.name;
    if ((element.type == "select-one") || (element.type == "select-multiple")){
```

Example 15-1. An HTML form containing all form elements (continued)

```
        value = " ";
        for(var i = 0; i < element.options.length; i++)
            if (element.options[i].selected)
                value += element.options[i].value + " ";
    }
    else if (element.type == "textarea") value = "...";
    else value = element.value;
    var msg = event + ": " + elmtname + ' (' + value + ')\n';
    var t = element.form.textarea;
    t.value = t.value + msg;
}

// This function adds a bunch of event handlers to every element in a form.
// It doesn't bother checking to see if the element supports the event handler,
// it just adds them all. Note that the event handlers call report( ) above.
// Note that we're defining event handlers by assigning functions to the
// properties of JavaScript objects rather than by assigning strings to
// the attributes of HTML elements.
function addhandlers(f) {
    // Loop through all the elements in the form
    for(var i = 0; i < f.elements.length; i++) {
        var e = f.elements[i];
        e.onclick = function( ) { report(this, 'Click'); }
        e.onchange = function( ) { report(this, 'Change'); }
        e.onfocus = function( ) { report(this, 'Focus'); }
        e.onblur = function( ) { report(this, 'Blur'); }
        e.onselect = function( ) { report(this, 'Select'); }
    }

    // Define some special-case event handlers for the three buttons:
    f.clearbutton.onclick = function( ) {
        this.form.textarea.value=''; report(this,'Click');
    }
    f.submitbutton.onclick = function ( ) {
        report(this, 'Click'); return false;
    }
    f.resetbutton.onclick = function( ) {
        this.form.reset( ); report(this, 'Click'); return false;
    }
}
// Finally, activate our form by adding all possible event handlers!
addhandlers(document.everything);
</script>
```

15.3 Scripting Form Elements

The previous section listed the form elements provided by HTML and explained how to embed these elements in your HTML documents. This section takes the next step and shows you how you can work with those elements in your JavaScript programs.

15.3.1 Naming Forms and Form Elements

Every form element has a name attribute that must be set in its HTML tag if the form is to be submitted to a server-side program. While form submission is not generally of interest to JavaScript programs, there is another useful reason to specify this name attribute, as you'll see shortly.

The <form> tag itself also has a name attribute that you can set. This attribute has nothing to do with form submission. It exists for the convenience of JavaScript programmers. If the name attribute is defined in a <form> tag, when the Form object is created for that form, it is stored as an element in the forms[] array of the Document object, as usual, and it is also stored in its own personal property of the Document object. The name of this newly defined property is the value of the name attribute. In Example 15-1, for instance, we defined a form with a tag like this:

```
<form name="everything">
```

This allowed us to refer to the Form object as:

```
document.everything
```

Often, you'll find this more convenient than the array notation:

```
document.forms[0]
```

Furthermore, using a form name makes your code position-independent: it works even if the document is rearranged so that forms appear in a different order.

<img>, <applet>, and other HTML tags also have name attributes that work the same as the name attribute of <form>. With forms, however, this style of naming goes a step further, because all elements contained within a form also have name attributes. When you give a form element a name, you create a new property of the Form object that refers to that element. The name of this property is the value of the attribute. Thus, you can refer to an element named "zipcode" in a form named "address" as:

```
document.address.zipcode
```

With reasonably chosen names, this syntax is much more elegant than the alternative, which relies on hardcoded (and position-dependent) array indices:

```
document.forms[1].elements[4]
```

In order for a group of Radio elements in an HTML form to exhibit mutually exclusive "radio-button" behavior, they must all be given the same name. In Example 15-1, for instance, we define three Radio elements that all have a name attribute of "browser". Although it is not strictly necessary, it is also common practice to define related groups of Checkbox elements with the same name attribute. Sharing a name attribute like this works naturally for server-side programming, but it is a little awkward on the client side. The solution is straightforward, though: when more than one element in a form has the same name attribute, JavaScript simply places those elements into an array with the specified name. The elements of the array are in the same order as they appear in the document. So, the Radio objects in Example 15-1 can be referred to as:

```
document.everything.browser[0]
document.everything.browser[1]
document.everything.browser[2]
```

15.3.2 Form Element Properties

All (or most) form elements have the following properties in common. Some elements have other special-purpose properties that are described later, when we consider the various types of form elements individually.

`type`
: A read-only string that identifies the type of the form element. The third column of Table 15-1 lists the value of this property for each form element.

`form`
: A read-only reference to the Form object in which this element is contained.

`name`
: A read-only string specified by the HTML `name` attribute.

`value`
: A read/write string that specifies the "value" contained or represented by the form element. This is the string that is sent to the web server when the form is submitted, and it is only sometimes of interest to JavaScript programs. For Text and Textarea elements, this property contains the text that the user entered. For Button elements, this property specifies the text displayed within the button, which is something that you might occasionally want to change from a script. For Radio and Checkbox elements, however, the `value` property is not edited or displayed to the user in any way. It is simply a string set by the HTML `value` attribute that is passed to the web server when the form is submitted. We'll discuss the `value` property when we consider the different categories of form elements later in this chapter.

15.3.3 Form Element Event Handlers

Most form elements support most of the following event handlers:

`onclick`
: Triggered when the user clicks the mouse on the element. This handler is particularly useful for Button and related form elements.

`onchange`
: Triggered when the user changes the value represented by the element by entering text or selecting an option, for example. Button and related elements typically do not support this event handler because they do not have an editable value. Note that this handler is not triggered every time the user types a key in a text field, for example. It is triggered only when the user changes the value of an element and then moves the input focus to some other form element. That is, the invocation of this event handler indicates a completed change.

`onfocus`
: Triggered when the form element receives the input focus.

`onblur`
: Triggered when the form element loses the input focus.

Example 15-1 shows how you can define these event handlers for form elements. The example is designed to report events as they occur by listing them in a large Textarea element. This makes the example a useful way to experiment with form elements and the event handlers they trigger.

An important thing to know about event handlers is that within the code of an event handler, the `this` keyword always refers to the document element that triggered the event. Since all form elements have a `form` property that refers to the containing form, the event handlers of a form element can always refer to the Form object as `this.form`. Going a step further, this means that an event handler for one form element can refer to a sibling form element named `x` as `this.form.x`.

Note that the four form element event handlers listed in this section are the ones that have particular significance for form elements. Form elements also support the various event handlers (such as `onmousedown`) that are supported by (nearly) all HTML elements. See Chapter 19 for a full discussion of events and event handlers.

15.3.4 Buttons

The Button form element is one of the most commonly used, because it provides a clear visual way to allow the user to trigger some scripted action. The Button object has no default behavior of its own, and it is never useful in a form unless it has an `onclick` (or other) event handler. The `value` property of a Button element controls the text that appears within the button itself. In fourth-generation browsers, you can set this property to change the text (plain text only, not HTML) that appears in the button, which can occasionally be a useful thing to do.

Note that hyperlinks provide the same `onclick` event handler that buttons do, and any button object can be replaced with a link that does the same thing when clicked. Use a button when you want an element that looks like a graphical push button. Use a link when the action to be triggered by the `onclick` handler can be conceptualized as "following a link."

Submit and Reset elements are just like Button elements, but they have default actions (submitting and resetting a form) associated with them. Because these elements have default actions, they can be useful even without an `onclick` event handler. On the other hand, because of their default actions, they are more useful for forms that are submitted to a web server than for pure client-side JavaScript programs. If the `onclick` event handler returns `false`, the default action of these buttons is not performed. You can use the `onclick` handler of a Submit element to perform form validation, but it is more common to do this with the `onsubmit` handler of the Form object itself.

In HTML 4, you can create Button, Submit, and Reset buttons with the <button> tag instead of the traditional <input> tag. <button> is more flexible, because instead of simply displaying the plain text specified by the value attribute, it displays any HTML content (formatted text and/or images) that appears between <button> and </button>. The Button objects created by a <button> tag are technically different from those created by an <input> tag, but they have the same value for the type field and otherwise behave quite similarly. The main difference is that because the <button> tag doesn't use its value attribute to define the appearance of the button, you can't change that appearance by setting the value property. In this book, we use the terms Button, Submit, and Reset to refer to objects created with either <input> or <button>.

15.3.5 Toggle Buttons

The Checkbox and Radio elements are toggle buttons, or buttons that have two visually distinct states: they can be checked or unchecked. The user can change the state of a toggle button by clicking on it. Radio elements are designed to be used in groups of related elements, all of which have the same value for the HTML name attribute. Radio elements created in this way are mutually exclusive—when you check one, the one that was previously checked becomes unchecked. Checkboxes are also often used in groups that share a name attribute, and when you refer to these elements by name, you must remember that the object you refer to by name is an array of same-named elements. In Example 15-1, we saw three Checkbox objects with the name "peripherals". In this example, we can refer to an array of these three Checkbox objects as:

```
document.everything.peripherals
```

To refer to an individual Checkbox element, we must index the array:

```
document.everything.peripherals[0]  // First form element named "peripherals"
```

Radio and Checkbox elements both define a checked property. This read/write boolean value specifies whether the element is currently checked. The defaultChecked property is a read-only boolean that has the value of the HTML checked attribute; it specifies whether the element was checked when the page was first loaded.

Radio and Checkbox elements do not display any text themselves and are typically displayed with adjacent HTML text (or, in HTML 4, with an associated <label> tag.) This means that setting the value property of a Checkbox or Radio element does not alter the visual appearance of the element, as it does for Button elements. You can set value, but this changes only the string that is sent to the web server when the form is submitted.

When the user clicks on a toggle button, the Radio or Checkbox element triggers its onclick event handler to notify the JavaScript program of the change of state. Newer web browsers also trigger the onchange handler for these elements. Both event handlers convey the same essential information, but the onclick handler is more portable.

15.3.6 Text Fields

The Text element is probably the most commonly used element in HTML forms and JavaScript programs. It allows the user to enter a short, single-line string of text. The `value` property represents the text the user has entered. You can set this property to specify explicitly the text that should be displayed in the field. The `onchange` event handler is triggered when the user enters new text or edits existing text and then indicates that he is finished editing by moving input focus out of the text field.

The Textarea element is just like the Text element, except that it allows the user to input (and your JavaScript programs to display) multiline text. Textarea elements are created with a `<textarea>` tag using a syntax significantly different from the `<input>` tag used to create a Text element. Nevertheless, the two types of element behave quite similarly, and Textarea can be considered to inherit from HTMLInputElement, even though it technically does not. You can use the `value` property and `onchange` event handler of a Textarea element just as you would for a Text element.

The Password element is a modified Text element that displays asterisks as the user types into it. As the name indicates, this is useful to allow the user to enter passwords without worrying about others reading over their shoulders. Password triggers its `onchange` event handler just as Text does, but there are some restrictions (or bugs) on the use of its `value` property. Some old browsers (such as Netscape 3) implement an ineffective security measure that prevents JavaScript from reading the value the user has entered into a Password element. In other browsers (such as Netscape 4), the `value` property may be set, but setting it does not cause any change to the visual appearance of the form element. Note that the Password element protects the user's input from prying eyes, but when the form is submitted, that input is not encrypted in any way (unless it is submitted over a secure HTTPS connection), and it may be visible as it is transmitted over the network.

Finally, the FileUpload object is designed to allow the user to enter the name of a file to be uploaded to the web server. It is essentially a Text element combined with a built-in button that pops up a file-chooser dialog box. FileUpload has an `onchange` event handler, like the Text element. Unlike Text, however, the `value` property of FileUpload is read-only. This prevents malicious JavaScript programs from tricking the user into uploading a file that should not be shared.

Netscape 4 and later and Internet Explorer 4 and later define `onkeypress`, `onkeydown`, and `onkeyup` event handlers (note, however, that they are not yet part of the DOM standard). These handlers can be specified for any Document object, but they are most useful (and, in Netscape 4, only useful) when specified on Text and related form elements that actually accept keyboard input. You may return `false` from the `onkeypress` or `onkeydown` event handlers to prevent the user's keystroke from being recorded. This can be useful, for example, when you want to force the user to enter only digits. See "HTMLElement" in the client-side and DOM reference sections for more details on these and other event handlers that are supported by all HTML elements.

15.3.7 Select and Option Elements

The Select element represents a set of options (represented by Option elements) from which the user can select. Browsers typically render Select elements in drop-down menus or list boxes. The Select element can operate in two very distinct ways, and the value of the type property depends on how it is configured. If the <select> tag has the multiple attribute, the user is allowed to select multiple options, and the type property of the Select object is "select-multiple". Otherwise, if the multiple attribute is not present, only a single item may be selected, and the type property is "select-one".

In some ways, a "select-multiple" element is like a set of Checkbox elements, and a "select-one" element is like a set of Radio elements. The Select element differs from the toggle-button elements in that a single Select element represents an entire set of options. These options are specified in HTML with the <option> tag, and they are represented in JavaScript by Option objects stored in the options[] array of the Select element. Because a Select element represents a set of choices, it does not have a value property, as all other form elements do. Instead, as we'll discuss shortly, each Option object contained by the Select element defines a value property.

When the user selects or deselects an option, the Select element triggers its onchange event handler. For "select-one" Select elements, the read/write selectedIndex property specifies by number which one of the options is currently selected. For "select-multiple" elements, the single selectedIndex property is not sufficient to represent the complete set of selected options. In this case, to determine which options are selected you must loop through the elements of the options[] array and check the value of the selected property for each Option object.

In addition to its selected property, the Option element has a text property that specifies the string of plain text that appears in the Select element for that option. You can set this property to change the text that is displayed to the user. The value property is also a read/write string that specifies the text to be sent to the web server when the form is submitted. Even if you are writing a pure client-side program and your form never gets submitted, the value property (or its corresponding HTML value attribute) can be a useful place to store any data that you'll need if the user selects a particular option. Note that the Option element does not define form-related event handlers; use the onchange handler of the containing Select element instead.

In addition to setting the text property of Option objects, there are other ways you can dynamically change the options displayed in a Select element. You can truncate the array of Option elements by setting options.length to the desired number of options, and you can remove all Option objects by setting options.length to zero. Suppose we have a Select object named "country" in a form named "address". We can remove all options from the element like this:

```
document.address.country.options.length = 0;  // Remove all options
```

We can remove an individual Option object from the Select element by setting its spot in the options[] array to null. This deletes the Option object, and any higher elements in the options[] array automatically get moved down to fill the empty spot:

```
// Remove a single Option object from the Select element
// The Option that was previously at options[11] gets moved to options[10]...
document.address.country.options[10] = null;
```

Finally, the Option element defines an Option() constructor that you can use (in JavaScript 1.1 and later) to dynamically create new Option elements, and you can append new options to a Select element by assigning them to the end of the options[] array. For example:

```
// Create a new Option object
var zaire = new Option("Zaire",  // The text property
                       "zaire",  // The value property
                       false,    // The defaultSelected property
                       false);   // The selected property

// Display it in a Select element by appending it to the options array:
var countries = document.address.country;  // Get the Select object
countries.options[countries.options.length] = zaire;
```

In HTML 4, you can use the <optgroup> tag to group related options within a Select element. The <optgroup> tag has a label attribute that specifies text to appear in the Select element. Despite its visual presence, however, an <optgroup> tag is not selectable by the user, and HTMLOptGroupElement objects never appear in the options[] array of the Select element.

15.3.8 Hidden Elements

As its name implies, the Hidden element has no visual representation in a form. It exists to allow arbitrary text to be transmitted to the server when a form is submitted. Server-side programs use this as a way to save state information that is passed back to them with form submission. Since they have no visual appearance, Hidden elements cannot generate events and have no event handlers. The value property allows to you read and write the text associated with a Hidden element, but, in general, Hidden elements are not commonly used in client-side JavaScript programming.

15.3.9 Fieldset Elements

The HTML 4 standard adds new <fieldset> and <label> tags to the set of elements that can appear within a form. In IE 5 and later, placing a <fieldset> in a form causes a corresponding object to be added to the form's elements[] array. Fieldset elements are not scriptable in interesting ways like other form elements are, and their objects do not have a type property like other form elements do. Therefore, the presence of Fieldset objects in the elements[] array seems like a mistaken design decision. This is particularly true since <label> tags do not cause corresponding objects to be added to the elements[] array. The Mozilla and Netscape 6 browsers have chosen to follow Microsoft's lead on this in order to be compatible with IE.

What this means is that if you define a form that contains fieldsets, the contents of the elements[] array differ in recent, HTML 4–capable browsers and in older, pre–HTML 4 browsers. In this situation, using position-based numeric indexes in the elements[] array is not portable, and you should define name attributes for all your form elements and refer to them by name.

15.4 Form Verification Example

We'll close our discussion of forms with an extended example that demonstrates several of the concepts we've been discussing. Example 15-2 shows how you might use the onsubmit event handler of the Form object to perform input validation so that you can notify the user and prevent the form from being submitted when it contains missing or invalid data. After studying this example, you may want to turn back to Example 1-3, the form-programming example we began this book with. The code of that example probably makes more sense now that you are a JavaScript expert!

Example 15-2 defines a verify() function suitable for use as a generic form validator. It checks for required fields that are empty. In addition, it can check that a numeric value is in fact numeric and also falls within a specified numeric range. This verify() function relies on the type property of a form element to determine which kind of element it is. The function also relies on additional user-defined properties to distinguish optional fields from required fields and to specify the allowed ranges for numeric fields. Note how the function reads the value property of an input field and uses the name property of a field when reporting errors.

Figure 15-2 shows an example form that uses this verification scheme, with the error message that is displayed when the user attempts to submit the form before correctly filling it in.

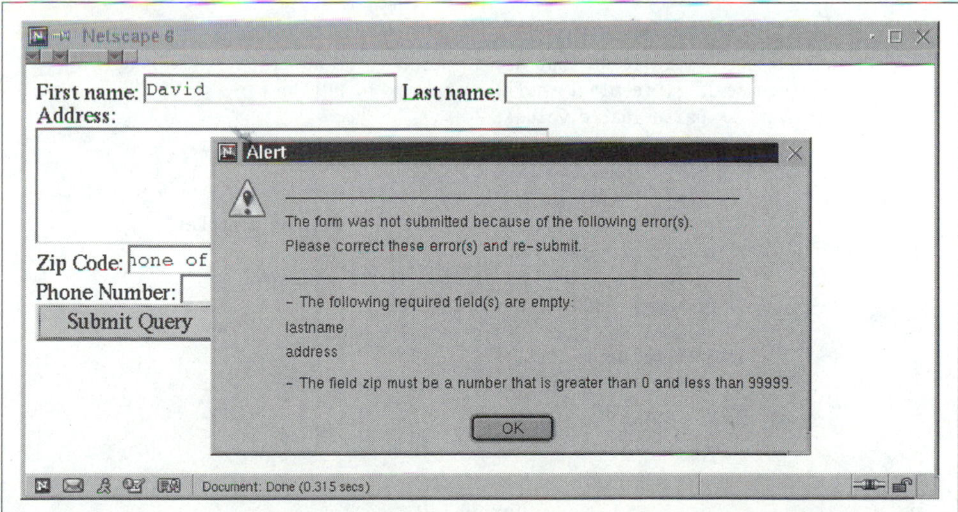

Figure 15-2. A form that failed validation

Example 15-2. Performing form validation

```
<script language="JavaScript1.1">
// A utility function that returns true if a string contains only
// whitespace characters
function isblank(s) {
    for(var i = 0; i < s.length; i++) {
        var c = s.charAt(i);
        if ((c != ' ') && (c != '\n') && (c != '')) return false;
    }
    return true;
}

// This is the function that performs form verification. It is invoked
// from the onsubmit event handler. The handler should return whatever
// value this function returns.
function verify(f) {
    var msg;
    var empty_fields = "";
    var errors = "";

    // Loop through the elements of the form, looking for all Text and
    // Textarea elements that don't have an "optional" property defined.
    // Then check for fields that are empty and make a list of them. Also, if
    // any of these elements have a "min" or a "max" property defined, verify
    // that they are numbers and are in the right range. If the element has a
    // "numeric" property defined, verify that it is a number, but don't check
    // its range. Put together error messages for fields that are wrong.
    for(var i = 0; i < f.length; i++) {
        var e = f.elements[i];
        if (((e.type == "text") || (e.type == "textarea")) && !e.optional) {
            // First check if the field is empty
            if ((e.value == null) || (e.value == "") || isblank(e.value)) {
                empty_fields += "\n          " + e.name;
                continue;
            }

            // Now check for fields that are supposed to be numeric
            if (e.numeric || (e.min != null) || (e.max != null)) {
                var v = parseFloat(e.value);
                if (isNaN(v) ||
                    ((e.min != null) && (v < e.min)) ||
                    ((e.max != null) && (v > e.max))) {
                    errors += "- The field " + e.name + " must be a number";
                    if (e.min != null)
                        errors += " that is greater than " + e.min;
                    if (e.max != null && e.min != null)
                        errors += " and less than " + e.max;
                    else if (e.max != null)
                        errors += " that is less than " + e.max;
                    errors += ".\n";
                }
            }
        }
    }
```

Example 15-2. Performing form validation (continued)

```
    // Now, if there were any errors, display the messages, and
    // return false to prevent the form from being submitted.
    // Otherwise, return true.
    if (!empty_fields && !errors) return true;

    msg  = "______________________________________________________\n\n"
    msg += "The form was not submitted because of the following error(s).\n";
    msg += "Please correct these error(s) and re-submit.\n";
    msg += "______________________________________________________\n\n"

    if (empty_fields) {
        msg += "- The following required field(s) are empty:"
                + empty_fields + "\n";
        if (errors) msg += "\n";
    }
    msg += errors;
    alert(msg);
    return false;
}
</script>

<!-----------------------------------------------------------------------
     Here's a sample form to test our verification. Note that we
     call verify() from the onsubmit event handler and return whatever
     value it returns. Also note that we use the onsubmit handler as
     an opportunity to set properties of the Form objects that verify()
     requires for the verification process.
------------------------------------------------------------------------>
<form onsubmit="
    this.firstname.optional = true;
    this.phonenumber.optional = true;
    this.zip.min = 0;
    this.zip.max = 99999;
    return verify(this);
">

First name: <input type="text" name="firstname">
Last name: <input type="text" name="lastname"><br>
Address:<br><textarea name="address" rows="4" cols="40"></textarea><br>
Zip Code: <input type="text" name="zip"><br>
Phone Number: <input type="text" name="phonenumber"><br>
<input type="submit">
</form>
```

CHAPTER 16
Scripting Cookies

The Document object contains a property named `cookie` that was not discussed in Chapter 14. On the surface, this property appears to be a simple string value; however, the `cookie` property controls a very important feature of the web browser and is important enough to warrant a complete chapter of its own.

16.1 An Overview of Cookies

A *cookie* is a small amount of named data stored by the web browser and associated with a particular web page or web site.* Cookies serve to give the web browser a memory, so that scripts and server-side programs can use data that was input on one page in another page, or so the browser can recall user preferences or other state variables when the user leaves a page and then returns. Cookies were originally designed for CGI programming, and at the lowest level, they are implemented as an extension to the HTTP protocol. Cookie data is automatically transmitted between the web browser and web server, so CGI scripts on the server can read and write cookie values that are stored on the client. As we'll see, JavaScript can also manipulate cookies using the `cookie` property of the Document object.

`cookie` is a string property that allows you to read, create, modify, and delete the cookie or cookies that apply to the current web page. Although `cookie` appears at first to be a normal read/write string property, its behavior is actually more complex. When you read the value of `cookie`, you get a string that contains the names and values of all the cookies that apply to the document. You create, modify, or delete a cookie by setting the value of the `cookie` property. Later sections of this chapter explain in detail how this works. To use the `cookie` property effectively, however, you need to know more about cookies and how they work.

* The name "cookie" does not have a lot of significance, but it is not used without precedent. In the obscure annals of computing history, the term "cookie" or "magic cookie" has been used to refer to a small chunk of data, particularly a chunk of privileged or secret data, akin to a password, that proves identity or permits access. In JavaScript, cookies are used to save state and can serve to establish a kind of identity for a web browser. Cookies in JavaScript do not use any kind of cryptography, however, and are not secure in any way.

In addition to a name and a value, each cookie has four optional attributes that control its lifetime, visibility, and security. The first attribute is `expires`, which specifies the cookie's lifetime. Cookies are transient by default—the values they store last for the duration of the web-browser session but are lost when the user exits the browser. If you want a cookie to last beyond a single browsing session, you use its `expires` attribute to specify an expiration date—this attribute causes the browser to save the cookie in a local file so that it can read it back in the next time the user visits the web page. Once the expiration date has passed, the cookie is automatically deleted from the cookie file.

The second attribute of a cookie is `path`, which specifies the web pages with which a cookie is associated. By default, a cookie is associated with, and accessible to, the web page that created it and any other web pages in the same directory or any subdirectories of that directory. If the web page *http://www.acme.com/catalog/index.html* creates a cookie, for example, that cookie is also visible to *http://www.acme.com/catalog/order.html* and *http://www.acme.com/catalog/widgets/index.html*, but it is not visible to *http://www.acme.com/about.html*.

This default visibility behavior is often exactly what you want. Sometimes, though, you'll want to use cookie values throughout a multipage web site, regardless of which page creates the cookie. For instance, if the user enters his mailing address in a form on one page, you may want to save that address to use as the default the next time he returns to the page and also as the default in an entirely unrelated form on another page where he is asked to enter a billing address. To allow this usage, you specify a `path` for the cookie. Then, any web page from the same web server that contains that path in its URL can share the cookies. For example, if a cookie set by *http://www.acme.com/catalog/widgets/index.html* has its path set to "/catalog", that cookie is also visible to *http://www.acme.com/catalog/order.html*. Or, if the path is set to "/", the cookie is visible to any page on the *www.acme.com* web server.

By default, cookies are accessible only to pages on the same web server from which they were set. Large web sites may want cookies to be shared across multiple web servers, however. For example, the server at *order.acme.com* may need to read cookie values set from *catalog.acme.com*. This is where the third cookie attribute, `domain`, comes in. If a cookie created by a page on *catalog.acme.com* sets its `path` attribute to "/" and its `domain` attribute to ".acme.com", that cookie is available to all web pages on *catalog.acme.com*, *orders.acme.com*, and any other server in the *acme.com* domain. If the `domain` attribute is not set for a cookie, the default is the hostname of the web server that serves the page. Note that you cannot set the domain of a cookie to a domain other than the domain of your server.

The fourth and final cookie attribute is a boolean attribute named secure that specifies how cookie values are transmitted over the network. By default, cookies are insecure, which means that they are transmitted over a normal, insecure HTTP connection. If a cookie is marked secure, however, it is transmitted only when the browser and server are connected via HTTPS or another secure protocol.

Note that the expires, path, domain, and secure attributes of a cookie are not JavaScript object properties. We'll see later in the chapter how you set these cookie atributes.

If you are interested in the complete technical details of how cookies work, see *http://www.netscape.com/newsref/std/cookie_spec.html*. This document is the original specification for HTTP cookies; it contains low-level details that are more suitable to CGI programming than to JavaScript programming. The following sections discuss how you can set and query cookie values in JavaScript and how you can specify the expires, path, domain, and secure attributes of a cookie.

16.2 Storing Cookies

To associate a transient cookie value with the current document, simply set the cookie property to a string of the form:

```
name=value
```

For example:

```
document.cookie = "version=" + escape(document.lastModified);
```

The next time you read the cookie property, the name/value pair you stored is included in the list of cookies for the document. Cookie values may not include semicolons, commas, or whitespace. For this reason, you may want to use the JavaScript escape( ) function to encode the value before storing it in the cookie. If you do this, you'll have to use the corresponding unescape( ) function when you read the cookie value.

A cookie written as described above lasts for the current web-browsing session but is lost when the user exits the browser. To create a cookie that can last across browser sessions, include an expiration date by setting the expires attribute. You can do this by setting the cookie property to a string of the form:

```
name=value; expires=date
```

When setting an expiration date like this, *date* should be a date specification in the format written by Date.toGMTString( ). For example, to create a cookie that persists for a year, you can use code like this:

```
var nextyear = new Date( );
nextyear.setFullYear(nextyear.getFullYear( ) + 1);
document.cookie = "version=" + document.lastModified +
                  "; expires=" + nextyear.toGMTString( );
```

Similarly, you can set the path, domain, and secure attributes of a cookie by appending strings of the following format to the cookie value before that value is written to the cookie property:

```
; path=path
; domain=domain
; secure
```

To change the value of a cookie, set its value again, using the same name and the new value. Use whatever values are appropriate for `expires`, `path`, and the other attributes. To delete a cookie, set it again using the same name, an arbitrary value, and an expiration date that has already passed. Note that the browser is not required to delete expired cookies immediately, so a cookie may remain in the browser's cookie file past its expiration date.

16.2.1 Cookie Limitations

Cookies are intended for infrequent storage of small amounts of data. They are not intended as a general-purpose communication or data-transfer mechanism, so you should use them in moderation. Web browsers are not required to retain more than 300 cookies total, 20 cookies per web server (for the entire server, not just for your page or site on the server), or 4 kilobytes of data per cookie (both name and value count toward this 4-kilobyte limit). The most restrictive of these is the 20 cookies per server limit. In order to avoid reaching that limit, you may want to avoid using a separate cookie for each state variable you want to save. Instead, you can encode several related state variables into a single named cookie. Example 16-1, later in this chapter, shows one way that this can be done.

16.3 Reading Cookies

When you use the `cookie` property in a JavaScript expression, the value it returns is a string that contains all the cookies that apply to the current document.[*] The string is a list of *name=value* pairs separated by semicolons, where *name* is the name of a cookie and *value* is its string value. This value does not include any of the attributes that may have been set for the cookie. To determine the value of a particular named cookie, you can use the `String.indexOf( )` and `String.substring( )` methods, or you can use `String.split( )` to break the string into individual cookies.

Once you have extracted the value of a cookie from the `cookie` property, you must interpret that value based on whatever format or encoding was used by the cookie's creator. For example, the cookie might store multiple pieces of information in colon-separated fields. In this case, you would have to use appropriate string methods to extract the various fields of information. Don't forget to use the `unescape( )` function on the cookie value if it was encoded using the `escape( )` function.

The following code shows how you might read the `cookie` property, extract a single cookie from it, and use the value of that cookie:

```
// Read the cookie property. This returns all cookies for this document.
var allcookies = document.cookie;
```

[*] In Internet Explorer 3, the `cookie` property works only for Document objects that were retrieved using the HTTP protocol. Documents retrieved from the local filesystem or via other protocols, such as FTP, cannot have cookies associated with them.

```
// Look for the start of the cookie named "version"
var pos = allcookies.indexOf("version=");

// If we find a cookie by that name, extract and use its value
if (pos != -1) {
    var start = pos + 8;                            // Start of cookie value
    var end = allcookies.indexOf(";", start);  // End of cookie value
    if (end == -1) end = allcookies.length;
    var value = allcookies.substring(start, end);  // Extract the value
    value = unescape(value);                        // Decode it

    // Now that we have the cookie value, we can use it.
    // In this case, the cookie was previously set to the modification
    // date of the document, so we can use it to see if the document has
    // changed since the user last visited.
    if (value != document.lastModified)
        alert("This document has changed since you were last here");
}
```

Note that the string returned when you read the value of the `cookie` property does not contain any information about the various cookie attributes. The `cookie` property allows you to set those attributes, but it does not allow you to read them.

16.4 Cookie Example

Example 16-1 brings together all the aspects of cookies we have discussed so far. First, the example defines a Cookie class. When you create a Cookie object, you specify a Document object, a name for the cookie, and, optionally, an expiration time, a path, a domain, and a boolean value that indicates whether the cookie should be secure. After creating a Cookie object, you can set arbitrary string properties on this object; the values of these properties are the values stored in the cookie.

The Cookie class defines three methods. The `store( )` method loops through all of the user-defined properties of the Cookie object and concatenates their names and values into a single string that serves as the value of the cookie. The `load( )` method of a Cookie object reads the `cookie` property of the Document object to obtain the values of all the cookies for the document. It searches this string to find the value of the named cookie and then parses this value into individual names and values, which it stores as properties of the Cookie object. Finally, the `remove( )` method of the Cookie object deletes the specified cookie from the document.

After defining the Cookie class, Example 16-1 demonstrates a useful and elegant way to use cookies. The code is somewhat complicated but is worth studying carefully. You may want to start with the test program at the end of the example; it shows a typical usage of the Cookie class.

Example 16-1. A utility class for working with cookies

```
<script language="JavaScript1.1">
// The constructor function: creates a Cookie object for the specified
```

Example 16-1. A utility class for working with cookies (continued)

```
// document, with a specified name and optional attributes.
// Arguments:
//   document: The Document object for which the cookie is stored. Required.
//   name:     A string that specifies a name for the cookie. Required.
//   hours:    An optional number that specifies the number of hours from now
//             after which the cookie should expire.
//   path:     An optional string that specifies the cookie path attribute.
//   domain:   An optional string that specifies the cookie domain attribute.
//   secure:   An optional boolean value that, if true, requests a secure cookie.
//
function Cookie(document, name, hours, path, domain, secure)
{
    // All the predefined properties of this object begin with '$'
    // to distinguish them from other properties, which are the values to
    // be stored in the cookie
    this.$document = document;
    this.$name = name;
    if (hours)
        this.$expiration = new Date((new Date()).getTime( ) + hours*3600000);
    else this.$expiration = null;
    if (path) this.$path = path; else this.$path = null;
    if (domain) this.$domain = domain; else this.$domain = null;
    if (secure) this.$secure = true; else this.$secure = false;
}

// This function is the store( ) method of the Cookie object
Cookie.prototype.store = function ( ) {
    // First, loop through the properties of the Cookie object and
    // put together the value of the cookie. Since cookies use the
    // equals sign and semicolons as separators, we'll use colons
    // and ampersands for the individual state variables we store
    // within a single cookie value. Note that we escape the value
    // of each state variable, in case it contains punctuation or other
    // illegal characters.
    var cookieval = "";
    for(var prop in this) {
        // Ignore properties with names that begin with '$' and also methods
        if ((prop.charAt(0) == '$') || ((typeof this[prop]) == 'function'))
            continue;
        if (cookieval != "") cookieval += '&';
        cookieval += prop + ':' + escape(this[prop]);
    }

    // Now that we have the value of the cookie, put together the
    // complete cookie string, which includes the name and the various
    // attributes specified when the Cookie object was created
    var cookie = this.$name + '=' + cookieval;
    if (this.$expiration)
        cookie += '; expires=' + this.$expiration.toGMTString( );
    if (this.$path) cookie += '; path=' + this.$path;
    if (this.$domain) cookie += '; domain=' + this.$domain;
    if (this.$secure) cookie += '; secure';
```

Example 16-1. A utility class for working with cookies (continued)

```
    // Now store the cookie by setting the magic Document.cookie property
    this.$document.cookie = cookie;
}

// This function is the load( ) method of the Cookie object
Cookie.prototype.load = function( ) {
    // First, get a list of all cookies that pertain to this document
    // We do this by reading the magic Document.cookie property
    var allcookies = this.$document.cookie;
    if (allcookies == "") return false;

    // Now extract just the named cookie from that list
    var start = allcookies.indexOf(this.$name + '=');
    if (start == -1) return false;   // Cookie not defined for this page
    start += this.$name.length + 1;  // Skip name and equals sign
    var end = allcookies.indexOf(';', start);
    if (end == -1) end = allcookies.length;
    var cookieval = allcookies.substring(start, end);

    // Now that we've extracted the value of the named cookie, we
    // must break that value down into individual state variable
    // names and values. The name/value pairs are separated from each
    // other by ampersands, and the individual names and values are
    // separated from each other by colons. We use the split( ) method
    // to parse everything.
    var a = cookieval.split('&');    // Break it into an array of name/value pairs
    for(var i=0; i < a.length; i++)  // Break each pair into an array
        a[i] = a[i].split(':');

    // Now that we've parsed the cookie value, set all the names and values
    // of the state variables in this Cookie object. Note that we unescape( )
    // the property value, because we called escape( ) when we stored it.
    for(var i = 0; i < a.length; i++) {
        this[a[i][0]] = unescape(a[i][1]);
    }

    // We're done, so return the success code
    return true;
}

// This function is the remove( ) method of the Cookie object
Cookie.prototype.remove = function( ) {
    var cookie;
    cookie = this.$name + '=';
    if (this.$path) cookie += '; path=' + this.$path;
    if (this.$domain) cookie += '; domain=' + this.$domain;
    cookie += '; expires=Fri, 02-Jan-1970 00:00:00 GMT';

    this.$document.cookie = cookie;
}
```

Example 16-1. A utility class for working with cookies (continued)

```
//===================================================================
//  The previous code is the definition of the Cookie class.
//  The following code is a sample use of that class.
//===================================================================

// Create the cookie we'll use to save state for this web page.
// Since we're using the default path, this cookie will be accessible
// to all web pages in the same directory as this file or "below" it.
// Therefore, it should have a name that is unique among those pages.
// Note that we set the expiration to 10 days in the future.
var visitordata = new Cookie(document, "name_color_count_state", 240);

// First, try to read data stored in the cookie. If the cookie is not
// defined, or if it doesn't contain the data we need, then query the
// user for that data.
if (!visitordata.load() || !visitordata.name || !visitordata.color) {
    visitordata.name = prompt("What is your name:", "");
    visitordata.color = prompt("What is your favorite color:", "");
}

// Keep track of how many times this user has visited the page:
if (visitordata.visits == null) visitordata.visits = 0;
visitordata.visits++;

// Store the cookie values, even if they were already stored, so that the
// expiration date will be reset to 10 days from this most recent visit.
// Also, store them again to save the updated visits state variable.
visitordata.store();

// Now we can use the state variables we read:
document.write('<font size="7" color="' + visitordata.color + '">' +
               'Welcome, ' + visitordata.name + '!' +
               '</font>' +
               '<p>You have visited ' + visitordata.visits + ' times.');
</script>

<form>
<input type="button" value="Forget My Name" onclick="visitordata.remove();">
</form>
```

CHAPTER 17
The Document Object Model

A *document object model* (DOM) is an application programming interface (API) for representing a document (such as an HTML document) and accessing and manipulating the various elements (such as HTML tags and strings of text) that make up that document. JavaScript-enabled web browsers have always defined a document object model; a web-browser DOM may specify, for example, that the forms in an HTML document are accessible through the `forms[]` array of the Document object.

In this chapter, we'll discuss the W3C DOM, a standard document object model defined by the World Wide Web Consortium and implemented (at least partially) by Netscape 6 and Internet Explorer 5 and 6. This DOM standard* is a full-featured superset of the traditional web-browser DOM. It represents HTML (and XML) documents in a tree structure and defines properties and methods for traversing the tree and examining and modifying its nodes. Other portions of the standard specify techniques for defining event handlers for the nodes of a document, working with the style sheets of a document, and manipulating contiguous ranges of a document.

This chapter begins with an overview of the DOM standard and then describes the core portions of the standard for working with HTML documents. The discussion of the core standard is followed by short sections that explain the DOM-like features of Internet Explorer 4 and Netscape 4. The chapter ends with an overview of two optional parts of the DOM standard that are closely related to the core. Later chapters cover advanced DOM features for working with style sheets and events.

17.1 An Overview of the DOM

The DOM API is not particularly complicated, but before we can begin our discussion of programming with the DOM, there are a number of things you should understand about the DOM architecture.

* Technically, the W3C issues "recommendations." These recommendations serve the same purpose and carry the same weight as international standards do, however, and are called "standards" in this book.

17.1.1 Representing Documents as Trees

HTML documents have a hierarchical structure that is represented in the DOM as a tree structure. The nodes of the tree represent the various types of content in a document. The tree representation of an HTML document primarily contains nodes representing elements or tags such as <body> and <p> and nodes representing strings of text. An HTML document may also contain nodes representing HTML comments.* Consider the following simple HTML document:

```
<html>
  <head>
    <title>Sample Document</title>
  </head>
  <body>
    <h1>An HTML Document</h1>
    <p>This is a <i>simple</i> document.
  </body>
</html>
```

The DOM representation of this document is the tree pictured in Figure 17-1.

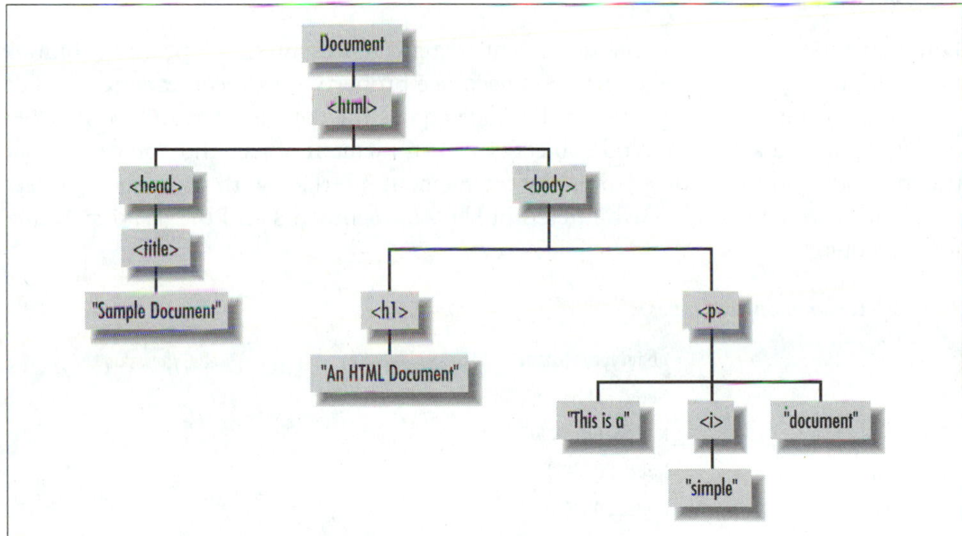

Figure 17-1. The tree representation of an HTML document

If you are not already familiar with tree structures in computer programming, it is helpful to know that they borrow terminology from family trees. The node directly

* The DOM can also be used to represent XML documents, which have a more complex syntax than HTML documents, and the tree representation of such a document may contain nodes that represent XML entity references, processing instructions, CDATA sections, and so on. Most client-side JavaScript programmers do not need to use the DOM with XML documents, and although the XML-specific features of the DOM are covered in the DOM reference section, they are not emphasized in this chapter.

above a node is the *parent* of that node. The nodes one level directly below another node are the *children* of that node. Nodes at the same level, and with the same parent, are *siblings*. The set of nodes any number of levels below another node are the *descendants* of that node. And the parent, grandparent, and all other nodes above a node are the *ancestors* of that node.

17.1.2 Nodes

The DOM tree structure illustrated in Figure 17-1 is represented as a tree of various types of Node objects. The Node interface* defines properties and methods for traversing and manipulating the tree. The `childNodes` property of a Node object returns a list of children of the node, and the `firstChild`, `lastChild`, `nextSibling`, `previousSibling`, and `parentNode` properties provide a way to traverse the tree of nodes. Methods such as `appendChild()`, `removeChild()`, `replaceChild()`, and `insertBefore()` enable you to add and remove nodes from the document tree. We'll see examples of the use of these properties and methods later in this chapter.

17.1.2.1 Types of nodes

Different types of nodes in the document tree are represented by specific subinterfaces of Node. Every Node object has a `nodeType` property that specifies what kind of node it is. If the `nodeType` property of a node equals the constant `Node.ELEMENT_NODE`, for example, you know the Node object is also an Element object and you can use all the methods and properties defined by the Element interface with it. Table 17-1 lists the node types commonly encountered in HTML documents and the `nodeType` value for each one.

Table 17-1. Common node types

Interface	nodeType constant	nodeType value
Element	Node.ELEMENT_NODE	1
Text	Node.TEXT_NODE	3
Document	Node.DOCUMENT_NODE	9
Comment	Node.COMMENT_NODE	8
DocumentFragment	Node.DOCUMENT_FRAGMENT_NODE	11
Attr	Node.ATTRIBUTE_NODE	2

The Node at the root of the DOM tree is a Document object. The `documentElement` property of this object refers to an Element object that represents the root element of

* The DOM standard defines interfaces, not classes. If you are not familiar with the term *interface* in object-oriented programming, you can think of it as an abstract kind of class. We'll describe the difference in more detail later in this DOM overview.

the document. For HTML documents, this is the <html> tag that is either explicit or implicit in the document. (The Document node may have other children, such as Comment nodes, in addition to the root element.) The bulk of a DOM tree consists of Element objects, which represent tags such as <html> and <i>, and Text objects, which represent strings of text. If the document parser preserves comments, those comments are represented in the DOM tree by Comment objects. Figure 17-2 shows a partial class hierarchy for these and other core DOM interfaces.

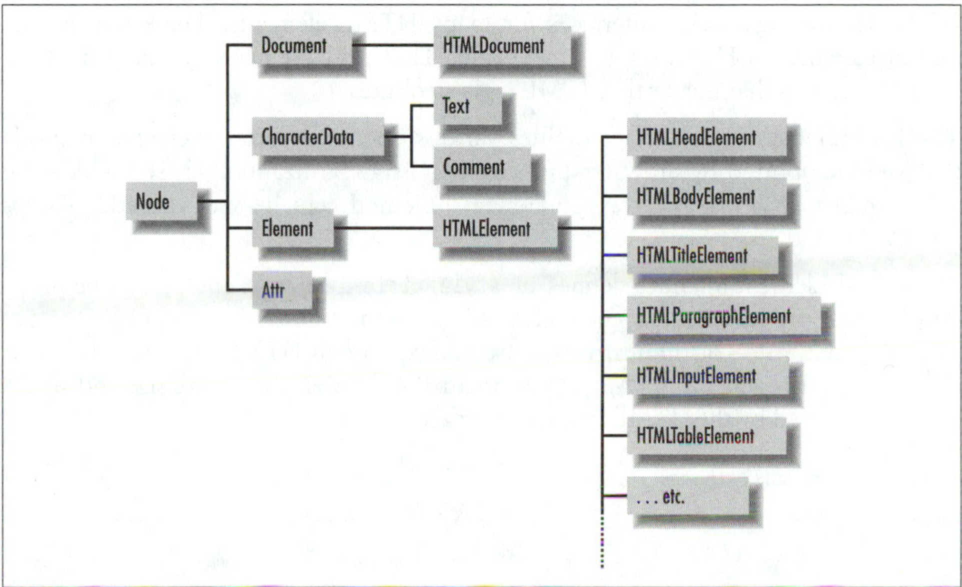

Figure 17-2. A partial class hierarchy of the core DOM API

17.1.2.2 Attributes

The attributes of an element (such as the `src` and `width` attributes of an <img> tag) may be queried, set, and deleted using the `getAttribute()`, `setAttribute()`, and `removeAttribute()` methods of the Element interface.

Another, more awkward way to work with attributes is with the `getAttributeNode()` method, which returns an Attr object representing an attribute and its value. (One reason to use this more awkward technique is that the Attr interface defines a `specified` property that allows you to determine whether the attribute is literally specified in the document, or whether its value is a default value.) The Attr interface appears in Figure 17-2, and it is a type of node. Note, however, that Attr objects do not appear in the `childNodes[]` array of an element and are not directly part of the document tree in the way that Element and Text nodes are. The DOM specification allows Attr nodes to be accessed through the `attributes[]` array of the Node interface, but Microsoft's Internet Explorer defines a different and incompatible `attributes[]` array that makes it impossible to use this feature portably.

17.1.3 The DOM HTML API

The DOM standard was designed for use with both XML and HTML documents. The core DOM API—the Node, Element, Document, and other interfaces—are relatively generic and apply to both types of documents. The DOM standard also includes interfaces that are specific to HTML documents. As you can see from Figure 17-2, HTMLDocument is an HTML-specific subinterface of Document, and HTMLElement is an HTML-specific subinterface of Element. Furthermore, the DOM defines tag-specific interfaces for many HTML elements. These tag-specific interfaces, such as HTMLBodyElement and HTMLTitleElement, typically define a set of properties that mirror the HTML tag's attributes.

The HTMLDocument interface defines various document properties and methods that were supported by browsers prior to W3C standardization. These include the `location` property, `forms[]` array, and `write()` method, which are described in Chapters 13, 14, and 15.

The HTMLElement interface defines `id`, `style`, `title`, `lang`, `dir`, and `className` properties. These properties allow convenient access to the values of the `id`, `style`, `title`, `lang`, `dir`, and `class` attributes, which are allowed on all HTML tags. A number of HTML tags, listed in Table 17-2, accept no attributes other than these six, and so are fully represented by the HTMLElement interface.

Table 17-2. Simple HTML tags

`<abbr>`	`<acronym>`	`<address>`	`<b>`	`<bdo>`
`<big>`	`<center>`	`<cite>`	`<code>`	`<dd>`
`<dfn>`	`<dt>`	`<em>`	`<i>`	`<kbd>`
`<noframes>`	`<noscript>`	`<s>`	`<samp>`	`<small>`
`<span>`	`<strike>`	`<strong>`	`<sub>`	`<sup>`
`<tt>`	`<u>`	`<var>`		

All other HTML tags have corresponding interfaces defined by the HTML portion of the DOM specification. For many HTML tags, these interfaces do nothing more than provide a set of properties that mirror their HTML attributes. For example, the `<ul>` tag has a corresponding HTMLUListElement interface, and the `<body>` tag has a corresponding HTMLBodyElement interface. Because these interfaces simply define properties that are standardized by the HTML standard, they are not documented in detail in this book. You can safely assume that the HTMLElement object that represents a particular HTML tag has properties for each of the standard attributes for that tag (but see the naming conventions described in the next section). Note that the DOM standard defines properties for HTML attributes as a "convenience" to script writers. The general (and possibly preferred) way to query and set attribute values is with the `getAttribute()` and `setAttribute()` methods of the Element object.

Some of the interfaces defined in the HTML DOM define additional properties or methods, other than those that mirror HTML attribute values. For example, the HTMLInputElement interface defines `focus()` and `blur()` methods, and the HTMLFormElement interface defines `submit()` and `reset()` methods and a `length` property. Methods and properties like these typically predate DOM standardization and have been made part of the DOM standard for backward compatibility with existing practice. Interfaces like these are documented in the DOM reference section. You can usually also find information about the "existing practice" portions of these interfaces in the client-side reference section, although this information is typically referenced under a name that also predates DOM standardization; for example, you can find information about HTMLFormElement and HTMLInputElement in the client-side reference section under "Form" and "Input."

17.1.3.1 HTML naming conventions

When working with the HTML-specific portions of the DOM standard, you should be aware of some simple naming conventions. Properties of the HTML-specific interfaces begin with lowercase letters. If the property name consists of multiple words, the first letters of the second and subsequent words are capitalized. Thus, the `maxlength` attribute of the `<input>` tag translates into the `maxLength` property of HTMLInputElement.

When an HTML attribute name conflicts with a JavaScript keyword, it is prefixed with the string "html" to avoid the conflict. Thus, the `for` attribute of the `<label>` tag translates to the `htmlFor` property of the HTMLLabelElement. An exception to this rule is the `class` attribute (which can be specified for any HTML element); it translates to the `className` property of HTMLElement.*

17.1.4 DOM Levels and Features

There are two versions, or "levels," of the DOM standard. DOM Level 1 was standardized in October, 1998. It defines the core DOM interfaces, such as Node, Element, Attr, and Document, and also defines various HTML-specific interfaces. DOM Level 2 was standardized in November, 2000.† In addition to some updates to the core interfaces, this new version of the DOM is greatly expanded to define standard APIs for working with document events and CSS style sheets and to provide additional tools for working with ranges of documents. As of this writing, the DOM Working Group at the W3C is working to standardize DOM Level 3. You may also

* The name `className` is misleading, because in addition to specifying a single class name, this property (and the HTML attribute it represents) can also specify a space-separated list of class names.

† Except for the HTML-specific portions of the standard, which are still at the "working draft" stage as of November 2001. Fortunately, the current working draft is presumed stable and includes only minor changes (documented in this book) from the HTML-specific portions of the Level 1 standard.

sometimes see a reference to DOM Level 0. This term does not refer to any formal standard but is used to refer informally to the common features of the HTML document object models implemented by Netscape and Internet Explorer prior to W3C standardization.

As of Level 2, the DOM standard has been "modularized." The core module, which defines the basic tree structure of a document with the Document, Node, Element, and Text interfaces (among others), is the only required module. All other modules are optional and may or may not be supported, depending on the needs of the implementation. The DOM implementation of a web browser would obviously support the HTML module, since web documents are written in HTML. Browsers that support CSS style sheets typically support the StyleSheets and CSS modules, because (as we'll see in Chapter 18) CSS styles play a crucial role in Dynamic HTML programming. Similarly, since almost all interesting client-side JavaScript programming requires event-handling capabilities, you would expect web browsers to support the Events module of the DOM specification. Unfortunately, the Events module was only recently defined by the DOM Level 2 specification and is not yet widely supported at the time of this writing. We'll see a complete list of DOM Level 2 modules in the next section.

17.1.5 DOM Conformance

At the time of this writing, no browser is completely conformant to the DOM standard. Recent releases of Mozilla come closest, and complete DOM Level 2 conformance is a goal of the Mozilla project. Netscape 6.1 does a good job of conforming to the most important Level 2 modules, and Netscape 6.0 does an adequate job but has gaps in its coverage. Internet Explorer 6 is mostly compliant (with at least one annoying exception) with the Level 1 DOM, but does not support many of the Level 2 modules—most notably the Events module, which is the topic of Chapter 19. Internet Explorer 5 and 5.5 have substantial gaps in their conformance but support key DOM Level 1 methods well enough to run most of the examples in this chapter. The Macintosh version of IE 5 has considerably better support for the DOM than the Windows version of IE 5.

In addition to Mozilla, Netscape, and Internet Explorer, several other browsers offer at least partial support for the DOM. The number of available browsers has become too large, and the rate of change in the area of standards support has grown too fast, for this book to even attempt to provide definitive statements about which browsers support which particular DOM features. Therefore, you'll have to rely on other information sources to determine exactly how conformant the DOM implementation in any particular web browser is.

One source for conformance information is the implementation itself. In a conformant implementation, the `implementation` property of the Document object refers to a DOMImplementation object that defines a method named `hasFeature()`. You can use this method (if it exists) to ask an implementation whether it supports a specific feature (or module) of the DOM standard. For example, to determine whether the DOM implementation in a web browser supports the basic DOM Level 1 interfaces for working with HTML documents, you could use the following code:

```
if (document.implementation &&
    document.implementation.hasFeature &&
    document.implementation.hasFeature("html", "1.0")) {
    // The browser claims to support Level 1 Core and HTML interfaces
}
```


The `hasFeature()` method takes two arguments: the first is the name of the feature to check, and the second is a version number, expressed as a string. It returns `true` if the specified version of the specified feature is supported. Table 17-3 lists the feature name/version number pairs that are defined by the DOM Level 1 and Level 2 standards. Note that the feature names are case-insensitive: you can capitalize them any way you choose. The fourth column of the table specifies what other features are required for support of a feature and are therefore implied by a return value of `true`. For example, if `hasFeature()` indicates that the MouseEvents module is supported, this implies that UIEvents is also supported, which in turn implies that the Events, Views, and Core modules are supported.

Table 17-3. Features that can be tested with hasFeature()

Feature name	Version	Description	Implies
HTML	1.0	Level 1 Core and HTML interfaces	
XML	1.0	Level 1 Core and XML interfaces	
Core	2.0	Level 2 Core interfaces	
HTML	2.0	Level 2 HTML interfaces	Core
XML	2.0	Level 2 XML-specific interfaces	Core
Views	2.0	AbstractView interface	Core
StyleSheets	2.0	Generic style-sheet traversal	Core
CSS	2.0	CSS styles	Core, Views
CSS2	2.0	CSS2Properties interface	CSS
Events	2.0	Event-handling infrastructure	Core
UIEvents	2.0	User-interface events (plus Events and Views)	Events, Views
MouseEvents	2.0	Mouse events	UIEvents
HTMLEvents	2.0	HTML events	Events
MutationEvents	2.0	Document mutation events	Events
Range	2.0	Document range interfaces	Core
Traversal	2.0	Document traversal interfaces	Core

In Internet Explorer 6 (on Windows), `hasFeature()` returns `true` only for the feature HTML and Version 1.0. It does not report compliance to any of the other features listed in Table 17-3 (although, as we'll see in Chapter 18, it supports the most common uses of the CSS2 module.) In Netscape 6.1, `hasFeature()` returns `true` for most feature names and version numbers, with the notable exceptions of the Traversal and MutationEvents features. It returns `false` for the Core and CSS2 features with Version 2.0, indicating incomplete support (even though support for these features is quite good).

This book documents the interfaces that make up all of the DOM modules listed in Table 17-3. The Core, HTML, Traversal, and Range modules are covered in this chapter. The StyleSheets, CSS, and CSS2 modules are covered in Chapter 18, and the various Event modules (except MutationEvents) are covered in Chapter 19. The DOM reference section includes complete coverage of all modules.

The `hasFeature()` method is not always perfectly reliable. As previously noted, IE 6 reports Level 1 compliance to HTML features even though there are some problems with its compliance. On the other hand, Netscape 6.1 reports noncompliance to the Level 2 Core feature even though it is mostly compliant. In both cases, you need more detailed information about exactly what is and is not compliant. This is exactly the type of information that is too voluminous and volatile to include in a printed book.

If you are an active web developer, you undoubtedly already know or will discover many browser-specific support details on your own. There are also resources on the Web that can help you. Most importantly, the W3C (in collaboration with the U.S. National Institute of Standards and Technology) is working on developing an open source test suite for DOM implementations. At the time of this writing, the test suite effort is just getting off the ground, but it ought to prove to be an invaluable resource for fine-grained compliance testing of DOM implementations. See *http://www.w3c.org/DOM/Test/* for details.

The Mozilla organization has a set of test suites for a variety of standards, including DOM Level 1 (available at *http://www.mozilla.org/quality/browser_sc.html*). Netscape has published a test suite that includes some DOM Level 2 tests (available at *http://developer.netscape.com/evangelism/tools/testsuites/*). Netscape has also published a partisan (and dated) comparison of DOM compliance of an early Mozilla release versus IE 5.5 (available at *http://home.netscape.com/browsers/future/standards.html*). Finally, you can also find compatibility and compliance information at independent sites on the Web. One notable site is published by Peter-Paul Koch. You can find a link to his DOM Compatibility Table from his main JavaScript page *(http://www.xs4all.nl/~ppk/js/)*.

17.1.5.1 DOM conformance in Internet Explorer

Because IE is the most widely used web browser, a few special notes about its compliance to the DOM specifications are appropriate here. IE 5 and later versions support the Level 1 Core and HTML features well enough to run the examples in this chapter, and they support the key Level 2 CSS features well enough to run most of the examples in Chapter 18. Unfortunately, IE 5, 5.5, and 6 do not support the DOM Level 2 Events module, even though Microsoft participated in the definition of this module and had ample time to implement it for IE 6. As we'll see in Chapter 19, event handling is crucial for client-side event handling, and IE's lack of support for the standard event model impedes the development of advanced client-side web applications.

Although IE 6 claims (through its `hasFeature()` method) to support the Core and HTML interfaces of the DOM Level 1 standard, this support is actually incomplete. The most egregious problem, and the one you are most likely to encounter, is a minor but annoying one: IE does not support the node-type constants defined by the Node interface. Recall that each node in a document has a `nodeType` property that specifies what type of node it is. The DOM specification also says that the Node interface defines constants that represent each of the defined node types. For example, the constant `Node.ELEMENT_NODE` represents an Element node. In IE (at least as high as version 6), these constants simply do not exist.

The examples in this chapter have been modified to work around this problem by using integer literals instead of the corresponding symbolic constants. For example, you'll see code like this:

```
if (n.nodeType == 1 /*Node.ELEMENT_NODE*/)  // Check if n is an Element
```

It is good programming style to use constants instead of hardcoded integer literals in your code, and if you'd like to do this portably, you can include the following code in your programs to define these constants if they are missing:

```
if (!window.Node) {
    var Node = {            // If there is no Node object, define one
        ELEMENT_NODE: 1,    // with the following properties and values.
        ATTRIBUTE_NODE: 2,  // Note that these are HTML node types only.
        TEXT_NODE: 3,       // For XML-specific nodes, you need to add
        COMMENT_NODE: 8,    // other constants here.
        DOCUMENT_NODE: 9,
        DOCUMENT_FRAGMENT_NODE: 11
    }
}
```

17.1.6 Language-Independent DOM Interfaces

Although the DOM standard grew out of a desire to have a common API for dynamic HTML programming, the DOM is not of interest only to web scripters. In fact, the standard is currently most heavily used by server-side Java and C++ programs that parse and manipulate XML documents. Because of its many uses, the DOM standard is defined to be language-independent. This book describes only the JavaScript binding of the DOM API, but you should be aware of a few other points. First, note that object properties in the JavaScript binding are typically mapped to pairs of get/set methods in other language bindings. Thus, when a Java programmer asks you about the getFirstChild( ) method of the Node interface, you need to understand that the JavaScript binding of the Node API doesn't define a getFirstChild( ) method. Instead, it simply defines a firstChild property, and reading the value of this property in JavaScript is equal to calling getFirstChild( ) in Java.

Another important feature of the JavaScript binding of the DOM API is that certain DOM objects behave like JavaScript arrays. If an interface defines a method named item( ), objects that implement that interface behave like read-only numerical arrays. For example, suppose you've obtained a NodeList object by reading the childNodes property of a node. You can obtain the individual Node objects in the list by passing the desired node number to the item( ) method, or, more simply, you can simply treat the NodeList object as an array and index it directly. The following code illustrates these two options:

```
var n = document.documentElement;  // This is a Node object.
var children = n.childNodes;       // This is a NodeList object.
var head = children.item(0);       // Here is one way to use a NodeList.
var body = children[1];            // But this way is easier!
```

Similarly, if a DOM object has a namedItem( ) method, passing a string to this method is the same as using the string as an array index for the object. For example, the following lines of code are all equivalent ways to access a form element:

```
var f = document.forms.namedItem("myform");
var g = document.forms["myform"];
var h = document.forms.myform;
```

Because the DOM standard may be used in a variety of ways, the architects of the standard were careful to define the DOM API in a way that would not restrict the ability of others to implement the API as they saw fit. Specifically, the DOM standard defines interfaces instead of classes. In object-oriented programming, a class is a fixed data type that must be implemented exactly as specified. An interface, on the other hand, is a collection of methods and properties that must be implemented together. Thus, an implementation of the DOM is free to define whatever classes it sees fit, but those classes must define the methods and properties of the various DOM interfaces.

This architecture has a couple of important implications. First, the class names used in an implementation might not correspond directly to the interface names used in the DOM standard (and in this book). Second, a single class may implement more than one interface. For example, consider the Document object. This object is an instance of some class defined by the web browser implementation. We don't know what the specific class is, but we do know that it implements the Document interface; that is, all methods and properties defined by Document are available to us through the Document object. Since web browsers work with HTML documents, we also know that the Document object implements the HTMLDocument interface and that all methods and properties defined by that interface are available to us as well. Furthermore, if a web browser supports CSS style sheets and implements the DOM CSS module, the

Document object also implements the DocumentStyle and DocumentCSS DOM interfaces. And if the web browser supports the Events and Views modules, Document implements the DocumentEvent and DocumentView interfaces as well.

Because the DOM is broken into independent modules, it defines a number of minor add-on interfaces, such as DocumentStyle, DocumentEvent, and DocumentView, that define only one or two methods each. Interfaces such as these are never implemented independently of the core Document interface, and for this reason, I do not document them independently. When you look up the Document interface in the DOM reference section, you'll find that it also lists the methods and properties of its various add-on interfaces. Similarly, if you look up one of the add-on interfaces, you'll simply find a cross-reference to the core interface with which it is associated. The exception to this rule is when the add-on interface is a complex one. For example, the HTMLDocument interface is always implemented by the same object that implements the Document object, but because it adds substantial new functionality, I have given it a reference page of its own.

Another important fact you need to understand is that since the DOM standard defines interfaces instead of classes, it does not define any constructor methods. If you want to create a new Text object to insert into a document, for example, you cannot simply say:

```
var t = new Text("this is a new text node");  // No such constructor!
```

Since it cannot define constructors, the DOM standard instead defines a number of useful *factory methods* for creating objects in the Document interface. So, to create a new Text node for a document, you would write the following:

```
var t = document.createTextNode("this is a new text node");
```

Factory methods defined by the DOM have names that begin with the word "create". In addition to the factory methods defined by Document, a few others are defined by DOMImplementation and available as `document.implementation`.

17.2 Using the Core DOM API

Now that we've studied the tree structure of documents and seen how the tree is composed of Node objects, we can move on to study the Node object and document trees in more detail. As I noted previously, the core DOM API is not terribly complex. The following sections contain examples that demonstrate how you can use it to accomplish common tasks.

17.2.1 Traversing a Document

As we've already discussed, the DOM represents an HTML document as a tree of Node objects. With any tree structure, one of the most common things to do is traverse the tree, examining each node of the tree in turn. Example 17-1 shows one way to do this. It is a JavaScript function that recursively examines a node and all its children, adding up the number of HTML tags (i.e., Element nodes) it encounters in the course of the traversal. Note the use of the `childNodes` property of a node. The value of this property is a NodeList object, which behaves (in JavaScript) like an array of Node objects. Thus, the function can enumerate all the children of a given node by looping through the elements of the `childNodes[]` array. By recursing, the function enumerates not just all children of a given node, but all nodes in the tree of nodes. Note that this function also demonstrates the use of the `nodeType` property to determine the type of each node.

Example 17-1. Traversing the nodes of a document

```
<head>
<script>
// This function is passed a DOM Node object and checks to see if that node
// represents an HTML tag; i.e., if the node is an Element object. It
// recursively calls itself on each of the children of the node, testing
// them in the same way. It returns the total number of Element objects
// it encounters. If you invoke this function by passing it the
// Document object, it traverses the entire DOM tree.
function countTags(n) {                             // n is a Node
    var numtags = 0;                                // Initialize the tag counter
    if (n.nodeType == 1 /*Node.ELEMENT_NODE*/)      // Check if n is an Element
        numtags++;                                  // Increment the counter if so
    var children = n.childNodes;                    // Now get all children of n
    for(var i=0; i < children.length; i++) {        // Loop through the children
        numtags += countTags(children[i]);          // Recurse on each one
    }
    return numtags;                                 // Return the total number of tags
}
</script>
</head>
<!-- Here's an example of how the countTags() function might be used -->
<body onload="alert('This document has ' + countTags(document) + ' tags')">
This is a <i>sample</i> document.
</body>
```

Another point to notice about Example 17-1 is that the `countTags()` function it defines is invoked from the `onload` event handler, so that it is not called until the document is completely loaded. This is a general requirement when working with the DOM: you cannot traverse or manipulate the document tree until the document has been fully loaded.

In addition to the `childNodes` property, the Node interface defines a few other useful properties. `firstChild` and `lastChild` refer to the first and last children of a node, and `nextSibling` and `previousSibling` refer to adjacent siblings of a node. (Two nodes are siblings if they have the same parent node.) These properties provide another way to loop through the children of a node, demonstrated in Example 17-2. This example counts the number of characters in all the Text nodes within the

<body> of the document. Notice the way the `countCharacters()` function uses the `firstChild` and `nextSibling` properties to loop through the children of a node.

Example 17-2. Another way to traverse a document

```
<head>
<script>
// This function is passed a DOM Node object and checks to see if that node
// represents a string of text; i.e., if the node is a Text object. If
// so, it returns the length of the string. If not, it recursively calls
// itself on each of the children of the node and adds up the total length
// of the text it finds. Note that it enumerates the children of a node
// using the firstChild and nextSibling properties. Note also that the
// function does not recurse when it finds a Text node, because Text nodes
// never have children.
function countCharacters(n) {                // n is a Node
    if (n.nodeType == 3 /*Node.TEXT_NODE*/)  // Check if n is a Text object
        return n.length;                     // If so, return its length
    // Otherwise, n may have children whose characters we need to count
    var numchars = 0;  // Used to hold total characters of the children
    // Instead of using the childNodes property, this loop examines the
    // children of n using the firstChild and nextSibling properties.
    for(var m = n.firstChild; m != null; m = m.nextSibling) {
        numchars += countCharacters(m);  // Add up total characters found
    }
    return numchars;                     // Return total characters
}
</script>
</head>
<!--
  The onload event handler is an example of how the countCharacters()
  function might be used. Note that we want to count only the characters
  in the <body> of the document, so we pass document.body to the function.
-->
<body onload="alert('Document length: ' + countCharacters(document.body))">
This is a sample document.<p>How long is it?
</body>
```

17.2.2 Finding Specific Elements in a Document

The ability to traverse all nodes in a document tree gives us the power to find specific nodes. When programming with the DOM API, it is quite common to need a particular node within the document or a list of nodes of a specific type within the document. Fortunately, the DOM API provides functions that make this easy for us.

In Example 17-2, we referred to the <body> element of an HTML document with the JavaScript expression `document.body`. The `body` property of the Document object is a convenient special-case property and is the preferred way to refer to the <body> tag of an HTML document. If this convenience property did not exist, however, we could also refer to the <body> tag like this:

```
document.getElementsByTagName("body")[0]
```

This expression calls the Document object's getElementsByTagName() method and selects the first element of the returned array. The call to getElementsByTagName() returns an array of all <body> elements within the document. Since HTML documents can have only one <body>, we know that we're interested in the first element of the returned array.*

You can use getElementsByTagName() to obtain a list of any type of HTML element. For example, to find all the tables within a document, you'd do this:

```
var tables = document.getElementsByTagName("table");
alert("This document contains " + tables.length + " tables");
```

Note that since HTML tags are not case-sensitive, the strings passed to getElementsByTagName() are also not case-sensitive. That is, the previous code finds <table> tags even if they are coded as <TABLE>. getElementsByTagName() returns elements in the order in which they appear in the document. Finally, if you pass the special string "*" to getElementsByTagName(), it returns a list of all the elements in the document, in the order in which they appear. (This special usage is not supported in IE 5 and IE 5.5. See instead the IE-specific Document.all[] array in the client-side reference section.)

Sometimes you don't want a list of elements but instead want to operate on a single specific element of a document. If you know a lot about the structure of the document, you may be able to use getElementsByTagName(). For example, if you want to do something to the fourth paragraph in a document, you might use this code:

```
var myParagraph = document.getElementsByTagName("p")[3];
```

This typically is not the best (nor the most efficient) technique, however, because it depends so heavily on the structure of the document; a new paragraph inserted at the beginning of the document would break the code. Instead, when you need to manipulate specific elements of a document, it is best to give those elements an id attribute that specifies a unique (within the document) name for the element. Then you can look up your desired element by its ID. For example, you might code the special fourth paragraph of your document with a tag like this:

```
<p id="specialParagraph">
```

You can then look up the node for that paragraph with JavaScript code like this:

```
var myParagraph = document.getElementById("specialParagraph");
```

Note that the getElementById() method does not return an array of elements like getElementsByTagName() does. Because the value of every id attribute is (or is supposed to be) unique, getElementById() returns only the single element with the matching id attribute. getElementById() is an important method, and its use is quite common in DOM programming.

* Technically, the DOM API specifies that getElementsByTagName() returns a NodeList object. In the JavaScript binding of the DOM, NodeList objects behave like arrays and are typically used that way.

getElementById( ) and getElementsByTagName( ) are both methods of the Document object. Element objects also define a getElementsByTagName( ) method, however. This method of the Element object behaves just like the method of the Document object, except that it returns only elements that are descendants of the element on which it is invoked. Instead of searching the entire document for elements of a specific type, it searches only within the given element. This makes it possible, for example, to use getElementById( ) to find a specific element and then to use getElementsByTagName( ) to find all descendants of a given type within that specific tag. For example:

```
// Find a specific Table element within a document and count its rows
var tableOfContents = document.getElementById("TOC");
var rows = tableOfContents.getElementsByTagName("tr");
var numrows = rows.length;
```

Finally, note that for HTML documents, the HTMLDocument object also defines a getElementsByName( ) method. This method is like getElementById( ), but it looks at the name attribute of elements rather than the id attribute. Also, because the name attribute is not expected to be unique within a document (for example, radio buttons within HTML forms usually have the same name), getElementsByName( ) returns an array of elements rather than a single element. For example:

```
// Find <a name="top">
var link = document.getElementsByName("top")[0];
// Find all <input type="radio" name="shippingMethod"> elements
var choices = document.getElementsByName("shippingMethod");
```

17.2.3 Modifying a Document

Traversing the nodes of a document can be useful, but the real power of the core DOM API lies in the features that allow you to use JavaScript to dynamically modify documents. The following examples demonstrate the basic techniques of modifying documents and illustrate some of the possibilities.

Example 17-3 includes a JavaScript function named reverse( ), a sample document, and an HTML button that, when pressed, calls the reverse( ) function, passing it the node that represents the <body> element of the document. (Note the use of getElementsByTagName( ) within the button's event handler to find the <body> element.) The reverse( ) function loops backward through the children of the supplied node and uses the removeChild( ) and appendChild( ) methods of the Node object to reverse the order of those children.

Example 17-3. Reversing the nodes of a document

```
<head><title>Reverse</title>
<script>
function reverse(n) {          // Reverse the order of the children of Node n
    var kids = n.childNodes;   // Get the list of children
    var numkids = kids.length; // Figure out how many children there are
    for(var i = numkids-1; i >= 0; i--) {  // Loop backward through the children
```

Example 17-3. Reversing the nodes of a document (continued)

```
        var c = n.removeChild(kids[i]);     // Remove a child
        n.appendChild(c);                   // Put it back at its new position
    }
}
</script>
</head>
<body>
<p>paragraph #1<p>paragraph #2<p>paragraph #3  <!-- A sample document -->
<p>                                     <!-- A button to call reverse()-->
<button onclick="reverse(document.body);"
>Click Me to Reverse</button>
</body>
```

The result of Example 17-3, illustrated in Figure 17-3, is that when the user clicks the button, the order of the paragraphs and of the button are reversed.

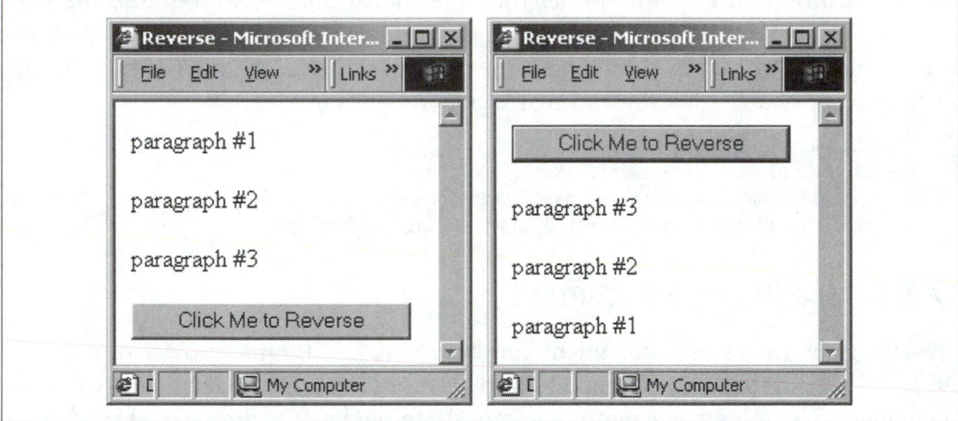

Figure 17-3. A document before and after being reversed

There are a couple of points worth noting about Example 17-3. First, if you pass a node that is already part of the document to `appendChild()` it first removes it, so we could have simplified our code by omitting the call to `removeChild()`. Second, keep in mind that the `childNodes` property (like all NodeList objects) is "live": when the document is modified, the modifications are immediately visible through the NodeList. This is an important features of the NodeList interface, but it can actually make some code trickier to write. A call to `removeChild()`, for example, changes the index of all the siblings that follow that child, so if you want to iterate through a NodeList and delete some of the nodes, you must write your looping code carefully.

Example 17-4 shows a variation on the `reverse()` function of the previous example. This one uses recursion to reverse not only the children of a specified node, but also all the node's descendants. In addition, when it encounters a Text node, it reverses the order of the characters within that node. Example 17-4 shows only the JavaScript code for this new reverse( ) function. It could easily be used in an HTML document like the one shown in Example 17-3, however.

Example 17-4. A recursive node-reversal function

```
// Recursively reverse all nodes beneath Node n and reverse Text nodes
function reverse(n) {
    if (n.nodeType == 3 /*Node.TEXT_NODE*/) {     // Reverse Text nodes
        var text = n.data;                        // Get content of node
        var reversed = "";
        for(var i = text.length-1; i >= 0; i--)  // Reverse it
            reversed += text.charAt(i);
        n.data = reversed;                        // Store reversed text
    }
    else {  // For non-Text nodes, recursively reverse the order of the children
        var kids = n.childNodes;
        var numkids = kids.length;
        for(var i = numkids-1; i >= 0; i--) {      // Loop through kids
            reverse(kids[i]);                      // Recurse to reverse kid
            n.appendChild(n.removeChild(kids[i])); // Move kid to new position
        }
    }
}
```

Example 17-4 shows one way to change the text displayed in a document: simply set the data field of the appropriate Text node. Example 17-5 shows another way. This example defines a function, uppercase( ), that recursively traverses the children of a given node. When it finds a Text node, the function replaces that node with a new Text node containing the text of the original node, converted to uppercase. Note the use of the document.createTextNode( ) method to create the new Text node and the use of Node's replaceChild( ) method to replace the original Text node with the newly created one. Note also that replaceChild( ) is invoked on the parent of the node to be replaced, not on the node itself. The uppercase( ) function uses Node's parentNode property to determine the parent of the Text node it replaces.

In addition to defining the uppercase( ) function, Example 17-5 includes two HTML paragraphs and a button. When the user clicks the button, one of the paragraphs is converted to uppercase. Each paragraph is identified with a unique name, specified with the id attribute of the <p> tag. The event handler on the button uses the getElementById( ) method to get the Element object that represents the desired paragraph.

Example 17-5. Replacing nodes with their uppercase equivalents

```
<script>
// This function recursively looks at Node n and its descendants,
// replacing all Text nodes with their uppercase equivalents.
function uppercase(n) {
    if (n.nodeType == 3 /*Node.TEXT_NODE*/) {
        // If the node is a Text node, create a new Text node that
```

Example 17-5. Replacing nodes with their uppercase equivalents (continued)

```
        // holds the uppercase version of the node's text, and use the
        // replaceChild( ) method of the parent node to replace the
        // original node with the new uppercase node.
        var newNode = document.createTextNode(n.data.toUpperCase( ));
        var parent = n.parentNode;
        parent.replaceChild(newNode, n);
    }
    else {
        // If the node is not a Text node, loop through its children
        // and recursively call this function on each child.
        var kids = n.childNodes;
        for(var i = 0; i < kids.length; i++) uppercase(kids[i]);
    }
}
</script>

<!-- Here is some sample text. Note that the <p> tags have id attributes. -->
<p id="p1">This <i>is</i> paragraph 1.</p>
<p id="p2">This <i>is</i> paragraph 2.</p>

<!-- Here is a button that invokes the uppercase( ) function defined above. -->
<!-- Note the call to document.getElementById( ) to find the desired node. -->
<button onclick="uppercase(document.getElementById('p1'));">Click Me</button>
```

The previous two examples show how to modify document content by replacing the text contained within a Text node and by replacing one Text node with an entirely new Text node. It is also possible to append, insert, delete, or replace text within a Text node with the `appendData( )`, `insertData( )`, `deleteData( )`, and `replaceData( )` methods. These methods are not directly defined by the Text interface, but instead are inherited by Text from CharacterData. You can find more information about them under "CharacterData" in the DOM reference section.

In the node-reversal examples, we saw how we could use the `removeChild( )` and `appendChild( )` methods to reorder the children of a Node. Note, however, that we are not restricted to changing the order of nodes within their parent node; the DOM API allows nodes in the document tree to be moved freely within the tree (only within the same document, however). Example 17-6 demonstrates this by defining a function named `embolden( )` that replaces a specified node with a new element (created with the `createElement( )` method of the Document object) that represents an HTML `<b>` tag and "reparents" the original node as a child of the new `<b>` node. In an HTML document, this causes any text within the node or its descendants to be displayed in boldface.

Example 17-6. Reparenting a node to a <b> element

```
<script>
// This function takes a Node n, replaces it in the tree with an Element node
// that represents an HTML <b> tag, and then makes the original node the
// child of the new <b> element.
```

Example 17-6. Reparenting a node to a <b> element (continued)

```
function embolden(node) {
    var bold = document.createElement("b");  // Create a new <b> element
    var parent = node.parentNode;            // Get the parent of the node
    parent.replaceChild(bold, node);         // Replace the node with the <b> tag
    bold.appendChild(node);                  // Make the node a child of the <b> tag
}
</script>

<!-- A couple of sample paragraphs -->
<p id="p1">This <i>is</i> paragraph #1.</p>
<p id="p2">This <i>is</i> paragraph #2.</p>

<!-- A button that invokes the embolden() function on the first paragraph -->
<button onclick="embolden(document.getElementById('p1'));">Embolden</button>
```


In addition to modifying documents by inserting, deleting, reparenting, and otherwise rearranging nodes, it is also possible to make substantial changes to a document simply by setting attribute values on document elements. One way to do this is with the `element.setAttribute()` method. For example:

```
var headline = document.getElementById("headline");  // Find named element
headline.setAttribute("align", "center");            // Set align='center'
```

The DOM elements that represent HTML attributes define JavaScript properties that correspond to each of their standard attributes (even deprecated attributes such as `align`), so you can also achieve the same effect with this code:

```
var headline = document.getElementById("headline");
headline.align = "center";  // Set alignment attribute.
```

17.2.4 Adding Content to a Document

The previous two examples showed how the contents of a Text node can be changed to uppercase and how a node can be reparented to be a child of a newly created <b> node. The `embolden()` function showed that it is possible to create new nodes and add them to a document. You can add arbitrary content to a document by creating the necessary Element nodes and Text nodes with `document.createElement()` and `document.createTextNode()` and by adding them appropriately to the document. This is demonstrated in Example 17-7, which defines a function named `debug()`. This function provides a convenient way to insert debugging messages into a program, and it serves as a useful alternative to using the built-in `alert()` function. A sample use of this `debug()` function is illustrated in Figure 17-4.

The first time `debug()` is called, it uses the DOM API to create a <div> element and insert it at the end of the document. The debugging messages passed to `debug()` on this first call and all subsequent calls are then inserted into this <div> element. Each debugging message is displayed by creating a Text node within a <p> element and inserting that <p> element at the end of the <div> element.

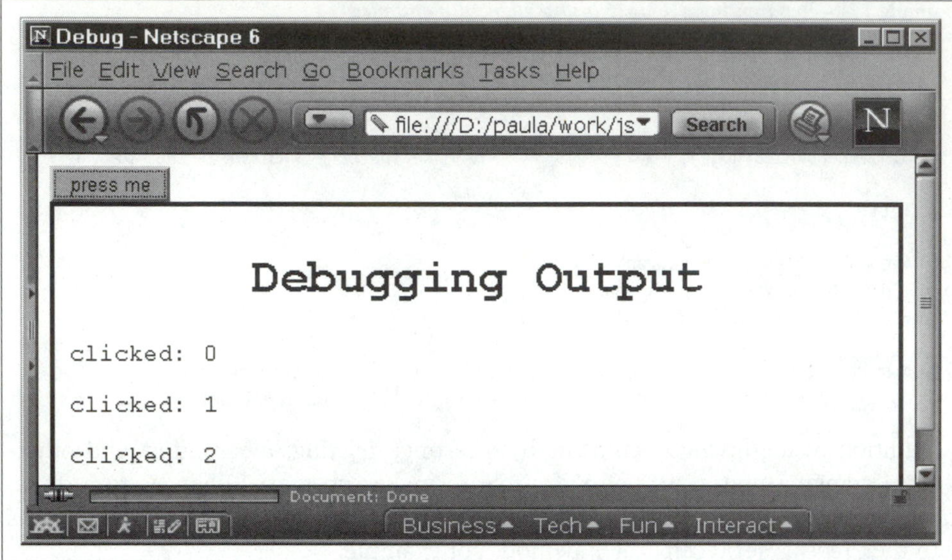

Figure 17-4. Output of the debug() function

Example 17-7 also demonstrates a convenient but nonstandard way to add new content to a document. The `<div>` element that contains the debugging messages displays a large, centered title. This title could be created and added to the document in the way that other content is, but in this example we instead use the `innerHTML` property of the `<div>` element. Setting this property of any element to a string of HTML text causes that HTML to be parsed and inserted as the content of the element. Although this property is not part of the DOM API, it is a useful shortcut that is supported by Internet Explorer 4 and later and Netscape 6. Although it is not standard, it is in common use and is included in this example for completeness.*

Example 17-7. Adding debugging output to a document

```
/**
 * This debug function displays plain-text debugging messages in a
 * special box at the end of a document. It is a useful alternative
 * to using alert( ) to display debugging messages.
 **/
function debug(msg) {
    // If we haven't already created a box within which to display
    // our debugging messages, then do so now. Note that to avoid
    // using another global variable, we store the box node as
    // a proprty of this function.
```

* The `innerHTML` property is particularly useful when you want to insert large or complex chunks of HTML text into a document. For simple fragments of HTML, using DOM methods is more efficient because no HTML parser is required. Note that appending bits of text to the `innerHTML` property with the `+=` operator is usually not efficient.

Example 17-7. Adding debugging output to a document (continued)

```
    if (!debug.box) {
        // Create a new <div> element
        debug.box = document.createElement("div");
        // Specify what it looks like using CSS style attributes
        debug.box.setAttribute("style",
                               "background-color: white; " +
                               "font-family: monospace; " +
                               "border: solid black 3px; " +
                               "padding: 10px;");

        // Append our new <div> element to the end of the document
        document.body.appendChild(debug.box);

        // Now add a title to our <div>. Note that the innerHTML property is
        // used to parse a fragment of HTML and insert it into the document.
        // innerHTML is not part of the W3C DOM standard, but it is supported
        // by Netscape 6 and Internet Explorer 4 and later. We can avoid
        // the use of innerHTML by explicitly creating the <h1> element,
        // setting its style attribute, adding a Text node to it, and
        // inserting it into the document, but this is a nice shortcut.
        debug.box.innerHTML = "<h1 style='text-align:center'>Debugging Output</h1>";
    }

    // When we get here, debug.box refers to a <div> element into which
    // we can insert our debugging message.
    // First create a <p> node to hold the message.
    var p = document.createElement("p");
    // Now create a text node containing the message, and add it to the <p>
    p.appendChild(document.createTextNode(msg));
    // And append the <p> node to the <div> that holds the debugging output
    debug.box.appendChild(p);
}
```

The `debug()` method listed in Example 17-7 can be used in HTML documents like the following, which is the document that was used to generate Figure 17-4:

```
<script src="Debug.js"></script>  <!-- Include the debug() function -->
<script>var numtimes=0;</script>  <!-- Define a global variable -->
<!-- Now use the debug() function in an event handler -->
<button onclick="debug('clicked: ' + numtimes++);">press me</button>
```

17.2.5 Working with Document Fragments

The core DOM API defines the DocumentFragment object as a convenient way of working with groups of Document nodes. A DocumentFragment is a special type of node that does not appear in a document itself but serves as a temporary container for a sequential collection of nodes and allows those nodes to be manipulated as a single object. When a DocumentFragment is inserted into a document (using any of the `appendChild()`, `insertBefore()`, or `replaceChild()` methods of the Node object), it is not the DocumentFragment itself that is inserted, but each of its children.

As an example, you can use a DocumentFragment to rewrite the reverse( ) method of Example 17-3 like this:

```
function reverse(n) {  // Reverses the order of the children of Node n
    var f = document.createDocumentFragment( );  // Get an empty DocumentFragment
    while(n.lastChild)                  // Loop backward through the children,
         f.appendChild(n.lastChild);    // moving each one to the DocumentFragment
    n.appendChild(f);                   // Then move them back (in their new order)
}
```

Once you have created a DocumentFragment, you can use it with code like this:

```
document.getElementsByTagName("p")[0].appendChild(fragment);
```

Note that when you insert a DocumentFragment into a document, the child nodes of the fragment are moved from the fragment into the document. After the insertion, the fragment is empty and cannot be reused unless you first add new children to it. We'll see the DocumentFragment object again later in this chapter, when we examine the DOM Range API.

17.2.6 Example: A Dynamically Created Table of Contents

The previous sections showed how you can use the core DOM API to traverse, modify, and add content to a document. Example 17-8, at the end of this section, puts all these pieces together into a single longer example. The example defines a single method, `maketoc( )`, which expects a Document node as its single argument. `maketoc( )` traverses the document, creates a table of contents (TOC) for it, and replaces the specified node with the newly created TOC. The TOC is generated by looking for `<h1>`, `<h2>`, `<h3>`, `<h4>`, `<h5>`, and `<h6>` tags within the document and assuming that these tags mark the beginnings of important sections within the document. In addition to creating a TOC, the `maketoc( )` function inserts named anchors (`<a>` elements with the `name` attribute set instead of the `href` attribute) before each section heading so that the TOC can link directly to each section. Finally, `maketoc( )` also inserts links at the beginning of each section back to the TOC; when the reader reaches a new section, she can either read that section or follow the link back to the TOC and choose a new section. Figure 17-5 shows what a TOC generated by the `maketoc( )` function looks like.

If you maintain and revise long documents that are broken into sections with `<h1>`, `<h2>`, and related tags, the `maketoc( )` function may be of interest to you. TOCs are quite useful in long documents, but when you frequently revise a document it can be difficult to keep the TOC in sync with the document itself. The TOC for this book was automatically created by postprocessing the content of the book. `maketoc( )` allows you to do something similar for your web documents. You can use the function in an HTML document like this one:

```
<script src="TOC.js"></script>  <!-- Load the maketoc( ) function -->
<!-- Call the maketoc( ) function when the document is fully loaded -->
<body onload="maketoc(document.getElementById('placeholder'))">
```

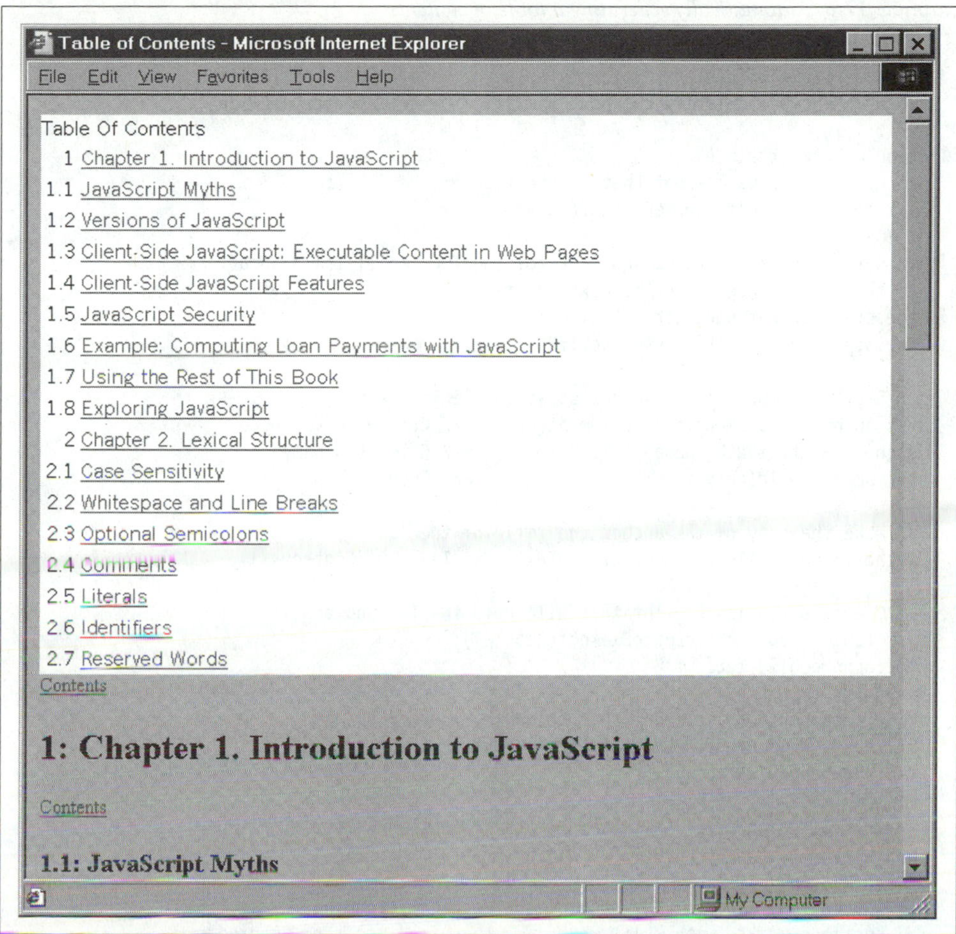

Figure 17-5. A dynamically created table of contents

```
<!-- This span element will be replaced by the generated TOC -->
<span id="placeholder">Table Of Contents</span>
// ... rest of document goes here ...
```

Another way to use the `maketoc()` function is to generate the TOC only when the reader requests it. You can do this by including a link (or button) that replaces itself with the generated TOC when the user clicks on it:

```
<a href="#" onclick="maketoc(this); return false;">Show Table Of Contents</a>
```

The code for the `maketoc()` function follows. Example 17-8 is long, but it is well commented and uses techniques that have already been demonstrated. It is worth studying as a practical example of the power of the DOM API. Note that the `maketoc()` function relies on two helper functions. For modularity, these helper functions are defined inside `maketoc()` itself. This prevents the addition of extra unnecessary functions to the global namespace.

Example 17-8. Automatically generating a table of contents

```
/**
 * Create a table of contents for this document, and insert the TOC into
 * the document by replacing the node specified by the replace argument.
 **/
function maketoc(replace) {
    // Create a <div> element that is the root of the TOC tree
    var toc = document.createElement("div");

    // Set a background color and font for the TOC. We'll learn about
    // the style property in the next chapter.
    toc.style.backgroundColor = "white";
    toc.style.fontFamily = "sans-serif";

    // Start the TOC with an anchor so we can link back to it
    var anchor = document.createElement("a");  // Create an <a> node
    anchor.setAttribute("name", "TOC");        // Give it a name
    toc.appendChild(anchor);                   // Insert it

    // Make the body of the anchor the title of the TOC
    anchor.appendChild(document.createTextNode("Table Of Contents"));

    // Create a <table> element that will hold the TOC and add it
    var table = document.createElement("table");
    toc.appendChild(table);

    // Create a <tbody> element that holds the rows of the TOC
    var tbody = document.createElement("tbody");
    table.appendChild(tbody);

    // Initialize an array that keeps track of section numbers
    var sectionNumbers = [0,0,0,0,0,0];

    // Recursively traverse the body of the document, looking for sections
    // sections marked with <h1>, <h2>, ... tags, and use them to create
    // the TOC by adding rows to the table
    addSections(document.body, tbody, sectionNumbers);

    // Finally, insert the TOC into the document by replacing the node
    // specified by the replace argument with the TOC subtree
    replace.parentNode.replaceChild(toc, replace);

    // This method recursively traverses the tree rooted at Node n, looking
    // looking for <h1> through <h6> tags, and uses the content of these tags
    // to build the table of contents by adding rows to the HTML table specified
    // by the toc argument. It uses the sectionNumbers array to keep track of
    // the current section number.
    // This function is defined inside of maketoc( ) so that it is not
    // visible from the outside. maketoc( ) is the only function exported
    // by this JavaScript module.
    function addSections(n, toc, sectionNumbers) {
        // Loop through all the children of n
        for(var m = n.firstChild; m != null; m = m.nextSibling) {
```

Example 17-8. Automatically generating a table of contents (continued)

```
// Check whether m is a heading element. It would be nice if we
// could just use (m instanceof HTMLHeadingElement), but this is
// not required by the specification and it does not work in IE.
// Therefore, we must check the tagname to see if it is H1-H6.
if ((m.nodeType == 1) &&  /* Node.ELEMENT_NODE */
    (m.tagName.length == 2) && (m.tagName.charAt(0) == "H")) {
    // Figure out what level heading it is
    var level = parseInt(m.tagName.charAt(1));
    if (!isNaN(level) && (level >= 1) && (level <= 6)) {
        // Increment the section number for this heading level
        sectionNumbers[level-1]++;
        // And reset all lower heading-level numbers to zero
        for(var i = level; i < 6; i++) sectionNumbers[i] = 0;
        // Now combine section numbers for all heading levels
        // to produce a section number like "2.3.1"
        var sectionNumber = "";
        for(var i = 0; i < level; i++) {
            sectionNumber += sectionNumbers[i];
            if (i < level-1) sectionNumber += ".";
        }

        // Create an anchor to mark the beginning of this section
        // This will be the target of a link we add to the TOC
        var anchor = document.createElement("a");
        anchor.setAttribute("name", "SECT"+sectionNumber);

        // Create a link back to the TOC and make it a
        // child of the anchor
        var backlink = document.createElement("a");
        backlink.setAttribute("href", "#TOC");
        backlink.appendChild(document.createTextNode("Contents"));
        anchor.appendChild(backlink);

        // Insert the anchor into the document right before the
        // section header
        n.insertBefore(anchor, m);

        // Now create a link to this section. It will be added
        // to the TOC below.
        var link = document.createElement("a");
        link.setAttribute("href", "#SECT" + sectionNumber);
        // Get the heading text using a function defined below
        var sectionTitle = getTextContent(m);
        // Use the heading text as the content of the link
        link.appendChild(document.createTextNode(sectionTitle));

        // Create a new row for the TOC
        var row = document.createElement("tr");
        // Create two columns for the row
        var col1 = document.createElement("td");
        var col2 = document.createElement("td");
        // Make the first column right-aligned and put the section
```

Example 17-8. Automatically generating a table of contents (continued)

```
                    // number in it
                    col1.setAttribute("align", "right");
                    col1.appendChild(document.createTextNode(sectionNumber));
                    // Put a link to the section in the second column
                    col2.appendChild(link);
                    // Add the columns to the row, and the row to the table
                    row.appendChild(col1);
                    row.appendChild(col2);
                    toc.appendChild(row);

                    // Modify the section header element itself to add
                    // the section number as part of the section title
                    m.insertBefore(document.createTextNode(sectionNumber+": "),
                                   m.firstChild);
                }
            }
            else {  // Otherwise, this is not a heading element, so recurse
                addSections(m, toc, sectionNumbers);
            }
        }
    }

    // This utility function traverses Node n, returning the content of
    // all Text nodes found and discarding any HTML tags. This is also
    // defined as a nested function, so it is private to this module.
    function getTextContent(n) {
        var s = '';
        var children = n.childNodes;
        for(var i = 0; i < children.length; i++) {
            var child = children[i];
            if (child.nodeType == 3 /*Node.TEXT_NODE*/) s += child.data;
            else s += getTextContent(child);
        }
        return s;
    }
}
```

17.2.7 Working with XML Documents

Web browsers display HTML documents, but XML documents are becoming more and more important as sources of data. Since the DOM allows us to traverse and manipulate both HTML and XML documents, we can use DOM methods to load an XML document, extract information from it, and dynamically create an HTML version of that information for display in a web browser. Example 17-9 shows how this can be done in Netscape 6.1 and Internet Explorer 6. It is an HTML file that consists mostly of JavaScript code. The file expects to be loaded through a URL that uses the URL query string to specify the relative URL of the data file to load. For example, you might invoke this example file with a URL like this:

```
file://C:/javascript/DisplayEmployeeData.html?data.xml
```

DisplayEmployeeData.html is the name of the example file, and *data.xml* is the name of the XML file it uses. The XML file must contain data formatted like this:

```
<employees>
  <employee name="J. Doe"><job>Programmer</job><salary>32768</salary></employee>
  <employee name="A. Baker"><job>Sales</job><salary>70000</salary></employee>
  <employee name="Big Cheese"><job>CEO</job><salary>1000000</salary></employee>
</employees>
```


The example contains two JavaScript functions. The first, `loadXML()`, is a generic function for loading any XML file. It contains standard DOM Level 2 code to load the XML document and also code that uses a proprietary Microsoft API to accomplish the same thing. The only really new thing in this example is the creation of a new Document object with the `DOMImplementation.createDocument()` method and the call to the `load()` method of that Document object. An important thing to notice here is that documents do not load instantaneously, so the call to `loadXML()` returns before the document is loaded. For this reason, we pass `loadXML()` a reference to another function that it should call when the document has finished loading.

The other function in the example is `makeTable()`. This is the function that we pass to `loadXML()`. When the XML file finishes loading, it passes the Document object representing the XML file and the URL of the file to `makeTable()`. `makeTable()` uses DOM methods we've seen before to extract information from the XML document and insert it into a table in the HTML document displayed by the browser. This function also illustrates the use of some table-related convenience methods defined by HTMLTableElement, HTMLTableRowElement, and related interfaces. See the DOM reference section for complete details about these table-specific interfaces and their methods. Although the DOM methods and properties used in this function are all straightforward, they are used in dense combinations. Study the code carefully and you should have no difficulty understanding it.

Example 17-9. Loading and reading data from an XML document

```
<head><title>Employee Data</title>
<script>
// This function loads the XML document from the specified URL and, when
// it is fully loaded, passes that document and the URL to the specified
// handler function. This function works with any XML document.
function loadXML(url, handler) {
    // Use the standard DOM Level 2 technique, if it is supported
    if (document.implementation && document.implementation.createDocument) {
        // Create a new Document object
        var xmldoc = document.implementation.createDocument("", "", null);
        // Specify what should happen when it finishes loading
        xmldoc.onload = function() { handler(xmldoc, url); }
        // And tell it what URL to load
        xmldoc.load(url);
    }
    // Otherwise, use Microsoft's proprietary API for Internet Explorer
```

Example 17-9. Loading and reading data from an XML document (continued)

```
    else if (window.ActiveXObject) {
        var xmldoc = new ActiveXObject("Microsoft.XMLDOM");   // Create doc
        xmldoc.onreadystatechange = function( ) {              // Specify onload
            if (xmldoc.readyState == 4) handler(xmldoc, url);
        }
        xmldoc.load(url);                                      // Start loading!
    }
}

// This function builds an HTML table of employees from data it reads from
// the XML document it is passed
function makeTable(xmldoc, url) {
    // Create a <table> object and insert it into the document
    var table = document.createElement("table");
    table.setAttribute("border", "1");
    document.body.appendChild(table);

    // Use convenience methods of HTMLTableElement and related interfaces
    // to define a table caption and a header that gives a name to each column
    var caption = "Employee Data from " + url;
    table.createCaption( ).appendChild(document.createTextNode(caption));
    var header = table.createTHead( );
    var headerrow = header.insertRow(0);
    headerrow.insertCell(0).appendChild(document.createTextNode("Name"));
    headerrow.insertCell(1).appendChild(document.createTextNode("Job"));
    headerrow.insertCell(2).appendChild(document.createTextNode("Salary"));

    // Now find all <employee> elements in our xmldoc document
    var employees = xmldoc.getElementsByTagName("employee");

    // Loop through these <employee> elements
    for(var i = 0; i < employees.length; i++) {
        // For each employee, get name, job, and salary data using standard DOM
        // methods. The name comes from an attribute. The other values are
        // in Text nodes within <job> and <salary> tags.
        var e = employees[i];
        var name = e.getAttribute("name");
        var job = e.getElementsByTagName("job")[0].firstChild.data;
        var salary = e.getElementsByTagName("salary")[0].firstChild.data;

        // Now that we have the employee data, use methods of the table to
        // create a new row and then use the methods of the row to create
        // new cells containing the data as Text nodes
        var row = table.insertRow(i+1);
        row.insertCell(0).appendChild(document.createTextNode(name));
        row.insertCell(1).appendChild(document.createTextNode(job));
        row.insertCell(2).appendChild(document.createTextNode(salary));
    }
}
</script>
</head>
```

Example 17-9. Loading and reading data from an XML document (continued)

```
<!--
The body of the document contains no static text; everything is dynamically
generated by the makeTable( ) function. The onload event handler starts
things off by calling loadXML( ) to load the XML data file. Note the use of
location.search to encode the name of the XML file in the query string. Load
this HTML file with a URL like this: DisplayEmployeeData.html?data.xml.
-->
<body onload="loadXML(location.search.substring(1), makeTable)">
</body>
```


17.3 DOM Compatibility with Internet Explorer 4

Although IE 4 is not DOM-compliant, it has features that are similar to the core DOM APIs. These features are not part of the DOM standard and are not compatible with Netscape, but they are compatible with later versions of IE. The features are summarized here; consult the client-side reference section of this book for more details.

17.3.1 Traversing a Document

The DOM standard specifies that all Node objects, which includes both the Document object and all Element objects, have a `childNodes[]` array that contains the children of that node. IE 4 does not support `childNodes[]`, but it provides a very similar `children[]` array on its Document and HTMLElement objects. Thus, it is easy to write a recursive function like the one shown in Example 17-1 to traverse the complete set of HTML elements within an IE 4 document.

There is one substantial difference between IE 4's `children[]` array and the standard DOM `childNodes[]` array, however. IE 4 does not have a Text node type and does not consider strings of text to be children. Thus, a `<p>` tag that contains only plain text with no markup has an empty `children[]` array in IE 4. As we'll see shortly, however, the textual content of a `<p>` tag is available through the IE 4 `innerText` property.

17.3.2 Finding Document Elements

IE 4 does not support the `getElementById( )` and `getElementsByTagName( )` methods of the Document object. Instead, the Document object and all document elements have an array property named `all[]`. As the name suggests, this array represents *all* the elements in a document or all the elements contained within another element. Note that `all[]` does not simply represent the children of the document or the element—it represents all descendants, no matter how deeply nested.

The `all[]` array can be used in several ways. If you index it with an integer *n*, it returns the *n+1*th element of the document or the parent element. For example:

```
var e1 = document.all[0];  // The first element of the document
var e2 = e1.all[4];        // The fifth element of element 1
```

Elements are numbered in the order in which they appear in the document source. Note the one big difference between the IE 4 API and the DOM standard: IE does not have a notion of Text nodes, so the all[] array contains only document elements, not the text that appears within them.

It is usually much more useful to be able to refer to document elements by name rather than number. The IE 4 equivalent to getElementbyId() is to index the all[] array with a string rather than a number. When you do this, IE 4 returns the element whose id or name attribute has the specified value. If there is more than one such element (which can happen, since it is common to have multiple form elements, such as radioboxes, with the same name attribute), the result is an array of those elements. For example:

```
var specialParagraph = document.all["special"];
var radioboxes = form.all["shippingMethod"];  // May return an array
```

JavaScript also allows us to write these expressions by expressing the array index as a property name:

```
var specialParagraph = document.all.special;
var radioboxes = form.all.shippingMethod;
```

Using the all[] array in this way provides the same basic functionality as getElementById() and getElementsByName(). The main difference is that the all[] array combines the features of these two methods, which can cause problems if you inadvertently use the same values for the id and name attributes of unrelated elements.

The all[] array has an unusual quirk: a tags() method that can be used to obtain an array of elements by tag name. For example:

```
var lists = document.all.tags("UL");  // Find all <ul> tags in the document
var items = lists[0].all.tags("LI");  // Find all <li> tags in the first <ul>
```

This IE 4 syntax provides essentially the same functionality as the DOM Document and Element objects' getElementsByTagName() method. Note that in IE 4, the tag name should be specified using all capital letters.

17.3.3 Modifying Documents

Like the DOM standard, IE 4 exposes the attributes of HTML tags as properties of the corresponding HTMLElement objects. Thus, it is possible to modify a document displayed in IE 4 by dynamically changing its HTML attributes. If an attribute modification changes the size of any element, the document "reflows" to accommodate its new size. The IE 4 HTMLElement object defines setAttribute(), getAttribute(), and removeAttribute() methods as well. These are similar to the methods of the same name defined by the Element object in the standard DOM API.

The DOM standard defines an API that makes it possible to create new nodes, insert nodes into the document tree, reparent nodes, and move nodes within the tree. IE 4 cannot do this. Instead, however, all HTMLElement objects in IE 4 define an innerHTML property. Setting this property to a string of HTML text allows you to replace the content of an element with whatever you want. Because this innerHTML property is so powerful, it has been implemented by Netscape 6 (and the Mozilla browser from which it is derived), even though it is not part of the DOM standard. innerHTML was demonstrated in Example 17-7.

IE 4 also defines several related properties and methods. The outerHTML property replaces an element's content and the entire element itself with a specified string of HTML text. The innerText and outerText properties are similar to innerHTML and outerHTML, except that they treat the string as plain text and do not parse it as HTML. Finally, the insertAdjacentHTML() and insertAdjacentText() methods leave the content of an element alone but insert new HTML or plain-text content near (before or after, inside or outside) it. These properties and functions are not as commonly used as innerHTML and have not been implemented by Netscape 6. For further details, see "HTMLElement" in the client-side reference section.

17.4 DOM Compatibility with Netscape 4

Netscape 4 does not even come close to implementing the DOM standard. In particular, Netscape 4 provides no way to access or set attributes on arbitrary elements of a document. Netscape 4 supports the Level 0 DOM API, of course, so elements such as forms and links can be accessed through the forms[] and links[] arrays, but there is no general way to traverse the children of these elements or set arbitrary attributes on them. Furthermore, Netscape 4 does not have the ability to "reflow" document content in response to changes in element size.

Despite these restrictions, Netscape 4 does provide an API that allows access to and manipulation of the crucial "dynamic elements" used to implement DHTML effects. In the Netscape 4 API, these elements are known as *layers*; they float above the rest of the document and can be moved, resized, and modified independently of the other elements of the document. Layers are typically implemented using CSS style sheets, and the Netscape 4 Layer API is discussed in detail in Chapter 18.

What follows is simply an overview that explains how you can create, access, and modify the content of individual layer elements within a document. Although Netscape 4 does not support anything like the DOM standard, its Layer API allows you to achieve some of the same dynamic effects that are possible with the standard API. Note that the Layer API was submitted to the W3C for consideration as part of the DOM standard, but no part of this API was ever standardized. Because Netscape 6 is based on a complete rewrite of Netscape 4, the Layer API has been abandoned and is not supported in Netscape 6 (or in Mozilla).

Layers can be created in a document using the <layer> tag, a proprietary Netscape extension to HTML. More commonly, however, you create a layer in a Netscape 4 document using standard CSS positioning attributes (which will be explained in detail in Chapter 18). Any element made dynamic with CSS style attributes is treated as a layer by Netscape 4 and can be manipulated using the Layer API. (Note, though, that Netscape 4 does not allow all elements to be made dynamic. To be safe, a `<div>` wrapper element is usually used around any element that is to be dynamic.) JavaScript can also dynamically create layers using the `Layer()` constructor, which you can read about in the client-side reference section of this book.

Once you've created dynamic elements, or layers, in your document, Netscape 4 allows you to access them via a simple extension of the Level 0 DOM API. Just as you access form elements through a `forms[]` array and image elements through an `images[]` array, so do you access layers through a `layers[]` array of the Document object. If the first layer in a document has a `name` attribute of "layer1", you can refer to that layer element with any of the following expressions:

```
document.layers[0]          // Index the array with a number
document.layers['layer1']  // Index the array with an element name
document.layer1             // Named layers become a document property
```

If a layer has no `name` attribute but has an `id` attribute, the value of this attribute is used as the layer name instead.

Layers in your documents are represented by Layer objects that define a number of useful properties and methods you can use to move, resize, show, hide, and set the stacking order of the layer. These properties and methods are related to CSS style attributes and will be discussed in Chapter 18. The most interesting thing about the Layer object is that it contains a Document object of its own: the content of a layer is treated as an entirely separate document from the document that contains the layer. This allows you to modify the content displayed by a layer by dynamically rewriting the content of the layer using the `document.write()` and `document.close()` methods. You can also dynamically load documents into a layer using Layer's `load()` method. Finally, note that layers may themselves contain layers, and you can refer to such nested layers with expressions like this:

```
// The second layer nested within the layer named "mylayer"
document.mylayer.document.layers[1];
```

17.5 Convenience Methods: The Traversal and Range APIs

So far in this chapter, we've discussed the core DOM API, which provides basic methods for document traversal and manipulation. The DOM standard also defines other optional API modules, the most important of which will be discussed in the chapters that follow. Two of the optional modules are essentially convenience APIs built on top of the core API. The Traversal API defines advanced techniques for traversing a document and filtering out nodes that are not of interest. The Range API defines methods for manipulating contiguous ranges of document content, even when that content does not begin or end at a node boundary. The Traversal and

Range APIs are briefly introduced in the sections that follow. See the DOM reference section for complete documentation. The Range API is implemented by Netscape 6.1 (and partially implemented by Netscape 6), and the Traversal API is expected to be fully supported by Mozilla 1.0, which means that a future release of Netscape will support it. At the time of this writing, IE does not support either of these APIs.

17.5.1 The DOM Traversal API

At the beginning of this chapter, we saw techniques for traversing the document tree by recursively examining each node in turn. This is an important technique, but it is often overkill; we do not typically want to examine every node of a document. We instead might want to examine only the `<img>` elements in a document, or to traverse only the subtrees of `<table>` elements. The Traversal API provides advanced techniques for this kind of selective document traversal. As noted previously, the Traversal API is optional and, at the time of this writing, is not implemented in major sixth-generation browsers. You can test whether it is supported by a DOM-compliant browser with the following:

```
document.implementation.hasFeature("Traversal", 2.0)  // True if supported
```

17.5.1.1 NodeIterator and TreeWalker

The Traversal API consists of two key objects, each of which provides a different filtered view of a document. The NodeIterator object provides a "flattened" sequential view of the nodes in a document and supports filtering. You could define a NodeIterator that filters out all document content except `<img>` tags and presents those image elements to you as a list. The `nextNode()` and `previousNode()` methods of the NodeIterator object allow you to move forward and backward through the list. Note that NodeIterator allows you to traverse selected parts of a document without recursion; you can simply use a NodeIterator within a loop, calling `nextNode()` repeatedly until you find the node or nodes in which you are interested, or until it returns `null`, indicating that it has reached the end of the document.

The other key object in the Traversal API is TreeWalker. This object also provides a filtered view of a document and allows you to traverse the filtered document by calling `nextNode()` and `previousNode()`, but it does not flatten the document tree. TreeWalker retains the tree structure of the document (although this tree structure may be dramatically modified by node filtering) and allows you to navigate the tree with the `firstChild()`, `lastChild()`, `nextSibling()`, `previousSibling()`, and `parentNode()` methods. You would use a TreeWalker instead of a NodeIterator when you want to traverse the filtered tree yourself, instead of simply calling `nextNode()` to iterate through it, or when you want to perform a more sophisticated traversal, skipping, for example, some subtrees.

The Document object defines createNodeIterator( ) and createTreeWalker( ) methods for creating NodeIterator and TreeWalker objects. A practical way to check whether a browser supports the Traversal API is to test for the existence of these methods:

```
if (document.createNodeIterator && document.createTreeWalker) {
    /* Safe to use Traversal API */
}
```

Both createNodeIterator( ) and createTreeWalker( ) are passed the same four arguments and differ only in the type of object they return. The first argument is the node at which the traversal is to begin. This should be the Document object if you want to traverse or iterate through the entire document, or any other node if you want to traverse only a subtree of the document. The second argument is a number that indicates the types of nodes NodeIterator or TreeWalker should return. This argument is formed by taking the sum of one or more of the SHOW_ constants defined by the NodeFilter object (discussed in the next section). The third argument to both methods is an optional function used to specify a more complex filter than simply including or rejecting nodes based on their type (again, see the next section). The final argument is a boolean value that specifies whether entity reference nodes in the document should be expanded during the traversal. This option can be useful when you're working with XML documents, but web programmers working with HTML documents can ignore it and pass false.

17.5.1.2 Filtering

One of the most important features of NodeIterator and TreeWalker is their selectivity, their ability to filter out nodes you don't care about. As described previously, you specify the nodes you are interested in with the second and (optionally) third arguments to createNodeIterator( ) and createTreeWalker( ). These arguments specify two levels of filtering. The first level simply accepts or rejects nodes based on their type. The NodeFilter object defines a numeric constant for each type of node, and you specify the types of nodes you are interested in by adding together (or by using the | bitwise OR operator on) the appropriate constants.

For example, if you are interested in only the Element and Text nodes of a document, you can use the following expression as the second argument:

```
NodeFilter.SHOW_ELEMENT + NodeFilter.SHOW_TEXT
```

If you are interested in only Element nodes, use:

```
NodeFilter.SHOW_ELEMENT
```

If you are interested in all nodes or do not want to reject any nodes simply on the basis of their types, use the special constant:

```
NodeFilter.SHOW_ALL
```

And if you are interested in all types of nodes except for comments, use:

```
~NodeFilter.SHOW_COMMENT
```

(See Chapter 5 if you've forgotten the meaning of the ~ operator.) Note that this first level of filtering applies to individual nodes but not to their children. If the second argument is `NodeFilter.SHOW_TEXT`, your NodeIterator or TreeWalker does not return element nodes to you, but it does not discard them entirely; it still traverses the subtree beneath the Element nodes to find the Text nodes you are interested in.

Any nodes that pass this type-based filtration may be put through a second level of filtering. This second filter is implemented by a function you define and can therefore perform arbitrarily complex filtering. If you do not need this kind of filtering, you can simply specify `null` as the value of the third argument to `create-NodeIterator( )` or `createTreeWalker( )`. But if you do want this kind of filtering, you must pass a function as the third argument.

The function should expect a single node argument, and it should evaluate the node and return a value that indicates whether the node should be filtered out. There are three possible return values, defined by three `NodeFilter` constants. If your filter function returns `NodeFilter.FILTER_ACCEPT`, the node is returned by the NodeIterator or TreeWalker. If your function returns `NodeFilter.FILTER_SKIP`, the node is filtered out and is not returned by the NodeIterator or TreeWalker. The children of the node are still traversed, however. If you are working with a TreeWalker, your filter function may also return the value `NodeFilter.FILTER_REJECT`, which specifies that the node should not be returned and that it should not even be traversed.

Example 17-10 demonstrates the creation and use of a NodeIterator and should clarify the previous discussion. Note, however, that at the time of this writing none of the major web browsers support the Traversal API, so this example is untested!

Example 17-10. Creating and using a NodeIterator

```
// Define a NodeFilter function to accept only <img> elements
function imgfilter(n) {
    if (n.tagName == 'IMG') return NodeFilter.FILTER_ACCEPT;
    else return NodeFilter.FILTER_SKIP;
}

// Create a NodeIterator to find <img> tags
var images = document.createNodeIterator(document,  // Traverse entire document
    /* Look only at Element nodes */     NodeFilter.SHOW_ELEMENT,
    /* Filter out all but <img> */       imgfilter,
    /* Unused in HTML documents */       false);

// Use the iterator to loop through all images and do something with them
var image;
while((image = images.nextNode( )) != null) {
    image.style.visibility = "hidden";  // Process the image here
}
```

17.5.2 The DOM Range API

The DOM Range API consists of a single interface, Range. A Range object represents a contiguous range* of document content, contained between a specified start position and a specified end position. Many applications that display text and documents allow the user to select a portion of the document by dragging with the mouse. Such a selected portion of a document is conceptually equivalent to a range.† When a node of a document tree falls within a range, we often say that the node is "selected," even though the Range object may not have anything to do with a selection action initiated by the end user. When the start and end positions of a range are the same, we say that the range is "collapsed." In this case, the Range object represents a single position or insertion point within a document.

The Range object provides methods for defining the start and end positions of a range, copying and deleting the contents of a range, and inserting nodes at the start position of a range. Support for the Range API is optional. At the time of this writing, it is supported by Netscape 6.1. IE 5 supports a proprietary API that is similar to, but not compatible with, the Range API. You can test for Range support with this code:

```
document.implementation.hasFeature("Range", "2.0");  // True if Range is supported
```

17.5.2.1 Start and end positions

The start and end positions of a range are each specified by two values. The first value is a document node, typically a Document, Element, or Text object. The second value is a number that represents a position within that node. When the node is a document or element, the number represents a position between the children of the document or the element. An offset of 0, for example, represents the position immediately before the first child of the node. An offset of 1 represents the position after the first child and before the second. When the specified node is a Text node (or another text-based node type, such as Comment), the number represents a position between the characters of text. An offset of 0 specifies the position before the first character of text, an offset of 1 specifies the position between the first and second characters, and so on. With start and end positions specified in this way, a range represents all nodes and/or characters between the start and end positions. The real power of the Range interface is that the start and end positions may fall within different nodes of the document, and therefore a range may span multiple (and fractional) Element and Text nodes.

* That is, a logically contiguous range. In bidirectional languages such as Arabic and Hebrew, a logically contiguous range of a document may be visually discontiguous when displayed.

† Although web browsers typically allow the user to select document content, the current DOM Level 2 standard does not make the contents of those ranges available to JavaScript, so there is no standard way to obtain a Range object that corresponds to a user's desired selection.

To demonstrate the action of the various range-manipulation methods, I'm going to adopt the notation used in the DOM specification for illustrating the document content represented by a range. Document contents are shown in the form of HTML source code, with the contents of a range in **bold**. For example, the following line represents a range that begins at position 0 within the <body> node and continues to position 8 within the Text node contained within the <h1> node:

```
<body><h1>Document Title</h1><body>
```

To create a Range object, call the `createRange()` method of the Document object:

```
var r = document.createRange();
```

Newly created ranges have both start and end points initialized to position 0 within the Document object. Before you can do anything interesting with a range, you must set the start and end positions to specify the desired document range. There are several ways you can do this. The most general way is to call the `setStart()` and `setEnd()` methods to specify the start and end points. Each is passed a node and a position within the node.

A higher-level technique for setting a start and/or end position is to call `setStartBefore()`, `setStartAfter()`, `setEndBefore()`, or `setEndAfter()`. These methods each take a single node as their argument. They set the start or end position of the Range to the position before or after the specified node within the parent of that node.

Finally, if you want to define a Range that represents a single Node or subtree of a document, you can use the `selectNode()` or `selectNodeContent()` method. Both methods take a single node argument. `selectNode()` sets the start and end positions before and after the specified node within its parent, defining a range that includes the node and all of its children. `selectNodeContent()` sets the start of the range to the position before the first child of the node and sets the end of the range to the position after the last child of the node. The resulting range contains all the children of the specified node, but not the node itself.

17.5.2.2 Manipulating ranges

Once you've defined a range, there are a number of interesting things you can do with it. To delete the document content within a range, simply call the `deleteContents()` method of the Range object. When a range includes partially selected Text nodes, the deletion operation is a little tricky. Consider the following range:

```
<p>This is <i>only</i> a test
```

After a call to `deleteContents()`, the affected portion of the document looks like this:

```
<p>This<i>ly</i> a test
```

Even though the <i> element was included (partially) in the Range, that element remains (with modified content) in the document tree after the deletion.

If you want to remove the content of a range from a document but also want to save the extracted content (for reinsertion as part of a paste operation, perhaps), you should use extractContents( ) instead of deleteContents( ). This method removes nodes from the document tree and inserts them into a DocumentFragment (introduced earlier in this chapter), which it returns. When a range includes a partially selected node, that node remains in the document tree and has its content modified as needed. A clone of the node (see Node.cloneNode( )) is made (and modified) to insert into the DocumentFragment. Consider the previous example again. If extractContents( ) is called instead of deleteContents( ), the effect on the document is the same as shown previously, and the returned DocumentFragment contains:

```
is <i>on</i>
```

extractContents( ) works when you want to perform the equivalent of a cut operation on the document. If instead you want to do a copy operation and extract content without deleting it from the document, use cloneContents( ) instead of extractContents( ).*

In addition to specifying the boundaries of text to be deleted or cloned, the start position of a range can be used to indicate an insertion point within a document. The insertNode( ) method of a range inserts the specified node (and all of its children) into the document at the start position of the range. If the specified node is already part of the document tree, it is moved from its current location and reinserted at the position specified by the range. If the specified node is a DocumentFragment, all the children of the node are inserted instead of the node itself.

Another useful method of the Range object is surroundContents( ). This method reparents the contents of a range to the specified node and inserts that node into the document tree at the position of the range. For example, by passing a newly created <i> node to surroundContents( ), you could transform this range:

```
This is only a test
```

into:

```
This is <i>only</i> a test
```

Note that because opening and closing tags must be properly nested in HTML files, surroundContents( ) cannot be used (and will throw an exception) for ranges that partially select any nodes other than Text nodes. The range used earlier to illustrate the deleteContents( ) method could not be used with surroundContents( ), for example.

The Range object has various other features as well. You can compare the boundaries of two different ranges with compareBoundaryPoints( ), clone a range with cloneRange( ), and extract a plain-text copy of the content of a range (not including

* Implementing word processor–style cut, copy, and paste operations is actually more complex than this. Simple range operations on a complex document tree do not always produce the desired cut-and-paste behavior in the linear view of the document.

any markup) with `toString()`. The start and end positions of a range are accessible through the read-only properties `startContainer`, `startOffset`, `endContainer`, and `endOffset`. The start and end points of all valid ranges share a common ancestor somewhere in the document tree, even if it is the Document object at the root of the tree. You can find out what this common ancestor is with the `commonAncestorContainer` property of the range.

CHAPTER 18

Cascading Style Sheets and Dynamic HTML

Cascading Style Sheets (CSS) is a standard for specifying the visual presentation* of HTML (or XML) documents. In theory, you use HTML markup to specify the structure of your document, resisting the temptation to use deprecated HTML tags such as `<font>` to specify how the document should look. Instead, you use CSS to define a style sheet that specifies how the structured elements of your document should be displayed. For example, you can use CSS to specify that the level-one headings defined by `<h1>` tags should be displayed in bold, sans-serif, centered, uppercase, 24-point letters.

CSS is a technology intended for use by graphic designers or anyone concerned with the precise visual display of HTML documents. It is of interest to client-side JavaScript programmers because the document object model allows the styles that are applied to the individual elements of a document to be scripted. Used together, CSS and JavaScript enable a variety of visual effects loosely referred to as Dynamic HTML (DHTML).†

The ability to script CSS styles allows you to dynamically change colors, fonts, and so on. More importantly, it allows you to set and change the position of elements and even to hide and show elements. This means that you can use DHTML techniques to create animated transitions where document content "slides in" from the right, for example, or an expanding and collapsing outline list in which the user can control the amount of information that is displayed.

This chapter begins with an overview of CSS style sheets and the use of CSS styles to specify the position and visibility of document elements. It then explains how CSS styles can be scripted using the API defined by the DOM Level 2 standard. Finally, it demonstrates the nonstandard, browser-specific APIs that can be used to achieve DHTML effects in Netscape 4 and Internet Explorer 4.

* And, in the CSS2 standard, also the aural presentation.

† Many advanced DHTML effects also involve the event-handling techniques we'll see in Chapter 19.

18.1 Styles and Style Sheets with CSS

Styles in CSS are specified as a semicolon-separated list of name/value attribute pairs, where each name and value are separated by colons. For example, the following style specifies bold, blue, underlined text:

```
font-weight: bold; color: blue; text-decoration: underline;
```


The CSS standard defines quite a few style attributes you can set. Table 18-1 lists all the attributes except for those used only in audio style sheets. You are not expected to understand or be familiar with all these attributes, their values, or their meanings. As you become familiar with CSS and use it in your documents and scripts, however, you may find this table a convenient quick reference. For more complete documentation on CSS, consult *Cascading Style Sheets: The Definitive Guide*, by Eric Meyer (O'Reilly), or *Dynamic HTML: The Definitive Guide*, by Danny Goodman (O'Reilly). Or read the specification itself—you can find it at *http://www.w3c.org/TR/REC-CSS2/*.

The second column of Table 18-1 shows the allowed values for each style attribute. It uses the grammar used by the CSS specification. Items in `fixed-width font` are keywords and should appear exactly as shown. Items in *italics* specify a data type such as a string or a length. Note that the *length* type is a number followed by a units specification such as px (for pixels). See a CSS reference for details on the other types. Items that appear in *`italic fixed-width font`* represent the set of values allowed by some other CSS attribute. In addition to the values shown in the table, each style attribute may have the value "inherit", to specify that it should inherit the value from its parent.

Values separated by a | are alternatives; you must specify exactly one. Values separated by || are options; you must specify at least one, but you may specify more than one, and they can appear in any order. Square brackets [] are used for grouping values. An asterisk (*) specifies that the previous value or group may appear zero or more times, a plus sign (+) specifies that the previous value or group may appear one or more times, and a question mark (?) specifies that the previous item is optional and may appear zero or one time. Numbers within curly braces specify a number of repetitions. For example, {2} specifies that the previous item must be repeated twice, and {1,4} specifies that the previous item must appear at least once and no more than four times. (This repetition syntax may seem familiar: it is the same one used by JavaScript regular expressions, discussed in Chapter 10.)

Table 18-1. CSS style attributes and their values

Name	Values
background	[*background-color* || *background-image* || *background-repeat* || *background-attachment* || *background-position*]
background-attachment	scroll | fixed
background-color	*color* | transparent
background-image	url(*url*) | none
background-position	[[*percentage* | *length*]{1,2} | [[top | center | bottom] || [left | center | right]]]

Table 18-1. CSS style attributes and their values (continued)

Name	Values
background-repeat	repeat | repeat-x | repeat-y | no-repeat
border	[*border-width* || *border-style* || *color*]
border-collapse	collapse | separate
border-color	*color*{1,4} | transparent
border-spacing	*length length?*
border-style	[none | hidden | dotted | dashed | solid | double | groove | ridge | inset | outset]{1,4}
border-top border-right border-bottom border-left	[*border-top-width* || *border-top-style* || *color*]
border-top-color border-right-color border-bottom-color border-left-color	*color*
border-top-style border-right-style border-bottom-style border-left-style	none | hidden | dotted | dashed | solid | double | groove | ridge | inset | outset
border-top-width border-right-width border-bottom-width border-left-width	thin | medium | thick | *length*
border-width	[thin | medium | thick | *length*]{1,4}
bottom	*length* | *percentage* | auto
caption-side	top | bottom | left | right
clear	none | left | right | both
clip	[rect([*length* | auto]{4})] | auto
color	*color*
content	[*string* | url(*url*) | *counter* | attr(*attribute-name*) | open-quote | close-quote | no-open-quote | no-close-quote]+
counter-increment	[*identifier integer?*]+ | none
counter-reset	[*identifier integer?*]+ | none
cursor	[[url(*url*) ,]* [auto | crosshair | default | pointer | move | e-resize | ne-resize | nw-resize | n-resize | se-resize | sw-resize | s-resize | w-resize | text | wait | help]]
direction	ltr | rtl
display	inline | block | list-item | run-in | compact | marker | table | inline-table | table-row-group | table-header-group | table-footer-group | table-row | table-column-group | table-column | table-cell | table-caption | none
empty-cells	show | hide

Table 18-1. CSS style attributes and their values (continued)

<table>
<tr><th>Name</th><th>Values</th></tr>
<tr><td>float</td><td>left | right | none</td></tr>
<tr><td>font</td><td>[[font-style || font-variant || font-weight]? font-size [/ line-height]? font-family] | caption | icon | menu | message-box | small-caption | status-bar</td></tr>
<tr><td>font-family</td><td>[[family-name | serif | sans-serif | monospace | cursive | fantasy],]+</td></tr>
<tr><td>font-size</td><td>xx-small | x-small | small | medium | large | x-large | xx-large | smaller | larger | length | percentage</td></tr>
<tr><td>font-size-adjust</td><td>number | none</td></tr>
<tr><td>font-stretch</td><td>normal | wider | narrower | ultra-condensed | extra-condensed | condensed | semi-condensed | semi-expanded | expanded | extra-expanded | ultra-expanded</td></tr>
<tr><td>font-style</td><td>normal | italic | oblique</td></tr>
<tr><td>font-variant</td><td>normal | small-caps</td></tr>
<tr><td>font-weight</td><td>normal | bold | bolder | lighter | 100 | 200 | 300 | 400 | 500 | 600 | 700 | 800 | 900</td></tr>
<tr><td>height</td><td>length | percentage | auto</td></tr>
<tr><td>left</td><td>length | percentage | auto</td></tr>
<tr><td>letter-spacing</td><td>normal | length</td></tr>
<tr><td>line-height</td><td>normal | number | length | percentage</td></tr>
<tr><td>list-style</td><td>[list-style-type || list-style-position || list-style-image]</td></tr>
<tr><td>list-style-image</td><td>url(url) | none</td></tr>
<tr><td>list-style-position</td><td>inside | outside</td></tr>
<tr><td>list-style-type</td><td>disc | circle | square | decimal | decimal-leading-zero | lower-roman | upper-roman | lower-greek | lower-alpha | lower-latin | upper-alpha | upper-latin | hebrew | armenian | georgian | cjk-ideographic | hiragana | katakana | hiragana-iroha | katakana-iroha | none</td></tr>
<tr><td>margin</td><td>[length | percentage | auto]{1,4}</td></tr>
<tr><td>margin-top
margin-right
margin-bottom
margin-left</td><td>length | percentage | auto</td></tr>
<tr><td>marker-offset</td><td>length | auto</td></tr>
<tr><td>marks</td><td>[crop || cross] | none</td></tr>
<tr><td>max-height</td><td>length | percentage | none</td></tr>
<tr><td>max-width</td><td>length | percentage | none</td></tr>
<tr><td>min-height</td><td>length | percentage</td></tr>
<tr><td>min-width</td><td>length | percentage</td></tr>
<tr><td>orphans</td><td>integer</td></tr>
<tr><td>outline</td><td>[outline-color || outline-style || outline-width]</td></tr>
<tr><td>outline-color</td><td>color | invert</td></tr>
</table>

Table 18-1. CSS style attributes and their values (continued)

<table>
<tr><th>Name</th><th>Values</th></tr>
<tr><td><code>outline-style</code></td><td><code>none</code> | <code>hidden</code> | <code>dotted</code> | <code>dashed</code> | <code>solid</code> | <code>double</code> | <code>groove</code> | <code>ridge</code> | <code>inset</code> | <code>outset</code></td></tr>
<tr><td><code>outline-width</code></td><td><code>thin</code> | <code>medium</code> | <code>thick</code> | length</td></tr>
<tr><td><code>overflow</code></td><td><code>visible</code> | <code>hidden</code> | <code>scroll</code> | <code>auto</code></td></tr>
<tr><td><code>padding</code></td><td>[length | percentage]{1,4}</td></tr>
<tr><td><code>padding-top</code>
<code>padding-right</code>
<code>padding-bottom</code>
<code>padding-left</code></td><td>length | percentage</td></tr>
<tr><td><code>page</code></td><td>identifier | <code>auto</code></td></tr>
<tr><td><code>page-break-after</code></td><td><code>auto</code> | <code>always</code> | <code>avoid</code> | <code>left</code> | <code>right</code></td></tr>
<tr><td><code>page-break-before</code></td><td><code>auto</code> | <code>always</code> | <code>avoid</code> | <code>left</code> | <code>right</code></td></tr>
<tr><td><code>page-break-inside</code></td><td><code>avoid</code> | <code>auto</code></td></tr>
<tr><td><code>position</code></td><td><code>static</code> | <code>relative</code> | <code>absolute</code> | <code>fixed</code></td></tr>
<tr><td><code>quotes</code></td><td>[string string]+ | <code>none</code></td></tr>
<tr><td><code>right</code></td><td>length | percentage | <code>auto</code></td></tr>
<tr><td><code>size</code></td><td>length{1,2} | <code>auto</code> | <code>portrait</code> | <code>landscape</code></td></tr>
<tr><td><code>table-layout</code></td><td><code>auto</code> | <code>fixed</code></td></tr>
<tr><td><code>text-align</code></td><td><code>left</code> | <code>right</code> | <code>center</code> | <code>justify</code> | string</td></tr>
<tr><td><code>text-decoration</code></td><td><code>none</code> | <code>[underline</code> || <code>overline</code> || <code>line-through</code> || <code>blink]</code></td></tr>
<tr><td><code>text-indent</code></td><td>length | percentage</td></tr>
<tr><td><code>text-shadow</code></td><td><code>none</code> | [color || length length length? ,]* [color || length length length?]</td></tr>
<tr><td><code>text-transform</code></td><td><code>capitalize</code> | <code>uppercase</code> | <code>lowercase</code> | <code>none</code></td></tr>
<tr><td><code>top</code></td><td>length | percentage | <code>auto</code></td></tr>
<tr><td><code>unicode-bidi</code></td><td><code>normal</code> | <code>embed</code> | <code>bidi-override</code></td></tr>
<tr><td><code>vertical-align</code></td><td><code>baseline</code> | <code>sub</code> | <code>super</code> | <code>top</code> | <code>text-top</code> | <code>middle</code> | <code>bottom</code> | <code>text-bottom</code> | percentage | length</td></tr>
<tr><td><code>visibility</code></td><td><code>visible</code> | <code>hidden</code> | <code>collapse</code></td></tr>
<tr><td><code>white-space</code></td><td><code>normal</code> | <code>pre</code> | <code>nowrap</code></td></tr>
<tr><td><code>widows</code></td><td>integer</td></tr>
<tr><td><code>width</code></td><td>length | percentage | <code>auto</code></td></tr>
<tr><td><code>word-spacing</code></td><td><code>normal</code> | length</td></tr>
<tr><td><code>z-index</code></td><td><code>auto</code> | integer</td></tr>
</table>

The CSS standard allows certain style attributes that are commonly used together to be combined using special shortcut attributes. For example, the `font-family`, `font-size`, `font-style`, and `font-weight` attributes can all be set at once using a single `font` attribute:

```
font: bold italic 24pt helvetica;
```

In fact, some of the attributes listed in Table 18-1 are themselves shortcuts. The `margin` and `padding` attributes are shortcuts for attributes that specify margins, padding, and borders for each of the individual sides of an element. Thus, instead of using the `margin` attribute, you can use `margin-left`, `margin-right`, `margin-top`, and `margin-bottom`, and similarly for `padding`.

18.1.1 Applying Style Rules to Document Elements

You can apply style attributes to the elements of a document in a number of ways. One way is to use them in the `style` attribute of an HTML tag. For example, to set the margins of an individual paragraph, you can use a tag like this:

```
<p style="margin-left: 1in; margin-right: 1in;">
```

One of the important goals of CSS is to separate document content and structure from document presentation. Specifying styles with the `style` attribute of individual HTML tags does not accomplish this (although it can be a useful technique for DHTML). To achieve the separation of structure from presentation, we use *style sheets*, which group all the style information into a single place. A CSS style sheet consists of a set of style rules. Each rule begins with a selector that specifies the document element or elements to which it applies, followed by a set of style attributes and their values within curly braces. The simplest kind of rule defines styles for one or more specific tag names. For example, the following rule sets the margins and background color for the `<body>` tag:

```
body { margin-left: 30px; margin-right: 15px; background-color: #ffffff }
```

The following rule specifies that text within `<h1>` and `<h2>` headings should be centered:

```
h1, h2 { text-align: center; }
```

In the previous example, note the use of a comma to separate the tag names to which the styles are to apply. If the comma is omitted, the selector specifies a contextual rule that applies only when one tag is nested within another. For example, the following rules specify that `<blockquote>` tags are displayed in an italic font, but text inside an `<i>` tag inside a `<blockquote>` is displayed in plain, nonitalic text:

```
blockquote { font-style: italic; }
blockquote i { font-style: normal; }
```

Another kind of style sheet rule uses a different selector to specify a *class* of elements to which its styles should be applied. The class of an element is defined by the `class` attribute of the HTML tag. For example, the following rule specifies that any tag with the attribute `class="attention"` should be displayed in bold:

```
.attention { font-weight: bold; }
```

Class selectors can be combined with tag name selectors. The following rule specifies that when a `<p>` tag has the `class="attention"` attribute, it should be displayed in red, in addition to being displayed in a bold font (as specified by the previous rule):

```
p.attention { color: red; }
```

Finally, style sheets can contain rules that apply only to individual elements that have a specified `id` attribute. The following rule specifies that the element with an `id` attribute equal to "p1" should not be shown:

```
#p1 { visibility: hidden; }
```

We've seen the `id` attribute before: it is used with the DOM function `getElementById( )` to return individual elements of a document. As you might imagine, this kind of element-specific style sheet rule is useful when we want to manipulate the style of an individual element. Given the previous rule, for example, a script might switch the value of the `visibility` attribute from `hidden` to `visible`, causing the element to dynamically appear.

18.1.2 Associating Style Sheets with Documents

You can incorporate a style sheet into an HTML document by placing it between `<style>` and `</style>` tags within the `<head>` of the document, or you can store the style sheet in a file of its own and reference it from the HTML document using a `<link>` tag. You can also combine these two techniques by creating a document-specific style sheet between `<style>` tags that references or imports a document-independent style sheet using the special `@import` "at-rule." Consult a CSS reference for details on `@import`.

18.1.3 The Cascade

Recall that the C in CSS stands for "cascading." This term indicates that the style rules that apply to any given element in a document can come from a cascade of different sources. Each web browser typically has its own default styles for all HTML elements and may allow the user to override these defaults with a user style sheet. The author of a document can define style sheets within `<style>` tags or in external files that are linked in or imported into other style sheets. The author may also define inline styles for individual elements with the HTML `style` attribute.

The CSS specification includes a complete set of rules for determining which rules from the cascade take precedence over the other rules. Briefly, however, what you need to know is that the user style sheet overrides the default browser style sheet, author style sheets override the user style sheet, and inline styles override everything. The exception to this general rule is that user style attributes whose values include the `!important` modifier override author styles. Within a style sheet, if more than one rule applies to an element, styles defined by the most specific rule override conflicting styles defined by less specific rules. Rules that specify an element `id` are the most specific. Rules that specify a `class` are next. Rules that specify only tag names are the least specific, but rules that specify multiple nested tag names are more specific than rules that specify only a single tag name.

18.1.4 Versions of CSS

At the time of this writing, there are two versions of the CSS standard. CSS1 was adopted in December, 1996 and defines attributes for specifying colors, fonts, margins, borders, and other basic styles. Netscape 4 and Internet Explorer 4 both implement at least partial support for CSS1. The second edition of the standard, CSS2, was adopted in May, 1998; it defines a number of more advanced features, most notably support for absolute positioning of elements. The advanced features of CSS2 are supported only in sixth-generation browsers. Fortunately, however, the crucial positioning features of CSS2 began the standardization process as part of a separate CSS-Positioning (CSS-P) effort, and therefore some of these DHTML-enabling features are available in fourth-generation browsers. Work continues on a third edition of the CSS standard. You can find the CSS specifications and working drafts at *http://www.w3.org/Style/CSS/*.

Client-Side JavaScript

18.1.5 CSS Example

Example 18-1 is an HTML file that defines and uses a style sheet. It demonstrates the previously described tag name, class, and ID-based style rules, and it also has an example of an inline style defined with the style attribute. Remember that this example is meant only as an overview of CSS syntax and capabilities. Full coverage of CSS is beyond the scope of this book.

Example 18-1. Defining and using Cascading Style Sheets

```
<head>
<style type="text/css">
/* Specify that headings display in blue italic text. */
h1, h2 { color: blue; font-style: italic }

/*
 * Any element of class="WARNING" displays in big bold text with large margins
 * and a yellow background with a fat red border.
 */
.WARNING {
          font-weight: bold;
          font-size: 150%;
          margin: 0 1in 0 1in; /* top right bottom left */
          background-color: yellow;
          border: solid red 8px;
          padding: 10px;       /* 10 pixels on all 4 sides */
}

/*
 * Text within an h1 or h2 heading within an element with class="WARNING"
 * should be centered, in addition to appearing in blue italics.
 */
.WARNING h1, .WARNING h2 { text-align: center }
```

Example 18-1. Defining and using Cascading Style Sheets (continued)

```
/* The single element with id="P23" displays in centered uppercase. */
#P23 {
      text-align: center;
      text-transform: uppercase;
}
</style>
</head>
<body>
<h1>Cascading Style Sheets Demo</h1>

<div class="WARNING">
<h2>Warning</h2>
This is a warning!
Notice how it grabs your attention with its bold text and bright colors.
Also notice that the heading is centered and in blue italics.
</div>

<p id="P23">
This paragraph is centered<br>
and appears in uppercase letters.<br>
<span style="text-transform: none">
Here we explicitly use an inline style to override the uppercase letters.
</span>
</p>
</body>
```

18.2 Element Positioning with CSS

For DHTML content developers, the most important feature of CSS is the ability to use ordinary CSS style attributes to specify the visibility, size, and precise position of individual elements of a document. In order to do DHTML programming, it is important to understand how these style attributes work. They are summarized in Table 18-2 and documented in more detail in the sections that follow.

Table 18-2. CSS positioning and visibility attributes

Attribute(s)	Description
`position`	Specifies the type of positioning applied to an element
`top`, `left`	Specifies the position of the top and left edges of an element
`bottom`, `right`	Specifies the position of the bottom and right edges of an element
`width`, `height`	Specifies the size of an element
`z-index`	Specifies the "stacking order" of an element relative to any overlapping elements; defines a third dimension of element positioning
`display`	Specifies how and whether an element is displayed
`visibility`	Specifies whether an element is visible
`clip`	Defines a "clipping region" for an element; only portions of the element within this region are displayed
`overflow`	Specifies what to do if an element is bigger than the space allotted for it

18.2.1 The Key to DHTML: The position Attribute

The CSS `position` attribute specifies the type of positioning applied to an element. The four possible values for this attribute are:

`static`
: This is the default value and specifies that the element is positioned according to the normal flow of document content (for most Western languages, this is left to right and top to bottom.) Statically positioned elements are not DHTML elements and cannot be positioned with the `top`, `left`, and other attributes. To use DHTML positioning techniques with a document element, you must first set its `position` attribute to one of the other three values.

`absolute`
: This value allows you to specify the position of an element relative to its containing element. Absolutely positioned elements are positioned independently of all other elements and are not part of the flow of statically positioned elements. An absolutely positioned element is positioned either relative to the `<body>` of the document or, if it is nested within another absolutely positioned element, relative to that element. This is the most commonly used positioning type for DHTML.

`fixed`
: This value allows you to specify an element's position with respect to the browser window. Elements with `fixed` positioning do not scroll with the rest of the document and thus can be used to achieve frame-like effects. Like absolutely positioned elements, fixed-position elements are independent of all others and are not part of the document flow. Fixed positioning is a CSS2 feature and is not supported by fourth-generation browsers. (It is supported in Netscape 6 and IE 5 for the Macintosh, but it is not supported by IE 5 or IE 6 for Windows).

`relative`
: When the `position` attribute is set to `relative`, an element is laid out according to the normal flow, and its position is then adjusted relative to its position in the normal flow. The space allocated for the element in the normal document flow remains allocated for it, and the elements on either side of it do not close up to fill in that space, nor are they "pushed away" from the new position of the element. Relative positioning can be useful for some static graphic design purposes, but it is not commonly used for DHTML effects.

18.2.2 Specifying the Position and Size of Elements

Once you have set the `position` attribute of an element to something other than `static`, you can specify the position of that element with some combination of the `left`, `top`, `right`, and `bottom` attributes. The most common positioning technique is to specify the `left` and `top` attributes, which specify the distance from the left edge of the containing element (usually the document itself) to the left edge of the element, and the distance from the top edge of the container to the top edge of the element. For example, to place an element 100 pixels from the left and 100 pixels from the top of the document, you can specify CSS styles in a style attribute as follows:

```
<div style="position: absolute; left: 100px; top: 100px;">
```

The containing element relative to which a dynamic element is positioned is not necessarily the same as the containing element within which the element is defined in the document source. Since dynamic elements are not part of normal element flow, their positions are not specified relative to the static container element within which they are defined. Most dynamic elements are positioned relative to the document (the <body> tag) itself. The exception is dynamic elements that are defined within other dynamic elements. In this case, the nested dynamic element is positioned relative to its nearest dynamic ancestor.

Although it is most common to specify the position of the upper-left corner of an element with left and top, you can also use right and bottom to specify the position of the bottom and right edges of an element relative to the bottom and right edges of the containing element. For example, to position an element so that its bottom-right corner is at the bottom-right of the document (assuming it is not nested within another dynamic element), use the following styles:

```
position: absolute; right: 0px; bottom: 0px;
```

To position an element so that its top edge is 10 pixels from the top of the window and its right edge is 10 pixels from the right of the window, you can use these styles:

```
position: fixed; right: 10px; top: 10px;
```

Note that the right and bottom attributes are newer additions to the CSS standard and are not supported by fourth-generation browsers, as top and left are.

In addition to the position of elements, CSS allows you to specify their size. This is most commonly done by providing values for the width and height style attributes. For example, the following HTML creates an absolutely positioned element with no content. Its width, height, and background-color attributes make it appear as a small blue square:

```
<div style="position: absolute; left: 10px; right: 10px;
            width: 10px; height: 10px; background-color: blue">
</div>
```

Another way to specify the width of an element is to specify a value for both the left and right attributes. Similarly, you can specify the height of an element by specifying both top and bottom. If you specify a value for left, right, and width, however, the width attribute overrides the right attribute; if the height of an element is overconstrained, height takes priority over bottom.

Bear in mind that it is not necessary to specify the size of every dynamic element. Some elements, such as images, have an intrinsic size. Furthermore, for dynamic elements that contain text or other flowed content, it is often sufficient to specify the desired width of the element and allow the height to be determined automatically by the layout of the element's content.

In the previous positioning examples, values for the position and size attributes were specified with the suffix "px". This stands for pixels. The CSS standard allows measurements to be done in a number of other units, including inches ("in"), centimeters ("cm"), points ("pt"), and ems ("em"—a measure of the line height for the current font). Pixel units are most commonly used with DHTML programming. Note that the CSS standard requires a unit to be specified. Some browsers may assume pixels if you omit the unit specification, but you should not rely on this behavior.

Instead of specifying absolute positions and sizes using the units shown above, CSS also allows you to specify the position and size of an element as a percentage of the size of the containing element. For example, the following HTML creates an empty element with a black border that is half as wide and half as high as the containing element (or the browser window) and centered within that element:

```
<div style="position: absolute; left: 25%; top: 25%; width: 50%; height: 50%;
            border: 2px solid black">
</div>
```

18.2.2.1 Element size and position details

It is important to understand some details about how the `left`, `right`, `width`, `top`, `bottom`, and `height` attributes work. First, `width` and `height` specify the size of an element's content area only; they do not include any additional space required for the element's padding, border, or margins. To determine the full onscreen size of an element with a border, you must add the left and right padding and left and right border widths to the element width, and you must add the top and bottom padding and top and bottom border widths to the element's height.

Since `width` and `height` specify the element content area only, you might think that `left` and `top` (and `right` and `bottom`) would be measured relative to the content area of the containing element. In fact, the CSS standard specifies that these values are measured relative to the outside edge of the containing element's padding (which is the same as the inside edge of the element's border).

Let's consider an example to make this clearer. Suppose you've created a dynamically positioned container element that has 10 pixels of padding all the way around its content area and a 5 pixel border all the way around the padding. Now suppose you dynamically position a child element inside this container. If you set the `left` attribute of the child to "0 px", you'll discover that the child is positioned with its left edge right up against the inner edge of the container's border. With this setting, the child overlaps the container's padding, which presumably was supposed to remain empty (since that is the purpose of padding). If you want to position the child element in the upper left corner of the container's content area, you should set both the `left` and `top` attributes to "10px". Figure 18-1 helps to clarify this.

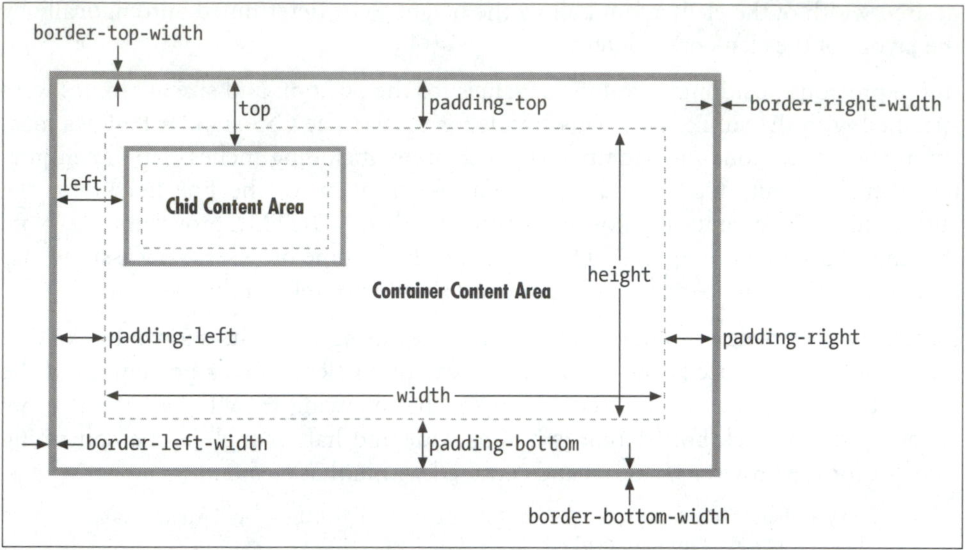

Figure 18-1. Dynamically positioned container and child elements with some CSS attributes

Now that you understand that `width` and `height` specify the size of an element's content area only and that the `left`, `top`, `right`, and `bottom` attributes are measured relative to the containing element's padding, there is one more detail you must be aware of: Internet Explorer Versions 4 through 5.5 for Windows (but not IE 5 for the Mac) implement the `width` and `height` attributes incorrectly and include an element's border and padding (but not its margins). For example, if you set the width of an element to 100 pixels and place a 10-pixel margin and a 5-pixel border on the left and right, the content area of the element ends up being only 70 pixels wide in these buggy versions of Internet Explorer.

In IE 6, the CSS position and size attributes work correctly when the browser is in standards mode and incorrectly (but compatibly with earlier versions) when the browser is in compatibility mode. Standards mode, and hence correct implementation of the CSS "box model," is triggered by the presence of a `<!DOCTYPE>` tag at the start of the document, declaring that the document adheres to the HTML 4.0 (or later) standard or some version of the XHTML standards. For example, any of the following three HTML document type declarations cause IE 6 to display documents in standards mode:

```
<!DOCTYPE HTML PUBLIC "-//W3C//DTD HTML 4.0//EN">
<!DOCTYPE HTML PUBLIC "-//W3C//DTD HTML 4.0 Strict//EN">
<!DOCTYPE HTML PUBLIC "-//W3C//DTD HTML 4.0 Transitional//EN"
    "http://www.w3.org/TR/html4/loose.dtd">
```

Netscape 6 and the Mozilla browser handle the `width` and `height` attributes correctly. But these browsers also have standards and compatibility modes, just as IE does. The absence of a `<!DOCTYPE>` declaration puts the Netscape browser in quirks mode, in which it mimics certain (relatively minor) nonstandard layout behaviors of

Netscape 4. The presence of <!DOCTYPE> causes the browser to break compatibility with Netscape 4 and correctly implement the standards.

18.2.3 The Third Dimension: z-index

We've seen that the `left`, `top`, `right`, and `bottom` attributes can be used to specify the X and Y coordinates of an element within the two-dimensional plane of the containing element. The `z-index` attribute defines a kind of third dimension: it allows you to specify the stacking order of elements and indicate which of two or more overlapping elements is drawn on top of the others. The `z-index` attribute is an integer. The default value is zero, but you may specify positive or negative values (although fourth-generation browsers may not support negative `z-index` values). When two or more elements overlap, they are drawn in order from lowest to highest `z-index`; the element with the highest `z-index` appears on top of all the others. If overlapping elements have the same `z-index`, they are drawn in the order in which they appear in the document, so the last overlapping element appears on top.

Note that `z-index` stacking applies only to sibling elements (i.e., elements that are children of the same container). If two elements that are not siblings overlap, setting their individual `z-index` attributes does not allow you to specify which one is on top. Instead, you must specify the `z-index` attribute for the two sibling containers of the two overlapping elements.

Nonpositioned elements are always laid out in a way that prevents overlaps, so the `z-index` attribute does not apply to them. Nevertheless, they have a default `z-index` of zero, which means that positioned elements with a positive `z-index` appear on top of the normal document flow, and positioned elements with a negative `z-index` appear beneath the normal document flow.

Note, finally, that some browsers do not honor the `z-index` attribute when it is applied to `<iframe>` tags, and you may find that inline frames float on top of other elements, regardless of the specified stacking order. You may have the same problem with other "windowed" elements such as `<select>` drop-down menus. Fourth-generation browsers may display all form-control elements on top of absolutely positioned elements, regardless of `z-index` settings.

18.2.4 Element Display and Visibility

There are two CSS attributes you can use to affect the visibility of a document element: `visibility` and `display`. The `visibility` attribute is simple: when the attribute is set to the value `hidden`, the element is not shown; when it is set to the value `visible`, the element is shown. The `display` attribute is more general and is used to specify the type of display an item receives. It specifies whether an element is a block element, an inline element, a list item, and so on. When `display` is set to `none`, however, the affected element is not displayed, or even laid out, at all.

The difference between the visibility and display style attributes has to do with their effect on elements that are not dynamically positioned. For an element that appears in the normal layout flow (with the position attribute set to static or relative), setting visibility to none makes the element invisible but reserves space for it in the document layout. Such an element can be repeatedly hidden and shown without changing the document layout. If an element's display attribute is set to none, however, no space is allocated for it in the document layout; elements on either side of it close up as if it were not there. (visibility and display have equivalent effects when used with absolute- or fixed-position elements, since these elements are never part of the document layout anyway.) You'll typically use the visibility attribute when you are working with dynamically positioned elements. The display attribute is useful when creating things like expanding and collapsing outlines.

Note that it doesn't make much sense to use visibility or display to make an element invisible unless you are going to use JavaScript to dynamically set these attributes and make the element visible at some point!* You'll see how you can do this later in the chapter.

18.2.5 Partial Visibility: overflow and clip

The visibility attribute allows you to completely hide a document element. The overflow and clip attributes allow you to display only part of an element. The overflow attribute specifies what happens when the content of an element exceeds the size specified (with the width and height style attributes, for example) for the element. The allowed values and their meanings for this attribute are as follows:

visible
: Content may overflow and be drawn outside of the element's box if necessary. This is the default.

hidden
: Content that overflows is clipped and hidden so that no content is ever drawn outside the region defined by the size and positioning attributes.

scroll
: The element's box has permanent horizontal and vertical scrollbars. If the content exceeds the size of the box, the scrollbars allow the user to scroll to view the extra content. This value is honored only when the document is displayed on a

* There is an exception: if you are creating a document that depends on CSS, you can warn users of browsers that do not support CSS with code like this:

```
<p style="display:none">
This document uses CSS, but your browser doesn't support it!
</p>
```

computer screen; when the document is printed on paper, for example, scrollbars obviously do not make sense.

`auto`
: Scrollbars are displayed only when content exceeds the element's size, rather than being permanently displayed.

While the `overflow` property allows you to specify what happens when an element's content is bigger than the element's box, the `clip` property allows you to specify exactly which portion of an element should be displayed, whether or not the element overflows. This attribute is especially useful for scripted DHTML effects in which an element is progressively displayed or uncovered.

The value of the `clip` property specifies the clipping region for the element. In CSS2 clipping regions are rectangular, but the syntax of the `clip` attribute leaves open the possibility that future versions of the standard will support clipping shapes other than rectangles. The syntax of the `clip` attribute is:

```
rect(top right bottom left)
```

The *`top`*, *`right`*, *`bottom`*, and *`left`* values specify the boundaries of the clipping rectangle relative to the upper-left corner of the element's box.* For example, to display only a 100 × 100-pixel portion of an element, you can give that element this `style` attribute:

```
style="clip: rect(0px 100px 100px 0px);"
```

Note that the four values within the parentheses are length values and must include a unit specification, such as "px" for pixels. Percentages are not allowed. Values may be negative to specify that the clipping region extends beyond the box specified for the element. You may also use the keyword `auto` for any of the four values to specify that that edge of the clipping region is the same as the corresponding edge of the element's box. For example, you can display just the leftmost 100 pixels of an element with this `style` attribute:

```
style="clip: rect(auto 100px auto auto);"
```

Note that there are no commas between the values, and the edges of the clipping region are specified in clockwise order from the top edge.

18.2.6 CSS Positioning Example

Example 18-2 is a nontrivial example using CSS style sheets and CSS positioning attributes. When this HTML document is displayed in a CSS-compliant browser, it

* As the CSS2 specification was originally written, these four values specified the offset of the edges of the clipping region from each of the corresponding edges of the element's box. All major browser implementations got it wrong, however, and interpreted the *`right`* and *`bottom`* values as offsets from the left and top edges. Because the implementations consistently disagree with the specification, the specification is being modified to match the implementations.

creates the visual effect of "subwindows" within the browser window. Figure 18-2 shows the effect created by the code in Example 18-2. Although the listing contains no JavaScript code, it is a useful demonstration of the powerful effects that can be achieved with CSS in general and the CSS positioning attributes in particular.

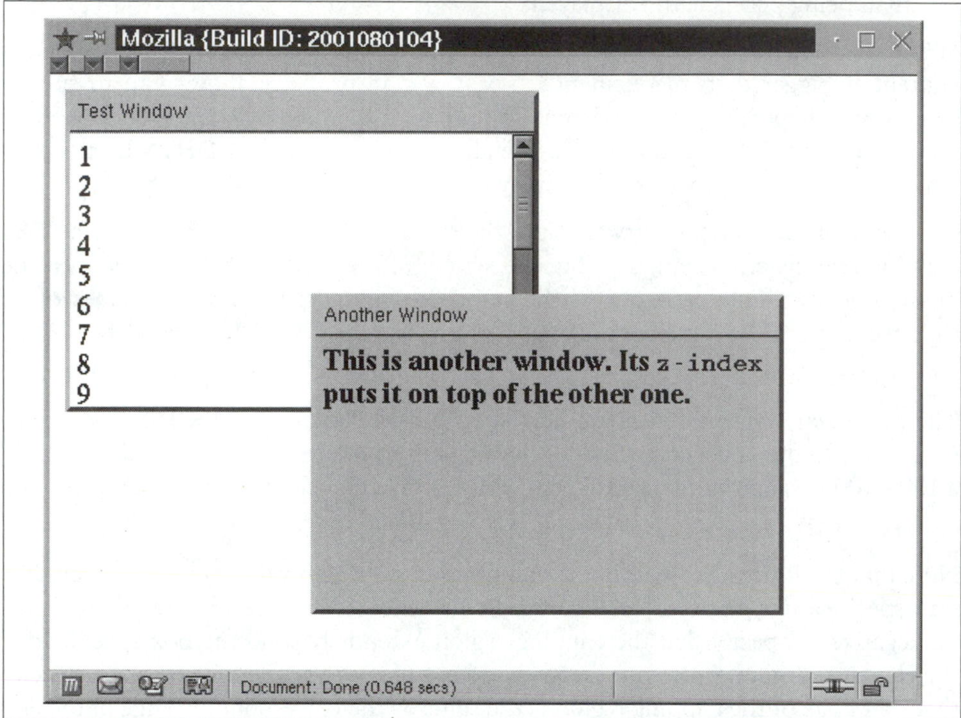

Figure 18-2. Windows created with CSS

Example 18-2. Displaying windows with CSS

```
<head>
<style type="text/css">
/**
 * This is a CSS style sheet that defines three style rules that we use
 * in the body of the document to create a "window" visual effect.
 * The rules use positioning attributes to set the overall size of the window
 * and the position of its components. Changing the size of the window
 * requires careful changes to positioning attributes in all three rules.
 **/
div.window {  /* Specifies size and border of the window */
    position: absolute;            /* The position is specified elsewhere */
    width: 300px; height: 200px;   /* Window size, not including borders */
    border: outset gray 3px;       /* Note 3D "outset" border effect */
}

div.titlebar {  /* Specifies position, size, and style of the titlebar */
```

Example 18-2. Displaying windows with CSS (continued)

```
    position: absolute;      /* It's a positioned element */
    top: 0px; height: 18px;  /* Titlebar is 18px + padding and borders */
    width: 290px;            /* 290 + 5px padding on left and right = 300 */
    background-color: ActiveCaption;  /* Use system titlebar color */
    border-bottom: groove black 2px;  /* Titlebar has border on bottom only */
    padding: 3px 5px 2px 5px;  /* Values clockwise: top, right, bottom, left */
    font: caption;             /* Use system font for titlebar */
}

div.content {  /* Specifies size, position and scrolling for window content */
    position: absolute;          /* It's a positioned element */
    top: 25px;                   /* 18px title+2px border+3px+2px padding */
    height: 165px;               /* 200px total - 25px titlebar - 10px padding */
    width: 290px;                /* 300px width - 10px of padding */
    padding: 5px;                /* Allow space on all four sides */
    overflow: auto;              /* Give us scrollbars if we need them */
    background-color: #ffffff;  /* White background by default */
}
</style>
</head>

<body>
<!-- Here is how we define a window: a "window" div with a titlebar and -->
<!-- content div nested between them. Note how position is specified with -->
<!-- a style attribute that augments the styles from the style sheet. -->
<div class="window" style="left: 10px; top: 10px; z-index: 10;">
<div class="titlebar">Test Window</div>
<div class="content">
1<br>2<br>3<br>4<br>5<br>6<br>7<br>8<br>9<br>0<br> <!-- Lots of lines to -->
1<br>2<br>3<br>4<br>5<br>6<br>7<br>8<br>9<br>0<br> <!-- demonstrate scrolling -->
</div>
</div>

<!-- Here's another window with different position, color, and font weight -->
<div class="window" style="left: 170px; top: 140px; z-index: 20;">
<div class="titlebar">Another Window</div>
<div class="content" style="background-color:#d0d0d0; font-weight:bold;">
This is another window. Its <tt>z-index</tt> puts it on top of the other one.
</div>
</div>
</body>
```

The major shortcoming of this example is that the style sheet specifies a fixed size for all windows. Because the titlebar and content portions of the window must be precisely positioned within the overall window, changing the size of a window requires changing the value of various positioning attributes in all three rules defined by the style sheet. This is difficult to do in a static HTML document, but it would not be so difficult if we could use a script to set all of the necessary attributes. We'll explore this topic in the next section.

18.3 Scripting Styles

The crux of DHTML is the ability to use JavaScript to dynamically change the style attributes applied to individual elements within a document. The DOM Level 2 standard defines an API that makes this quite easy to do. In Chapter 17, we saw how to use the DOM API to obtain references to document elements either by tag name or ID or by recursively traversing the entire document. Once you've obtained a reference to the element whose styles you want to manipulate, you use the element's `style` property to obtain a CSS2Properties object for that document element. This JavaScript object has JavaScript properties corresponding to each of the CSS1 and CSS2 style attributes. Setting these properties has the same effect as setting the corresponding styles in a `style` attribute on the element. Reading these properties returns the CSS attribute value, if any, that was set in the `style` attribute of the element. It is important to understand that the CSS2Properties object you obtain with the `style` property of an element specifies only the inline styles of the element. You cannot use the properties of the CSS2Properties object to obtain information about the style-sheet styles that apply to the element. By setting properties on this object, you are defining inline styles that effectively override style-sheet styles.

Consider the following script, for example. It finds all `<img>` elements in the document and loops through them looking for ones that appear (based on their size) to be banner advertisements. When it finds an ad, it uses the `style.visibility` property to set the CSS `visibility` attribute to `hidden`, making the ad invisible:

```
var imgs = document.getElementsByTagName("img");  // Find all images
for(var i = 0; i < imgs.length; i++) {            // Loop through them
    var img=imgs[i];
    if (img.width == 468 && img.height == 60)     // If it's a 468x60 banner...
        img.style.visibility = "hidden";          // hide it!
}
```

I've transformed this simple script into a "bookmarklet" by converting it to a `javascript:` URL and bookmarking it in my browser. I take subversive pleasure in using the bookmarklet to immediately hide distracting animated ads that won't stop animating. Here's a version of the script suitable for bookmarking:

```
javascript:a=document.getElementsByTagName("img");for(n=0;n<a.length;n++){
i=a[n];if(i.width==468&&i.height==60)i.style.visibility="hidden";}void 0;
```

The bookmarklet is written with very compact code and is intended to be formatted on a single line. The `javascript:` at the beginning of this bookmarklet identifies it as a URL whose body is a string of executable content. The `void 0` statement at the end causes the code to return an undefined value, which means that the browser continues to display the current web page (minus its banner ads, of course!). Without the `void 0`, the browser would overwrite the current web page with the return value of the last JavaScript statement executed.

18.3.1 Naming Conventions: CSS Attributes in JavaScript

Many CSS style attributes, such as `font-family`, contain hyphens in their names. In JavaScript, a hyphen is interpreted as a minus sign, so it is not possible to write an expression like:

```
element.style.font-family = "sans-serif";
```

Therefore, the names of the properties of the CSS2Properties object are slightly different from the names of actual CSS attributes. If a CSS attribute name contains one or more hyphens, the CSS2Properties property name is formed by removing the hyphens and capitalizing the letter immediately following each hyphen. Thus, the `border-left-width` attribute is accessed through the `borderLeftWidth` property, and you can access the `font-family` attribute with code like this:

```
element.style.fontFamily = "sans-serif";
```

There is one other naming difference between CSS attributes and the JavaScript properties of CSS2Properties. The word "float" is a keyword in Java and other languages, and although it is not currently used in JavaScript, it is reserved for possible future use. Therefore, the CSS2Properties object cannot have a property named `float` to correspond to the CSS `float` attribute. The solution to this problem is to prefix the `float` attribute with the string "css" to form the property name `cssFloat`. Thus, to set or query the value of the `float` attribute of an element, use the `cssFloat` property of the CSS2Properties object.

18.3.2 Working with Style Properties

When working with the style properties of the CSS2Properties object, remember that all values must be specified as strings. In a style sheet or `style` attribute, you can write:

```
position: absolute; font-family: sans-serif; background-color: #ffffff;
```

To accomplish the same thing for an element `e` with JavaScript, you have to quote all of the values:

```
e.style.position = "absolute";
e.style.fontFamily = "sans-serif";
e.style.backgroundColor = "#ffffff";
```

Note that the semicolons go outside the strings. These are just normal JavaScript semicolons; the semicolons you use in CSS style sheets are not required as part of the string values you set with JavaScript.

Furthermore, remember that all the positioning properties require units. Thus, it is not correct to set the `left` property like this:

```
e.style.left = 300;    // Incorrect: this is a number, not a string
e.style.left = "300";  // Incorrect: the units are missing
```

Units are required when setting style properties in JavaScript, just as they are when setting style attributes in style sheets. The correct way to set the value of the left property of an element e to 300 pixels is:

```
e.style.left = "300px";
```

If you want to set the left property to a computed value, be sure to append the units at the end of the computation:

```
e.style.left = (x0 + left_margin + left_border + left_padding) + "px";
```

As a side effect of appending the units, the addition of the unit string converts the computed value from a number to a string.

You can also use the CSS2Properties object to query the values of the CSS attributes that were explicitly set in the style attribute of an element or to read any inline style values previously set by JavaScript code. Once again, however, you must remember that the values returned by these properties are strings, not numbers, so the following code (which assumes that the element e has its margins specified with inline styles) does not do what you might expect it to:

```
var totalMarginWidth = e.style.marginLeft + e.style.marginRight;
```

Instead, you should use code like this:

```
var totalMarginWidth = parseInt(e.style.marginLeft) + parseInt(e.style.marginRight);
```

This expression simply discards the unit specifications returned at the ends of both strings. It assumes that both the marginLeft and marginRight properties were specified using the same units. If you exclusively use pixel units in your inline styles, you can usually get away with discarding the units like this.

Recall that some CSS attributes, such as margin, are shortcuts for other properties, such as margin-top, margin-right, margin-bottom, and margin-left. The CSS2Properties object has properties that correspond to these shortcut attributes. For example, you might set the margin property like this:

```
e.style.margin = topMargin + "px " + rightMargin + "px " +
                 bottomMargin + "px " + leftMargin + "px";
```

Arguably, it is easier to set the four margin properties individually:

```
e.style.marginTop = topMargin + "px";
e.style.marginRight = rightMargin + "px";
e.style.marginBottom = bottomMargin + "px";
e.style.marginLeft = leftMargin + "px";
```

You can also query the values of shortcut properties, but this is rarely worthwhile, because typically you must then parse the returned value to break it up into its component parts. This is usually difficult to do, and it is much simpler to query the component properties individually.

Finally, let me emphasize again that when you obtain a CSS2Properties object from the style property of an HTMLElement, the properties of this object represent the values of inline style attributes for the element. In other words, setting one of these properties is like setting a CSS attribute in the style attribute of the element: it affects only that one element, and it takes precedence over conflicting style settings from all other sources in the CSS cascade. This precise control over individual elements is exactly what we want when using JavaScript to create DHTML effects.

When you read the values of these CSS2Properties properties, however, they return meaningful values only if they've previously been set by your JavaScript code or if the HTML element with which you are working has an inline style attribute that sets the desired property. For example, your document may include a style sheet that sets the left margin for all paragraphs to 30 pixels, but if you read the leftMargin property of one of your paragraph elements, you'll get the empty string unless that paragraph has a style attribute that overrides the style sheet setting. Thus, although the CSS2Properties object is useful for setting styles that override any other styles, it does not provide a way to query the CSS cascade and determine the complete set of styles that apply to a given element. Later in this chapter we will briefly consider the getComputedStyle( ) method, which does provide this ability.

18.3.3 Example: Dynamic Bar Charts

When adding graphs and charts to your HTML documents, you typically implement them as static, inline images. Because the CSS layout model is heavily based on rectangular boxes, however, it is possible to dynamically create bar charts using JavaScript, HTML, and CSS. Example 18-3 shows how this can be done. This example defines a function makeBarChart( ) that makes it simple to insert bar charts into your HTML documents.

The code for Example 18-3 uses the techniques shown in Chapter 17 to create new <div> elements and add them to the document and the techniques discussed in this chapter to set style properties on the elements it creates. No text or other content is involved; the bar chart is just a bunch of rectangles carefully sized and positioned within another rectangle. CSS border and background-color attributes are used to make the rectangles visible.

The example includes some simple math to compute the height in pixels of each bar based on the values of the data to be charted. The JavaScript code that sets the position and size of the chart and its bars also includes some simple arithmetic to account for the presence of borders and padding. With the techniques shown in this example, you should be able to modify Example 18-2 to include a JavaScript function that dynamically creates windows of any specified size.

Figure 18-3 shows a bar chart created using the makeBarChart( ) function as follows:

```
<html>
<head>
<title>BarChart Demo</title>
<script src="BarChart.js"></script>
```

```
</head>
<body>
<h1>y = 2<sup>n</sup></h1>
<script>makeBarChart([2,4,8,16,32,64,128,256,512], 600, 250, "red");</script>
<i>Note that each bar is twice as tall as the one before it,
the result of rapid exponential growth.</i>
</body>
</html>
```

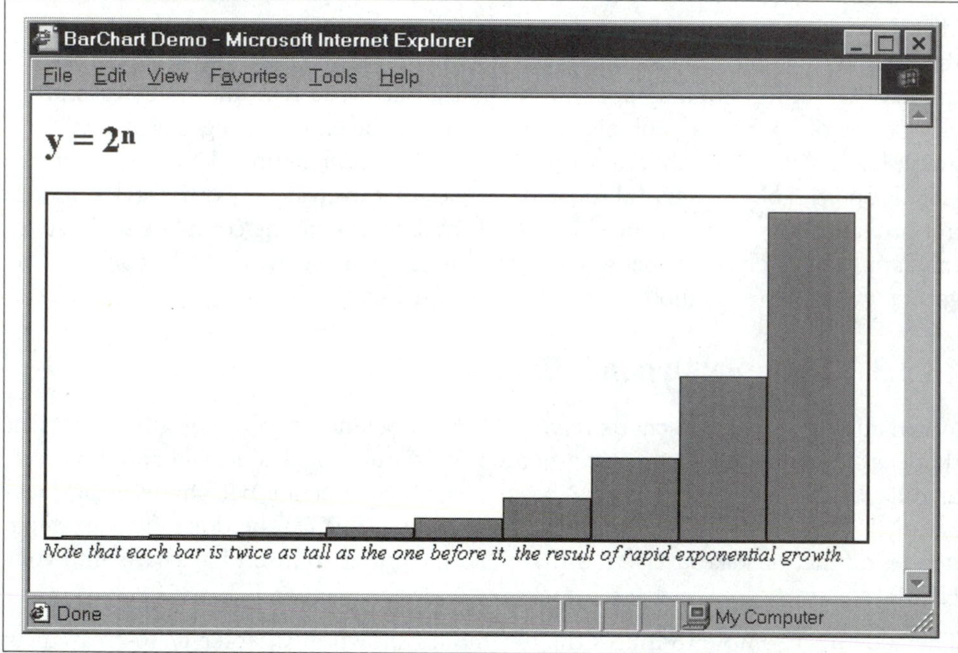

Figure 18-3. A dynamically created bar chart

Example 18-3. Dynamically creating bar charts

```
/**
 * BarChart.js:
 * This file defines makeBarChart(), a function that creates a bar chart to
 * display the numbers from the data[] array. The chart is a block element
 * inserted at the current end of the document. The overall size of the chart
 * is specified by the optional width and height arguments, which include the
 * space required for the chart borders and internal padding. The optional
 * barcolor argument specifies the color of the bars. The function returns the
 * chart element it creates, so the caller can further manipulate it by
 * setting a margin size, for example.
 *
 * Import this function into an HTML file with code like this:
 *    <script src="BarChart.js"></script>
 * Use this function in an HTML file with code like this:
 *    <script>makeBarChart([1,4,9,16,25], 300, 150, "yellow");</script>
 **/
function makeBarChart(data, width, height, barcolor) {
```

Example 18-3. Dynamically creating bar charts (continued)

```
    // Provide default values for the optional arguments
    if (!width) width = 500;
    if (!height) height = 350;
    if (!barcolor) barcolor = "blue";

    // The width and height arguments specify the overall size of the
    // generated chart. We have to subtract the border and padding
    // sizes to get the size of the element we create.
    width -= 24;   // Subtract 10px padding and 2px left and right border
    height -= 14;  // Subtract 10px top padding and 2px top and bottom border

    // Now create an element to hold the chart. Note that we make the chart
    // relatively positioned so that it can have absolutely positioned children,
    // but it still appears in the normal element flow.
    var chart = document.createElement("DIV");
    chart.style.position = "relative";          // Set relative positioning
    chart.style.width = width + "px";           // Set the chart width
    chart.style.height = height + "px";         // Set the chart height
    chart.style.border = "solid black 2px";     // Give it a border
    chart.style.paddingLeft = "10px";           // Add padding on the left,
    chart.style.paddingRight = "10px";          // on the right,
    chart.style.paddingTop = "10px";            // and on the top,
    chart.style.paddingBottom = "0px";          // but not on the bottom
    chart.style.backgroundColor = "white";      // Make the chart background white

    // Compute the width of each bar
    var barwidth = Math.floor(width/data.length);
    // Find the largest number in data[]. Note the clever use of Function.apply( ).
    var maxdata = Math.max.apply(this, data);
    // The scaling factor for the chart: scale*data[i] gives the height of a bar
    var scale = height/maxdata;

    // Now loop through the data array and create a bar for each datum
    for(var i = 0; i < data.length; i++) {
        var bar = document.createElement("div");   // Create div for bar
        var barheight = data[i] * scale;           // Compute height of bar
        bar.style.position = "absolute";           // Set bar position and size
        bar.style.left = (barwidth*i+1+10)+"px";   // Add bar border and chart pad
        bar.style.top = height-barheight+10+"px";  // Add chart padding
        bar.style.width = (barwidth-2) + "px";     // -2 for bar border
        bar.style.height = (barheight-1) + "px";   // -1 for bar top border
        bar.style.border = "solid black 1px";      // Bar border style
        bar.style.backgroundColor = barcolor;      // Bar color
        bar.style.fontSize = "1px";                // IE bug workaround
        chart.appendChild(bar);                    // Add bar to chart
    }

    // Now add the chart we've built to the document body
    document.body.appendChild(chart);

    // Finally, return the chart element so the caller can manipulate it
    return chart;
}
```

18.3.4 DHTML Animations

Some of the most powerful DHTML techniques you can achieve with JavaScript and CSS are animations. There is nothing particularly special about DHTML animations; all you have to do is periodically change one or more style properties of an element or elements. For example, to slide an image into place from the left, you increment the image's `style.left` property repeatedly, until it reaches the desired position. Or you can repeatedly modify the `style.clip` property to "unveil" the image pixel by pixel.

Example 18-4 contains a simple HTML file that defines a `div` element to be animated and a short script that changes the background color of the element every 500 milliseconds. Note that the color change is done simply by assigning a value to a CSS style property. What makes it an animation is that the color is changed repeatedly, using the `setInterval( )` function of the Window object. (You'll need to use `setInterval( )` or `setTimeout( )` for all DHTML animations; you may want to refresh your memory by reading about these functions in the client-side reference section.) Finally, note the use of the modulo (remainder) operator `%` to cycle through the colors. Consult Chapter 5 if you've forgotten how that operator works.

Example 18-4. A simple color-changing animation

```
<!-- This div is the element we are animating -->
<div id="urgent"><h1>Red Alert!</h1>The Web server is under attack!</div>
<!-- This is the animation script for the element -->
<script>
var e = document.getElementById("urgent");          // Get Element object
var colors = ["white", "yellow", "orange", "red"]  // Colors to cycle through
var nextColor = 0;                                  // Position in the cycle
// Evaluate the following expression every 500 milliseconds
// to animate the background color of the div element
setInterval("e.style.backgroundColor=colors[nextColor++%colors.length];", 500);
</script>
```

Example 18-4 produces a very simple animation. In practice, CSS animations typically involve modifications to two or more style properties (such as `top`, `left`, and `clip`) at the same time. Setting up complex animations using a technique like that shown in Example 18-4 can get quite complicated. Furthermore, in order to avoid becoming annoying, animations should typically run for a short while and then stop, but there is no way to stop the animation produced by Example 18-4.

Example 18-5 shows a JavaScript file that defines a CSS animation function that makes it much easier to set up animations, even complex ones. The `animateCSS( )` function defined in this example is passed five arguments. The first specifies the HTMLElement object to be animated. The second and third arguments specify the number of frames in the animation and the length of time each frame should be displayed. The fourth argument is a JavaScript object that specifies the animation to be performed. And the fifth argument is an optional function that should be invoked once when the animation is complete.

The fourth argument to animateCSS( ) is the crucial one. Each property of the JavaScript object must have the same name as a CSS style property, and the value of each property must be a function that returns a legal value for the named style. Every time a new frame of the animation is displayed, each of these functions is called to generate a new value for each of the style properties. Each function is passed the frame number and the total elapsed time and can use these arguments to help it return an appropriate value.

An example should make the use of animateCSS( ) much clearer. The following code moves an element up the screen while gradually uncovering it by enlarging its clipping region:

```
// Animate the element with id "title" for 40 frames of 50 milliseconds each
animateCSS(document.getElementById("title"), 40, 50,
           { // Set top and clip style properties for each frame as follows:
               top:  function(f,t) { return 300-f*5 + "px"; }
               clip: function(f,t) {return "rect(auto "+f*10+"px auto auto)";},
           });
```

The next code fragment uses animateCSS( ) to move a Button object in a circle. It uses the optional fifth argument to animateCSS( ) to change the button text to "Done" when the animation is complete. Note that the element being animated is passed as the argument to the function specified by the fifth argument:

```
// Move a button in a circle, then change the text it displays
animateCSS(document.forms[0].elements[0], 40, 50,  // Button, 40 frames, 50ms
           {  // This trigonometry defines a circle of radius 100 at (200,200):
               left: function(f,t){ return 200 + 100*Math.cos(f/8) + "px"},
               top:  function(f,t){ return 200 + 100*Math.sin(f/8) + "px"}
           },
function(button) { button.value = "Done"; });
```

The code in Example 18-5 is fairly straightforward; all the real complexity is embedded in the properties of the animation object that you pass to animateCSS( ), as we'll see shortly. animateCSS( ) defines a nested function called displayNextFrame( ) and does little more than use setInterval( ) to arrange for displayNextFrame( ) to be called repeatedly. displayNextFrame( ) loops through the properties of the animation object and invokes the various functions to compute the new values of the style properties.

Note that because displayNextFrame( ) is defined inside animateCSS( ), it has access to the arguments and local variables of animateCSS( ), even though displayNextFrame( ) is invoked after animateCSS( ) has already returned! This works even if animateCSS( ) is called more than once to animate more than one element at a time. (If you don't understand why this works, you may want to review Section 11.4, "Lexical Scoping and Nested Functions.")

Example 18-5. A framework for CSS-based animations

```
/**
 * AnimateCSS.js:
 * This file defines a function named animateCSS( ), which serves as a framework
 * for creating CSS-based animations. The arguments to this function are:
 *
 *     element: The HTML element to be animated.
 *     numFrames: The total number of frames in the animation.
 *     timePerFrame: The number of milliseconds to display each frame.
 *     animation: An object that defines the animation; described below.
 *     whendone: An optional function to call when the animation finishes.
 *               If specified, this function is passed element as its argument.
 *
 * The animateCSS( ) function simply defines an animation framework. It is
 * the properties of the animation object that specify the animation to be
 * done. Each property should have the same name as a CSS style property. The
 * value of each property must be a function that returns values for that
 * style property.  Each function is passed the frame number and the total
 * amount of elapsed time, and it can use these to compute the style value it
 * should return for that frame.  For example, to animate an image so that it
 * slides in from the upper left, you might invoke animateCSS as follows:
 *
 *  animateCSS(image, 25, 50,  // Animate image for 25 frames of 50ms each
 *             {  // Set top and left attributes for each frame as follows:
 *               top: function(frame,time) { return frame*8 + "px"; },
 *               left: function(frame,time) { return frame*8 + "px"; }
 *             });
 *
 **/
function animateCSS(element, numFrames, timePerFrame, animation, whendone) {
    var frame = 0;  // Store current frame number
    var time = 0;   // Store total elapsed time

    // Arrange to call displayNextFrame( ) every timePerFrame milliseconds.
    // This will display each of the frames of the animation.
    var intervalId = setInterval(displayNextFrame, timePerFrame);

    // The call to animateCSS( ) returns now, but the line above ensures that
    // the nested function defined below will be invoked once for each frame
    // of the animation.  Because this function is defined inside
    // animateCSS( ), it has access to the arguments and local variables of
    // animateCSS( ) even though it is invoked after that function has returned!
    function displayNextFrame( ) {
        if (frame >= numFrames) {             // First, see if we're done
            clearInterval(intervalId);        // If so, stop calling ourselves
            if (whendone) whendone(element);  // Invoke whendone function
            return;                           // And we're finished
        }

        // Now loop through all properties defined in the animation object
        for(var cssprop in animation) {
            // For each property, call its animation function, passing the
            // frame number and the elapsed time. Use the return value of the
```

Example 18-5. A framework for CSS-based animations (continued)

```
                // function as the new value of the corresponding style property
                // of the specified element. Use try/catch to ignore any
                // exceptions caused by bad return values.
                try {
                    element.style[cssprop] = animation[cssprop](frame, time);
                } catch(e) {}
            }

            frame++;               // Increment the frame number
            time += timePerFrame;  // Increment the elapsed time
        }
    }
```


18.4 DHTML in Fourth-Generation Browsers

Internet Explorer 4 and Netscape 4 were the browsers that introduced DHTML technology to the Internet. Both browsers include partial support for the CSS1 standard and support the CSS positioning attributes (which were integrated into the CSS2 standard) that are critical to DHTML. Unfortunately, the DOM standard did not exist when these fourth-generation browsers were being developed, so they do not conform to that standard. Nevertheless, it is possible to achieve DHTML effects in both browsers.

18.4.1 DHTML in Internet Explorer 4

As we saw in Chapter 17, IE 4 does not support the `document.getElementById()` method, nor does it support an API for dynamically creating new nodes and inserting them into a document. Instead, it provides the `document.all[]` array as a way of locating arbitrary elements of the document and allows document content to be altered with the `innerHTML` property of document elements. IE 4 does not conform to the standards here, but it provides adequate alternatives.

Although traversing and modifying documents is an important part of DHTML, the focus of this chapter is on the dynamic use of CSS styles. The good news is that the DOM API described earlier for setting CSS style attributes through the `style` property was adopted from the IE 4 API. Thus, once you've used `document.all[]` to locate the document element you want to modify, you can script the styles of that element just as you would in a browser that fully supports the DOM API. (Remember, though, that IE 4 does not fully support CSS, so you should not expect all style properties to be scriptable.)

The CSS2 standard specifies that the `position` attribute can be used to specify absolute or relative positioning for any element in a document. IE 4 was implemented before CSS2 was complete, however, and it supports absolute positioning for only a certain subset of elements. Therefore, when using absolute positioning in IE 4, you should wrap the content you want to position or animate in <div> or <span> tags, which do honor the CSS `position` attribute.

18.4.2 DHTML in Netscape 4

Creating DHTML effects with Netscape 4 is a more complicated affair. Netscape 4 does not support a full object model, so it does not allow JavaScript programs to refer to arbitrary HTML elements. It cannot, therefore, allow access to the inline styles of arbitrary elements. Instead, it defines a special Layer object.* Any element that is absolutely positioned (that is, any element that has its `position` style set to `absolute`) is placed in a separate layer from the rest of the document. This layer can be independently positioned, hidden, shown, lowered below or raised above other layers, and so on. The Layer API was proposed to the W3C for standardization but was never standardized. For this reason, it has been dropped by the Mozilla project and is not supported in Mozilla or in Netscape 6. Thus, the techniques described in this section are useful only in the 4.x series of browsers from Netscape.

Each independently positioned layer in a document is represented by a Layer object, and, not surprisingly, the `layers[]` array of the Document object contains the complete set of Layer objects in a document. (Layer objects appear in this array in the order in which they appear in the document.) Additionally, any layer that is given a name with the `name` or `id` attribute can be accessed by name. For example, if a layer specifies `id="L2"`, you can refer to it in Netscape as `document.L2` or as `document.layers["L2"]`. Although Netscape 4 does not provide a way to refer to arbitrary document elements, this `layers[]` array provides a way to refer to the most important dynamic elements.

A layer is something like a separate window or frame. Although the Layer object is not the same as the Window object, it does have a `document` property, just as windows and frames do. The `document` property of a Layer object refers to a Document object: each layer has its own totally independent HTML document. Layers can even be nested; we can output some HTML text into a nested layer with code like this:

```
document.layers[1].document.layers[0].document.write("Layers Are Fun!");
document.layers[1].document.layers[0].document.close( );
```

Netscape 4 does not allow us to create or manipulate the nodes of the document tree, and it does not even support the `innerHTML` property of Internet Explorer. However, the fact that layers contain independent documents does provide a technique for dynamically modifying document content.

* Layers were introduced in Chapter 17, when we discussed Netscape 4 compatibility with the core DOM API. Here we expand that introduction and discuss how layers provide an alternative to the core DOM API and an alternative to the DOM API for accessing CSS styles.

Although Netscape 4 defines a layer as an element with the CSS position style set, it does not define any way to script the styles of a layer element directly. Instead, the Layer object defines properties and methods that we can use to dynamically position layers.

The properties of the Layer object have names that are similar to important CSS style attributes, but these layer properties are not exactly the same as style properties. For example, the left and top properties of the Layer object specify the pixel position of the layer; setting these properties of a layer is like setting the left and top style properties of an element, except that the Layer properties expect numeric pixel values instead of strings that include a numeric value and a unit specification. The visibility property of a layer specifies whether the contents of the layer should be visible; it is a lot like the style property with the same name, except that it expects a value of show or hide instead of the CSS standard visible or hidden. The Layer object also supports a zIndex property that works just like the zIndex style property. Table 18-3 lists key CSS style properties and the Layer property that is most closely equivalent to each. Note that these are the only style properties that Netscape 4 allows to be scripted.

Table 18-3. Layer properties in Netscape 4

CSS property	Equivalent Layer property	Layer notes
left, top	left, top	Specify pixels without units. See also moveTo( ) and moveBy( ).
zIndex	zIndex	See also moveAbove( ), moveBelow( ).
visibility	visibility	Layer returns show or hide even if you set this property to the standard visible and hidden values.
clip	clip.bottom, clip.height, clip.left, clip.right, clip.top, clip.width	Specify pixels without units.
backgroundColor	bgColor	
backgroundImage	background.src	Set to a URL string.

As you can see from Table 18-3, the Layer object supports a couple of useful properties that are not related to dynamic positioning. The background.src property specifies a background image for the layer, and the bgColor property specifies a background color for the layer. These properties correspond to the backgroundImage and backgroundColor style properties.

In addition to its properties, the Layer object offers a number of convenient methods. moveBy( ) and moveTo( ) move a layer by a relative amount or to an absolute position. moveAbove( ) and moveBelow( ) set the zIndex of a layer relative to that of some other layer. See the client-side reference section of this book for a complete list of Layer properties and methods.

Because every layer contains an independent document, you can dynamically update the contents of a layer with the `open()`, `write()`, and `close()` methods of the Document object, as we saw in Chapter 14. In addition, the `src` property of a layer specifies the URL of the document that it displays. By setting this property, you can force the browser to load an entirely new document for display in the layer. The `load()` method is similar; it loads a new URL and changes the layer's width at the same time. Because layers often contain dynamically generated content, you may find it convenient to use `javascript:` URLs with the `src` property and `load()` method.

We've seen that Netscape 4 automatically creates a Layer object for any element that has its `position` style property set to `absolute`. The Netscape 4 API also allows layers to be created in other, less standards-compliant ways. For example, Netscape 4 defines an HTML `<layer>` tag that allows layers to be defined directly in HTML. `<layer>` remains a proprietary Netscape 4 extension; it was not included in the HTML 4 standard and is not supported in Mozilla or Netscape 6. More importantly, though, Netscape 4 supports a `Layer()` constructor that allows Layer objects to be dynamically created, as needed within a program. See the client-side reference section of this book for details.

18.4.3 Example: A Cross-Platform DHTML Animation

Despite the differences between the DOM API, the IE 4 API, and the Netscape Layer API, it is still possible to create DHTML effects that work in DOM-compliant browsers, in pre-DOM versions of IE, and in Netscape 4. Example 18-6 shows one way it can be done. This script displays the word "Hello" and animates it in a straight line from one point in the browser window to another.

Note the compatibility technique used in this example: we test for the existence of key functions, arrays, and properties before using them. If the Document object has a property named `getElementById`, we assume that we have a DOM-compliant browser with that property referring to the `getElementById()` method. Similarly, if the Document object has a property named `all`, we assume that we're running in Internet Explorer and use the `document.all[]` array to locate the element to be animated.

Example 18-6. A cross-browser DHTML animation script

```
<!-- This is the dynamic element we will animate. We wrap the h1 tag in a -->
<!-- div because IE 4 won't move the h1 without a div or a span container. -->
<div id="title" style="position:absolute"><h1>Hello</h1></div>

<!-- This is the JavaScript code that performs the animation -->
<script>
// These variables set the parameters for our animation:
var id = "title";                     // Name of the element to animate
var numFrames = 30;                   // How many frames to display
var interval = 100;                   // How long to display each frame
var x0 = 100, y0 = 100;               // The element's starting position
```

Example 18-6. A cross-browser DHTML animation script (continued)

```
var x1 = 500, y1 = 500;             // The element's ending position
var dx = (x1 - x0)/(numFrames-1);   // Distance to horizontally move each frame
var dy = (y1 - y0)/(numFrames-1);   // Distance to vertically move each frame
var frameNum = 0;                   // Frame we are at now
var element = null;                 // The element to be animated

// First, we find the element to be animated. Use a DOM-compliant technique
// if the browser supports it; otherwise, fall back on browser-specific code.
if (document.getElementById) {                 // If this is a DOM-compliant browser,
    element = document.getElementById(id);     // use the DOM method
}
else if (document.all) {              // Otherwise, if the IE API is supported,
    element = document.all[id];       // use the all[] array to find the element
}
else if (document.layers) {           // Else, if the Netscape API is supported,
    element = document.layers[id];    // use the layers[] array to get the element
}

// If we found the element to animate using one of the previous techniques,
// start animating it by calling nextFrame() every interval milliseconds
if (element) {
    var intervalId = setInterval("nextFrame()", interval);
}

// This function is repeatedly called to display each frame of the animation.
// It moves the element using either the DOM API for setting CSS style
// properties or, if the browser does not support that API, the Netscape
// Layer API.
function nextFrame() {
    if (element.style) {
        // If the browser supports it, move the element by setting CSS
        // style properties. Note the inclusion of the units string.
        element.style.left = x0 + dx*frameNum + "px";
        element.style.top = y0 + dy*frameNum + "px";
    }
    else {
        // Otherwise, assume that element is a layer, and move it by
        // setting its properties. We could also use element.moveTo().
        element.left = x0 + dx*frameNum;
        element.top = y0 + dy*frameNum;
    }

    // Increment the frame number, and stop if we've reached the end
    if (++frameNum >= numFrames) clearInterval(intervalId);
}
</script>
```

18.5 Other DOM APIs for Styles and Style Sheets

So far in this chapter, we've discussed a simple DOM API for working with CSS styles: every HTMLElement in a document has a style property that represents the inline style attributes of that element. The style property refers to a CSS2Properties object that defines a JavaScript property for each CSS style attribute defined by the CSS2 standard.

Although we've made extensive use of it, the CSS2Properties object is just one part of the DOM API for CSS.* This section provides a quick overview of the rest of the DOM API for working with CSS style sheets. Note, however, that at the time of this writing, much of the CSS API is not well supported by current (sixth-generation) browsers. You should test carefully before relying on any of the APIs described here.

18.5.1 Style Declarations

The CSS2Properties interface is a subinterface of CSSStyleDeclaration. Thus, the `style` property of each document element also implements the properties and methods of CSSStyleDeclaration. The methods include `setProperty()` and `getPropertyValue()`, which you can use as an alternative to setting and querying the individual style properties of CSS2Properties. For example, these two lines of code accomplish the same thing:

```
element.style.fontFamily = "sans-serif";
element.style.setProperty("font-family", "sans-serif", "");
```

Other features of the CSSStyleDeclaration interface are the `removeProperty()` method, which deletes a named style, and the `cssText` property, which returns a text representation of all the style attributes and their values. Since CSSStyleDeclaration objects represent a set of style attributes and their values, they can also be used as arrays to iterate through the names of the style attributes.

18.5.2 Computed Styles

As I emphasized earlier in this chapter, the `style` property of a document element represents the `style` attribute for that element, and it does not contain any information about other styles (from style sheets) that affect that element. To determine the complete set of styles that apply to an element, use the `getComputedStyle()` method of the Window object (this method is defined by the AbstractView interface: see the "AbstractView.getComputedStyle()" entry in the DOM reference section). The return value of this method is a CSSStyleDeclaration object that describes all the styles that apply to the specified element. You can assume that the returned object also implements the CSS2Properties interface, just as the `style` property of an element does.

* In fact, the CSS2Properties object is optional. A DOM implementation may support CSS without supporting CSS2Properties. In practice, however, this is the most commonly used API for working with styles, and DOM implementations in web browsers are effectively required to support it.

To illustrate the difference between an element's inline style and its computed style, consider an element e. To determine whether e has a font specified in its inline style attribute, you can do this:

```
var inlinefont = e.style.fontFamily;
```

But to determine what font family e is displayed in (regardless of whether this is specified by an inline style or by a style sheet), do this instead:

```
var fontfamily = window.getComputedStyle(e, null).fontFamily;
```

You may prefer to use getComputedStyle( ) in a way that makes it clearer that it is defined by the AbstractView interface:

```
var fontfamily = document.defaultView.getComputedStyle(e, null).fontFamily;
```

The style values returned by getComputedStyle( ) are read-only, since they come from various places in the style cascade. Setting any of the attributes has no effect on the style of the element. The getComputedStyle( ) method should also be considered "expensive," since it must traverse the entire cascade and build a large CSSStyleDeclaration representing the many style attributes that apply to the element.

Finally, note that IE 5 and later define a nonstandard but useful currentStyle property in addition to the style property for all HTML elements. currentStyle refers to a CSS2Properties object that holds the computed style for that element.

18.5.3 Override Styles

The CSS standard specifies that a web browser have a default style sheet that defines the basic display styles of HTML elements. The browser may allow the user to specify a user style sheet that represents the user's style preferences and overrides styles specified in the default style sheet. Author style sheets are style sheets defined by a document's author—that is, the styles included in or linked into a document. Author style sheets override the browser's default styles and the user's styles (except for !important styles). Inline styles specified with the style attribute of an element can be considered part of the author style sheet.

The DOM standard introduces the notion of an override style sheet that overrides the author style sheet, including inline styles. By setting styles for an element in the override style sheet, you can change the displayed style of an element without modifying the document's style sheets or the inline style of that element. To obtain the override style of an element, use the getOverrideStyle( ) method of the Document object:

```
var element = document.getElementById("title");
var override = document.getOverrideStyle(element, null);
```

This method returns a CSSStyleDeclaration object (which also implements CSS2Properties) that you can use to change the displayed style of an element. Note the difference between setting an override style and an inline style:

```
override.backgroundColor = "yellow";      // Sets an override style
element.style.backgroundColor = "pink";  // Sets an inline style
```

18.5.4 Creating Style Sheets

The DOMImplementation object (accessed as `document.implementation`) defines a `createCSSStyleSheet()` method for creating CSSStyleSheet objects. The CSSStyleSheet object defines an `insertRule()` method that you can use to add style rules to the style sheet. Unfortunately, DOM Level 2 does not define any way to associate a created style sheet with a document, so there is currently no point in using this method. Future versions of the DOM standard may remedy this.

18.5.5 Traversing Style Sheets

The core DOM API makes it possible to traverse an HTML (or XML) document and examine every element, attribute, and Text node of the document. Similarly, the style sheets and CSS modules of the DOM make it possible to examine all the style sheets in or linked into a document and to traverse those style sheets, examining all the rules, selectors, and style attributes that comprise them.

For scripters who want to create DHTML, it is usually sufficient simply to work within the inline styles of elements using the API shown earlier in this chapter, and it is not typically necessary to traverse style sheets. Nevertheless, this section briefly introduces the DOM API for style-sheet traversal. You can find further details on the API in the DOM reference section. At the time of this writing this API is not well supported, but support in Mozilla is expected soon. Note also that IE 5 defines a proprietary and incompatible API for traversing style sheets.

The style sheets that are included in or linked into a document are accessible through the `document.styleSheets[]` array. For example:

```
var ss = document.styleSheets[0];
```

The elements of this array are StyleSheet objects. StyleSheet represents a generic style sheet. In HTML documents using CSS style sheets, these objects all implement the subinterface CSSStyleSheet, which provides CSS-specific properties and methods. A CSSStyleSheet object has a `cssRules[]` array that contains the rules of the style sheet. For example:

```
var firstRule = document.styleSheets[0].cssRules[0]
```

The CSSStyleSheet interface also defines `insertRule()` and `deleteRule()` methods for adding and removing rules from the style sheet:

```
document.styleSheets[0].insertRule("H1 { text-weight: bold; }", 0);
```

The elements of the `CSSStyleSheet.cssRules[]` array are CSSRule objects. CSS style sheets may contain a number of different types of rules. In addition to the basic style rules that we've seen in this chapter, there are various "at-rules," which are specified with keywords like `@import` and `@page`. You can read about these special types of CSS rules in a CSS reference.

The CSSRule interface is a generic one that can represent any type of rule and has subinterfaces that represent the specific rule types. The type property of CSSRule specifies the specific rule type. Most rules in a CSS style sheet are basic style rules, such as:

```
h1 { font-family: sans-serif; font-weight: bold; font-size: 24pt; }
```

Rules of this type have a type property of `CSSRule.STYLE_RULE` and are represented by CSSRule objects that additionally implement the CSSStyleRule interface. CSSStyle-Rule objects define a `selectorText` property that contains the rule selector (the string "h1" in the previous rule) and a `style` property that contains the rule's style attributes and values (such as the font attributes in the previous rule). For example:

```
var rule = document.styleSheets[0].cssRules[0]
var styles;
if (rule.type == CSSRule.STYLE_RULE) styles = rule.style;
```

The value of the `CSSStyleRule.style` property is a CSSStyleDeclaration object. We've already encountered this object: it is the same type of object that is used to represent the inline styles of document elements. It defines methods such as `setProperty()`, `removeProperty()`, and `getPropertyValue()`. As discussed previously, CSSStyleDeclaration objects typically also implement the CSS2Properties interface and therefore define a property that corresponds to each CSS attribute.

The properties of CSS2Properties and the `getPropertyValue()` method of CSSStyle-Declaration return the values of CSS style attributes as strings. As discussed earlier in this chapter, this means that when you query the value of an attribute such as `font-size` (or when you read the `fontSize` property of CSS2Properties), what you get back is a number and a units value. This might be "24pt" or a (probably less useful) value like "10mm". In general, when you get the value of a CSS attribute as a string, you have to parse it in some way to extract the data you want from it. This is particularly true of attributes like `clip`, which have a complex string syntax.

As an alternative to parsing strings, CSSStyleDeclaration provides another method, `getPropertyCSSValue()`, that returns the value of a CSS attribute as a CSSValue object instead of a string. The `cssValueType` property of the CSSValue object specifies a sub-interface that the object also implements. If an attribute has more than one value, the CSSValue object implements CSSValueList and behaves like an array of CSSValue objects. Otherwise, the CSSValue. object is typically a "primitive" value and implements the CSSPrimitiveValue interface. CSSPrimitiveValue objects have a property named `primitiveType` that specifies the type of the value or the units that apply to the value. There are 26 possible types, all represented by constants like `CSSPrimitiveValue.CSS_PERCENTAGE`, `CSSPrimitiveValue.CSS_PX`, and `CSSPrimitive-Value.CSS_RGBCOLOR`. In addition to the `primitiveType` property and the various type constants, CSSPrimitiveValue defines various methods for setting and querying the value represented by the object. If the CSSPrimitiveValue object represents a length or percentage, for example, you call `getFloatValue()` to obtain the length. If the `primitiveType` property indicates that the value represents a color, you use `getRGBColorValue( )` to query the color value.

Finally, the DOM CSS API also defines a few special object types to represent attribute values: RGBColor objects represent color values, Rect objects represent rectangle values (such as the value of the `clip` attribute), and Counter objects represent CSS2 counters. See the DOM reference section for details.

CHAPTER 19
Events and Event Handling

As we saw in Chapter 12, interactive JavaScript programs use an event-driven programming model. In this style of programming, the web browser generates an *event* whenever something interesting happens to the document or to some element of it. For example, the web browser generates an event when it finishes loading a document, when the user moves the mouse over a hyperlink, or when the user clicks on the **Submit** button of a form. If a JavaScript application cares about a particular type of event for a particular document element, it can register an *event handler*—a JavaScript function or snippet of code—for that type of event on the element of interest. Then, when that particular event occurs, the browser invokes the handler code. All applications with graphical user interfaces are designed this way: they sit around waiting for the user to do something interesting (i.e., they wait for events to occur) and then they respond.

As an aside, it is worth noting that timers and error handlers (both of which are described in Chapter 13) are related to the event-driven programming model. Like the event handlers described in this chapter, timers and error handlers work by registering a function with the browser and allowing the browser to call that function when the appropriate event occurs. In these cases, however, the event of interest is the passage of a specified amount of time or the occurrence of a JavaScript error. Although timers and error handlers are not discussed in this chapter, it is useful to think of them as related to event handling, and I encourage you to reread Section 13.4, "Timeouts and Intervals," and Section 13.5, "Error Handling," in the context of this chapter.

Most nontrivial JavaScript programs rely heavily on event handlers. We've already seen a number of JavaScript examples that use simple event handlers. This chapter fills in all the missing details about events and event handling. Unfortunately, these details are more complex than they ought to be, because there are four distinct and incompatible event-handling models in use. These models are:

The original event model. This is the simple event-handling scheme that we've used (but not thoroughly documented) so far in this book. It was codified, to a limited extent, by the HTML 4 standard, and is informally considered to be part of the DOM Level 0 API. Although its features are limited, it is supported by all JavaScript-enabled web browsers and is therefore portable.

The standard event model. This powerful and full-featured event model was standardized by the DOM Level 2 standard. It is supported by the Netscape 6 and Mozilla browsers.

The Internet Explorer event model. This event model is implemented by IE 4 and later and has some, but not all, of the advanced features of the standard event model. Although Microsoft participated in the creation of the DOM Level 2 event model and had plenty of time to implement this standard event model in IE 5.5 and IE 6, they have stuck with their proprietary event model instead. This means that JavaScript programmers who want to used advanced event-handling features must write special code for IE browsers.

The Netscape 4 event model. This event model was implemented in Netscape 4 and continues to be (mostly, but not fully) supported in Netscape 6, although it has been superseded by the standard event model. It has some, but not all, of the advanced features of the standard event model. JavaScript programmers who want to use advanced event-handling features and retain compatibility with Netscape 4 need to understand this model.

The rest of this chapter documents each of these event models in turn.

19.1 Basic Event Handling

In the code we've seen so far in this book, event handlers have been written as strings of JavaScript code that are used as the values of certain HTML attributes, such as `onclick`. Although this is the key to the original event model, there are a number of additional details, described in the following sections, that you should understand.

19.1.1 Events and Event Types

Different types of occurrences generate different types of events. When the user moves the mouse over a hyperlink, it causes a different type of event than when the user clicks the mouse on the **Submit** button of a form. Even the same occurrence can generate different types of events based on context: when the user clicks the mouse over a **Submit** button, for example, it generates a different event than when the user clicks the mouse over the **Reset** button of a form.

In the original event model, an event is an abstraction internal to the web browser, and JavaScript code cannot manipulate an event directly. When we speak of an *event type* in the original event model, what we really mean is the name of the event handler that is invoked in response to the event. In this model, event-handling code is specified using the attributes of HTML elements (and the corresponding properties of the associated JavaScript objects). Thus, if your application needs to know when the user moves the mouse over a specific hyperlink, you use the `onmouseover` attribute of the

<a> tag that defines the hyperlink. And if the application needs to know when the user clicks the **Submit** button, you use the onclick attribute of the <input> tag that defines the button or the onsubmit attribute of the <form> element that contains that button.

There are quite a few different event handler attributes that you can use in the original event model. They are listed in Table 19-1, which also specifies when these event handlers are triggered and which HTML elements support the handler attributes.

As client-side JavaScript programming has evolved, so has the event model it supports. With each new browser version, new event handler attributes have been added. Finally, the HTML 4 specification codified a standard set of event handler attributes for HTML tags. The third column of Table 19-1 specifies which HTML elements support each event handler attribute, and it also specifies which browser versions support that event handler for that tag and whether the event handler is a standard part of HTML 4 for that tag. In this third column, "N" is an abbreviation for Netscape and "IE" is an abbreviation for Internet Explorer. Each browser version is backward compatible with previous versions, so "N3," for example, means Netscape 3 and all later versions.

If you study the various event handler attributes in Table 19-1 closely, you can discern two broad categories of events. One category is *raw events* or *input events*. These are the events that are generated when the user moves or clicks the mouse or presses a key on the keyboard. These low-level events simply describe a user's gesture and have no other meaning. The second category of events are *semantic events*. These higher-level events have a more complex meaning and can typically occur only in specific contexts: when the browser has finished loading the document or a form is about to be submitted, for example. A semantic event often occurs as a side effect of a lower-level event. For example, when the user clicks the mouse over a **Submit** button, three input handlers are triggered: onmousedown, onmouseup, and onclick. And, as a result of this mouse-click, the HTML form that contains the button generates an onsubmit event.

One final note about Table 19-1 is required. For raw mouse event handlers, column three specifies that the handler attribute is supported (in HTML 4, at least) by "most elements." The HTML elements that do not support these event handlers are typically elements that belong in the <head> of a document or do not have a graphical representation of their own. The tags that do not support the nearly universal mouse event handler attributes are: <applet>, <bdo>, <br>, <font>, <frame>, <frameset>, <head>, <html>, <iframe>, <isindex>, <meta>, and <style>.

Table 19-1. Event handlers and the HTML elements that support them

Handler	Triggered when	Supported by
onabort	Image loading interrupted.	N3, IE4: <img>
onblur	Element loses input focus.	HTML4, N2, IE3: <button>, <input>, <label>, <select>, <textarea> N3, IE4: <body>

Table 19-1. Event handlers and the HTML elements that support them (continued)

Handler	Triggered when	Supported by
onchange	Selection in a <select> element or other form element loses focus and its value has changed since it gained focus.	HTML4, N2, IE3: <input>, <select>, <textarea>
onclick	Mouse press and release; follows mouseup event. Return false to cancel default action (i.e., follow link, reset, submit).	N2, IE3: <a>, <area>, <input> HTML4, N6, IE4: most elements
ondblclick	Double-click.	HTML4, N6, IE4: most elements
onerror	Error when loading image.	N3, IE4: <img>
onfocus	Element gains input focus.	HTML4, N2, IE3: <button>, <input>, <label>, <select>, <textarea> N3, IE4: <body>
onkeydown	Key pressed down. Return false to cancel.	N4: <input>, <textarea> HTML4, N6, IE4: form elements and <body>
onkeypress	Key pressed and released. Return false to cancel.	N4: <input>, <textarea> HTML4, N6, IE4: form elements and <body>
onkeyup	Key released.	N4: <input>, <textarea> HTML4, N6, IE4: form elements and <body>
onload	Document load complete.	HTML4, N2, IE3: <body>, <frameset> N3, IE4: <img> N6, IE4: <iframe>, <object>
onmousedown	Mouse button pressed.	N4: <a>, <area>, <img> HTML4, N6, IE4: most elements
onmousemove	Mouse moved.	HTML4, N6, IE4: most elements
onmouseout	Mouse moves off element.	N3: <a>, <area> HTML4, N6, IE4: most elements
onmouseover	Mouse moves over element. For links, return true to prevent URL from appearing in status bar.	N2, IE3: <a>, <area> HTML4, N6, IE4: most elements
onmouseup	Mouse button released.	N4: <a>, <area>, <img> HTML4, N6, IE4: most elements
onreset	Form reset requested. Return false to prevent reset.	HTML4, N3, IE4: <form>
onresize	Window size changes.	N4, IE4: <body>, <frameset>
onselect	Text selected.	HTML4, N6, IE3: <input>, <textarea>
onsubmit	Form submission requested. Return false to prevent submission.	HTML4, N3, IE4: <form>
onunload	[illegible] frameset unloaded.	HTML4, N2, IE3: <body>, <frameset>

19.1.2 Event Handlers as Attributes

As we've seen in a number of examples prior to this chapter, event handlers are specified (in the original event model) as strings of JavaScript code used for the values of

HTML attributes. So, for example, to execute JavaScript code when the user clicks a button, specify that code as the value of the `onclick` attribute of the `<input>` tag:

```
<input type="button" value="Press Me" onclick="alert('thanks');">
```

The value of an event handler attribute is an arbitrary string of JavaScript code. If the handler consists of multiple JavaScript statements, the statements *must* be separated from each other by semicolons. For example:

```
<input type="button" value="Click Here"
       onclick="if (window.numclicks) numclicks++; else numclicks=1;
                this.value='Click # ' + numclicks;">
```

When an event handler requires multiple statements, it is usually easier to define them in the body of a function and then use the HTML event handler attribute to invoke that function. For example, if you want to validate a user's form input before submitting the form, you can use the `onsubmit` attribute of the `<form>` tag. Form validation typically requires several lines of code, at a minimum, so instead of cramming all this code into one long attribute value, it makes more sense to define a form-validation function and simply use the `onclick` attribute to invoke that function. For example, if you defined a function named `validateForm()` to perform validation, you could invoke it from an event handler like this:

```
<form action="processform.cgi" onsubmit="return validateForm();">
```

Remember that HTML is case-insensitive, so you can capitalize event handler attributes any way you choose. One common convention is to use mixed-case capitalization, with the initial "on" prefix in lowercase: `onClick`, `onLoad`, `onMouseOut`, and so on. In this book, I've chosen to use all lowercase, however, for compatibility with XHTML, which is case-sensitive.

The JavaScript code in an event handler attribute may contain a `return` statement, and the return value may have special meaning to the browser. This is discussed shortly. Also, note that the JavaScript code of an event handler runs in a different scope (see Chapter 4) than global JavaScript code. This, too, is discussed in more detail later in this section.

19.1.3 Event Handlers as Properties

We've seen that each HTML element in a document has a corresponding JavaScript object in the document tree, and the properties of this JavaScript object correspond to the attributes of the HTML element. In JavaScript 1.1 and later, this applies to event handler attributes as well. So if an `<input>` tag has an `onclick` attribute, the event handler it contains can be referred to with the `onclick` property of the form element object. (JavaScript is case-sensitive, so regardless of the capitalization used for the HTML attribute, the JavaScript property must be all lowercase.)

Technically, the DOM specification does not support the original event model we've described here and does not define JavaScript attributes that correspond to the event handler attributes standardized by HTML 4. Despite the lack of formal standardization by the DOM, this event model is so widely used that all JavaScript-enabled web browsers allow event handlers to be referred to as JavaScript properties.

Since the value of an HTML event handler attribute is a string of JavaScript code, you might expect the value of the corresponding JavaScript property to be a string as well. This is not the case: when accessed through JavaScript, event handler properties are functions. You can verify this with a simple example:

```
<input type="button" value="Click Here" onclick="alert(typeof this.onclick);">
```

If you click the button, it displays a dialog box containing the word "function," not the word "string." (Note that in event handlers, the `this` keyword refers to the object on which the event occurred. We'll discuss the `this` keyword shortly.)

To assign an event handler to a document element using JavaScript, simply set the event handler property to the desired function. For example, consider the following HTML form:

```
<form name="f1">
<input name="b1" type="button" value="Press Me">
</form>
```

The button in this form can be referred to as `document.f1.b1`, which means that an event handler can be assigned with a line of JavaScript like this one:

```
document.f1.b1.onclick=function( ) { alert('Thanks!'); };
```

An event handler can also be assigned like this:

```
function plead( ) { window.status = "Please Press Me!"; }
document.f1.b1.onmouseover = plead;
```

Pay particular attention to that last line: there are no parentheses after the name of the function. To define an event handler, we are assigning the function itself to the event handler property, not the result of invoking the function. This is an area that often trips up beginning JavaScript programmers.

There are a couple of advantages to expressing event handlers as JavaScript properties. First, it reduces the intermingling of HTML and JavaScript, promoting modularity and cleaner, more maintainable code. Second, it allows event handler functions to be dynamic. Unlike HTML attributes, which are a static part of the document and can be set only when the document is created, JavaScript properties can be changed at any time. In complex interactive programs, it can sometimes be useful to dynamically change the event handlers registered for HTML elements. One minor disadvantage to defining event handlers in JavaScript is that it separates the handler from the element to which it belongs. If the user interacts with a document element before the document is fully loaded (and before all its scripts have executed), the event handlers for the document element may not yet be defined.

Example 19-1 shows how you can specify a single function to be the event handler for many document elements. The example is a simple function that defines an onclick event handler for every link in a document. The event handler asks for the user's confirmation before allowing the browser to follow the hyperlink on which the user has just clicked. The event handler function returns false if the user does not confirm, which prevents the browser from following the link. Event handler return values will be discussed shortly.

Example 19-1. One function, many event handlers

```
// This function is suitable for use as an onclick event handler for <a> and
// <area> elements. It uses the this keyword to refer to the document element
// and may return false to prevent the browser from following the link.
function confirmLink( ) {
  return confirm("Do you really want to visit " + this.href + "?");
}

// This function loops through all the hyperlinks in a document and assigns
// the confirmLink function to each one as an event handler. Don't call it
// before the document is parsed and the links are all defined. It is best
// to call it from the onload event handler of a <body> tag.
function confirmAllLinks( ) {
  for(var i = 0; i < document.links.length; i++) {
    document.links[i].onclick = confirmLink;
  }
}
```


19.1.3.1 Explicitly invoking event handlers

Because the values of JavaScript event handler properties are functions, we can use JavaScript to invoke event handler functions directly. For example, if we've used the onsubmit attribute of a <form> tag to define a form-validation function and we want to validate the form at some point before the user attempts to submit it, we can use the onsubmit property of the Form object to invoke the event handler function. The code might look like this:

```
document.myform.onsubmit( );
```

Note, however, that invoking an event handler is not a way to simulate what happens when the event actually occurs. If we invoke the onclick method of a Link object, for example, it does not make the browser follow the link and load a new document. It merely executes whatever function we've defined as the value of that property. To make the browser load a new document, we have to set the location property of the Window object, as we saw in Chapter 13. The same is true of the onsubmit method of a Form object or the onclick method of a Submit object: invoking the method runs the event handler function but does not cause the form to be submitted. (To actually submit the form, we call the submit( ) method of the Form object.)

One reason that you might want to explicitly invoke an event handler function is if you want to use JavaScript to augment an event handler that is (or may be) already defined by HTML code. Suppose you want to take a special action when the user clicks a button, but you do not want to disrupt any onclick event handler that may have been defined in the HTML document itself. (This is one of the problems with the code in Example 19-1—by adding a handler for each hyperlink, it overwrites any `onclick` handlers that were already defined for those hyperlinks.) You might accomplish this with code like the following:

```
var b = document.myform.mybutton;  // This is the button we're interested in
var oldHandler = b.onclick;        // Save the HTML event handler
function newHandler( ) { /* My event-handling code goes here */ }
// Now assign a new event handler that calls both the old and new handlers
b.onclick = function() { oldHandler(); newHandler( ); }
```

19.1.4 Event Handler Return Values

In many cases, an event handler (whether specified by HTML attribute or JavaScript property) uses its return value to indicate the disposition of the event. For example, if you use the `onsubmit` event handler of a Form object to perform form validation and discover that the user has not filled in all the fields, you can return `false` from the handler to prevent the form from actually being submitted. You can ensure that a form is not submitted with an empty text field like this:

```
<form action="search.cgi"
      onsubmit="if (this.elements[0].value.length == 0) return false;">
<input type="text">
</form>
```

Generally, if the web browser performs some kind of default action in response to an event, you can return `false` to prevent the browser from performing that action. In addition to `onsubmit`, other event handlers from which you can return `false` to prevent the default action include `onclick`, `onkeydown`, `onkeypress`, `onmousedown`, `onmouseup`, and `onreset`. The second column of Table 19-1 contains a note about the return values for these event handlers.

There is one exception to the rule about returning `false` to cancel: when the user moves the mouse over a hyperlink (or image map), the browser's default action is to display the link's URL in the status line. To prevent this from happening, you must return `true` from the `onmouseover` event handler. For example, you can display a message other than a URL with code like this:

```
<a href="help.htm" onmouseover="window.status='Help!!'; return true;">Help</a>
```

There is no good reason for this exception: it is this way simply because that is always the way it has been.

Note that event handlers are never required to explicitly return a value. If you don't return a value, the default behavior occurs.

19.1.5 Event Handlers and the this Keyword

Whether you define an event handler with an HTML attribute or with a JavaScript property, what you are doing is assigning a function to a property of a document element. In other words, you're defining a new method of the document element. When your event handler is invoked, it is invoked as a method of the element on which the event occurred, so the `this` keyword refers to that target element. This behavior is useful and unsurprising.

Be sure, however, that you understand the implications. Suppose you have an object `o` with a method `mymethod`. You might register an event handler like this:

```
button.onclick= o.mymethod;
```

This statement makes `button.onclick` refer to the same function that `o.mymethod` does. This function is now a method of both `o` and `button`. When the browser triggers this event handler, it invokes the function as a method of the `button` object, not as a method of `o`. The `this` keyword refers to the Button object, not to your object `o`. Do not make the mistake of thinking you can trick the browser into invoking an event handler as a method of some other object. If you want to do that, you must do it explicitly, like this:

```
button.onclick = function() { o.mymethod(); }
```

19.1.6 Scope of Event Handlers

As we discussed in Chapter 11, functions in JavaScript are lexically scoped. This means that they run in the scope in which they were defined, not in the scope from which they are called. When you define an event handler by setting the value of an HTML attribute to a string of JavaScript code, you are implicitly defining a JavaScript function (as you can see when you examine the type of the corresponding event handler property in JavaScript). It is important to understand that the scope of an event handler function defined in this way is not the same as the scope of other normally defined global JavaScript functions. This means that event handlers defined as HTML attributes execute in a different scope than other functions.*

Recall from the discussion in Chapter 4 that the scope of a function is defined by a scope chain, or list of objects, that is searched, in turn, for variable definitions. When a variable `x` is looked up or resolved in a normal function, JavaScript first looks for a local variable or argument by checking the call object of the function for a property of that name. If no such property is found, JavaScript proceeds to the next object in the scope chain: the global object. It checks the properties of the global object to see if the variable is a global variable.

Event handlers defined as HTML attributes have a more complex scope chain than this. The head of the scope chain is the call object. Any arguments passed to the event handler are defined here (we'll see later in this chapter that in some advanced event models, event handlers are passed an argument), as are any local variables

* It is important to understand this, and while the discussion that follows is interesting, it is also dense. You may want to skip it on your first time through this chapter and come back to it later.

declared in the body of the event handler. The next object in an event handler's scope chain isn't the global object, however; it is the object that triggered the event handler. So, for example, suppose you use an `<input>` tag to define a Button object in an HTML form and then use the `onclick` attribute to define an event handler. If the code for the event handler uses a variable named `form`, that variable is resolved to the `form` property of the Button object. This can be a useful shortcut when writing event handlers as HTML attributes.

The scope chain of an event handler does not stop with the object that defines the handler: it proceeds up the containment hierarchy. For the `onclick` event handler described earlier, the scope chain begins with the call object of the handler function. Then it proceeds to the Button object, as we've discussed. After that, it continues up the HTML element containment hierarchy and includes, at a minimum, the HTML `<form>` element that contains the button and the Document object that contains the form. The precise composition of the scope chain has never been standardized and is implementation-dependent. Netscape 6 and Mozilla include all containing objects (even things such as `<div>` tags), while IE 6 sticks to a more minimal set that includes the target element, plus the containing Form object (if any) and the Document object. Regardless of the browser, the final object in the scope chain is the Window object, as it always is in client-side JavaScript.

Having the target object in the scope chain of an event handler can be a useful shortcut. But having an extended scope chain that includes other document elements can be a nuisance. Consider, for example, that both the Window and Document objects define methods named `open()`. If you use the identifier `open` without qualification, you are almost always referring to the `window.open()` method. In an event handler defined as an HTML attribute, however, the Document object is in the scope chain before the Window object, and using `open` by itself refers to the `document.open()` method. Similarly, consider what would happen if you added a property named `window` to a Form object (or defined an input field with `name="window"`). Then, if you define an event handler within the form that uses the expression `window.open()`, the identifier `window` resolves to the property of the Form object rather than the global Window object, and event handlers within the form have no easy way to refer to the global Window object or to call the `window.open()` method!

The moral is that you must be careful when defining event handlers as HTML attributes. Your safest bet is to keep any such handlers very simple. Ideally, they should just call a global function defined elsewhere and perhaps return the result:

```
<script>
function validateForm( ) {
  /* Form validation code here */
  return true;
}
</script>
<input type="submit" onclick="return validateForm( );">
```

A simple event handler like this is still executed using an unusual scope chain, and you can subvert it by defining a `validateForm()` method on one of the containing elements. But, assuming that the intended global function does get called, that function executes in the normal global scope. Once again, remember that functions are executed using the scope in which they were defined, not the scope from which they are invoked. So, even though our `validateForm()` method is invoked from an unusual scope, it is still executed in its own global scope with no possibility for confusion.

Furthermore, since there is no standard for the precise composition of the scope chain of an event handler, it is safest to assume that it contains only the target element and the global Window object. For example, use `this` to refer to the target element, and when the target is an `<input>` element, feel free to use `form` to refer to the containing Form object. But don't rely on the Form or Document objects being in the scope chain. For example, don't use the unqualified identifier `write` to refer to the Document's `write()` method. Instead, spell out that you mean `document.write()`.

Keep in mind that this entire discussion of event-handler scope applies only to event handlers defined as HTML attributes. If you specify an event handler by assigning a function to an appropriate JavaScript event handler property, there is no special scope chain involved, and your function executes in the scope in which it was defined. This is almost always the global scope, unless it is a nested function, in which case the scope chain can get interesting again!

19.2 Advanced Event Handling with DOM Level 2

The event-handling techniques we've seen so far in this chapter are part of the Level 0 DOM: the de facto standard API that is supported by every JavaScript-enabled browser. The DOM Level 2 standard defines an advanced event-handling API that is significantly different (and quite a bit more powerful) than the Level 0 API. The Level 2 standard does not incorporate the existing API into the standard DOM, but there is no danger of the Level 0 API being dropped. For basic event-handling tasks, you should feel free to continue to use the simple API.

The Level 2 DOM Events module is supported by Mozilla and Netscape 6, but is not supported by Internet Explorer 6.

19.2.1 Event Propagation

In the Level 0 event model, the browser dispatches events to the document elements on which they occur. If that object has an appropriate event handler, that handler is run. There is nothing more to it. The situation is more complex in the Level 2 DOM. In this advanced event model, when an event occurs on a Document node (known as the event *target*), the target's event handler or handlers are triggered, but in addition, each of the target's ancestor nodes has one or two opportunities to handle that event. Event propagation proceeds in three phases. First, during the *capturing* phase, events propagate from the Document object down through the document tree to the target node. If any of the ancestors of the target (but not the target itself) has a specially registered capturing event handler, those handlers are run during this phase of event propagation. (We'll learn how both regular and capturing event handlers are registered shortly.)

The next phase of event propagation occurs at the target node itself: any appropriate event handlers registered directly on the target are run. This is akin to the kind of event handling provided by the Level 0 event model.

The third phase of event propagation is the *bubbling* phase, in which the event propagates or bubbles back up the document hierarchy from the target element up to the Document object. Although all events are subject to the capturing phase of event propagation, not all types of events bubble: for example, it does not make sense for a submit event to propagate up the document beyond the `<form>` element to which it is directed. On the other hand, generic events such as mousedown events can be of interest to any element in the document, so they do bubble up through the document hierarchy, triggering any appropriate event handlers on each of the ancestors of the target element. In general, raw input events bubble, while higher-level semantic events do not. (See Table 19-3, later in this chapter, for a definitive list of which events bubble and which do not.)

During event propagation, it is possible for any event handler to stop further propagation of the event by calling the `stopPropagation()` method of the Event object that represents the event. We'll see more about the Event object and its `stopPropagation()` method later in this chapter.

Some events cause an associated default action to be performed by the web browser. For example, when a click event occurs on an `<a>` tag, the browser's default action is to follow the hyperlink. Default actions like these are performed only after all three phases of event propagation complete, and any of the handlers invoked during event propagation have the opportunity to prevent the default action from occurring by calling the `preventDefault()` method of the Event object.

Although this kind of event propagation may seem convoluted, it provides an important means of centralizing your event-handling code. The Level 1 DOM exposes all document elements and allows events (such as mouseover events) to occur on any of those elements. This means that there are many, many more places for event handlers to be registered than there were with the old Level 0 event model. Suppose you want to trigger an event handler whenever the user moves the mouse over a `<p>` element in your document. Instead of registering an `onmouseover` event handler for each `<p>` tag, you can instead register a single event handler on the Document object and handle these events during either the capturing or bubbling phase of event propagation.

There is one other important detail about event propagation. In the Level 0 model, you can register only a single event handler for a particular type of event for a particular object. In the Level 2 model, however, you can register any number of handler functions for a particular event type on a particular object. This applies also to ancestors of an event target whose handler function or functions are invoked during the capturing or bubbling phases of event propagation.

19.2.2 Event Handler Registration

In the Level 0 API, you register an event handler by setting an attribute in your HTML or an object property in your JavaScript code. In the Level 2 event model, you register an event handler for a particular element by calling the `addEventListener()` method of that object. (The DOM standard uses the term "listener" in its API, but we'll continue to use the synonymous word "handler" in our discussion.) This method takes three arguments. The first is the name of the event type for which the handler is being registered. The event type should be a string that contains the lowercase name of the HTML handler attribute, with the leading "on" removed. Thus, if you use an `onmousedown` HTML attribute or `onmousedown` property in the Level 0 model, you'd use the string "mousedown" in the Level 2 event model.

The second argument to `addEventListener()` is the handler (or listener) function that should be invoked when the specified type of event occurs. When your function is invoked, it is passed an Event object as its only argument. This object contains details about the event (such as which mouse button was pressed) and defines methods such as `stopPropagation()`. We'll learn more about the Event interface and its subinterfaces later.

The final argument to `addEventListener()` is a boolean value. If `true`, the specified event handler is used to capture events during the capturing phase of event propagation. If the argument is `false`, the event handler is a normal event handler and is triggered when the event occurs directly on the object or on a descendant of the element and subsequently bubbles up to the element.

For example, you might use `addEventListener()` as follows to register a handler for submit events on a `<form>` element:

```
document.myform.addEventListener("submit",
                                 function(e) { validate(e.target); }
                                 false);
```

Or, if you wanted to capture all mousedown events that occur within a particular named `<div>` element, you might use `addEventListener()` like this:

```
var mydiv = document.getElementById("mydiv");
mydiv.addEventListener("mousedown", handleMouseDown, true);
```

Note that these examples assume that you've defined functions named `validate()` and `handleMouseDown()` elsewhere in your JavaScript code.

Event handlers registered with `addEventListener()` are executed in the scope in which they are defined. They are not invoked with the augmented scope chain that is used for event handlers defined as HTML attributes. (See Section 19.1.6, "Scope of Event Handlers.")

Because event handlers are registered in the Level 2 model by invoking a method rather than by setting an attribute or property, we can register more than one event handler for a given type of event on a given object. If you call `addEventListener()` multiple times to register more than one handler function for the same event type on the same object, all of the functions you've registered are invoked when an event of that type occurs on (or bubbles up to, or is captured by) that object. It is important to understand that the DOM standard makes no guarantees about the order in which the handler functions of a single object are invoked, so you should not rely on them being called in the order in which you registered them. Also note that if you register the same handler function more than once on the same element, all registrations after the first are ignored.

Why would you want to have more than one handler function for the same event on the same object? This can be quite useful for modularizing your software. Suppose, for example, that you've written a reusable module of JavaScript code that uses mouseover events on images to perform image rollovers. Now suppose that you have another module that wants to use the same mouseover events to display additional information about the image (or the link that the image represents) in the browser's status line. With the Level 0 API, you'd have to merge your two modules into one, so that they could share the single `onmouseover` property of the Image object. With the Level 2 API, on the other hand, each module can register the event handler it needs without knowing about or interfering with the other module.

`addEventListener()` is paired with a `removeEventListener()` method that expects the same three arguments but removes an event handler function from an object rather than adding it. It is often useful to temporarily register an event handler and then remove it soon afterward. For example, when you get a mousedown event, you might register temporary capturing event handlers for mousemove and mouseup events so you can see if the user drags the mouse. You'd then deregister these handlers when the mouseup event arrives. In such a situation, your event-handler removal code might look as follows:

```
document.removeEventListener("mousemove", handleMouseMove, true);
document.removeEventListener("mouseup", handleMouseUp, true);
```

Both the `addEventListener()` and `removeEventListener()` methods are defined by the EventTarget interface. In web browsers that support the Level 2 DOM Event API, all Document nodes implement this interface. For more information about these event-handler registration and deregistration methods, look up the EventTarget interface in the DOM reference section.

One final note about event-handler registration: in the Level 2 DOM, event handlers are not restricted to document elements; you can also register handlers for Text nodes. In practice, however, you may find it simpler to register handlers on containing elements and allow Text node events to bubble up and be handled at the container level.

19.2.3 addEventListener( ) and the this Keyword

In the original Level 0 event model, when a function is registered as an event handler for a document element, it becomes a method of that document element (as discussed previously in "Event Handlers and the this Keyword"). When the event handler is invoked, it is invoked as a method of the element, and, within the function, the `this` keyword refers to the element on which the event occurred.

In Mozilla and Netscape 6, when you register an event handler function with `addEventListener( )`, it is treated the same way: when the browser invokes the function, it invokes it as a method of the document element for which it was registered. Note, however, that this is implementation-dependent behavior, and the DOM specification does not require that this happen. Thus, you should not rely on the value of the `this` keyword in your event handler functions when using the Level 2 event model. Instead, use the `currentTarget` property of the Event object that is passed to your handler functions. As we'll see when we consider the Event object later in this chapter, the `currentTarget` property refers to the object on which the event handler was registered but does so in a portable way.

19.2.4 Registering Objects as Event Handlers

`addEventListener( )` allows us to register event handler functions. As discussed in the previous section, whether these functions are invoked as methods of the objects for which they are registered is implementation-dependent. For object-oriented programming, you may prefer to define event handlers as methods of a custom object and then have them invoked as methods of that object. For Java programmers, the DOM standard allows exactly this: it specifies that event handlers are objects that implement the EventListener interface and a method named `handleEvent( )`. In Java, when you register an event handler, you pass an object to `addEventListener( )`, not a function. For simplicity, the JavaScript binding of the DOM API does not require us to implement an EventListener interface and instead allows us to pass function references directly to `addEventListener( )`.

If you are writing an object-oriented JavaScript program and prefer to use objects as event handlers, you might use a function like this to register them:

```
function registerObjectEventHandler(element, eventtype, listener, captures) {
    element.addEventListener(eventtype,
                             function(event) { listener.handleEvent(event); }
                             captures);
}
```

Any object can be registered as an event listener with this function, as long as it defines a method named `handleEvent( )`. That method is invoked as a method of the listener object, and the this keyword refers to the listener object, not to the document element that generated the event. This function works because it uses a nested function literal to capture and remember the listener object in its scope chain. (If this doesn't make sense to you, you may want to review Section 11.4, "Lexical Scoping and Nested Functions.")

Although it is not part of the DOM specification, Mozilla 0.9.1 and Netscape 6.1 (but not Netscape 6.0 or 6.01) allow event listener objects that define a handleEvent() method to be passed directly to addEventListener() instead of a function reference. For these browsers, a special registration function like the one we just defined is not necessary.

19.2.5 Event Modules and Event Types

As I've noted before, the Level 2 DOM is modularized, so an implementation can support parts of it and omit support for other parts. The Events API is one such module. You can test whether a browser supports this module with code like this:

```
document.implementation.hasFeature("Events", "2.0")
```

The Events module contains only the API for the basic event-handling infrastructure, however. Support for specific types of events is delegated to submodules. Each submodule provides support for a category of related event types and defines an Event type that is passed to event handlers for each of those types. For example, the submodule named MouseEvents provides support for mousedown, mouseup, click, and related event types. It also defines the MouseEvent interface. An object that implements this interface is passed to the handler function for any event type supported by the module.

Table 19-2 lists each event module, the event interface it defines, and the types of events it supports. Note that the Level 2 DOM does not standardize any type of keyboard event, so no module of key events is listed here. Support for this type of event is expected in the DOM Level 3 standard.

Table 19-2. Event modules, interfaces, and types

Module name	Event interface	Event types
HTMLEvents	Event	abort, blur, change, error, focus, load, reset, resize, scroll, select, submit, unload
MouseEvents	MouseEvent	click, mousedown, mousemove, mouseout, mouseover, mouseup
UIEvents	UIEvent	DOMActivate, DOMFocusIn, DOMFocusOut
MutationEvents	MutationEvent	DOMAttrModified, DOMCharacterDataModified, DOMNodeInserted, DOMNodeInsertedIntoDocument, DOMNodeRemoved, DOMNode-RemovedFromDocument, DOMSubtreeModified

As you can see from Table 19-2, The HTMLEvents and MouseEvents modules define event types that are familiar from the Level 0 event module. The UIEvents module defines event types that are similar to the focus, blur, and click events supported by HTML form elements but are generalized so that they can be generated by any document element that can receive focus or be activated in some way. The MutationEvents module defines events that are generated when the document changes (is mutated) in some way. These are specialized event types and are not commonly used.

As I noted earlier, when an event occurs, its handler is passed an object that implements the Event interface associated with that type of event. The properties of this object provide details about the event that may be useful to the handler. Table 19-3 lists the standard events again, but this time organizes them by event type, rather than by event module. For each event type, this table specifies the kind of event object that is passed to its handler, whether this type of event bubbles up the document hierarchy during event propagation (the "B" column), and whether the event has a default action that is cancelable with the `preventDefault()` method (the "C" column). For events in the HTMLEvents module, the fifth column of the table specifies which HTML elements can generate the event. For all other event types, the fifth column specifies which properties of the event object contain meaningful event details (these properties are documented in the next section). Note that the properties listed in this column do not include the properties that are defined by the basic Event interface, which contain meaningful values for all event types.

It is useful to compare Table 19-3 with Table 19-1, which lists the Level 0 event handlers defined by HTML 4. The event types supported by the two models are largely the same (excluding the UIEvents and MutationEvents modules). The DOM Level 2 standard adds support for the abort, error, resize, and scroll event types that were not standardized by HTML 4, and it does not support the dblclick event type that is part of the HTML 4 standard. (Instead, as we'll see shortly, the `detail` property of the object passed to a `click` event handler specifies the number of consecutive clicks that have occurred.)

Table 19-3. Event types

Event type	Interface	B	C	Supported by/detail properties
abort	Event	yes	no	`<img>`, `<object>`
blur	Event	no	no	`<a>`, `<area>`, `<button>`, `<input>`, `<label>`, `<select>`, `<textarea>`
change	Event	yes	no	`<input>`, `<select>`, `<textarea>`
click	MouseEvent	yes	yes	`screenX`, `screenY`, `clientX`, `clientY`, `altKey`, `ctrlKey`, `shiftKey`, `metaKey`, `button`, `detail`
error	Event	yes	no	`<body>`, `<frameset>`, `<img>`, `<object>`
focus	Event	no	no	`<a>`, `<area>`, `<button>`, `<input>`, `<label>`, `<select>`, `<textarea>`

Table 19-3. Event types (continued)

Event type	Interface	B	C	Supported by/detail properties
load	Event	no	no	`<body>`, `<frameset>`, `<iframe>`, `<img>`, `<object>`
mousedown	MouseEvent	yes	yes	`screenX`, `screenY`, `clientX`, `clientY`, `altKey`, `ctrlKey`, `shiftKey`, `metaKey`, `button`, `detail`
mousemove	MouseEvent	yes	no	`screenX`, `screenY`, `clientX`, `clientY`, `altKey`, `ctrlKey`, `shiftKey`, `metaKey`
mouseout	MouseEvent	yes	yes	`screenX`, `screenY`, `clientX`, `clientY`, `altKey`, `ctrlKey`, `shiftKey`, `metaKey`, `relatedTarget`
mouseover	MouseEvent	yes	yes	`screenX`, `screenY`, `clientX`, `clientY`, `altKey`, `ctrlKey`, `shiftKey`, `metaKey`, `relatedTarget`
mouseup	MouseEvent	yes	yes	`screenX`, `screenY`, `clientX`, `clientY`, `altKey`, `ctrlKey`, `shiftKey`, `metaKey`, `button`, `detail`
reset	Event	yes	no	`<form>`
resize	Event	yes	no	`<body>`, `<frameset>`, `<iframe>`
scroll	Event	yes	no	`<body>`
select	Event	yes	no	`<input>`, `<textarea>`
submit	Event	yes	yes	`<form>`
unload	Event	no	no	`<body>`, `<frameset>`
DOMActivate	UIEvent	yes	yes	`detail`
DOMAttrModified	MutationEvent	yes	no	`attrName`, `attrChange`, `prevValue`, `newValue`, `relatedNode`
DOMCharacterDataModified	MutationEvent	yes	no	`prevValue`, `newValue`
DOMFocusIn	UIEvent	yes	no	none
DOMFocusOut	UIEvent	yes	no	none
DOMNodeInserted	MutationEvent	yes	no	`relatedNode`
DOMNodeInsertedIntoDocument	MutationEvent	no	no	none
DOMNodeRemoved	MutationEvents	yes	no	`relatedNode`
DOMNodeRemovedFromDocument	MutationEvent	no	no	none
DOMSubtreeModified	MutationEvent	yes	no	none

19.2.6 Event Interfaces and Event Details

When an event occurs, the DOM Level 2 API provides additional details about the event (such as when and where it occurred) as properties of an object that is passed to the event handler. Each event module has an associated event interface that specifies details appropriate to that type of event. Table 19-2 (earlier in this chapter) lists four different event modules and four different event interfaces.

These four interfaces are actually related to one another and form a hierarchy. The Event interface is the root of the hierarchy; all event objects implement this most basic event interface. UIEvent is a subinterface of Event: any event object that implements UIEvent also implements all the methods and properties of Event. The MouseEvent interface is a subinterface of UIEvent. This means, for example, that the event object passed to an event handler for a click event implements all the methods and properties defined by each of the MouseEvent, UIEvent, and Event interfaces. Finally, the MutationEvent interface is a subinterface of Event.

The following sections introduce each of the event interfaces and highlight their most important properties and methods. You will find complete details about each interface in the DOM reference section of this book.

19.2.6.1 Event

The event types defined by the HTMLEvents module use the Event interface. All other event types use subinterfaces of this interface, which means that Event is implemented by all event objects and provides detailed information that applies to all event types. The Event interface defines the following properties (note that these properties, and the properties of all Event subinterfaces, are read-only):

`type`
: The type of event that occurred. The value of this property is the name of the event type and is the same string value that was used when registering the event handler (e.g., "click" or "mouseover").

`target`
: The node on which the event occurred, which may not be the same as `currentTarget`.

`currentTarget`
: The node at which the event is currently being processed (i.e., the node whose event handler is currently being run). If the event is being processed during the capturing or bubbling phase of propagation, the value of this property is different from the value of the `target` property. As discussed earlier, you should use this property instead of the `this` keyword in your event handler functions.

`eventPhase`
: A number that specifies what phase of event propagation is currently in process. The value is one of the constants `Event.CAPTURING_PHASE`, `Event.AT_TARGET`, or `Event.BUBBLING_PHASE`.

`timeStamp`
: A Date object that specifies when the event occurred.

`bubbles`
: A boolean that specifies whether this event (and events of this type) bubbles up the document tree.

`cancelable`
: A boolean that specifies whether the event has a default action associated with it that can be canceled with the `preventDefault()` method.

In addition to these seven properties, the Event interface defines two methods that are also implemented by all event objects: `stopPropagation()` and `preventDefault()`. Any event handler can call `stopPropagation()` to prevent the event from being propagated beyond the node at which it is currently being handled. Any event handler can call `preventDefault()` to prevent the browser from performing a default action associated with the event. Calling `preventDefault()` in the DOM Level 2 API is like returning `false` in the Level 0 event model.

19.2.6.2 UIEvent

The UIEvent interface is a subinterface of Event. It defines the type of event object passed to events of type DOMFocusIn, DOMFocusOut, and DOMActivate. These event types are not commonly used; what is more important about the UIEvent interface is that it is the parent interface of MouseEvent. UIEvent defines two properties in addition to those defined by Event:

`view`
: The Window object (known as a "view" in DOM terminology) within which the event occurred.

`detail`
: A number that may provide additional information about the event. For click, mousedown, and mouseup events, this field is the click count: 1 for a single-click, 2 for a double-click, and 3 for a triple-click. (Note that each click generates an event, but if multiple clicks are close enough together, the `detail` value indicates that. That is, a mouse event with a `detail` of 2 is always preceded by a mouse event with a `detail` of 1.) For DOMActivate events, this field is 1 for a normal activation or 2 for a hyperactivation, such as a double-click or **Shift-Enter** combination.

19.2.6.3 MouseEvent

The MouseEvent interface inherits the properties and methods of Event and UIEvent and defines the following additional properties:

`button`
: A number that specifies which mouse button changed state during a mousedown, mouseup, or click event. A value of 0 indicates the left button, 1 indicates the middle button, and 2 indicates the right button. This property is used only

when a button changes state: it is not used to report whether a button is held down during a mousemove event, for example. Note also that Netscape 6 gets this wrong and uses the values 1, 2, and 3, instead of 0, 1, and 2. This problem is fixed in Netscape 6.1.

`altKey`, `ctrlKey`, `metaKey`, `shiftKey`
: These four boolean fields indicate whether the **Alt**, **Ctrl**, **Meta**, or **Shift** keys were held down when a mouse event occurred. Unlike the `button` property, these key properties are valid for any type of mouse event.

`clientX`, `clientY`
: These two properties specify the X and Y coordinates of the mouse pointer, relative to the client area or browser window. Note that these coordinates do not take document scrolling into account: if an event occurs at the very top of the window, `clientY` is 0, regardless of how far down the document has been scrolled. Unfortunately, the Level 2 DOM does not provide a standard way to translate these window coordinates to document coordinates. In Netscape 6, you can add `window.pageXOffset` and `window.pageYOffset`, and in Internet Explorer, you can add `document.body.scrollLeft` and `document.body.scrollTop`.

`screenX`, `screenY`
: These two properties specify the X- and Y-coordinates of the mouse pointer relative to the upper-left corner of the user's monitor. These values are useful if you plan to open a new browser window at or near the location of the mouse event.

`relatedTarget`
: This property refers to a node that is related to the target node of the event. For mouseover events, it is the node that the mouse left when it moved over the target. For mouseout events, it is the node that the mouse entered when leaving the target. It is unused for other event types.

19.2.6.4 MutationEvent

The MutationEvent interface is a subinterface of Event, and is used to provide event details for the event types defined by the MutationEvents module. These event types are not commonly used in DHTML programming, so details on the interface are not provided here. See the DOM reference section for details.

19.2.7 Example: Dragging Document Elements

Now that we've discussed event propagation, event-handler registration, and the various event object interfaces for the DOM Level 2 event model, we can finally look at how they work. Example 19-2 shows a JavaScript function, `beginDrag()`, that, when invoked from a `mousedown` event handler, allows a document element to be dragged by the user.

beginDrag( ) takes two arguments. The first is the element that is to be dragged. This may be the element on which the mousedown event occurred or a containing element (e.g., you might allow the user to drag on the titlebar of a window to move the entire window). In either case, however, it must refer to a document element that is absolutely positioned using the CSS position attribute, and the left and top CSS attributes must be explicitly set to pixel values in a style attribute. The second argument is the event object associated with the triggering mousedown event.

beginDrag( ) records the position of the mousedown event and then registers event handlers for the mousemove and mouseup events that will follow the mousedown event. The handler for the mousemove event is responsible for moving the document element, and the handler for the mouseup event is responsible for deregistering itself and the mousemove handler. It is important to note that the mousemove and mouseup handlers are registered as capturing event handlers, because the user can move the mouse faster than the document element can follow it, and some of these events occur outside of the original target element. Also, note that the moveHandler( ) and upHandler( ) functions that are registered to handle these events are defined as functions nested within beginDrag( ). Because they are defined in this nested scope, they can use the arguments and local variables of beginDrag( ), which considerably simplifies their implementation.

Example 19-2. Dragging with the DOM Level 2 event model

```
/**
 * Drag.js:
 * This function is designed to be called from a mousedown event handler.
 * It registers temporary capturing event handlers for the mousemove and
 * mouseup events that will follow and uses these handlers to "drag" the
 * specified document element. The first argument must be an absolutely
 * positioned document element. It may be the element that received the
 * mousedown event or it may be some containing element. The second
 * argument must be the event object for the mousedown event.
 **/
function beginDrag(elementToDrag, event) {
    // Figure out where the element currently is
    // The element must have left and top CSS properties in a style attribute
    // Also, we assume they are set using pixel units
    var x = parseInt(elementToDrag.style.left);
    var y = parseInt(elementToDrag.style.top);

    // Compute the distance between that point and the mouse-click
    // The nested moveHandler function below needs these values
    var deltaX = event.clientX - x;
    var deltaY = event.clientY - y;

    // Register the event handlers that will respond to the mousemove
    // and mouseup events that follow this mousedown event. Note that
    // these are registered as capturing event handlers on the document.
    // These event handlers remain active while the mouse button remains
    // pressed and are removed when the button is released.
```

Example 19-2. Dragging with the DOM Level 2 event model (continued)

```
    document.addEventListener("mousemove", moveHandler, true);
    document.addEventListener("mouseup", upHandler, true);

    // We've handled this event. Don't let anybody else see it.
    event.stopPropagation( );
    event.preventDefault( );

    /**
     * This is the handler that captures mousemove events when an element
     * is being dragged. It is responsible for moving the element.
     **/
    function moveHandler(event) {
        // Move the element to the current mouse position, adjusted as
        // necessary by the offset of the initial mouse-click
        elementToDrag.style.left = (event.clientX - deltaX) + "px";
        elementToDrag.style.top = (event.clientY - deltaY) + "px";

        // And don't let anyone else see this event
        event.stopPropagation( );
    }

    /**
     * This is the handler that captures the final mouseup event that
     * occurs at the end of a drag
     **/
    function upHandler(event) {
        // Unregister the capturing event handlers
        document.removeEventListener("mouseup", upHandler, true);
        document.removeEventListener("mousemove", moveHandler, true);
        // And don't let the event propagate any further
        event.stopPropagation( );
    }
}
```

You can use `beginDrag( )` in an HTML file like the following (which is a simplified version of Example 19-2 with the addition of dragging):

```
<script src="Drag.js"></script> <!-- Include the Drag.js script -->
<!-- Define the element to be dragged -->
<div style="position:absolute; left:100px; top:100px;
            background-color: white; border: solid black;">
<!-- Define the "handle" to drag it with. Note the onmousedown attribute. -->
<div style="background-color: gray; border-bottom: dotted black;
            padding: 3px; font-family: sans-serif; font-weight: bold;"
     onmousedown="beginDrag(this.parentNode, event);">
Drag Me  <!-- The content of the "titlebar" -->
</div>
<!-- Content of the dragable element -->
<p>This is a test. Testing, testing, testing.<p>This is a test.<p>Test.
</div>
```

The key here is the `onmousedown` attribute of the inner `<div>` element. Although `beginDrag( )` uses the DOM Level 2 event model, we register it here using the Level 0 model for convenience. As we'll discuss in the next section, the event models can be mixed, and when an event handler is specified as an HTML attribute, the event object is available using the event keyword. (This is not part of the DOM standard but is a convention of the Netscape 4 and IE event models, which are described later.)

Here's another simple example of using beginDrag(); it defines an image that the user can drag, but only if the **Shift** key is held down:

```
<script src="Drag.js"></script>
<img src="plus.gif" width="20" height="20"
style="position:absolute; left:0px; top:0px;"
onmousedown="if (event.shiftKey) beginDrag(this, event);">
```

Note the differences between the onmousedown attribute here and the one in the previous example.

19.2.8 Mixing Event Models

So far, we've discussed the traditional Level 0 event model and the new standard DOM Level 2 model. For backward compatibility, browsers that support the Level 2 model will continue to support the Level 0 event model. This means that you can mix event models within a document, as we did in the HTML fragments used to demonstrate the element-dragging script in the previous section.

It is important to understand that web browsers that support the Level 2 event model always pass an event object to event handlers—even handlers registered by setting an HTML attribute or a JavaScript property using the Level 0 model. When an event handler is defined as an HTML attribute, it is implicitly converted to a function that has an argument named event. This means that such an event handler can use the identifier event to refer to the event object.

The DOM standard never formalized the Level 0 event model. It does not even require properties like onclick for HTML elements that support an onclick attribute. However, the standard recognizes that the Level 0 event model will remain in use and specifies that implementations that support the Level 0 model treat handlers registered with that model as if they were registered using addEventListener(). That is, if you assign a function f to the onclick property of a document element e (or set the corresponding HTML onclick attribute), it is equivalent to registering that function as follows:

```
e.addEventListener("click", f, false);
```

When f() is invoked, it is passed an event object as its argument, even though it was registered using the Level 0 model. Furthermore, if you change the value of the onclick property from function f to function g, it is equivalent to this code:

```
e.removeEventListener("click", f, false);
e.addEventListener("click", g, false);
```

Note, however, that the Level 2 specification does not say whether an event handler registered by assigning to the onclick property can be removed by calling `removeEventListener()`. At the time of this writing, the Mozilla/Netscape implementation does not allow this.

19.2.9 Synthesizing Events

The DOM Level 2 standard includes an API for creating and dispatching synthetic events. This API allows events to be generated under program control rather than under user control. Although this is not a commonly needed feature, it can be useful, for example, to produce regression tests that subject a DHTML application to a known sequence of events and verify that the result is the same. It could also be used to implement a macro playback facility to automate commonly performed user-interface actions. On the other hand, the synthetic event API is not suitable for producing self-running demo programs: you can create a synthetic mousemove event and deliver it to the appropriate event handlers in your application, but this does not actually cause the mouse pointer to move across the screen!

Unfortunately, at the time of this writing, the synthetic event API is not supported by Netscape 6, nor by the current version of Mozilla.

To generate a synthetic event, you must complete three steps:

- Create an appropriate event object.
- Initialize the fields of the event object.
- Dispatch the event object to the desired document element.

To create an event object, call the `createEvent()` method of the Document object. This method takes a single argument, which is the name of the event module for which an event object should be created. For example, to create an event object suitable for use with a click event, call the method as follows:

```
document.createEvent("HTMLEvents");
```

To create an event object suitable for use with any of the mouse event types, call it like this instead:

```
document.createEvent("MouseEvents");
```

Note that the argument to `createEvent()` is plural. This is counterintuitive, but it is the same string that you'd pass to the `hasFeature()` method to test whether a browser supports an event module.

After creating an event object, the next step is to initialize its properties. The properties of event objects are always read-only, however, so you cannot directly assign values to them. Instead, you must call a method to perform the initialization. Although the earlier descriptions of the Event, MouseEvent, and other event objects mentioned only properties, each object also defines a single method for initializing the properties of the event. This initialization method has a name that depends on the type of event object to be initialized and is passed as many arguments as there are properties to be set. Note that you can call an event initialization method only before dispatching a synthetic event: you cannot use these methods to modify the properties of an event object that is passed to an event handler.

Let's look at a couple of examples. As you know, click events are part of the HTMLEvents module and use event objects of type Event. These objects are initialized with an `initEvent( )` method, as follows:

```
e.initEvent("click", "true", "true");
```

On the other hand, mousedown events are part of the MouseEvents module and use event objects of the MouseEvent type. These objects are initialized with an `initMouseEvent( )` method that takes many more arguments:

```
e.initMouseEvent("mousedown", true, false,  // Event properties
                 window, 1,                 // UIEvent properties
                 0, 0, 0, 0,                // MouseEvent properties
                 false, false, false, false,
                 0, null);
```

Note that you pass only the event module name to `createEvent( )`. The name of the actual event type is passed to the event initialization method. The DOM standard does not require that you use one of the predefined names. You may create events using any event type name you choose, as long as it does not begin with a digit or with the prefix "DOM" (in uppercase, lowercase, or mixed case). If you initialize a synthetic event with a custom event type name, you must register event handlers with that event type name as well.

After creating and initializing an event object, you can dispatch it by passing it to the `dispatchEvent( )` method of the appropriate document element. `dispatchEvent( )` is defined by the EventTarget interface, so it is available as a method of any document node that supports the `addEventListener( )` and `removeEventListener( )` methods. The element to which you dispatch an event becomes the event target, and the event object goes through the usual sequence of event propagation. At each stage of event propagation, the event object you created is passed to any event handlers that were registered for the event type you specified when you initialized the event. Finally, when event propagation finishes, your call to `dispatchEvent( )` returns. The return value is `false` if any of the event handlers called the `preventDefault( )` method on your event object and is `true` otherwise.

19.3 The Internet Explorer Event Model

The event model supported by Internet Explorer 4, 5, 5.5, and 6 is an intermediate model, halfway between the original Level 0 model and the standard DOM Level 2 model. The IE event model includes an Event object that provides details about events that occur. Instead of being passed to event handler functions, however, the Event object is made available as a property of the Window object. The IE model supports event propagation by bubbling, but not by capturing, as the DOM model does. In IE 4, event handlers are registered in the same way as they are in the original

Level 0 model. In IE 5 and later, however, multiple handlers may be registered with special (but nonstandard) registration functions.

The following sections provide more detail about this event model and document it by comparison to the original Level 0 event model and the standard Level 2 event model. Therefore, you should be sure you understand those two event models before reading about the IE model.

19.3.1 The IE Event Object

Like the standard DOM Level 2 event model, the IE event model provides details about each event that occurs in the properties of an Event object. The Event objects defined in the standard model were in fact modeled on the IE Event object, so you'll notice a number of similarities between the properties of the IE Event object and the properties of the DOM Event, UIEvent, and MouseEvent objects.

The most important properties of the IE Event object are:

`type`
: A string that specifies the type of event that occurred. The value of this property is the name of the event handler with the leading "on" removed (e.g., "click" or "mouseover"). Compatible with the `type` property of the DOM Event object.

`srcElement`
: The document element on which the event occurred. Comparable to the `target` property of the DOM Event object.

`button`
: An integer that specifies the mouse button that was pressed. A value of 1 indicates the left button, 2 indicates the right button, and 4 indicates the middle button. If multiple buttons are pressed, these values are added together—the left and right buttons together produce a value of 3, for example. Compare this with the `button` property of the DOM Level 2 MouseEvent object, but note that although the property names are the same, the interpretation of the property values differs.

`clientX`, `clientY`
: These integer properties specify the mouse coordinates at the time of the event, relative to the upper-left corner of the containing window. Note that for documents that are larger than the window, these coordinates are not the same as the position within the document, and you may want to add the values `document.body.scrollLeft` and `document.body.scrollTop`, respectively, to account for scrolling. These properties are compatible with the DOM Level 2 MouseEvent properties of the same name.

`offsetX`, `offsetY`
: These integer properties specify the position of the mouse pointer relative to the source element. They enable you to determine which pixel of an Image object

was clicked on, for example. These properties have no equivalent in the DOM Level 2 event model.

`altKey`, `ctrlKey`, `shiftKey`
: These boolean properties specify whether the **Alt**, **Ctrl**, and **Shift** keys were held down when the event occurred. These properties are compatible with the properties of the same name in the DOM Level 2 MouseEvent object. Note, however, that the IE Event object does not have a `metaKey` property.

`keyCode`
: This integer property specifies the key code for keydown and keyup events and the Unicode character code for keypress events. Use `String.fromCharCode( )` to convert character codes to strings. The DOM Level 2 event model does not standardize key events (although DOM Level 3 is working on this) and has no equivalent to these properties.

`fromElement`, `toElement`
: `fromElement` specifies the document element that the mouse used to be over for mouseover events. `toElement` specifies the document element that the mouse has moved to for mouseout events. Comparable to the `relatedTarget` property of the DOM Level 2 MouseEvent object.

`cancelBubble`
: A boolean property that, when set to `true`, prevents the current event from bubbling any further up the element containment hierarchy. Comparable to the `stopPropagation( )` method of the DOM Level 2 Event object.

`returnValue`
: A boolean property that can be set to `false` to prevent the browser from performing the default action associated with the event. This is an alternative to the traditional technique of returning `false` from the event handler. Comparable to the `preventDefault( )` method of the DOM Level 2 Event object.

You can find complete documentation for the IE Event object in the client-side reference section of this book.

19.3.2 The IE Event Object as a Global Variable

Although the IE event model provides event details in an Event object, it never passes Event objects as arguments to event handlers. Instead, it makes the Event object available as the `event` property of the global Window object. This means that an event handling function in IE can refer to the Event object as `window.event` or simply as `event`. Although it seems strange to use a global variable where a function argument would do, the IE scheme works because it is implicit in the event-driven programming model that only one event is ever being processed at a time. Since two events are never handled concurrently, it is safe to use a global variable to store details on the event that is currently being processed.

The fact that the Event object is a global variable is incompatible with the standard DOM Level 2 event model, but there is a one-line workaround. If you want to write an event handler function that works with either event model, write the function so that it expects an argument, and then, if no argument is passed, initialize the argument from the global variable. For example:

```
function portableEventHandler(e) {
    if (!e) e = window.event;  // Get event details for IE

    // Body of the event handler goes here
}
```


19.3.3 Event Bubbling in IE

The IE event model does not have any notion of event capturing, as the DOM Level 2 model does. However, events do bubble up through the containment hierarchy in the IE model, just as they do in the Level 2 model. As with the Level 2 model, event bubbling applies only to raw or input events (primarily mouse and keyboard events), not to higher-level semantic events. The primary difference between event bubbling in the IE and DOM Level 2 event models is the way that you stop bubbling. The IE Event object does not have a `stopPropagation()` method, as the DOM Event object does. To prevent an event from bubbling or stop it from bubbling any further up the containment hierarchy, an IE event handler must set the `cancelBubble` property of the Event object to `true`:

```
window.event.cancelBubble = true;
```

Note that setting `cancelBubble` applies only to the current event. When a new event is generated, a new Event object is assigned to `window.event`, and `cancelBubble` is restored to its default value of `false`.

19.3.4 IE Event-Handler Registration

In IE 4, event handlers are registered in the same way they are in the original Level 0 event model: by specifying them as HTML attributes or assigning functions to the event handler properties of document elements. The only difference is that IE 4 allows access to (and event-handler registration on) all of the elements in a document, instead of just the form, image, and link elements that are accessible with the Level 0 DOM.

IE 5 and later introduce the `attachEvent()` and `detachEvent()` methods, which provide a way to register more than one handler function for a given event type on a given object. These methods work like `addEventListener()` and `removeEventListener()`, except that since the IE event model does not support event capturing, they expect only two arguments: the event type and the handler function. Also, unlike with the Level 2 event model, the event handler names passed to the IE method should include the "on" prefix: use "onclick" instead of just "click". You can use `attachEvent()` to register an event handler as follows:

```
function highlight( ) { /* Event-handler code goes here */ }
document.getElementById("myelt").attachEvent("onmouseover", highlight);
```

Another difference between `attachEvent()` and `addEventListener()` is that functions registered with `attachEvent()` are invoked as global functions, rather than as methods of the document element on which the event occurred. That is, when an event handler registered with `attachEvent()` executes, the `this` keyword refers to the Window object, not to the event's target element.

19.3.5 Example: Dragging with the IE Event Model

Example 19-3 is a modified version of the `beginDrag()` function that was presented in Example 19-2. This version includes code that makes it work with the IE event model, in addition to the DOM Level 2 event model. The design and intended usage of this version of `beginDrag()` are the same as in Example 19-2, so if you understood that example, you should have no trouble understanding this one. What makes this example interesting is that it juxtaposes two event models, clearly highlighting their differences.

The biggest difference in the IE version of the code is that it must rely on event bubbling rather than event capturing. This usually works, but it is not the ideal solution for this problem. Another important difference to note is that IE event handlers are not passed an Event object. Note that the code in this example also distinguishes between IE 5 and later, which support `attachEvent()`, and IE 4, which does not. See the discussion of Example 19-2 for a sample HTML document that is designed to use this `beginDrag()` function.

Example 19-3. Dragging with the IE event model

```
/**
 * PortableDrag.js:
 * beginDrag( ) is designed to be called from an onmousedown event handler.
 * elementToDrag may be the element that received the mousedown event, or it
 * may be some containing element. event must be the Event object for the
 * mousedown event. This implementation works with both the DOM Level 2
 * event model and the IE event model.
 **/
function beginDrag(elementToDrag, event) {
    // Compute the distance between the upper-left corner of the element
    // and the mouse-click. The moveHandler function below needs these values.
    var deltaX = event.clientX - parseInt(elementToDrag.style.left);
    var deltaY = event.clientY - parseInt(elementToDrag.style.top);

    // Register the event handlers that will respond to the mousemove events
    // and the mouseup event that follow this mousedown event.
    if (document.addEventListener) {  // DOM Level 2 Event Model
```

Example 19-3. Dragging with the IE event model (continued)

```
        // Register capturing event handlers
        document.addEventListener("mousemove", moveHandler, true);
        document.addEventListener("mouseup", upHandler, true);
    }
    else if (document.attachEvent) {  // IE 5+ Event Model
        // In the IE event model, we can't capture events, so these handlers
        // are triggered only if the event bubbles up to them.
        // This assumes that there aren't any intervening elements that
        // handle the events and stop them from bubbling.
        document.attachEvent("onmousemove", moveHandler);
        document.attachEvent("onmouseup", upHandler);
    }
    else {  // IE 4 Event Model
        // In IE 4 we can't use attachEvent( ), so assign the event handlers
        // directly after storing any previously assigned handlers, so they
        // can be restored. Note that this also relies on event bubbling.
        var oldmovehandler = document.onmousemove;
        var olduphandler = document.onmouseup;
        document.onmousemove = moveHandler;
        document.onmouseup = upHandler;
    }

    // We've handled this event. Don't let anybody else see it.
    if (event.stopPropagation) event.stopPropagation( );  // DOM Level 2
    else event.cancelBubble = true;                       // IE

    // Now prevent any default action.
    if (event.preventDefault) event.preventDefault( );   // DOM Level 2
    else event.returnValue = false;                      // IE

    /**
     * This is the handler that captures mousemove events when an element
     * is being dragged. It is responsible for moving the element.
     **/
    function moveHandler(e) {
        if (!e) e = window.event;  // IE Event Model

        // Move the element to the current mouse position, adjusted as
        // necessary by the offset of the initial mouse-click.
        elementToDrag.style.left = (e.clientX - deltaX) + "px";
        elementToDrag.style.top = (e.clientY - deltaY) + "px";

        // And don't let anyone else see this event.
        if (e.stopPropagation) e.stopPropagation( );  // DOM Level 2
        else e.cancelBubble = true;                   // IE
    }

    /**
     * This is the handler that captures the final mouseup event that
     * occurs at the end of a drag.
     **/
```

Example 19-3. Dragging with the IE event model (continued)

```
    function upHandler(e) {
        if (!e) e = window.event;  // IE Event Model

        // Unregister the capturing event handlers.
        if (document.removeEventListener) {  // DOM Event Model
            document.removeEventListener("mouseup", upHandler, true);
            document.removeEventListener("mousemove", moveHandler, true);
        }
        else if (document.detachEvent) {  // IE 5+ Event Model
            document.detachEvent("onmouseup", upHandler);
            document.detachEvent("onmousemove", moveHandler);
        }
        else {  // IE 4 Event Model
            document.onmouseup = olduphandler;
            document.onmousemove = oldmovehandler;
        }

        // And don't let the event propagate any further.
        if (e.stopPropagation) e.stopPropagation( );  // DOM Level 2
        else e.cancelBubble = true;                    // IE
    }
}
```

19.4 The Netscape 4 Event Model

The Netscape 4 event model is like the original Level 0 event model, except that it provides event details in an Event object that is passed as an argument to handler functions. It also supports special methods to enable event capturing. These features are explained in the sections that follow.

19.4.1 The Netscape 4 Event Object

The Netscape 4 event model defines an Event object that contains details about the event that occurred. Like the DOM Level 2 model, it passes an Event object as an argument to all event handlers. Unfortunately, however, the properties of the Netscape 4 Event object are almost entirely different than those of the IE Event object and the various DOM Level 2 event objects. The key Event properties in the Netscape 4 event model are:

`type`
: A string that specifies the type of event that occurred. This string is the name of the event handler, minus the "on" prefix (e.g., "click" or "mousedown"). This property is compatible with the IE and DOM Level 2 Event objects.

`target`
: The document element on which the event occurred. This property is compatible with the `target` property of the DOM Level 2 Event object and comparable to `srcElement` in the IE Event object.

pageX, pageY
: These properties specify the pixel coordinates at which the event occurred, relative to the upper-left corner of the window. For documents that are larger than the window, you need to add in the offsets `window.pageXOffset` and `window.pageYOffset` to convert these to document coordinates. Comparable to the `clientX` and `clientY` properties of the DOM Level 2 MouseEvent object and the IE Event object.

which
: An integer that specifies which mouse button or key was pressed. For mouse events, the left, middle, and right buttons are specified by the values 1, 2, and 3, respectively. Compare this to the (mutually incompatible) `button` properties of the DOM Level 2 MouseEvent object and the IE Event object. For keyboard events, this property contains the Unicode encoding of the key that was pressed. Compare this to the `keyCode` property of the IE Event object.

modifiers
: An integer that specifies which keyboard modifier keys were pressed when the event occurred. The value is a bitmask comprised of any of the following values: `Event.ALT_MASK`, `Event.CONTROL_MASK`, `Event.META_MASK`, and `Event.SHIFT_MASK`. Comparable to the `altKey`, `ctrlKey`, `metaKey`, and `shiftKey` properties of the DOM Level 2 MouseEvent object and the IE Event object.

In the Netscape 4 event model, an Event object is passed to all event handlers. When an event handler is defined as a string of JavaScript code in an HTML attribute, that code is implicitly converted to a function with an argument named `event`. This means that HTML event handlers can refer to the Event object with the identifier `event`. (Compare this to the IE model, in which the `event` identifier refers to the global Event object. The implementations are quite different, but the practical result is the same.)

For backward compatibility, the Event objects used by Mozilla and Netscape 6 implement most of the properties of the Netscape 4 Event object, with the notable exception, at the time of this writing, of the `modifiers` property.

19.4.2 Event Capturing in Netscape 4

The Netscape 4 event model does not support event bubbling, as the IE event model does, but it does support a limited form of event capturing, like the DOM Level 2 model does. (In fact, the event-propagation model for the DOM standard is a combination of the Netscape capturing and IE bubbling models.) Although Netscape 4 supports a form of event capturing, the way it works is quite different from that defined by the DOM Level 2 event model.

In Netscape 4, the Window, Document, and Layer objects may request the opportunity to preview certain types of events before they are processed by the elements that generated them. Such a request is made with the `captureEvents()` method of these objects. The argument to this method specifies the type of events to be captured; it is a bitmask composed of constants defined as static properties of the Event constructor. So, for example, if a program wants all mousedown and mouseup events to be routed to the Window object before being handled by the object for which they were intended, it can call `captureEvents()` like this:

```
window.captureEvents(Event.MOUSEDOWN | Event.MOUSEUP);
```

Having made this request to receive the events, the program then has to register event handlers for those events:

```
window.onmousedown = function(event) { ... };
window.onmouseup = function(event) { ... };
```

When one of these capturing event handlers receives an event, it gets to decide what should happen to it next. In some programs, a captured event is handled and propagates no further. In other circumstances, however, the program wants to pass the event along. If you pass the event to the `routeEvent()` method of the Window, Document, and Layer objects, the method passes the event to the next Window, Document, or Layer object that has used `captureEvents()` to specify interest in that type of event. Or, if there is no other capturing object to which to route the event, it is routed to its original source object and the appropriate event handler of that object is invoked. For example:

```
function clickHandler(event) {
  if (event.which == 3) {  // It is the right mouse button
    // Handle the event here, and do nothing else
    // The event will not propagate any further
  }
  else {  // It is not the right mouse button
    // We're not interested in this event, so let it propagate on
    // to some element that is interested in it
    window.routeEvent(event);
  }
}
```

An alternative to calling `routeEvent()` is to simply pass the Event object to the `handleEvent()` method of the object to which you want the event delivered. The `handleEvent()` method passes the event to the appropriate event handler of that object.

When a Window, Document, or Layer object no longer wishes to capture events, it should call the `releaseEvents()` method, specifying the same argument it passed to `captureEvents()`.

The Netscape 4 event-capturing model is fundamentally incompatible with the DOM Level 2 event-capturing model. For example, the DOM model propagates captured events by default, but the Netscape model does not. Mozilla and Netscape 6 implement the Netscape 4 event-capturing API, but the API appears to be nonfunctional.

19.4.3 Example: Dragging with the Netscape 4 Event Model

Example 19-4 is an implementation of our familiar beginDrag() method, using the Netscape 4 event model (and the Netscape 4 Layer-based DOM). It demonstrates how events are captured and how event handlers are written for this event model. This example includes both JavaScript code and a simple HTML document that uses the beginDrag() method to define an image that the user can drag. Compare this implementation of beginDrag() to the two we've seen previously. Note that this example defines its nested event handler functions at the beginning of the beginDrag() function instead of at the end. This is a bug workaround: if the nested functions are placed at the end of beginDrag(), they do not work in Netscape 4. Also note the onmousedown handler at the end of the example: it allows dragging only if the **Shift** key is held down and tests for this modifier key using the Netscape 4 Event object API, which is significantly different from the DOM Level 2 and IE APIs.*

Example 19-4. Dragging in Netscape 4

```
<script>
/**
 * This function is intended for use in a mousedown event handler of an object
 * within a layer. The first argument must be a Layer object. The second
 * argument must be the Event object for the mousedown event.
 **/
function beginDrag(layerToDrag, event) {
    // This nested function responds to mousemove events and moves the layer
    function moveHandler(event) {
        // Move the element to the current mouse position, adjusted as
        // necessary by the offset of the initial mouse-click
        layerToDrag.moveTo(event.pageX - deltaX, event.pageY-deltaY);

        // Don't take any default action, and don't propagate further
        return false;
    }

    // This nested function handles mouseup events
    // It stops capturing events and deregisters the handlers
    function upHandler(event) {
        // Stop capturing and handling drag events
        document.releaseEvents(Event.MOUSEMOVE | Event.MOUSEUP);
        document.onmousemove = null;
        document.onmouseup = null;

        // Don't take any default action, and don't propagate further
```

* At the time of this writing, Mozilla and Netscape 6 have not retained compatibility with the modifiers property of the Netscape 4 Event object, so the onmousedown handler shown here works only in Netscape 4, not in Netscape 6.

Example 19-4. Dragging in Netscape 4 (continued)

```
        return false;
    }

    // Compute the distance between the upper-left corner of the layer and
    // the mouse-click. The moveHandler function below needs these values.
    var deltaX = event.pageX - layerToDrag.left;
    var deltaY = event.pageY - layerToDrag.top;

    // Arrange to capture mousemove and mouseup events
    // Then arrange to handle them using the functions defined below
    document.captureEvents(Event.MOUSEMOVE | Event.MOUSEUP);
    document.onmousemove = moveHandler;
    document.onmouseup = upHandler;
}
</script>
<!-- Here's how we might use beginDrag( ) in Netscape 4 -->
<!-- Define a layer using CSS attributes -->
<div id="div1" style="position:absolute; left:100px; top:100px;">
<!-- Give the layer some content and a mousedown event handler -->
<img src="plus.gif" width="20" height="20"
     onmousedown="if (event.modifiers & Event.SHIFT_MASK)
                      beginDrag(window.document.div1, event);">
</div>
```

CHAPTER 20

Compatibility Techniques

JavaScript, like Java, is one of a new breed of platform-independent languages. That is, you can develop a program in JavaScript and expect to run it unchanged in a JavaScript-enabled web browser running on any type of computer with any type of operating system. Though this is the ideal, we live in an imperfect world and have not yet reached that state of perfection.

There are, and probably always will be, compatibility problems that JavaScript programmers must bear in mind. The one fact that we must always remember is that it is a heterogeneous network out there. Your JavaScript programs may run on three or more operating systems, using three or more versions of browsers from at least two different vendors. This can be difficult to keep in mind for those of us who come from the nonportable past, when programs were developed on a platform-specific basis. Remember: which platform you develop a program on doesn't matter. It may work fine on that platform, but the real test is whether it works (or fails gracefully) on *all* platforms on which it is used.

The compatibility issues fall into two broad categories: platform-specific, browser-specific, and version-specific features on one hand; and bugs and language-level incompatibilities, including the incompatibility of JavaScript with non-JavaScript browsers, on the other. This chapter discusses techniques for coping with compatibility issues in both of these areas. If you've worked your way through all the previous chapters in this book, you are probably an expert JavaScript programmer, and you may already be writing serious JavaScript programs. Don't release those programs on the Internet (or onto a heterogeneous intranet) before you've read this chapter, though!

20.1 Platform and Browser Compatibility

When developing production-quality JavaScript code, testing and knowledge of platform-specific, vendor-specific, and version-specific incompatibilities are your chief allies. If you know, for example, that Netscape 2 on Macintosh platforms always gets the time wrong by about an hour, you can take steps to deal with this problem. If you know that Netscape 2 and 3 on Windows platforms do not automatically clear your setting of the status line when the mouse moves off a hypertext link, you can provide an appropriate event handler to explicitly clear the status line. If you know that Internet Explorer 4 and Netscape 4 support vastly different Dynamic HTML models, you can write pages that use the appropriate mechanism depending on the browser in use.

Knowledge of existing incompatibilities is crucial to writing compatible code. Unfortunately, producing a definitive listing of all known vendor, version, and platform incompatibilities would be an enormous task. It is beyond the scope and mission of this book, and it has apparently never even been seriously attempted. You may find some assistance on the Internet, but you will have to rely primarily on your own experience and testing. Once you have identified an area of incompatibility, however, there are a number of basic approaches you can take to coping with it, as described in the following sections.

20.1.1 The Least-Common-Denominator Approach

One technique for dealing with incompatibilities is to avoid them like the plague. For example, the Date object is notoriously buggy in Netscape 2. If you want Netscape 2 users to be able to use your programs, you can simply avoid relying on the Date object at all.*

As another example, Netscape 3 and IE 3 both support the opener property of the Window object, but Netscape 2 does not. The least-common-denominator approach says that you should not use this property if compatibility with Netscape 2 is a goal. Instead, you can create an equivalent property of your own whenever you open a new window:

```
newwin = window.open("", "new", "width=500, height=300");
newwin.creator = self;
```

If you consistently set a creator property for each new window you create, you can rely on that property instead of the nonportable opener property. (Another alternative, as we'll see later, is to give up on compatibility with Netscape 2 and require a browser that supports JavaScript 1.1 or later, as all such browsers support the opener property.)

With this technique, you use only features that are known to work on all your target platforms. It doesn't allow you to write cutting-edge programs or push the envelope, but it results in portable, safe programs that can serve many important functions.

* I don't actually recommend doing this. At the time of this writing, Netscape 2 is so far out of date that it is safe to ignore it.

20.1.2 Defensive Coding

With the defensive coding approach to compatibility, you write code that contains platform-independent workarounds for platform-specific incompatibilities. For example, if you set the `status` property of a Window object from the `onmouseover` event handler to display a custom message in the status line, the status line is cleared when you move the mouse off the hyperlink, except in Windows versions of Netscape 2 and 3. To correct for this problem, you could get in the habit of including an `onmouseout` event handler to clear the status line. This precaution fixes the bug in current (and future) platforms that have it and doesn't do any harm on platforms that don't have the bug.

Client-Side JavaScript

20.1.3 Feature Testing

Feature testing is a powerful technique for coping with incompatibilities. If you want to use a feature that may not be supported by all browsers, include code in your script that tests to see whether that feature is supported. If the desired feature is not supported on the current platform, either do not use it on that platform or provide alternative code that works on all platforms.

Consider again the `opener` property. In the least-common-denominator approach, we simply avoided the use of this property and used an alternative on all platforms. With the feature-testing approach, we provide the alternative only when the current platform does not support `opener`:

```
newwin = window.open("", "new", "width=500, height=300");
if (!newwin.opener) newwin.opener = self;
```

Note how we tested for the existence of the `opener` property. The same technique works to test for the existence of methods. For example, the `split()` method of the String object exists only for JavaScript 1.1 implementations. We can write our own version of this function that works in all versions of JavaScript, but for efficiency we'd like to use the fast, built-in method on those platforms that do support it. Thus, our feature-testing code to `split()` a string might end up looking like this:

```
if (s.split)              // Check if the method exists, without invoking it
    a = s.split(":");     // If it does exist, it is safe to invoke it
else                      // Otherwise:
    a = mysplit(s, ":");  // use our alternative implementation
```

Feature testing is commonly used for performing DHTML effects that are supported only on some browsers or are implemented differently in different browsers. For example, if you are designing a site that includes image rollover effects, you can use feature testing with code like this:

```
if (document.images) {  // If the browser defines an images[] array,
                        // we include image rollover code here
}
// Otherwise, we simply omit the image rollover effect
```

As another example, suppose we want to work with a dynamically positioned document element. Different browsers have different APIs for doing this, so we first use feature testing to see which API is supported by the current browser with code like this:

```
if (document.getElementById) {  // If the W3C DOM API is supported,
    // do our DHTML using the W3C DOM API
}
else if (document.all) {        // If the IE 4 API is supported,
    // do our DHTML using the IE 4 API
}
else if (document.layers) {     // If the Netscape 4 API is supported,
    // do the DHTML effect (as best we can) using the Netscape 4 API
}
else {                          // Otherwise, DHTML is not supported,
    // so provide a static alternative to DHTML, if we can
}
```

The nice thing about the feature-testing technique is that it results in code that is not tied to a specific list of browser vendors or browser version numbers. It works with the set of browsers that exist today and should continue to work with future browsers, whatever feature sets they implement.

20.1.4 Platform-Specific Workarounds

Feature testing is well suited to checking for support of large functional areas. You can use it to determine whether a browser supports image rollovers or the W3C DOM API, for example. On the other hand, sometimes you may need to work around individual bugs or quirks in a particular browser, and there may be no easy way to test for the existence of the bug. In this case, you will need to create a platform-specific workaround that is tied to a particular browser vendor, version, or operating system (or some combination of the three).

Recall from Chapter 13 that the `navigator` property of the Window object provides information about the vendor and version of the browser and the operating system on which it is running. You can use this information to insert platform-specific code into your program.

An example of a platform-specific workaround involves the `bgColor` property of the Document object. On Windows and Macintosh platforms, you can set this property at runtime to change the background color of a document. Unfortunately, when you do this on Unix versions of Netscape 2 and 3, the color changes but the document contents temporarily disappear. If you wanted to create a special effect using a changing background color, you could use the Netscape object to test for Unix platforms and simply skip the special effect for those platforms. The code could look like this:

```
// Check whether we're running Netscape 2 or 3 on a Unix platform
var nobg = (parseInt(navigator.appVersion) < 4) &&          // Version
           (navigator.appName.indexOf("Netscape") != -1) &&  // Vendor
           (navigator.appVersion.indexOf("X11") != -1);      // OS
```

```
// If we're not, then go ahead and animate the page background color
if (!nobg) animate_bg_color();
```

When writing platform-specific workarounds, it is common to use "client-sniffer" code to determine what the current platform is, based (typically) on the properties of the navigator object. You run your client-sniffer code once, and it sets variables that describe the current platform. Then you don't have to reparse the properties of navigator for each platform-specific bit of code you write; you can simply use the variables set by the sniffer code. A simple sniffer that may be sufficient for many purposes might look like this:

```
var browserVersion = parseInt(navigator.appVersion);
var isNetscape = navigator.appName.indexOf("Netscape") != -1;
var isIE = navigator.appName.indexOf("Microsoft") != -1;
var agent = navigator.userAgent.toLowerCase();
var isWindows = agent.indexOf("win") != -1;
var isMac = agent.indexOf("mac") != -1;
var isUnix = agent.indexOf("X11") != -1;
```

With variables like these defined, you might write code like the following:

```
if (isNetscape && browserVersion < 4 && isUnix) {
    // Work around a bug in Netscape 3 on Unix platforms here
}
```

A variety of prewritten client sniffers are available on the Internet. You can find a thorough one (along with a helpful discussion of its use) at *http://www.mozilla.org/docs/web-developer/sniffer/browser_type.html.*

20.1.5 Compatibility Through Server-Side Scripts

Another platform-specific approach to compatibility is possible if your web application includes the use of server-side scripts, such as CGI scripts or server-side JavaScript. A program on the server side can inspect the User-Agent field of the HTTP request header, which allows it to determine exactly what browser the user is running. With this information, the program can generate customized JavaScript code that is known to work correctly on that browser. Or, if the server-side script detects that the user's browser does not support JavaScript, it can generate web pages that do not require JavaScript at all. An important drawback to this approach is that a server-side script cannot detect when a user has disabled JavaScript support in her browser.

Note that the topics of CGI programming and server-side scripting in general are beyond the scope of this book.

20.1.6 Ignore the Problem

An important question to ask when considering any incompatibility is, how important is it? If the incompatibility is minor or cosmetic, affects a browser or platform that is not widely used, or affects only an out-of-date version of a browser, you might simply decide to ignore the problem and let the users affected by it cope with it on their own.

For example, earlier I suggested defining an `onmouseout` event handler to correct for the fact that Netscape 2 and 3 for Windows do not correctly clear the status line. Unfortunately, the `onmouseout` event handler is not supported in Netscape 2, so this workaround won't work for that platform. If you expect your application to have a lot of users who use Netscape 2 on Windows and you think that it is really important to get that status line cleared, you'll have to develop some other workaround. You could use `setTimeout()` in your `onmouseover` event handler to arrange for the status line to be cleared in two seconds. But this solution brings problems with it: what if the mouse is still over the hypertext link and the status line shouldn't be cleared in two seconds? In this case, a simpler approach might be to simply ignore the problem. This approach can easily be justified, because Netscape 2 is by now well out of date; any users still relying on it should be encouraged to upgrade.

20.1.7 Fail Gracefully

Finally, there are some incompatibilities that cannot be ignored and cannot be worked around. In these cases, your program should work correctly on all platforms, browsers, and versions that provide the needed features and fail gracefully on all others. Failing gracefully means recognizing that the required features are not available and informing the user that he will not be able to use your JavaScript program.

For example, the image-replacement technique we saw during the discussion of images in Chapter 14 does not work in Netscape 2 or Internet Explorer 3, and there is really no workaround that can simulate it. Therefore, we should not even attempt to run the program on those platforms; instead, we should politely notify the user of the incompatibility.

Failing gracefully can be harder than it sounds. Much of the rest of this chapter explains techniques for doing so.

20.2 Language Version Compatibility

The previous section discussed general compatibility techniques that are useful for coping with incompatibilities between different versions of browsers from different vendors running on different platforms. This section addresses another compatibility concern: how to use new features of the JavaScript language in a way that does not cause errors on browsers that do not support those features. Our goals are simple: we need to prevent JavaScript code from being interpreted by browsers that don't understand it, and we need to display special messages on those browsers that inform users that their browsers cannot run the scripts.

20.2.1 The language Attribute

The first goal is easy. As we saw in Chapter 12, we can prevent a browser from attempting to run code that it cannot understand by setting the language attribute of the <script> tag appropriately. For example, the following <script> tag specifies that the code it contains uses features of JavaScript 1.1 and that browsers that do not support that version of the scripting language should not attempt to run it:

```
<script language="JavaScript1.1">
    // JavaScript 1.1 code goes here
</script>
```

Note that the use of the language attribute is a general technique. When set to the string "JavaScript1.2", the attribute prevents JavaScript 1.0 or 1.1 browsers from attempting to run the code. At the time of this writing, the latest browsers (Netscape 6 and IE 6) support language versions 1.0, 1.1, 1.2, 1.3, 1.4, and 1.5. If you write JavaScript code that includes the try/catch exception-handling statement, for example, you should include it in a <script> tag with language="JavaScript1.5" to prevent browsers that do not understand this statement from trying to run it.

Unfortunately, the language attribute is marred by the fact that specifying language="JavaScript1.2" causes Netscape to behave in ways that are incompatible with the ECMA-262 standard. For example, as we saw in Chapter 5, setting the language attribute to this value causes the == operator to perform equality comparisons without doing any type conversions. And as we saw in Chapter 8, specifying "JavaScript1.2" also causes the toString() method to behave quite differently. Unless you explicitly want these new, incompatible behaviors, or unless you can carefully avoid all incompatible features, you should avoid the use of language="JavaScript1.2".

Note that the version numbers used by the language attribute match the version numbers of Netscape's (and now Mozilla's) JavaScript interpreter. Microsoft's interpreter has more or less followed the evolution of Netscape's, but bear in mind that the language attribute is still somewhat vendor-specific: the language features supported by different vendors for a given version number are not guaranteed to be the same. This is particularly so for language="JavaScript1.2", but caution is advisable for other versions as well. Unfortunately, there is no way to specify a specification version with the language attribute. That is, you *cannot* write:

```
<script language="ECMAScript3">...</script>
```

20.2.2 Explicit Version Testing

The language attribute provides at least a partial solution to the problem of language version compatibility, but it solves only half of the problem. We also need to be able to fail gracefully for browsers that do not support the desired version of JavaScript. If we require JavaScript 1.1, we'd like to be able to notify users of JavaScript 1.0 browsers that they cannot use the page. Example 20-1 shows how we can do this.

Example 20-1. A message for browsers that do not support JavaScript 1.1

```
<!-- Set a variable to determine what version of JavaScript we support -->
<!-- This technique can be extended to any number of language versions -->
<script language="JavaScript"> var _version = 1.0; </script>
<script language="JavaScript1.1">  _version = 1.1; </script>
<script language="JavaScript1.2">  _version = 1.2; </script>

<!-- Run this code on any JavaScript-enabled browser -->
<!-- If the version is not high enough, display a message -->
<script language="JavaScript">
  if (_version < 1.1) {
    document.write('<hr><h1>This Page Requires JavaScript 1.1</h1>');
    document.write('Your JavaScript 1.0 browser cannot run this page.<hr>');
  }
</script>

<!-- Now run the actual program only on JavaScript 1.1 browsers -->
<script language="JavaScript1.1">
   // The actual JavaScript 1.1 code goes here
</script>
```

20.2.3 Suppressing Version-Related Errors

Example 20-1 showed how we can write JavaScript 1.1 code that JavaScript 1.0 browsers do not attempt to execute. What if we wanted to write JavaScript 1.2 code that JavaScript 1.1 browsers do not attempt to execute? We could use the `language` attribute to explicitly specify "JavaScript1.2", but as we discussed earlier, this causes Netscape to behave incompatibly. Unfortunately, JavaScript 1.2 adds a lot of new syntax to the language. If you write code that uses a `switch` statement, an object initializer, or a function literal and then run that code on a JavaScript 1.1 browser, you'll cause runtime syntax errors.

One way to work around this problem is simply to suppress any errors that occur on JavaScript 1.1 browsers. Example 20-2 shows how this can be done using the `onerror` error handler of the Window object (which was described in Chapter 13).

Example 20-2. Suppressing version-related errors

```
<!-- Check whether JavaScript 1.2 is supported -->
<script language="JavaScript1.2">var _js12_ = 1.2</script>

<!-- Now avoid the problems with JavaScript 1.2 on Netscape by running -->
<!-- the following code on any browser that supports JavaScript 1.1. If -->
<!-- the browser does not support JavaScript 1.2, however, we'll display -->
<!-- an error message and suppress any syntax errors that occur. -->
<script language="JavaScript1.1">
// If JavaScript 1.2 is not supported, fail gracefully
```

Example 20-2. Suppressing version-related errors (continued)

```
function supressErrors( ) { return true; }
if (!_js12_) {
    window.onerror = supressErrors;
    alert("This program requires a browser with JavaScript 1.2 support");
}

// Now proceed with the JavaScript 1.2 code
</script>
```


20.2.4 Loading a New Page for Compatibility

Another approach to version compatibility is to load a web page that requires a specific level of JavaScript support only after determining whether the browser provides that level of support. Example 20-3 shows how this might be done with a short script that tests whether JavaScript 1.2 is supported. If the browser supports this version, the script uses the `Location.replace( )` method to load in a new web page that requires JavaScript 1.2. If JavaScript 1.2 is not supported, the script displays a message saying that it is required.

Example 20-3. A web page to test for JavaScript compatibility

```
<head>
<script language="JavaScript1.2">
// If JavaScript 1.2 is supported, extract a new URL from the portion of
// our URL following the question mark, and load in that new URL
location.replace(location.search.substring(1));

// Enter a really long, empty loop, so that the body of this document
// doesn't get displayed while the new document is loading
for(var i = 0; i < 10000000; i++);
</script>
</head>
<body>
<hr size="4">
<h1>This Page Requires JavaScript 1.2</h1>
Your browser cannot run this page. Please upgrade to a browser that
supports JavaScript 1.2, such as Netscape 4 or Internet Explorer 4.
<hr size="4">
</body>
```

The most interesting thing about this example is that it is a generic one—the name of the JavaScript 1.2 file to be loaded is encoded in the search portion of the original URL; that file is loaded only if JavaScript 1.2 is supported. Thus, if the file in this example has the name *testjs12.html*, you can use it in URLs like the one shown in this hyperlink:

```
<a href="http://my.isp.net/~david/utils/testjs12.html?../js/cooljs12.html">
Visit my cool JavaScript 1.2 page!
</a>
```

The other thing to note about Example 20-3 is that calling `Location.replace()` starts a new page loading but does not immediately stop the current page from loading. Therefore, the JavaScript code in this example enters a long, empty loop after it calls `replace()`. This prevents the rest of the document from being parsed and displayed, so that users of JavaScript 1.2 browsers do not see the message intended for users of browsers that do not support JavaScript 1.2.

Finally, note that the technique shown in Example 20-3 is useful not only to distinguish one version of JavaScript from another, but also to distinguish between browsers that support JavaScript and those that do not. The next section discusses other compatibility techniques that are useful with non-JavaScript browsers.

20.3 Compatibility with Non-JavaScript Browsers

The previous section discussed compatibility with browsers that do not support a particular version of JavaScript. This section considers compatibility with browsers that do not support JavaScript at all. These are either browsers that have no JavaScript capability or browsers in which the user has disabled JavaScript (which some users do because of security concerns). Because a number of such browsers are still in use, you should design your web pages to fail gracefully when read into browsers that do not understand JavaScript. There are two parts to doing this: first, you must take care to ensure that your JavaScript code does not appear as if it were HTML text; and second, you should arrange to display a message informing the visitor that her browser cannot correctly handle the page.

20.3.1 Hiding Scripts from Old Browsers

Web browsers that support JavaScript execute the JavaScript statements that appear between the `<script>` and `</script>` tags. Browsers that don't support JavaScript but recognize the `<script>` tag simply ignore everything between `<script>` and `</script>`. This is as it should be. Really old browsers, however (and there are still some out there), do not even recognize the `<script>` and `</script>` tags. This means that they ignore the tags themselves and treat all the JavaScript between them as HTML text to be displayed. Unless you take steps to prevent it, users of these old browsers see your JavaScript code formatted into big meaningless paragraphs and presented as web page content!

To prevent this, enclose the body of your script within an HTML comment, using the format shown in Example 20-4.

Example 20-4. A script hidden from old browsers

```
<script language="JavaScript">
<!-- Begin HTML comment that hides the script
```

```
        // JavaScript statements go here
        //              .
        //              .
// End HTML comment that hides the script -->
</script>
```

Browsers that do not understand the <script> and </script> tags simply ignore them. Thus, lines one and seven in Example 20-4 have no effect on these browsers. They'll ignore lines two through six as well, because the first four characters on line two begin an HTML comment and the last three characters on line six end that comment—everything in between is ignored by the HTML parser.

This script-hiding technique also works for browsers that *do* support JavaScript. Lines one and seven indicate the beginning and end of a script. Client-side JavaScript interpreters recognize the HTML comment-opening string `<!--` but treat it as a single-line comment. Thus, a browser with JavaScript support treats line two as a single-line comment. Similarly, line six begins with the `//` single-line comment string, so that line is ignored by JavaScript-enabled browsers as well. This leaves lines three through five, which are executed as JavaScript statements.

While it takes a little getting used to, this simple and elegant mix of HTML and JavaScript comments does exactly what we need: it prevents JavaScript code from being displayed by browsers that do not support JavaScript. Although a declining number of browsers require this type of commenting, it is still quite common to see it used in JavaScript code on the Internet. The comments need not be as verbose as in Example 20-4, of course. It is common to see scripts like this:

```
<script language="JavaScript">
<!--
  document.write(new Date());
// -->
</script>
```

This commenting technique has solved the problem of hiding our JavaScript code from browsers that can't run it. The next step in failing gracefully is to display a message to the user to let him know that the page cannot run.

20.3.2 <noscript>

The <noscript> and </noscript> tags enclose an arbitrary block of HTML text that should be displayed by any browser that does not support JavaScript. These tags can be employed to let a user know that his browser cannot correctly display your pages that require JavaScript. For example:

```
<script language="JavaScript1.1">
  // Your JavaScript code here
</script>
<noscript>
```

```
<hr size="4">
<h1>This Page Requires JavaScript 1.1</h1>
This page requires a browser that supports JavaScript 1.1.<p>
Your browser either does not support JavaScript, or it has JavaScript
support disabled. If you want to correctly view this page, please
upgrade your browser or enable JavaScript support.
<hr size="4">
</noscript>
```

There is one problem with the `<noscript>` tag. It was introduced into HTML by Netscape with the release of Netscape 3. Thus, it is not supported in Netscape 2. Since Netscape 2 does not support `<noscript>` and `</noscript>`, it ignores the tags and displays the text that appears between them, even though it does support scripting. In the previous code, however, this works out to our advantage, because we've specified that the code requires JavaScript 1.1 support.

CHAPTER 21

JavaScript Security

Because of the wide-open nature of the Internet, security is an important issue. This is particularly true with the introduction of languages such as Java and JavaScript, because they allow executable content to be embedded in otherwise static web pages. Since loading a web page can cause arbitrary code to be executed on your computer, stringent security precautions are required to prevent malicious code from doing any damage to your data or your privacy. This chapter discusses Internet security issues related to JavaScript. Note that this chapter does *not* cover any of the many other issues involved in web security, such as the authentication and cryptographic technologies used to keep the contents of web documents and HTML forms private while they traverse the Web.

21.1 JavaScript and Security

JavaScript's first line of defense against malicious code is that the language simply does not support certain capabilities. For example, client-side JavaScript does not provide any way to write or delete files or directories on the client computer. With no File object and no file access functions, a JavaScript program cannot delete a user's data or plant viruses on the user's system.

Similarly, client-side JavaScript has no networking primitives of any type. A JavaScript program can load URLs and can send HTML form data to web servers, CGI scripts, and email addresses, but it cannot establish a direct connection to any other hosts on the network. This means, for example, that a JavaScript program cannot use a client's machine as an attack platform from which to attempt to crack passwords on another machine. (This would be a particularly dangerous possibility if the JavaScript program had been loaded from the Internet through a firewall and could then attempt to break into the intranet protected by the firewall.)

Although the core JavaScript language and the basic client-side object model lack the filesystem and networking features that most malicious code requires, the situation is not quite as simple as it appears. In many web browsers, JavaScript is used as a "script engine" for other software components, such as ActiveX controls in Internet Explorer and plugins in Netscape. These components may have filesystem and network capabilities, and the fact that JavaScript programs can control them clouds the picture and raises security concerns. This is particularly true with ActiveX controls, and Microsoft has at times had to release security patches to prevent JavaScript code from exploiting the capabilities of scriptable ActiveX objects. We'll touch on this issue again briefly at the end of this chapter.

While this intentional lack of features in client-side JavaScript provides a basic level of security against the most egregious attacks, other security issues remain. These are primarily privacy issues—JavaScript programs must not be allowed to export information about the user of a browser when that information is supposed to be private.

When you browse the Web, one of the pieces of information you are by default consenting to release about yourself is which web browser you use. As a standard part of the HTTP protocol, a string identifying your browser, its version, and its vendor is sent with every request for a web page. This information is public, as is the IP address of your Internet connection, for example. Other information, however, should not be public: this includes your email address, which should not be released unless you choose to do so by sending an email message or authorizing an automated email message to be sent under your name.

Similarly, your browsing history (the record of which sites you've already visited) and the contents of your bookmarks list should remain private. Your browsing history and bookmarks say a lot about your interests; this is information that direct marketers and others pay good money for so that they can target sales pitches to you more effectively. You can be sure that if a web browser or JavaScript allowed this valuable private information to be stolen, some people would steal it every time you visited their sites, and it would be on the market only seconds later. Most web users would be uncomfortable knowing that any site they visited could find out that they were cat fanciers, for example, who were also interested in women's footwear and the Sierra Club.

Even assuming that we have no embarrassing fetishes to hide, there are plenty of good reasons to be concerned about data privacy. One such reason is a pragmatic concern about receiving electronic junk mail (spam) and the like. Another is a legitimate concern about keeping secrets. We don't want a JavaScript program loaded from the Internet and running in one web browser window to be able to start examining the contents of other browser windows that contain pages loaded from the company intranet behind the firewall. The remainder of this chapter explains how JavaScript defends itself against such abuses.

21.2 Restricted Features

As I've already mentioned, the first line of defense against malicious scripts in client-side JavaScript is that the language simply omits certain capabilities. The second line of defense is that JavaScript imposes restrictions on certain features that it does support. For example, client-side JavaScript supports a `close()` method for the Window object, but most (hopefully all) web-browser implementations restrict this method so that a script can close only a window that was opened by a script from the same web server. In particular, a script cannot close a window that the user opened; if it tries to do so, the user is presented with a confirmation box asking if he really wants to close the window.

The most important of these security restrictions is known as the *same-origin policy* and is described in the next section. The following is a list of the other security restrictions found in most implementations of client-side JavaScript. This is not a definitive list. Each browser may have a slightly different set of restrictions, and the proprietary features of each browser may well have proprietary security restrictions to go along with them.

- The History object was originally designed as an array of URLs that represented the complete browsing history of the browser. Once the privacy implications of this became apparent, however, all access to the actual URLs was restricted, and the History object was left with only its `back()`, `forward()`, and `go()` methods to move the browser through the history array without revealing the contents of the array.
- The `value` property of the FileUpload object cannot be set. If this property could be set, a script could set it to any desired filename and cause the form to upload the contents of any specified file (such as a password file) to the server.
- A script cannot submit a form (using the `submit()` method of the Form object, for example) to a `mailto:` or `news:` URL without the user's explicit approval through a confirmation dialog box. Such a form submission would contain the user's email address, which should not be made public without obtaining the user's permission.
- A JavaScript program cannot close a browser window without user confirmation unless it opened the window itself. This prevents malicious scripts from calling `self.close()` to close the user's browsing window, thereby causing the program to exit.
- A script cannot open a window that is smaller than 100 pixels on a side or cause a window to be resized to smaller than 100 pixels on a side. Similarly, such a script cannot move a window off the screen, or create a window that is larger than the screen. This prevents scripts from opening windows that the user cannot see or could easily overlook; such windows could contain scripts that keep running after the user thinks they have stopped. Also, a script may not create a browser window without a titlebar, because such a window could be made to spoof an operating-system dialog box and trick the user into entering a sensitive password, for example.

- A script may not cause a window or frame to display an `about:` URL, such as `about:cache`, because these URLs can expose system information, such as the contents of the browser's cache.
- A script cannot set any of the properties of an Event object. This prevents scripts from spoofing events. A script cannot register event listeners within for or capture events for documents loaded from different sources than the script. This prevents scripts from snooping on the user's input (such as the keystrokes that constitute a password entry) to other pages.

21.3 The Same-Origin Policy

There is one far-reaching security restriction in JavaScript that deserves its own section. This restriction is known as the same-origin policy: a script can read only the properties of windows and documents that have the same origin (i.e., that were loaded from the same host, through the same port, and by the same protocol) as the script itself.

The same-origin policy does not actually apply to all properties of all objects in a window from a different origin. But it does apply to many of them, and in particular, it applies to practically all of the properties of the Document object. For all intents and purposes, you should consider all predefined properties of all client-side objects with different origins off-limits to your scripts. User-defined properties of objects with different origins may also be restricted, although this may vary from implementation to implementation.

The same-origin policy is a fairly severe restriction, but it is necessary to prevent scripts from stealing proprietary information. Without this restriction, an untrusted script (perhaps a script loaded through a firewall into a browser on a secure corporate intranet) in one window could use DOM methods to read the contents of documents in other browser windows, which might contain private information.

Still, there are circumstances in which the same-origin policy is too restrictive. It poses particular problems for large web sites that use more than one server. For example, a script from *home.netscape.com* might legitimately want to read properties of a document loaded from *developer.netscape.com*, or scripts from *orders.acme.com* might need to read properties from documents on *catalog.acme.com*. To support large web sites of this sort, JavaScript 1.1 introduced the `domain` property of the Document object. By default, the `domain` property contains the hostname of the server from which the document was loaded. You can set this property, but only to a string that is a valid domain suffix of itself. Thus, if `domain` is originally the string "home.netscape.com", you can set it to the string "netscape.com", but not to "home.netscape" or "cape.com", and certainly not to "microsoft.com". (The `domain` value must have at least one dot in it; you cannot set it to "com" or any other top-level domain.)

If two windows (or frames) contain scripts that set `domain` to the same value, the same-origin policy is relaxed for these two windows and each of the windows may read properties from the other. For example, cooperating scripts in documents loaded from *orders.acme.com* and *catalog.acme.com* might set their `document.domain` properties to "acme.com", thereby making the documents appear to have the same origin and enabling each document to read properties of the other.

21.4 Security Zones and Signed Scripts

A one-size-fits-all security policy is never entirely satisfactory. If the policy is too restrictive, trusted scripts don't have the ability to do the interesting and useful things we would like them to do. On the other hand, if the policy is too permissive, untrusted scripts may cause havoc! The ideal solution is to allow the security policy to be configured so that trusted scripts are subject to fewer security restrictions than untrusted scripts. The two major browser vendors, Microsoft and Netscape, have taken different approaches to allowing configurable security; their approaches are briefly described in this section.

Internet Explorer defines "security zones" in which you can list web sites whose scripts you trust and web sites whose scripts you do not trust. You can then configure the security policies of these two zones separately, giving more privileges to and placing fewer restrictions on the trusted sites. (You may also separately configure the privileges of internet and intranet sites that are not explicitly listed in either of the other two zones.)

Unfortunately, this is not a complete or fine-grained solution for JavaScript security, because most of the security options that IE allows you to configure are not directly related to JavaScript. In IE 6 beta, for example, you can specify whether scripts are allowed to control ActiveX objects and Java applets, and whether they can perform paste (as in cut-and-paste) operations. You are not given the option, for example, of disabling the same-origin policy for a trusted site or of allowing scripts from trusted sites to send email messages without a user confirmation.

Netscape 4 and Netscape 6 implement configurable security with an approach known as "signed scripts." Signed scripts provide complete fine-grained configurability of security policies and do it in a way that is cryptographically secure and theoretically very compelling. Unfortunately, since Microsoft has no compatible technology, the process of creating signed scripts is cumbersome for script authors, and the use of signed scripts can be confusing for end users, the use of this promising technology has never really caught on.

Briefly, a signed script bears an unforgeable digital signature that specifies the person or organization that wrote or otherwise takes responsibility for the script. When a signed script needs to circumvent one of the security restrictions described earlier, it first requests a special "privilege" that allows it to do so. When a script requests a privilege, the browser defers to the user. The user is told who the signer of the script is and is asked whether she wants to grant the requested privilege to a script written by that person or organization. Once the user makes the decision, she can have the browser remember it so that she doesn't get asked the same question in the future. In effect, this procedure allows a user to configure a fine-grained customized security policy on the fly, as the need arises.

As I've already mentioned, the process of creating signed scripts is somewhat cumbersome. Also, the details of how it is done have change between Netscape 4 and Netscape 6. Those details are beyond the scope of this book, but you can learn more online at *http://developer.netscape.com/docs/manuals/signedobj/trust/index.htm* and *http://www.mozilla.org/projects/security/components/*.

CHAPTER 22

Using Java with JavaScript

As we discussed in Chapter 14, Netscape 3 and later and Internet Explorer 4 and later both allow JavaScript programs to read and write the public fields and invoke the public methods of Java applets embedded in HTML documents. Netscape supports JavaScript interaction with Java applets through a technology known as LiveConnect. Internet Explorer instead treats every Java object (including applets) as an ActiveX control and uses its ActiveX scripting technology to allow JavaScript programs to interact with Java. Because Netscape's technology is specifically designed for communication between JavaScript and Java, it has some features that IE's ActiveX technology cannot provide. In practice, however, the two technologies are fairly compatible. Although this chapter is based on Netscape's LiveConnect, the key features it describes work in IE as well.*

This chapter begins with a discussion of how you can use JavaScript to script Java applets, how your Java applets can invoke JavaScript code, and how (in Netscape only) you can use JavaScript to work directly with Java system classes. It then documents the nitty-gritty details of how LiveConnect works. It assumes you have at least a basic familiarity with Java programming (see *Java in a Nutshell*, by David Flanagan, and *Learning Java*, by Patrick Niemeyer and Jonathan Knudsen, both published by O'Reilly).

22.1 Scripting Java Applets

As discussed in Chapter 14, all Java applets embedded in a web page become part of the `Document.applets[]` array. Also, if given a `name` or `id`, an applet can be accessed directly as a property of the Document object. For example, the applet created by an `<applet>` tag with a `name` attribute of "chart" can be referred to as `document.chart`.

* Note that Netscape 6 was released with poor support for LiveConnect but that it is fully implemented in Netscape 6.1 and later.

The public fields and methods of every applet are accessible to JavaScript as if they were the properties and methods of a JavaScript object. For example, if an applet named "chart" defines a field named `lineColor` whose type is `String`, a JavaScript program can query and set this field with code like this:

```
var chartcolor = document.chart.lineColor;  // Read an applet field
document.chart.lineColor = "#ff00ff";       // Set an applet field
```

JavaScript can even query and set the values of fields that are arrays. Suppose that the chart applet defines two fields declared as follows (Java code):

```
public int numPoints;
public double[] points;
```

A JavaScript program might use these fields with code like this:

```
for(var i = 0; i < document.chart.numPoints; i++)
    document.chart.points[i] = i*i;
```

This example illustrates the tricky thing about connecting JavaScript and Java: type conversion. Java is a strongly typed language with a fair number of distinct primitive types. JavaScript is loosely typed and has only a single numeric type. In the previous example, a Java integer is converted to a JavaScript number and various JavaScript numbers are converted to Java `double` values. There is a lot of work going on behind the scenes to ensure that these values are properly converted as needed. Later in this chapter, we'll consider the topic of data type conversion in detail.

In addition to querying and setting the fields of a Java applet, JavaScript can also invoke the methods of an applet. Suppose, for example, that the chart applet defines a method named `redraw()`. This method takes no arguments and simply serves to notify the applet that its `points[]` array has been modified and it should redraw itself. JavaScript can invoke this method just as if it was a JavaScript method:

```
document.chart.redraw();
```

JavaScript can also call methods that take arguments and return values. The underlying LiveConnect or ActiveX scripting technology does the work of converting JavaScript argument values into legal Java values and converting Java return values into legal JavaScript values. Suppose the chart applet defines Java methods like these:

```
public void setDomain(double xmin, double xmax);
public void setChartTitle(String title);
public String getXAxisLabel();
```

JavaScript can call these methods with code like this:

```
document.chart.setDomain(0, 20);
document.chart.setChartTitle("y = x*x");
var label = document.chart.getXAxisLabel();
```

Finally, note that Java methods can return Java objects as their return values, and JavaScript can read and write the public fields and invoke the public methods of these objects as well. JavaScript can also use Java objects as arguments to Java methods. Suppose the Java applet defines a method named getXAxis() that returns a Java object that is an instance of a class named Axis and a method named setYAxis() that takes an argument of the same type. Now, suppose further that Axis has a method named setTitle(). We might use these methods with JavaScript code like this:

```
var xaxis = document.chart.getXAxis();  // Get an Axis object
var newyaxis = xaxis.clone();            // Make a copy of it
newyaxis.setTitle("Y");                  // Call a method of it...
document.chart.setYAxis(newyaxis);       // and pass it to another method
```


There is one complication when we use JavaScript to invoke the methods of a Java object. Java allows two or more methods to have the same name, as long as they have different argument types. For example, a Java object could declare these two methods:

```
public String convert(int i);     // Convert an integer to a string
public String convert(double d);  // Convert a floating-point number
```

JavaScript has only one numeric type and doesn't distinguish between integers and floating-point values, so when you use JavaScript to pass a number to the method named "convert", it cannot tell which one you intended to call. In practice, this problem doesn't arise often, and it is usually possible to work around it by simply renaming the methods as needed. The latest versions of LiveConnect (in Netscape 6.1 and later) also allow you to disambiguate cases like this by including the argument types in the method name. For example, if the two methods above were defined by document.applets[0], you could disambiguate them like this:

```
var iconvert = document.applets[0]["convert(int)"];  // Get int method
iconvert(3);  // Invoke the method like this
```

22.2 Using JavaScript from Java

Having explored how to control Java from JavaScript code, we now turn to the opposite problem: how to control JavaScript from Java code. This control is accomplished primarily through the Java *netscape.javascript.JSObject* class, which represents a JavaScript object within a Java program. The JavaScript-to-Java capabilities described in the previous section typically work well in both Netscape and Internet Explorer. In contrast, the Java-to-JavaScript techniques described here are not as robustly supported, and you may well encounter bugs in both Netscape and IE.

22.2.1 The JSObject Class

All Java interactions with JavaScript are handled through an instance of the *netscape.javascript.JSObject* class. An instance of this class is a wrapper around a single JavaScript object. The class defines methods that allow you to read and write property values and array elements of the JavaScript object and to invoke methods of the object. Here is a synopsis of this class:

```
public final class JSObject extends Object {
    // Static method to obtain initial JSObject for applet's browser window
    public static JSObject getWindow(java.applet.Applet applet);
    public Object getMember(String name);                    // Read object property
    public Object getSlot(int index);                        // Read array element
    public void setMember(String name, Object value);        // Set object property
    public void setSlot(int index, Object value);            // Set array element
    public void removeMember(String name);                   // Delete property
    public Object call(String methodName, Object args[]);    // Invoke method
    public Object eval(String s);                            // Evaluate string
    public String toString();                                // Convert to string
    protected void finalize();
}
```

Because all JavaScript objects appear in a hierarchy rooted in the current browser window, JSObject objects must also appear in a hierarchy. To interact with any JavaScript objects, a Java applet must first obtain a JSObject that represents the browser window (or frame) in which the applet appears. The JSObject class does not define a constructor method, so we cannot simply create an appropriate JSObject. Instead, we must call the static `getWindow()` method. When passed a reference to an applet, this method returns a JSObject that represents the browser window that contains the applet. Thus, every applet that interacts with JavaScript includes a line that looks something like this:

```
JSObject jsroot = JSObject.getWindow(this);  // "this" is the applet itself
```

Having obtained a JSObject that refers to the root window of the JavaScript object hierarchy, you can use instance methods of the JSObject to read the values of properties of the JavaScript object that it represents. Most of these properties have values that are themselves JavaScript objects, so you can continue the process and read their properties as well. The JSObject `getMember()` method returns the value of a named property, while the `getSlot()` method returns the value of a numbered array element of the specified JavaScript object. You might use these methods as follows:

```
import netscape.javascript.JSObject;  // This must be at the top of the file
    ...
JSObject jsroot = JSObject.getWindow(this);                        // self
JSObject document = (JSObject) jsroot.getMember("document");       //  .document
JSObject applets = (JSObject) document.getMember("applets");      //    .applets
Applet applet0 = (Applet) applets.getSlot(0);                      //      [0]
```

You should note two things about this code fragment. First, `getMember()` and `getSlot()` both return a value of type "Object", which generally must be cast to some more specific value, such as a JSObject. Second, the value read from slot 0 of the `applets` array can be cast to an Applet, rather than a JSObject. This is because the elements of the JavaScript `applets[]` array are JavaObject objects that represent Java Applet objects. When Java reads a JavaScript JavaObject, it unwraps that object and returns the Java object that it contains (in this case, an Applet). The data conversion that occurs through the JSObject interface is documented later in this chapter.

The JSObject class also supports methods for setting properties and array elements of JavaScript objects. `setMember()` and `setSlot()` are analogous to the `getMember()` and `getSlot()` methods. These methods set the value of a named property or a numbered array element to a specified value. Note, however, that the value to be set must be a Java object. If you want to set a value of a primitive type, use the corresponding Java wrapper class: use an Integer object instead of an `int` value, for example. Finally, the `removeMember()` method allows you to delete the value of a named property from a JavaScript object.

In addition to reading and writing properties and array elements from JavaScript objects, the JSObject class allows you to invoke methods of JavaScript objects. The JSObject `call()` method invokes a named method of the specified JavaScript object and passes a specified array of Java objects as arguments to that method. As we saw when setting JavaScript properties, it is not possible to pass primitive Java values as arguments to a JavaScript method; instead you must use the corresponding Java object types. For example, you might use the `call()` method in Java code like the following to open a new browser window:

```
public JSObject newwin(String url, String window_name)
{
    Object[] args = { url, window_name };
    JSObject win = JSObject.getWindow(this);
    return (JSObject) win.call("open", args);
}
```

The JSObject class has one more important method: `eval()`. This Java method works just like the JavaScript function of the same name—it executes a string that contains JavaScript code. You'll find that using `eval()` is often much easier than using the various other methods of the JSObject class. Since all the code is passed as a string, you can use string representations of the data types you want—you do not have to convert Java primitive types to their corresponding object types. For example, compare the following two lines of code that set properties of the main browser window:

```
jsroot.setMember("i", new Integer(0));
jsroot.eval("self.i = 0");
```

The second line is obviously easier to understand. As another example, consider the following use of `eval()` to write a particular frame being displayed in the browser window:

```
JSObject jsroot = JSObject.getWindow(this);
jsroot.eval("parent.frames[1].document.write('Hello from Java!')");
```

To do the equivalent without the `eval()` method is a lot harder:

```
JSObject jsroot = JSObject.getWindow(this);
JSObject parent = (JSObject) jsroot.getMember("parent");
```

```
JSObject frames = (JSObject) parent.getMember("frames");
JSObject frame1 = (JSObject) frames.getSlot(1);
JSObject document = (JSObject) frame1.getMember("document");
Object[] args = { "Hello from Java!" };
document.call("write", args);
```

22.2.2 Using JSObjects in Applets

Example 22-1 shows the `init( )` method of an applet that uses LiveConnect to interact with JavaScript.

Example 22-1. Using JavaScript from an applet method

```
import netscape.javascript.*

public void init( )
{
    // Get the JSObject representing the applet's browser window.
    JSObject win = JSObject.getWindow(this);

    // Run JavaScript with eval( ). Careful with those nested quotes!
    win.eval("alert('The CPUHog applet is now running on your computer. " +
             "You may find that your system slows down a bit.');");
}
```

In order to use any applet, you must compile it and then embed it in an HTML file. When the applet interacts with JavaScript, special instructions are required for both of these steps.

22.2.2.1 Compiling applets that use the JSObject class

Any applet that interacts with JavaScript uses the *netscape.javascript.JSObject* class. To compile such an applet, therefore, your Java compiler must know where to find a definition of this class. Because the class is defined and shipped by Netscape and not by Sun, the *javac* compiler from Sun does not know about it. This section explains how to enable your compiler to find this required class. If you are not using the JDK from Sun, you may have to do something a little different—see the documentation from the vendor of your Java compiler or Java development environment.

To tell the JDK compiler where to find classes, you set the `CLASSPATH` environment variable. This environment variable specifies a list of directories and JAR files (or ZIP files) that the compiler should search for class definitions (in addition to its standard directory of system classes). The trick is to figure out which JAR file on your system holds the definition of the *netscape.javascript.JSObject* class. In Netscape 6.1, the file is *plugins/java2/javaplugin.jar*, under the Netscape installation directory. In Netscape 4, the file is *java/classes/java40.jar*, under the installation directory. For Netscape 4 on a Windows system, for example, you would probably find *java40.jar* at *C:\Program Files\Netscape\Communicator\Program\Java\Classes\java40.jar*.

For Internet Explorer, the class definition you need is usually in one of the ZIP files in *c:\Windows\Java\Packages*. The trouble is that this directory contains a bunch of ZIP files, all of whose names are gibberish and change from release to release! The largest of the files is typically the one you need. You can use an unzip utility to verify that it contains the file *netscape/javascript/JSObject.class*.

Once you have found the JAR or ZIP file you need, you can tell the compiler about it by setting the CLASSPATH environment variable. For a Unix system, set a path like this:

```
setenv CLASSPATH .:/usr/local/netscape/plugins/java2/javaplugin.jar
```

And for a Windows system, set a path like this:

```
set CLASSPATH=.;C:\Windows\Java\Packages\5fpnnz7t.zip
```

With CLASSPATH set, you should be able to compile your applet with *javac* as you would normally.

22.2.2.2 The mayscript attribute

There is an additional requirement for running an applet that interacts with JavaScript. As a security precaution, an applet is not allowed to use JavaScript unless the web page author (who may not be the applet author) explicitly gives the applet permission to do so. To give this permission, you must include the new mayscript attribute in the applet's <applet> tag in the HTML file.

Example 22-1 showed a fragment of an applet that used JavaScript to display an alert dialog box. Once you have successfully compiled this applet, you might include it in an HTML file as follows:

```
<applet code="CPUHog.class" width="300" height="300" mayscript></applet>
```

If you do not remember to include the mayscript attribute, the applet is not allowed to use the JSObject class.

22.3 Using Java Classes Directly

As described in the previous two sections, both Netscape and Internet Explorer allow JavaScript code to interact with Java applets and Java applets to interact with JavaScript. Netscape's LiveConnect technology also allows JavaScript programs to instantiate their own Java objects and use them, even in the absence of any applets. Internet Explorer does not have any analogous capability.

In Netscape, the Packages object provides access to all the Java packages that Netscape knows about. The expression Packages.java.lang refers to the *java.lang* package, and the expression Packages.java.lang.System refers to the *java.lang.System* class. For convenience, java is a shortcut for Packages.java. In Netscape, JavaScript code might invoke a static method of this *java.lang.System* class as follows:

```
// Invoke the static Java method System.getProperty()
var javaVersion = java.lang.System.getProperty("java.version");
```

This use of LiveConnect is not limited to system classes, because LiveConnect allows us to use the JavaScript `new` operator to create new instances of Java classes (just as we would in Java). Example 22-2 shows JavaScript code that uses standard Java classes (the JavaScript code looks almost identical to Java code, in fact) to pop up a window and display some text. The result is shown in Figure 22-1.

Figure 22-1. A Java window created from JavaScript

Example 22-2. Scripting the built-in Java classes

```
var f = new java.awt.Frame("Hello World");
var ta = new java.awt.TextArea("hello, world", 5, 20);
f.add("Center", ta);
f.pack( );
f.show( );
```

The code in Example 22-2 creates a simple Java user interface. What is missing, however, is any form of event handling or user interaction. A program like the one shown here is restricted to doing output, since it doesn't include any way for JavaScript to be notified when the user interacts with the Java window. It is possible, though complicated, to use JavaScript to define a Java user interface that responds to events. In Java 1.1 and later, notification of an event is performed by invoking a method of an EventListener object. Since Java applets can execute arbitrary strings of JavaScript code, it is possible to define a Java class that implements the appropriate EventListener interface and invokes a specified string of JavaScript code when it is notified that an event has occurred. If you create an applet with a method that allows you to create such EventListener objects, you can use JavaScript to piece together Java GUIs that include event handlers defined in JavaScript.

Note that LiveConnect does not give complete and unrestricted access to the Java system; in other words, there are some things we cannot do with LiveConnect. For example, LiveConnect does not give us the capability to define new Java classes or subclasses from within JavaScript, nor does it give us the ability to create Java arrays.* In addition to these limitations, access to the standard Java classes is restricted for

* JavaScript programs can create arrays indirectly, using the Java 1.1 method `java.lang.reflect.Array.newInstance( )`.

security reasons. An untrusted JavaScript program cannot use the *java.io.File* class, for example, because that would give it the power to read, write, and delete files on the host system. Untrusted JavaScript code can use Java only in the ways that untrusted applets can.

22.4 LiveConnect Data Types

To understand how LiveConnect does its job of connecting JavaScript to Java, you have to understand the JavaScript data types that LiveConnect uses. The following sections explain these JavaScript data types. Although Internet Explorer uses a different technology, an understanding of how LiveConnect works will also help you understand the workings of IE. Some of the LiveConnect data types described here have analogs in IE.

22.4.1 The JavaPackage Class

A *package* in Java is collection of related Java classes. The JavaPackage class is a JavaScript data type that represents a Java package. The properties of a JavaPackage are the classes that the package contains (classes are represented by the JavaClass class, which we'll see shortly), as well as any other packages that the package contains. There is a restriction on the JavaPackage class: you cannot use a JavaScript `for/in` loop to obtain a complete list of all packages and classes that a JavaPackage contains. This restriction is the result of an underlying restriction in the Java virtual machine.

All JavaPackage objects are contained within a parent JavaPackage; the Window property named `Packages` is a top-level JavaPackage that serves as the root of this package hierarchy. It has properties such as `java`, `sun`, and `netscape`, which are JavaPackage objects that represent the various hierarchies of Java classes that are available to the browser. For example, the JavaPackage `Packages.java` contains the JavaPackage `Packages.java.awt`. For convenience, every Window object also has `java`, `sun`, and `netscape` properties that are shortcuts to `Packages.java`, `Packages.sun`, and `Packages.netscape`. Thus, instead of typing `Packages.java.awt`, you can simply type `java.awt`.

To continue with the example, `java.awt` is a JavaPackage object that contains JavaClass objects such as `java.awt.Button`, which represents the *java.awt.Button* class. But it also contains yet another JavaPackage object, `java.awt.image`, which represents the *java.awt.image* package in Java.

As you can see, the property naming scheme for the JavaPackage hierarchy mirrors the naming scheme for Java packages. Note, however, that there is one big difference between the JavaPackage class and the actual Java packages that it represents. Packages in Java are collections of classes, not collections of other packages. That is, *java.lang* is the name of a Java package, but *java* is not. So the JavaPackage object named `java` does not actually represent a package in Java—it is simply a convenient placeholder in the package hierarchy for other JavaPackage objects that do represent real Java packages.

On most systems, Java classes are installed in files in a directory hierarchy that corresponds to their package names. For example, the *java.lang.String* class is stored in the file *java/lang/String.class*. Actually, this file is usually contained in a ZIP file, but the directory hierarchy is still there, encoded within the archive. Therefore, instead of thinking of a JavaPackage object as representing a Java package, you may find it clearer to think of it as representing a directory or subdirectory in the directory hierarchy of Java classes.

The JavaPackage class has a few shortcomings. There is no way for LiveConnect to tell in advance whether a property of a JavaPackage refers to a Java class or to another Java package, so JavaScript assumes that it is a class and tries to load a class. Thus, when you use an expression like `java.awt`, LiveConnect first looks for a class file *java/awt.class*. It may even search for this class over the network, causing the web server to log a "404 File Not Found" error. If LiveConnect does not find a class, it assumes that the property refers to a package, but it has no way to ascertain that the package actually exists and has real classes in it. This causes the second shortcoming: if you misspell a class name, LiveConnect happily treats it as a package name, rather than telling you that the class you are trying to use does not exist.

22.4.2 The JavaClass Class

The JavaClass class is a JavaScript data type that represents a Java class. A JavaClass object does not have any properties of its own—all of its properties represent (and have the same name as) the public static fields and methods of the represented Java class. These public static fields and methods are sometimes called *class fields* and *class methods*, to indicate that they are associated with a class rather than an object instance. Unlike the JavaPackage class, JavaClass does allow the use of the `for/in` loop to enumerate its properties. Note that JavaClass objects do not have properties representing the instance fields and methods of a Java class—individual instances of a Java class are represented by the JavaObject class, which is documented in the next section.

As we saw earlier, JavaClass objects are contained in JavaPackage objects. For example, `java.lang` is a JavaPackage that contains a `System` property. Thus, `java.lang.System` is a JavaClass object, representing the Java class *java.lang.System*. This JavaClass object, in turn, has properties such as `out` and `in` that represent static fields of the *java.lang.System* class. You can use JavaScript to refer to any of the standard Java system classes in this same way. The *java.lang.Double* class is named `java.lang.Double` (or `Packages.java.lang.Double`), for example, and the *java.awt.Button* class is `java.awt.Button`.

Another way to obtain a JavaClass object in JavaScript is to use the getClass() function. Given any JavaObject object, you can obtain a JavaClass object that represents the class of that Java object by passing the JavaObject to getClass().*

Once you have a JavaClass object, there are several things you can do with it. The JavaClass class implements the LiveConnect functionality that allows JavaScript programs to read and write the public static fields of Java classes and invoke the public static methods of Java classes. For example, java.lang.System is a JavaClass. We can read the value of a static field of java.lang.System like this:

```
var java_console = java.lang.System.out;
```

Similarly, we might invoke a static method of java.lang.System with a line like this one:

```
var java_version = java.lang.System.getProperty("java.version");
```

Recall that Java is a typed language—all fields and method arguments have types. If you attempt to set a field or pass an argument of the wrong type, an exception is thrown. (Or, in versions of JavaScript prior to 1.5, a JavaScript error occurs.)

There is one more important feature of the JavaClass class. You can use JavaClass objects with the JavaScript new operator to create new instances of Java classes—i.e., to create JavaObject objects. The syntax for doing so is just as it is in JavaScript (and just as it is in Java):

```
var d = new java.lang.Double(1.23);
```

Finally, having created a JavaObject in this way, we can return to the getClass() function and show an example of its use:

```
var d = new java.lang.Double(1.23);     // Create a JavaObject
var d_class = getClass(d);              // Obtain the JavaClass of the JavaObject
if (d_class == java.lang.Double) ...;   // This comparison will be true
```

When working with standard system classes like this, you can typically use the name of the system class directly rather than calling getClass(). The getClass() function is more useful in obtaining the class of a non-system object, such as an applet instance.

Instead of referring to a JavaClass with a cumbersome expression like java.lang.Double, you can define a variable that serves as a shortcut:

```
var Double = java.lang.Double;
```

This mimics the Java import statement and can improve the efficiency of your program, since LiveConnect does not have to look up the lang property of java and the Double property of java.lang.

* Don't confuse the JavaScript getClass() function, which returns a JavaClass object, with the Java getClass() method, which returns a java.lang.Class object.

22.4.3 The JavaObject Class

The JavaObject class is a JavaScript data type that represents a Java object. The JavaObject class is, in many ways, analogous to the JavaClass class. As with JavaClass, a JavaObject has no properties of its own—all of its properties represent (and have the same names as) the public instance fields and public instance methods of the Java object it represents. As with JavaClass, you can use a JavaScript `for/in` loop to enumerate all the properties of a JavaObject object. The JavaObject class implements the LiveConnect functionality that allows us to read and write the public instance fields and invoke the public methods of a Java object.

For example, if `d` is a JavaObject that represents an instance of the *java.lang.Double* class, we can invoke a method of that Java object with JavaScript code like this:

```
n = d.doubleValue( );
```

Similarly, we saw earlier that the *java.lang.System* class has a static field `out`. This field refers to a Java object of class *java.io.PrintStream*. In JavaScript, we can refer to the corresponding JavaObject as:

```
java.lang.System.out
```

and we can invoke a method of this object like this:*

```
java.lang.System.out.println("Hello world!");
```

A JavaObject object also allows us to read and write the public instance fields of the Java object it represents. Neither the *java.lang.Double* class nor the *java.io.PrintStream* class used in the preceding examples has any public instance fields, however. But suppose we use JavaScript to create an instance of the *java.awt.Rectangle* class:

```
r = new java.awt.Rectangle( );
```

Then we can read and write its public instance fields with JavaScript code like the following:

```
r.x = r.y = 0;
r.width = 4;
r.height = 5;
var perimeter = 2*r.width + 2*r.height;
```

The beauty of LiveConnect is that it allows a Java object, `r`, to be used just as if it were a JavaScript object. Some caution is required, however: `r` is a JavaObject and does not behave identically to regular JavaScript objects. The differences will be detailed later. Also, remember that unlike JavaScript, the fields of Java objects and the arguments of their methods are typed. If you do not specify JavaScript values of the correct types, you cause JavaScript errors or exceptions.

* The output of this line of code doesn't appear in the web browser itself, but rather in the Java Console. In Netscape 6, select **Tasks** → **Tools** → **Java Console** to see this window.

In Netscape 6.1 and later the JavaObject class makes methods available by name and by name plus argument type, which is useful when there are two or methods that share the same name but expect different types of arguments. As we saw earlier in this chapter, if a JavaObject `o` represents an object that has two methods named "convert", the `convert` property of `o` may refer to either of those methods. In recent versions of LiveConnect, however, `o` also defines properties that include the argument types, and you can specify which version of the method you want by including this type information:

```
var iconvert = o["convert(int)"];  // Get the method we want
iconvert(3);                        // Invoke it
```

Because the name of the property includes parentheses, you can't use the regular "." notation to access it and must express it as a string within square brackets. The JavaClass type has the same capability for overridden static methods.

22.4.4 The JavaArray Class

The final LiveConnect data type for JavaScript is the JavaArray class. As you might expect by now, instances of this class represent Java arrays and provide the LiveConnect functionality that allows JavaScript to read the elements of Java arrays. Like JavaScript arrays (and like Java arrays), a JavaArray object has a `length` property that specifies the number of elements it contains. The elements of a JavaArray object are read with the standard JavaScript `[]` array index operator. They can also be enumerated with a `for/in` loop. You can use JavaArray objects to access multidimensional arrays (actually arrays of arrays), just as in JavaScript or Java.

For example, suppose we create an instance of the *java.awt.Polygon* class:

```
p = new java.awt.Polygon( );
```

The JavaObject `p` has properties `xpoints` and `ypoints` that are JavaArray objects representing Java arrays of integers. (To learn the names and types of these properties, look up the documentation for *java.awt.Polygon* in a Java reference manual.) We can use these JavaArray objects to randomly initialize the Java polygon with code like this:

```
for(var i = 0; i < p.xpoints.length; i++)
    p.xpoints[i] = Math.round(Math.random( )*100);
for(var i = 0; i < p.ypoints.length; i++)
    p.ypoints[i] = Math.round(Math.random( )*100);
```

22.4.5 Java Methods

The JavaClass and JavaObject classes allow us to invoke static methods and instance methods, respectively. In Netscape 3, Java methods were internally represented by a JavaMethod object. In Netscape 4, however, Java methods are simply native methods, like the methods of built-in JavaScript objects such as String and Date.

When you're using Java methods, remember that they expect a fixed number of arguments of fixed types. If you pass the wrong number of arguments, or an argument of the wrong type, you cause a JavaScript error.

22.5 LiveConnect Data Conversion

Java is a strongly typed language with a relatively large number of data types, while JavaScript is an untyped language with a relatively small number of types. Because of this major structural difference between the two languages, one of the central responsibilities of LiveConnect is data conversion. When JavaScript sets a Java class or instance field or passes an argument to a Java method, a JavaScript value must be converted to an equivalent Java value, and when JavaScript reads a Java class or instance field or obtains the return value of a Java method, that Java value must be converted into a compatible JavaScript value.*

Figures 22-2 and 22-3 illustrate how data conversion is performed when JavaScript writes Java values and when it reads them, respectively.

Notice the following points about the data conversions illustrated in Figure 22-2:

- Figure 22-2 does not show all possible conversions between JavaScript types and Java types. This is because JavaScript-to-JavaScript type conversions can occur before the JavaScript-to-Java conversion takes place. For example, if you pass a JavaScript number to a Java method that expects a *java.lang.String* argument, JavaScript first converts that number to a JavaScript string, which can then be converted to a Java string.
- A JavaScript number can be converted to any of the primitive Java numeric types. The actual conversion performed depends, of course, on the type of the Java field being set or the method argument being passed. Note that you can lose precision doing this, for example, when you pass a large number to a Java field of type `short` or when you pass a floating-point value to a Java integral type.
- A JavaScript number can also be converted to an instance of the Java class *java.lang.Double* but not to an instance of a related class, such as *java.lang.Integer* or *java.lang.Float*.
- JavaScript does not have any representation for character data, so a JavaScript number may also be converted to the Java primitive `char` type.
- A JavaObject in JavaScript is "unwrapped" when passed to Java—that is, it is converted to the Java object it represents. Note, however, that JavaClass objects

* In addition, data conversion must happen when Java reads or writes a JavaScript field or invokes a JavaScript method. These conversions are done differently, however, and are described later in this chapter, when we discuss how to use JavaScript from Java. For now, we're considering only the data conversion that happens when JavaScript code interacts with Java, not the other way around.

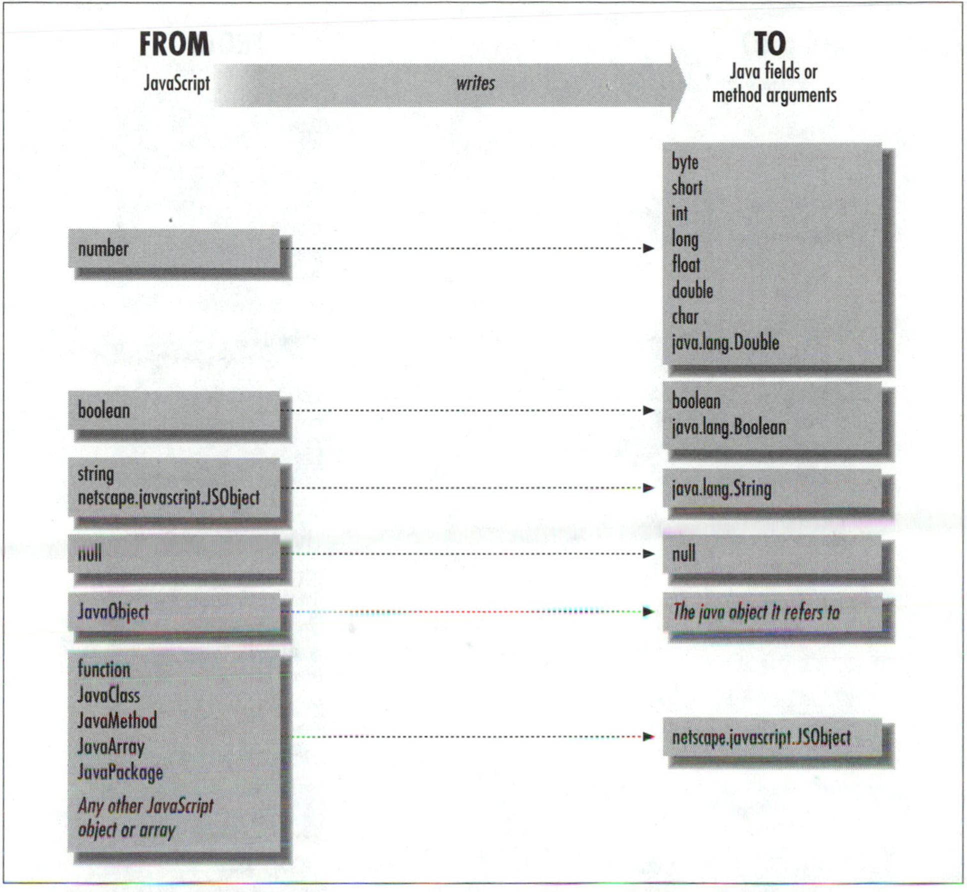

Figure 22-2. Data conversions performed when JavaScript writes Java values

in JavaScript are not converted to instances of *java.lang.Class*, as might be expected.

- JavaScript arrays are not converted to Java arrays.

Also notice these points about the conversions illustrated in Figure 22-3:

- Since JavaScript does not have a type for character data, the Java primitive `char` type is converted to a JavaScript number, not a string, as might be expected.
- A Java instance of *java.lang.Double*, *java.lang.Integer*, or a similar class is not converted to a JavaScript number. Like any Java object, it is converted to a JavaObject object in JavaScript.
- A Java string is an instance of *java.lang.String*, so like any other Java object, it is converted to a JavaObject object rather than to an actual JavaScript string.
- Any type of Java array is converted to a JavaArray object in JavaScript.

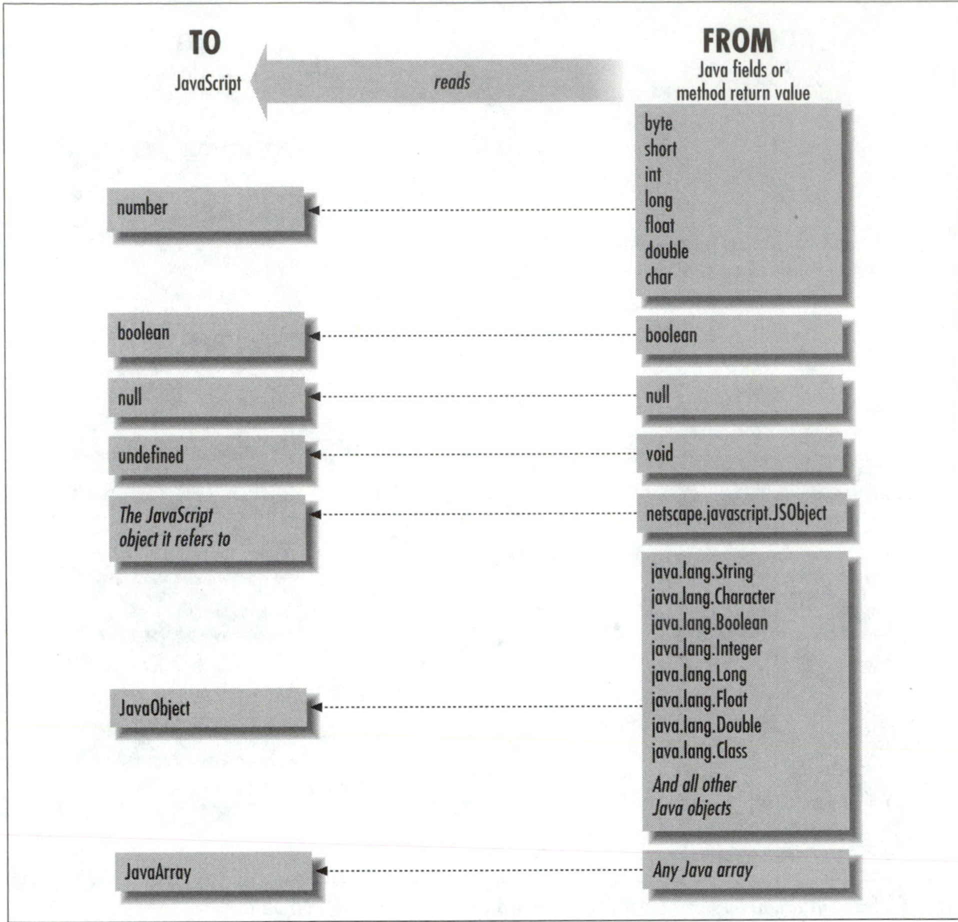

Figure 22-3. Data conversions performed when JavaScript reads Java values

22.5.1 Wrapper Objects

Another important concept that you must grasp in order to fully understand Figures 22-2 and 22-3 is the idea of wrapper objects. While conversions between most JavaScript and Java primitive types are possible, conversions between object types are generally not possible. This is why LiveConnect defines the JavaObject object in JavaScript—it represents a Java object that cannot be directly converted to a JavaScript object. In a sense, a JavaObject is a JavaScript wrapper around a Java object. When JavaScript reads a Java value (a field or the return value of a method), any Java objects are wrapped and JavaScript sees a JavaObject.

A similar thing happens when JavaScript writes a JavaScript object into a Java field or passes a JavaScript object to a Java method. There is no way to convert the JavaScript object to a Java object, so the object gets wrapped. The Java wrapper for a JavaScript object is the Java class *netscape.javascript.JSObject*.

Things get interesting when these wrapper objects are passed back. If JavaScript writes a JavaObject into a Java field or passes it to a Java method, LiveConnect first unwraps the object, converting the JavaObject back into the Java object that it represents. Similarly, if JavaScript reads a Java field or gets the return value of a Java method that is an instance of *netscape.javascript.JSObject*, that JSObject is also unwrapped to reveal and return the original JavaScript object.

22.5.2 LiveConnect Data Conversion in Netscape 3

In Netscape 3, there was a bug in the way that LiveConnect converted Java values to JavaScript values: the value of a primitive field of a Java object was incorrectly returned as a JavaScript object, rather than as a JavaScript primitive value. For example, if JavaScript read the value of a field of type `int`, LiveConnect in Netscape 3 converted that value to a Number object, rather than to a primitive numeric value. Similarly, LiveConnect converted the value of Java `boolean` fields to JavaScript Boolean objects, rather than primitive JavaScript boolean values. Note that this bug occurred only when querying the values of Java fields. It did not occur when LiveConnect converted the return value of a Java method.

Number and Boolean objects in JavaScript behave almost, but not exactly, the same as primitive number and boolean values. One important difference is that Number objects, like all JavaScript objects, use the + operator for string concatenation rather than for addition. As a result, code like the following that uses LiveConnect in Netscape 3 can yield unexpected results:

```
var r = new java.awt.Rectangle(0,0,5,5);
var w = r.width;     // This is a Number object, not a primitive number.
var new_w = w + 1;   // Oops! new_w is now "51", not 6, as expected.
```

To work around this problem, you can explicitly call the `valueOf( )` method to convert a Number object to its corresponding numeric value. For example:

```
var r = new java.awt.Rectangle(0,0,5,5);
var w = r.width.valueOf( );  // Now we've got a primitive number.
var new_w = w + 1;           // This time, new_w is 6, as desired.
```

22.6 JavaScript Conversion of JavaObjects

Having worked your way through the previous dense section, you may hope that we are done with the topic of data conversion. Unfortunately, there is more to be discussed on the topic of how JavaScript converts JavaObject objects to various JavaScript primitive types. Notice in Figure 22-3 that quite a few Java data types, including Java strings (instances of *java.lang.String*), are converted to JavaObject objects in JavaScript rather than being converted to actual JavaScript primitive types, such as strings. This means that when you use LiveConnect, you'll often be working with JavaObject objects.

Refer back to Table 11-1, which shows how various JavaScript data types are converted when used in various contexts. For example, when a number is used in a string context, it is converted to a string, and when an object is used in a boolean context, it is converted to the value `false` if it is `null` and `true` otherwise. These conversion rules don't apply to JavaObject objects, which are converted using their own rules, as follows:

- When a JavaObject is used in a numeric context, it is converted to a number by invoking the `doubleValue()` method of the Java object it represents. If the Java object does not define this method, a JavaScript error occurs.
- When a JavaObject is used in a boolean context, it is converted to a boolean value by invoking the `booleanValue()` method of the Java object it represents. If the Java object does not define this method, a JavaScript error occurs.
- When a JavaObject is used in a string context, it is converted to a string value by invoking the `toString()` method of the Java object it represents. All Java objects define or inherit this method, so this conversion always succeeds.
- When a JavaObject is used in an object context, no conversion is necessary, since it is already a JavaScript object.

Because of these different conversion rules, and for other reasons as well, JavaObject objects behave differently than other JavaScript objects, and there are some common pitfalls that you need to recognize. First, it is not uncommon to work with a JavaObject that represents an instance of *java.lang.Double* or some other numeric object. In many ways, such a JavaObject behaves like a primitive number value, but be careful when using the + operator. When you use a JavaObject (or any JavaScript object) with +, you are specifying a string context, so the object is converted to a string for string concatenation instead of being converted to a number for addition.

When you want to explicitly convert a JavaScript object to a primitive value, you usually call its `valueOf()` method. Note that this does not work with JavaObject objects. As we discussed earlier, the JavaObject class defines no properties of its own; all of its properties represent fields and methods of the Java object it represents. This means that JavaObject objects don't support common JavaScript methods, such as `valueOf()`. In the case of our JavaObject-wrapped `java.lang.Double` object, you should call the Java `doubleValue()` method when you need to force the object into a primitive value.

Another difference between JavaObject objects and other JavaScript data types is that JavaObjects can be used in a boolean context only if they define a `booleanValue()` method. Suppose `button` is a JavaScript variable that may contain `null` or may hold a

JavaObject that represents an instance of the *java.awt.Button* class. If you want to check whether the variable contains `null`, you might write code like this, out of habit:

```
if (!button) { ... }
```

If `button` is `null`, this works fine. But if `button` actually contains a JavaObject representing a *java.awt.Button* instance, LiveConnect tries to invoke the `booleanValue( )` method. When it discovers that the *java.awt.Button* class doesn't define one, it causes a JavaScript error. The workaround in this case is to be explicit about what you are testing for, to avoid using the JavaObject in a boolean context:

```
if (button != null) { ... }
```

This is a good habit to get into, in any case, since it makes your code easier to read and understand.

22.7 Java-to-JavaScript Data Conversion

In the last two sections, we discussed the rules by which values are converted when JavaScript reads and writes Java fields and invokes Java methods. Those rules explained how the JavaScript JavaObject, JavaArray, and JavaClass objects convert data; they apply only to the case of JavaScript manipulating Java. When Java manipulates JavaScript, the conversion is performed by the Java JSObject class, and the conversion rules are different. Figure 22-4 and Figure 22-5 illustrate these conversions.

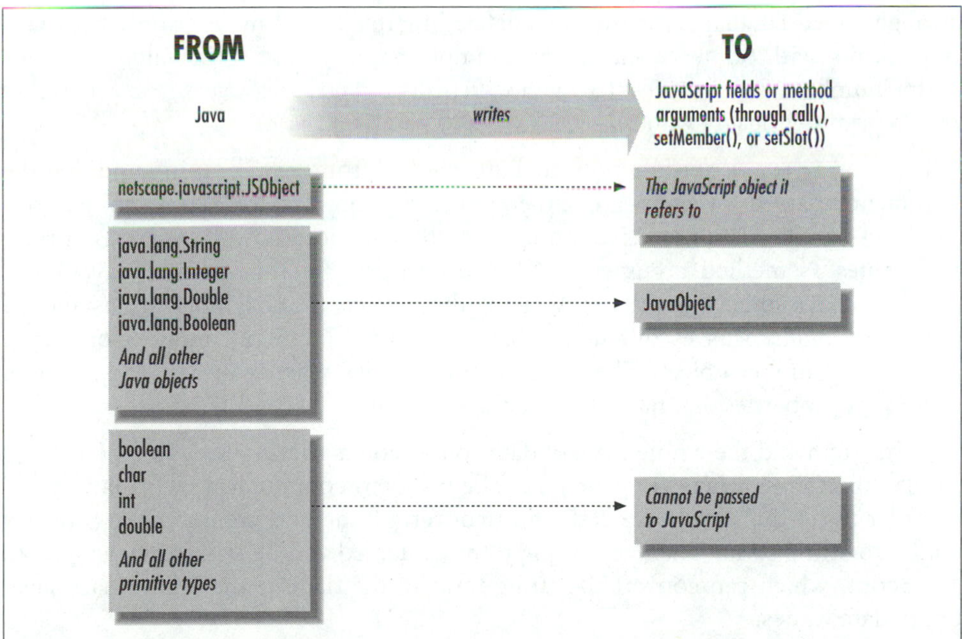

Figure 22-4. Data conversions performed when Java writes JavaScript values

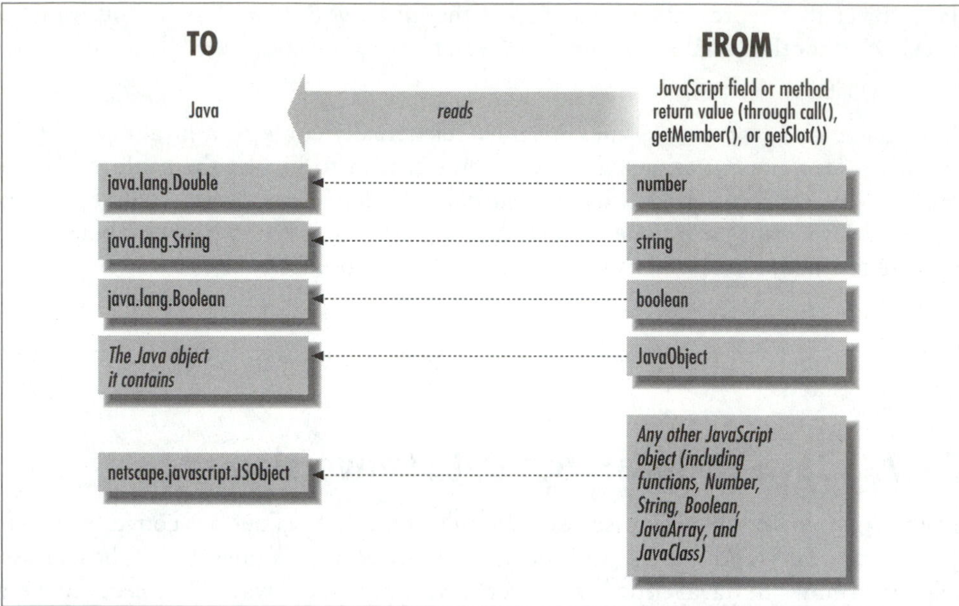

Figure 22-5. Data conversions performed when Java reads JavaScript values

The point to remember when studying these figures is that Java can interact with JavaScript only through the API provided by the JSObject class. Because Java is a strongly typed language, the methods defined by this class can work only with Java objects, not with primitive values. For example, when you read the value of a JavaScript number, the `getMember()` method returns a `java.lang.Double` object, rather than a primitive `double` value.

When writing JavaScript functions that are invoked from Java, bear in mind that the arguments passed by Java are either JavaScript objects from unwrapped Java JSObjects, or JavaObjects. LiveConnect simply does not allow Java to pass primitive values as method arguments. As we saw earlier in this chapter, JavaObject objects behave somewhat differently than other objects. For example, an instance of *java.lang.Double* behaves differently than a primitive JavaScript number or even a JavaScript Number object. The same caution applies when you are working with JavaScript properties that have their values set by Java.

One way to avoid the whole issue of data conversion is to use the `eval()` method of the JSObject class whenever your Java code wants to communicate with JavaScript. In order to do this, your Java code must convert all method arguments or property values to string form. Then, the string to be evaluated can be passed unchanged to JavaScript, which can convert the string form of the data to the appropriate JavaScript data values.

PART III

Core JavaScript Reference

This part of the book is a complete reference to all of the objects, properties, functions, methods, and event handlers in the core JavaScript language. The first few pages of this part explain how to use this reference material.

Core JavaScript Reference

This part of the book is a reference section that documents the classes, methods, and properties defined by the core JavaScript language. The introduction and sample reference page explain how to use and get the most out of this reference section. Take the time to read this material carefully, and you will find it easier to locate and use the information you need!

This reference section is arranged alphabetically. The reference pages for the methods and properties of classes are alphabetized by their full names, which include the names of the classes that define them. For example, if you want to read about the `replace()` method of the String class, you would look under "String.replace," not just "replace."

Core JavaScript defines some global functions and properties, such as `eval()` and `NaN`. Technically, these are properties of a global object. Since the global object has no name, however, they are listed in this reference section under their own unqualified names. For convenience, the full set of global functions and properties in core JavaScript is summarized in a special reference page named "Global" (even though there is no object or class by that name).

Sometimes you may find that you don't know the name of the class or interface that defines the method or property want to look up, or you may not be sure which of the three reference sections to look up a class or interface in. Part VI of this book is a special index designed to help with these situations. Look up the name of a class, method, or property, and it will tell you which reference section to look in and which class to look under in that section. For example, if you look up "Date," it will tell you that the Date class is documented in this core reference section. And if you look up the name "match," it will tell you that `match()` is a method of the String class and is also documented in this section.

Once you've found the reference page you're looking for, you shouldn't have much difficulty finding the information you need. Still, you'll be able to make better use of this reference section if you understand how the reference pages are written and organized. What follows is a sample reference page titled "Sample Entry" that demonstrates the structure of each reference page and tells you where to find various types of information within the pages. Take the time to read this page before diving into the rest of the reference material.

Sample Entry

Availability

how to read core JavaScript reference pages

Inherits from/Overrides

Title and Short Description

Every reference entry begins with a four-part title block like that above. The entries are alphabetized by title. The short description, shown below the title, gives you a quick summary of the item documented in the entry; it can help you quickly decide if you're interested in reading the rest of the page.

Availability

The availability information is shown in the upper-right corner of the title block. This information tells you which version of Netscape's JavaScript interpreter and Microsoft's JScript interpreter the item (class, method, or property) was introduced in. If the item has been standardized in ECMAScript, it tells you which version of the standard introduced it. You can assume that anything available in one version of JavaScript is also available in later versions. Note, however, that if this section says the item is deprecated it may be removed in the future and you should avoid using it.

Inherits from/Overrides

If a class inherits from a superclass or a method overrides a method in a superclass, that information is shown in the lower-right corner of the title block.

As described in Chapter 8, JavaScript classes can inherit properties and methods from other classes. For example, the String class inherits from Object, and the RangeError class inherits from Error, which in turn inherits from Object. When you see this inheritance information, you may also want to look up the listed superclasses.

When a method has the same name as a method in a superclass, the method overrides the superclass's method. See "Array.toString()" for an example.

Constructor

If the reference page documents a class, it usually has a "Constructor" section that shows you how to use the constructor method to create instances of the class. Since constructors are a type of method, the "Constructor" section looks a lot like the "Synopsis" section of a method's reference page.

Synopsis

Reference pages for functions, methods, and properties have a "Synopsis" section that shows how you might use the function, method, or property in your code. For example, the synopsis for the `Array.concat()` method is:

```
array.concat(value, ...)
```

The *italic* font indicates text that is to be replaced with something else. *array* should be replaced with a variable or JavaScript expression that holds or evaluates to an array. And *value* simply represents an arbitrary value that is to be concatenated to the array. The ellipsis (`...`) indicates that this method can take any number of *value* arguments. Because the terms `concat` and the open and close parentheses are not in *italics*, you must include them exactly as shown in your JavaScript code.

Arguments

If a reference page documents a function, a method, or a class with a constructor method, the "Constructor" or "Synopsis" section is followed by an "Arguments" subsection that describes the arguments to the method, function, or constructor. If there are no arguments, this subsection is simply omitted.

arg1
: The arguments are described in a list here. This is the description for argument *arg1*, for example.

arg2
: And this is the description for argument *arg2*.

Returns

If a constructor, function, or method has a return value, this subsection explains that value.

Throws

If a constructor, function, or method can throw an exception, this subsection lists the types of exceptions that may be thrown and explains the circumstances under which this can occur.

Properties

If the reference page documents a class, the "Properties" section lists the properties defined by the class and provides short explanations of each. In this core reference section, each property also has a complete reference page of its own. For example, the reference page for the Array class lists the `length` property in this section and gives a brief explanation of it, but the property is fully documented in the "Array.length" reference page. The property listing looks like this:

`prop1`
: This is a summary of property `prop1`, including its type, its purpose or meaning, and whether it is read-only or read/write.

`prop2`
: This is the same for `prop2`.

Methods

The reference page for a class that defines methods includes a "Methods" section. It is just like the "Properties" section, except that it summarizes methods instead of properties. All methods also have reference pages of their own.

Description

Most reference pages contain a "Description" section, which is the basic description of the class, method, function, or property that is being documented. This is the heart of the reference page. If you are learning about a class, method, or property for the first time, you may want to skip directly to this section and then go back and look at previous sections such as "Arguments," "Properties," and "Methods." If you are already familiar with a class, method, or property, you probably won't need to read this section and instead will just want to quickly look up some specific bit of information (for example, from the "Arguments" or "Properties" sections).

In some entries, this section is no more than a short paragraph. In others, it may occupy a page or more. For some simple methods, the "Arguments" and "Returns" sections document the method sufficiently by themselves, so the "Description" section is omitted.

Example

Some pages include an example that shows typical usage. Most pages do not contain examples, however—you'll find those in first half of this book.

Bugs

When an item doesn't work quite right, this section describes the bugs. Note, however, that this book does not attempt to catalog every bug in every version and implementation of JavaScript.

See Also

Many reference pages conclude with cross-references to related reference pages that may be of interest. Sometimes reference pages also refer back to one of the main chapters of the book.

arguments[] JavaScript 1.1; JScript 2.0; ECMAScript v1

an array of function arguments

Synopsis

```
arguments
```

Description

The `arguments[]` array is defined only within a function body. Within the body of a function, `arguments` refers to the Arguments object for the function. This object has numbered properties and serves as an array containing all arguments passed to the function. The `arguments` identifier is essentially a local variable automatically declared and initialized within every function. It refers to an Arguments object only within the body of a function and is undefined in global code.

See Also

Arguments; Chapter 7

Arguments

JavaScript 1.1; JScript 2.0; ECMAScript v1

arguments and other properties of a function

Inherits from Object

Synopsis

```
arguments
arguments[n]
```

Elements

The Arguments object is defined only within a function body. Although it is not technically an array, the Arguments object has numbered properties that function as array elements and a `length` property that specifies the number of array elements. Its elements are the values that were passed as arguments to the function. Element 0 is the first argument, element 1 is the second argument, and so on. All values passed as arguments become array elements of the Arguments object, whether or not those arguments are given names in the function declaration.

Properties

`callee`
: A reference to the function that is currently executing.

`length`
: The number of arguments passed to the function and the number of array elements in the Arguments object.

Description

When a function is invoked, an Arguments object is created for it and the local variable `arguments` is automatically initialized to refer to that Arguments object. The main purpose of the Arguments object is to provide a way to determine how many arguments were passed to the function and to refer to unnamed arguments. In addition to the array elements and `length` property, however, the `callee` property allows an unnamed function to refer to itself.

For most purposes, the Arguments object can be thought of as an array with the addition of the `callee` property. However, it is not an instance of Array, and the `Arguments.length` property does not have any of the special behaviors of the `Array.length` property and cannot be used to change the size of the array.

The Arguments object has one *very* unusual feature. When a function has named arguments, the array elements of the Arguments object are synonyms for the local variables that hold the function arguments. The Arguments object and the argument names provide two different ways of referring to the same variable. Changing the value of an argument with an argument name changes the value that is retrieved through the Arguments object, and changing the value of an argument through the Arguments object changes the value that is retrieved by the argument name.

See Also

Function; Chapter 7

Arguments.callee

JavaScript 1.2; JScript 5.5; ECMAScript v1

the function that is currently running

Synopsis

`arguments.callee`

Description

`arguments.callee` refers to the function that is currently running. It provides a way for an unnamed function to refer to itself. This property is defined only within a function body.

Example

```
// An unnamed function literal uses the callee property to refer
// to itself so that it can be recursive
var factorial = function(x) {
    if (x < 2) return 1;
    else return x * arguments.callee(x-1);
}
var y = factorial(5);  // Returns 120
```

Arguments.length

JavaScript 1.1; JScript 2; ECMAScript v1

the number of arguments passed to a function

Synopsis

`arguments.length`

Description

The `length` property of the Arguments object specifies the number of arguments passed to the current function. This property is defined only within a function body.

Note that this property specifies the number of arguments actually passed, not the number expected. See "Function.length" for the number of declared arguments. Note also that this property does not have any of the special behavior of the `Array.length` property.

Example

```
// Use an Arguments object to check that correct # of args were passed
function check(args) {
    var actual = args.length;           // The actual number of arguments
    var expected = args.callee.length;  // The expected number of arguments
    if (actual != expected) {           // Throw exception if they don't match
        throw new Error("Wrong number of arguments: expected: " +
                         expected + "; actually passed " + actual);
    }
}
// A function that demonstrates how to use the function above
function f(x, y, z) {
    check(arguments);  // Check for correct number of arguments
    return x + y + z;  // Now do the rest of the function normally
}
```

See Also

Array.length, Function.length

Array

JavaScript 1.1; JScript 2.0; ECMAScript v1

built-in support for arrays

Inherits from Object

Constructor

```
new Array()
new Array(size)
new Array(element0, element1, ..., elementn)
```

Arguments

size

The desired number of elements in the array. The returned array has its `length` field set to *size*.

element0, ... elementn

An argument list of two or more arbitrary values. When the `Array()` constructor is invoked with these arguments, the newly created array is initialized with the specified argument values as its elements and its `length` field set to the number of arguments.

Returns

The newly created and initialized array. When `Array()` is invoked with no arguments, the returned array is empty and has a `length` field of 0. When invoked with a single numeric argument, the constructor returns an array with the specified number of undefined elements. When invoked with any other arguments, the constructor initializes the array with the values specified by the arguments. When the `Array()` constructor is called as a function, without the `new` operator, it behaves exactly as it does when called with the `new` operator.

Throws

`RangeError`

When a single integer *size* argument is passed to the `Array()` constructor, a `RangeError` exception is thrown if *size* is negative or is larger than $2^{32}-1$.

Literal Syntax

ECMAScript v3 specifies and JavaScript 1.2 and JScript 3.0 implement an array literal syntax. You may also create and initialize an array by placing a comma-separated list of expressions within square brackets. The values of these expressions become the elements of the array. For example:

```
var a = [1, true, 'abc'];
var b = [a[0], a[0]*2, f(x)];
```

Properties

`length`

A read/write integer specifying the number of elements in the array or, when the array does not have contiguous elements, a number one larger than the index of the last element in the array. Changing the value of this property truncates or extends the array.

Methods

`concat( )`	Concatenates elements to an array.
`join( )`	Converts all array elements to strings and concatenate them.
`pop( )`	Removes an item from the end of an array.
`push( )`	Pushes an item onto the end of an array.
`reverse( )`	Reverses, in place, the order of the elements of an array.
`shift( )`	Shifts an element off the beginning of an array.
`slice( )`	Returns a subarray slice of an array.
`sort( )`	Sorts, in place, the elements of an array.
`splice( )`	Inserts, deletes, or replaces array elements.
`toLocaleString( )`	Converts an array to a localized string.
`toString( )`	Converts an array to a string.
`unshift( )`	Inserts elements at the beginning of an array.

Description

Arrays are a basic feature of JavaScript and are documented in detail in Chapter 9.

See Also

Chapter 9

Array.concat( ) — JavaScript 1.2; JScript 3.0; ECMAScript v3

concatenate arrays

Synopsis

array.concat(*value*, ...)

Arguments

value, ...
: Any number of values to be concatenated with *array*.

Returns

A new array, which is formed by concatenating each of the specified arguments to *array*.

Description

`concat( )` creates and returns a new array that is the result of concatenating each of its arguments to *array*. It does not modify *array*. If any of the arguments to `concat( )` is itself an array, the elements of that array are concatenated, rather than the array itself.

Example

```
var a = [1,2,3];
a.concat(4, 5)          // Returns [1,2,3,4,5]
a.concat([4,5]);        // Returns [1,2,3,4,5]
a.concat([4,5],[6,7])   // Returns [1,2,3,4,5,6,7]
a.concat(4, [5,[6,7]])  // Returns [1,2,3,4,5,[6,7]]
```

See Also

Array.join(), Array.push(), Array.splice()

Array.join( )

JavaScript 1.1; JScript 2.0; ECMAScript v1

concatenate array elements to form a string

Synopsis

array.join( )
array.join(*separator*)

Arguments

separator
: An optional character or string used to separate one element of the array from the next in the returned string. If this argument is omitted, a comma is used.

Returns

The string that results from converting each element of *array* to a string and then concatenating them together, with the *separator* string between elements.

Description

`join( )` converts each of the elements of an array to a string and then concatenates those strings, inserting the specified *separator* string between the elements. It returns the resulting string.

You can perform a conversion in the opposite direction—splitting a string up into array elements—with the `split( )` method of the String object. See the "String.split()" reference page for details.

Example

```
a = new Array(1, 2, 3, "testing");
s = a.join("+");  // s is the string "1+2+3+testing"
```

See Also

String.split()

Array.length

JavaScript 1.1, JScript 2.0; ECMAScript v1

the size of an array

Synopsis

array.length

Description

The `length` property of an array is always one larger than the highest element defined in the array. For traditional "dense" arrays that have contiguous elements and begin with element 0, the `length` property specifies the number of elements in the array.

The length property of an array is initialized when the array is created with the Array( ) constructor method. Adding new elements to an array updates the length, if necessary:

```
a = new Array();                      // a.length initialized to 0
b = new Array(10);                    // b.length initialized to 10
c = new Array("one", "two", "three"); // c.length initialized to 3
c[3] = "four";                        // c.length updated to 4
c[10] = "blastoff";                   // c.length becomes 11
```

You can set the value of the length property to change the size of an array. If you set length to be smaller than its previous value, the array is truncated and elements at the end are lost. If you set length to be larger than its previous value, the array becomes bigger and the new elements added at the end of the array have the undefined value.

Array.pop( )

JavaScript 1.2; JScript 5.5; ECMAScript v3

remove and return the last element of an array

Synopsis

array.pop( )

Returns

The last element of *array*.

Description

pop( ) deletes the last element of *array*, decrements the array length, and returns the value of the element that it deleted. If the array is already empty, pop( ) does not change the array and returns the undefined value.

Example

pop( ), and its companion method push( ), provide the functionality of a first-in, last-out stack. For example:

```
var stack = [];       // stack: []
stack.push(1, 2);     // stack: [1,2]     Returns 2
stack.pop();          // stack: [1]       Returns 2
stack.push([4,5]);    // stack: [1,[4,5]] Returns 2
stack.pop()           // stack: [1]       Returns [4,5]
stack.pop();          // stack: []        Returns 1
```

See Also

Array.push()

Array.push( )

JavaScript 1.2; JScript 5.5; ECMAScript v3

append elements to an array

Synopsis

array.push(*value*, ...)

Arguments

value, ...

One or more values to be appended to the end of *array*.

Returns

The new length of the array, after the specified values are appended to it.

Description

push( ) appends its arguments, in order, to the end of *array*. It modifies *array* directly, rather than creating a new array. push( ), and its companion method pop( ), use arrays to provide the functionality of a first in, last out stack. See "Array.pop()" for an example.

Bugs

In Netscape's implementations of JavaScript, when the language version is explicitly set to 1.2 this function returns the last value appended, rather than returning the new array length.

See Also

Array.pop()

Array.reverse( ) — JavaScript 1.1; JScript 2.0; ECMAScript v1

reverse the elements of an array

Synopsis

array.reverse( )

Description

The reverse( ) method of an Array object reverses the order of the elements of an array. It does this "in place"—it rearranges the elements of the specified *array*, without creating a new array. If there are multiple references to *array*, the new order of the array elements is visible through all references.

Example

```
a = new Array(1, 2, 3);   // a[0] == 1, a[2] == 3;
a.reverse();              // Now a[0] == 3, a[2] == 1;
```

Array.shift( ) — JavaScript 1.2; JScript 5.5; ECMAScript v3

shift array elements down

Synopsis

array.shift( )

Returns

The former first element of the array.

Description

`shift( )` removes and returns the first element of *array*, shifting all subsequent elements down one place to occupy the newly vacant space at the start of the array. If the array is empty, `shift( )` does nothing and returns the `undefined` value. Note that `shift( )` does not create a new array; instead, it modifies *array* directly.

`shift( )` is similar to `Array.pop( )`, except it operates on the beginning of an array rather than the end. `shift( )` is often used in conjunction with `unshift( )`.

Example

```
var a = [1, [2,3], 4]
a.shift( );  // Returns 1; a = [[2,3], 4]
a.shift( );  // Returns [2,3]; a = [4]
```

See Also

Array.pop( ), Array.unshift( )

Array.slice( )

JavaScript 1.2; JScript 3.0; ECMAScript v3

return a portion of an array

Synopsis

array.slice(*start*, *end*)

Arguments

start

The array index at which the slice is to begin. If negative, this argument specifies a position measured from the end of the array. That is, –1 indicates the last element, –2 indicates the second from last element, and so on.

end

The array index immediately after the end of the slice. If not specified, the slice includes all array elements from the *start* to the end of the array. If this argument is negative, it specifies an array element measured from the end of the array.

Returns

A new array that contains the elements of *array* from the element specified by *start*, up to, but not including, the element specified by *end*.

Description

`slice( )` returns a slice, or subarray, of *array*. The returned array contains the element specified by *start* and all subsequent elements up to, but not including, the element specified by *end*. If *end* is not specified, the returned array contains all elements from the *start* to the end of *array*.

Note that `slice( )` does not modify the array. If you want to actually remove a slice of an array, use `Array.splice( )`.

Example

```
var a = [1,2,3,4,5];
a.slice(0,3);    // Returns [1,2,3]
a.slice(3);      // Returns [4,5]
a.slice(1,-1);   // Returns [2,3,4]
a.slice(-3,-2);  // Returns [3]; buggy in IE 4: returns [1,2,3]
```

Bugs

`start` cannot be a negative number in Internet Explorer 4.

See Also

Array.splice()

Array.sort( )

JavaScript 1.1; JScript 2.0; ECMAScript v1

sort the elements of an array

Synopsis

`array``.sort( )`
`array``.sort(`*`orderfunc`*`)`

Arguments

`orderfunc`

An optional function used to specify the sorting order.

Returns

A reference to the array. Note that the array is sorted in place and no copy is made.

Description

The `sort( )` method sorts the elements of *array* in place—no copy of the array is made. If `sort( )` is called with no arguments, the elements of the array are arranged in alphabetical order (more precisely, the order determined by the character encoding). To do this, elements are first converted to strings, if necessary, so that they can be compared.

If you want to sort the array elements in some other order, you must supply a comparison function that compares two values and returns a number indicating their relative order. The comparison function should take two arguments, *a* and *b*, and should return one of the following:

- A value less than zero, if, according to your sort criteria, *a* is "less than" *b* and should appear before *b* in the sorted array.
- Zero, if *a* and *b* are equivalent for the purposes of this sort.
- A value greater than zero, if *a* is "greater than" *b* for the purposes of the sort.

Note that undefined elements of an array are always sorted to the end of the array. This is true even if you provide a custom ordering function: undefined values are never passed to the *`orderfunc`* you supply.

Example

The following code shows how you might write a comparison function to sort an array of numbers in numerical, rather than alphabetical order:

```
// An ordering function for a numerical sort
function numberorder(a, b) { return a - b; }

a = new Array(33, 4, 1111, 222);
a.sort();             // Alphabetical sort: 1111, 222, 33, 4
a.sort(numberorder);  // Numerical sort: 4, 33, 222, 1111
```

Array.splice( )

JavaScript 1.2; JScript 5.5; ECMAScript v3

insert, remove, or replace array elements

Synopsis

array.splice(*start*, *deleteCount*, *value*, ...)

Arguments

start
: The array element at which the insertion and/or deletion is to begin.

deleteCount
: The number of elements, starting with and including *start*, to be deleted from *array*. This argument is optional; if not specified, splice( ) deletes all elements from *start* to the end of the array.

value, ...
: Zero or more values to be inserted into *array*, beginning at the index specified by *start*.

Returns

An array containing the elements, if any, deleted from *array*. Note, however, that due to a bug, the return value is not always an array in the Netscape implementation of JavaScript 1.2.

Description

splice( ) deletes zero or more array elements starting with and including the element *start* and replaces them with zero or more values specified in the argument list. Array elements that appear after the insertion or deletion are moved as necessary so that they remain contiguous with the rest of the array. Note that, unlike the similarly named slice( ), splice( ) modifies *array* directly.

Example

The operation of splice( ) is most easily understood through an example:

```
var a = [1,2,3,4,5,6,7,8]
a.splice(4);        // Returns [5,6,7,8]; a is [1,2,3,4]
a.splice(1,2);      // Returns [2,3]; a is [1,4]
a.splice(1,1);      // Netscape/JavaScript 1.2 returns 4 instead of [4]
a.splice(1,0,2,3);  // Netscape/JavaScript 1.2 returns undefined instead of []
```

Bugs

splice( ) is supposed to return an array of deleted elements in all cases. However, in Netscape's JavaScript 1.2 interpreter, when a single element is deleted it returns that element rather than an array containing the element. Also, if no elements are deleted, it returns nothing instead of returning an empty array. Netscape implementions of JavaScript emulate this buggy behavior whenever Version 1.2 of the language is explicitly specified.

See Also

Array.slice( )

Array.toLocaleString( )

JavaScript 1.5; JScript 5.5; ECMAScript v1

convert an array to a localized string

Overrides Object.toLocaleString( )

Core JavaScript Reference

Synopsis

```
array.toLocaleString( )
```

Returns

A localized string representation of *array*.

Throws

TypeError

If this method is invoked on an object that is not an Array.

Description

The toString( ) method of an array returns a localized string representation of an array. It does this by calling the toLocaleString( ) method of all of the array elements, then concatenating the resulting strings using a locale-specific separator character.

See Also

Array.toString( ), Object.toLocaleString( )

Array.toString( )

JavaScript 1.1; JScript 2.0; ECMAScript v1

convert an array to a string

Overrides Object.toString( )

Synopsis

```
array.toString( )
```

Returns

A string representation of *array*.

Throws

TypeError

If this method is invoked on an object that is not an Array.

Description

The `toString( )` method of an array converts an array to a string and returns the string. When an array is used in a string context, JavaScript automatically converts it to a string by calling this method. On some occasions, however, you may want to call `toString( )` explicitly.

`toString( )` converts an array to a string by first converting each of the array elements to strings (by calling their `toString( )` methods). Once each element is converted to a string, it outputs them in a comma-separated list. This return value is the same string that would be returned by the `join( )` method with no arguments.

Bugs

In Netscape implementations, when Version 1.2 of the language is explicitly specified, `toString( )` returns its list of comma-and-space-separated array elements within square brackets using array literal notation. This occurs, for example, when the `language` attribute of a `<script>` tag is explicitly specified as "JavaScript1.2".

See Also

Array.toLocaleString( ), Object.toString( )

Array.unshift( )

JavaScript 1.2; JScript 5.5; ECMAScript v3

insert elements at the beginning of an array

Synopsis

array.unshift(*value*, ...)

Arguments

value, ...

One or more values that are to be inserted at the start of *array*.

Returns

The new length of the array.

Description

`unshift( )` inserts its arguments at the beginning of *array*, shifting the existing elements to higher indexes to make room. The first argument to `shift( )` becomes the new element 0 of the array, the second argument, if any, becomes the new element 1, and so on. Note that `unshift( )` does not create a new array; it modifies *array* directly.

Example

`unshift( )` is often used in conjunction with `shift( )`. For example:

```
var a = [];              // a:[]
a.unshift(1);            // a:[1]          Returns: 1
a.unshift(22);           // a:[22,1]       Returns: 2
```

```
a.shift();            // a:[1]         Returns: 22
a.unshift(33,[4,5]);  // a:[33,[4,5],1] Returns: 3
```

See Also

Array.shift()

Boolean

JavaScript 1.1; JScript 2.0; ECMAScript v1

support for boolean values

Inherits from Object

Constructor

```
new Boolean(value)  // Constructor function
Boolean(value)      // Conversion function
```

Arguments

value
The value to be held by the Boolean object or to be converted to a boolean value.

Returns

When invoked as a constructor with the new operator, Boolean( ) converts its argument to a boolean value and returns a Boolean object that contains that value. When invoked as a function, without the new operator, Boolean( ) simply converts its argument to a primitive boolean value and returns that value.

The values 0, NaN, null, the empty string "", and the undefined value are all converted to false. All other primitive values, except false (but including the string "false"), and all objects and arrays are converted to true.

Methods

toString( )
Returns true or false, depending on the boolean value represented by the Boolean object.

valueOf( )
Returns the primitive boolean value contained in the Boolean object.

Description

Boolean values are a fundamental data type in JavaScript. The Boolean object is an object wrapper around the boolean value. This Boolean object type exists primarily to provide a toString( ) method to convert boolean values to strings. When the toString( ) method is invoked to convert a boolean value to a string (and it is often invoked implicitly by JavaScript) JavaScript internally converts the boolean value to a transient Boolean object, on which the method can be invoked.

See Also

Object

Boolean.toString( )

JavaScript 1.1; JScript 2.0; ECMAScript v1

convert a boolean value to a string

Overrides Object.toString( )

Synopsis

```
b.toString( )
```

Returns

The string "true" or "false", depending on the value of the primitive boolean value or Boolean object *b*.

Throws

`TypeError`
: If this method is invoked on an object that is not a Boolean.

Boolean.valueOf( )

JavaScript 1.1; JScript 2.0; ECMAScript v1

the boolean value of a Boolean object

Overrides Object.valueOf( )

Synopsis

```
b.valueOf( )
```

Returns

The primitive boolean value held by the Boolean object *b*.

Throws

`TypeError`
: If this method is invoked on an object that is not a Boolean.

Date

JavaScript 1.0; JScript 1.0; ECMAScript v1

manipulate dates and times

Inherits from Object

Constructor

```
new Date( )
new Date(milliseconds)
new Date(datestring)
new Date(year, month, day, hours, minutes, seconds, ms)
```

With no arguments, the `Date( )` constructor creates a Date object set to the current date and time. When one numeric argument is passed, it is taken as the internal numeric representation of the date in milliseconds, as returned by the `getTime( )` method. When one string argument is passed, it is a string representation of a date, in the format accepted by the `Date.parse( )` method. Otherwise, the constructor is passed between two and seven numeric arguments that specify the individual fields of the date and time. All but the first two arguments—the year and month fields—are optional. Note that these date and time fields are specified using local time, not UTC (similar to GMT) time. See the static `Date.UTC( )` method for an alternative.

`Date()` may also be called as a function, without the `new` operator. When invoked in this way, `Date()` ignores any arguments passed to it and returns a string representation of the current date and time.

Arguments

milliseconds
: The number of milliseconds between the desired date and midnight on January 1, 1970 (UTC). For example, passing the argument 5000 would create a date that represents five seconds past midnight on 1/1/70.

datestring
: A single argument that specifies the date and, optionally, the time as a String. The string should be in a format accepted by `Date.parse()`.

year
: The year, in four-digit format. For example, specify `2001` for the year 2001. For compatibility with early implementations of JavaScript, if this argument is between 0 and 99, 1900 is added to it.

month
: The month, specified as an integer from 0 (January) to 11 (December).

day
: The day of the month, specified as an integer from 1 to 31. Note that this argument uses 1 as its lowest value, while other arguments use 0 as their lowest value. Optional.

hours
: The hour, specified as an integer from 0 (midnight) to 23 (11 p.m.). Optional.

minutes
: The minutes in the hour, specified as an integer from 0 to 59. Optional.

seconds
: The seconds in the minute, specified as an integer from 0 to 59. Optional.

ms
: The milliseconds in the second, specified as an integer from 0 to 999. Optional.

Methods

The Date object has no properties that can be read and written directly; instead, all access to date and time values is done through methods. Most methods of the Date object come in two forms: one that operates using local time, and one that operates using universal (UTC or GMT) time. If a method has "UTC" in its name, it operates using universal time. These pairs of methods are listed together below. For example, the listing for `get[UTC]Day()` refers to both the methods `getDay()` and `getUTCDay()`.

Date methods may be invoked only on Date objects and throw a TypeError exception if you attempt to invoke them on any other type of object.

`get[UTC]Date()`
: Returns the day of the month of a Date object, in local or universal time.

`get[UTC]Day()`
: Returns the day of the week of a Date object, in local or universal time.

`get[UTC]FullYear()`
: Returns the year of the date in full four-digit form, in local or universal time.

`get[UTC]Hours()`
: Returns the hours field of a Date object, in local or universal time.

`get[UTC]Milliseconds()`
: Returns the milliseconds field of a Date object, in local or universal time.

`get[UTC]Minutes()`
: Returns the minutes field of a Date object, in local or universal time.

`get[UTC]Month()`
: Returns the month field of a Date object, in local or universal time.

`get[UTC]Seconds()`
: Returns the seconds field of a Date object, in local or universal time.

`getTime()`
: Returns the internal, millisecond representation of a Date object. Note that this value is independent of time zone, and therefore, there is not a separate `getUTCTime()` method.

`getTimezoneOffset()`
: Returns the difference, in minutes, between the local and UTC representations of this date. Note that the value returned depends on whether daylight savings time is or would be in effect at the specified date.

`getYear()`
: Returns the year field of a Date object. Deprecated in favor of `getFullYear()`.

`set[UTC]Date()`
: Sets the day of the month field of the date, using local or universal time.

`set[UTC]FullYear()`
: Sets the year (and optionally month and day) of the date, using local or universal time.

`set[UTC]Hours()`
: Sets the hour (and optionally the minutes, seconds, and milliseconds fields) of the date, using local or universal time.

`set[UTC]Milliseconds()`
: Sets the milliseconds field of a date, using local or universal time.

`set[UTC]Minutes()`
: Sets the minutes field (and optionally the seconds and milliseconds fields) of a date, using local or universal time.

`set[UTC]Month()`
: Sets the month field (and optionally the day of the month) of a date, using local or universal time.

`set[UTC]Seconds()`
: Sets the seconds field (and optionally the milliseconds field) of a date, using local or universal time.

`setTime()`
: Sets the fields of a Date object using the millisecond format.

`setYear()`
: Sets the year field of a Date object. Deprecated in favor of `setFullYear()`.

`toDateString()`
: Returns a string that represents the date portion of the date, expressed in the local time zone.

`toGMTString()`
: Converts a Date to a string, using the GMT time zone. Deprecated in favor of `toUTCString()`.

`toLocaleDateString()`
: Returns a string that represents the date portion of the date, expressed in the local time zone, using the local date formatting conventions.

`toLocaleString()`
: Converts a Date to a string, using the local time zone and the local date formatting conventions.

`toLocaleTimeString()`
: Returns a string that represents the time portion of the date, expressed in the local time zone, using the local time formatting conventions.

`toString()`
: Converts a Date to a string using the local time zone.

`toTimeString()`
: Returns a string that represents the time portion of the date, expressed in the local time zone.

`toUTCString()`
: Converts a Date to a string, using universal time.

`valueOf()`
: Converts a Date to its internal millisecond format.

Static Methods

In addition to the many instance methods listed above, the Date object also defines two static methods. These methods are invoked through the `Date()` constructor itself, not through individual Date objects:

`Date.parse()`
: Parses a string representation of a date and time and returns the internal millisecond representation of that date.

`Date.UTC()`
: Returns the millisecond representation of the specified UTC date and time.

Description

The Date object is a data type built into the JavaScript language. Date objects are created with the `new Date()` syntax shown in the preceding "Constructor" section.

Once a Date object is created, there are a number of methods that allow you to operate on it. Most of the methods simply allow you to get and set the year, month, day, hour, minute, second, and millisecond fields of the object, using either local time or UTC (universal, or GMT) time. The `toString()` method and its variants convert dates to human-readable strings. `getTime()` and `setTime()` convert to and from the internal representation of the Date object—the number of milliseconds since midnight (GMT) on January 1, 1970. In this standard millisecond format, a date and time are represented by a single integer, which makes date arithmetic particularly easy. The ECMAScript standard requires the Date object to be able to represent any date and time, to millisecond precision, within 100 million days before or after 1/1/1970. This is a range of plus or minus 273,785 years, so the JavaScript clock will not "roll over" until the year 275755.

Example

Once you create a Date object, there are a variety of methods you can use to operate on it:

```
d = new Date( );  // Get the current date and time
document.write('Today is: " + d.toLocaleDateString( ) + '. ');  // Display date
document.write('The time is: ' + d.toLocaleTimeString( ));      // Display time
var dayOfWeek = d.getDay( );                                  // What weekday is it?
var weekend = (dayOfWeek == 0) || (dayOfWeek == 6);  // Is it a weekend?
```

Another common use of the Date object is to subtract the millisecond representations of the current time from some other time to determine the difference between the two times. The following client-side example shows two such uses:

```
<script language="JavaScript">
today = new Date( );         // Make a note of today's date
christmas = new Date( );  // Get a date with the current year
christmas.setMonth(11);  // Set the month to December...
christmas.setDate(25);    // and the day to the 25th

// If Christmas hasn't already passed, compute the number of
// milliseconds between now and Christmas, convert this
// to a number of days and print a message
if (today.getTime( ) < christmas.getTime( )) {
    difference = christmas.getTime( ) - today.getTime( );
    difference = Math.floor(difference / (1000 * 60 * 60 * 24));
    document.write('Only ' + difference + ' days until Christmas!<p>');
}
</script>

// ... rest of HTML document here ...

<script language="JavaScript">
// Here we use Date objects for timing
// We divide by 1000 to convert milliseconds to seconds
now = new Date( );
document.write('<p>It took ' +
    (now.getTime( )-today.getTime( ))/1000 +
    'seconds to load this page.');
</script>
```

See Also

Date.parse( ), Date.UTC( )

Date.getDate( ) — JavaScript 1.0; JScript 1.0; ECMAScript v1

return the day of the month

Synopsis

date.getDate( )

Returns

The day of the month of the specified Date object *date*, using local time. Return values are between 1 and 31.

Date.getDay( )

JavaScript 1.0; JScript 1.0; ECMAScript v1

return the day of the week

Synopsis

```
date.getDay( )
```

Returns

The day of the week of the specified Date object *date*, using local time. Return values are between 0 (Sunday) and 6 (Saturday).

Date.getFullYear( )

JavaScript 1.2; JScript 3.0; ECMAScript v1

return the year

Synopsis

```
date.getFullYear( )
```

Returns

The year that results when *date* is expressed in local time. The return value is a full four-digit year, including the century, not a two-digit abbreviation.

Date.getHours( )

JavaScript 1.0; JScript 1.0; ECMAScript v1

return the hours field of a Date

Synopsis

```
date.getHours( )
```

Returns

The hours field, expressed in local time, of the specified Date object *date*. Return values are between 0 (midnight) and 23 (11 p.m.).

Date.getMilliseconds( )

JavaScript 1.2; JScript 3.0; ECMAScript v1

return the milliseconds field of a Date

Synopsis

```
date.getMilliseconds( )
```

Returns

The milliseconds field, expressed in local time, of *date*.

Date.getMinutes( )

JavaScript 1.0; JScript 1.0; ECMAScript v1

return the minutes field of a Date

Synopsis

date.getMinutes( )

Returns

The minutes field, expressed in local time, of the specified Date object *date*. Return values are between 0 and 59.

Date.getMonth( )

JavaScript 1.0; JScript 1.0; ECMAScript v1

return the month of a Date

Synopsis

date.getMonth( )

Returns

The month field, expressed in local time, of the specified Date object *date*. Return values are between 0 (January) and 11 (December).

Date.getSeconds( )

JavaScript 1.0; JScript 1.0; ECMAScript v1

return the seconds field of a Date

Synopsis

date.getSeconds( )

Returns

The seconds field, expressed in local time, of the specified Date object *date*. Return values are between 0 and 59.

Date.getTime( )

JavaScript 1.0; JScript 1.0; ECMAScript v1

return a Date in milliseconds

Synopsis

date.getTime( )

Returns

The millisecond representation of the specified Date object *date*; that is, the number of milliseconds between midnight (GMT) on 1/1/1970 and the date and time specified by *date*.

Description

`getTime( )` converts a date and time to a single integer. This is useful when you want to compare two Date objects or to determine the time elapsed between two dates. Note that the millisecond representation of a date is independent of the time zone, so there is no `getUTCTime()` method in addition to this one. Don't confuse this `getTime()` method with the `getDay()` and `getDate()` methods, which return the day of the week and the day of the month, respectively.

`Date.parse()` and `Date.UTC()` allow you to convert a date and time specification to millisecond representation without going through the overhead of first creating a Date object.

See Also

Date, Date.parse(), Date.setTime(), Date.UTC()

Date.getTimezoneOffset()

JavaScript 1.0; JScript 1.0; ECMAScript v1

determine the offset from GMT

Synopsis

```
date.getTimezoneOffset()
```

Returns

The difference, in minutes, between Greenwich Mean Time (GMT) and local time.

Description

`getTimezoneOffset()` returns the number of minutes difference between the GMT or UTC time and the local time. In effect, this function tells you what time zone the JavaScript code is running in and whether or not daylight savings time is (or would be) in effect at the specified *date*.

The return value is measured in minutes, rather than hours, because some countries have time zones that are not at even one-hour intervals.

Date.getUTCDate()

JavaScript 1.2; JScript 3.0; ECMAScript v1

return the day of the month (universal time)

Synopsis

```
date.getUTCDate()
```

Returns

The day of the month (a value between 1 and 31) that results when *date* is expressed in universal time.

Date.getUTCDay()

JavaScript 1.2; JScript 3.0; ECMAScript v1

return the day of the week (universal time)

Synopsis

```
date.getUTCDay()
```

Returns

The day of the week that results when *date* is expressed in universal time. Return values are between 0 (Sunday) and 6 (Saturday).

Date.getUTCFullYear( )

JavaScript 1.2; JScript 3.0; ECMAScript v1

return the year (universal time)

Synopsis

```
date.getUTCFullYear( )
```

Returns

The year that results when *date* is expressed in universal time. The return value is a full four-digit year, not a two-digit abbreviation.

Date.getUTCHours( )

JavaScript 1.2; JScript 3.0; ECMAScript v1

return the hours field of a Date (universal time)

Synopsis

```
date.getUTCHours( )
```

Returns

The hours field, expressed in universal time, of *date*. The return value is an integer between 0 (midnight) and 23 (11 p.m.).

Date.getUTCMilliseconds( )

JavaScript 1.2; JScript 3.0; ECMAScript v1

return the milliseconds field of a Date (universal time)

Synopsis

```
date.getUTCMilliseconds( )
```

Returns

The milliseconds field, expressed in universal time, of *date*.

Date.getUTCMinutes( )

JavaScript 1.2; JScript 3.0; ECMAScript v1

return the minutes field of a Date (universal time)

Synopsis

```
date.getUTCMinutes( )
```

Returns

The minutes field, expressed in universal time, of *date*. The return value is an integer between 0 and 59.

Date.getUTCMonth( )

JavaScript 1.2; JScript 3.0; ECMAScript v1

return the month of the year (universal time)

Synopsis

date.getUTCMonth( )

Returns

The month of the year that results when *date* is expressed in universal time. The return value is an integer between 0 (January) and 11 (December). Note that the Date object represents the first day of the month as 1 but represents the first month of the year as 0.

Date.getUTCSeconds( )

JavaScript 1.2; JScript 3.0; ECMAScript v1

return the seconds field of a Date (universal time)

Synopsis

date.getUTCSeconds( )

Returns

The seconds field, expressed in universal time, of *date*. The return value is an integer between 0 and 59.

Date.getYear( )

JavaScript 1.0; JScript 1.0; ECMAScript v1; deprecated by ECMAScript v3

return the year field of a Date

Synopsis

date.getYear( )

Returns

The year field of the specified Date object *date* minus 1900.

Description

getYear( ) returns the year field of a specified Date object minus 1900. As of ECMAScript v3, it is not required in conforming JavaScript implementations; use getFullYear( ) instead.

Bugs

Netscape implementations of JavaScript 1.0 through 1.2 subtract 1900 only for years between 1900 and 1999.

Date.parse( )

JavaScript 1.0; JScript 1.0; ECMAScript v1

parse a date/time string

Synopsis

Date.parse(*date*)

Arguments

date

A string containing the date and time to be parsed.

Returns

The number of milliseconds between the specified date and time and midnight GMT on January 1, 1970.

Description

`Date.parse( )` is a static method of Date. It is always invoked through the `Date` constructor as `Date.parse( )`, not through a Date object as *`date`*`.parse( )`. `Date.parse( )` takes a single string argument. It parses the date contained in this string and returns it in millisecond format, which can be used directly, used to create a new Date object, or used to set the date in an existing Date object with `Date.setTime( )`.

The ECMAScript standard does not specify the format of the strings that can be parsed by `Date.parse( )` except to say that this method can parse the strings returned by the `Date.toString( )` and `Date.toUTCString( )` methods. Unfortunately, these functions format dates in an implementation-dependent way, so it is not in general possible to write dates in a way that is guaranteed to be understood by all JavaScript implementations.

See Also

Date, Date.setTime( ), Date.toGMTString( ), Date.UTC( )

Date.setDate( ) JavaScript 1.0; JScript 1.0; ECMAScript v1

set the day of the month

Synopsis

`date``.setDate(`*`day_of_month`*`)`

Arguments

day_of_month

An integer between 1 and 31 that is used as the new value (in local time) of the day-of-month field of *date*.

Returns

The millisecond representation of the adjusted date. Prior to ECMAScript standardization, this method returns nothing.

Date.setFullYear( ) JavaScript 1.2; JScript 3.0; ECMAScript v1

set the year and, optionally, the month and date

Synopsis

```
date.setFullYear(year)
date.setFullYear(year, month)
date.setFullYear(year, month, day)
```

Arguments

year

The year, expressed in local time, to be set in *date*. This argument should be an integer that includes the century, such as 1999; it should not be an abbreviation, such as 99.

month

An optional integer, between 0 and 11 that is used as the new value (in local time) of the month field of *date*.

day

An optional integer, between 1 and 31 that is used as the new value (in local time) of the day-of-month field of *date*.

Returns

The internal millisecond representation of the adjusted date.

Date.setHours( )

JavaScript 1.0; JScript 1.0; ECMAScript v1

set the hours, minutes, seconds, and milliseconds fields of a Date

Synopsis

```
date.setHours(hours)
date.setHours(hours, minutes)
date.setHours(hours, minutes, seconds)
date.setHours(hours, minutes, seconds, millis)
```

Arguments

hours

An integer between 0 (midnight) and 23 (11 p.m.) local time that is set as the new hours value of *date*.

minutes

An optional integer, between 0 and 59, that is used as the new value (in local time) of the minutes field of *date*. This argument is not supported prior to ECMAScript standardization.

seconds

An optional integer, between 0 and 59, that is used as the new value (in local time) of the seconds field of *date*. This argument is not supported prior to ECMAScript standardization.

millis

An optional integer, between 0 and 999, that is used as the new value (in local time) of the milliseconds field of *date*. This argument is not supported prior to ECMAScript standardization.

Returns

The millisecond representation of the adjusted date. Prior to ECMAScript standardization, this method returns nothing.

Date.setMilliseconds( )

JavaScript 1.2; JScript 3.0; ECMAScript v1

set the milliseconds field of a Date

Synopsis

```
date.setMilliseconds(millis)
```

Arguments

millis
: The milliseconds field, expressed in local time, to be set in *date*. This argument should be an integer between 0 and 999.

Returns

The millisecond representation of the adjusted date.

Date.setMinutes( )

JavaScript 1.0; JScript 1.0; ECMAScript v1

set the minutes and seconds fields of a Date

Synopsis

```
date.setMinutes(minutes)
date.setMinutes(minutes, seconds)
date.setMinutes(minutes, seconds, millis)
```

Arguments

minutes
: An integer between 0 and 59 that is set as the minutes value (in local time) of the Date object *date*.

seconds
: An optional integer, between 0 and 59, that is used as the new value (in local time) of the seconds field of *date*. This argument is not supported prior to ECMAScript standardization.

millis
: An optional integer, between 0 and 999, that is used as the new value (in local time) of the milliseconds field of *date*. This argument is not supported prior to ECMAScript standardization.

Returns

The millisecond representation of the adjusted date. Prior to ECMAScript standardization, this method returns nothing.

Date.setMonth( )

JavaScript 1.0; JScript 1.0; ECMAScript v1

set the month and day fields of a Date

Synopsis

```
date.setMonth(month)
date.setMonth(month, day)
```

Arguments

month

An integer between 0 (January) and 11 (December) that is set as the month value (in local time) for the Date object *date*. Note that months are numbered beginning with 0, while days within the month are numbered beginning with 1.

day

An optional integer, between 1 and 31 that is used as the new value (in local time) of the day-of-month field of *date*. This argument is not supported prior to ECMAScript standardization.

Returns

The millisecond representation of the adjusted date. Prior to ECMAScript standardization, this method returns nothing.

Date.setSeconds( )

JavaScript 1.0; JScript 1.0; ECMAScript v1

set the seconds and milliseconds fields of a Date

Synopsis

```
date.setSeconds(seconds)
date.setSeconds(seconds, millis)
```

Arguments

seconds

An integer between 0 and 59 that is set as the seconds value for the Date object *date*.

millis

An optional integer, between 0 and 999, that is used as the new value (in local time) of the milliseconds field of *date*. This argument is not supported prior to ECMAScript standardization.

Returns

The millisecond representation of the adjusted date. Prior to ECMAScript standardization, this method returns nothing.

Date.setTime( )

JavaScript 1.0; JScript 1.0; ECMAScript v1

set a Date in milliseconds

Synopsis

```
date.setTime(milliseconds)
```

Arguments

milliseconds

The number of milliseconds between the desired date and time and midnight GMT on January 1, 1970. A millisecond value of this type may also be passed to the `Date( )` constructor and may be obtained by calling the `Date.UTC( )` and `Date.parse( )` methods. Representing a date in this millisecond format makes it independent of time zone.

Returns

The *milliseconds* argument. Prior to ECMAScript standardization, this method returns nothing.

Date.setUTCDate( )

JavaScript 1.2; JScript 3.0; ECMAScript v1

set the day of the month (universal time)

Synopsis

```
date.setUTCDate(day_of_month)
```

Arguments

day_of_month
: The day of the month, expressed in universal time, to be set in *date*. This argument should be an integer between 1 and 31.

Returns

The internal millisecond representation of the adjusted date.

Date.setUTCFullYear( )

JavaScript 1.2; JScript 3.0; ECMAScript v1

set the year, month, and day (universal time)

Synopsis

```
date.setUTCFullYear(year)
date.setUTCFullYear(year, month)
date.setUTCFullYear(year, month, day)
```

Arguments

year
: The year, expressed in universal time, to be set in *date*. This argument should be an integer that includes the century, such as 1999, not be an abbreviation, such as 99.

month
: An optional integer, between 0 and 11 that is used as the new value (in universal time) of the month field of *date*.

day
: An optional integer, between 1 and 31 that is used as the new value (in universal time) of the day-of-month field of *date*.

Returns

The internal millisecond representation of the adjusted date.

Date.setUTCHours( )

JavaScript 1.2; JScript 3.0; ECMAScript v1

set the hours, minutes, seconds, and milliseconds fields of a Date (universal time)

Synopsis

```
date.setUTCHours(hours)
date.setUTCHours(hours, minutes)
date.setUTCHours(hours, minutes, seconds)
date.setUTCHours(hours, minutes, seconds, millis)
```

Arguments

hours
: The hours field, expressed in universal time, to be set in *date*. This argument should be an integer between 0 (midnight) and 23 (11 p.m.).

minutes
: An optional integer, between 0 and 59, that is used as the new value (in universal time) of the minutes field of *date*.

seconds
: An optional integer, between 0 and 59, that is used as the new value (in universal time) of the seconds field of *date*.

millis
: An optional integer, between 0 and 999, that is used as the new value (in universal time) of the milliseconds field of *date*.

Returns

The millisecond representation of the adjusted date.

Date.setUTCMilliseconds( )

JavaScript 1.2; JScript 3.0; ECMAScript v1

set the milliseconds field of a Date (universal time)

Synopsis

```
date.setUTCMilliseconds(millis)
```

Arguments

millis
: The milliseconds field, expressed in universal time, to be set in *date*. This argument should be an integer between 0 and 999.

Returns

The millisecond representation of the adjusted date.

Date.setUTCMinutes( )

JavaScript 1.2; JScript 3.0; ECMAScript v1

set the minutes and seconds fields of a Date (universal time)

Synopsis

```
date.setUTCMinutes(minutes)
date.setUTCMinutes(minutes, seconds)
date.setUTCMinutes(minutes, seconds, millis)
```

Arguments

minutes
: The minutes field, expressed in universal time, to be set in *date*. This argument should be an integer between 0 and 59.

seconds
: An optional integer, between 0 and 59, that is used as the new value (in universal time) of the seconds field of *date*.

millis
: An optional integer, between 0 and 999, that is used as the new value (in universal time) of the milliseconds field of *date*.

Returns

The millisecond representation of the adjusted date.

Date.setUTCMonth( )

JavaScript 1.2; JScript 3.0; ECMAScript v1

set the month and day fields of a Date (universal time)

Synopsis

```
date.setUTCMonth(month)
date.setUTCMonth(month, day)
```

Arguments

month
: The month, expressed in universal time, to be set in *date*. This argument should be an integer between 0 (January) and 11 (December). Note that months are numbered beginning with 0, while days within the month are numbered beginning with 1.

day
: An optional integer, between 1 and 31 that is used as the new value (in universal time) of the day-of-month field of *date*.

Returns

The millisecond representation of the adjusted date.

Date.setUTCSeconds( )

JavaScript 1.2; JScript 3.0; ECMAScript v1

set the seconds and milliseconds fields of a Date (universal time)

Synopsis

```
date.setUTCSeconds(seconds)
date.setUTCSeconds(seconds, millis)
```

Arguments

seconds
: The seconds field, expressed in universal time, to be set in *date*. This argument should be an integer between 0 and 59.

millis
: An optional integer, between 0 and 999, that is used as the new value (in universal time) of the milliseconds field of *date*.

Returns

The millisecond representation of the adjusted date.

Date.setYear( )

JavaScript 1.0; JScript 1.0; ECMAScript v1; deprecated by ECMAScript v3

set the year field of a Date

Synopsis

```
date.setYear(year)
```

Arguments

year
: An integer that is set as the year value (in local time) for the Date object *date*. If this value is between 0 and 99, inclusive, 1900 is added to it and it is treated as a year between 1900 and 1999.

Returns

The millisecond representation of the adjusted date. Prior to ECMAScript standardization, this method returns nothing.

Description

`setYear( )` sets the year field of a specified Date object, with special behavior for years between 1900 and 1999.

As of ECMAScript v3, this function is no longer required in conforming JavaScript implementations; use `setFullYear( )` instead.

Date.toDateString( )

JavaScript 1.5; JScript 5.5; ECMAScript v3

return the date portion of a Date as a string

Synopsis

`date.toDateString( )`

Returns

An implementation-dependent human-readable string representation of the date portion of *date*, expressed in the local time zone.

See Also

Date.toLocaleDateString( ), Date.toLocaleString( ), Date.toLocaleTimeString( ), Date.toString( ), Date.toTimeString( )

Date.toGMTString( )

JavaScript 1.0; JScript 1.0; ECMAScript v1; deprecated by ECMAScript v3

convert a Date to a universal time string

Synopsis

`date.toGMTString( )`

Returns

A string representation of the date and time specified by the Date object *date*. The date is converted from the local time zone to the GMT time zone before being converted to a string.

Description

`toGMTString( )` is deprecated in favor of the identical method `Date.toUTCString( )`.

As of ECMAScript v3, conforming implementations of JavaScript are no longer required to provide this method; use `toUTCString( )` instead.

See Also

Date.toUTCString()

Date.toLocaleDateString( )

JavaScript 1.5; JScript 5.5; ECMAScript v3

return the date portion of a Date as a locally formatted string

Synopsis

`date.toLocaleDateString( )`

Returns

An implementation-dependent human-readable string representation of the date portion of *date*, expressed in the local time zone and formatted according to local conventions.

See Also

Date.toDateString( ), Date.toLocaleString( ), Date.toLocaleTimeString( ), Date.toString( ), Date.toTimeString( )

Date.toLocaleString( )

JavaScript 1.0; JScript 1.0; ECMAScript v1

convert a Date to a locally formatted string

Synopsis

```
date.toLocaleString( )
```

Returns

A string representation of the date and time specified by *date*. The date and time are represented in the local time zone and formatted using locally appropriate conventions.

Usage

`toLocaleString( )` converts a date to a string, using the local time zone. This method also uses local conventions for date and time formatting, so the format may vary from platform to platform and from country to country. `toLocaleString( )` returns a string formatted in what is likely the user's preferred date and time format.

See Also

Date.toLocaleDateString( ), Date.toLocaleTimeString( ), Date.toString( ), Date.toUTCString( )

Date.toLocaleTimeString( )

JavaScript 1.5; JScript 5.5; ECMAScript v3

return the time portion of a Date as a locally formatted string

Synopsis

```
date.toLocaleTimeString( )
```

Returns

An implementation-dependent human-readable string representation of the time portion of *date*, expressed in the local time zone and formatted according to local conventions.

See Also

Date.toDateString( ), Date.toLocaleDateString( ), Date.toLocaleString( ), Date.toString( ), Date.toTimeString( )

Date.toString( )

JavaScript 1.0; JScript 1.0; ECMAScript v1

convert a Date to a string

Overrides Object.toString( )

Synopsis

```
date.toString( )
```

Returns

A human-readable string representation of *date*, expressed in the local time zone.

Description

`toString( )` returns a human-readable, implementation-dependent string representation of *date*. Unlike `toUTCString( )`, `toString( )` expresses the date in the local time zone. Unlike `toLocaleString( )`, `toString( )` may not represent the date and time using locale-specific formatting.

See Also

Date.parse(), Date.toDateString(), Date.toLocaleString(), Date.toTimeString(), Date.toUTCString()

Date.toTimeString( )

JavaScript 1.5; JScript 5.5; ECMAScript v3

return the time portion of a Date as a string

Synopsis

```
date.toTimeString( )
```

Returns

A implementation-dependent human-readable string representation of the time portion of *date*, expressed in the local time zone.

See Also

Date.toString(), Date.toDateString(), Date.toLocaleDateString(), Date.toLocaleString(), Date.toLocaleTimeString()

Date.toUTCString( )

JavaScript 1.2; JScript 3.0; ECMAScript v1

convert a Date to a string (universal time)

Synopsis

```
date.toUTCString( )
```

Returns

A human-readable string representation, expressed in universal time, of *date*.

Description

`toUTCString( )` returns an implementation-dependent string that represents *date* in universal time.

See Also

Date.toLocaleString(), Date.toString()

Date.UTC( )

JavaScript 1.0; JScript 1.0; ECMAScript v1

convert a Date specification to milliseconds

Synopsis

```
Date.UTC(year, month, day, hours, minutes, seconds, ms)
```

Arguments

year
: The year in four-digit format. If this argument is between 0 and 99, inclusive, 1900 will be added to it and it will be treated as a year between 1900 and 1999.

month
: The month, specified as an integer from 0 (January) to 11 (December).

day
: The day of the month, specified as an integer from 1 to 31. Note that this argument uses 1 as its lowest value, while other arguments use 0 as their lowest value. This argument is optional.

hours
: The hour, specified as an integer from 0 (midnight) to 23 (11 p.m.). This argument is optional.

minutes
: The minutes in the hour, specified as an integer from 0 to 59. This argument is optional.

seconds
: The seconds in the minute, specified as an integer from 0 to 59. This argument is optional.

ms
: The number of milliseconds. This argument is optional and is ignored prior to ECMAScript standardization.

Returns

The millisecond representation of the specified universal time. That is, this method returns the number of milliseconds between midnight GMT on January 1, 1970 and the specified time.

Description

`Date.UTC( )` is a static method; it is invoked through the `Date( )` constructor, not through an individual Date object.

The arguments to `Date.UTC( )` specify a date and time and are understood to be in UTC (Universal Coordinated Time)—they are in the GMT time zone. The specified UTC time is converted to the millisecond format, which can be used by the `Date( )` constructor method and by the `Date.setTime( )` method.

The `Date( )` constructor method can accept date and time arguments identical to those that `Date.UTC( )` accepts. The difference is that the `Date( )` constructor assumes local time, while

`Date.UTC( )` assumes universal time (GMT). To create a Date object using a UTC time specification, you can use code like this:

```
d = new Date(Date.UTC(1996, 4, 8, 16, 30));
```

See Also

Date, Date.parse(), Date.setTime()

Date.valueOf( )

JavaScript 1.1; ECMAScript v1

convert a Date to millisecond representation — **Overrides Object.valueOf( )**

Synopsis

date`.valueOf( )`

Returns

The millisecond representation of *date*. The value returned is the same as that returned by `Date.getTime( )`.

decodeURI( )

JavaScript 1.5; JScript 5.5; ECMAScript v3

unescape characters in a URI

Synopsis

`decodeURI(`*uri*`)`

Arguments

uri
: A string that contains an encoded URI or other text to be decoded.

Returns

A copy of *uri*, with any hexadecimal escape sequences replaced with the characters they represent.

Throws

`URIError`
: Indicates that one or more of the escape sequences in *uri* is malformed and cannot be correctly decoded.

Description

`decodeURI( )` is a global function that returns a decoded copy of its *uri* argument. It reverses the encoding performed by `encodeURI( )`; see that function for details.

See Also

decodeURIComponent(), encodeURI(), encodeURIComponent(), escape(), unescape()

decodeURIComponent( )

JavaScript 1.5; JScript 5.5; ECMAScript v3

unescape characters in a URI component

Synopsis

```
decodeURI(s)
```

Arguments

s A string that contains an encoded URI component or other text to be decoded.

Returns

A copy of *s*, with any hexadecimal escape sequences replaced with the characters they represent.

Throws

`URIError`
Indicates that one or more of the escape sequences in *s* is malformed and cannot be correctly decoded.

Description

`decodeURIComponent( )` is a global function that returns a decoded copy of its *s* argument. It reverses the encoding performed by `encodeURIComponent( )`. See that function's reference page for details.

See Also

decodeURI( ), encodeURI( ), encodeURIComponent( ), escape( ), unescape( )

encodeURI( )

JavaScript 1.5; JScript 5.5; ECMAScript v3

escape characters in a URI

Synopsis

```
encodeURI(uri)
```

Arguments

uri
A string that contains the URI or other text to be encoded.

Returns

A copy of *uri*, with certain characters replaced by hexadecimal escape sequences.

Throws

`URIError`
Indicates that *uri* contains malformed Unicode surrogate pairs and cannot be encoded.

Description

encodeURI( ) is a global function that returns an encoded copy of its *uri* argument. ASCII letters and digits are not encoded, nor are the following ASCII punctuation characters:

```
- _ . ! ~ * ' ( )
```

Because encodeURI( ) is intended to encode complete URIs, the following ASCII punctuation characters, which have special meaning in URIs, are not escaped either:

```
; / ? : @ & = + $ , #
```

Any other characters in *uri* are replaced by converting the character to its UTF-8 encoding and then encoding each of the resulting one, two, or three bytes with a hexadecimal escape sequence of the form %xx. In this encoding scheme, ASCII characters are replaced with a single %xx escape, characters with encodings between \u0080 and \u07ff are replaced with two escape sequences, and all other 16-bit Unicode characters are replaced with three escape sequences.

If you use this method to encode a URI, you should be certain that none of the components of the URI (such as the query string) contain URI separator characters such as ? and #. If the components may contain these characters, you should encode each component separately with encodeURIComponent( ).

Use decodeURI( ) to reverse the encoding applied by this method. Prior to ECMAScript v3, you can use escape( ) and unescape( ) methods (which are now deprecated) to perform a similar kind of encoding and decoding.

Example

```
// Returns http://www.isp.com/app.cgi?arg1=1&arg2=hello%20world
encodeURI("http://www.isp.com/app.cgi?arg1=1&arg2=hello world");
encodeURI("\u00a9");  // The copyright character encodes to %C2%A9
```

See Also

decodeURI( ), decodeURIComponent( ), encodeURIComponent( ), escape( ), unescape( )

encodeURIComponent( )

JavaScript 1.5; JScript 5.5; ECMAScript v3

escape characters in a URI component

Synopsis

```
encodeURIComponent(s)
```

Arguments

s A string that contains a portion of a URI or other text to be encoded.

Returns

A copy of *s*, with certain characters replaced by hexadecimal escape sequences.

Throws

URIError

Indicates that *s* contains malformed Unicode surrogate pairs and cannot be encoded.

Description

`encodeURIComponent()` is a global function that returns an encoded copy of its *s* argument. ASCII letters and digits are not encoded, nor are the following ASCII punctuation characters:

```
- _ . ! ~ * ' ( )
```

All other characters, including punctuation characters such as /, :, # that serve to separate the various components of a URI, are replaced with one or more hexadecimal escape sequences. See "encodeURI()" for a description of the encoding scheme used.

Note the difference between `encodeURIComponent()` and `encodeURI()`: `encodeURIComponent()` assumes that its argument is a portion (such as the protocol, hostname, path, or query string) of a URI. Therefore it escapes the punctuation characters that are used to separate the portions of a URI.

Example

```
encodeURIComponent("hello world?");  // Returns hello%20world%3F
```

See Also

decodeURI(), decodeURIComponent(), encodeURI(), escape(), unescape()

Error JavaScript 1.5; JScript 5.5; ECMAScript v3

a generic exception Inherits from Object

Constructor

```
new Error()
new Error(message)
```

Arguments

`message`
: An optional error message that provides details about the exception.

Returns

A newly constructed Error object. If the *`message`* argument is specified, the Error object will use it as the value of its `message` property; otherwise, it will use an implementation-defined default string as the value of that property. When the `Error()` constructor is called as a function, without the `new` operator, it behaves just as it does when called with the `new` operator.

Properties

`message`
: An error message that provides details about the exception. This property holds the string passed to the constructor or an implementation-defined default string.

`name`
: A string that specifies the type of the exception. For instances of the Error class and all of its subclasses, this property specifies the name of the constructor used to create the instance.

Methods

`toString( )`
: Returns an implementation-defined string that represents this Error object.

Description

Instances of the Error class represent errors or exceptions and are typically used with the `throw` and `try/catch` statements. The `name` property specifies the type of the exception, and the `message` property can be used to provide human-readable details about the exception.

The JavaScript interpreter never throws Error object directly; instead, it throws instances of one of the Error subclasses such as SyntaxError or RangeError. In your own code you may find it convenient to throw Error objects to signal exceptions, or you may prefer to simply throw an error message or error code as a primitive string or number value.

Note that the ECMAScript specification defines a `toString( )` method for the Error class (it is inherited by each of the subclasses of Error) but that it does not require this `toString( )` method to return a string that contains the contents of the `message` property. Therefore, you should not expect the `toString( )` method to convert an Error object to convert to a meaningful human-readable string. To display an error message to a user, you should explicitly use the `name` and `message` properties of the Error object.

Example

You might signal an exception with code like the following:

```
function factorial(x) {
    if (x < 0) throw new Error("factorial: x must be >= 0");
    if (x <= 1) return 1; else return x * factorial(x-1);
}
```

And if you catch an exception, you might display its to the user with code like the following (which uses the client-side `Window.alert( )` method):

```
try { &*(&/* an error is thrown here */ }
catch(e) {
    if (e instanceof Error) {  // Is it an instance of Error or a subclass?
        alert(e.name + ": " + e.message);
    }
}
```

See Also

EvalError, RangeError, ReferenceError, SyntaxError, TypeError, URIError

Error.message

JavaScript 1.5; JScript 5.5; ECMAScript v3

a human-readable error message

Synopsis

error.message

Description

The message property of an Error object (or of an instance of any subclass of Error) is intended to contain a human-readable string that provides details about the error or exception that occurred. If a message argument is passed to the `Error( )` constructor, this message becomes the value of the message property. If no message argument is passed, an Error object inherits an implementation-defined default value (which may be the empty string) for this property.

Error.name — JavaScript 1.5; JScript 5.5; ECMAScript v3

the type of an error

Synopsis

error.name

Description

The name property of an Error object (or of an instance of any subclass of Error) specifies the type of error or exception that occurred. All Error objects inherit this property from their constructor. The value of the property is the same as the name of the constructor. Thus SyntaxError objects have a name property of "SyntaxError" and EvalError objects have a name of "EvalError".

Error.toString( ) — JavaScript 1.5; JScript 5.5; ECMAScript v3

convert an Error object to a string — Overrides Object.toString( )

Synopsis

error.toString( )

Returns

An implementation-defined string. The ECMAScript standard does not specify anything about the return value of this method, except that it is a string. Notably, it does not require the returned string to contain the error name or the error message.

escape( ) — JavaScript 1.0; JScript 1.0; ECMAScript v1; deprecated in ECMAScript v3

encode a string

Synopsis

escape(*s*)

Arguments

s The string that is to be "escaped" or encoded.

Returns

An encoded copy of s in which certain characters have been replaced by hexadecimal escape sequences.

Description

escape() is a global function. It returns a new string that contains an encoded version of s. The string s itself is not modified.

escape() returns a string in which all characters of s other than ASCII letters, digits, and the punctuation characters @, *, _, +, –, ., and / have been replaced by escape sequences of the form %*xx* or %u*xxxx* (where *x* represents a hexadecimal digit). Unicode characters \u0000 to \u00ff are replaced with the %*xx* escape sequence, and all other Unicode characters are replaced with the %u*xxxx* sequence.

Use the unescape() function to decode a string encoded with escape().

In client-side JavaScript, a common use of escape() is to encode cookie values, which have restrictions on the punctuation characters they may contain. See the "Document.cookie" reference page in the client-side reference section.

Although the escape() function was standardized in the first version of ECMAScript, it has been deprecated and removed from the standard by ECMAScript v3. Implementations of ECMAScript are likely to implement this function, but they are not required to. In JavaScript 1.5 and JScript 5.5 and later, you should use encodeURI() and encodeURIComponent() instead of escape().

Example

```
escape("Hello World!");  // Returns "Hello%20World%21"
```

See Also

encodeURI(), encodeURIComponent(), String, unescape(); Document.cookie in the client-side reference section

eval()

JavaScript 1.0; JScript 1.0; ECMAScript v1

execute JavaScript code from a string

Synopsis

eval(*code*)

Arguments

code

A string that contains the JavaScript expression to be evaluated or the statements to be executed.

Returns

The value of the evaluated *code*, if any.

Throws

SyntaxError
: Indicates that *code* does not contain legal JavaScript.

EvalError
: Indicates that eval( ) was called illegally, through an identifier other than "eval", for example. See the restrictions on this function described below.

Other exception
: If the JavaScript code passed to eval( ) generates an exception, eval( ) will pass that exception on to the caller.

Description

eval( ) is a global method that evaluates a string containing JavaScript code. If *code* contains an expression, eval evaluates the expression and returns its value. If *code* contains a JavaScript statement or statements, eval( ) executes those statements and returns the value, if any, returned by the last statement. If *code* does not return any value, eval( ) returns undefined. Finally, if *code* throws an exception, eval( ) passes that exception on to the caller.

eval( ) provides a very powerful capability to the JavaScript language, but its use is infrequent in real-world programs. Obvious uses are to write programs that act as recursive JavaScript interpreters and to write programs that dynamically generate and evaluate JavaScript code.

Most JavaScript functions and methods that expect string arguments accept arguments of other types as well and simply convert those argument values to strings before proceeding. eval( ) does not behave like this. If the *code* argument is not a primitive string, it is simply returned unchanged. Be careful, therefore, that you do not inadvertently pass a String object to eval( ) when you intended to pass a primitive string value.

For purposes of implementation efficiency, the ECMAScript v3 standard places an unusual restriction on the use of eval( ). An ECMAScript implementation is allowed to throw an EvalError exception if you attempt to overwrite the eval property or if you assign the eval( ) method to another property and attempt to invoke it through that property.

Example

```
eval("1+2");  // Returns 3

// This code uses client-side JavaScript methods to prompt the user to
// enter an expression and to display the results of evaluating it.
// See the client-side methods Window.alert( ) and Window.prompt( ) for details.
try {
    alert("Result: " +  eval(prompt("Enter an expression:","")));
}
catch(exception) {
    alert(exception);
}

var myeval = eval;  // May throw an EvalError
myeval("1+2");      // May throw an EvalError
```

EvalError

JavaScript 1.5; JScript 5.5; ECMAScript v3

thrown when eval( ) is used improperly

Inherits from Error

Constructor

```
new EvalError( )
new EvalError(message)
```

Arguments

message

An optional error message that provides details about the exception. If specified, this argument is used as the value for the `message` property of the EvalError object.

Returns

A newly constructed EvalError object. If the *message* argument is specified, the Error object will use it as the value of its `message` property; otherwise, it will use an implementation-defined default string as the value of that property. When the `EvalError( )` constructor is called as a function, without the `new` operator, it behaves just as it does when called with the `new` operator.

Properties

`message`

An error message that provides details about the exception. This property holds the string passed to the constructor or an implementation-defined default string. See "Error.message" for details.

`name`

A string that specifies the type of the exception. All EvalError objects inherit the value "EvalError" for this property.

Description

An instance of the EvalError class may be thrown when the global function `eval( )` is invoked under any other name. See "eval()" for an explanation of the restrictions on how this function may be invoked. See "Error" for details about throwing and catching exceptions.

See Also

Error, Error.message, Error.name

Function

JavaScript 1.0; JScript 1.0; ECMAScript v1

a JavaScript function

Inherits from Object

Synopsis

```
function functionname(argument_name_list)  // Function definition statement
{
    body
}
function (argument_name_list) { body }  // Unnamed function literal; JavaScript 1.2
functionname(argument_value_list)       // Function invocation
```

Constructor

```
new Function(argument_names..., body)  // JavaScript 1.1 and later
```

Arguments

argument_names...
: Any number of string arguments, each naming one or more arguments of the Function object being created.

body
: A string that specifies the body of the function. It may contain any number of JavaScript statements, separated with semicolons, and may refer to any of the argument names specified by previous arguments to the constructor.

Returns

A newly created Function object. Invoking the function executes the JavaScript code specified by *body*.

Throws

`SyntaxError`
: Indicates that there was a JavaScript syntax error in the *body* argument or in one of the *argument_names* arguments.

Properties

`arguments[]`
: An array of arguments that were passed to the function. Deprecated.

`caller`
: A reference to the Function object that invoked this one, or `null` if the function was invoked from top-level code. Deprecated.

`length`
: The number of named arguments specified when the function was declared.

`prototype`
: An object which, for a constructor function, defines properties and methods shared by all objects created with that constructor function.

Methods

`apply()`
: Invokes a function as a method of a specified object, passing a specified array of arguments.

`call()`
: Invokes a function as a method of a specified object, passing the specified arguments.

`toString()`
: Returns a string representation of the function.

Description

A function is a fundamental data type in JavaScript. Chapter 7 explains how to define and use functions, and Chapter 8 covers the related topics of methods, constructors, and the `prototype` property of functions. See those chapters for complete details. Note that although function objects may be created with the `Function( )` constructor described here, this is not efficient, and the preferred way to define functions, in most cases, is with a function definition statement or a function literal.

In JavaScript 1.1 and later, the body of a function is automatically given a local variable, named *`arguments`*, that refers to an Arguments object. This object is an array of the values passed as arguments to the function. Don't confuse this with the deprecated `arguments[]` property listed above. See the "Arguments" reference page for details.

See Also

Arguments; Chapter 7; Chapter 8

Function.apply( )

JavaScript 1.2; JScript 5.5; ECMAScript v3

invoke a function as a method of an object

Synopsis

`function``.apply(`*`thisobj`*`, `*`args`*`)`

Arguments

`thisobj`
: The object to which *`function`* is to be applied. In the body of the function, *`thisobj`* becomes the value of the `this` keyword.

`args`
: An array of values to be passed as arguments to *`function`*.

Returns

Whatever value is returned by the invocation of *`function`*.

Throws

`TypeError`
: If this method is invoked on an object that is not a function or if this method is invoked with an *`args`* argument that is not an array or an Arguments object.

Description

`apply( )` invokes the specified *`function`* as if it were a method of *`thisobj`*, passing it the arguments contained in the *`args`* array. It returns the value returned by the function invocation. Within the body of the function, the `this` keyword refers to the *`thisobj`* object.

The *`args`* argument must be an array or an Arguments object. Use `Function.call( )` instead if you want to specify the arguments to pass to the function individually instead of as array elements.

Example

```
// Apply the default Object.toString( ) method to an object that
// overrides it with its own version of the method. Note no arguments.
Object.prototype.toString.apply(o);
```

```
// Invoke the Math.max( ) method with apply to find the largest
// element in an array. Note that first argument doesn't matter
// in this case.
var data = [1,2,3,4,5,6,7,8];
Math.max.apply(null, data);
```

See Also

Function.call( )

Function.arguments[] JavaScript 1.0; JScript 1.0; ECMAScript v1; deprecated by ECMAScript v3

arguments passed to a function

Synopsis

function.arguments[*i*]
function.arguments.length

Description

The `arguments` property of a Function object is an array of the arguments that are passed to a function. It is only defined while the function is executing. `arguments.length` specifies the number of elements in the array.

This property is deprecated in favor of the Arguments object. Although ECMAScript v1 supports the `Function.arguments` property, it has been removed from ECMAScript v3 and conforming implementations may no longer support this property. Therefore, it should never be used in new JavaScript code.

See Also

Arguments

Function.call( ) JavaScript 1.5; JScript 5.5; ECMAScript v3

invoke a function as a method of an object

Synopsis

function.call(*thisobj*, *args*...)

Arguments

thisobj
: The object on which *function* is to be invoked. In the body of the function, *thisobj* becomes the value of the `this` keyword.

args...
: Any number of arguments, which will be passed as arguments to *function*.

Returns

Whatever value is returned by the invocation of *function*.

Throws

`TypeError`
: If this method is invoked on an object that is not a function.

Description

`call()` invokes the specified *`function`* as if it were a method of *`thisobj`*, passing it any arguments that follow *`thisobj`* in the argument list. The return value of `call()` is the value returned by the function invocation. Within the body of the function, the `this` keyword refers to the *`thisobj`* object.

Use `Function.apply()` instead if you want to specify the arguments to pass to the function in an array.

Example

```
// Call the default Object.toString() method on an object that
// overrides it with its own version of the method. Note no arguments.
Object.prototype.toString.call(o);
```

See Also

Function.apply()

Function.caller

JavaScript 1.0, JScript 2.0; deprecated by ECMAScript

the function that called this one

Synopsis

`function``.caller`

Description

In early versions of JavaScript, the `caller` property of a Function object is a reference to the function that invoked the current one. If the function was invoked from the top level of a JavaScript program, `caller` is `null`. This property may only be used from within the function (i.e., the `caller` property is only defined for a function while that function is executing).

`Function.caller` is not part of the ECMAScript standard and is not required in conforming implementations. It should not be used.

Function.length

JavaScript 1.1; JScript 2.0; ECMAScript v1

the number of declared arguments

Synopsis

`function``.length`

Description

The `length` property of a function specifies the number of named arguments declared when the function was defined. The function may actually be invoked with more than or fewer than this number of arguments. Don't confuse this property of a Function object with the `length` property of the Arguments object which specifies the number of arguments actually passed to the function. See "Arguments.length" for an example.

See Also

Arguments.length

Function.prototype

JavaScript 1.1; JScript 2.0; ECMAScript v1

the prototype for a class of objects

Synopsis

function.prototype

Description

The `prototype` property is used when a function is used as a constructor. It refers to an object that serves as the prototype for an entire class of objects. Any object created by the constructor inherits all properties of the object referred to by the `prototype` property.

See Chapter 8 for a full discussion of constructor functions, the `prototype` property, and the definition of classes in JavaScript.

Bugs

JavaScript 1.1 requires a constructor to be used once before anything can be assigned to its prototype object.

See Also

Chapter 8

Function.toString( )

JavaScript 1.0; JScript 2.0; ECMAScript v1

convert a function to a string

Synopsis

function.toString( )

Returns

A string that represents the function.

Throws

`TypeError`
If this method is invoked on an object that is not a Function.

Description

The `toString( )` method of the Function object converts a function to a string in an implementation-dependent way. In Netscape implementations, this method returns a string of valid JavaScript code—code that includes the `function` keyword, argument list, the complete body of the function, and so on.

Global

JavaScript 1.0; JScript 1.0; ECMAScript v1

the global object

Synopsis

```
this
```

Global Properties

The global object is not a class, so the following global properties have individual reference entries under their own name. That is, you can find details on the `undefined` property listed under the name "undefined," not under "Global.undefined." Note that all top-level variables are also properties of the global object.

`Infinity`
A numeric value that represents positive infinity.

`NaN`
The not-a-number value.

`undefined`
The `undefined` value.

Global Functions

The global object is an object, not a class. The global functions listed below are not methods of any object, and their reference entries appear under the function name. For example, you'll find details on the `parseInt()` function under "parseInt()," not "Global.parseInt()."

`decodeURI()`
Decodes a string escaped with encodeURI().

`decodeURIComponent()`
Decodes a string escaped with encodeURIComponent().

`encodeURI`
Encodes a URI by escaping certain characters.

`encodeURIComponent`
Encodes a URI component by escaping certain characters.

`escape()`
Encodes a string by replacing certain characters with escape sequences.

`eval()`
Evaluates a string of JavaScript code and return the result.

`isFinite()`
Tests whether a value is a finite number.

`isNaN`
Tests whether a value is the not-a-number value.

`parseFloat()`
Parses a number from a string.

`parseInt()`
Parses an integer from a string.

`unescape()`
Decodes a string encoded with escape().

Global Objects

In addition to the global properties and functions listed above, the global object also defines properties that refer to all the other predefined JavaScript objects. All of these properties are constructor functions that define classes except for `Math`, which is a reference to an object that is not a constructor.

`Array`
The `Array()` constructor.

`Boolean`
The `Boolean()` constructor.

`Date`	The `Date()` constructor.
`Error`	The `Error()` constructor.
`EvalError`	The `EvalError()` constructor.
`Function`	The `Function()` constructor.
`Math`	A reference to an object that defines mathematical functions.
`Number`	The `Number()` constructor.
`Object`	The `Object()` constructor.
`RangeError`	The `RangeError()` constructor.
`ReferenceError`	The `ReferenceError()` constructor.
`RegExp`	The `RegExp()` constructor.
`String`	The `String()` constructor.
`SyntaxError`	The `SyntaxError()` constructor.
`TypeError`	The `TypeError()` constructor.
`URIError`	The `URIError()` constructor.

Description

The global object is a predefined object that serves as a placeholder for the global properties and functions of JavaScript. All other predefined objects, functions, and properties are accessible through the global object. The global object is not a property of any other object, so it does not have a name. (The title of this reference page was chosen simply for organizational convenience and does not indicate that the global object is named "Global"). In top-level JavaScript code, you can refer to the global object with the keyword `this`. It is rarely necessary to refer to the global object in this way, however, because the global object serves as the top of the scope chain, which means that unqualified variable and function names are looked up as properties of the object. When JavaScript code refers to the `parseInt()` function, for example, it is referring to the `parseInt` property of the global object. The fact that the global object is the top of the scope chain also means that all variables declared in top-level JavaScript code become properties of the global object.

The global object is simply an object, not a class. There is no `Global()` constructor, and there is no way to instantiate a new global object.

When JavaScript is embedded in a particular environment, the global object is usually given additional properties that are specific to that environment. In fact, the type of the global object is not specified by the ECMAScript standard, and an implementation or embedding of JavaScript may use an object of any type as the global object, as long as the object defines the basic properties and functions listed here. In client-side JavaScript, for example, the global object is a Window object and represents the web browser window within which the JavaScript code is running.

Example

In core JavaScript, none of the predefined properties of the global object are enumerable, so you can list all implicitly and explicitly declared global variables with a `for/in` loop like this:

```
var variables = ""
for(var name in this)
    variables += name + "\n";
```

See Also

Window in the client-side reference section; Chapter 4

Infinity

JavaScript 1.3; JScript 3.0; ECMAScript v1

a numeric property that represents infinity

Synopsis

```
Infinity
```

Description

`Infinity` is a global property that contains the special numeric value representing positive infinity. The `Infinity` property is not enumerated by `for/in` loops and cannot be deleted with the `delete` operator. Note that `Infinity` is not a constant and can be set to any other value, something that you should take care not to do. (`Number.POSITIVE_INFINITY` is a constant, however.)

See Also

isFinite( ), NaN, Number.POSITIVE_INFINITY

isFinite( )

JavaScript 1.2; JScript 3.0; ECMAScript v1

determine whether a number is finite

Synopsis

```
isFinite(n)
```

Arguments

n The number to be tested.

Returns

`true` if *n* is (or can be converted to) a finite number or `false` if *n* is `NaN` (not a number) or positive or negative infinity.

See Also

Infinity, isNaN(), NaN, Number.NaN, Number.NEGATIVE_INFINITY, Number.POSITIVE_INFINITY

isNaN( )

JavaScript 1.1; JScript 1.0; ECMAScript v1

check for not-a-number

Synopsis

```
isNaN(x)
```

Arguments

x The value to be tested.

Returns

`true` if *x* is (or can be converted to) the special not-a-number value; `false` if *x* is any other value.

Description

`isNaN()` tests its argument to determine whether it is the value `NaN`, which represents an illegal number (such as the result of division by zero). This function is required, because comparing a `NaN` with any value, including itself, always returns `false`, so it is not possible to test for `NaN` with the `==` or `===` operators.

A common use of `isNaN()` is to test the results of `parseFloat()` and `parseInt()` to determine if they represent legal numbers. You can also use `isNaN()` to check for arithmetic errors, such as division by zero.

Example

```
isNaN(0);                  // Returns false
isNaN(0/0);                // Returns true
isNaN(parseInt("3"));      // Returns false
isNaN(parseInt("hello"));  // Returns true
isNaN("3");                // Returns false
isNaN("hello");            // Returns true
isNaN(true);               // Returns false
isNaN(undefined);          // Returns true
```

See Also

isFinite(), NaN, Number.NaN, parseFloat(), parseInt()

Math JavaScript 1.0; JScript 1.0; ECMAScript v1

mathematical functions and constants

Synopsis

```
Math.constant
Math.function()
```

Constants

`Math.E`	The constant *e*, the base of the natural logarithms.
`Math.LN10`	The natural logarithm of 10.
`Math.LN2`	The natural logarithm of 2.
`Math.LOG10E`	The base-10 logarithm of *e*.
`Math.LOG2E`	The base-2 logarithm of *e*.
`Math.PI`	The constant π.

`Math.SQRT1_2`	1 divided by the square root of 2.
`Math.SQRT2`	The square root of 2.

Static Functions

`Math.abs( )`	Computes an absolute value.
`Math.acos( )`	Computes an arc cosine.
`Math.asin( )`	Computes an arc sine.
`Math.atan( )`	Computes an arc tangent.
`Math.atan2( )`	Computes the angle from the X-axis to a point.
`Math.ceil( )`	Rounds a number up.
`Math.cos( )`	Computes a cosine.
`Math.exp( )`	Computes an exponent of *e*.
`Math.floor( )`	Rounds a number down.
`Math.log( )`	Computes a natural logarithm.
`Math.max( )`	Returns the larger of two numbers.
`Math.min( )`	Returns the smaller of two numbers.
`Math.pow( )`	Computes x^y.
`Math.random( )`	Computes a random number.
`Math.round( )`	Rounds to the nearest integer.
`Math.sin( )`	Computes a sine.
`Math.sqrt( )`	Computes a square root.
`Math.tan( )`	Computes a tangent.

Description

Math is an object that defines properties that refer to useful mathematical functions and constants. These functions and constants are conveniently grouped by this Math object and are invoked with syntax like this:

```
y = Math.sin(x);
area = radius * radius * Math.PI;
```

Math is not a class of objects like Date and String are. There is no `Math( )` constructor, and functions like `Math.sin( )` are simply functions, not methods that operate on an object.

See Also

Number

Math.abs( ) — JavaScript 1.0; JScript 1.0; ECMAScript v1

compute an absolute value

Synopsis

```
Math.abs(x)
```

Arguments

x Any number.

Returns

The absolute value of *x*.

Math.acos()

JavaScript 1.0; JScript 1.0; ECMAScript v1

compute an arc cosine

Synopsis

```
Math.acos(x)
```

Arguments

x A number between –1.0 and 1.0.

Returns

The arc cosine, or inverse cosine, of the specified value *x*. This return value is between 0 and π radians.

Math.asin()

JavaScript 1.0; JScript 1.0; ECMAScript v1

compute an arc sine

Synopsis

```
Math.asin(x)
```

Arguments

x A number between –1.0 and 1.0.

Returns

The arc sine of the specified value *x*. This return value is between –π/2 and π/2 radians.

Math.atan()

JavaScript 1.0; JScript 1.0; ECMAScript v1

compute an arc tangent

Synopsis

```
Math.atan(x)
```

Arguments

x Any number.

Returns

The arc tangent of the specified value *x*. This return value is between –π/2 and π/2 radians.

Math.atan2( )

JavaScript 1.0; JScript 1.0; ECMAScript v1

compute the angle from the X-axis to a point

Synopsis

```
Math.atan2(y, x)
```

Arguments

y The Y-coordinate of the point.

x The X-coordinate of the point.

Returns

A value between $-\pi$ and π radians that specifies the counterclockwise angle between the positive X-axis and the point (*x*, *y*).

Description

The `Math.atan2( )` function computes the arc tangent of the ratio *y*/*x*. The *y* argument can be considered the Y-coordinate (or "rise") of a point, and the *x* argument can be considered the X-coordinate (or "run") of the point. Note the unusual order of the arguments to this function: the Y-coordinate is passed before the X-coordinate.

Math.ceil( )

JavaScript 1.0; JScript 1.0; ECMAScript v1

round a number up

Synopsis

```
Math.ceil(x)
```

Arguments

x Any numeric value or expression.

Returns

The closest integer greater than or equal to *x*.

Description

`Math.ceil( )` computes the ceiling function—i.e., it returns the closest integer value that is greater than or equal to the function argument. `Math.ceil( )` differs from `Math.round( )` in that it always rounds up, rather than rounding up or down to the closest integer. Also note that `Math.ceil( )` does not round negative numbers to larger negative numbers; it rounds them up toward zero.

Example

```
a = Math.ceil(1.99);   // Result is 2.0
b = Math.ceil(1.01);   // Result is 2.0
c = Math.ceil(1.0);    // Result is 1.0
d = Math.ceil(-1.99);  // Result is -1.0
```

Math.cos( ) JavaScript 1.0; JScript 1.0; ECMAScript v1

compute a cosine

Synopsis

```
Math.cos(x)
```

Arguments

x An angle, measured in radians. To convert degrees to radians, multiply the degree value by 0.017453293 (2π/360).

Returns

The cosine of the specified value *x*. This return value is between –1.0 and 1.0.

Math.E JavaScript 1.0; JScript 1.0; ECMAScript v1

the mathematical constant *e*

Synopsis

```
Math.E
```

Description

`Math.E` is the mathematical constant *e*, the base of the natural logarithms, with a value of approximately 2.71828.

Math.exp( ) JavaScript 1.0; JScript 1.0; ECMAScript v1

compute e^x

Synopsis

```
Math.exp(x)
```

Arguments

x A numeric value or expression to be used as the exponent.

Returns

e^x, *e* raised to the power of the specified exponent *x*, where *e* is the base of the natural logarithms, with a value of approximately 2.71828.

Math.floor( ) JavaScript 1.0; JScript 1.0; ECMAScript v1

round a number down

Synopsis

```
Math.floor(x)
```

Arguments

x Any numeric value or expression.

Returns

The closest integer less than or equal to *x*.

Description

`Math.floor( )` computes the floor function—in other words, it returns the nearest integer value that is less than or equal to the function argument.

`Math.floor( )` rounds a floating-point value down to the closest integer. This behavior differs from that of `Math.round( )`, which rounds up or down to the nearest integer. Also note that `Math.floor( )` rounds negative numbers down (i.e., to be more negative), not up (i.e., closer to zero).

Example

```
a = Math.floor(1.99);     // Result is 1.0
b = Math.floor(1.01);     // Result is 1.0
c = Math.floor(1.0);      // Result is 1.0
d = Math.floor(-1.01);    // Result is -2.0
```

Math.LN10 JavaScript 1.0; JScript 1.0; ECMAScript v1

the mathematical constant $\log_e 10$

Synopsis

```
Math.LN10
```

Description

`Math.LN10` is $\log_e 10$, the natural logarithm of 10. This constant has a value of approximately 2.3025850929940459011.

Math.LN2 JavaScript 1.0; JScript 1.0; ECMAScript v1

the mathematical constant $\log_e 2$

Synopsis

```
Math.LN2
```

Description

`Math.LN2` is $\log_e 2$, the natural logarithm of 2. This constant has a value of approximately 0.69314718055994528623.

Math.log( )

JavaScript 1.0; JScript 1.0; ECMAScript v1

compute a natural logarithm

Synopsis

`Math.log(x)`

Arguments

x Any numeric value or expression greater than zero.

Returns

The natural logarithm of *x*.

Description

`Math.log()` computes $\log_e x$, the natural logarithm of its argument. The argument must be greater than zero.

You can compute the base-10 and base-2 logarithms of a number with these formulas:

$$\log_{10} x = \log_{10} e \cdot \log_e x$$
$$\log_2 x = \log_2 e \cdot \log_e x$$

These formulas translate into the following JavaScript functions:

```
function log10(x) { return Math.LOG10E * Math.log(x); }
function log2(x) { return  Math.LOG2E * Math.log(x); }
```

Math.LOG10E

JavaScript 1.0; JScript 1.0; ECMAScript v1

the mathematical constant $\log_{10} e$

Synopsis

`Math.LOG10E`

Description

`Math.LOG10E` is $\log_{10} e$, the base-10 logarithm of the constant *e*. It has a value of approximately 0.43429448190325181667.

Math.LOG2E

JavaScript 1.0; JScript 1.0; ECMAScript v1

the mathematical constant $\log_2 e$

Synopsis

`Math.LOG2E`

Description

`Math.LOG2E` is $\log_2 e$, the base-2 logarithm of the constant *e*. It has a value of approximately 1.442695040888963387.

Math.max( )

JavaScript 1.0; JScript 1.0; ECMAScript v1; enhanced in ECMAScript v3

return the largest argument

Synopsis

```
Math.max(args...)
```

Arguments

`args...`
: Zero or more values. Prior to ECMAScript v3, this method expects exactly two arguments.

Returns

The largest of the arguments. Returns `-Infinity` if there are no arguments. Returns `NaN` if any of the arguments is `NaN` or is a non-numeric value that cannot be converted to a number.

Math.min( )

JavaScript 1.0; JScript 1.0; ECMAScript v1; enhanced in ECMAScript v3

return the smallest argument

Synopsis

```
Math.min(args...)
```

Arguments

`args...`
: Any number of arguments. Prior to ECMAScript v3, this function expects exactly two arguments.

Returns

The smallest of the specified arguments. Returns `Infinity` if there are no arguments. Returns `NaN` if any argument is `NaN` or is a non-numeric value that cannot be converted to a number.

Math.PI

JavaScript 1.0; JScript 1.0; ECMAScript v1

the mathematical constant π

Synopsis

```
Math.PI
```

Description

`Math.PI` is the constant π or pi, the ratio of the circumference of a circle to its diameter. It has a value of approximately 3.14159265358979.

Math.pow( )

JavaScript 1.0; JScript 1.0; ECMAScript v1

compute x^y

Synopsis

```
Math.pow(x, y)
```

Arguments

x The number to be raised to a power.

y The power that *x* is to be raised to.

Returns

x to the power of *y*, x^y.

Description

`Math.pow( )` computes *x to* the power of *y*. Any values of *x* and *y* may be passed to `Math.pow( )`. However, if the result is an imaginary or complex number, `Math.pow( )` returns `NaN`. In practice, this means that if *x* is negative, *y* should be a positive or negative integer. Also, bear in mind that large exponents can easily cause floating-point overflow and return a value of `Infinity`.

Math.random( )

JavaScript 1.1; JScript 1.0; ECMAScript v1

return a pseudorandom number

Synopsis

```
Math.random( )
```

Returns

A pseudorandom number between 0.0 and 1.0.

Math.round( )

JavaScript 1.0; JScript 1.0; ECMAScript v1

round to the nearest integer

Synopsis

```
Math.round(x)
```

Arguments

x Any number.

Returns

The integer closest to *x*.

Description

`Math.round( )` rounds its argument up or down to the nearest integer. It rounds .5 up. For example, it rounds 2.5 to 3 and rounds –2.5 to –2.

Math.sin( )

JavaScript 1.0; JScript 1.0; ECMAScript v1

compute a sine

Synopsis

`Math.sin(x)`

Arguments

x An angle, in radians. To convert degrees to radians, multiply by 0.017453293 (2π/360).

Returns

The sine of *x*.

Math.sqrt( )

JavaScript 1.0; JScript 1.0; ECMAScript v1

compute a square root

Synopsis

`Math.sqrt(x)`

Arguments

x A numeric value greater than or equal to zero.

Returns

The square root of *x*. Returns `NaN` if *x* is less than zero.

Description

`Math.sqrt( )` computes the square root of a number. Note, however, that you can compute arbitrary roots of a number with `Math.pow( )`. For example:

```
Math.cuberoot = function(x){ return Math.pow(x,1/3); }
Math.cuberoot(8);  // Returns 2
```

Math.SQRT1_2

JavaScript 1.0; JScript 1.0; ECMAScript v1

the mathematical constant $1/\sqrt{2}$

Synopsis

`Math.SQRT1_2`

Description

`Math.SQRT1_2` is $1/\sqrt{2}$, the reciprocal of the square root of 2. This constant has a value of approximately 0.7071067811865476.

Math.SQRT2 — JavaScript 1.0; JScript 1.0; ECMAScript v1

the mathematical constant $\sqrt{2}$

Synopsis

```
Math.SQRT2
```

Description

`Math.SQRT2` is the constant $\sqrt{2}$, the square root of 2. This constant has a value of approximately 1.414213562373095.

Math.tan( ) — JavaScript 1.0; JScript 1.0; ECMAScript v1

compute a tangent

Synopsis

```
Math.tan(x)
```

Arguments

x An angle, measured in radians. To convert degrees to radians, multiply the degree value by 0.017453293 ($2\pi/360$).

Returns

The tangent of the specified angle *x*.

NaN — JavaScript 1.3; JScript 3.0; ECMAScript v1

the not-a-number property

Synopsis

```
NaN
```

Description

`NaN` is global property that refers to the special numeric not-a-number value. The `NaN` property is not enumerated by `for/in` loops and cannot be deleted with the `delete` operator. Note that `NaN` is not a constant and can be set to any other value, something that you should take care not to do.

To determine if a value is not a number, use `isNaN( )`, since `NaN` always compares non-equal to any other value, including itself!

See Also

Infinity, isNaN(), Number.NaN

Number

JavaScript 1.1; JScript 2.0; ECMAScript v1

support for numbers

Inherits from Object

Constructor

```
new Number(value)
Number(value)
```

Arguments

value

The numeric value of the Number object being created, or a value to be converted to a number.

Returns

When `Number()` is used with the `new` operator as a constructor, it returns a newly constructed Number object. When `Number()` is invoked as a function without the `new` operator, it converts its argument to a primitive numeric value and returns that value (or `NaN` if the conversion failed).

Constants

`Number.MAX_VALUE`
: The largest representable number.

`Number.MIN_VALUE`
: The smallest representable number.

`Number.NaN`
: Not-a-number value.

`Number.NEGATIVE_INFINITY`
: Negative infinite value; returned on overflow.

`Number.POSITIVE_INFINITY`
: Infinite value; returned on overflow.

Methods

`toString()`
: Converts a number to a string, using a specified radix (base).

`toLocaleString()`
: Converts a number to a string, using local number formatting conventions.

`toFixed()`
: Converts a number to a string that contains a specified number of digits after the decimal place.

`toExponential()`
: Converts a number to a string using exponential notation with the specified number of digits after the decimal place.

toPrecision( )
: Converts a number to a string using the specified number of significant digits. Uses exponential or fixed-point notation depending on the size of the number and the number of significant digits specified.

Description

Numbers are a basic, primitive data type in JavaScript. In JavaScript 1.1, however, JavaScript also supports the Number object, which is a wrapper object around a primitive numeric value. JavaScript automatically converts between the primitive and object forms as necessary. In JavaScript 1.1, you can explicitly create a Number object with the `Number( )` constructor, although there is rarely any need to do so.

The `Number( )` constructor can also be used without the `new` operator, as a conversion function. When invoked in this way, it attempts to convert its argument to a number and returns the primitive numeric value (or NaN) that results from the conversion.

The `Number( )` constructor is also used as a placeholder for five useful numeric constants: the largest and smallest representable numbers; positive and negative infinity; and the special not-a-number value. Note that these values are properties of the `Number( )` constructor function itself, not of individual number objects. For example, you can use the `MAX_VALUE` property as follows:

```
var biggest = Number.MAX_VALUE
```

but *not* like this:

```
var n = new Number(2);
var biggest = n.MAX_VALUE
```

By contrast, the `toString( )` and other methods of the Number object are methods of each Number object, not of the `Number( )` constructor function. As noted earlier, JavaScript automatically converts from primitive numeric values to Number objects whenever necessary. This means that we can use the Number methods with primitive numeric values as well as with Number objects.

```
var value = 1234;
var binary_value = n.toString(2);
```

See Also

Infinity, Math, NaN

Number.MAX_VALUE

JavaScript 1.1; JScript 2.0, ECMAScript v1

the maximum numeric value

Synopsis

```
Number.MAX_VALUE
```

Description

`Number.MAX_VALUE` is the largest number representable in JavaScript. Its value is approximately 1.79E+308.

Number.MIN_VALUE

JavaScript 1.1; JScript 2.0, ECMAScript v1

the minimum numeric value

Synopsis

```
Number.MIN_VALUE
```

Description

`Number.MIN_VALUE` is the smallest (closest to zero, not most negative) number representable in JavaScript. Its value is approximately 5E–324.

Number.NaN

JavaScript 1.1; JScript 2.0, ECMAScript v1

the special not-a-number value

Synopsis

```
Number.NaN
```

Description

`Number.NaN` is a special value that indicates that the result of some mathematical operation (such as taking the square root of a negative number) is not a number. `parseInt()` and `parseFloat()` return this value when they cannot parse the specified string, and you might use `Number.NaN` in a similar way to indicate an error condition for some function that normally returns a valid number.

JavaScript prints the `Number.NaN` value as `NaN`. Note that the `NaN` value always compares unequal to any other number, including `NaN` itself. Thus, you cannot check for the not-a-number value by comparing to `Number.NaN`. Use the `isNaN()` function instead. In ECMAScript v1 and later, you can also use the predefined global constant `NaN` instead of using `Number.NaN`.

See Also

isNaN(), NaN

Number.NEGATIVE_INFINITY

JavaScript 1.1; JScript 2.0, ECMAScript v1

negative infinity

Synopsis

```
Number.NEGATIVE_INFINITY
```

Description

`Number.NEGATIVE_INFINITY` is a special numeric value that is returned when an arithmetic operation or mathematical function generates a negative value greater than the largest representable number in JavaScript (i.e., more negative than `-Number.MAX_VALUE`).

JavaScript displays the `NEGATIVE_INFINITY` value as `-Infinity`. This value behaves mathematically like infinity; for example, anything multiplied by infinity is infinity and anything divided by infinity is zero. In ECMAScript v1 and later, you can also use `-Infinity` instead of `Number.NEGATIVE_INFINITY`.

See Also

Infinity, isFinite( )

Number.POSITIVE_INFINITY

JavaScript 1.1; JScript 2.0, ECMAScript v1

infinity

Synopsis

```
Number.POSITIVE_INFINITY
```

Description

`Number.POSITIVE_INFINITY` is a special numeric value returned when an arithmetic operation or mathematical function overflows or generates a value greater than the largest representable number in JavaScript (i.e., greater than `Number.MAX_VALUE`). Note that when numbers "underflow," or become less than `Number.MIN_VALUE`, JavaScript converts them to zero.

JavaScript displays the `POSITIVE_INFINITY` value as `Infinity`. This value behaves mathematically like infinity; for example, anything multiplied by infinity is infinity and anything divided by infinity is zero. In ECMAScript v1 and later, you can also use the predefined global constant `Infinity` instead of `Number.POSITIVE_INFINITY`.

See Also

Infinity, isFinite( )

Number.toExponential( )

JavaScript 1.5; JScript 5.5, ECMAScript v3

format a number using exponential notation

Synopsis

`number``.toExponential(`*`digits`*`)`

Arguments

`digits`

The number of digits that will appear after the decimal point. This may be a value between 0 and 20, inclusive, and implementations may optionally support a larger range of values. If this argument is omitted, as many digits as necessary will be used.

Returns

A string representation of *`number`*, in exponential notation, with one digit before the decimal place and *`digits`* digits after the decimal place. The fractional part of the number is rounded, or padded with zeros, as necessary, so that it has the specified length.

Throws

RangeError
: If *digits* is too small or too large. Values between 0 and 20, inclusive, will not cause a RangeError. Implementations are allowed to support larger and smaller values as well.

TypeError
: If this method is invoked on an object that is not a Number.

Example

```
var n = 12345.6789;
n.toExponential(1);     // Returns 1.2e+4
n.toExponential(5);     // Returns 1.23457e+4
n.toExponential(10);    // Returns 1.2345678900e+4
n.toExponential( );     // Returns 1.23456789e+4
```

See Also

Number.toFixed( ), Number.toLocaleString( ), Number.toPrecision( ), Number.toString( )

Number.toFixed( ) — JavaScript 1.5; JScript 5.5, ECMAScript v3

format a number using fixed-point notation

Synopsis

number.toFixed(*digits*)

Arguments

digits
: The number of digits to appear after the decimal point; this may be a value between 0 and 20, inclusive, and implementations may optionally support a larger range of values. If this argument is omitted, it is treated as 0.

Returns

A string representation of *number* that does not use exponential notation and has exactly *digits* digits after the decimal place. The number is rounded if necessary, and the fractional part is padded with zeros if necessary so that it has the specified length. If *number* is greater than 1e+21, this method simply calls `Number.toString( )` and returns a string in exponential notation.

Throws

RangeError
: If *digits* is too small or too large. Values between 0 and 20, inclusive, will not cause a RangeError. Implementations are allowed to support larger and smaller values as well.

TypeError
: If this method is invoked on an object that is not a Number.

Example

```
var n = 12345.6789;
n.toFixed( );           // Returns 12346: note rounding, no fractional part
n.toFixed(1);           // Returns 12345.7: note rounding
n.toFixed(6);           // Returns 12345.678900: note added zeros
(1.23e+20).toFixed(2);  // Returns 123000000000000000000.00
(1.23e-10).toFixed(2)   // Returns 0.00
```

See Also

Number.toExponential( ), Number.toLocaleString( ), Number.toPrecision( ), Number.toString( )

Number.toLocaleString( ) JavaScript 1.5; JScript 5.5, ECMAScript v3

convert a number to a locally formatted string

Synopsis

number.toLocaleString( )

Returns

An implementation-dependent string representation of the number, formatted according to local conventions, which may affect such things as the punctuation characters used for the decimal point and the thousands separator.

Throws

TypeError
: If this method is invoked on an object that is not a Number.

See Also

Number.toExponential( ), Number.toFixed( ), Number.toPrecision( ), Number.toString( )

Number.toPrecision( ) JavaScript 1.5; JScript 5.5, ECMAScript v3

format the significant digits of a number

Synopsis

number.toPrecision(*precision*)

Arguments

precision
: The number of significant digits to appear in the returned string. This may be a value between 1 and 21, inclusive. Implementations are allowed to optionally support larger and smaller values of *precision*. If this argument is omitted, the toString( ) method is used instead to convert the number to a base-10 value.

Returns

A string representation of *number* that contains *precision* significant digits. If *precision* is large enough to include all the digits of the integer part of *number*, the returned string uses fixed-point notation. Otherwise, exponential notation is used with one digit before the decimal place and *precision*–1 digits after the decimal place. The number is rounded or padded with zeros as necessary.

Throws

`RangeError`
: If *digits* is too small or too large. Values between 1 and 21, inclusive, will not cause a RangeError. Implementations are allowed to support larger and smaller values as well.

`TypeError`
: If this method is invoked on an object that is not a Number.

Example

```
var n = 12345.6789;
n.toPrecision(1);   // Returns 1e+4
n.toPrecision(3);   // Returns 1.23e+4
n.toPrecision(5);   // Returns 12346: note rounding
n.toPrecision(10);  // Returns 12345.67890: note added zero
```

See Also

Number.toExponential( ), Number.toFixed( ), Number.toLocaleString( ), Number.toString( )

Number.toString( )

JavaScript 1.1; JScript 2.0, ECMAScript v1

convert a number to a string

Overrides Object.toString( )

Synopsis

number.toString(*radix*)

Arguments

radix
: An optional argument that specifies the radix, or base, between 2 and 36, in which the number should be represented. If omitted, base 10 is used. Note, however, that the ECMAScript specification allows an implementation to return any value if this argument is specified as any value other than 10.

Returns

A string representation of the number.

Throws

`TypeError`
: If this method is invoked on an object that is not a Number.

Description

The `toString()` method of the Number object converts a number to a string. When the *`radix`* argument is omitted or is specified as 10, the number is converted to a base-10 string. If *`radix`* is any other value, this method returns an implementation-defined string. Netscape implementations and Microsoft implementations after JScript 3.0 honor the *`radix`* argument and return a string representation of the number in the specified base.

See Also

Number.toExponential(), Number.toFixed(), Number.toLocaleString(), Number.toPrecision()

Number.valueOf( )

JavaScript 1.1; JScript 2.0, ECMAScript v1

return the primitive number value — **Overrides Object.valueOf( )**

Synopsis

`number``.valueOf( )`

Returns

The primitive number value of this Number object. It is rarely necessary to call this method explicitly.

Throws

`TypeError`

If this method is invoked on an object that is not a Number.

See Also

Object.valueOf()

Object

JavaScript 1.0; JScript 1.0; ECMAScript v1

a superclass that contains features of all JavaScript objects

Constructor

```
new Object( )
new Object(value)
```

Arguments

`value`

This optional argument specifies a primitive JavaScript value—a number, boolean, or string—that is to be converted to a Number, Boolean, or String object. This object is not supported prior to JavaScript 1.1 and ECMAScript v1.

Returns

If no *value* argument is passed, this constructor returns a newly created Object instance. If a primitive *value* argument is specified, the constructor creates and returns a Number, Boolean, or String object wrapper for the primitive value. When the `Object()` constructor is called as a function, without the `new` operator, it behaves just as it does when used with the `new` operator.

Properties

`constructor`
: A reference to the JavaScript function that was the constructor for the object.

Methods

`hasOwnProperty()`
: Checks whether an object has a locally defined (noninherited) property with a specified name.

`isPrototypeOf()`
: Checks whether this object is the prototype object of a specified object.

`propertyIsEnumerable()`
: Checks whether a named property exists and would be enumerated by a `for/in` loop.

`toLocaleString()`
: Returns a localized string representation of the object. The default implementation of this method simply calls `toString()`, but subclasses may override it to provide localization.

`toString()`
: Returns a string representation of the object. The implementation of this method provided by the Object class is quite generic and does not provide much useful information. Subclasses of Object typically override this method by defining their own `toString()` method which produces more useful output.

`valueOf()`
: Returns the primitive value of the object, if any. For objects of type Object, this method simply returns the object itself. Subclasses of Object, such as Number and Boolean, override this method to return the primitive value associated with the object.

Description

The Object class is a built-in data type of the JavaScript language. It serves as the superclass for all other JavaScript objects; therefore, methods and behavior of the Object class are inherited by all other objects. The basic behavior of objects in JavaScript is explained in Chapter 8.

In addition to the `Object()` constructor shown above, objects can also be created and initialized using the Object literal syntax described in Chapter 8.

See Also

Array, Boolean, Function, Function.prototype, Number, String; Chapter 8

Object.constructor

JavaScript 1.1; JScript 2.0; ECMAScript v1

an object's constructor function

Synopsis

object.constructor

Description

The constructor property of any object is a reference to the function that was used as the constructor for that object. For example, if you create an array a with the Array( ) constructor, a.constructor is an Array:

```
a = new Array(1,2,3);    // Create an object
a.constructor == Array   // Evaluates to true
```

One common use of the constructor property is to determine the type of unknown objects. Given an unknown value, you can use the typeof operator to determine whether it is a primitive value or an object. If it is an object, you can use the constructor property to determine what type of object it is. For example, the following function determines whether a given value is an array:

```
function isArray(x) {
    return ((typeof x == "object") && (x.constructor == Array));
}
```

Note, however, that while this technique works for the objects built-in to core JavaScript, it is not guaranteed to work with "host objects" such as the Window object of client-side JavaScript. The default implementation of the Object.toString( ) method provides another way to determine the type of an unknown object.

See Also

Object.toString( )

Object.hasOwnProperty( )

JavaScript 1.5; JScript 5.5; ECMAScript v3

check whether a property is inherited

Synopsis

object.hasOwnProperty(*propname*)

Arguments

propname

A string that contains the name of a property of *object*.

Returns

true if *object* has a noninherited property with the name specified by *propname*. Returns false if *object* does not have a property with the specified name or if it inherits that property from its prototype object.

Description

As explained in Chapter 8, JavaScript objects may have properties of their own, and they may also inherit properties from their prototype object. The `hasOwnProperty( )` method provides a way to distinguish between inherited properties and noninherited local properties.

Example

```
var o = new Object( );             // Create an object
o.x = 3.14;                        // Define a noninherited local property
o.hasOwnProperty("x");             // Returns true: x is a local property of o
o.hasOwnProperty("y");             // Returns false: o doesn't have a property y
o.hasOwnProperty("toString");      // Returns false: toString property is inherited
```

See Also

Function.prototype, Object.propertyIsEnumerable( ); Chapter 8

Object.isPrototypeOf( )

JavaScript 1.5; JScript 5.5; ECMAScript v3

is one object the prototype of another?

Synopsis

`object``.isPrototypeOf(`*`o`*`)`

Arguments

o Any object.

Returns

`true` if *`object`* is the prototype of *o*. Returns `false` if *o* is not an object or if *`object`* is not the prototype of *o*.

Description

As explained in Chapter 8, JavaScript objects inherit properties from their prototype object. The prototype of an object is referred to by the `prototype` property of the constructor function used to create and initialize the object. The `isPrototypeOf( )` method provides a way to determine if one object is the prototype of another. This technique can be used to determine the class of an object.

Example

```
var o = new Object( );                           // Create an object
Object.prototype.isPrototypeOf(o)                // true: o is an object
Function.prototype.isPrototypeOf(o.toString);    // true: toString is a function
Array.prototype.isPrototypeOf([1,2,3]);          // true: [1,2,3] is an array

// Here is a way to perform a similar test
(o.constructor == Object);  // true: o was created with Object( ) constructor
(o.toString.constructor == Function);  // true: o.toString is a function
```

```
// Prototype objects themselves have prototypes. The following call
// returns true, showing that function objects inherit properties
// from Function.prototype and also from Object.prototype.
Object.prototype.isPrototypeOf(Function.prototype);
```

See Also

Function.prototype, Object.constructor; Chapter 8

Object.propertyIsEnumerable( )

JavaScript 1.5; JScript 5.5; ECMAScript v3

will property be seen by a for/in loop?

Synopsis

object.propertyIsEnumerable(*propname*)

Arguments

propname

A string that contains the name of a property of *object*.

Returns

true if *object* has a noninherited property with the name specified by *propname* and if that property is "enumerable," which means that it would be enumerated by a for/in loop on *object*.

Description

The for/in statement loops through the "enumerable" properties of an object. Not all properties of an object are enumerable, however: properties added to an object by Java-Script code are enumerable, but the predefined properties (such as methods) of built-in objects are not usually enumerable. The propertyIsEnumerable( ) method provides a way to distinguish between enumerable and nonenumerable properties. Note, however, that the ECMAScript specification states that propertyIsEnumerable( ) does not examine the prototype chain, which means that it only works for local properties of an object and does not provide any way to test the enumerability of inherited properties.

Example

```
var o = new Object( );                // Create an object
o.x = 3.14;                           // Define a property
o.propertyIsEnumerable("x");          // true: property x is local and enumerable
o.propertyIsEnumerable("y");          // false: o doesn't have a property y
o.propertyIsEnumerable("toString");   // false: toString property is inherited
Object.prototype.propertyIsEnumerable("toString");  // false: nonenumerable
```

Bugs

The specification is apparently in error when it restricts propertyIsEnumerable( ) to check only noninherited properties. Internet Explorer 5.5 implements this method as specified. Netscape 6.0 implements it so that it does consider the prototype chain. Although this is the way the method was probably intended to work, it violates the specification, and Netscape 6.1 has been modified to match the IE 5.5. Because of the error in the specification, this method is less useful than it should be.

See Also

Function.prototype, Object.hasOwnProperty(); Chapter 8

Object.toLocaleString( )

JavaScript 1.5; JScript 5.5; ECMAScript v3

return an object's localized string representation

Synopsis

```
object.toString( )
```

Returns

A string representing the object.

Description

This method is intended to return a string representation of the object, localized as appropriate for the current locale. The default `toLocaleString( )` method provided by the Object class simply calls the `toString( )` method and returns the nonlocalized string that it returns. Note, however, that other classes, including Array, Date, and Number, define their own versions of this method to perform localized string conversions. When defining your own classes, you may want to override this method as well.

See Also

Array.toLocaleString( ), Date.toLocaleString( ), Number.toLocaleString( ), Object.toString( )

Object.toString( )

JavaScript 1.0; JScript 2.0; ECMAScript v1

define an object's string representation

Synopsis

```
object.toString( )
```

Returns

A string representing the object.

Description

The `toString( )` method is not one you often call explicitly in your JavaScript programs. Instead, you define this method in your objects, and the system calls it whenever it needs to convert your object to a string.

The JavaScript system invokes the `toString( )` method to convert an object to a string whenever the object is used in a string context. For example, if an object is converted to a string when it is passed to a function that expects a string argument:

```
alert(my_object);
```

Similarly, objects are converted to strings when they are concatenated to strings with the + operator:

```
var msg = 'My object is: ' + my_object;
```

The `toString( )` method is invoked without arguments and should return a string. To be useful, the string you return should be based, in some way, on the value of the object for which the method was invoked.

When you define a custom class in JavaScript, it is good practice to define a `toString( )` method for the class. If you do not, the object inherits the default `toString( )` method from the Object class. This default method returns a string of the form:

```
[object class]
```

where *`class`* is the class of the object: a value such as "Object", "String", "Number", "Function", "Window", "Document", and so on. This behavior of the default `toString( )` method is occasionally useful to determine the type or class of an unknown object. Because most objects have a custom version of `toString( )`, however, you must explicitly invoke the `Object.toString( )` method on an object `o` with code like this:

```
Object.prototype.toString.apply(o);
```

Note that this technique for identifying unknown objects works only for built-in objects. If you define your own object class, it will have a *`class`* of "Object". In this case, you can use the `Object.constructor` property to obtain more information about the object.

The `toString( )` method can be quite useful when you are debugging JavaScript programs—it allows you to print objects and see their value. For this reason alone, it is a good idea to define a `toString( )` method for every object class you create.

Although the `toString( )` method is usually invoked automatically by the system, there are times when you may invoke it yourself. For example, you might want to do an explicit conversion of an object to a string in a situation where JavaScript does not do it automatically for you:

```
y = Math.sqrt(x);       // Compute a number
ystr = y.toString( );  // Convert it to a string
```

Note in this example that numbers have a built-in `toString( )` method that you can use to force a conversion.

In other circumstances, you might choose to use a `toString( )` call even in a context where JavaScript would do the conversion automatically. Using `toString( )` explicitly can help to make your code clearer:

```
alert(my_obj.toString( ));
```

See Also

Object.constructor( ), Object.toLocaleString( ), Object.valueOf( )

Object.valueOf( )

JavaScript 1.1; JScript 2.0; ECMAScript v1

the primitive value of the specified object

Synopsis

object.valueOf( )

Returns

The primitive value associated with the *object*, if any. If there is no value associated with *object*, returns the object itself.

Description

The valueOf( ) method of an object returns the primitive value associated with that object, if there is one. For objects of type Object there is no primitive value, and this method simply returns the object itself.

For objects of type Number, however, valueOf( ) returns the primitive numeric value represented by the object. Similarly, it returns the primitive boolean value associated with a Boolean object and the string associated with a String object.

It is rarely necessary to invoke the valueOf( ) method yourself. JavaScript does this automatically whenever an object is used where a primitive value is expected. In fact, because of this automatic invocation of the valueOf( ) method, it is difficult to even distinguish between primitive values and their corresponding objects. The typeof operator shows you the difference between strings and String objects for example, but in practical terms, you can use them equivalently in your JavaScript code.

The valueOf( ) methods of the Number, Boolean, and String objects convert these wrapper objects to the primitive values they represent. The Object( ) constructor performs the opposite operation when invoked with a number, boolean, or string argument: it wraps the primitive value in an appropriate object wrapper. JavaScript performs this primitive-to-object conversion for you in almost all circumstances, so it is rarely necessary to invoke the Object( ) constructor in this way.

In some circumstances, you may want to define a custom valueOf( ) method for your own objects. For example, you might define a JavaScript object type to represent complex numbers (a real number plus an imaginary number). As part of this object type, you would probably define methods for performing complex addition, multiplication, and so on. But you might also want the ability to treat your complex numbers like ordinary real numbers by discarding the imaginary part. To achieve this, you might do something like the following:

```
Complex.prototype.valueOf = new Function("return this.real");
```

With this valueOf( ) method defined for your Complex object type, you could then do things like pass one of your complex number objects to Math.sqrt( ), which would compute the square root of the real portion of the complex number.

See Also

Object.toString( )

parseFloat( )

JavaScript 1.0; JScript 1.0; ECMAScript v1

convert a string to a number

Synopsis

```
parseFloat(s)
```

Arguments

s The string to be parsed and converted to a number.

Returns

The parsed number, or `NaN` if *s* does not begin with a valid number. In JavaScript 1.0, `parseFloat( )` returns 0 instead of `NaN` when *s* cannot be parsed as a number.

Description

`parseFloat( )` parses and returns the first number that occurs in *s*. Parsing stops, and the value is returned, when `parseFloat( )` encounters a character in *s* that is not a valid part of the number. If *s* does not begin with a number that `parseFloat( )` can parse, the function the not-a-number value `NaN`. Test for this return value with the `isNaN( )` function. If you want to parse only the integer portion of a number, use `parseInt( )` instead of `parseFloat( )`.

Bugs

`NaN` is not supported in JavaScript 1.0, so in that version of the language, `parseFloat( )` returns 0 when it cannot parse *s*. This means that in JavaScript 1.0, if the return value of `parseFloat( )` is 0, you must perform additional tests on *s* to determine whether it really represents the number zero or does not represent a number at all.

See Also

isNaN(), parseInt()

parseInt( )

JavaScript 1.0; JScript 1.1; ECMAScript v1

convert a string to an integer

Synopsis

```
parseInt(s)
parseInt(s, radix)
```

Arguments

s

The string to be parsed.

radix

An optional integer argument that represents the radix (i.e., base) of the number to be parsed. If this argument is omitted or is 0, the number is parsed in base 10, or in base 16 if it begins with "0x" or "0X". If this argument is less than 2 or greater than 36, `parseInt( )` returns `NaN`.

Returns

The parsed number, or `NaN` if *s* does not begin with a valid integer. In JavaScript 1.0, `parseInt()` returns 0 instead of `NaN` when it cannot parse *s*.

Description

`parseInt()` parses and returns the first number (with an optional leading minus sign) that occurs in *s*. Parsing stops, and the value is returned, when `parseInt()` encounters a character in *s* that is not a valid digit for the specified *radix*. If *s* does not begin with a number that `parseInt()` can parse, the function returns the not-a-number value `NaN`. Use the `isNaN()` function to test for this return value.

The *radix* argument specifies the base of the number to be parsed. Specifying 10 makes the `parseInt()` parse a decimal number. The value 8 specifies that an octal number (using digits 0 through 7) is to be parsed. The value 16 specifies a hexadecimal value, using digits 0 through 9 and letters A through F. *radix* can be any value between 2 and 36.

If *radix* is 0 or is not specified, `parseInt()` tries to determine the radix of the number from *s*. If *s* begins (after an optional minus sign) with `0x`, `parseInt()` parses the remainder of *s* as a hexadecimal number. If *s* begins with a `0`, the ECMAScript v3 standard allows an implementation of `parseInt()` to interpret the following characters as an octal number or as a decimal number. Otherwise, if *s* begins with a digit from `1` through `9`, `parseInt()` parses it as a decimal number.

Example

```
parseInt("19", 10);  // Returns 19  (10 + 9)
parseInt("11", 2);   // Returns 3   (2 + 1)
parseInt("17", 8);   // Returns 15  (8 + 7)
parseInt("1f", 16);  // Returns 31  (16 + 15)
parseInt("10");      // Returns 10
parseInt("0x10");    // Returns 16
parseInt("010");     // Ambiguous: returns 10 or 8
```

Bugs

When no *radix* is specified, ECMAScript v3 allows an implementation to parse a string that begins with "0" (but not "0x" or "0X") as an octal or as a decimal number. To avoid this ambiguity, you should explicitly specify a radix or leave the radix unspecified only when you are sure that all numbers to be parsed will be decimal or hexadecimal numbers with the "0x" or "0X" prefix.

In JavaScript 1.0, `NaN` is not supported, and `parseInt()` returns 0 instead of `NaN` when it cannot parse *s*. In this version of the language, `parseInt()` cannot distinguish between malformed input and a the legal input "0".

See Also

isNaN(), parseFloat()

RangeError

JavaScript 1.5; JScript 5.5; ECMAScript v3

thrown when a number is out of its legal range — **Inherits from Error**

Constructor

```
new RangeError( )
new RangeError(message)
```

Arguments

message
: An optional error message that provides details about the exception. If specified, this argument is used as the value for the `message` property of the RangeError object.

Returns

A newly constructed RangeError object. If the *message* argument is specified, the Error object will use it as the value of its `message` property; otherwise, it will use an implementation-defined default string as the value of that property. When the `RangeError( )` constructor is called as a function, without the `new` operator, it behaves just as it does when called with the `new` operator.

Properties

`message`
: An error message that provides details about the exception. This property holds the string passed to the constructor, or an implementation-defined default string. See "Error.message" for details.

`name`
: A string that specifies the type of the exception. All RangeError objects inherit the value "RangeError" for this property.

Description

An instance of the RangeError class is thrown when a numeric value is not in its legal range. For example, setting the length of an array is set to a negative number causes a RangeError to be thrown. See "Error" for details about throwing and catching exceptions.

See Also

Error, Error.message, Error.name

ReferenceError

JavaScript 1.5; JScript 5.5; ECMAScript v3

thrown when reading a variable that does not exist — **Inherits from Error**

Constructor

```
new ReferenceError( )
new ReferenceError(message)
```

Arguments

message

An optional error message that provides details about the exception. If specified, this argument is used as the value for the `message` property of the ReferenceError object.

Returns

A newly constructed ReferenceError object. If the *message* argument is specified, the Error object will use it as the value of its `message` property; otherwise, it will use an implementation-defined default string as the value of that property. When the `ReferenceError()` constructor is called as a function, without the `new` operator, it behaves just as it does when called with the `new` operator.

Properties

`message`

An error message that provides details about the exception. This property holds the string passed to the constructor, or an implementation-defined default string. See "Error.message" for details.

`name`

A string that specifies the type of the exception. All ReferenceError objects inherit the value "ReferenceError" for this property.

Description

An instance of the ReferenceError class is thrown when you attempt to read the value of a variable that does not exist. See "Error" for details about throwing and catching exceptions.

See Also

Error, Error.message, Error.name

RegExp

JavaScript 1.2; JScript 3.0; ECMAScript v3

regular expressions for pattern matching

Literal Syntax

```
/pattern/attributes
```

Constructor

```
new RegExp(pattern, attributes)
```

Arguments

pattern

A string that specifies the pattern of the regular expression, or another regular expression.

attributes

An optional string containing any of the "g", "i", and "m" attributes that specify global, case-insensitive, and multiline matches. The "m" attribute is not available prior to ECMAScript standardization. If the *pattern* argument is a regular expression instead of a string, this argument must be omitted.

Returns

A new `RegExp` object, with the specified pattern and flags. If the *pattern* argument is a regular expression rather than a string, the `RegExp()` constructor creates a new RegExp object using the same pattern and flags as the specified RegExp. If `RegExp()` is called as a function without the `new` operator, it behaves just as it would with the `new` operator, except when *pattern* is a regular expression; in that case, it simply returns *pattern* instead of creating a new RegExp object.

Throws

`SyntaxError`
: If *pattern* is not a legal regular expression or if *attributes* contains characters other than "g", "i", and "m".

`TypeError`
: If *pattern* is a RegExp object and the *attributes* argument is not omitted.

Instance Properties

`global`
: Whether the RegExp has the `g` attribute.

`ignoreCase`
: Whether the RegExp has the `i` attribute.

`lastIndex`
: The character position of the last match; used for finding multiple matches in a string.

`multiline`
: Whether the RegExp has the `m` attribute.

`source`
: The source text of the regular expression.

Methods

`exec()`
: Performs powerful, general-purpose pattern matching.

`test()`
: Tests whether a string contains a pattern.

Description

The RegExp object represents a regular expression, a powerful tool for performing pattern matching on strings. See Chapter 10 for complete details on regular expression syntax and use.

See Also

Chapter 10

RegExp.exec( )

JavaScript 1.2; JScript 3.0; ECMAScript v3

general-purpose pattern matching

Synopsis

regexp.exec(*string*)

Arguments

string
    The string to be searched.

Returns

An array containing the results of the match, or null if no match was found. The format of the returned array is described below.

Throws

TypeError
    If this method is invoked on an object that is not a RegExp.

Description

exec( ) is the most powerful of all the RegExp and String pattern matching methods. It is a general-purpose method that is somewhat more complex to use than RegExp.test( ), String.search( ), String.replace( ), and String.match( ).

exec( ) searches *string* for text that matches *regexp*. If it finds a match, it returns an array of results; otherwise, it returns null. Element 0 of the returned array is the matched text. Element 1 is the text that matched the first parenthesized subexpression, if any, within *regexp*. Element 2 contains the text that matched the second subexpression, and so on. The array length property specifies the number of elements in the array, as usual. In addition to the array elements and the length property, the value returned by exec( ) also has two other properties. The index property specifies the character position of the first character of the matched text. The input property refers to *string*. This returned array is the same as the array that is returned by the String.match( ) method, when invoked on a nonglobal RegExp object.

When exec( ) is invoked on a nonglobal pattern, it performs the search and returns the result described above. When *regexp* is a global regular expression, however, exec( ) behaves in a slightly more complex way. It begins searching *string* at the character position specified by the lastIndex property of *regexp*. When it finds a match, it sets lastIndex to the position of the first character after the match. This means that you can invoke exec( ) repeatedly in order to loop through all matches in a string. When exec( ) cannot find any more matches, it returns null and resets lastIndex to zero. If you begin searching a new string immediately after successfully finding a match in another string, you must be careful to manually reset lastIndex to zero.

Note that exec( ) always includes full details of every match in the array it returns, whether or not *regexp* is a global pattern. This is where exec( ) differs from String.match( ), which returns much less information when used with global patterns. Calling the exec( ) method repeatedly in a loop is the only way to obtain complete pattern matching information for a global pattern.

Example

You can use exec( ) in a loop to find all matches within a string. For example:

```
var pattern = /\bJava\w*\b/g;
var text = "JavaScript is more fun than Java or JavaBeans!";
var result;
while((result = pattern.exec(text)) != null) {
    alert("Matched `" + result[0] +
          "' at position " + result.index +
          " next search begins at position " + pattern.lastIndex);
}
```

Bugs

In JScript 3.0, exec( ) does not properly set or use the lastIndex property, so it cannot be used with global patterns in the kind of loop shown in the example above.

See Also

RegExp.lastIndex, RegExp.test( ), String.match( ), String.replace( ), String.search( ); Chapter 10

RegExp.global — JavaScript 1.2; JScript 5.5; ECMAScript v3

whether a regular expression matches globally

Synopsis

regexp.global

Description

global is a read-only boolean property of RegExp objects. It specifies whether a particular regular expression performs global matching; i.e., whether it was created with the g attribute.

RegExp.ignoreCase — JavaScript 1.2; JScript 5.5; ECMAScript v3

whether a regular expression is case-insensitive

Synopsis

regexp.ignoreCase

Description

ignoreCase is a read-only boolean property of RegExp objects. It specifies whether a particular regular expression performs case-insensitive matching; i.e.,whether it was created with the i attribute.

RegExp.lastIndex

JavaScript 1.2; JScript 5.5; ECMAScript v3

the starting position of the next match

Synopsis

`regexp.lastIndex`

Description

`lastIndex` is a read/write property of RegExp objects. For regular expressions with the `g` attribute set, it contains an integer that specifies the character position immediately following the last match found by the `RegExp.exec()` and `RegExp.test()` methods. These methods use this property as the starting point for the next search they conduct. This allows you to call those methods repeatedly, to loop through all matches in a string. Note that `lastIndex` is not used by RegExp objects that do not have the `g` attribute and do not represent global patterns.

This property is read/write, so you can set it at any time to specify where in the target string the next search should begin. `exec()` and `test()` automatically reset `lastIndex` to 0 when they fail to find a match (or another match). If you begin to search a new string after a successful match of some other string, you have to explicitly set this property to 0.

See Also

RegExp.exec(), RegExp.test()

RegExp.source

JavaScript 1.2; JScript 3.0; ECMAScript v3

the text of the regular expression

Synopsis

`regexp.source`

Description

`source` is a read-only string property of RegExp objects. It contains the text of the RegExp pattern. This text does not include the delimiting slashes used in regular expression literals, and it does not include the `g`, `i`, and `m` attributes.

RegExp.test( )

JavaScript 1.2; JScript 3.0; ECMAScript v3

test whether a string matches a pattern

Synopsis

`regexp.test(string)`

Arguments

string
: The string to be tested.

Returns

true if *string* contains text that matches *regexp*; `false` otherwise.

Throws

`TypeError`
    If this method is invoked on an object that is not a RegExp.

Description

`test()` tests *string* to see if it contains text that matches *regexp*. If so, it returns `true`; otherwise, it returns `false`. Calling the test method of a RegExp *r* and passing it the string *s* is equivalent to the following expression:

```
(r.exec(s) != null)
```

Example

```
var pattern = /java/i;
pattern.test("JavaScript");   // Returns true
pattern.test("ECMAScript");   // Returns false
```

See Also

RegExp.exec(), RegExp.lastIndex, String.match(), String.replace(), String.substring(); Chapter 10

RegExp.toString()

JavaScript 1.2; JScript 3.0; ECMAScript v3

convert a regular expression to a string

Overrides Object.toString()

Synopsis

regexp`.toString()`

Returns

A string representation of *regexp*.

Throws

`TypeError`
    If this method is invoked on an object that is not a RegExp.

Description

The `RegExp.toString()` method returns a string representation of a regular expression in the form of a regular expression literal.

Note that implementations are not required to add escape sequences to ensure that the returned string is a legal regular expression literal. Consider the regular expression created by the expression `new RegExp("/", "g")`. An implementation of `RegExp.toString()` could return `///g` for this regular expression, or it could also add an escape sequence and return `/\//g`.

String

JavaScript 1.0; JScript 1.0; ECMAScript v1

support for strings

Inherits from Object

Constructor

```
new String(s)  // Constructor function
String(s)      // Conversion function
```

Arguments

s The value to be stored in a String object or converted to a primitive string.

Returns

When `String()` is used as a constructor with the `new` operator, it returns a String object, which holds the string *s* or the string representation of *s*. When the `String()` constructor is used without the `new` operator, it simply converts *s* to a primitive string and returns the converted value.

Properties

`length`	The number of characters in the string.

Methods

`charAt()`	Extracts the character at a given position from a string.
`charCodeAt()`	Returns the encoding of the character at a given position in a string.
`concat()`	Concatenates one or more values to a string.
`indexOf()`	Searches the string for a character or substring.
`lastIndexOf()`	Searches the string backward for a character or substring.
`match()`	Performs pattern matching with a regular expression.
`replace()`	Performs a search-and-replace operation with a regular expression.
`search()`	Searches a string for a substring that matches a regular expression.
`slice()`	Returns a slice or substring of a string.
`split()`	Splits a string into an array of strings, breaking at a specified delimiter string or regular expression.
`substring()`	Extracts a substring of a string.
`substr()`	Extracts a substring of a string. A variant of `substring()`.
`toLowerCase()`	Returns a copy of the string, with all characters converted to lowercase.
`toString()`	Returns the primitive string value.
`toUpperCase()`	Returns a copy of the string, with all characters converted to uppercase.
`valueOf()`	Returns the primitive string value.

Static Methods

`String.fromCharCode()`
Creates a new string using the character codes passed as arguments.

HTML Methods

Since JavaScript 1.0 and JScript 1.0, the String class has defined a number of methods that return a string modified by placing it within HTML tags. These methods have never been standardized by ECMAScript but can be useful in both client-side and server-side JavaScript code that dynamically generates HTML. If you are willing to use nonstandard methods, you might create the HTML source for a bold, red hyperlink, with code like this:

```
var s = "click here!";
var html = s.bold().link("javascript:alert('hello')").fontcolor("red");
```

Because these methods are not standardized, they do not have individual reference entries in the pages that follow:

anchor(*name*)	Returns a copy of the string, in an <a name=> environment.
big()	Returns a copy of the string, in a <big> environment.
blink()	Returns a copy of the string, in a <blink> environment.
bold()	Returns a copy of the string, in a <b> environment.
fixed()	Returns a copy of the string, in a <tt> environment.
fontcolor(*color*)	Returns a copy of the string, in a <font color=> environment.
fontsize(*size*)	Returns a copy of the string, in a <font size=> environment.
italics()	Returns a copy of the string, in a <i> environment.
link(*url*)	Returns a copy of the string, in a <a href=> environment.
small()	Returns a copy of the string, in a <small> environment.
strike()	Returns a copy of the string, in a <strike> environment.
sub()	Returns a copy of the string, in a <sub> environment.
sup()	Returns a copy of the string, in a <sup> environment.

Description

Strings are a primitive data type in JavaScript. The String class type exists to provide methods for operating on primitive string values. The length property of a String object specifies the number of characters in the string. The String class defines a number of methods for operating on strings: there are methods for extracting a character or a substring from the string or searching for a character or a substring, for example. Note that JavaScript strings are *immutable*: none of the methods defined by the String class allows you to change the contents of a string. Instead, methods like String.toUpperCase() return an entirely new string, without modifying the original.

In Netscape implementations of JavaScript 1.2 and later, strings behave like read-only arrays of characters. For example, to extract the 3rd character from a string s, you could write s[2] instead of the more standard s.charAt(2). In addition, when the for/in statement is applied to a string, it enumerates these array indexes for each character in the string. (Note, however, that the length property is not enumerated, as per the ECMAScript specification.) Because this string-as-array behavior of Netscape's implementations is not standard, you should usually avoid using it.

See Also

Chapter 3

String.charAt( )

JavaScript 1.0; JScript 1.0, ECMAScript v1

get the *n*th character from a string

Synopsis

```
string.charAt(n)
```

Arguments

n The index of the character that should be returned from *string*.

Returns

The *n*th character of *string*.

Description

`String.charAt( )` returns the *n*th character of the string *string*. The first character of the string is numbered 0. If *n* is not between 0 and *string.length*–1, this method returns an empty string. Note that JavaScript does not have a character data type that is distinct from the string type, so the returned character is a string of length 1.

See Also

String.charCodeAt( ), String.indexOf( ), String.lastIndexOf( )

String.charCodeAt( )

JavaScript 1.2; JScript 5.5; ECMAScript v1

get the *n*th character code from a string

Synopsis

```
string.charCodeAt(n)
```

Arguments

n The index of the character whose encoding is to be returned.

Returns

The Unicode encoding of the *n*th character within *string*. This return value is a 16-bit integer between 0 and 65535.

Description

`charCodeAt( )` is like `charAt( )` except that it returns the character encoding at a specific location, rather than returning a substring that contains the character itself. If *n* is negative or greater than or equal to the string length, `charCodeAt( )` returns `NaN`.

See "String.fromCharCode( )" for a way to create a string from Unicode encodings.

Bugs

JavaScript 1.2 (as implemented by Netscape 4.0, for example) does not have full support for 16-bit Unicode characters and strings.

See Also

String.charAt( ), String.fromCharCode( )

String.concat( )

JavaScript 1.2; JScript 3.0; ECMAScript v3

concatenate strings

Synopsis

string.concat(*value*, ...)

Arguments

value, ...
: One or more values to be concatenated to *string*.

Returns

A new string that results from concatenating each of the arguments to *string*.

Description

concat( ) converts each of its arguments to a string (if necessary) and appends them, in order, to the end of *string*. It returns the resulting concatenation. Note that *string* itself is not modified.

String.concat( ) is an analog to Array.concat( ). Note that it is often easier to use the + operator to perform string concatenation.

See Also

Array.concat( )

String.fromCharCode( )

JavaScript 1.2; JScript 3.0; ECMAScript v1

create a string from character encodings

Synopsis

String.fromCharCode(*c1*, *c2*, ...)

Arguments

c1, *c2*, ...
: Zero or more integers that specify the Unicode encodings of the characters in the string to be created.

Returns

A new string containing characters with the specified encodings.

Description

This static method provides a way to create a string by specifying the individual numeric Unicode encodings of its characters. Note that as a static method, fromCharCode( ) is a property of the `String( )` constructor and is not actually a method of strings or String objects.

`String.charCodeAt( )` is a companion instance method that provides a way to obtain the encodings of the individual characters of a string.

Example

```
// Create the string "hello"
var s = String.fromCharCode(104, 101, 108, 108, 111);
```

Bugs

JavaScript 1.2 (as implemented by Netscape 4.0, for example) does not have full support for 16-bit Unicode characters and strings.

See Also

String.charCodeAt()

String.indexOf( )

JavaScript 1.0; JScript 1.0, ECMAScript v1

search a string

Synopsis

`string``.indexOf(`*`substring`*`)`
`string``.indexOf(`*`substring`*`, `*`start`*`)`

Arguments

`substring`
: The substring that is to be searched for within *`string`*.

`start`
: An optional integer argument that specifies the position within *`string`* at which the search is to start. Legal values are 0 (the position of the first character in the string) to *`string`*`.length−1` (the position of the last character in the string). If this argument is omitted, the search begins at the first character of the string.

Returns

The position of the first occurrence of *`substring`* within *`string`* that appears after the *`start`* position, if any, or −1 if no such occurrence is found.

Description

`String.indexOf( )` searches the string *`string`* from beginning to end to see if it contains an occurrence of *`substring`*. The search begins at position *`start`* within *`string`*, or at the beginning of *`string`* if *`start`* is not specified. If an occurrence of *`substring`* is found, `String.indexOf( )` returns the position of the first character of the first occurrence of *`substring`* within *`string`*. Character positions within *`string`* are numbered starting with zero.

If no occurrence of *`substring`* is found within *`string`*, `String.indexOf( )` returns −1.

Bugs

In JavaScript 1.0 and 1.1, if *start* is greater than the length of *string*, `indexOf( )` returns the empty string, rather than –1.

See Also

String.charAt( ), String.lastIndexOf( ), String.substring( )

String.lastIndexOf( )

JavaScript 1.0; JScript 1.0, ECMAScript v1

search a string backward

Synopsis

```
string.lastIndexOf(substring)
string.lastIndexOf(substring, start)
```

Arguments

substring
: The substring that is to be searched for within *string*.

start
: An optional integer argument that specifies the position within *string* where the search is to start. Legal values are from 0 (the position of the first character in the string) to *string*.`length`–1 (the position of the last character in the string). If this argument is omitted, the search begins with the last character of the string.

Returns

The position of the last occurrence of *substring* within *string* that appears before the *start* position, if any, or –1 if no such occurrence is found within *string*.

Description

`String.lastIndexOf( )` searches the string from end to beginning to see if it contains an occurrence of *substring*. The search begins at position *start* within *string*, or at the end of *string* if *start* is not specified. If an occurrence of *substring* is found, `String.lastIndexOf( )` returns the position of the first character of that occurrence. Since this method searches from end to beginning of the string, the first occurrence found is the last one in the string that occurs before the *start* position.

If no occurrence of *substring* is found, `String.lastIndexOf( )` returns –1.

Note that although `String.lastIndexOf( )` searches *string* from end to beginning, it still numbers character positions within *string* from the beginning. The first character of the string has position 0 and the last has position *string*.`length`–1.

See Also

String.charAt( ), String.indexOf( ), String.substring( )

String.length

JavaScript 1.0; JScript 1.0, ECMAScript v1

the length of a string

Synopsis

string.length

Description

The `String.length` property is a read-only integer that indicates the number of characters in the specified *string*. For any string `s`, the index of the last character is `s.length–1`. The `length` property of a string is not enumerated by a `for/in` loop and may not be deleted with the `delete` operator.

String.localeCompare( )

JavaScript 1.5; JScript 5.5; ECMAScript v3

compare one string to another, using locale-specific ordering

Synopsis

string.localeCompare(*target*)

Arguments

target
: A `string` to be compared, in a locale-sensitive fashion, with *string*.

Returns

A number that indicates the result of the comparison. If *string* is "less than" *target*, `localeCompare( )` returns a number less than zero. If *string* is "greater than" *target*, the method returns a number greater than zero. And if the strings are identical or indistinguishable according to the locale ordering conventions, the method returns 0.

Description

When the < and > operators are applied to strings, they compare those strings using only the Unicode encodings of those characters and do not consider the collation order of the current locale. The ordering produced in this way is not always correct. Consider Spanish, for example, in which the letters "ch" are traditionally sorted as if they were a single letter that appeared between the letters "c" and "d".

`localeCompare( )` provides a way to compare strings that does take the collation order of the default locale into account. The ECMAScript standard does not specify how the locale-specific comparison is done; it merely specifies that this function utilizes the collation order provided by the underlying operating system.

Example

You can use code like the following to sort an array of strings into a locale-specific ordering:

```
var strings;  // The array of strings to sort; initialized elsewhere
strings.sort(function(a,b) { return a.localeCompare(b) });
```

String.match( )

JavaScript 1.2; JScript 3.0; ECMAScript v3

find one or more regular expression matches

Synopsis

string.match(*regexp*)

Arguments

regexp
: A RegExp object that specifies the pattern to be matched. If this argument is not a RegExp, it is first converted to one by passing it to the RegExp( ) constructor.

Returns

An array containing the results of the match. The contents of the array depend on whether *regexp* has the global g attribute set. Details on this return value are given below.

Description

match( ) searches *string* for one or more matches of *regexp*. The behavior of this method depends significantly on whether *regexp* has the g attribute or not. See Chapter 10 for full details on regular expressions.

If *regexp* does not have the g attribute, match( ) searches *string* for a single match. If no match is found, match( ) returns null. Otherwise, it returns an array containing information about the match that it found. Element 0 of the array contains the matched text. The remaining elements contain the text that matched any parenthesized subexpressions within the regular expression. In addition to these normal array elements, the returned array also has two object properties. The index property of the array specifies the character position within *string* of the start of the matched text. Also, the input property of the returned array is a reference to *string* itself.

If *regexp* has the g flag, match( ) does a global search, searching *string* for all matching substrings. It returns null if no match is found, and it returns an array if one or more matches are found. The contents of this returned array are quite different for global matches, however. In this case, the array elements contain each of the matched substrings within *string*. The returned array does not have index or input properties in this case. Note that for global matches, match( ) does not provide information about parenthesized subexpressions, nor does it specify where within *string* each match occurred. If you need to obtain this information for a global search, you can use RegExp.exec( ).

Example

The following global match finds all numbers within a string:

```
"1 plus 2 equals 3".match(/\d+/g)  // Returns ["1", "2", "3"]
```

The following nonglobal match uses a more complex regular expression with several parenthesized subexpressions. It matches a URL, and its subexpressions match the protocol, host, and path portions of the URL:

```
var url = /(\w+):\/\/([\w.]+)\/(\S*)/;
var text = "Visit my home page at http://www.isp.com/~david";
```

```
    var result = text.match(url);
    if (result != null) {
        var fullurl = result[0];    // Contains "http://www.isp.com/~david"
        var protocol = result[1];   // Contains "http"
        var host = result[2];       // Contains "www.isp.com"
        var path = result[3];       // Contains "~david"
    }
```

See Also

RegExp, RegExp.exec( ), RegExp.test( ), String.replace( ), String.search( ); Chapter 10

String.replace( ) JavaScript 1.2; JScript 3.0; ECMAScript v3

replace substring(s) matching a regular expression

Synopsis

string.replace(*regexp*, *replacement*)

Arguments

regexp
: The RegExp object that specifies the pattern to be replaced. If this argument is a string, it is used as a literal text pattern to be searched for; it is not first converted to a RegExp object.

replacement
: A string that specifies the replacement text, or a function that is invoked to generate the replacement text. See the "Description" section for details.

Returns

A new string, with the first match, or all matches, of *regexp* replaced with *replacement*.

Description

replace( ) performs a search-and-replace operation on *string*. It searches *string* for one or more substrings that match *regexp* and replaces them with *replacement*. If *regexp* has the global g attribute specified, replace( ) replaces all matching substrings. Otherwise, it replaces only the first matching substring.

replacement may be a string or a function. If it is a string, each match is replaced by the string. Except, however, that the $ character has special meaning within the *replacement* string. As shown in the following table, it indicates that a string derived from the pattern match is to be used in the replacement.

Characters	Replacement
$1, $2, ... $99	The text that matched the 1st through 99th parenthesized subexpression within *regexp*
$&	The substring that matched *regexp*
$`	The text to the left of the matched substring
$'	The text to the right of the matched substring
$$	A literal dollar sign

ECMAScript v3 specifies that the *replacement* argument to replace( ) may be a function instead of a string, and this feature is implemented in JavaScript 1.2 and JScript 5.5. In this case, the function is invoked for each match and the string it returns is used as the replacement text. The first argument to the function is the string that matched the pattern. The next arguments are the strings that matched any parenthesized subexpressions within the pattern. There may be zero or more of these arguments. The next argument is an integer that specifies the position within *string* at which the match occurred, and the final argument to the *replacement* function is *string* itself.

Example

To ensure that the capitalization of the word "JavaScript" is correct:

```
text.replace(/javascript/i, "JavaScript");
```

To convert a single name from "Doe, John" format to "John Doe" format:

```
name.replace(/(\w+)\s*,\s*(\w+)/, "$2 $1");
```

To replace all double quotes with double back and forward single quotes:

```
text.replace(/"([^"]*)"/g, "``$1''");
```

To capitalize the first letter of all words in a string:

```
text.replace(/\b\w+\b/g, function(word) {
                           return word.substring(0,1).toUpperCase( ) +
                                  word.substring(1);
                         });
```

See Also

RegExp, RegExp.exec( ), RegExp.test( ), String.match( ), String.search( ); Chapter 10

String.search( )

JavaScript 1.2; JScript 3.0; ECMAScript v3

search for a regular expression

Synopsis

string.search(*regexp*)

Arguments

regexp
: A RegExp object that specifies the pattern to be searched for in *string*. If this argument is not a RegExp, it is first converted to one by passing it to the RegExp( ) constructor.

Returns

The position of the start of the first substring of *string* that matches *regexp*, or –1 if no match was found.

Description

search( ) looks for a substring matching *regexp* within *string* and returns the position of the first character of the matching substring, or –1 if no match was found.

search( ) does not do global matches; it ignores the g flag. It also ignores the lastIndex property of *regexp* and always searches from the beginning of the string, which means that it always returns the position of the first match in *string*.

Example

```
var s = "JavaScript is fun";
s.search(/script/i)  // Returns 4
s.search(/a(.)a/)    // Returns 1
```

See Also

RegExp, RegExp.exec( ), RegExp.test( ), String.match( ), String.replace( ); Chapter 10

String.slice( )

JavaScript 1.2; JScript 3.0; ECMAScript v3

extract a substring

Synopsis

string.slice(*start*, *end*)

Arguments

start

The string index where the slice is to begin. If negative, this argument specifies a position measured from the end of the string. That is, –1 indicates the last character, –2 indicates the second from last character, and so on.

end

The string index immediately after the end of the slice. If not specified, the slice includes all characters from *start* to the end of the string. If this argument is negative, it specifies a position measured from the end of the string.

Returns

A new string that contains all the characters of *string* from and including *start* and up to but not including *end*.

Description

slice( ) returns a string containing a slice, or substring, of *string*. It does not modify *string*.

The String methods slice( ), substring( ), and the deprecated substr( ) all return specified portions of a string. slice( ) is more flexible than substring( ) because it allows negative argument values. slice( ) differs from substr( ) in that it specifies a substring with two character positions, while substr( ) uses one position and a length. Note also that String.slice( ) is an analog of Array.slice( ).

Example

```
var s = "abcdefg";
s.slice(0,4)    // Returns "abcd"
s.slice(2,4)    // Returns "cd"
```

```
s.slice(4)       // Returns "efg"
s.slice(3,-1)    // Returns "def"
s.slice(3,-2)    // Returns "de"
s.slice(-3,-1)   // Should return "ef"; returns "abcdef" in IE 4
```

Bugs

Negative values for *start* do not work in JScript 3.0 (Internet Explorer 4). Instead of specifying a character position measured from the end of the string, they specify character position 0.

See Also

Array.slice( ), String.substring( )

String.split( )

JavaScript 1.1; JScript 3.0; ECMAScript v1; enhanced in ECMAScript v3

break a string into an array of strings

Synopsis

string.split(*delimiter*, *limit*)

Arguments

delimiter
: The string or regular expression at which the *string* splits. The use of a regular expression as a delimiter is standardized by ECMAScript v3 and implemented in JavaScript 1.2 and JScript 3.0; it is not implemented in JavaScript 1.1.

limit
: This optional integer specifies the maximum length of the returned array. If specified, no more than this number of substrings will be returned. If not specified, the entire string will be split, regardless of its length. This argument is standardized by ECMAScript v3 and implemented in JavaScript 1.2 and JScript 3.0; it is not implemented in JavaScript 1.1.

Returns

An array of strings, created by splitting *string* into substrings at the boundaries specified by *delimiter*. The substrings in the returned array do not include *delimiter* itself, except in the case noted below.

Description

The split( ) method creates and returns an array of as many as *limit* substrings of the specified string. These substrings are created by searching the string from start to end for text that matches *delimiter* and breaking the string before and after that matching text. The delimiting text is not included in any of the returned substrings, except as noted below. Note that if the delimiter matches the beginning of the string, the first element of the returned array will be an empty string—the text that appears before the delimiter. Similarly, if the delimiter matches the end of the string, the last element of the array (assuming no conflicting *limit*) will be the empty string.

If no *delimiter* is specified, the string is not split at all, and the returned array contains only a single, unbroken string element. If *delimiter* is the empty string or a regular expression that matches the empty string, the string is broken between each character, and the returned array has the same length as the string does, assuming no smaller *limit* is specified. (Note that this is a special case since the empty string before the first character and after the last character is not matched.)

We said above that the substrings in the array returned by this method do not contain the delimiting text used to split the string. However, if *delimiter* is a regular expression that contains parenthesized subexpressions, the substrings that match those parenthesized subexpressions (but not the text that matches the regular expression as a whole) are included in the returned array.

Note that the `String.split( )` method is the inverse of the `Array.join( )` method.

Example

The `split( )` method is most useful when you are working with highly structured strings. For example:

```
"1:2:3:4:5".split(":");  // Returns ["1","2","3","4","5"]
"|a|b|c|".split("|");    // Returns ["", "a", "b", "c", ""]
```

Another common use of the `split( )` method is to parse commands and similar strings by breaking them down into words delimited by spaces:

```
var words = sentence.split(' ');
```

See the "Bugs" section for details on a special case when *delimiter* is a single space. It is easier to split a string into words using a regular expression as a delimiter:

```
var words = sentence.split(/\s+/);
```

To split a string into an array of characters, use the empty string as the delimiter. Use the *limit* argument if you only want to split a prefix of the string into an array of characters:

```
"hello".split("");     // Returns ["h","e","l","l","o"]
"hello".split("", 3);  // Returns ["h","e","l"]
```

If you want the delimiters, or one or more portions of the delimiter included in the returned array, use a regular expression with parenthesized subexpressions. For example, the following code breaks a string at HTML tags and includes those tags in the returned array:

```
var text = "hello <b>world</b>";
text.split(/(<[^>]*>)/);  // Returns ["hello ","<b>","world","</b>",""]
```

Bugs

In Netscape's implementations of JavaScript, when language Version 1.2 is explicitly requested (with the `language` attribute of a `<script>` tag, for example), the `split( )` method has one special-case behavior: if *delimiter* is a single space, the method splits the string at spaces but ignores any white space at the beginning and end of the string. See Section 11.6, "Netscape's JavaScript 1.2 Incompatibilities," for further details.

See Also

Array.join(), RegExp; Chapter 10

String.substr( )

JavaScript 1.2; JScript 3.0; deprecated

extract a substring

Synopsis

string.substr(*start*, *length*)

Arguments

start
: The start position of the substring. If this argument is negative, it specifies a position measured from the end of the string: –1 specifies the last character, –2 specifies the second-to-last character, and so on.

length
: The number of characters in the substring. If this argument is omitted, the returned substring includes all characters from the starting position to the end of the string.

Returns

A copy of the portion of *string* starting at and including the character specified by *start* and continuing for *length* characters, or to the end of the string if *length* is not specified.

Description

substr( ) extracts and returns a substring of *string*. It does not modify *string*.

Note that substr( ) specifies the desired substring with a character position and a length. This provides a useful alternative to String.substring( ) and String.splice( ), which specify a substring with two character positions. Note, however, that this method has not been standardized by ECMAScript and is therefore deprecated.

Example

```
var s = "abcdefg";
s.substr(2,2);   // Returns "cd"
s.substr(3);     // Returns "defg"
s.substr(-3,2);  // Should return "ef"; returns "ab" in IE 4
```

Bugs

Negative values for *start* do not work in JScript 3.0 (IE 4). Instead of specifying a character position measured from the end of the string, they specify character position 0.

See Also

String.slice( ), String.substring( )

String.substring( )

JavaScript 1.0; JScript 1.0, ECMAScript v1

return a substring of a string

Synopsis

string.substring(*from*, *to*)

Arguments

from

An integer that specifies the position within *string* of the first character of the desired substring.

to

An optional integer that is one greater than the position of the last character of the desired substring. If this argument is omitted, the returned substring runs to the end of the string.

Returns

A new string, of length *to–from*, which contains a substring of *string*. The new string contains characters copied from positions *from* to *to*–1 of *string*.

Description

`String.substring( )` returns a substring of *string* consisting of the characters between positions *from* and *to*. The character at position *from* is included, but the character at position *to* is not included.

If *from* equals *to*, this method returns an empty (length 0) string. If *from* is greater than *to*, this method first swaps the two arguments and then returns the substring between them.

It is important to remember that the character at position *from* is included in the substring but that the character at position *to* is not included in the substring. While this may seem arbitrary or counterintuitive, a notable feature of this system is that the length of the returned substring is always equal to *to–from*.

Note that `String.slice( )` and the nonstandard `String.substr( )` can also be used to extract substrings from a string.

Bugs

In Netscape's implementations of JavaScript, when language Version 1.2 is explicitly requested (with the `language` attribute of a `<script>` tag, for example), this method does not correctly swap its arguments if *from* is greater than *to*. Instead it returns the empty string.

See Also

String.charAt( ), String.indexOf( ), String.lastIndexOf( ), String.slice( ), String.substr( )

String.toLocaleLowerCase( )

JavaScript 1.5; JScript 5.5, ECMAScript v3

convert a string to lowercase

Synopsis

```
string.toLocaleLowerCase( )
```

Returns

A copy of *string*, converted to lowercase letters in a locale-specific way. Only a few languages, such as Turkish, have locale-specific case mappings, so this method usually returns the same value as `toLowerCase( )`.

See Also

String.toLocaleUpperCase( ), String.toLowerCase( ), String.toUpperCase( )

String.toLocaleUpperCase( )

JavaScript 1.5; JScript 5.5, ECMAScript v3

convert a string to uppercase

Synopsis

```
string.toLocaleUpperCase( )
```

Returns

A copy of *string*, converted to uppercase letters in a locale-specific way. Only a few languages, such as Turkish, have locale-specific case mappings, so this method usually returns the same value as `toUpperCase( )`.

See Also

String.toLocaleLowerCase( ), String.toLowerCase( ), String.toUpperCase( )

String.toLowerCase( )

JavaScript 1.0; JScript 1.0, ECMAScript v1

convert a string to lowercase

Synopsis

```
string.toLowerCase( )
```

Returns

A copy of *string*, with each uppercase letter converted to its lowercase equivalent, if it has one.

String.toString( )

JavaScript 1.0; JScript 1.0, ECMAScript v1

return the string

Overrides Object.toString( )

Synopsis

```
string.toString( )
```

Returns

The primitive string value of *string*. It is rarely necessary to call this method.

Throws

`TypeError`
: If this method is invoked on an object that is not a String.

See Also

String.valueOf( )

String.toUpperCase( )

JavaScript 1.0; JScript 1.0, ECMAScript v1

convert a string to uppercase

Synopsis

```
string.toUpperCase( )
```

Returns

A copy of *string*, with each lowercase letter converted to its uppercase equivalent, if it has one.

String.valueOf( )

JavaScript 1.0; JScript 1.0, ECMAScript v1

return the string

Overrides Object.valueOf( )

Synopsis

```
string.valueOf( )
```

Returns

The primitive string value of *string*.

Throws

`TypeError`
: If this method is invoked on an object that is not a String.

See Also

String.toString( )

SyntaxError

JavaScript 1.5; JScript 5.5; ECMAScript v3

thrown to signal a syntax error

Inherits from Error

Constructor

```
new SyntaxError( )
new SyntaxError(message)
```

Arguments

message
: An optional error message that provides details about the exception. If specified, this argument is used as the value for the `message` property of the SyntaxError object.

Returns

A newly constructed SyntaxError object. If the *message* argument is specified, the Error object will use it as the value of its `message` property; otherwise, it will use an implementation-defined default string as the value of that property. When the `SyntaxError( )` constructor is called as a function, without the `new` operator, it behaves just as it does when called with the `new` operator.

Properties

`message`
: An error message that provides details about the exception. This property holds the string passed to the constructor, or an implementation-defined default string. See "Error.message" for details.

`name`
: A string that specifies the type of the exception. All SyntaxError objects inherit the value "SyntaxError" for this property.

Description

An instance of the SyntaxError class is thrown to signal a syntax error in JavaScript code. The `eval()` method, the `Function()` constructor, and the `RegExp()` constructor may all throw exceptions of this type. See "Error" for details about throwing and catching exceptions.

See Also

Error, Error.message, Error.name

TypeError

JavaScript 1.5; JScript 5.5; ECMAScript v3

thrown when a value is of the wrong type — **Inherits from Error**

Constructor

```
new TypeError()
new TypeError(message)
```

Arguments

`message`
: An optional error message that provides details about the exception. If specified, this argument is used as the value for the `message` property of the TypeError object.

Returns

A newly constructed TypeError object. If the *`message`* argument is specified, the Error object will use it as the value of its `message` property; otherwise, it will use an implementation-defined default string as the value of that property. When the `TypeError()` constructor is called as a function, without the `new` operator, it behaves just as it does when called with the `new` operator.

Properties

`message`
: An error message that provides details about the exception. This property holds the string passed to the constructor, or an implementation-defined default string. See "Error.message" for details

`name`
: A string that specifies the type of the exception. All TypeError objects inherit the value "TypeError" for this property.

Description

An instance of the TypeError class is thrown when a value is not of the type expected. This happens most often when you attempt to access a property of a `null` or undefined value. It can also occur if you invoke a method defined by one class on an object that is an instance of some other class or if you use the `new` operator with a value that is not a constructor function, for example. JavaScript implementations are also permitted to throw `TypeError` objects when a built-in function or method is called with more arguments than expected. See "Error" for details about throwing and catching exceptions.

See Also

Error, Error.message, Error.name

undefined — JavaScript 1.5; JScript 5.5; ECMAScript v3

the undefined value

Synopsis

```
undefined
```

Description

`undefined` is a global property that holds the JavaScript `undefined` value. This is the same value that is returned when you attempt to read the value of a nonexistent object property. The `undefined` property is not enumerated by `for/in` loops and cannot be deleted with the `delete` operator. Note that `undefined` is not a constant and can be set to any other value, something that you should take care not to do.

When testing a value to see whether it is undefined, use the `===` operator, because the `==` operator treats the `undefined` value as equal to `null`.

unescape( ) — JavaScript 1.0; JScript 1.0; ECMAScript v1; deprecated in ECMAScript v3

decode an escaped string

Synopsis

```
unescape(s)
```

Arguments

s The string that is to be decoded or "unescaped."

Returns

A decoded copy of *s*.

Description

`unescape( )` is a global function that decodes a string encoded with `escape( )`. It decodes *s* by finding and replacing character sequences of the form `%`*xx* and `%u`*xxxx* (where *x* represents a hexadecimal digit) with the Unicode characters `\u00`*xx* and `\u`*xxxx*.

Although unescape( ) was standardized in the first version of ECMAScript, it has been deprecated and removed from the standard by ECMAScript v3. Implementations of ECMAScript are likely to implement this function, but they are not required to. In JavaScript 1.5 and JScript 5.5 and later, you should use decodeURI( ) and decodeURIComponent( ) instead of unescape( ). See "escape()" for more details and an example.

See Also

decodeURI( ), decodeURIComponent( ), escape( ), String

URIError

JavaScript 1.5; JScript 5.5; ECMAScript v3

thrown by URI encoding and decoding methods

Inherits from Error

Constructor

```
new URIError( )
new URIError(message)
```

Arguments

message

An optional error message that provides details about the exception. If specified, this argument is used as the value for the message property of the URIError object.

Returns

A newly constructed URIError object. If the *message* argument is specified, the Error object will use it as the value of its message property; otherwise, it will use an implementation-defined default string as the value of that property. When the URIError( ) constructor is called as a function without the new operator, it behaves just as it does when called with the new operator.

Properties

message

An error message that provides details about the exception. This property holds the string passed to the constructor, or an implementation-defined default string. See "Error.message" for details.

name

A string that specifies the type of the exception. All URIError objects inherit the value "URIError" for this property.

Description

An instance of the URIError class is thrown by decodeURI( ) and decodeURIComponent( ) if the specified string contains illegal hexadecimal escapes. It can also be thrown by encodeURI( ) and encodeURIComponent( ) if the specified string contains illegal Unicode surrogate pairs. See "Error" for details about throwing and catching exceptions.

See Also

Error, Error.message, Error.name

PART IV

Client-Side JavaScript Reference

This part of the book is a complete reference to all of the objects, properties, functions, methods, and event handlers in client-side JavaScript. The first few pages of this part explain how to use this reference material.

Client-Side JavaScript Reference

This part of the book is a reference section that documents the classes, methods, properties, and event handlers defined by web browsers that support client-side JavaScript. These classes, methods, and properties form the de facto standard called the DOM Level 0 API. Beginning scripters and programmers writing with backward compatibility in mind will use this reference section in conjunction with the core JavaScript reference of Part III. The introduction and sample reference page explain how to use and get the most out of this reference section. Take the time to read this material carefully, and you will find it easier to locate and use the information you need!

This reference section is arranged alphabetically. The reference pages for the methods and properties of classes are alphabetized by their full names, which include the names of the classes that define them. For example, if you want to read about the `submit()` method of the Form class, you would look under "Form.submit," not just "submit."

To save space in this enlarged fourth edition of the book, most properties in this reference section do not have reference pages of their own (all methods and event handlers do have their own reference pages, however). Instead, simple properties are completely documented in the reference page for the class that defines them. For example, you can read about the `images[]` property of the Document class in the "Document" reference page. Nontrivial properties that require substantial explanation do have reference pages of their own, and you'll find a cross-reference to these pages within the reference page of the class or interface that defines the properties. For example, when you look up the `cookie` property in the "Document" reference page or the `status` property in the "Window" reference page, you'll find a short description of the property and a reference to pages named "Document.cookie" and "Window.status."

Client-side JavaScript has a number of global properties and functions, such as `window`, `history`, and `alert()`. In client-side JavaScript, a Window object serves as the global object, and the "global" properties and functions of client-side JavaScript are actually properties of the Window class. Therefore, in this client-side reference section, global properties and functions are documented in the "Window" reference page or under names such as "Window.alert()."

Sometimes you may find that you don't know the name of the class or interface that defines the method or property you want to look up, or you may not be sure which of the three reference sections to look up a class or interface in. Part VI of this book is a special index designed to help with these situations. Look up the name of a class, method, or property, and it will tell you which reference section to look in and which class to look under in that section. For example, if you look up "Button," it will tell you that the Button class is documented in this client-side reference section. And if you look up the name "alert," it will tell you that `alert()` is a method of the client-side Window class.

Once you've found the reference page you're looking for, you shouldn't have much difficulty finding the information you need. Still, you'll be able to make better use of this reference section if you understand how the reference pages are written and organized. What follows is a sample reference page titled "Sample Entry" that demonstrates the structure of each reference page and tells you where to find various types of information within the pages. Take the time to read this page before diving into the rest of the reference material.

Sample Entry — Availability

how to read client-side reference pages — Inherits from

Title and Short Description

Every reference entry begins with a four-part title block like that above. The entries are alphabetized by title. The short description, shown below the title, gives you a quick summary of the item documented in the entry; it can help you quickly decide if you're interested in reading the rest of the page.

Availability

The availability information is shown in the upper-right corner of the title block. This information tells you when a class, method, or event handler was introduced. For some less portable items, this section specifies which versions of Netscape and Internet Explorer support it. If the item is well supported by web browsers and support was added by Netscape and IE within the same browser generation, this section specifies its availability in terms of a version of core JavaScript. You can use the tables in Chapter 1 to determine the particular releases of Netscape and Internet Explorer to which these versions correspond. Of course, since most properties do not have their own reference pages, they do not have availability information. If the availability of a property is different from the availability of the class that defines it, however, this fact is noted in the description of the property.

Inherits from

If a class inherits from a superclass, that information is shown in the lower-right corner of the title block. As described in Chapter 8, JavaScript classes can inherit properties and methods from other classes. For example, the Button class inherits from Input, which in turn inherits from HTMLElement. When you see this inheritance information, you may also want to look up the listed superclasses.

Synopsis

Every reference page has a "Synopsis" section that shows how you might use the class, method, or event handler in your code. For example, the synopsis for the Form class is:

```
document.form_name
document.forms[form_number]
```

This synopsis shows two different ways of referring to a Form object. Text in `this font` must be typed exactly as shown. The *`italic`* font indicates text that is to be replaced with something else. *`form_name`* should be replaced with the name of a form, and *`form_number`* should be replaced with the index of the form in the `forms[]` array. Similarly, *`document`* should be replaced in these synopses with a reference to a Document object. By looking at the "Synopsis" section of the "Document" reference page, we discover that it also has two forms:

```
document
window.document
```

That is, you can replace *`document`* with the literal `document` or with *`window`*`.document`. If you choose the latter, you'll need to look up the synopsis of the Window class to find out how to refer to a Window—that is, what to replace *`window`* with.

Arguments

If a reference page documents a method, the "Synopsis" section is followed by an "Arguments" subsection that describes the arguments to the method. If the method has no arguments, this subsection is simply omitted.

`arg1`
: The arguments are described in a list here. This is the description for argument *`arg1`*, for example.

`arg2`
: And this is the description for argument *`arg2`*.

Returns

This section explains the method's return value. If the method does not return a value, this subsection is omitted.

Constructor

If the reference page documents a class that has a constructor method, this section shows you how to use the constructor method to create instances of the class. Since constructors are a type of method, the "Constructor" section looks a lot like the "Synopsis" section of a method's reference page and has an "Arguments" subsection as well.

Properties

If the reference page documents a class, the "Properties" section lists and documents the properties defined by that class. In this client-side reference section, only particularly complex properties have reference pages of their own.

`prop1`
: This is documentation for property `prop1`, including its type, its purpose or meaning, and whether it is read-only or read/write.

`prop2`
: This is the same for `prop2`.

Methods

The reference page for a class that defines methods includes a "Methods" section that lists the names of the methods and provides a short description of each. Full documentation for each method is found in a separate reference page.

Event Handlers

The reference page for a class that defines event handlers includes an "Event Handlers" section that lists the names of the handlers and provides a short description of each. Full documentation for each event handler is found in a separate reference page.

HTML Syntax

A number of client-side JavaScript classes have analogs in HTML. The reference pages for these classes include a section that shows the annotated HTML syntax used to create an HTML element that corresponds to a JavaScript object.

Description

Most reference pages contain a "Description" section, which is the basic description of the class, method, or event handler that is being documented. This is the heart of the reference page. If you are learning about a class, method, or handler for the first time, you may want to skip directly to this section and then go back and look at previous sections such as "Arguments," "Properties," and "Methods." If you are already familiar with an item, you probably won't need to read this section and instead will just want to quickly look up some specific bit of information (for example, from the "Arguments" or "Properties" sections).

In some entries, this section is no more than a short paragraph. In others, it may occupy a page or more. For some simple methods, the "Arguments" and "Returns" sections document the method sufficiently by themselves, so the "Description" section is omitted.

Example

A few pages include an example that shows typical usage. Most pages do not contain examples, however—you'll find those in first half of this book.

Bugs

When an item doesn't work quite right, this section describes the bugs. Note, however, that this book does not attempt to catalog every bug in every version and implementation of client-side JavaScript.

See Also

Many reference pages conclude with cross-references to related reference pages that may be of interest. Most of these cross references are to other reference pages in this client-side reference section. Some are to individual property descriptions contained within a class reference page, however, and others are to related reference pages in the DOM reference section or to chapters in the first two parts of the book.

Anchor

JavaScript 1.2

the target of a hypertext link

Inherits from HTMLElement

Synopsis

```
document.anchors[i]
document.anchors.length
```

Properties

Anchor inherits properties from HTMLElement and defines or overrides the following:

`name`

Contains the name of an Anchor object. The value of this property is initially set by the `name` attribute of the `<a>` tag.

`text` *[Netscape 4]*

This property specifies the plain text, if any, between the `<a>` and `</a>` tags of an anchor. Note that this property works correctly only if there are no intervening HTML tags between the `<a>` and `</a>` tags. If there are other HTML tags, the `text` property may contain only a portion of the anchor text.

`HTMLElement.innerText` provides the IE 4 equivalent of this Netscape-specific property.

HTML Syntax

An Anchor object is created by any standard HTML `<a>` tag that contains a `name` attribute:

```
<a
  name="name"  // Links may refer to this anchor by this name
>
text
</a>
```

Description

An anchor is a named location within an HTML document. Anchors are created with an `<a>` tag that has a `name` attribute specified. The Document object has an `anchors[]` array property that contains Anchor objects that represent each of the anchors in the document. This `anchors[]` array has existed since JavaScript 1.0, but the Anchor object was not implemented until JavaScript 1.2. Therefore, the elements of `anchors[]` were `null` until JavaScript 1.2.

Note that the `<a>` tag used to create anchors is also used to create hypertext links. Although hypertext links are often called anchors in HTML parlance, they are represented in JavaScript with the Link object, not with the Anchor object. In the DOM reference section of this book, however, both anchors and links are documented under HTMLAnchorElement.

See Also

`anchors[]` property of the Document object, Link; HTMLAnchorElement in the DOM reference section

Applet

JavaScript 1.1

an applet embedded in a web page

Synopsis

```
document.applets[i]
document.appletName
```

Properties

The properties of an Applet object are the same as the public fields of the Java applet it represents.

Methods

The methods of an Applet object are the same as the public methods of the Java applet it represents.

Description

The Applet object represents a Java applet embedded in an HTML document. The properties of the Applet object represent the public fields of the applet, and the methods of the Applet object represent the public methods of the applet. LiveConnect technology in Netscape and ActiveX technology in Internet Explorer allow JavaScript programs to use the Applet object to read and write the fields and invoke the methods of the corresponding Java applet. See Chapter 22 for details.

Remember that Java is a strongly typed language. This means that each field of an applet has been declared to have a specific data type, and setting it to a value of some other type causes a runtime error. The same is true of applet methods: each argument has a specific type, and arguments cannot be omitted as they can be in JavaScript.

See Also

JavaObject; Chapter 22

Area

see Link

Button

JavaScript 1.0; enhanced in JavaScript 1.1

a graphical push button

Inherits from Input, HTMLElement

Synopsis

```
form.button_name
form.elements[i]
```

Properties

Button inherits properties from Input and HTMLElement and defines or overrides the following:

`value`
: A string property that specifies the text that appears in the button. The value of this property is specified by the `value` attribute of the HTML `<input>` tag that creates the button. In browsers that cannot reflow document content, this property may be read-only.

Methods

Button inherits methods from Input and HTMLElement.

Event Handlers

Button inherits event handlers from Input and HTMLElement and defines or overrides the following:

`onclick`
: Invoked when the button is clicked.

HTML Syntax

A Button element is created with a standard HTML `<input>` tag:

```
<form>
   ...
  <input
    type="button"          // Specifies that this is a button
    value="label"          // The text that is to appear within the button
                           // Specifies the value property
    [ name="name" ]        // A name you can use later to refer to the button
                           // Specifies the name property
    [ onclick="handler" ]  // JavaScript statements to be executed when the button
                           // is clicked
  >
    ...
</form>
```

Button objects can also be created with the HTML 4 `<button>` tag:

```
<button id="name"
        onclick="handler">
label
</button>
```

Description

The Button element represents a graphical push button in a form within an HTML document. The `value` property contains the text displayed by the button. The `name` property is the name the button may be referred to as. The `onclick` event handler is invoked when the user clicks on the button.

Usage

Use a Button element whenever you want to allow the user to trigger some action on your web page. You can sometimes use a Link object for the same purpose, but unless the desired action is to follow a hypertext link, a Button is a better choice than a Link, because it makes it more explicit to the user that there is something to be triggered.

Note that the Submit and Reset elements are types of Buttons that submit a form and reset a form's values. Often these default actions are sufficient for a form, and you do not need to create any other types of buttons.

Example

```
<form name="form1">
    <input type="button"
        name="press_me_button"
        value="Press Me"
        onclick="username = prompt('What is your name?',"")"
    >
</form>
```

See Also

Form, HTMLElement, Input, Reset, Submit; HTMLInputElement in the DOM reference section

Button.onclick

JavaScript 1.0

the handler invoked when a Button is clicked

Synopsis

```
<input type="button" value="button-text" onclick="handler">
button.onclick
```

Description

The `onclick` property of a Button object refers to an event handler function that is invoked when the user clicks on the button. See "HTMLElement.onclick" for complete details. Note, however, that `Button.onclick` has been supported since JavaScript 1.0, unlike the generalized `HTMLElement.onclick` handler.

See Also

HTMLElement.onclick; Chapter 19; EventListener, EventTarget, and MouseEvent in the DOM reference section

Checkbox

JavaScript 1.0; enhanced in JavaScript 1.1

a graphical checkbox

Inherits from Input, HTMLElement

Synopsis

A single Checkbox element with a unique name may be referenced in either of these ways:

```
form.checkbox_name
form.elements[i]
```

When a form contains a group of checkboxes with the same name, they are placed in an array and may be referenced as follows:

```
form.checkbox_name[j]
form.checkbox_name.length
```

Properties

Checkbox inherits properties from Input and HTMLElement and defines or overrides the following:

`checked`
: A read/write boolean property. If the checkbox is checked, the `checked` property is `true`. If the checkbox is not checked, `checked` is `false`.

  If you set `checked` to `true`, the checkbox appears checked. Similarly, if you set this property to `false`, the checkbox appears unchecked. Note that setting the `checked` property does not cause the Checkbox element's `onclick` event handler to be invoked.

`defaultChecked`
: A read-only boolean that specifies the initial state of the checkbox. It is `true` if the checkbox is initially checked—i.e., if the `checked` attribute appears in the checkbox's HTML `<input>` tag. If this attribute does not appear, the checkbox is initially unchecked and `defaultChecked` is `false`.

`value`
: A read/write string property that specifies the text passed to the web server if the checkbox is checked when the form is submitted. The initial value of `value` is specified by the `value` attribute of the checkbox's HTML `<input>` tag. If no `value` attribute is specified, the default `value` string is "on".

  Note that the `value` field does not specify whether the checkbox is selected; the `checked` property specifies the current state of the checkbox. When defining a group of related checkboxes that share the same name in a form that is submitted to the server, it is important that each be given a distinct `value` attribute.

Methods

Checkbox inherits the methods of Input and HTMLElement.

Event Handlers

Checkbox inherits event handlers from Input and HTMLElement and defines or overrides the following:

`onclick`
: Invoked when the checkbox is clicked.

HTML Syntax

A Checkbox element is created with a standard HTML `<input>` tag. Multiple Checkbox elements are often created in groups by specifying multiple `<input>` tags that have the same `name` attribute.

```
<form>
   ...
  <input
    type="checkbox"          // Specifies that this is a checkbox
```

```
      [ name="name" ]           // A name you can use later to refer to this checkbox
                                // or to the group of checkboxes with this name
                                // Specifies the name property
      [ value="value" ]         // The value returned when this checkbox is selected
                                // Specifies the value property
      [ checked ]               // Specifies that the checkbox is initially checked
                                // Specifies the defaultChecked property
      [ onclick="handler" ]     // JavaScript statements to be executed
    >                           // when the checkbox is clicked
  label                         // The HTML text that should appear next to the checkbox
    ...
  </form>
```

Description

The Checkbox element represents a single graphical checkbox in an HTML form. Note that the text that appears next to the checkbox is not part of the Checkbox element itself and must be specified externally to the Checkbox's HTML `<input>` tag.

The `onclick` event handler allows you to specify JavaScript code to be executed when the checkbox is checked or unchecked. You can examine the `checked` property to determine the state of the checkbox and set this property to check or uncheck the checkbox. Note that setting `checked` changes the graphical appearance of the checkbox but does not invoke the `onclick` event handler.

It is good programming style to specify the `name` attribute for a checkbox; this is mandatory if the checkbox is part of a form that submits data to a CGI script running on a web server. Specifying a `name` attribute sets the `name` property and allows you to refer to the checkbox by name (instead of as a member of the form `elements` array) in your JavaScript code, which makes the code more modular and portable.

For example, if the `name` attribute of a checkbox in form `f` is "opts", `f.opts` refers to the Checkbox element. Checkbox elements are often used in related groups, however, and each member of the group is given the same `name` attribute (the shared name defines the members of the group). In this case, JavaScript places each Checkbox element in the group in an array, and the array is given the shared name. If, for example, each of a group of checkboxes in form `f` has its `name` attribute set to "opts", `f.opts` is an array of Checkbox elements, and `f.opts.length` is the number of elements in the array.

You can set the `value` attribute or the `value` property of a checkbox to specify the string that is passed to the server if the checkbox is checked when the form is submitted. For a single checkbox used alone, the default `value` of "on" is usually adequate. When multiple checkboxes with the same name are used, each should specify a distinct `value` so a list of values from selected checkboxes can be passed to the server.

Usage

Checkbox elements can present the user with one or more options. This element type is suitable for presenting non-mutually exclusive choices. Use the Radio element for mutually exclusive lists of options.

See Also

Form, HTMLElement, Input, Radio; HTMLInputElement in the DOM reference section

Checkbox.onclick

JavaScript 1.0

the handler invoked when a checkbox is selected

Synopsis

```
<input type="checkbox" onclick="handler">
checkbox.onclick
```

Description

The onclick property of a Checkbox object refers to an event handler function that is invoked when the user clicks on the checkbox. See "HTMLElement.onclick" for complete details. Note, however, that Checkbox.onclick has been supported since JavaScript 1.0, unlike the generalized HTMLElement.onclick handler.

See Also

HTMLElement.onclick; Chapter 19; EventListener, EventTarget, and MouseEvent in the DOM reference section

Document

JavaScript 1.0; enhanced in JavaScript 1.1, Netscape 4, and IE 4

represents an HTML document

Inherits from HTMLElement

Synopsis

```
window.document
document
```

Properties

Document inherits properties from HTMLElement and defines the following properties. Netscape and Internet Explorer both define a number of incompatible Document properties that are used mostly for DHTML; they are listed separately after these properties.

`alinkColor`

: alinkColor is a string property that specifies the color of activated links in *document*. Browsers may display this color between the times that the user presses and releases the mouse button over the link. The alink attribute of the <body> HTML tag specifies the initial value of this property. This property may be set, but only in the <head> of the document. See also the color properties of HTMLBodyElement in the DOM reference section.

`anchors[]`

: An array of Anchor objects, one for each anchor that appears in *document*. An anchor is a named position within the document that can serve as the target of a hypertext link. The anchors[] array has anchors.length elements, numbered from zero to anchors.length–1. Do not confuse anchors with hypertext links, which are represented in JavaScript by the Link objects in the Document.links[] array.

  Prior to JavaScript 1.2, the Anchor object was unimplemented, and the elements of anchors[] were all null.

`applets[]` *[JavaScript 1.1]*

An array of Applet objects, one for each applet that appears in the document. You can use the Applet object to read and write all public variables in the applet, and you can invoke all of the applet's public methods. If an `<applet>` tag has a `name` attribute, the applet may also be referred to by using the name as a property of `document` or as an index into the `applets` array. Thus, if the first applet in a document has `name="animator"`, you can refer to it in any of these ways:

```
document.applets[0]
document.animator
document.applets["animator"]
```

`bgColor`

A string property that specifies the background color of *`document`*. The initial value of this property comes from the `bgcolor` attribute of the `<body>` tag. The background color may be changed by assigning a value to `bgColor`. Unlike the other color properties, `bgColor` can be set at any time. See also the color properties of HTMLBodyElement in the DOM reference section.

`cookie`

A string that is the value of a cookie associated with this document. See the "Document.cookie" reference page.

`domain`

A string that specifies the document's Internet domain. Used for security purposes. JavaScript 1.1 and higher. See the "Document.domain" reference page.

`embeds[]` *[JavaScript 1.1]*

An array of objects that represent data embedded in the document with the `<embed>` tag. The objects in the `embeds[]` array do not refer to the embedded data directly but refer instead to the object that displays that data. You can use the objects in the `embeds[]` array to interact with embedded data. The way you do this, however, is specific to the type of embedded data and the plugin or ActiveX control used to display it. Consult the developer's documentation for the plugin or ActiveX control to learn whether it can be scripted from JavaScript and, if so, what the supported APIs are.

`Document.plugins[]` is a synonym for `Document.embeds[]`. Do not confuse it with `Navigator.plugins[]`.

`fgColor`

A string property that specifies the default color of text in *`document`*. The initial value of this property is from the `text` attribute of the `<body>` tag, and you can set the value of this property from a script within the `<head>` of the document. See also the color properties of HTMLBodyElement in the DOM reference section.

`forms[]`

An array of Form objects, one for each HTML form that appears in *`document`*. The `forms[]` array has `forms.length` elements, numbered from zero to `forms.length`–1.

`images[]` *[JavaScript 1.1]*

An array of Image objects, one for each image that is embedded in the document with the HTML `<img>` tag. If the `name` attribute is specified in the `<img>` tag for an Image, a reference to that image is also stored in a property of the Document object. This property has the same name as the image. So if an image has a `name="toggle"` attribute, you can refer to the image with `document.toggle`.

`lastModified`
: A read-only string that specifies the date of the most recent change to the document (as reported by the web server). See the "Document.lastModified" reference page.

`linkColor`
: A string property that specifies the color of unvisited links in the document. The value of this property is set by the `link` attribute of the `<body>` tag, and it may also be set by a script in the `<head>` of the document. See also the color properties of HTMLBodyElement in the DOM reference section.

`links[]`
: An array of Link objects, one for each hypertext link that appears in the document. The `links[]` array has `links.length` elements, numbered from zero to `links.length–1`.

`location` *[Deprecated]*
: A Location object that contains the complete URL of the current document; a synonym for the `Window.location` property. In JavaScript 1.0, this property was instead a read-only string object that served the same purpose as the `Document.URL` property.

`plugins[]` *[JavaScript 1.1]*
: A synonym for the `embeds[]` array. Refers to an array of objects that represent the plugins or ActiveX controls used to display embedded data in a document. The `embeds` property is the preferred way to access this array, since it avoids confusion with the `Navigator.plugins[]` array.

`referrer`
: A read-only string property that contains the URL of the document, if any, from which the current document was reached. For example, if the user follows a link in document A to document B, the `Document.referrer` property in document B contains the URL of document A. On the other hand, if the user types the URL of document B directly and does not follow any link to get there, the `Document.referrer` property for document B is an empty string.

`title`
: A read-only string property that specifies the title of the current document. The title is any text that appears between the `<title>` and `</title>` tags in the `<head>` of the document.

`URL`
: A read-only string that specifies the URL of the document. See the "Document.URL" reference page.

`vlinkColor`
: A string property that specifies the color of visited links in *`document`*. The value of this property is set by the `vlink` attribute of the `<body>` tag, and you can also set it from a script within the `<head>` of the document. See also the color properties of HTMLBodyElement in the DOM reference section.

Netscape Properties

`height` *[Netscape 4]*
: The height, in pixels, of the document.

`layers[]` *[Netscape 4 only]*
An array of Layer objects that represent the layers contained within a document. Each Layer object contains its own subdocument, accessible through the `document` property of the Layer object. This property is available only in Netscape 4; it has been discontinued in Netscape 6.

`width` *[Netscape 4]*
The width, in pixels, of the document.

Internet Explorer Properties

`activeElement` *[IE 4]*
A read-only property that refers to the input element within the document that is currently active (i.e., has the input focus).

`all[]` *[IE 4]*
An array of all elements within the document. See the "Document.all" reference page.

`charset` *[IE 4]*
The character set of the document.

`children[]` *[IE 4]*
An array that contains the HTML elements, in source order, that are direct children of the document. Note that this is different than the `all[]` array that contains all elements in the document, regardless of their position in the containment hierarchy.

`defaultCharset` *[IE 4]*
The default character set of the document.

`expando` *[IE 4]*
This property, if set to `false`, prevents client-side objects from being expanded. That is, it causes a runtime error if a program attempts to set the value of a nonexistent property of a client-side object. Setting `expando` to `false` can sometimes catch bugs caused by property misspellings, which can otherwise be difficult to detect. This property can be particularly helpful for programmers who are switching to JavaScript after becoming accustomed to case-insensitive languages. Although `expando` works only in IE 4, it can be set safely (if ineffectively) in Netscape.

`parentWindow` *[IE 4]*
The window that contains the document.

`readyState`
Specifies the loading status of a document. It has one of the following four string values:

`uninitialized`
The document has not started loading.

`loading`
The document is loading.

`interactive`
The document has loaded sufficiently for the user to interact with it.

`complete`
The document is completely loaded.

Methods

Document inherits methods from HTMLElement and defines the following methods. Netscape and IE both define a number of incompatible Document methods that are used mostly for DHTML; they are listed separately.

`clear()`
: Erases the contents of the document. This method is deprecated in JavaScript 1.1.

`close()`
: Closes a document stream opened with the `open()` method.

`open()`
: Opens a stream to which document contents may be written.

`write()`
: Inserts the specified string or strings into the document currently being parsed or into a document stream opened with `open()`.

`writeln()`
: Identical to `write()`, except that it appends a newline character to the output.

Netscape Methods

`captureEvents()`
: Requests events of specified types.

`getSelection()`
: Returns the currently selected document text.

`releaseEvents`
: Stops capturing specified event types.

`routeEvent()`
: Routes a captured event to the next interested element. See "Window.routeEvent()."

Internet Explorer Methods

`elementFromPoint()`
: Returns the element located at a given (X-coordinate, Y-coordinate) point.

Event Handlers

The <body> tag has `onload` and `onunload` attributes. Technically, however, the `onload` and `onunload` event handlers belong to the Window object rather than the Document object. See "Window.onload" and "Window.onunload."

HTML Syntax

The Document object obtains values for a number of its properties from attributes of the HTML <body> tag. Also, the HTML contents of a document appear between the <body> and </body> tags:

```
<body
  [ background="imageURL" ]  // A background image for the document
  [ bgcolor="color" ]        // A background color for the document
  [ text="color" ]           // The foreground color for the document's text
```

```
    [ link="color" ]            // The color for unvisited links
    [ alink="color" ]           // The color for activated links
    [ vlink="color" ]           // The color for visited links
    [ onload="handler" ]        // JavaScript to run when the document is loaded
    [ onunload="handler" ]      // JavaScript to run when the document is unloaded
  >
  // HTML document contents go here
  </body>
```

Description

The Document object represents the HTML document displayed in a browser window or frame (or layer, in Netscape 4). The properties of this object provide details about many aspects of the document, from the colors of the text, background, and anchors, to the date on which the document was last modified. The Document object also contains a number of arrays that describe the contents of the document. The `links[]` array contains one Link object for each hypertext link in the document. Similarly, the `applets[]` array contains one object for each Java applet embedded in the document, and the `forms[]` array contains one Form object for each HTML form that appears in the document.

The `write()` method of the Document object is especially notable. When invoked in scripts that are run while the document is loading, you can call `document.write()` to insert dynamically generated HTML text into the document.

See Chapter 14 for an overview of the Document object and of many of the JavaScript objects to which it refers. See Chapter 17 for an overview of the DOM standard.

See Also

Form, the `document` property of the Window object; Chapter 14; Document, HTMLDocument, and HTMLBodyElement in the DOM reference section

Document.all[] — Internet Explorer 4

all HTML elements in a document

Synopsis

```
document.all[i]
document.all[name]
document.all.tags(tagname)
```

Description

`all[]` is a versatile array that contains all the HTML elements in a document. `all[]` contains the elements in source order, and you can extract them directly from the array if you know their exact numeric position within the array. It is more common, however, to use the `all[]` array to retreive elements by the value of their `name` or `id` HTML attributes. If more than one element has the specified name, using that name as an index into the `all[]` returns an array of elements that share the name.

`all.tags()` is passed a tag name and returns an array of HTML elements of the specified type.

See Also

HTMLElement

Document.captureEvents( )

see Window.captureEvents( )

Document.clear( ) — JavaScript 1.0; deprecated

clear a document

Synopsis

```
document.clear( )
```

Description

The `clear( )` method of the Document object is deprecated and should not be used. To clear a document, you should simply open a new one with `Document.open( )`.

See Also

Document.close( ), Document.open( ), Document.write( )

Document.close( ) — JavaScript 1.0

close an output stream

Synopsis

```
document.close( )
```

Description

This method displays any output to *document* that has been written but not yet displayed and closes the output stream to *document*. When generating complete HTML pages with `Document.write( )`, you should invoke `Document.close( )` when you reach the end of the page.

After *document*`.close( )` has been called, if any further output is written to *document* (e.g., with *document*`.write( )`), the document is implicitly cleared and reopened, erasing all the output that was written prior to calling the `close( )` method.

See Also

Document.open( ), Document.write( )

Document.cookie — JavaScript 1.0

the cookie(s) of the document

Synopsis

```
document.cookie
```

Description

cookie is a string property that allows you to read, create, modify, and delete the cookie or cookies that apply to the current document. A *cookie* is a small amount of named data stored by the web browser. It gives web browsers a "memory" so they can use data input on one page in another page or recall user preferences across web browsing sessions. Cookie data is automatically transmitted between web browser and web server when appropriate so CGI scripts on the server end can read and write cookie values. Client-side JavaScript code can also read and write cookies with this property.

The `Document.cookie` property does not behave like a normal read/write property. You may both read and write the value of `Document.cookie`, but the value you read from this property is, in general, not the same as the value you write. For complete details on the use of this particularly complex property, see Chapter 16.

Usage

Cookies are intended for infrequent storage of small amounts of data. They are not intended as a general-purpose communication or programming mechanism, so use them in moderation. Note that web browsers are not required to retain the value of more than 20 cookies per web server (for the entire server, not just for your site on the server), nor to retain a cookie *name/value* pair of more than 4 KB in length.

See Also

Chapter 16

Document.domain — JavaScript 1.1

the security domain of a document

Synopsis

```
document.domain
```

Description

For security reasons, an unsigned script running in one window is not allowed to read properties of another window unless that window comes from the same web server as the host. This causes problems for large web sites that use multiple servers. For example, a script on the host *www.oreilly.com* might want to share properties with a script from the host *search.oreilly.com*.

The `domain` property helps to address this problem. Initially, this string property contains the hostname of the web server from which the document was loaded. You can set this property, but only in a very restricted way: it can be set only to a domain suffix of itself. For example, a script loaded from *search.oreilly.com* could set its own `domain` property to "oreilly.com". If a script from *www.oreilly.com* is running in another window, and it also sets its `domain` property to "oreilly.com", these two scripts can share properties, even though they did not originate on the same server.

Note, however, that a script from *search.oreilly.com* cannot set its `domain` property to "search.oreilly". And, more importantly, a script from *snoop.spam.com* cannot set its domain to "oreilly.com", which might allow it to determine, for example, which search keywords you use.

See Also

Chapter 21

Document.elementFromPoint( )

Internet Explorer 4

determine which HTML element is at a given point

Synopsis

```
document.elementFromPoint(x, y)
```

Arguments

x The X-coordinate.

y The Y-coordinate.

Returns

The HTML element that appears at point (*x*, *y*) in *document*.

Document.getSelection( )

Netscape 4

return the selected text

Synopsis

```
document.getSelection( )
```

Returns

The text, if any, that is currently selected within the document. This returned text has HTML formatting tags removed.

Document.handleEvent( )

see Window.handleEvent( )

Document.lastModified

JavaScript 1.0

the modification date of a document

Synopsis

```
document.lastModified
```

Description

`lastModified` is a read-only string property that contains the date and time at which *document* was most recently modified. This data is derived from HTTP header data sent by the web server. The web server generally obtains the last-modified date by examining the modification date of the file itself.

Web servers are not required to provide last-modified dates for the documents they serve. When a web server does not provide a last-modified date, JavaScript assumes 0, which translates to a date of midnight, January 1, 1970, GMT. The following example shows how you can test for this case.

Example

It is a good idea to let readers know how recent the information you provide on the Web is. You can include an automatic timestamp in your documents by placing the following script at the end of each HTML file. Doing this means you do not need to update the modification time by hand each time you make a change to the file. Note that this script tests that the supplied date is valid before displaying it:

```
<script>
if (Date.parse(document.lastModified) != 0)
    document.write('<p><hr><small><i>Last modified: '
                   + document.lastModified
                   + '</i></small>');
</script>
```

See Also

The Document `location`, `referrer`, and `title` properties

Document.links[] — JavaScript 1.0

the Link objects in a document

Synopsis

`document``.links`
`document``.links.length`

Description

The `links` property is an array of Link objects—one object for each hypertext link that appears in *`document`*. The `links[]` array has `links.length` elements, numbered from zero to `links.length–1`.

See Also

Link

Document.open( ) — JavaScript 1.0

begin a new document

Synopsis

`document``.open( )`
`document``.open(`*`mimetype`*`)`

Arguments

mimetype

An optional string argument that specifies the type of data to be written to and displayed in *document*. The value of this argument should be one of the standard MIME types that the browser understands ("text/html", "text/plain", "image/gif", "image/jpeg", and "image/x-bitmap" for Netscape) or some other MIME type that can be handled by an installed plugin. If this argument is omitted, it is taken to be "text/html". This argument is ignored by IE 3, which always assumes a document of type "text/html". This argument is also not supported in the standard W3C DOM version of this method. See the "HTMLDocument.open()" entry in the DOM reference section.

Description

The *document*.`open( )` method opens a stream to *document* so subsequent *document*.`write( )` calls can append data to the document. The optional *mimetype* argument specifies the type of data to be written and tells the browser how to interpret that data.

If any existing document is displayed when the `open( )` method is called, it is automatically cleared by the call to `open( )` or by the first call to `write( )` or `writeln( )`. After opening a document with `open( )` and writing data to it with `write( )`, you should complete the document by calling `close( )`.

Usage

You usually call `Document.open( )` with no argument to open an HTML document. Occasionally, a "text/plain" document is useful, for example, for a pop-up window of debugging messages.

See Also

Document.close(), Document.write(); HTMLDocument.open() in the DOM reference section

Document.releaseEvents( )

see Window.releaseEvents( )

Document.routeEvent( )

see Window.routeEvent( )

Document.URL

JavaScript 1.1

the URL of the current document

Synopsis

document.`URL`

Description

`URL` is a read-only string property that contains the complete URL of the current *document*.

document.URL is usually equal to *window*.location.href for the *window* that contains *document*. These two are not always equal, however, because the Document.URL property may be modified through URL redirection—Window.location contains the requested URL, and Document.URL specifies the actual URL where it was found.

Usage

Some web authors like to include the URL of a document somewhere within the document so, for example, if the document is cut-and-pasted to a file or printed out, there is still a reference to its location online. The following script, when appended to a document, automatically adds the document's URL:

```
<script>
document.write('<p><hr><small><i>URL: ' + document.URL
    + '</i></small>');
</script>
```

See Also

The lastModified, location, referrer, and title properties of the Document object; the location property of the Window object

Document.write( )

JavaScript 1.0

append data to a document

Synopsis

document.write(*value*, ...)

Arguments

value

An arbitrary JavaScript value to be appended to *document*. If the value is not a string, it is converted to one before being appended.

...

Any number (zero or higher) of additional values to be appended (in order) to *document*.

Description

document.write( ) appends each of its arguments, in order, to *document*. Any arguments that are not strings are converted to strings before they are written to the end of the document.

Document.write( ) is usually used in one of two ways. First, it can be invoked on the current document within a <script> tag or within a function that is executed while the document is being parsed. In this case, the write( ) method writes its HTML output as if that output appeared literally in the file at the location of the code that invoked the method.

Second, you can use Document.write( ) to dynamically generate the contents of a document for a window other than the current window. In this case, the target document is never in the process of being parsed, and so the output cannot appear "in place" as it does in the case just described. In order for `write()` to output text into a document, that document must be open. You can open a document by explicitly calling the `Document.open()` method. In most cases this is unnecessary, however, because when `write()` is invoked on a document that is closed, it implicitly opens the document. When a document is opened, any contents that previously appeared in that document are discarded and replaced with a blank document.

Once a document is open, `Document.write()` can append any amount of output to the end of the document. When a new document has been completely generated by this technique, the document should be closed by calling `Document.close()`. Note that although the call to `open()` is usually optional, the call to `close()` is never optional.

The results of calling `Document.write()` may not be immediately visible in the targeted web browser window or frame. This is because a web browser may buffer up data to output in larger chunks. Calling `Document.close()` is the only way to explicitly force all buffered output to be "flushed" and displayed in the browser window.

See Also

Document.close(), Document.open(), Document.writeln(); Chapter 14

Document.writeln() JavaScript 1.0

append data and a newline to a document

Synopsis

document.writeln(*value*, ...)

Arguments

value

An arbitrary JavaScript value to be appended to *document*. If the value is not a string, it is converted to one before being appended.

...

Any number (zero or higher) of additional values to be appended (in order) to *document*.

Description

`Document.writeln()` behaves just like `Document.write()` except that after appending all of its arguments to *document*, it also appends a newline character. See the "Document.write()" reference page for more information on this method.

Newline characters are not usually displayed in HTML documents, so `Document.writeln()` is generally useful only when writing text to appear in a `<pre>` environment, or when writing to a document opened with a MIME type of "text/plain".

See Also

Document.close(), Document.open(), Document.write()

Element

see Input

Event

JavaScript 1.2; incompatible versions supported by Netscape 4 and IE 4

details about an event

Synopsis

```
function handler(event) { ... } // Event handler argument in Netscape 4
window.event                    // Window property in IE 4
```

Constants

In Netscape 4, the Event object defines bitmask constants for each of the supported event types. These static properties are used to form the bitmasks that are passed to `captureEvents()` and `releaseEvents()`. The available constants are:

`Event.ABORT`	`Event.BLUR`	`Event.CHANGE`	`Event.CLICK`
`Event.DBLCLICK`	`Event.DRAGDROP`	`Event.ERROR`	`Event.FOCUS`
`Event.KEYDOWN`	`Event.KEYPRESS`	`Event.KEYUP`	`Event.LOAD`
`Event.MOUSEDOWN`	`Event.MOUSEMOVE`	`Event.MOUSEOUT`	`Event.MOUSEOVER`
`Event.MOUSEUP`	`Event.MOVE`	`Event.RESET`	`Event.RESIZE`
`Event.SELECT`	`Event.SUBMIT`	`Event.UNLOAD`	

Netscape 4 Properties

`height`
: Set only in events of type "resize". Specifies the new height of the window or frame that was resized.

`layerX, layerY`
: Specify the X- and Y-coordinates, relative to the enclosing layer, at which an event occurred.

`modifiers`
: Specifies which keyboard modifier keys were held down when the event occurred. This numeric value is a bitmask consisting of any of the constants `Event.ALT_MASK`, `Event.CONTROL_MASK`, `Event.META_MASK`, or `Event.SHIFT_MASK`. Due to a bug, this property is not defined in Netscape 6 or 6.1.

`pageX, pageY`
: Specify the X- and Y-coordinates, relative to the web browser page, at which the event occurred. Note that these coordinates are relative to the top-level page, not to any enclosing layers.

`screenX, screenY`
: Specify the X- and Y-coordinates, relative to the screen, at which the event occurred. Note that, unlike most Event properties, these properties are supported by and have the same meaning in both Netscape 4 and Internet Explorer 4.

`target`
: Specifies the Window, Document, Layer, or HTMLElement object on which the event occurred.

`type`
: A string property that specifies the type of the event. Its value is the name of the event handler minus the "on" prefix. So when the `onclick()` event handler is invoked, the `type` property of the Event object is "click".

`which`
: For keyboard and mouse events, `which` specifies which key or mouse button was pressed or released. For keyboard events, this property contains the character encoding of the key that was pressed. For mouse events, it contains 1, 2, or 3, indicating the left, middle, or right buttons.

`width`
: Set only in events of type "resize". Specifies the new width of the window or frame that was resized.

`x, y`
: Specify the X- and Y-coordinates at which the event occurred. In Netscape 4, these properties are synonyms for `layerX` and `layerY` and specify the position relative to the containing layer (if any). Their meaning is different in Internet Explorer (see below).

Internet Explorer 4 Properties

`altKey`
: A boolean value that specifies whether the **Alt** key was held down when the event occurred.

`button`
: For mouse events, `button` specifies which mouse button or buttons were pressed. This read-only integer is a bitmask: the 1 bit is set if the left button was pressed; the 2 bit is set if the right button was pressed; and the 4 bit is set if the middle button (of a three-button mouse) was pressed.

`cancelBubble`
: If an event handler wants to stop an event from being propagated up to containing objects, it must set this property to `true`.

`clientX, clientY`
: Specify the X- and Y-coordinates, relative to the web browser page, at which the event occurred.

`ctrlKey`
: A boolean value that specifies whether the **Ctrl** key was held down when the event occurred.

`fromElement`
: For mouseover and mouseout events, `fromElement` refers to the object from which the mouse pointer is moving.

`keyCode`
: For keyboard events, `keyCode` specifies the Unicode character code generated by the key that was struck.

`offsetX, offsetY`
: Specify the X- and Y-coordinates at which the event occurred within the coordinate system of the event's source element (see `srcElement`).

`reason`
: For the `datasetcomplete` event, `reason` contains a code that specifies the status of the data transfer. A value of 0 indicates a successful transfer. A value of 1 indicates that the transfer was aborted. A value of 2 indicates that an error occurred during data transfer.

`returnValue`
: If this property is set, its value takes precedence over the value actually returned by an event handler. Set this property to `false` to cancel the default action of the source element on which the event occurred.

`screenX, screenY`
: Specify the X- and Y-coordinates, relative to the screen, at which the event occurred. Note that, unlike most Event properties, these two properties are supported by and have the same meaning in both Netscape 4 and Internet Explorer 4.

`shiftKey`
: A boolean value that specifies whether the **Shift** key was held down when the event occurred.

`srcElement`
: A reference to the Window, Document, or HTMLElement object that generated the event.

`srcFilter`
: For filterchange events, `srcFilter` specifies the filter that changed.

`toElement`
: For mouseover and mouseout events, `toElement` refers to the object into which the mouse pointer is moving.

`type`
: A string property that specifies the type of the event. Its value is the name of the event handler minus the "on" prefix. So when the `onclick()` event handler is invoked, the `type` property of the Event object is "click".

`x, y`
: Specify the X- and Y-coordinates at which the event occurred. In Internet Explorer 4, this property specifies the X position relative to the innermost containing element that is dynamically positioned using CSS. The interpretation of these properties is different in Netscape 4 (see the previous section).

Description

The Event object provides details about an event that has occurred. Unfortunately, these details are not standardized, and Netscape 4 and IE 4 define Event objects that are almost entirely incompatible. Besides having different properties, Netscape 4 and IE 4 provide access to Event objects in different ways. In Netscape, an Event object is passed as an argument to every event handler. For event handlers defined by HTML attributes, the name of the event argument is `event`. In IE, the Event object of the most recent event is instead stored in the `event` property of the Window object.

In addition to the incompatibility between the Netscape 4 Event object and the IE Event object, the W3C DOM defines its own Event object that is incompatible with both. See the "Event," "UIEvent," and "MouseEvent" entries in the DOM reference section.

See Also

Chapter 19; Event, UIEvent, and MouseEvent in the DOM reference section

FileUpload

JavaScript 1.0

a file upload field for form input — **Inherits from Input, HTMLElement**

Synopsis

```
form.name
form.elements[i]
```

Properties

FileUpload inherits properties from Input and HTMLElement and defines or overrides the following:

`value` *[JavaScript 1.1]*

A read-only string that specifies the filename entered by the user into the FileUpload object. The user may enter a filename either by typing it directly or by using the directory browser associated with the FileUpload object.

To prevent malicious programs from uploading arbitrary files from the client, this property may not be set by JavaScript code. Similarly, the `value` attribute of the `<input>` tag does not specify the initial value for this property.

Methods

FileUpload inherits methods from Input and HTMLElement.

Event Handlers

FileUpload inherits event handlers from Input and HTMLElement and defines or overrides the following:

`onchange`

Invoked when the user changes the value in the FileUpload element and moves the keyboard focus elsewhere. This event handler is not invoked for every keystroke in the FileUpload element, but only when the user completes an edit.

HTML Syntax

A FileUpload element is created with a standard HTML `<input>` tag:

```
<form enctype="multipart/form-data"
      method="post">          // Required attributes
    ...
  <input
    type="file"               // Specifies that this is a FileUpload element
```

```
    [ name="name" ]          // A name you can use later to refer to this element
                             // Specifies the name property
    [ size="integer" ]       // How many characters wide the element is
    [ maxlength="integer" ]  // Maximum allowed number of input characters
    [ onblur="handler" ]     // The onblur( ) event handler
    [ onchange="handler" ]   // The onchange( ) event handler
    [ onfocus="handler" ]    // The onfocus( ) event handler
  >
    ...
```

Description

The FileUpload element represents a file upload input element in a form. In many respects, this input element is much like the Text element. On the screen, it appears like a text input field with the addition of a **Browse** button that opens a directory browser. Entering a filename into a FileUpload element (either directly or through the browser) causes Netscape to submit the contents of that file along with the form. For this to work, the form must use "multipart/form-data" encoding and the POST method.

The FileUpload element does not have a `defaultValue` property and does not recognize the value HTML attribute to specify an initial value for the input field. Similarly, the value property of the FileUpload element is read-only. Only the user may enter a filename; JavaScript may not enter text into the FileUpload field in any way. This is to prevent malicious JavaScript programs from uploading arbitrary files (such as password files) from the user's machine.

See Also

Form, HTMLElement, Input, Text; HTMLInputElement in the DOM reference section

FileUpload.onchange — JavaScript 1.0

the handler invoked when input value changes

Synopsis

```
<input type="file" onchange="handler" ...>
fileupload.onchange
```

Description

The onchange property of a FileUpload element specifies an event handler function that is invoked when the user changes the value in the input field (either by typing directly or using the **Browse** button) and then moves input focus elsewhere. This handler is intended to process a complete change to the input value and therefore is not invoked on a keystroke-by-keystroke basis.

The initial value of this property is a function that contains the semicolon-separated JavaScript statements specified by the onchange attribute of the HTML tag that defined the object. When an event handler function is defined by an HTML attribute, it is executed in the scope of *element* rather than in the scope of the containing window.

In the Netscape 4 event model, the onchange handler function is passed an Event object as an argument. In the IE event model, no argument is passed, but the applicable Event object is available as the event property of the Window object that contains the *element*.

See Also

Input.onchange; Chapter 19; Event, EventListener, and EventTarget in the DOM reference section

Form — JavaScript 1.0

an HTML input form — Inherits from HTMLElement

Synopsis

document.form_name
document.forms[*form_number*]

Properties

Form inherits properties from HTMLElement and defines or overrides the following:

`action`
: A read/write string (read-only in IE 3) that specifies the URL to which the form data is sent when the form is submitted. The initial value of this property is specified by the `action` attribute of the `<form>` HTML tag. Usually, this URL specifies the address as a CGI script, although it can also be a `mailto:` or `news:` address.

`elements[]`
: An array of input elements that appear in the form. Each element is a Button, Checkbox, Hidden, Password, Radio, Reset, Select, Submit, Text, or Textarea object. See the "Form.elements" reference page.

`encoding`
: A read/write string (read-only in IE 3) that specifies how form data is encoded for transmission when the form is submitted. The initial value of this property is specified by the `enctype` attribute of the `<form>` tag. The default value is "application/x-www-form-urlencoded", which is sufficient for almost all purposes. Other values may sometimes be necessary. For example, a value of "text/plain" is convenient when the form is submitted by email to a `mailto:` URL. See *CGI Programming on the World Wide Web*, by Shishir Gundavaram (O'Reilly), for further information.

`length`
: The number of elements in the form. Equivalent to `elements.length`.

`method`
: A read/write string (read-only in IE 3) that specifies the method by which form data is submitted. The initial value of this property is specified by the `method` attribute of the `<form>` tag. The two legal values are `get` and `post`.

: The `get` method is the default. It is usually used for form submissions such as database queries that do not have side effects. With this method, the encoded form data is appended to the URL specified by the `Form.action` property. The `post` method is appropriate for form submissions, such as additions to databases, that have side effects. With this method, encoded form data is sent in the body of the HTTP request.

`name`
: Specifies the name of the form. The initial value of this read/write string property is the value of the `name` attribute of the `<form>` tag.

`target`
: A read/write string that specifies the name of the frame or window in which the results of submitting a form should be displayed. Initially specified by the `target` attribute. The special names `"_top"`, `"_parent"`, `"_self"`, and `"_blank"` are also supported for the `target` property and the `target` attribute. See the "Form.target" reference page.

Methods

Form inherits methods from HTMLElement and defines the following:

`reset()`
: Resets each of the input elements of the form to their default values.

`submit()`
: Submits the form.

Event Handlers

Form inherits event handlers from HTMLElement and defines the following:

`onreset`
: Invoked just before the elements of the form are reset. Specified in HTML by the `onreset` attribute.

`onsubmit`
: Invoked just before the form is submitted. Specified in HTML by the `onsubmit` attribute. This event handler allows form entries to be validated before being submitted.

HTML Syntax

A Form object is created with a standard HTML `<form>` tag. The form contains any input elements created with the `<input>`, `<select>`, and `<textarea>` tags between `<form>` and `</form>`:

```
<form
    [ name="form_name" ]        // Used to name the form in JavaScript
    [ target="window_name" ]    // The name of the window for responses
    [ action="url" ]            // The URL to which the form is submitted
    [ method=("get"|"post") ]   // The method of form submission
    [ enctype="encoding" ]      // How the form data is encoded
    [ onreset="handler" ]       // A handler invoked when form is reset
    [ onsubmit="handler" ]      // A handler invoked when form is submitted
>
// Form text and input elements go here
</form>
```

Description

The Form object represents an HTML `<form>` in a document. Each form in a document is represented as an element of the `Document.forms[]` array. Named forms are also represented by the *form_name* property of their document, where *form_name* is the name specified in the `name` attribute of the `<form>` tag.

The elements of a form (buttons, input fields, checkboxes, and so on) are collected in the `Form.elements[]` array. Named elements, like named forms, can also be referenced directly by name—the element name is used as a property name of the Form object. Thus, to refer to a Text object element named `phone` within a form named `questionnaire`, you might use the JavaScript expression:

```
document.questionnaire.phone
```

See Also

Button, Checkbox, FileUpload, Hidden, Input, Password, Radio, Reset, Select, Submit, Text, Textarea; Chapter 15; HTMLFormElement in the DOM reference section

Form.elements[] JavaScript 1.0

the input elements of the form

Synopsis

```
form.elements[i]
form.elements.length
```

Description

form`.elements[]` is an array of the form input objects in *form*. The array has `elements.length` items in it. These items may be of any of the form input element types: Button, Checkbox, Hidden, Password, Radio, Reset, Select, Submit, Text, and Textarea. These form input objects appear in the array in the same order that they appear in the HTML source code for the form.

Usage

If an item in the *form*`.elements[]` array has been given a name with the `name="`*name*`"` attribute of its HTML `<input>` tag, that item's name becomes a property of *form*, and this property refers to the item. Thus, it is possible to refer to input objects by name instead of by number:

```
form.name
```

Referring to elements by name is usually easier, so it is a good idea to specify the `name` attribute for all form elements.

See Also

Button, Checkbox, Form, Hidden, Input, Password, Radio, Reset, Select, Submit, Text, Textarea

Form.onreset

JavaScript 1.1

the handler invoked when a form is reset

Synopsis

```
<form ... onreset="handler" ... >
form.onreset
```

Description

The onreset property of a Form object specifies an event handler function that is invoked when the user clicks on a **Reset** button in the form or when Form.reset( ) is called.

The initial value of this property is a function that contains the semicolon-separated JavaScript statements specified by the onreset attribute of the HTML <form> tag. When an event handler function is defined by an HTML attribute, it is executed in the scope of *element* rather than the scope of the containing window.

In the Netscape 4 event model, the onreset handler function is passed an Event object as an argument. In the IE event model, no argument is passed, but the applicable Event object is available as the event property of the Window object that contains the *element*.

If the onreset handler returns false, the elements of the form are not reset.

Example

You could use the following event handler to ask the user to confirm that they really want to reset the form:

```
<form ...
    onreset="return confirm('Really erase all entered data?')"
>
```

See Also

Form.onsubmit, Form.reset(); Chapter 19; Event, EventListener, and EventTarget in the DOM reference section

Form.onsubmit

JavaScript 1.0

invoked when a form is submitted

Synopsis

```
<form ... onsubmit="handler" ... >
form.onsubmit
```

Description

The onsubmit property of a Form object specifies an event handler function that is invoked when the user submits a form by clicking on a **Submit** button in the form. Note that this event handler is not invoked when the Form.submit( ) method is called.

The initial value of this property is a function that contains the semicolon-separated JavaScript statements specified by the onsubmit attribute of the HTML <form> tag. When an event handler function is defined by an HTML attribute, it is executed in the scope of *`element`* rather than the scope of the containing window.

In the Netscape 4 event model, the `onsubmit` handler function is passed an Event object as an argument. In the IE event model, no argument is passed, but the applicable Event object is available as the `event` property of the Window object that contains the *`element`*.

If the `onsubmit` handler returns `false`, the elements of the form are not submitted. If the handler returns any other value or returns nothing, the form is submitted normally. Because the `onsubmit` handler can cancel form submission, it is ideal for performing form data validation.

See Also

Form.onreset, Form.submit(); Chapter 19; Event, EventListener, and EventTarget in the DOM reference section

Form.reset( ) JavaScript 1.1

reset the elements of a form

Synopsis

`form``.reset( )`

Description

The `reset( )` method resets the specified form, restoring each element of the form to its default value, exactly as if a **Reset** button had been pressed by the user. The form's `onreset( )` event handler is first invoked and may prevent the reset from occurring by returning the value `false`.

Form.submit( ) JavaScript 1.0

submit a form

Synopsis

`form``.submit( )`

Description

The `submit( )` method submits the specified *`form`*, almost as if a **Submit** button had been pressed by the user. The form is submitted as specified by the `action`, `method`, and `encoding` properties of *`form`* (or the `action`, `method`, and `enctype` attributes of the `<form>` tag), and the results are displayed in the window or frame specified by the `target` property or the `target` attribute.

The one important difference between the `submit( )` method and form submission by the user is that the `onsubmit( )` event handler is not invoked when `submit( )` is called. If you use `onsubmit( )` to perform input validation, for example, you'll have to do that validation explicitly before calling `submit( )`.

Usage

It is more common to use a **Submit** button that allows the user to submit the form than to call the `submit()` method yourself.

Form.target

JavaScript 1.0; read-only in Internet Explorer 3

the window for form results

Synopsis

```
form.target
```

Description

`target` is a read/write string property of the Form object. It specifies the name of the frame or window in which the results of the submission of *form* should be displayed. The initial value of this property is specified by the `target` attribute of the `<form>` tag. If unset, the default is that form submission results appear in the same window as the form.

Note that the value of `target` is the *name* of a frame or window, not the actual frame or window itself. The name of a frame is specified by the `name` attribute of the `<frame>` tag. The name of a window is specified when the window is created with a call to the `Window.open()` method. If `target` specifies the name of a window that does not exist, the browser automatically opens a new window to display the results of form submission, and any future forms with the same `target` name use the same newly created window.

Four special target names are supported. The target named `"_blank"` specifies that a new, empty browser window should be created and used to display the results of the form submission. The target `"_self"` is the default; it specifies that the form submission results should be displayed in the same frame or window as the form itself. The target `"_parent"` specifies that the results should be displayed in the parent frame of the frame that contains the form. Finally, the `"_top"` target specifies that the results should be displayed in the topmost frame—in other words, all frames should be removed, and the results should occupy the entire browser window.

You can set this property in IE 3, but doing so has no effect on the actual target of the form.

See Also

Link.target

Frame

JavaScript 1.0

a type of Window object

Synopsis

```
window.frames[i]
window.frames.length
frames[i]
frames.length
```

Description

Though the Frame object is sometimes referred to, there is, strictly speaking, no such object. All frames within a browser window are instances of the Window object, and they contain the same properties and support the same methods and event handlers as the Window object. See the Window object and its properties, methods, and event handlers for details.

There are a few practical differences between Window objects that represent top-level browser windows and those that represent frames within a browser window, however:

- When the `defaultStatus` property is set for a frame, the specified status message is visible only when the mouse is within that frame.
- The `top` and `parent` properties of a top-level browser window always refer to the top-level window itself. These properties are really useful only for frames.
- The `close()` method is not useful for Window objects that are frames.

See Also

Window

getClass()

Netscape 3 LiveConnect

return the JavaClass of a JavaObject

Synopsis

`getClass(`*`javaobj`*`)`

Arguments

`javaobj`

A JavaObject object.

Returns

The JavaClass object of *`javaobj`*.

Description

`getClass()` is a function that takes a JavaObject object (*`javaobj`*) as an argument. It returns the JavaClass object of that JavaObject. That is, it returns the JavaClass object that represents the Java class of the Java object represented by the specified JavaObject.

Usage

Don't confuse the JavaScript `getClass()` function with the *getClass* method of all Java objects. Similarly, don't confuse the JavaScript JavaClass object with the Java *java.lang.Class* class.

Consider the Java Rectangle object created with the following line:

```
var r = new java.awt.Rectangle();
```

`r` is a JavaScript variable that holds a JavaObject object. Calling the JavaScript function `getClass()` returns a JavaClass object that represents the *java.awt.Rectangle* class:

```
var c = getClass(r);
```

You can see this by comparing this JavaClass object to `java.awt.Rectangle`:

```
if (c == java.awt.Rectangle) ...
```

The Java `getClass()` method is invoked differently and performs an entirely different function:

```
c = r.getClass();
```

After executing the above line of code, `c` is a JavaObject that represents a `java.lang.Class` object. This `java.lang.Class` object is a Java object that is a Java representation of the *java.awt.Rectangle* class. See your Java documentation for details on what you can do with the *java.lang.Class* class.

To summarize, you can see that the following expression always evaluates to `true` for any JavaObject `o`:

```
(getClass(o.getClass()) == java.lang.Class)
```

See Also

JavaArray, JavaClass, JavaObject, JavaPackage, the `java` property of the Window object; Chapter 22

Hidden

JavaScript 1.0; enhanced in JavaScript 1.1

hidden data for client/server communication

Inherits from Input, HTMLElement

Synopsis

```
form.name
form.elements[i]
```

Properties

Hidden inherits properties from Input and HTMLElement and defines or overrides the following:

`value`

A read/write string that specifies arbitrary data passed to the web server when the form containing the Hidden object is submitted. The initial value of `value` is specified by the `value` attribute of the `<input>` tag that defines the Hidden object.

HTML Syntax

A Hidden element is created with a standard HTML `<input>` tag:

```
<form>
  ...
  <input
    type="hidden"      // Specifies that this is a Hidden element
    [ name="name" ]    // A name you can use later to refer to this element
                       // Specifies the name property
    [ value="value" ]  // The value transmitted when the form is submitted
                       // Specifies the initial value of the value property
  >
  ...
</form>
```

Description

The Hidden element is an invisible form element that allows arbitrary data to be transmitted to the server when the form is submitted. You can use a Hidden element when you want to transmit information other than the user's input data to the server.

When an HTML document is generated on the fly by a server, another use of Hidden form elements is to transmit data from the server to the client for later processing by JavaScript on the user's side. For example, the server might transmit raw data to the client in a compact, machine-readable form by specifying the data in the `value` attribute of a Hidden element or elements. On the client side, a JavaScript program (transmitted along with the data or in another frame) could read the `value` property of the Hidden element or elements and process, format, and display that data in a less compact, human-readable (and perhaps user-configurable) format.

Hidden elements can also be useful for communication between CGI scripts, even without the intervention of JavaScript on the client side. In this usage, one CGI script generates a dynamic HTML page containing hidden data, which is then submitted to a second CGI script. This hidden data can communicate state information, such as the results of the submission of a previous form.

Cookies can also be used to transmit data from client to server. An important difference between Hidden form elements and cookies, however, is that cookies are persistent on the client side.

See Also

Document.cookie, Form, HTMLElement, Input; HTMLInputElement in the DOM reference section

History — JavaScript 1.0

the URL history of the browser

Synopsis

```
window.history
frame.history
history
```

Properties

`length`
: This numeric property specifies the number of URLs in the browser's history list. Since there is no way to determine the index of the currently displayed document within this list, knowing the size of this list is not particularly helpful.

Methods

`back()`	Goes backward to a previously visited URL.
`forward()`	Goes forward to a previously visited URL.
`go()`	Goes to a previously visited URL.

Description

The History object represents the browsing history of a window—it maintains a list of recently visited web pages. For security and privacy reasons, however, the contents of this list are not accessible to scripts. Although scripts cannot access the URLs represented by the History object, they can use the `length` property to determine the number of URLs in the list and the `back( )`, `forward( )`, and `go( )` methods to cause the browser to revisit any of the URLs in the array.

Example

The following line performs the same action as clicking a browser's **Back** button:

```
history.back( );
```

The following performs the same action as clicking the **Back** button twice:

```
history.go(-2);
```

See Also

The `history` property of the Window object, Location

History.back( ) JavaScript 1.0

return to the previous URL

Synopsis

```
history.back( )
```

Description

`back( )` causes the window or frame to which the History object belongs to revisit the URL (if any) that was visited immediately before the current one. Calling this method has the same effect as clicking on the browser's **Back** button. It is also equivalent to:

```
history.go(-1);
```

History.forward( ) JavaScript 1.0

visit the next URL

Synopsis

```
history.forward( )
```

Description

`forward( )` causes the window or frame to which the History object belongs to revisit the URL (if any) that was visited immediately after the current one. Calling this method has the same effect as clicking on the browser's **Forward** button. It is also equivalent to:

```
history.go(1);
```

Note that if the user has not used the **Back** button or the **Go** menu to move backward through the history, and if JavaScript has not invoked the `History.back( )` or `History.go( )`

methods, the `forward()` method has no effect because the browser is already at the end of its list of URLs, and there is no URL to go forward to.

History.go( )

JavaScript 1.0; enhanced in JavaScript 1.1

revisit a URL

Synopsis

```
history.go(relative_position)
history.go(target_string)
```

Arguments

relative_position
: The relative position in the History list of the URL to be visited. In IE 3, this argument must be 1, 0, or –1.

target_string
: A substring of the URL to be visited. This version of the `go()` method was added in JavaScript 1.1.

Description

The first form of the `History.go()` method takes an integer argument and causes the browser to visit the URL that is the specified number of positions distant in the history list maintained by the History object. Positive arguments move the browser forward through the list, and negative arguments move it backward. Thus, calling `history.go(-1)` is equivalent to calling `history.back()` and produces the same effect as clicking on the **Back** button. Similarly, `history.go(3)` revisits the same URL that would be visited by calling `history.forward()` three times. Calling `go()` with an argument of 0 causes the current page to be reloaded (although in Netscape 3, the `Location.reload()` provides a better way of doing this). This form of the method is buggy in multiframe documents in Netscape 3, and in Internet Explorer it can be called only with the values 1, 0, and –1.

The second form of the `History.go()` method was implemented in JavaScript 1.1. It takes a string argument and causes the browser to revisit the first (i.e., most recently visited) URL that contains the specified string.

HTMLElement

JavaScript 1.2

the superclass of all HTML elements

Synopsis

HTMLElement is the superclass of all classes that represent HTML elements. Therefore, HTMLElement objects are used in many contexts in client-side JavaScript and are available in all of the following ways:

```
document.images[i]
document.links[i]
document.anchors[i]
document.forms[i]
document.forms[i].elements[j]
```

```
document.elementName
document.formName.elementName
document.all[i]
```

Properties

`all[]` *[IE 4]*
: The complete list of elements contained within this element, in source order. This property behaves exactly like the `Document.all[]` property. See the "Document.all[]" reference page.

`children[]` *[IE 4]*
: The elements that are direct children of this element.

`className` *[IE 4, Netscape 6]*
: A read/write string that specifies the value of the `class` attribute of an element. This property is used in conjunction with Cascading Style Sheets.

`document` *[IE 4]*
: A reference to the containing Document object.

`id` *[IE 4, Netscape 6]*
: A read/write string that specifies the value of the `id` attribute of an element. This property is used to assign a unique name to an element.

`innerHTML` *[IE 4, Netscape 6]*
: A read/write string that specifies the HTML text that is contained within the element, not including the opening and closing tags of the element itself. Setting this property replaces the content of the element with the specified HTML text. Note that you cannot set this property while the document is loading.

`innerText` *[IE 4]*
: A read/write string that specifies the plain text contained within the element, not including the opening and closing tags of the element itself. Setting this property replaces the content of the element with unparsed plain text. Note that you cannot set this property while the document is loading.

`lang` *[IE 4, Netscape 6]*
: A read/write string that specifies the value of the `lang` HTML attribute of the *`element`*.

`offsetHeight` *[IE 4]*
: The height, in pixels, of the element and all its content.

`offsetLeft` *[IE 4]*
: The X-coordinate of the element relative to the `offsetParent` container element.

`offsetParent` *[IE 4]*
: Specifies the container element that defines the coordinate system in which `offsetLeft` and `offsetTop` are measured. For most elements, `offsetParent` is the Document object that contains them. However, if an element has a dynamically positioned container, the dynamically positioned element is the `offsetParent`. Similarly, table cells are positioned relative to the row in which they are contained.

`offsetTop` *[IE 4]*
: The Y-coordinate of the element, relative to the `offsetParent` container element.

`offsetWidth` *[IE 4]*
: The width, in pixels, of the element and all its content.

`outerHTML` *[IE 4]*
: A read/write property that specifies the HTML text of an element, including its start and end tags. Setting this property to a string of HTML text completely replaces `element` and its contents. Note that you cannot set this property while the document is loading.

`outerText` *[IE 4]*
: A read/write property that specifies the plain text of an element, including its start and end tags. Setting this property completely replaces `element` and its contents with the specified plain text. Note that you cannot set this property while the document is loading.

`parentElement` *[IE 4]*
: The element that is the direct parent of this element. This property is read-only.

`sourceIndex` *[IE 4]*
: The index of the element in the `Document.all[]` array of the document that contains it.

`style` *[IE 4, Netscape 6]*
: The inline CSS style attributes for this element. Setting properties of this Style object changes the display style of the element. See Chapter 18.

`tagName` *[IE 4, Netscape 6]*
: A read-only string that specifies the name of the HTML tag that defined *`element`*.

`title` *[IE 4, Netscape 6]*
: A read/write string that specifies the value of the `title` attribute of the HTML tag that defined *`element`*. Most browsers use this string as a "tool tip" for the element.

Methods

`contains()`	Determines whether the element contains a specified element.
`getAttribute()`	Gets the value of a named attribute.
`handleEvent()`	Passes an Event object to the appropriate event handler.
`insertAdjacentHTML()`	Inserts HTML text into the document near this element.
`insertAdjacentText()`	Inserts plain text into the document near this element.
`removeAttribute()`	Deletes an attribute and its value from the element.
`scrollIntoView()`	Scrolls the document so the element is visible at the top or bottom of the window.
`setAttribute()`	Sets the value of an attribute of the element.

Event Handlers

`onclick`	Invoked when the user clicks on the element.
`ondblclick`	Invoked when the user double-clicks on the element.
`onhelp`	Invoked when the user requests help. IE 4 only.
`onkeydown`	Invoked when the user presses a key.
`onkeypress`	Invoked when the user presses and releases a key.
`onkeyup`	Invoked when the user releases a key.
`onmousedown`	Invoked when the user presses a mouse button.
`onmousemove`	Invoked when the user moves the mouse.
`onmouseout`	Invoked when the user moves the mouse off the element.

`onmouseover`	Invoked when the user moves the mouse over an element.
`onmouseup`	Invoked when the user releases a mouse button.

Description

HTMLElement is the superclass of all JavaScript classes that represent HTML elements: Anchor, Form, Image, Input, Link, and so on. HTMLElement defines event handlers that are implemented by all elements in both IE 4 and Netscape 4. Because The IE 4 document object model exposes all HTML elements in a document, it defines quite a few properties and methods for those elements. Netscape 4 implements none of these IE properties and methods (except `handleEvent( )`, which is Netscape-specific), but Netscape 6 implements those that have been standardized by the W3C DOM. See the DOM reference section for complete information on the standard properties and methods of HTML elements.

See Also

Anchor, Form, Image, Input, Link; Chapter 17; Chapter 19; Element, HTMLElement, and Node in the DOM reference section

HTMLElement.contains( ) — Internet Explorer 4

whether one element is contained in another

Synopsis

`element``.contains(`*`target`*`)`

Arguments

`target`

An HTMLElement object.

Returns

`true` if *`element`* contains *`target`*; `false` if it does not.

HTMLElement.getAttribute( ) — Internet Explorer 4, Netscape 6

get an attribute value

Synopsis

`element``.getAttribute(`*`name`*`)`

Arguments

`name`

The name of the attribute.

Returns

The value of the named attribute of *`element`* or `null` if *`element`* does not have an attribute named *`name`*.

HTMLElement.handleEvent( )

see Window.handleEvent( )

HTMLElement.insertAdjacentHTML( ) Internet Explorer 4

insert HTML text around an element

Synopsis

```
element.insertAdjacentHTML(where, text)
```

Arguments

where

A string specifying where the text is to be inserted. The value "BeforeBegin" specifies that *text* is to be inserted before the start tag of *element*. "AfterBegin" specifies that *text* is to be inserted immediately after the start tag of *element*. "BeforeEnd" specifies that *text* is to be inserted immediately before the end tag of *element*. "AfterEnd" specifies that *text* is to be inserted immediately after the end tag of *element*.

text

The HTML text to insert.

Description

`insertAdjacentHTML( )` inserts the HTML *text* at a position within or next to *element*, as specified by the argument *where*.

HTMLElement.insertAdjacentText( ) Internet Explorer 4

insert plain text before or after an element

Synopsis

```
element.insertAdjacentText(where, text)
```

Arguments

where

A string that specifies where the text is to be inserted. The value "BeforeBegin" specifies that *text* is to be inserted before the start tag of *element*. "AfterBegin" specifies that *text* is to be inserted immediately after the start tag of *element*. "BeforeEnd" specifies that *text* is to be inserted immediately before the end tag of *element*. "AfterEnd" specifies that *text* is to be inserted immediately after the end tag of *element*.

text

The plain text to insert.

Description

`insertAdjacentText( )` inserts the plain text *text* at a position within or next to *element*, as specified by the argument *where*.

HTMLElement.onclick

JavaScript 1.2; HTML 4.0

the handler invoked when the user clicks on an element

Synopsis

```
<element onclick="handler" ... >
element.onclick
```

Description

The `onclick` property of an HTMLElement object specifies an event handler function that is invoked when the user clicks on the *element*. Note that onclick is different than `onmousedown`. A click event does not occur unless a mousedown event and the subsequent mouseup event both occur over the same *element*.

The initial value of this property is a function that contains the JavaScript statements specified by the `onclick` attribute of the HTML tag that defined the object. When an event handler function is defined by an HTML attribute, it is executed in the scope of *element* rather than in the scope of the containing window.

In the Netscape 4 event model, the `onclick` handler function is passed an Event object as an argument. In the IE event model, no argument is passed, but the applicable Event object is available as the `event` property of the Window object that contains the *element*.

In Netscape 4, the `Event.which` property specifies which mouse button was pressed. In IE 4, the `Event.button` property specifies the button number.

See Also

Event, Input.onclick; Chapter 19; EventListener, EventTarget, and MouseEvent in the DOM reference section

HTMLElement.ondblclick

JavaScript 1.2; HTML 4.0

the handler invoked when the user double-clicks on an element

Synopsis

```
<element ondblclick="handler" ... >
element.ondblclick
```

Description

The `ondblclick` property of an HTMLElement object specifies an event handler function that is invoked when the user double-clicks on the *element*.

The initial value of this property is a function that contains the JavaScript statements specified by the `ondblclick` attribute of the HTML tag that defined the object. When an event handler function is defined by an HTML attribute, it is executed in the scope of *element* rather than in the scope of the containing window.

In the Netscape 4 event model, the `ondblclick` handler function is passed an Event object as an argument. In the IE event model, no argument is passed, but the applicable Event object is available as the `event` property of the Window object that contains the *element*.

See Also

Event; Chapter 19; EventListener, EventTarget, and MouseEvent in the DOM reference section

HTMLElement.onhelp

Internet Explorer 4

the handler invoked when the user presses F1

Synopsis

```
<element onhelp="handler" ... >
element.onhelp
```

Description

The `onhelp` property of *`element`* specifies an event handler function that is invoked when the user presses the **F1** key while *`element`* has keyboard focus.

The initial value of this property is a function that contains the JavaScript statements specified by the `onhelp` attribute of the HTML tag that defined the element. When an event handler function is defined by an HTML attribute, it is executed in the scope of *`element`* rather than in the scope of the containing window.

After the `onhelp` handler function is invoked, Internet Explorer 4 displays the built-in help window.

Client-Side JavaScript Reference

HTMLElement.onkeydown

JavaScript 1.2; HTML 4.0

the handler invoked when the user presses a key

Synopsis

```
<element onkeydown="handler" ... >
element.onkeydown
```

Description

The `onkeydown` property of an HTMLElement object specifies an event handler function that is invoked when the user presses a key over the *`element`*.

The initial value of this property is a function that contains the JavaScript statements specified by the `onkeydown` attribute of the HTML tag that defined the object. When an event handler function is defined by an HTML attribute, it is executed in the scope of *`element`* rather than in the scope of the containing window.

In the Netscape 4 event model, the `onkeydown` handler function is passed an Event object as an argument. In the IE event model, no argument is passed, but the applicable Event object is available as the event property of the Window object that contains the *`element`*.

The character code of the key pressed is contained in the `which` property of the Event object in Netscape and in the `keyCode` property of the Event object in IE. You can convert this keycode to a string with `String.fromCharCode()`. The modifier keys in effect can be determined from the `Event.modifiers` property in Netscape or with `Event.shiftKey()` and related methods in IE.

In the Netscape event model, you can cancel processing of the keystroke by returning `false` from this handler. In the IE event model, you cancel processing by setting `Event.returnValue` to `false`. In IE, this handler may return an alternate keycode that is used in place of the key actually pressed by the user.

You can often use the `onkeypress` event handler instead of the `onkeydown` and `onkeyup` handlers.

See Also

Event, HTMLElement.onkeypress; Chapter 19

HTMLElement.onkeypress — JavaScript 1.2; HTML 4.0

the handler invoked when the user presses a key

Synopsis

```
<element onkeypress="handler" ... >
element.onkeypress
```

Description

The `onkeypress` property of an HTMLElement object specifies an event handler function that is invoked when the user presses a key over the *`element`*. A keypress event is generated after a key down event and before the corresponding key up event. The keypress and key down events are similar. Unless you care about receiving individual key up events, you should use `onkeypress` instead of `onkeydown`.

The initial value of this property is a function that contains the JavaScript statements specified by the `onkeypress` attribute of the HTML tag that defined the object. When an event handler function is defined by an HTML attribute, it is executed in the scope of *`element`* rather than in the scope of the containing window.

In the Netscape 4 event model, the `onkeypress` handler function is passed an Event object as an argument. In the IE event model, no argument is passed, but the applicable Event object is available as the `event` property of the Window object that contains the *`element`*.

The character code of the key pressed is contained in the `which` property of the Event object in Netscape and in the `keyCode` property of the Event object in IE. You can convert this keycode to a string with `String.fromCharCode()`. The modifier keys in effect can be determined from the `Event.modifiers` property in Netscape or with `Event.shiftKey()` and related methods in IE.

In Netscape, you can cancel processing of the keystroke by returning `false` from this handler. In IE, you cancel processing by setting `Event.returnValue` to `false`. In IE, this handler may return an alternate keycode that is used in place of the key actually pressed by the user.

See Also

Event; Chapter 19

HTMLElement.onkeyup

JavaScript 1.2; HTML 4.0

the handler invoked when the user releases a key

Synopsis

```
<element onkeyup="handler" ... >
element.onkeyup
```

Description

The onkeyup property of an HTMLElement object specifies an event handler function that is invoked when the user releases a key over the *element*.

The initial value of this property is a function that contains the JavaScript statements specified by the onkeyup attribute of the HTML tag that defined the object. When an event handler function is defined by an HTML attribute, it is executed in the scope of *element* rather than in the scope of the containing window.

In the Netscape 4 event model, the onkeyup handler function is passed an Event object as an argument. In the IE event model, no argument is passed, but the applicable Event object is available as the event property of the Window object that contains the *element*.

See Also

Event, HTMLElement.onkeydown; Chapter 19

HTMLElement.onmousedown

JavaScript 1.2; HTML 4.0

the handler invoked when the user presses a mouse button

Synopsis

```
<element onmousedown="handler" ... >
element.onmousedown
```

Description

The onmousedown property of an HTMLElement object specifies an event handler function that is invoked when the user presses a mouse button over *element*.

The initial value of this property is a function that contains the JavaScript statements specified by the onmousedown attribute of the HTML tag that defined the object. When an event handler function is defined by an HTML attribute, it is executed in the scope of *element* rather than in the scope of the containing window.

In the Netscape 4 event model, the onmousedown handler function is passed an Event object as an argument. In the IE event model, no argument is passed, but the applicable Event object is available as the event property of the Window object that contains the *element*.

In Netscape, the Event.which property specifies which mouse button was pressed. In IE, the Event.button property specifies the button number.

See Also

Event, HTMLElement.onclick; Chapter 19; EventListener, EventTarget, and MouseEvent in the DOM reference section

HTMLElement.onmousemove JavaScript 1.2; HTML 4.0

the handler invoked when the mouse moves within an element

Synopsis

```
<element onmousemove="handler" ... >
element.onmousemove
```

Description

The onmousemove property of an HTMLElement object specifies an event handler function that is invoked when the user moves the mouse pointer within the *element*.

The initial value of this property is a function that contains the JavaScript statements specified by the onmousemove attribute of the HTML tag that defined the object. When an event handler function is defined by an HTML attribute, it is executed in the scope of *element* rather than in the scope of the containing window.

In the Netscape 4 event model, the onmousemove handler function is passed an Event object as an argument. In the IE event model, no argument is passed, but the applicable Event object is available as the event property of the Window object that contains the *element*.

If you define an onmousemove event handler, mouse motion events are generated and reported in huge quantities when the mouse is moved within *element*. Keep this in mind when writing the function to be invoked by the event handler.

In Netscape 4, you cannot define this event handler on individual elements; instead, you must explicitly register your interest in mouse motion events by capturing them with the captureEvents() method of a Window, Document, or Layer object.

See Also

Event, Window.captureEvents(); Chapter 19; EventListener, EventTarget, and MouseEvent in the DOM reference section

HTMLElement.onmouseout JavaScript 1.2; HTML 4.0

the handler invoked when mouse moves out of an element

Synopsis

```
<element onmouseout="handler" ... >
element.onmouseout
```

Description

The onmouseout property of an HTMLElement object specifies an event handler function that is invoked when the user moves the mouse pointer out of the *element*.

The initial value of this property is a function that contains the JavaScript statements specified by the `onmouseout` attribute of the HTML tag that defined the object. When an event handler function is defined by an HTML attribute, it is executed in the scope of *element* rather than in the scope of the containing window.

In the Netscape 4 event model, the `onmouseout` handler function is passed an Event object as an argument. In the IE event model, no argument is passed, but the applicable Event object is available as the event property of the Window object that contains the *element*.

See Also

Event, Link.onmouseout; Chapter 19; EventListener, EventTarget, and MouseEvent in the DOM reference section

HTMLElement.onmouseover — JavaScript 1.2; HTML 4.0

the handler invoked when the mouse moves over an element

Synopsis

```
<element onmouseover="handler" ... >
element.onmouseover
```

Description

The `onmouseover` property of an HTMLElement object specifies an event handler function that is invoked when the user moves the mouse pointer over the *element*.

The initial value of this property is a function that contains the JavaScript statements specified by the `onmouseover` attribute of the HTML tag that defined the object. When an event handler function is defined by an HTML attribute, it is executed in the scope of *element* rather than in the scope of the containing window.

In Netscape 4, the `onmouseover` handler function is passed an Event object as an argument. In IE 4, no argument is passed, but the applicable Event object is available as the event property of the Window object that contains the *element*.

See Also

Event, Link.onmouseover; Chapter 19

HTMLElement.onmouseup — JavaScript 1.2; HTML 4.0

the handler invoked when the user releases a mouse button

Synopsis

```
<element onmouseup="handler" ... >
element.onmouseup
```

Description

The `onmouseup` property of an HTMLElement object specifies an event handler function that is invoked when the user releases a mouse button over the *element*.

The initial value of this property is a function that contains the JavaScript statements specified by the `onmouseup` attribute of the HTML tag that defined the object. When an event handler function is defined by an HTML attribute, it is executed in the scope of *`element`* rather than in the scope of the containing window.

In the Netscape 4 event model, the `onmouseup` handler function is passed an Event object as an argument. In the IE event model, no argument is passed, but the applicable Event object is available as the `event` property of the Window object that contains the *`element`*.

In Netscape 4, the `Event.which` property specifies which mouse button was pressed. In IE, the `Event.button` property specifies the button number.

See Also

Event, HTMLElement.onclick; Chapter 19; EventListener, EventTarget, and MouseEvent in the DOM reference section

HTMLElement.removeAttribute( )

Internet Explorer 4, Netscape 6

delete an attribute

Synopsis

```
element.removeAttribute(name)
```

Arguments

name
: The name of the attribute to be deleted.

Returns

`true` on success; `false` on failure.

Description

`removeAttribute( )` deletes the attribute *name* from *`element`*. If *`element`* does not have an attribute named *name*, this method returns `false`.

HTMLElement.scrollIntoView( )

Internet Explorer 4

make an element visible

Synopsis

```
element.scrollIntoView(top)
```

Arguments

top
: An optional boolean argument that specifies whether the element should be scrolled to the top or bottom of the screen. If `true` or omitted, `element` appears at the top of the screen. If `false`, *`element`* appears at the bottom of the screen.

Description

`scrollIntoView()` scrolls the document containing *element* so the top of *element* is aligned with the top of the display area or the bottom of *element* is aligned with the bottom of the display area.

HTMLElement.setAttribute( ) — Internet Explorer 4, Netscape 6

set the value of an attribute

Synopsis

```
element.setAttribute(name, value)
```

Arguments

name
: The name of the attribute to set.

value
: The value to set it to.

Description

`setAttribute()` sets the attribute *name* of *element* to *value*.

Image — JavaScript 1.1

an image in an HTML document — Inherits from HTMLElement

Synopsis

```
document.images[i]
document.images.length
document.image-name
```

Constructor

```
new Image(width, height)
```

Arguments

width, height
: An optionally specified width and height for the image.

Properties

Image inherits properties from HTMLElement and defines the following properties, most of which correspond to the HTML attributes of the `<img>` tag. In JavaScript 1.1 and later, the `src` and `lowsrc` properties are read/write and may be set to change the displayed image. In browsers that do not allow document reflow, such as IE 3 and Netscape 4, the other properties are read-only.

`border`
An integer that specifies the width, in pixels, of the border around an image. Its value is set by the `border` attribute. Images have borders only when they are within hyperlinks.

`complete`
A read-only boolean value that specifies whether an image is completely loaded or, more accurately, whether the browser has completed its attempt to load the image. If an error occurs during loading, or if the load is aborted, the `complete` property is still set to `true`.

`height`
An integer that specifies the height, in pixels, of the image. Its value is set by the `height` attribute.

`hspace`
An integer that specifies the amount of extra horizontal space, in pixels, inserted on the left and right of the image. Its value is set by the `hspace` attribute.

`lowsrc`
A read/write string that specifies the URL of an alternate image (usually a smaller one) to display when the user's browser is running on a low-resolution monitor. The initial value is specified by the `lowsrc` attribute of the `<img>` tag.

Setting this property has no immediate effect. If the `src` property is set, however, a new image is loaded, and on low-resolution systems, the current value of the `lowsrc` property is used instead of the newly updated value of `src`.

`name`
A string value, specified by the HTML `name` attribute, that specifies the name of the image. When an image is given a name with the `name` attribute, a reference to the image is placed in the *`image-name`* property of the document in addition to being placed in the `document.images[]` array.

`src`
A read/write string that specifies the URL of the image to be displayed by the browser. The initial value of this property is specified by the `src` attribute of the `<img>` tag. When you set this property to the URL of a new image, the browser loads and displays that new image (or, on low-resolution systems, the image specified by the `lowsrc` property). This is useful for updating the graphical appearance of your web pages in response to user actions and can also be used to perform simple animation.

`vspace`
An integer that specifies the amount of extra vertical space, in pixels, inserted above and below the image. Its value is set by the `vspace` attribute.

`width`
An integer that specifies the width, in pixels, of the image. Its value is set by the `width` attribute.

Event Handlers

Image inherits event handlers from HTMLElement and defines the following:

`onabort`
Invoked if the user aborts the download of an image.

`onerror`
Invoked if an error occurs while downloading the image.

`onload`
Invoked when the image successfully finishes loading.

HTML Syntax

The Image object is created with a standard HTML `<img>` tag. Some `<img>` attributes have been omitted from the following syntax because they are not used by or accessible from JavaScript:

```
<img src="url"                  // The image to display
     width="pixels"             // The width of the image
     height="pixels"            // The height of the image
     [ name="image_name" ]      // A property name for the image
     [ lowsrc="url" ]           // Alternate low-resolution image
     [ border="pixels" ]        // Width of image border
     [ hspace="pixels" ]        // Extra horizontal space around image
     [ vspace="pixels" ]        // Extra vertical space around image
     [ onload="handler" ]       // Invoked when image is fully loaded
     [ onerror="handler" ]      // Invoked if error in loading
     [ onabort="handler" ]      // Invoked if user aborts load
>
```


Description

The Image objects in the `document.images[]` array represent the images embedded in an HTML document using the `<img>` tag. The `src` property is the most interesting one; when you set this property, the browser loads and displays the image specified by the new value.

You can create Image objects dynamically in your JavaScript code using the `Image()` constructor function. Note that this constructor method does not have an argument to specify the image to be loaded. As with images created from HTML, you tell the browser to load an image by setting the `src` property of any images you create explicitly. There is no way to display an Image object in the web browser. All you can do is force the Image object to download an image by setting the `src` property. This is useful, however, because it loads an image into the browser's cache. Later, if that same image URL is specified for one of the images in the `images[]` array, it is preloaded and displays quickly. You can do this with the following lines:

```
document.images[2].src = preloaded_image.src;
document.toggle_image.src = toggle_off.src;
```

Usage

Setting the `src` property of an Image object is a way to implement simple animations in your web pages. It is also an excellent technique for changing the graphics on a page as the user interacts with the page. For example, you can create your own **Submit** button using an image and a hypertext link. The button will start out with a disabled graphic and remain that way until the user correctly enters all the required information into the form, at which point the graphic changes, and the user is able to submit the form.

Image.onabort

JavaScript 1.1

the handler invoked when the user aborts image loading

Synopsis

```
<img ... onabort="handler" ... >
image.onabort
```

Description

The onabort property of an Image object specifies an event handler function that is invoked when the user aborts the loading of an image (for example, by clicking the **Stop** button).

The initial value of this property is a function that contains the JavaScript statements specified by the onabort attribute of the <img> tag that defined the Image object. When an event handler function is defined by an HTML attribute, it is executed in the scope of *element* rather than in the scope of the containing window.

In the Netscape 4 event model, the onabort handler function is passed an Event object as an argument. In the IE event model, no argument is passed, but the applicable Event object is available as the event property of the Window object that contains the *element*.

Image.onerror

JavaScript 1.1

the handler invoked when an error occurs during image loading

Synopsis

```
<img ... onerror="handler" ... >
image.onerror
```

Description

The onerror property of an Image object specifies an event handler function that is invoked when an error occurs during the loading of an image.

The initial value of this property is a function that contains the JavaScript statements specified by the onerror attribute of the <img> tag that defined the Image object. When an event handler function is defined by an HTML attribute, it is executed in the scope of *element* rather than in the scope of the containing window.

In the Netscape 4 event model, the onerror handler function is passed an Event object as an argument. In the IE event model, no argument is passed, but the applicable Event object is available as the event property of the Window object that contains the *element*.

Image.onload

JavaScript 1.1

the handler invoked when an image finishes loading

Synopsis

```
<img ... onload="handler" ... >
image.onload
```

Description

The onload property of an Image object specifies an event handler function that is invoked when an image loads successfully.

The initial value of this property is a function that contains the JavaScript statements specified by the onload attribute of the <img> tag that defined the Image object. When an event handler function is defined by an HTML attribute, it is executed in the scope of *element* rather than in the scope of the containing window.

In the Netscape 4 event model, the onload handler function is passed an Event object as an argument. In the IE event model, no argument is passed, but the applicable Event object is available as the event property of the Window object that contains the *element*.

See Also

Chapter 19; Event, EventListener, and EventTarget in the DOM reference section

Input

JavaScript 1.0; enhanced in JavaScript 1.1

an input element in an HTML form — **Inherits from HTMLElement**

Synopsis

```
form.elements[i]
form.name
```

Properties

Input inherits properties from HTMLElement and defines or overrides the following:

`checked`
: A read/write boolean that specifies whether a Checkbox or Radio form element is currently checked. You can set the state of these button elements by setting the value of this property. This property is not used by other form elements.

`defaultChecked`
: A read-only boolean value that specifies whether a Checkbox or Radio element is checked by default. This property is used to restore the Checkbox or Radio element to its default value when the form is reset and has no meaning for other form elements. defaultChecked corresponds to the checked attribute in the HTML <input> tag that created the form element. If checked was present, defaultChecked is true. Otherwise, defaultChecked is false.

`defaultValue`
: Specifies the initial text that appears in the form element and the value that is restored to that element when the form is reset. This property is used only by the Text, Textarea, and Password elements. For security reasons, it is not used by the File-Upload element. For Checkbox and Radio elements, the equivalent property is defaultChecked.

`form`
: A read-only reference to the Form object that contains the element. The form property allows the event handlers of one form element to easily refer to sibling elements

in the same form. When an event handler is invoked, the this keyword refers to the form element for which it was invoked. Thus, an event handler can use the expression this.form to refer to the form that contains it. From there, it can refer to sibling elements by name or use the elements[] array of the Form object to refer to them by number.

length
: For the Select form element, this property specifies the number of options or choices (each represented by an Option object) that are contained within the options[] array of the element. See the "Select" reference page.

name
: A read-only string, specified by the HTML name attribute, that specifies the name of this element. This name may be used to refer to the element, as shown in the preceding "Synopsis" section. See the "Input.name" reference page.

options[]
: For the Select form element, this array contains Option objects that represent the options or choices displayed by the Select object. The number of elements in the array is specified by the length property of the Select element. See the "Select" reference page.

selectedIndex
: For the Select form element, this integer specifies which option displayed by the Select object is currently selected. In JavaScript 1.1, this property is read/write. In JavaScript 1.0, it is read-only. See the "Select" reference page.

type *[JavaScript 1.1]*
: A read-only string that specifies the type of the form element. See the "Input.type" reference page.

value
: A string that specifies the value displayed by the element and/or to be sent to the server for this element when the form that contains it is submitted. See the "Input.value" reference page.

Methods

Input inherits methods from HTMLElement and defines or overrides the following:

blur()
: Removes keyboard focus from the element.

click()
: Simulates a mouse-click on the form element.

focus()
: Gives keyboard focus to the element.

select()
: For form elements that display editable text, selects the text that appears in the element.

Event Handlers

Input inherits event handlers from HTMLElement and defines or overrides the following:

`onblur`
: Invoked when the user takes keyboard focus away from the element.

`onchange`
: For form elements that are not buttons, this event handler is invoked when the user enters or selects a new value.

`onclick`
: For form elements that are buttons, this event handler is invoked when the user clicks or selects the button.

`onfocus`
: Invoked when the user gives keyboard focus to the element.

Description

Form elements are stored in the `elements[]` array of the Form object. The contents of this array are Input objects, which represent the individual buttons, input fields, and other controls that appear within the form. Many types of input elements are created with the `<input>` tag; others are created with the `<select>` and `<option>` tags and the `<textarea>` tag. The various form input elements share quite a few properties, methods, and event handlers, which are described on this reference page. Specific behaviors for specific types of form elements are described on their own pages.

The Input object defines many shared properties, methods, and event handlers, but not all of them are shared by all types of form elements. For example, the Button object triggers the `onclick` event handler but not the `onchange` handler, while the Text object triggers `onchange` but not `onclick`. The following figure shows all of the form elements and the properties associated with them.

ELEMENT / PROPERTY	checked	defaultChecked	defaultValue	form	length	name	options	selectedIndex	type	value	blur()	click()	focus()	select()	onblur	onchange	onclick	onfocus
Button				●		●			●	●	●	●	●		●		●	●
Checkbox	●	●		●		●			●	●	●	●	●		●		●	●
Radio	●	●		●		●			●	●	●	●	●		●		●	●
Reset				●		●			●	●	●	●	●		●		●	●
Submit				●		●			●	●	●	●	●		●		●	●
Text			●	●		●			●	●	●		●	●	●	●		●
Textarea			●	●		●			●	●	●		●	●	●	●		●
Password			●	●		●			●	●	●		●	●	●	●		●
FileUpload			●	●		●			●	●	●		●	●	●	●		●
Select				●	●	●	●	●	●		●	●	●		●	●		●
Hidden				●		●			●	●								

There are two broad categories of form elements. The first is the buttons: Button, Checkbox, Radio, Reset, and Submit. These elements have an `onclick` event handler but not an onchange handler. Similarly, they respond to the `click( )` method but not to the `select( )` method. The second category contains those elements that display text: Text, Textarea, Password, and FileUpload. These elements have an onchange event handler rather than an `onclick` handler, and they respond to the `select( )` method but not to the `click( )` method.

The Select element is a special case. It is created with the `<select>` tag and is less like the `<input>` elements than the other form elements. Although the Select element is technically represented by a different object type, it is still convenient to consider it an Input object.

See Also

Button, Checkbox, FileUpload, Form, Hidden, Password, Radio, Reset, Select, Submit, Text, Textarea; Chapter 15; HTMLInputElement in the DOM reference section

Input.blur( ) JavaScript 1.0

remove keyboard focus from a form element

Synopsis

```
input.blur( )
```

Description

The `blur( )` method of a form element removes keyboard focus from that element without invoking the `onblur` event handler; it is essentially the opposite of the `focus( )` method. The `blur( )` method does not transfer keyboard focus anywhere, however, so the only time that it is actually useful to call this method right before you transfer keyboard focus elsewhere with the `focus( )` method, when you don't want to trigger the `onblur` event handler. That is, by removing focus explicitly from the element, you won't be notified when it is removed implicitly by a `focus( )` call on another element.

All form elements other than Hidden support the `blur( )` method. Unfortunately, not all platforms support keyboard navigation equally well. In Netscape 2 and 3 for Unix platforms, the `blur( )` method is functional only for those form elements that display text: Text, Textarea, Password, and FileUpload.

Input.click( ) JavaScript 1.0

simulate a mouse-click on a form element

Synopsis

```
input.click( )
```

Description

The `click( )` method of a form element simulates a mouse-click on the form element but does not invoke the `onclick` event handler of the element.

The click( ) method is not often useful. Because it does not invoke the onclick event handler, it is not useful to call this method on Button elements—they don't have any behavior other than that defined by the onclick handler. Calling click( ) on a Submit or Reset element submits or resets a form, but this can be more directly achieved with the submit( ) and reset( ) method of the Form object itself.

Input.focus( ) — JavaScript 1.0

give keyboard focus to a form element

Synopsis

```
input.focus( )
```

Description

The focus( ) method of a form element transfers keyboard focus to that element without calling the onfocus event handler. That is, it makes the element active with respect to keyboard navigation and keyboard input. Thus, if you call focus( ) for a Text element, any text the user types appears in that text element. Or, if you call focus( ) for a Button element, the user can invoke that button from the keyboard.

All form elements except the Hidden element support the focus( ) method. Unfortunately, not all platforms support keyboard navigation equally well. In Unix versions of Netscape, focus( ) is functional only for those form elements that display text: Text, Textarea, Password, and FileUpload.

Input.name — JavaScript 1.0

the name of a form element

Synopsis

```
input.name
```

Description

name is a read-only string property of every form element. The value of this property is set by the name attributes of the HTML <input> tag that defines the form element.

The name of a form element is used for two purposes. First, it is used when the form is submitted. Data for each element in the form is usually submitted in the format:

```
name=value
```

where *name* and *value* are encoded as necessary for transmission. If a name is not specified for a form element, the data for that element cannot be submitted to a web server.

The second use of the name property is to refer to a form element in JavaScript code. The name of an element becomes a property of the form that contains the element. The value of this property is a reference to the element. For example, if address is a form that contains a text input element with the name zip, address.zip refers to that text input element.

With Radio and Checkbox form elements, it is common to define more than one related object, each of which have the same `name` property. In this case, data is submitted to the server with this format:

```
name=value1,value2,...,valuen
```

Similarly, in JavaScript, each of the elements that shares a name becomes an element of an array with that name. Thus, if four Checkbox objects in the form `order` share the name `options`, they are available in JavaScript as elements of the array `order.options[]`.

Input.onblur JavaScript 1.0

the handler invoked when a form element loses focus

Synopsis

```
<input type="type" onblur="handler">
input.onblur
```

Description

The `onblur` property of an Input object specifies an event handler function that is invoked when the user transfers keyboard focus away from that input element. Calling `blur()` to remove focus from an element does not invoke `onblur` for that object. Note, however, that calling `focus()` to transfer focus to some other element causes the `onblur` event handler to be invoked for whichever element currently has the focus.

The initial value of this property is a function that contains the semicolon-separated JavaScript statements specified by the `onblur` attribute of the HTML tag that defined the object. When an event handler function is defined by an HTML attribute, it is executed in the scope of *`element`* rather than in the scope of the containing window.

In the Netscape 4 event model, the `onblur` handler function is passed an Event object as an argument. In the IE event model, no argument is passed, but the applicable Event object is available as the event property of the Window object that contains the *`element`*.

The `onblur` event handler is available for all form elements except the Hidden element. In Netscape on Unix platforms, however, it is invoked only for the text-entry elements: Text, Textarea, Password, and FileUpload. Note that in JavaScript 1.1, the Window object also defines an `onblur` event handler.

See Also

Window.onblur; Chapter 19; Event, EventListener, and EventTarget in the DOM reference section

Input.onchange JavaScript 1.0

the handler invoked when a form element's value changes

Synopsis

```
<input type="type" onchange="handler">
input.onchange
```

Description

The onchange property of an Input object specifies an event handler function that is invoked when the user changes the value displayed by a form element. Such a change may be an edit to the text displayed in Text, Textarea, Password, or FileUpload elements, or the selection or deselection of an option in a Select element. Note that this event handler is only invoked when the user makes such a change—it is not invoked if a JavaScript program changes the value displayed by an element.

Also note that the onchange handler is not invoked every time the user enters or deletes a character in a text-entry form element. onchange is not intended for that type of character-by-character event handling. Instead, onchange is invoked when the user's edit is complete. The browser assumes that the edit is complete when keyboard focus is moved from the current element to some other element—for example, when the user clicks on the next element in the form. See the "HTMLElement.onkeypress" reference page for character-by-character event notification.

The onchange event handler is not used by the Hidden element or by any of the button elements. Those elements—Button, Checkbox, Radio, Reset, and Submit—use the onclick event handler instead.

The initial value of this property is a function that contains the semicolon-separated JavaScript statements specified by the onchange attribute of the HTML tag that defined the object. When an event handler function is defined by an HTML attribute, it is executed in the scope of *element* rather than in the scope of the containing window.

In the Netscape 4 event model, the onchange handler function is passed an Event object as an argument. In the IE event model, no argument is passed, but the applicable Event object is available as the event property of the Window object that contains the *element*.

See Also

HTMLElement.onkeypress; Chapter 19; Event, EventListener, and EventTarget in the DOM reference section

Input.onclick

JavaScript 1.0; enhanced in JavaScript 1.1

the handler invoked when a form element is clicked

Synopsis

```
<input type="type" onclick="handler">
input.onclick
```

Description

The onclick property of an Input object specifies an event handler function that is invoked when the user clicks on the input element. It is not invoked when the click() method is called for the element.

Only form elements that are buttons invoke the onclick event handler. These are the Button, Checkbox, Radio, Reset, and Submit elements. Other form elements use the onchange event handler instead of onclick.

The initial value of the onclick property is a function containing the semicolon-separated JavaScript statements specified by the onclick attribute of the HTML tag that defined the object. When an event handler function is defined by an HTML attribute, it is executed in the scope of *element* rather than in the scope of the containing window.

In the Netscape 4 event model, the onclick handler function is passed an Event object as an argument. In the IE event model, no argument is passed, but the applicable Event object is available as the event property of the Window object that contains the *element*.

Note that the Reset and Submit elements perform a default action when clicked: they reset and submit, respectively, the form that contains them. You can use the onclick event handlers of each of these elements to perform actions in addition to these default actions. In JavaScript 1.1, you can also prevent these default actions by returning false. That is, if the onclick handler of a **Reset** button returns false, the form is not reset, and if the onclick handler of a **Submit** button returns false, the form is not submitted. Note that you do similar things with the onsubmit and onreset event handlers of the Form object itself.

Finally, note that the Link object also defines an onclick event handler.

See Also

Link.onclick; Chapter 19; EventListener, EventTarget, and MouseEvent in the DOM reference section

Input.onfocus

JavaScript 1.0

the handler invoked when a form element gains focus

Synopsis

```
<input type="type" onfocus="handler">
input.onfocus
```

Description

The onfocus property of an Input object specifies an event handler function that is invoked when the user transfers keyboard focus to that input element. Calling focus( ) to set focus to an element does not invoke onfocus for that object.

The initial value of this property is a function that contains the semicolon-separated JavaScript statements specified by the onfocus attribute of the HTML tag that defined the object. When an event handler function is defined by an HTML attribute, it is executed in the scope of *element* rather than in the scope of the containing window.

In the Netscape 4 event model, the onfocus handler function is passed an Event object as an argument. In the IE event model, no argument is passed, but the applicable Event object is available as the event property of the Window object that contains the *element*.

The onfocus event handler is available for all form elements except the Hidden element. In Netscape on Unix platforms, however, it is invoked only for the text-entry elements: Text, Textarea, Password, and FileUpload. Note that in JavaScript 1.1, the Window object also defines an onfocus event handler.

See Also

Window.onfocus; Chapter 19; Event, EventListener, and EventTarget in the DOM reference section

Input.select( )

JavaScript 1.0

select the text in a form element

Synopsis

```
input.select( )
```

Description

The `select( )` method selects the text displayed in a Text, Textarea, Password, or File-Upload element. The effects of selecting text may vary from platform to platform, but typically, invoking this method produces the same result as the user dragging the mouse across all the text in the specified Text object. On most platforms, this produces the following effects:

- The text is highlighted, often displayed with colors reversed.
- If the text remains selected the next time the user types a character, the selected text is deleted and replaced with the newly typed character.
- On some platforms, the text becomes available for cut-and-paste.

The user can usually deselect text by clicking in the Text object or by moving the cursor. Once deselected, the user can add and delete individual characters without replacing the entire text value.

Input.type

JavaScript 1.1

the type of a form element

Synopsis

```
input.type
```

Description

`type` is a read-only string property of all form elements that specifies the type of the form element. The value of this property for each possible form element is given in the following table.

Object type	HTML tag	type property
Button	`<input type="button">`	"button"
Checkbox	`<input type="checkbox">`	"checkbox"
FileUpload	`<input type="file">`	"file"
Hidden	`<input type="hidden">`	"hidden"

Object type	HTML tag	type property
Password	`<input type="password">`	"password"
Radio	`<input type="radio">`	"radio"
Reset	`<input type="reset">`	"reset"
Select	`<select>`	"select-one"
Select	`<select multiple>`	"select-multiple"
Submit	`<input type="submit">`	"submit"
Text	`<input type="text">`	"text"
Textarea	`<textarea>`	"textarea"

Note that the Select element has two possible type values, depending on whether it allows single or multiple selection. Also note that unlike other input element properties, type is not available in JavaScript 1.0.

Input.value

Netscape 2; buggy in Internet Explorer 3

the value displayed or submitted by a form element

Synopsis

```
input.value
```

Description

value is a read/write string property of all form elements that specifies the value displayed by the form element and/or submitted for the element when the form is submitted. The value property of the Text element, for example, is the user's input, which is also the value submitted with the form. For the Checkbox object, on the other hand, the value property specifies a string that is not displayed but is submitted with the form if the Checkbox element is checked when the form is submitted.

The initial value of the value property is specified by the value attribute of the HTML tag that defines the form element.

For Button, Submit, and Reset objects, the value property specifies the text that appears within the button. On some platforms, changing the value property of these elements actually changes the text displayed by the buttons onscreen. This does not work on all platforms, however, and is not an advisable technique. Changing the label of a button may change the size of the button, causing it to overlap and obscure other portions of the document.

The Select element has a value property, like all form elements, but does not use it. Instead, the value submitted by this element is specified by the value property of the Option objects it contains.

For security reasons, the value property of the FileUpload element is read-only.

JavaArray

Netscape 3 LiveConnect

JavaScript representation of a Java array

Synopsis

```
javaarray.length  // The length of the array
javaarray[index]  // Read or write an array element
```

Properties

`length`

A read-only integer that specifies the number of elements in the Java array represented by the JavaArray object.

Description

The JavaArray object is a JavaScript representation of a Java array that allows JavaScript code to read and write the elements of the array using familiar JavaScript array syntax. In addition, the JavaArray object has a `length` field that specifies the number of elements in the Java array.

When reading and writing values from array elements, data conversion between JavaScript and Java representations is automatically handled by the system. See Chapter 22 for full details.

Usage

Note that Java arrays differ from JavaScript arrays in a couple of important aspects. First, Java arrays have a fixed length that is specified when they are created. For this reason, the JavaArray `length` field is read-only. The second difference is that Java arrays are *typed* (i.e., their elements must all be of the same type of data). Attempting to set an array element to a value of the wrong type results in a JavaScript error or exception.

Example

`java.awt.Polygon` is a JavaClass object. We can create a JavaObject representing an instance of the class like this:

```
p = new java.awt.Polygon();
```

The object `p` has properties `xpoints` and `ypoints`, which are JavaArray objects representing Java arrays of integers. We can initialize the contents of these arrays with JavaScript code like the following:

```
for(int i = 0; i < p.xpoints.length; i++)
    p.xpoints[i] = Math.round(Math.random()*100);
for(int i = 0; i < p.ypoints.length; i++)
    p.ypoints[i] = Math.round(Math.random()*100);
```

See Also

getClass(), JavaClass, JavaObject, JavaPackage, the java property of the Window object; Chapter 22

JavaClass

Netscape 3 LiveConnect

JavaScript representation of a Java class

Synopsis

```
javaclass.static_member  // Read or write a static Java field or method
new javaclass(...)       // Create a new Java object
```

Properties

Each JavaClass object contains properties that have the same names as the public static fields and methods of the Java class it represents. These properties allow you to read and write the static fields of the class and invoke the static methods of the class. Each JavaClass object has different properties; you can use a `for/in` loop to enumerate them for any given JavaClass object.

Description

The JavaClass object is a JavaScript representation of a Java class. The properties of a JavaClass object represent the public static fields and methods (sometimes called class fields and class methods) of the represented class. Note that the JavaClass object does not have properties representing the *instance* fields of a Java class—individual instances of a Java class are represented by the JavaObject object.

The JavaClass object implements the LiveConnect functionality that allows JavaScript programs to read and write the static variables of Java classes using normal JavaScript syntax. It also provides the functionality that allows JavaScript to invoke the static methods of a Java class.

In addition to allowing JavaScript to read and write Java variable and method values, the JavaClass object allows JavaScript programs to create Java objects (represented by a JavaObject object) by using the `new` keyword and invoking the constructor method of a JavaClass.

The data conversion required for communication between JavaScript and Java through the JavaClass object is handled automatically by LiveConnect. See Chapter 22 for full details.

Usage

Bear in mind that Java is a *typed* language. This means that each of the fields of an object has a specific data type that is set to values of only that type. Attempting to set a field to a value that is not of the correct type results in a JavaScript error or exception. Attempting to invoke a method with arguments of the wrong type also causes an error or exception.

Example

`java.lang.System` is a JavaClass object that represents the *java.lang.System* class in Java. You can read a static field of this class with code like the following:

```
var java_console = java.lang.System.out;
```

You can invoke a static method of this class with a line like this one:

```
var version = java.lang.System.getProperty("java.version");
```

Finally, the JavaClass object also allows you to create new Java objects:

```
var java_date = new java.lang.Date();
```

See Also

getClass(), JavaArray, JavaObject, JavaPackage, the java property of the Window object; Chapter 22

JavaObject

Netscape 3 LiveConnect

JavaScript representation of a Java object

Synopsis

```
javaobject.member  // Read or write an instance field or method
```

Properties

Each JavaObject object contains properties that have the same names as the public instance fields and methods (but not the static or class fields and methods) of the Java object it represents. These properties allow you to read and write the value of public fields and invoke the public methods. The properties of a given JavaObject object obviously depend on the type of Java object it represents. You can use the for/in loop to enumerate the properties of any given JavaObject.

Description

The JavaObject object is a JavaScript representation of a Java object. The properties of a JavaObject object represent the public instance fields and public instance methods defined for the Java object. (The class or static fields and methods of the object are represented by the JavaClass object.)

The JavaObject object implements the LiveConnect functionality that allows JavaScript programs to read and write the public instance fields of a Java object using normal JavaScript syntax. It also provides the functionality that allows JavaScript to invoke the methods of a Java object. Data conversion between JavaScript and Java representations is handled automatically by LiveConnect. See Chapter 22 for full details.

Usage

Bear in mind that Java is a *typed* language. This means that each of the fields of an object has a specific data type, and you can set it only to values of that type. For example, the width field of a java.awt.Rectangle object is an integer field, and attempting to set it to a string causes a JavaScript error or exception.

Example

java.awt.Rectangle is a JavaClass that represents the *java.awt.Rectangle* class. We can create a JavaObject that represents an instance of this class like this:

```
var r = new java.awt.Rectangle(0,0,4,5);
```

We can then read the public instance variables of this JavaObject r with code like this:

```
var perimeter = 2*r.width + 2*r.height;
```

We can also set the value of public instance variables of `r` using JavaScript syntax:

```
r.width = perimeter/4;
r.height = perimeter/4;
```

See Also

getClass(), JavaArray, JavaClass, JavaPackage, the `java` property of the Window object; Chapter 22

JavaPackage

Netscape 3 LiveConnect

JavaScript representation of a Java package

Synopsis

```
package.package_name   // Refers to another JavaPackage
package.class_name     // Refers to a JavaClass object
```

Properties

The properties of a JavaPackage object are the names of the JavaPackage objects and JavaClass objects that it contains. These properties are different for each individual JavaPackage. Note that it is not possible to use the JavaScript `for/in` loop to iterate over the list of property names of a Package object. Consult a Java reference manual to determine the packages and classes contained within any given package.

Description

The JavaPackage object is a JavaScript representation of a Java package. A package in Java is a collection of related classes. In JavaScript, a JavaPackage can contain classes (represented by the JavaClass object) and other JavaPackage objects.

The Window object has properties `java`, `netscape`, and `sun` that represent the *java.**, *netscape.**, and *sun.** package hierarchies. These JavaPackage objects define properties that refer to other JavaPackage objects. For example, `java.lang` and `java.net` refer to the *java.lang* and *java.net* packages. The `java.awt` JavaPackage contains properties named `Frame` and `Button`, which are both references to JavaClass objects and represent the classes *java.awt.Frame* and *java.awt.Button*.

The Window object also defines a property named `Packages`, which is the root JavaPackage whose properties refer to the roots of all known package hierarchies. For example, the expression `Packages.java.awt` is the same as `java.awt`.

It is not possible to use the `for/in` loop to determine the names of the packages and classes contained within a JavaPackage. You must have this information in advance. You can find it in any Java reference manual or by examining the Java class hierarchy.

See Chapter 22 for further details on working with Java packages, classes, and objects.

See Also

JavaArray, JavaClass, JavaObject; the `java`, `netscape`, `sun`, and `Packages` properties of the Window object; Chapter 22

JSObject

Netscape 3, Internet Explorer 4

Java representation of a JavaScript object

Synopsis

```
public final class netscape.javascript.JSObject extends Object
```

Methods

`call( )`	Invokes a method of the JavaScript object.
`eval( )`	Evaluates a string of JavaScript code in the context of the JavaScript object.
`getMember( )`	Gets the value of a property of the JavaScript object.
`getSlot( )`	Gets the value of an array element of the JavaScript object.
`getWindow( )`	Gets a "root" JSObject that represents the JavaScript Window object of the web browser.
`removeMember( )`	Deletes a property from the JavaScript object.
`setMember( )`	Sets the value of a property of the JavaScript object.
`setSlot( )`	Sets the value of an array element of the JavaScript object.
`toString( )`	Invokes the JavaScript `toString( )` method of the JavaScript object and returns its result.

Description

The JSObject is a Java class, not a JavaScript object; it cannot be used in your JavaScript programs. Instead, the JSObject is used by Java applets that wish to communicate with JavaScript by reading and writing JavaScript properties and array elements, invoking JavaScript methods, and evaluating and executing arbitrary strings of JavaScript code. Obviously, since JSObject is a Java class, you must understand Java programming in order to use it.

Full details on programming with the JSObject can be found in Chapter 22.

See Also

Chapter 22

JSObject.call( )

Netscape 3, Internet Explorer 4

invoke a method of a JavaScript object

Synopsis

```
public Object call(String methodName, Object args[])
```

Arguments

methodName

The name of the JavaScript method to be invoked.

args[]

An array of Java objects to be passed as arguments to the method.

Returns

A Java object that represents the return value of the JavaScript method.

Description

The `call()` method of the Java JSObject class invokes a named method of the JavaScript object represented by the JSObject. Arguments are passed to the method as an array of Java objects, and the return value of the JavaScript method is returned as a Java object.

Chapter 22 describes the data conversion of the method arguments from Java objects to JavaScript values and the method return value from a JavaScript value to a Java object.

JSObject.eval() — Netscape 3, Internet Explorer 4

evaluate a string of JavaScript code

Synopsis

```
public Object eval(String s)
```

Arguments

s A string that contains arbitrary JavaScript statements separated by semicolons.

Returns

The JavaScript value of the last expression evaluated in *s*, converted to a Java object.

Description

The `eval()` method of the Java JSObject class evaluates the JavaScript code contained in the string *s* in the context of the JavaScript object specified by the JSObject. The behavior of the `eval()` method of the Java JSObject class is much like that of the JavaScript global `eval()` function.

The argument *s* may contain any number of JavaScript statements separated by semicolons; these statements are executed in the order in which they appear. The return value of `eval()` is the value of the last statement or expression evaluated in *s*.

JSObject.getMember() — Netscape 3, Internet Explorer 4

read a property of a JavaScript object

Synopsis

```
public Object getMember(String name)
```

Arguments

name

The name of the property to be read.

Returns

A Java object that contains the value of the named property of the specified JSObject.

Description

The `getMember( )` method of the Java JSObject class reads and returns to Java the value of a named property of a JavaScript object. The return value may be another JSObject object or a Double, Boolean, or String object, but it is returned as a generic Object, which you must cast as necessary.

JSObject.getSlot( )

Netscape 3, Internet Explorer 4

read an array element of a JavaScript object

Synopsis

```
public Object getSlot(int index)
```

Arguments

`index`
The index of the array element to be read.

Returns

The value of the array element at the specified *`index`* of a JavaScript object.

Description

The `getSlot( )` method of the Java JSObject class reads and returns to Java the value of an array element at the specified *`index`* of a JavaScript object. The return value may be another JSObject object or a Double, Boolean, or String object, but it is returned as a generic Object, which you must cast as necessary.

JSObject.getWindow( )

Netscape 3, Internet Explorer 4

return initial JSObject for browser window

Synopsis

```
public static JSObject getWindow(java.applet.Applet applet)
```

Arguments

`applet`
An Applet object running in the web browser window for which a JSObject is to be obtained.

Returns

A JSObject that represents the JavaScript Window object for the web browser window that contains the specified *`applet`*.

Description

The `getWindow( )` method is the first JSObject method that any Java applet calls. JSObject does not define a constructor, and the static `getWindow( )` method provides the only way to obtain an initial "root" JSObject from which other JSObjects may be obtained.

JSObject.removeMember( ) — Netscape 3, Internet Explorer 4

delete a property of a JavaScript object

Synopsis

```
public void removeMember(String name)
```

Arguments

name
: The name of the property to be deleted from the JSObject.

Description

The `removeMember( )` method of the Java JSObject class deletes a named property from the JavaScript object represented by the JSObject.

JSObject.setMember( ) — Netscape 3, Internet Explorer 4

set a property of a JavaScript object

Synopsis

```
public void setMember(String name, Object value)
```

Arguments

name
: The name of the property to be set in the JSObject.

value
: The value to which the named property should be set.

Description

The `setMember( )` method of the Java JSObject class sets the value of a named property of a JavaScript object from Java. The specified *value* may be any Java Object. Primitive Java values may not be passed to this method. In JavaScript, the specified *value* is accessible as a JavaObject object.

JSObject.setSlot( ) — Netscape 3, Internet Explorer 4

set an array element of a JavaScript object

Synopsis

```
public void setSlot(int index, Object value)
```

Arguments

index
: The index of the array element to be set in the JSObject.

value
: The value to which the specified array element should be set.

Description

The `setSlot()` method of the Java JSObject class sets the value of a numbered array element of a JavaScript object from Java. The specified *value* may be any Java Object. Primitive Java values may not be passed to this method. In JavaScript, the specified *value* is accessible as a JavaObject object.

JSObject.toString()

Netscape 3, Internet Explorer 4

return the string value of a JavaScript object

Synopsis

```
public String toString()
```

Returns

The string returned by invoking the `toString()` method of the JavaScript object represented by the specified Java JSObject.

Description

The `toString()` method of the Java JSObject class invokes the JavaScript `toString()` method of the JavaScript object represented by a JSObject and returns the result of that method.

Layer

Netscape 4 only; discontinued in Netscape 6

an independent layer in a DHTML document

Synopsis

```
document.layers[i]
```

Constructor

```
new Layer(width, parent)
```

Arguments

width
: The width of the new layer, in pixels.

parent
: The Layer or Window that should be the parent of this newly created layer. This argument is optional; if omitted, the new layer is a child of the current window.

Notes

The `Layer()` constructor creates a new Layer object and returns it. You can set its size, position, and other attributes with the various Layer properties and methods described in the following lists. In particular, you must set the `hidden` property to `false` to make the new layer visible. See the `src` property and `load()` methods in particular for ways to set the content of a layer. Alternatively, you can dynamically generate content for the layer by writing to its `document` property.

Note that you can only call the `Layer()` constructor once the current document and all of its layers have finished loading.

Properties

`above`
: A read-only property that refers to the Layer object immediately above *`layer`* in the stacking order. If there is no such layer, `above` is `null`.

`background`
: An Image object that specifies the image displayed in the background of the layer. The initial value of this property is specified by the `background` attribute of the `<layer>` tag. You can change the image displayed in the background of the layer by setting the `background.src` property. If set to `null`, no image is displayed, and the background color (specified by `bgColor`) is displayed instead.

`below`
: A read-only property that refers to the Layer object immediately below *`layer`* in the stacking order. If there is no such layer, `below` is `null`.

`bgColor`
: A read/write string property that specifies the background color of *`layer`*. The initial value of this property is specified by the `bgcolor` attribute of the `<layer>` tag. Note that *`layer`*`.background` takes precedence over *`layer`*`.bgColor`, so the color specified by this property appears only if the `background.src` property of *`layer`* is `null`.

`clip.bottom`
: The Y-coordinate of the bottom edge of the layer's clipping area, relative to *`layer`*`.top`.

`clip.height`
: The height of the layer's clipping area. Setting this property also sets the value of *`layer`*`.clip.bottom`.

`clip.left`
: Specifies the X-coordinate of the left edge of the layer's clipping area. This value is relative to *`layer`*`.left`.

`clip.right`
: Specifies the X-coordinate of the right edge of the layer's clipping area. This value is relative to *`layer`*`.left`.

`clip.top`
: Specifies the Y-coordinate of the top edge of the layer's clipping area. This value is relative to *`layer`*`.top`.

`clip.width`
: Specifies the width of the layer's clipping area. Setting this property also sets the value of *`layer`*`.clip.right`.

`document`
: A read-only reference to the Document object contained within that layer.

`hidden`
: Specifies whether a layer is hidden (`true`) or visible (`false`). Setting this property to `true` hides the layer, and setting it to `false` makes the layer visible.

`layers[]`
: An array that contains any child Layer objects of this layer. It is the same as the `document.layers[]` array of a layer.

`left`
: A read/write integer that specifies the X-coordinate, relative to the containing layer or document, of this layer. Setting this property moves the layer to the left or right. `left` is a synonym for `x`.

`name`
: A read/write string that specifies the name of a layer. The initial value of this property is specified by the `name` or `id` attributes of the HTML tag used to create the layer and is also used as the name of the Document property that refers to the Layer object.

`pageX, pageY`
: Read/write integers that specify the X- and Y-coordinates of this layer relative to the top-level document. Note that these coordinates are relative to the top-level page, not relative to any containing layer.

`parentLayer`
: A read-only reference to the Layer or Window object that contains (is the parent of) this layer.

`siblingAbove, siblingBelow`
: Refer to the sibling Layer object (i.e., a child of the same parent Layer) immediately above or below this layer in the stacking order. If there is no such layer, these properties are `null`.

`src`
: A read/write string that specifies the URL, if any, of the contents of a layer. Setting this property to a new URL causes the browser to read the contents of that URL and display them in the layer. Note, however, that this does not work while the current document is being parsed. For this reason, you should not set `src` in a top-level script; instead, set it in an event handler or a function called from an event handler.

`top`
: A read/write integer that specifies the Y-coordinate of this layer relative to the containing layer or document. Setting this property moves the layer up or down. `top` is a synonym for `y`.

`visibility`
: A read/write string that specifies the visibility of the layer. There are three possible legal values: `"show"` specifies that the layer should be visible; `"hide"` specifies that the layer should not be visible; `"inherit"` specifies that the layer should inherit the visibility of its parent layer.

`window`
: Refers to the Window object that contains the layer, regardless of how deeply nested the layer is within other layers.

`x, y`
: The X- and Y-coordinates of the layer, relative to the containing layer or document. Setting these properties move the layer. `x` is a synonym for the `left` property, and `y` is a synonym for the `top` property.

zIndex
Specifies the position of the layer in the z-order, or stacking order, of layers. When two layers overlap, the one with the higher zIndex appears on top and obscures the one with the lower zIndex. If two sibling layers have the same zIndex, the one that appears later in the layers[] array of the containing document is displayed later and overlaps any that appear earlier.

zIndex is a read/write property. Setting this property changes the stacking order and redisplays the layers in the new order. Setting this property may reorder the layers[] array of the containing document.

Methods

captureEvents()	Specifies event types to be captured.
handleEvent()	Dispatches an event to the appropriate handler.
load()	Loads a new URL and resize.
moveAbove()	Moves this layer above another.
moveBelow()	Moves this layer below another.
moveBy()	Moves the layer to a relative position.
moveTo()	Moves the layer to a position relative to its containing layer.
moveToAbsolute()	Moves the layer to a position relative to the page.
offset()	A synonym for moveBy().
releaseEvents()	Stops capturing specified event types.
resizeBy()	Resizes the layer by the specified amounts.
resizeTo()	Resizes the layer to the specified size.
routeEvent()	Routes an event to the next interested handler.

HTML Syntax

A Layer object can be created with the Netscape-specific <layer> tag in HTML:

```
<layer
    [ id="layername" ]              // Layer name
    [ left="x" ]                    // Position relative to containing layer
    [ top="y" ]
    [ pagex="x" ]                   // Position relative to top-level document
    [ pagey="y" ]
    [ width="w" ]                   // Size of layer
    [ height="h" ]
    [ src="url" ]                   // URL of layer contents
    [ clip="x,y,w,h" ]              // Clipping rectangle for layer
    [ clip="w,h" ]                  // Alternate syntax: x,y default to 0
    [ zindex="z" ]                  // Stacking order
    [ above="layername" ]           // Alternative ways of specifying stacking
    [ below="layername" ]
    [ visibility="vis" ]            // "show", "hide", or "inherit"
    [ bgcolor="color" ]             // Background color of layer
    [ background="url" ]            // Background image of layer
    [ onmouseover="handler" ]       // Invoked when mouse enters layer
    [ onmouseout="handler" ]        // Invoked when mouse leaves layer
```

```
        [ onfocus="handler" ]       // Invoked when layer gets focus
        [ onblur="handler" ]        // Invoked when layer loses focus
        [ onload="handler" ]        // Invoked when layer's contents are loaded
    >
```

Description

The Layer object is Netscape 4's technique for supporting dynamically positionable HTML elements. Note, however, that the Layer object was never standardized and is no longer supported in Netscape 6. A Layer object can be created in three ways: with the `<layer>` tag; with the `Layer()` constructor; or, most portably, with CSS style attributes on HTML elements, as explained in Chapter 18.

See Also

Window; Chapter 18

Layer.captureEvents( )

see Window.captureEvents( )

Layer.handleEvent( )

see Window.handleEvent( )

Layer.load( )

Netscape 4 only

change layer contents and width

Synopsis

layer.load(*src*, *width*)

Arguments

src

A string that specifies the URL of the document to be loaded into *layer*.

width

An integer that specifies a new width, in pixels, for *layer*.

Description

`load()` loads a new document into *layer* and specifies a *width* at which the lines of that document are wrapped.

Note, however, that `load()` does not work while the current document is being parsed. For this reason, you should not call `load()` in a top-level script; instead, call it in an event handler or a function called from an event handler.

See Also

The `src` property of the Layer object

Layer.moveAbove( ) Netscape 4 only

move one layer above another

Synopsis

```
layer.moveAbove(target)
```

Arguments

target
: The reference Layer object above which *layer* is to be placed.

Description

`moveAbove( )` changes the stacking order so *layer* appears on top of *target*. *layer* becomes a sibling of *target* if it is not one already. *layer* is given the same *zIndex* as *target* and is placed after *target* in the `layers[]` array of the containing document.

Layer.moveBelow( ) Netscape 4 only

move one layer below another

Synopsis

```
layer.moveBelow(target)
```

Arguments

target
: The reference Layer object below which *layer* is to be placed.

Description

`moveBelow( )` changes the stacking order so *layer* appears beneath *target*. *layer* becomes a sibling of *target* if it is not one already. *layer* is given the same *zIndex* as *target* and is placed before *target* in the `layers[]` array of the containing document.

Layer.moveBy( ) Netscape 4 only

move a Layer to a relative position

Synopsis

```
layer.moveBy(dx, dy)
```

Arguments

dx The number of pixels to move the layer to the right (may be negative).

dy The number of pixels to move the layer down (may be negative).

Description

`moveBy( )` moves *layer* *dx* pixels to the right and *dy* pixels down from its current position.

Layer.moveTo( )

Netscape 4 only

move a Layer

Synopsis

layer.moveTo(*x*, *y*)

Arguments

x The desired X-coordinate of the layer.

y The desired Y-coordinate of the layer.

Description

`moveTo( )` moves the upper-left corner of *layer* to the coordinates specified by *x* and *y*. Note that these coordinates are expressed relative to the containing layer or document.

Layer.moveToAbsolute( )

Netscape 4 only

move a Layer to page coordinates

Synopsis

layer.moveToAbsolute(*x*, *y*)

Arguments

x The desired X-coordinate of the layer.

y The desired Y-coordinate of the layer.

Description

`moveToAbsolute( )` moves the upper-left corner of *layer* to the document coordinates specified by *x* and *y*. Note that these coordinates are expressed relative to the page or top-level document, not relative to any containing layers.

Layer.offset( )

Netscape 4 only; deprecated

move a Layer to a relative position

Synopsis

layer.offset(*dx*, *dy*)

Arguments

dx The number of pixels to move the layer to the right (may be negative).

dy The number of pixels to move the layer down (may be negative).

Description

`offset( )` moves a layer relative to its current position. `offset( )` is deprecated in favor of `moveBy( )`.

Layer.releaseEvents( )

see Window.releaseEvents( )

Layer.resizeBy( ) Netscape 4 only

resize a Layer by a relative amount

Synopsis

```
layer.resizeBy(dw, dh)
```

Arguments

dw The number of pixels by which to increase the width of the window (may be negative).

dh The number of pixels by which to increase the height of the window (may be negative).

Description

`resizeBy( )` resizes *layer* by incrementing its `clip.width` and `clip.height` properties by *dw* and *dh*. It does not cause the contents of the layer to be reformatted, so making a layer smaller may clip the layer's contents.

Layer.resizeTo( ) Netscape 4 only

resize a Layer

Synopsis

```
layer.resizeTo(width, height)
```

Arguments

width
The desired width of the layer.

height
The desired height of the layer.

Description

`resizeTo( )` resizes *layer* by setting its `clip.width` and `clip.height` properties to *width* and *height*. It does not cause the contents of the layer to be reformatted, so making a layer smaller may clip the layer's contents.

Layer.routeEvent( )

see Window.routeEvent( )

Link

JavaScript 1.0; enhanced in JavaScript 1.1

a hypertext link

Inherits from HTMLElement

Synopsis

```
document.links[]
document.links.length
```

Properties

Link inherits properties from HTMLElement and defines the following properties. Many of the properties represent portions of a URL. For each of these properties, the example given is a portion of the following (fictitious) URL:

```
http://www.oreilly.com:1234/catalog/search.html?q=JavaScript&m=10#results
```

`hash`
: A read/write string property that specifies the anchor portion of the Link's URL, including the leading hash (#) mark. For example: "#result". This anchor portion of a URL refers to a named position within the document referenced by the Link. In HTML files, positions are named with anchors created with the `<a name="anchor_name">` tag.

`host`
: A read/write string property that specifies the hostname and port portions of a Link's URL. For example, "www.oreilly.com:1234".

`hostname`
: A read/write string property that specifies the hostname portion of a Link's URL. For example "www.oreilly.com".

`href`
: A read/write string property that specifies the complete text of the Link's URL, unlike other Link URL properties that specify only portions of the URL.

`pathname`
: A read/write string property that specifies the pathname portion of a Link's URL. For example "/catalog/search.html".

`port`
: A read/write string (not a number) property that specifies the port portion of a Link's URL. For example "1234".

`protocol`
: A read/write string property that specifies the protocol portion of a Link's URL, including the trailing colon. For example, "http:".

`search`
: A read/write string property that specifies the query portion of a Link's URL, including the leading question mark. For example, "?q=JavaScript&m=10".

`target`
: A read/write string property that specifies the name of a Window object (i.e., a frame or a top-level browser window) in which the linked document should be displayed. See the "Link.target" reference page for details.

`text` *[Netscape 4]*
Specifies the plain text, if any, between the `<a>` and `</a>` tags of a link. Note that this property works correctly only if there are no intervening HTML tags between the `<a>` and `</a>` tags. If there are other HTML tags, the `text` property may contain only a portion of the link text. `HTMLElement.innerText` provides the IE 4 equivalent of this Netscape-specific property.

Methods

Link inherits the methods of HTMLElement.

Event Handlers

Link inherits the event handlers of HTMLElement and defines special behavior for the following:

`onclick`
Invoked when the user clicks on the link. In JavaScript 1.1, this event handler may prevent the link from being followed by returning `false`. On Windows platforms in Netscape 3, this event handler does not work for links created with the `<area>` tag.

`onmouseout`
Invoked when the user moves the mouse off the link. Available in JavaScript 1.1 and later.

`onmouseover`
Invoked when the user moves the mouse over the link. The `status` property of the current window may be set here. May return `true` to tell the browser not to display the URL of the link.

HTML Syntax

A Link object is created with standard `<a>` and `</a>` tags. The `href` attribute is required for all Link objects. If the `name` attribute is also specified, an Anchor object is also created:

```
<a href="url"                    // The destination of the link
    [ name="anchor_tag" ]        // Creates an Anchor object
    [ target="window_name" ]     // Where the new document should be displayed
    [ onclick="handler" ]        // Invoked when link is clicked
    [ onmouseover="handler" ]    // Invoked when mouse is over link
    [ onmouseout="handler" ]     // Invoked when mouse leaves link
>
link text or image               // The visible part of the link
</a>
```

In JavaScript 1.1 and later, a Link object is also created by each `<area>` tag within a client-side image map. This is also standard HTML:

```
<map name="map_name">
    <area shape="area_shape"
        coords="coordinates"
        href="url"                   // The destination of the link
        [ target="window_name" ]     // Where the new document should be displayed
        [ onclick="handler" ]        // Invoked when area is clicked
```

```
        [ onmouseover="handler" ]  // Invoked when mouse is over area
        [ onmouseout="handler" ]   // Invoked when mouse leaves area
>
    ...
</map>
```

Description

The Link object represents a hypertext link or a clickable area of a client-side image map in an HTML document. All links created with the <a> and <area> tags are represented by Link objects and stored in the `links[]` array of the Document object. Note that links created by both the <a> and <area> tags are stored in the same array—there is no distinction between them.

The destination of a hypertext link is a URL, of course, and many of the properties of the Link object specify the contents of that URL. The Link object is similar to the Location object, which also has a full set of URL properties. In the case of the Location object, these properties describe the URL of the currently displayed document.

In addition to its properties, the Link object has three event handlers. The `onmouseover()`, `onclick()`, and `onmouseout()` event handlers specify code to be executed when the mouse passes over the hypertext link, clicks on it, and moves off or out of the link's region of the screen.

See Also

Anchor, Location; HTMLAnchorElement in the DOM reference section

Link.onclick

JavaScript 1.0; enhanced in JavaScript 1.1

the handler invoked when a Link is clicked

Synopsis

```
<a ... onclick="handler" ... >
<area ... onclick="handler" ... >
link.onclick
```

Description

The `onclick` property of a Link object specifies an event handler function that is invoked when the user clicks on the link. The initial value of this property is a function that contains the JavaScript statements specified by the `onclick` attribute of the <a> or <area> tag that defined the Link object. When an event handler function is defined in this way by an HTML attribute, it is executed in the scope of *`element`* rather than in the scope of the containing window.

The `onclick` event handler is invoked before the browser follows the clicked hypertext link. This allows you to dynamically set `href`, `target`, and other properties of the link (using the `this` keyword to refer to the clicked link). You may also use the methods `Window.alert()`, `Window.confirm()`, and `Window.prompt()` from this event handler.

Client-Side JavaScript Reference

In JavaScript 1.1, you may prevent the browser from following the link by returning `false`. If you return `true`, any other value, or nothing, the browser follows the link as soon as `onclick` returns. You might stop the browser from following a link if you use the `Window.confirm()` method to ask the user if he really wants to follow the link and the user chooses the **Cancel** button, for example. In general, if you want a link that performs some action but does not cause a new URL to be displayed, it is better to use the `onclick` event handler of a Button object instead of the `onclick` handler of a Link object.

Note that while the `onclick` event handler returns `false` to tell the browser not to perform its default action (following a link), the `onmouseover` event handler must return `true` to tell the browser not to take its default action (displaying the URL of the link). This incompatibility exists for historical reasons. The standard for Form and form element event handlers is to return `false` to prevent the browser from performing a default action.

In the Netscape 4 event model, the `onclick` handler function is passed an Event object as an argument. In the IE event model, no argument is passed, but the applicable Event object is available as the event property of the Window object that contains the hypertext link.

Bugs

In Netscape 3, the `onclick` event handler of the `<area>` does not work on Windows platforms. A workaround is to specify a `javascript:` URL as the value of the `href` attribute of the `<area>` tag.

See Also

Chapter 19; EventListener, EventTarget, and MouseEvent in the DOM reference section

Link.onmouseout — JavaScript 1.1

the handler invoked when the mouse leaves a link

Synopsis

```
<a ... onmouseout="handler" ... >
<area ... onmouseout="handler" ... >
link.onmouseout
```

Description

The `onmouseout` property of a Link object specifies an event handler function that is invoked when the user moves the mouse off a hypertext link. The initial value of this property is a function that contains the JavaScript statements specified by the `onmouseout` attribute of the `<a>` or `<area>` tag that defined the Link object. When an event handler function is defined in this way by an HTML attribute, it is executed in the scope of *`element`* rather than in the scope of the containing window.

In the Netscape 4 event model, the `onmouseout` handler function is passed an Event object as an argument. In the IE event model, no argument is passed, but the applicable Event object is available as the event property of the Window object that contains the hypertext link.

See Also

Chapter 19; EventListener, EventTarget, and MouseEvent in the DOM reference section

Link.onmouseover

JavaScript 1.0

the handler invoked when the mouse goes over a link

Synopsis

```
<a ... onmouseover="handler" ... >
<area ... onmouseover="handler" ... >
link.onmouseover
```

Description

The `onmouseover` property of a Link object specifies an event handler function that is invoked when the user moves the mouse over a hypertext link. The initial value of this property is a function that contains the JavaScript statements specified by the `onmouseover` attribute of the `<a>` or `<area>` tag that defined the Link object. When an event handler function is defined in this way by an HTML attribute, it is executed in the scope of *`element`* rather than in the scope of the containing window.

By default, the browser displays the URL that a hypertext link refers to in the status line whenever the mouse goes over the link. The `onmouseover` event handler is invoked before the URL is displayed. If the handler returns `true`, the browser does not display the URL. Thus, an event handler function that returns `true` can display a custom message in the status line by setting the `Window.status` property to any desired value.

Note that while this event handler returns `true` to tell the browser not to perform its default action (displaying the URL of a link), the `onclick` event handler of the Link object must return `false` to tell the browser not to take its default action (following the link). This incompatibility exists for historical reasons. The standard for Form and form element event handlers is to return `false` to prevent the browser from performing a default action.

In the Netscape 4 event model, the `onmouseover` handler function is passed an Event object as an argument. In the IE event model, no argument is passed, but the applicable Event object is available as the `event` property of the Window object that contains the hypertext link.

See Also

Chapter 19; EventListener, EventTarget, and MouseEvent in the DOM reference section

Link.target

JavaScript 1.0

the target window of a hypertext link

Synopsis

```
link.target
```

Description

target is a read/write string property of the Link object. It specifies the name of the frame or window in which the URL referred to by the Link object should be displayed. The initial value of this property is specified by the `target` attribute of the `<a>` tag that creates the Link object. If this attribute is unset, the default is that the window containing the link is used, so following a hypertext link overwrites the document that contains the link.

Note that the value of *target* is the *name* of a frame or window, not an actual JavaScript reference to the frame or window itself. The name of a frame is specified by the `name` attribute of the `<frame>` tag. The name of a window is specified when the window is created with a call to the `Window.open()` method. If `target` specifies the name of a window that does not exist, the browser automatically opens a new window to display the URL, and any future links with the same `target` name use that freshly created window.

Four special target names are supported. The target named `"_blank"` specifies that a new, empty browser window should be created and used to display the new URL. The target `"_self"` is the default; it specifies that the new URL should be displayed in the same frame or window as the link. The target `"_parent"` specifies that the results should be displayed in the parent frame of the frame that contains the link. Finally, the `"_top"` target specifies that the new URL should be displayed in the topmost frame—in other words, all frames should be removed, and the new URL should occupy the entire browser window.

See Also

Form.target

Location — JavaScript 1.0; enhanced in JavaScript 1.1

represents and controls browser location

Synopsis

```
location
window.location
```

Properties

The properties of a Location object refer to the various portions of the current document's URL. In each of the following property descriptions, the example given is a portion of this (fictitious) URL:

```
http://www.oreilly.com:1234/catalog/search.html?q=JavaScript&m=10#results
```

`hash`

A read/write string property that specifies the anchor portion of the URL, including the leading hash (#) mark. For example: "#result". This portion of the document URL specifies the name of an anchor within the document.

`host`

A read/write string property that specifies the hostname and port portions of the URL. For example, "www.oreilly.com:1234".

`hostname`
: A read/write string property that specifies the hostname portion of a URL. For example "www.oreilly.com".

`href`
: A read/write string property that specifies the complete text of the document's URL, unlike other Location properties which specify only portions of the URL. Setting this property to a new URL causes the browser to read and display the contents of the new URL.

`pathname`
: A read/write string property that specifies the pathname portion of a URL. For example "/catalog/search.html".

`port`
: A read/write string (not a number) property that specifies the port portion of a URL. For example "1234".

`protocol`
: A read/write string property that specifies the protocol portion of a URL, including the trailing colon. For example, "http:".

`search`
: A read/write string property that specifies the query portion of a URL, including the leading question mark. For example, "?q=JavaScript&m=10".

Methods

`reload()`
: Reloads the current document from the cache or the server. This method was added in JavaScript 1.1.

`replace()`
: Replaces the current document with a new one without generating a new entry in the browser's session history. This method was added in JavaScript 1.1.

Description

The Location object is stored in the `location` property of the Window object and represents the web address (the "location") of the document currently displayed in that window. The `href` property contains the complete URL of that document, and the other properties of the Location object each describe a portion of that URL. These properties are much like the URL properties of the Link object.

While the Link object represents a hyperlink in a document, the Location object represents the URL, or location, currently displayed by the browser. But the Location object does more than that: it also *controls* the location displayed by the browser. If you assign a string containing a URL to the Location object or to its `href` property, the web browser responds by loading the newly specified URL and displaying the document it refers to.

Instead of setting `location` or `location.href` to replace the current URL with a completely new one, you can also modify just a portion of the current URL by assigning strings to the other properties of the Location object. This creates a new URL with one new portion, which the browser loads and displays. For example, if you set the hash property of the Location object, you can cause the browser to move to a named location within the current document. Similarly, if you set the search property, you can cause the browser to reload the current URL with a new query string appended. If the URL refers to a server-side program, the document resulting from the new query string may be quite different from the original document.

In addition to its URL properties, the Location object also defines two methods. The reload( ) method reloads the current document, and the replace( ) method loads a new document without creating a new history entry for it—the new document replaces the current one in the browser's history list.

See Also

Link, the location property of the Window object

Location.reload( )

JavaScript 1.1

reload the current document

Synopsis

location.reload( )
location.reload(*force*)

Arguments

force
A boolean argument that specifies whether the document should be reloaded, even if the server reports that it has not been modified since it was last loaded. If this argument is omitted, or if it is false, the method reloads the full page only if it has changed since last loaded.

Description

The reload( ) method of the Location object reloads the document that is currently displayed in the window of the Location object. When called with no arguments or with the argument false, it uses the If-Modified-Since HTTP header to determine whether the document has changed on the web server. If the document has changed, reload reloads the document from the server, and if not, it reloads the document from the cache. This is the same action that occurs when the user clicks on the browser's **Reload** button.

When reload( ) is called with the argument true, it always bypasses the cache and reloads the document from the server, regardless of the last-modified time of the document. This is the same action that occurs when the user **Shift**-clicks on the browser's **Reload** button.

Location.replace( )

JavaScript 1.1

replace one displayed document with another

Synopsis

location.replace(*url*)

Arguments

url
: A string that specifies the URL of the new document that is to replace the current one.

Description

The `replace()` method of the Location object loads and displays a new document. Loading a document in this way is different from simply setting *`location`* or *`location`*`.href` in one important respect: the `replace()` method does not generate a new entry in the History object. When you use `replace()`, the new URL overwrites the current entry in the History object. After calling `replace()`, the browser's **Back** button does not return you to the previous URL; it returns you to the URL before that one.

Usage

When you are working with multiple frames and/or JavaScript-generated documents, you sometimes end up with quite a few temporary documents. If there are more than just a few of these documents, backing out of your web site with the **Back** button can be annoying. If you use the `replace()` method to load these documents, however, you can prevent this problem.

See Also

History

MimeType — Netscape 3

represents a MIME data type

Synopsis

```
navigator.mimeTypes[i]
navigator.mimeTypes["type"]
navigator.mimeTypes.length
```

Properties

`description`
: A read/only string that provides a human-readable description (in English) of the data type described by the MimeType. This description is more explicit and understandable than the `name` property.

`enabledPlugin`
: A read-only reference to a Plugin object that represents the installed and enabled plugin that handles the specified MIME type. If the MIME type is not handled by any plugins, the value of this property is `null`.

: The `navigator.mimeType[]` array tells you whether a given MIME type is supported by the browser. The `enabledPlugin` property of the MimeType object, however, tells you whether a particular supported type is supported with a plugin (MIME types can also be supported with helper applications, or directly by the browser). If a MIME type is supported by a plugin, data of that type can be embedded in a web page with the `<embed>` tag.

`suffixes`
: A read-only string that contains a comma-separated list of filename suffixes (not including the "." character) that are commonly used with files of the specified MIME type. For example, the suffixes for the `text/html` MIME type are "html, htm".

`type`
: A read-only string that specifies the name of the MIME type. This is a unique string such as "text/html" or "image/jpeg" that distinguishes this MIME type from all others. It describes the general type of data and the data format used. The value of the type property can also be used as an index to access the elements of the `navigator.mimeTypes[]` array.

Description

The MimeType object represents a MIME type (i.e., a data format) supported by Netscape. The format may be supported directly by the browser or through an external helper application or a plugin for embedded data.

Usage

The `navigator.mimeTypes[]` array may be indexed numerically or with the name of the desired MIME type (which is the value of the type property). To check which MIME types are supported by Netscape, you can loop through each element in the array numerically. Or, if you just want to check whether a specific type is supported, you can write code like the following:

```
var show_movie = (navigator.mimeTypes["video/mpeg"] != null);
```

See Also

Navigator, Plugin

Navigator

JavaScript 1.0; enhanced in JavaScript 1.1 and 1.2

information about the browser in use

Synopsis

```
navigator
```

Properties

`appCodeName`
: A read-only string that specifies the code name of the browser. In all Netscape browsers, this is "Mozilla". For compatibility, this property is "Mozilla" in Microsoft browsers as well.

`appName`
: A read-only string property that specifies the name of the browser. For Netscape, the value of this property is "Netscape". In IE, the value of this property is "Microsoft Internet Explorer".

`appVersion`
A read-only string that specifies version and platform information for the browser. The first part of this string is a version number. Pass the string to `parseInt()` to obtain only the major version number or to `parseFloat()` to obtain the major and minor version numbers as a floating-point value. The remainder of the string value of this property provides other details about the browser version, including the operating system it is running on. Unfortunately, however, the format of this information varies widely from browser to browser.

`cookieEnabled` *[IE 4, Netscape6]*
A read-only boolean that is `true` if the browser has cookies enabled and `false` if they are disabled.

`language` *[Netscape 4]*
A read-only string that specifies the default language of the browser version. The value of this property is either a standard two-letter language code, such as "en" for English or "fr" for French, or a five-letter string that indicates a language and a regional variant, such as "fr_CA" for French, as spoken in Canada. Note that IE 4 provides two different language-related properties.

`mimeTypes[]` *[Netscape 3]*
An array of MimeType objects, each of which represents one of the MIME types (e.g., "text/html" and "image/gif") supported by the browser. The `mimeTypes[]` array is defined by IE 4 but is always empty because IE 4 does not support the MimeType object.

`platform` *[JavaScript 1.2]*
A read-only string that specifies the operating system and/or hardware platform on which the browser is running. Although there is no standard set of values for this property, some typical values are "Win32", "MacPPC", and "Linux i586".

`plugins[]` *[Netscape 3]*
An array of Plugin objects, each of which represents one plugin that was installed with the browser. The Plugin object provides information about the plugin, including a list of MIME types it supports. A *plugin* is the Netscape name for a software package that is invoked by the browser to display specific data types within the browser window.

The `plugins[]` array is defined by IE 4 but is always empty because IE 4 does not support plugins or the Plugin object.

`systemLanguage` *[IE 4]*
A read-only string that specifies the default language of the operating system using the same standard codes used by the Netscape-specific `language` property.

`userAgent`
A read-only string that specifies the value the browser uses for the user-agent header in HTTP requests. Typically, this is the value of `navigator.appCodeName` followed by a slash and the value of `navigator.appVersion`. For example:

```
Mozilla/4.0 (compatible; MSIE 4.01; Windows 95)
```

`userLanguage` *[IE 4]*
A read-only string that specifies the user's preferred language using the same standard codes used by the Netscape-specific `language` property.

Functions

`navigator.javaEnabled( )`
: Tests whether Java is supported and enabled in the current browser. Added in JavaScript 1.1.

`navigator.plugins.refresh( )`
: Checks for newly installed plugins, enters them in the `plugins[]` array, and optionally reloads documents using those plugins. Added in Netscape 3.

Description

The Navigator object contains properties that describe the web browser in use. You can use its properties to perform platform-specific customization. The name of this object obviously refers to the Netscape Navigator browser, but other browsers that implement JavaScript support this object as well.

There is only a single instance of the Navigator object, which you can reference through the `navigator` property of any Window object. Because of the implicit window reference, you can always refer to the Navigator object simply as `navigator`.

See Also

MimeType, Plugin

Navigator.javaEnabled( ) — JavaScript 1.1

test whether Java is available

Synopsis

```
navigator.javaEnabled( )
```

Returns

`true` if Java is supported by and enabled on the current browser; `false` otherwise.

Description

You can use `navigator.javaEnabled( )` to check whether the current browser supports Java and can therefore display applets.

Navigator.plugins.refresh( ) — Netscape 3

make newly installed plugins available

Synopsis

```
navigator.plugins.refresh([reload])
```

Arguments

`reload`
: An optional boolean argument that, if `true`, specifies that `refresh( )` should reload any pages that contain `<embed>` tags and use plugins. Defaults to `false` if omitted.

Description

The `refresh()` method causes Netscape to check whether any new plugins have been installed. If so, the `plugins[]` array is updated ("refreshed") to include the newly installed plugins. If the *reload* argument is specified and is `true`, Netscape also reloads any currently displayed documents that contain `<embed>` tags and use plugins.

Note the unusual synopsis for this method. `refresh()` is a method of the `plugins[]` array, not of the Navigator object. For almost all purposes, however, it is simpler to consider it a method of the Navigator object, which is why it is grouped here with the methods and properties of that object.

Option — JavaScript 1.0; enhanced in JavaScript 1.1

an option in a Select box — Inherits from HTMLElement

Synopsis

select.options[*i*]

Constructor

In JavaScript 1.1, Option objects can be dynamically created with the `Option()` constructor, as follows:

```
new Option(text, value, defaultSelected, selected)
```

Arguments

text
: An optional string argument that specifies the text property of the Option object.

value
: An optional string argument that specifies the `value` property of the Option object.

defaultSelected
: An optional boolean argument that specifies the `defaultSelected` property of the Option object.

selected
: An optional boolean argument that specifies the `selected` property of the Option object.

Properties

Option inherits the properties of HTMLElement and defines the following:

`defaultSelected`
: A boolean that specifies whether the option is initially selected when the Select object that contains it is created. This value is used to restore a Select object to its initial state when the containing form is reset. The initial value of this property is specified by the `selected` attribute of the `<option>` tag.

`index`
: A read-only integer that specifies the position or index of the option within the `options[]` array of the Select object that contains it. The first Option object in the array has its `index` property set to 0. The second Option has an `index` of 1, and so on.

`selected`

A read/write boolean value that specifies whether an option is currently selected. You can use this property to test whether a given option is selected and to select (by setting it to `true`) or deselect (by setting it to `false`) a given option. Note that when you select or deselect an option in this way the `Select.onchange()` event handler is not invoked.

`text`

A string that specifies the text for the option that appears to the user. The initial value of this property is whatever plain text (without HTML tags) appears after the `<option>` tag and before the next `<option>`, `</option>`, or `</select>` tag.

In JavaScript 1.0, the `text` property is read-only. In JavaScript 1.1, it is read/write. By setting a new value for this property, you can change the text that appears for the option within its Select object. Note that if you plan to set this property in a browser that cannot reflow document content, you should ensure that changing the option label does not make the Select object wider. If the object must become wider, ensure that no information to the right of the Select object becomes obscured when it grows.

`value`

A read/write string that specifies the text passed to the web server if the *`option`* is selected when the form is submitted. The initial value of `value` is specified by the `value` attribute of the `<option>` tag. If the form is designed to be submitted to a server (as opposed to simply being used by JavaScript on the client side), each Option object within a Select object should have a distinct `value`.

HTML Syntax

An Option object is created by an `<option>` tag within a `<select>`, which is within a `<form>`. Multiple `<option>` tags typically appear within the `<select>`:

```
<form ...>
  <select  ...>
   <option
       [ value="value" ]  // The value returned when the form is submitted
       [ selected ] >     // Specifies whether this option is initially selected
   plain_text_label       // The text to display for this option
   [ </option> ]
       ...
  </select>
       ...
</form>
```

Description

The Option object describes a single option displayed within a Select object. The properties of this object specify whether it is selected by default, whether it is currently selected, the position it has in the `options[]` array of its containing Select object, the text it displays, and the value it passes to the server if it is selected when the containing form is submitted.

Note that although the text displayed by this option is specified outside of the `<option>` tag, it must be plain, unformatted text without any HTML tags so it can be properly displayed in list boxes and drop-down menus that do not support HTML formatting.

In JavaScript 1.1, you can dynamically create new Option objects for display in a Select object with the `Option()` constructor. Once a new Option object is created, it can be appended to the list of options in a Select object *s* by assigning it to:

```
s.options[options.length]
```

See the "Select.options[]" reference page for details.

See Also

Select, Select.options[ ]; HTMLOptionElement and HTMLSelectElement in the DOM reference section

Password — JavaScript 1.0; enhanced in JavaScript 1.1

a text input field for sensitive data — Inherits from Input, HTMLElement

Synopsis

```
form.name
form.elements[i]
```

Properties

Password inherits properties from Input and HTMLElement and defines or overrides the following:

`value`

A read/write string that specifies the password entered by the user. It is the value sent over the Net when the form is submitted. The initial value of this property is specified by the `value` attribute of the `<input>` element that defined the Password object. Note that because of the sensitive nature of password input, security restrictions may protect the `value` property. In some browsers, the string returned when querying this property may not match the text entered by the user, and setting the property may have no effect on either the displayed value or the value submitted upon form submission.

Methods

Password inherits methods from Input and HTMLElement.

Event Handlers

Password inherits event handlers from Input and HTMLElement.

HTML Syntax

A Password element is created with a standard HTML `<input>` tag:

```
<form>
    ...
  <input
    type="password"      // Specifies that this is a Password element
    [ name="name" ]      // A name you can use later to refer to this element
                         // Specifies the name property
```

```
    [ value="default" ]  // The default value transmitted when the form is submitted
    [ size="integer" ]   // How many characters wide the element is
  >
    ...
</form>
```

Description

The Password element is a text input field intended for input of sensitive data, such as passwords. As the user types characters, only asterisks appear. This prevents bystanders from reading the input value over the user's shoulder. As a further security precaution, there are limitations on how JavaScript can read and write the `value` property of a Password element. See the "Text" and "Input" reference pages for more information.

See Also

Input, Text; HTMLInputElement in the DOM reference section

Plugin **Netscape 3**

describes an installed plugin

Synopsis

```
navigator.plugins[i]
navigator.plugins['name']
```

Properties

`description`
: A read-only string that contains a human-readable description of the specified plugin. The text of this description is provided by the creators of the plugin and may contain vendor and version information as well as a brief description of the plugin's function.

`filename`
: A read-only string that specifies the name of the file on disk that contains the plugin program itself. This name may vary from platform to platform. The `name` property is more useful than `filename` for identifying a plugin.

`length`
: Each Plugin object contains MimeType array elements that specify the data formats supported by the plugin. As with all arrays, the `length` property specifies the number of elements in the array.

`name`
: The `name` property of a Plugin object is a read-only string that specifies the name of the plugin. Each plugin should have a name that uniquely identifies it. The name of a plugin can be used as an index into the `navigator.plugins[]` array. You can use this fact to determine easily whether a particular named plugin is installed in the current browser:

```
var sw_installed = (navigator.plugins["Shockwave"] != null);
```

Elements

The array elements of the Plugin object are MimeType objects that specify the data formats supported by the plugin.

Description

A *plugin* is a software module that can be invoked by Netscape to display specialized types of embedded data within the browser window. In Netscape 3, plugins are represented by the Plugin object. This object is somewhat unusual in that it has both regular object properties and array elements. The properties of the Plugin object provide various pieces of information about the plugin, and its array elements are MimeType objects that specify the embedded data formats that the plugin supports.

Plugin objects are obtained from the `plugins[]` array of the Navigator object. `navigator.plugins[]` may be indexed numerically when you want to loop through the complete list of installed plugins, looking for one that meets your needs (for example, one that supports the MIME type of the data you want to embed in your web page). This array can also be indexed by plugin name, however. That is, if you want to check whether a specific plugin is installed in the user's browser, you might use code like this:

```
document.write( navigator.plugins("Shockwave") ?
                "<embed src="movie.dir' height=100 width=100>" :
                "You don't have the Shockwave plugin!" );
```

The name used as an array index with this technique is the same name that appears as the value of the `name` property of the Plugin.

Don't confuse the fact that Plugin objects are stored in an array of the Navigator object with the fact that each Plugin object is itself an array of MimeType objects. Because there are two arrays involved, you may end up with code that looks like this:

```
navigator.plugins[i][j]            // The jth MIME type of the ith plugin
navigator.plugins["LiveAudio"][0]  // First MIME type of LiveAudio plugin
```

Finally, note that while the array elements of a Plugin object specify the MIME types supported by that plugin, you can also determine which plugin supports a given MIME type with the `enabledPlugin` property of the MimeType object.

See Also

Navigator, MimeType

Radio

JavaScript 1.0; enhanced in JavaScript 1.1

a graphical radio button

Inherits from Input, HTMLElement

Synopsis

The Radio button element is usually used in groups of mutually exclusive options that have the same name. To reference one Radio element within a group, use this syntax:

```
form.radio_name[j]
form.radio_name.length
```

Properties

Radio inherits properties from Input and HTMLElement and defines or overrides the following:

`checked`
: A read/write boolean that is `true` if the radio button is checked or `false` otherwise. If you set `checked` to `true`, the radio button is selected, and the previously selected button is deselected. Note, however, that setting the `checked` property of a radio button to `false` has no effect, because at least one button must always be selected; you cannot deselect a radio button except by selecting some other button. Note also that setting the `checked` property does not cause the Radio button element's `onclick` event handler to be invoked. If you want to invoke that event handler, you must do so explicitly.

`defaultChecked`
: A boolean property that is `true` if the radio button is initially selected, but only if the `checked` attribute appears in the button's HTML `<input>` tag. If this tag does not appear, the radio button is initially deselected, and `defaultChecked` is `false`.

`value`
: A read/write string that specifies the text passed to the web server if the radio button is checked when the form is submitted. The initial value of this property is specified by the `value` attribute of the button's `<input>` tag. If the form is designed to be submitted to a server (as opposed to simply being used by JavaScript on the client side), each radio button in a group should have a distinct `value`. Note that the `value` field does not specify whether the radio button is currently selected; the `checked` property specifies the current state of the Radio object.

Methods

Radio inherits methods from Input and HTMLElement.

Event Handlers

Radio inherits event handlers from Input and HTMLElement and defines or overrides the following:

`onclick`
: Invoked when the radio button is clicked.

HTML Syntax

A Radio element is created with a standard HTML `<input>` tag. Radio elements are created in groups by specifying multiple `<input>` tags that have the same `name` attribute:

```
<form>
    ...
  <input
    type="radio"            // Specifies that this is a radio button

    [ name="name" ]         // A name you can use later to refer to this button
                            // or to the group of buttons with this name
```

```
                                    // Specifies the name property
      [ value="value" ]             // The value returned when this button is selected
                                    // Specifies the value property
      [ checked ]                   // Specifies that the button is initially checked
                                    // Specifies the defaultChecked property
      [ onclick="handler" ]         // JavaScript statements to be executed when the button
                                    // is clicked
  >
label                               // The HTML text that should appear next to the button
    ...
</form>
```

Description

The Radio element represents a single graphical radio button in an HTML form. A *radio button* is one button in a group of buttons that represents mutually exclusive choices. When one button is selected, the previously selected button is deselected. The `onclick` event handler allows you to specify JavaScript code to be executed when the button is selected.

You can examine the `checked` property to determine the state of the button and set this property to select or deselect the button. Note that setting `checked` changes the graphical appearance of the button but does not invoke the `onclick` event handler. The initial value of the `checked` property and the value of the `defaultChecked` property are determined by the `checked` attribute. Only one Radio element in a group may contain this attribute—it sets the `checked` and `defaultChecked` properties `true` for that element and `false` for all other radio buttons in the group. If none of the elements has the `checked` attribute, the first one in the group is `checked` (and `defaultChecked`) by default.

Note that the text that appears next to a radio button is not part of the Radio element itself and must be specified externally to the Radio's HTML `<input>` tag.

Radio elements are used in groups of mutually exclusive options. A mutually exclusive group is defined as the set of all Radio elements within a form that have the same name. If the shared name of a group of Radio elements in form `f` is `opts`, `f.opts` is an array of Radio elements, and `f.opts.length` is the number of elements in the array.

You can set the `value` attribute or the `value` property of a Radio element to specify the string that is passed to the server if the Radio element is checked when the form is submitted. Each Radio element in a group should specify a distinct `value` so a script on the server can determine which one was checked when the form was submitted.

Usage

Radio elements can present the user with a list of multiple mutually-exclusive options. Use the Checkbox element to present a single option or a list of options that are not mutually exclusive.

See Also

Checkbox, Form, Input; HTMLInputElement in DOM reference section

Radio.onclick

JavaScript 1.0

the handler invoked when a radio button is selected

Synopsis

```
<input type="radio" onclick="handler" ... >
radio.onclick
```

Description

The onclick property of a Radio object refers to an event handler function that is invoked when the user clicks on the checkbox. See the "HTMLElement.onclick" reference page for complete details. Note, however, that Radio.onclick has been supported since JavaScript 1.0, unlike the generalized HTMLElement.onclick handler.

See Also

HTMLElement.onclick; Chapter 19; EventListener, EventTarget, and MouseEvent in the DOM reference section

Reset

JavaScript 1.0; enhanced in JavaScript 1.1

a button to reset a form's values

Inherits from Input, HTMLElement

Synopsis

```
form.name
form.elements[i]
```

Properties

Reset inherits properties from Input and HTMLElement and defines or overrides the following:

`value`
: A string that specifies the text that appears within the **Reset** button. It is specified by the value attribute of the <input> tag that created the button. If no value attribute is specified, the default value is "Reset" (or the equivalent in the browser's default language). In browsers that cannot reflow document content, this property may be read-only.

Methods

Reset inherits the methods of Input and HTMLElement.

Event Handlers

Reset inherits the event handlers of Input and HTMLElement and defines or overrides the following:

`onclick`
: Invoked when the **Reset** button is clicked.

HTML Syntax

A Reset element is created with a standard HTML <input> tag:

```
<form>
  ...
  <input
    type="reset"            // Specifies that this is a Reset button
    [ value="label" ]       // The text that is to appear within the button
                            // Specifies the value property
    [ name="name" ]         // A name you can use later to refer to the button
                            // Specifies the name property
    [ onclick="handler" ]   // JavaScript statements to be executed when the button
                            // is clicked
  >
    ...
</form>
```

Reset objects can also be created with the HTML 4 <button> tag:

```
<button id="name"
        type="reset"
        onclick="handler">
label
</button>
```

Description

The Reset element has the same properties and methods as the Button element but has a more specialized purpose. When a Reset element is clicked, the values of all input elements in the form that contains it are reset to their initial default values. (For most elements, this means to the value specified by the HTML `value` attribute.) If no initial value was specified, a click on the **Reset** button clears any user input from those elements.

Usage

If no `value` attribute is specified for a Reset element, it is labeled "Reset". In some forms, it may be better to label the button "Clear Form" or "Defaults".

In JavaScript 1.1, you can simulate the action of a **Reset** button with the `reset()` method of the Form object. Also in JavaScript 1.1, the `onreset` event handler of the Form object is invoked before the form is reset. This event handler can cancel the reset by returning `false`.

See Also

Button, Form, HTMLElement, Input; HTMLInputElement in the DOM reference section

Reset.onclick

JavaScript 1.0; enhanced in JavaScript 1.1

the handler invoked when a Reset button is clicked

Synopsis

```
<input type="reset" onclick="handler" ... >
reset.onclick
```

Description

The onclick property of a Reset object refers to an event handler function that is invoked when the user clicks on the **Reset** button. See the "HTMLElement.onclick" reference page for complete details. Note, however, that `Reset.onclick` has been supported since JavaScript 1.0, unlike the generalized `HTMLElement.onclick` handler.

The **Reset** button has the special function of resetting all form elements to their default value. The `onclick` event handler may add any additional functionality to the **Reset** button. In JavaScript 1.1, the `onclick` handler may return `false` to prevent the Reset object from resetting the form. (For example, the `onclick` handler could use `confirm()` to ask the user to confirm the reset and return `false` if it was not confirmed.)

See Also

Form.onreset, Form.reset(), HTMLElement.onclick; Chapter 19; EventListener, EventTarget, and MouseEvent in the DOM reference section

Screen — JavaScript 1.2

provides information about the display

Synopsis

```
screen
```

Properties

`availHeight`
: Specifies the available height, in pixels, of the screen on which the web browser is displayed. On operating systems such as Windows, this available height does not include vertical space allocated to semipermanent features, such as the task bar at the bottom of the screen.

`availLeft` *[Netscape 4]*
: Specifies the leftmost X-coordinate that is not allocated to a semipermanent display feature, such as an application shortcut bar or the Windows 95 task bar.

`availTop [Netscape 4]`
: Specifies the topmost Y-coordinate that is not allocated to a semipermanent display feature, such as an application shortcut bar or the Windows 95 task bar.

`availWidth`
: Specifies the available width, in pixels, of the screen on which the web browser is displayed. On operating systems such as Windows, this available width does not include horizontal space allocated to semipermanent features, such as application shortcut bars.

`colorDepth`
: Specifies the base-2 logarithm of the number of colors allocated by the web browser and available for displaying images. For example, if a browser preallocates 128 colors, `screen.colorDepth` would be 7. On systems that do not allocate color palettes, this value is the same as the number of bits-per-pixel for the screen.

In IE 4, `colorDepth` specifies the color depth of the screen in bits-per-pixel, rather than the depth of a preallocated color palette. The `screen.pixelDepth` property provides this value in Netscape.

`height`
: Specifies the total height, in pixels, of the screen on which the web browser is displayed. See also `availHeight`.

`pixelDepth` *[Netscape 4]*
: Specifies the color depth, in bits-per-pixel, of the screen on which the web browser is displayed. Contrast with `colorDepth`.

`width`
: Specifies the total width, in pixels, of the screen on which the web browser is displayed. See also `availWidth`.

Description

The `screen` property of every Window refers to a Screen object. The static properties of this global object contain information about the screen on which the browser is displayed. JavaScript programs can use this information to optimize their output to match the user's display capabilities. For example, a program can choose between large and small images based on the display size and between 16-bit color images and 8-bit color images based on the screen's color depth. A JavaScript program can also use the information about the size of the screen to center new browser windows on the screen.

See Also

The `screen` property of the Window object

Select

JavaScript 1.0; enhanced in JavaScript 1.1

a graphical selection list

Inherits from Input, HTMLElement

Synopsis

```
form.element_name
form.elements[i]
```

Properties

Select inherits properties from Input and HTMLElement and defines or overrides the following:

`length`
: A read-only integer that specifies the number of elements in the `options[]` array. The value of this property is the same as `options.length`.

`options`
: An array of Option objects, each of which describes one of the options displayed within the Select element. See the "Select.options[]" reference page for details about this array, including techniques for modifying the options displayed by the Select object.

`selectedIndex`
An integer that specifies the index of the selected option within the Select object. If no option is selected, `selectedIndex` is –1. If more than one option is selected, `selectedIndex` specifies the index of the first one only.

In JavaScript 1.0, `selectedIndex` is a read-only property. In JavaScript 1.1, it is read/write. Setting the value of this property selects the specified option and deselects all other options, even if the Select object has the `multiple` attribute specified. When you're doing list-box selection (instead of drop-down menu selection), you can deselect all options by setting `selectedIndex` to –1. Note that changing the selection in this way does not trigger the `onchange()` event handler.

`type` *[JavaScript 1.1]*
A read-only string property shared by all form elements; it specifies the type of the element. The Select object is unusual in that there are two possible values for the `type` property. If the Select object allows only a single selection (i.e., if the `multiple` attribute does not appear in the object's HTML definition), the value of the `type` property is "select-one". If the `multiple` attribute does appear, the value of the `type` attribute is "select-multiple". See also the "Input.type" reference page.

Methods

Select inherits the methods of Input and HTMLElement.

Event Handlers

Select inherits event handlers from Input and HTMLElement and defines or overrides the following:

`onchange`
Invoked when the user selects or deselects an item.

HTML Syntax

A Select element is created with a standard HTML `<select>` tag. Options to appear within the Select element are created with the `<option>` tag:

```
<form>
    ...
<select
    name="name"  // A name that identifies this element; specifies name property
    [ size="integer" ]       // Number of visible options in Select element
    [ multiple ]             // Multiple options may be selected, if present
    [ onchange="handler" ]   // Invoked when the selection changes
>
<option value="value1" [selected]> option_label1
<option value="value2" [selected]> option_label2

// Other options here
</select>
   ...
</form>
```

Description

The Select element represents a graphical list of choices for the user. If the `multiple` attribute is present in the HTML definition of the element, the user may select any number of options from the list. If that attribute is not present, the user may select only one option, and options have a radio button behavior—selecting one deselects whichever was previously selected.

The options in a Select element may be displayed in two distinct ways. If the `size` attribute has a value greater than 1, or if the `multiple` attribute is present, they are displayed in a list box which is `size` lines high in the browser window. If `size` is smaller than the number of options, the list box includes a scrollbar so all the options are accessible. On the other hand, if `size` is specified as 1 and `multiple` is not specified, the currently selected option is displayed on a single line, and the list of other options is made available through a drop-down menu. The first presentation style displays the options clearly but requires more space in the browser window. The second style requires minimal space but does not display alternative options as explicitly.

The `options[]` property of the Select element is the most interesting. This is the array of Option objects that describe the choices presented by the Select element. The `length` property specifies the length of this array (as does `options.length`). See the documentation of the Option object for details.

In JavaScript 1.1, the options displayed by the Select element may be dynamically modified. You can change the text displayed by an Option object simply by setting its `text` property. You can change the number of options displayed by the Select element by setting the `options.length` property. And you can create new options for display with the `Option()` constructor function. See the "Select.options[]" and "Option" reference pages for details.

Note that the Select object is a kind of Input object and inherits from Input, despite the fact that Select objects are not created with HTML `<input>` tags.

See Also

Form, HTMLElement, Input, Option; HTMLSelectElement in the DOM reference section

Select.onchange — JavaScript 1.0

the handler invoked when the selection changes

Synopsis

```
<select ... onchange="handler" ... >
select.onchange
```

Description

The onchange property of a Select object refers to an event handler function that is invoked when the user selects or deselects an option. See the "Input.onchange" reference page for further details on this event handler.

See Also

Input.onchange, Option; Chapter 19; Event, EventListener, and EventTarget in the DOM reference section

Select.options[] JavaScript 1.0; enhanced in JavaScript 1.1

the choices in a Select object

Synopsis

```
select.options[i]
select.options.length
```

Description

The `options[]` property contains an array of Option objects, each of which describes one of the selection options presented within the Select object *select*. The `options.length` property specifies the number of elements in the array, as does the *select*`.length` property. See the Option object for further details.

In JavaScript 1.1, you can modify the options displayed in a Select object in any of the following ways:

- If you set `options.length` to 0, all options in the Select object are cleared.
- If you set `options.length` to a value less than the current value, the number of options in the Select object is decreased, and those at the end of the array disappear.
- If you set an element in the `options[]` array to `null`, that option is removed from the Select object, and the elements above it in the array are moved down, changing their indices to occupy the new space in the array.
- If you create a new Option object with the `Option()` constructor (see the "Option" reference entry), you can add that option to the end of list of options in the Select object by assigning the newly created option to a position at the end of the `options[]` array. To do this, set `options[options.length]`.

See Also

Option

Style Internet Explorer 4, Netscape 6

Cascading Style Sheet attributes

Synopsis

```
htmlElement.style
```

Properties

The Style object has properties corresponding to each of the CSS attributes supported by the browser.

Description

The properties of the Style object correspond directly to the CSS attributes supported by the browser. For compatibility with JavaScript syntax, however, hyphenated CSS attribute names are written with mixed capitalization with the hyphen removed. So, for example, the CSS `color` attribute is represented by the `color` property of the Style object, while the CSS `background-color` attribute is represented by the `backgroundColor` property of the Style object. See Chapter 18 for more information about element styles.

See Also

HTMLElement.style; Chapter 18; CSSStyleDeclaration and CSS2Properties in the DOM reference section.

Submit

JavaScript 1.0; enhanced in JavaScript 1.1

a button to submit a form

Inherits from Input, HTMLElement

Synopsis

```
form.name
form.elements[i]
form.elements['name']
```

Properties

Submit inherits properties from Input and HTMLElement and defines or overrides the following:

`value`

A read-only string that specifies the text that appears within the **Submit** button. It is specified by the `value` attribute of the `<input>` tag that created the button. If no `value` attribute is specified, the default `value` is "Submit Query" or some similar string in the browser's default language. In browsers that cannot reflow document content, this property may be read-only.

Methods

Submit inherits methods from Input and HTMLElement.

Event Handlers

Submit inherits event handlers from Input and HTMLElement and defines or overrides the following:

`onclick`

Invoked when the **Submit** button is clicked.

HTML Syntax

A Submit object is created with a standard HTML `<input>` tag:

```
<form>
   ...
```

```
  <input
    type="submit"              // Specifies that this is a Submit button
    [ value="label" ]          // The text that is to appear within the button
                               // Specifies the value property
    [ name="name" ]            // A name you can use later to refer to the button
                               // Specifies the name property
    [ onclick="handler" ]      // JavaScript statements to be executed when the button
                               // is clicked
  >
    ...
</form>
```

Submit objects can also be created with the HTML 4 <button> tag:

```
<button id="name"
        type="submit"
        value="value"
        onclick="handler">label
</button>
```

Description

The Submit element has the same properties and methods as the Button object but has a more specialized purpose. When a **Submit** button is clicked, it submits the data in the form that contains the button to the server specified by the form's `action` attribute and loads the resulting HTML page sent back by that server. In JavaScript 1.1, the exception is that the form is not submitted if either the `Submit.onclick` or `Form.onsubmit` event handler returns `false`.

Note that in JavaScript 1.1 the `Form.submit()` method provides an alternative way to submit a form.

If no `value` attribute is specified for a Submit object, it is typically labeled "Submit Query". In some forms, it may make more sense to label the button "Submit", "Done", or "Send".

See Also

Button, Form.onsubmit, Form.submit(), HTMLElement, Input; HTMLInputElement in the DOM reference section

Submit.onclick

JavaScript 1.0; enhanced in JavaScript 1.1

invoked when a Submit button is clicked

Synopsis

```
<input type="submit" onclick="handler" ... >
submit.onclick
```

Description

The `onclick` property of a Submit object refers to an event handler function that is invoked when the user clicks on the **Submit** button. See the "HTMLElement.onclick" reference page for complete details. Note, however, that `Submit.onclick` has been supported since JavaScript 1.0, unlike the generalized `HTMLElement.onclick` handler.

The **Submit** button has the special function of submitting the form to a server. The `onclick` event handler may add any additional functionality to the **Submit** button. In JavaScript 1.1 the `onclick` handler may return `false` to prevent the Submit object from submitting the form. (For example, the `onclick` handler could perform form validation and return `false` if required fields in the form are not filled in.)

See Also

Form.onsubmit, Form.submit(), HTMLElement.onclick; Chapter 19; EventListener, EventTarget, and MouseEvent in the DOM reference section

Text

JavaScript 1.0; enhanced in JavaScript 1.1

a graphical text input field

Inherits from Input, HTMLElement

Synopsis

```
form.name
form.elements[i]
```

Properties

Text inherits properties from Input and HTMLElement and defines or overrides the following:

`value`
: A read/write string that specifies the text displayed in the text input field. This text may have been entered by the user, or it may be a default value specified by the document or by a script. The initial value of this property is specified by the `value` attribute of the `<input>` tag that defines the Text object. When the user types characters into the Text object, the `value` property is updated to match the user's input. If you set the `value` property explicitly, the string you specify is displayed in the Text object. This property also specifies the string that is sent to the server when the form is submitted.

Methods

Text inherits the methods of Input and HTMLElement.

Event Handlers

Text inherits the event handlers of Input and HTMLElement and defines or overrides the following:

`onchange`
: Invoked when the user changes the value in the Text element and moves the keyboard focus elsewhere. This event handler is not invoked for every keystroke in the Text element, but only when the user completes an edit.

HTML Syntax

A Text element is created with a standard HTML `<input>` tag:

```
<form>
    ...
```

```
    <input
      type="text"                  // Specifies that this is a Text element
      [ name="name" ]              // A name you can use later to refer to this element
                                   // Specifies the name property
      [ value="default" ]          // Default value transmitted when the form is submitted
                                   // Specifies the defaultValue property
      [ size="integer" ]           // How many characters wide the element is
      [ maxlength="integer" ]      // Maximum allowed number of input characters
      [ onchange="handler" ]       // The onchange() event handler
    >
      ...
  </form>
```

Description

The Text element represents a text input field in a form. The `size` attribute specifies the width, in characters, of the input field as it appears on the screen, and the `maxlength` attribute specifies the maximum number of characters the user is allowed to enter.

Besides these HTML attributes, value is the main property of interest for the Text element. You can read this property to obtain the user's input or set it to display arbitrary (unformatted) text in the input field.

Usage

Use the Password element instead of the Text element when the value you are asking the user to enter is sensitive information, such as a password that should not be displayed openly on the screen. Use a Textarea element to allow the user to enter multiple lines of text.

When a form contains only one Text or Password element, the form is automatically submitted if the user strikes the **Return** key in that Text or Password element. In many forms, this is a useful shortcut. In some, however, it can be confusing if the user strikes **Return** and submits the form before entering input into other form elements, such as Checkboxes and Radio buttons. You can sometimes minimize this confusion by placing Text elements with their default submission action at the bottom of the form.

See Also

Form, Input, Password, Textarea; HTMLInputElement in the DOM reference section

Text.onchange — JavaScript 1.0

the handler invoked when input value changes

Synopsis

```
<input type="text" onchange="handler" ... >
text.onchange
```

Description

The onchange property of a Text element refers to an event handler function that is invoked when the user changes the value in the input field and then "commits" those changes by moving keyboard focus (i.e., by clicking the mouse elsewhere or pressing **Tab** or **Return**).

Note that the onchange event handler is *not* invoked when the value property of a Text object is set by JavaScript. Also note that this handler is intended to process a complete change to the input value, and therefore it is not invoked on a keystroke-by-keystroke basis. See the "HTMLElement.onkeypress" reference page for information on receiving notification of every key press event.

See "Input.onchange" for complete details about the onchange event handler.

See Also

HTMLElement.onkeypress, Input.onchange; Chapter 19; Event, EventListener, and Event-Target in the DOM reference section

Textarea

JavaScript 1.0; enhanced in JavaScript 1.1

a multiline text input area — **Inherits from Input, HTMLElement**

Synopsis

```
form.name
form.elements[i]
```

Properties

Textarea inherits the properties of Input and HTMLElement and defines or overrides the following:

`value`

A read/write string property. The initial value of this property is the same as the `defaultValue` property: the plain text (i.e., without any HTML tags) that appears between the `<textarea>` and `</textarea>` tags. When the user types characters into the Textarea object, the `value` property is updated to match the user's input. If you set the `value` property explicitly, the string you specify is displayed in the Textarea object. This `value` property contains the string that is sent to the server when the form is submitted.

Methods

Textarea inherits the methods of Input and HTMLElement.

Event Handlers

Textarea inherits the event handlers of Input and HTMLElement and defines or overrides the following:

`onchange`

Invoked when the user changes the value in the Textarea element and moves the keyboard focus elsewhere. This event handler is not invoked for every keystroke in the Textarea element, but only when the user completes an edit.

HTML Syntax

A Textarea element is created with standard HTML `<textarea>` and `</textarea>` tags:

```
<form>
    ...
```

```
    <textarea
      [ name="name" ]           // A name that can be used to refer to this element
      [ rows="integer" ]        // How many lines tall the element is
      [ cols="integer" ]        // How many characters wide the element is
      [ onchange="handler" ]    // The onchange( ) event handler
    >
      plain_text                // The initial text; specifies defaultValue
    </textarea>
      ...
  </form>
```

Description

The Textarea element represents a text input field in a form. The `name` attribute specifies a name for the element. This is mandatory if the form is to be submitted, and it also provides a convenient way to refer to the Textarea element from JavaScript code. The `cols` attribute specifies the width, in characters, of the element as it appears on the screen, and the `rows` attribute specifies the height, in lines of text, of the element. The `wrap` attribute specifies how long lines should be handled: the value `off` specifies that they should be left as-is, the value `virtual` specifies that they should be displayed with line breaks but transmitted without them, and the value `physical` specifies that they should be displayed and transmitted with line breaks inserted.

In addition to these HTML attributes, `value` is the main property of interest for the Textarea element. You can read this property to obtain the user's input or set it to display arbitrary (unformatted) text in the Textarea. The initial value of the `value` property (and the permanent value of the `defaultValue` property) is the text that appears between the `<textarea>` and `</textarea>` tags.

Note that the Textarea object is a kind of Input object and inherits from Input, despite the fact that Textarea objects are not created with HTML `<input>` tags.

Usage

If you need only a single line of input text, use the Text element. If the text to be input is sensitive information, such as a password, use the Password element.

See Also

Form, HTMLElement, Input, Password, Text; HTMLTextAreaElement in the DOM reference section

Textarea.onchange — JavaScript 1.0

the handler invoked when input value changes

Synopsis

```
<textarea onchange="handler" ... >
  ...
</textarea>
textarea.onchange
```

Description

The onchange property of a Textarea element refers to an event handler function that is invoked when the user changes the value in the text area and then "commits" those changes by moving keyboard focus elsewhere.

Note that the onchange event handler is *not* invoked when the value property of a Text object is set by JavaScript. Also note that this handler is intended to process a complete change to the input value, and therefore it is not invoked on a keystroke-by-keystroke basis. See the "HTMLElement.onkeypress" reference page for information on receiving notification of every key press event.

See "Input.onchange" for complete details about the onchange event handler.

See Also

HTMLElement.onkeypress, Input.onchange; Chapter 19; Event, EventListener, and Event-Target in the DOM reference section

URL

see Link, Location, or Document.URL

Window

JavaScript 1.0; enhanced in JavaScript 1.1 and 1.2

a web browser window or frame

Synopsis

```
self
window
window.frames[i]
```

Properties

The Window object defines the following properties. Nonportable, browser-specific properties are listed separately after this list.

`closed`
: A read-only boolean value that specifies whether the window has been closed. When a browser window closes, the Window object that represents it does not simply disappear. The Window object continues to exist, but its `closed` property is set to `true`.

`defaultStatus`
: A read/write string that specifies the default message that appears in the status line. See the "Window.defaultStatus" reference page.

`document`
: A read-only reference to the Document object that describes the document contained in this window or frame. See the Document object for details.

`frames[]`
: An array of Window objects, one for each frame contained within the this window. The `frames.length` property contains the number of elements in the `frames[]` array.

Note that frames referenced by the `frames[]` array may themselves contain frames and may have a `frames[]` array of their own.

`history`
A read-only reference to the History object of this window or frame. See the History object for details.

`length`
The number of frames contained in this window or frame. `length` also specifies the number of elements in the `frames[]` array.

`location`
The Location object for this window or frame. This object specifies the URL of the currently loaded document. Setting this property to a new URL string causes the browser to load and display the contents of that URL. See the Location object for further details.

`Math`
A reference to an object holding various mathematical functions and constants. See the Math object for details.

`name`
A string that contains the name of the window. The name is optionally specified when the window is created with the `open()` method. Read-only in JavaScript 1.0; read/write in JavaScript 1.1. See the "Window.name" reference page.

`navigator`
A read-only reference to the Navigator object, which provides version and configuration information about the web browser. See the Navigator object for details.

`opener` *[JavaScript 1.1]*
A read/write reference to the Window object that contained the script that called `open()` to open this top-level browser window. This property is valid only for Window objects that represent top-level windows, not those that represent frames. The `opener` property is useful so that a newly created window can refer to variables and functions defined in the window that created it.

`parent`
A read-only reference to the Window object that contains this window or frame. If this window is a top-level window, `parent` refers to the window itself. If this window is a frame, the `parent` property refers to the window or frame that contains it.

`screen` *[JavaScript 1.2]*
The Screen object that is shared by all windows in a browser. This Screen object contains properties that specify information about the screen: the number of available pixels and the number of available colors. See the Screen object for details.

`self`
A read-only reference to this window itself. This is a synonym for the `window` property.

`status`
A read/write string that specifies the current contents of the browser's status line. See the "Window.status" reference page for details.

`top`
A read-only reference to the top-level window that contains this window. If this window is a top-level window itself, the `top` property simply contains a reference to the

window itself. If this window is a frame, the top property refers to the top-level window that contains the frame. Contrast with the parent property.

window
: The window property is identical to the self property; it contains a reference to this window.

Netscape Properties

innerHeight, innerWidth *[Netscape 4]*
: Read/write properties that specify the height and width, in pixels, of the document display area of this window. These dimensions do not include the height of the menu bar, toolbars, scrollbars, and so on. As a security restriction, you are not allowed to set either of these properties to less than 100 pixels.

java *[Netscape 3]*
: A reference to the JavaPackage object that is the top of the package name hierarchy for the core *java.** packages that comprise the Java language. See the "JavaPackage" reference page.

locationbar.visible *[Netscape 4]*
: A read-only boolean that specifies whether the window displays a location bar. See window features in the "Window.open()" reference page.

menubar.visible *[Netscape 4]*
: A read-only boolean that specifies whether the window displays a menu bar. See window features in the "Window.open()" reference page.

netscape *[Netscape 3]*
: A reference to the JavaPackage object which is the top of the Java package name hierarchy for the *netscape.** Java packages from Netscape. See the "JavaPackage" reference page.

outerHeight, outerWidth *[Netscape 4]*
: Read/write integers that specify the total height and width, in pixels, of the window. These dimensions include the height and width of the menu bar, toolbars, scrollbars, window borders, and so on.

Packages *[Netscape 3]*
: A reference to a JavaPackage object that represents the top of the Java package name hierarchy. For example, use Packages.java.lang to refer to the *java.lang* package. See the "JavaPackage" reference page.

pageXOffset, pageYOffset *[Netscape 4]*
: Read-only integers that specify the number of pixels that the current document has been scrolled to the right (pageXOffset) and down (pageYOffset).

personalbar.visible *[Netscape 4]*
: A read-only boolean that specifies whether this window displays a "personal bar" of bookmarks. See window features in the "Window.open()" reference page.

screenX, screenY *[Netscape 4]*
: Read-only integers that specify the X- and Y-coordinates of the upper-left corner of the window on the screen. If this window is a frame, these properties specify the X- and Y-coordinates of the top-level window that contains the frame.

`scrollbars.visible` *[Netscape 4]*
: A read-only boolean that specifies whether the scroll bars are visible in this window, or would be visible if the document was long enough or wide enough to require them. What this property really specifies is whether scrolling is enabled in this window. See window features in the "Window.open()" reference page.

`statusbar.visible` *[Netscape 4]*
: A read-only boolean that specifies whether this window has a status line. See window features in the "Window.open()" reference page.

`sun` *[Netscape 3]*
: A reference to the JavaPackage object which is the top of the Java package name hierarchy for the *sun.** Java packages from Sun Microsystems. See the "JavaPackage" reference page.

`toolbar.visible` *[Netscape 4]*
: A read-only boolean that specifies whether this window displays a toolbar. See window features in the "Window.open()" reference page.

Internet Explorer Properties

`clientInformation` *[IE 4]*
: An IE-specific synonym for the `navigator` property. Both refer to a Navigator object. Despite the fact that `clientInformation` has a better name and is less Netscape-specific than `navigator`, it is not supported by Netscape and is therefore not portable.

`event` *[IE 4]*
: An Event object that contains the details of the most recent event to occur within *`window`*. In the Netscape 4 event model and the DOM standard event model, an Event object describing the event is passed as an argument to every event handler. In the IE event model, however, no Event object is passed, and event handlers must obtain information about the event from the event property of the Window object.

Methods

The Window object has the following portable methods. Nonportable, browser-specific methods are listed separately after this list.

`alert()`	Displays a simple message in a dialog box.
`blur()`	Takes keyboard focus from the top-level browser window; this sends the window to the background on most platforms.
`clearInterval()`	Cancels periodic execution of code.
`clearTimeout()`	Cancels a pending timeout operation.
`close()`	Closes a window.
`confirm()`	Asks a yes-or-no question with a dialog box.
`focus()`	Gives the top-level browser window keyboard focus; this brings the window to the front on most platforms.
`moveBy()`	Moves the window by a relative amount.
`moveTo()`	Moves the window to an absolute position.
`open()`	Creates and opens a new window.

`print()`	Simulates a click on the browser's **Print** button. IE 5 and Netscape 4 only.
`prompt()`	Asks for simple string input with a dialog box.
`resizeBy()`	Resizes the window by a specified amount.
`resizeTo()`	Resizes the window to a specified size.
`scroll()`	Scrolls the document displayed in the window.
`scrollBy`	Scrolls the window by a specified amount.
`scrollTo()`	Scrolls the window to a specified position.
`setInterval()`	Executes code at periodic intervals.
`setTimeout()`	Executes code after a specified amount of time elapses.

Netscape Methods

`back()`	Behaves as if the user clicked the **Back** button.
`captureEvents()`	Specifies event types to be routed directly to the window.
`forward()`	Simulates a click on the browser's **Forward** button.
`handleEvent()`	Invokes the appropriate event handler for a given Event object.
`home()`	Displays the browser's home page.
`releaseEvents()`	Specifies types of events that will no longer be captured.
`routeEvent()`	Passes an Event to the appropriate handler of the next interested object.
`stop()`	Simulates a click on the browser's **Stop** button.

Internet Explorer Methods

`navigate()`	Loads and displays the specified URL.

Event Handlers

`onblur`	Invoked when the window loses focus.
`onerror`	Invoked when a JavaScript error occurs.
`onfocus`	Invoked when the window gains focus.
`onload`	Invoked when the document (or frameset) is fully loaded.
`onmove`	Invoked when the window is moved. Netscape 4 only.
`onresize`	Invoked when the window is resized.
`onunload`	Invoked when the browser leaves the current document or frameset.

Description

The Window object represents a browser window or frame. It is documented in detail in Chapter 13. In client-side JavaScript, the Window serves as the "global object," and all expressions are evaluated in the context of the current Window object. This means that no special syntax is required to refer to the current window, and you can use the properties of that window object as if they were global variables. For example, you can write `document` rather than *`window`*`.document`. Similarly, you can use the methods of the current window object as if they were functions: e.g., `alert()` instead of *`window`*`.alert()`.

The Window object does have `window` and `self` properties that refer to the window object itself. You can use these to make the current window reference explicit rather than implicit. In addition to these two properties, the `parent` and `top` properties and the `frames[]` array refer to other Window objects related to the current one.

To refer to a frame within a window, use:

```
frames[i] or self.frames[i]  // Frames of current window
window.frames[i]             // Frames of specified window
```

To refer to the parent window (or frame) of a frame, use:

```
parent or self.parent  // Parent of current window
window.parent          // Parent of specified window
```

To refer to the top-level browser window from any frame contained within it, use:

```
top or self.top  // Top window of current frame
window.top       // Top window of specified frame
```

New top-level browser windows are created with the `Window.open()` method. When you call this method, save the return value of the `open()` call in a variable and use that variable to reference the new window. In JavaScript 1.1, the `opener` property of the new window is a reference to the window that opened it.

In general, the methods of the Window object manipulate the browser window or frame in some way. The `alert()`, `confirm()`, and `prompt()` methods are notable: they interact with the user through simple dialog boxes.

See Chapter 13 for an in-depth overview of the Window object, and see the individual reference pages for complete details on all the Window properties, methods, and event handlers.

See Also

Document; Chapter 13; AbstractView in the DOM reference section

Window.alert( ) — JavaScript 1.0

display a message in a dialog box

Synopsis

window.alert(*message*)

Arguments

message
: The plain-text (not HTML) string to display in a dialog box popped up over *window*.

Description

The `alert()` method displays the specified *message* to the user in a dialog box. The dialog box contains an **OK** button that the user can click to dismiss the dialog box.

On Windows platforms, the dialog box displayed by `alert()` is modal, and JavaScript execution pauses until the user dismisses it. In Netscape 4 on Unix platforms, however, the `alert()` dialog box is nonmodal, and execution continues uninterrupted.

Usage

Perhaps the most common use of the `alert( )` method is to display error messages when the user's input to some form element is invalid in some way. The alert dialog box can inform the user of the problem and explain what needs to be corrected to avoid the problem in the future.

The appearance of the `alert( )` dialog box is platform-dependent, but it generally contains graphics that indicate an error, warning, or alert message of some kind. While `alert( )` can display any desired message, the alert graphics of the dialog box mean that this method is not appropriate for simple informational messages like "Welcome to my home page" or "You are the 177th visitor this week!"

Note that the *`message`* displayed in the dialog box is a string of plain text, not formatted HTML. You can use the newline character "\n" in your strings to break your message across multiple lines. You can also do some rudimentary formatting using spaces and can approximate horizontal rules with underscore characters, but the results depend greatly on the font used in the dialog box, and thus are system-dependent.

See Also

Window.confirm(), Window.prompt()

Window.back( ) — Netscape 4

go back to previous document

Synopsis

```
window.back( )
```

Description

Calling `back( )` makes the browser display the document previously displayed in *`window`*, exactly as if the user had clicked on the window's **Back** button.

Note that for framed documents, there may be differences between the behavior of `Window.back( )` and `History.back( )`.

Window.blur( ) — JavaScript 1.1

remove keyboard focus from a top-level window

Synopsis

```
window.blur( )
```

Description

The `blur( )` method removes keyboard focus from the top-level browser window specified by the Window object. If the Window object is a frame, keyboard focus is given to the top-level window that contains that frame. On most platforms, a top-level window is sent to the background (i.e., to the bottom of the window stack) when keyboard focus is taken from it.

See Also

Window.focus()

Window.captureEvents( ) Netscape 4

specify event types to be captured

Synopsis

```
window.captureEvents(eventmask)
document.captureEvents(eventmask)
layer.captureEvents(eventmask)
```

Arguments

eventmask
An integer that specifies the type of events that the window, document, or layer should capture. This value should be one of the static event type constants defined by the Event class, or it should be a group of event type constants combined with the bitwise-OR (|) or addition operators.

Description

`captureEvents( )` is a method of the Window, Document, and Layer classes. Its purpose is the same for all three: in the Netscape 4 event model, `captureEvents( )` specifies that all events of a given type or types occurring within the specified *window*, *document*, or *layer* should be passed to the window, document, or layer instead of to the object on which they actually occurred.

The type of the events to be captured is specified by *eventmask*, a bitmask comprised of static constants defined by the Event class. See the "Event.TYPE" reference page for a full list of these bitmask constants.

See Also

Event, Window.handleEvent(), Window.releaseEvents(), Window.routeEvent(); Chapter 19; EventTarget.addEventListener() in the DOM reference section

Window.clearInterval( ) JavaScript 1.2

stop periodically executing code

Synopsis

```
window.clearInterval(intervalId)
```

Arguments

intervalId
The value returned by the corresponding call to `setInterval( )`.

Description

clearInterval() stops the repeated execution of code that was started by a call to setInterval(). *intervalId* must be the value that was returned by a call to setInterval().

See Also

Window.setInterval()

Window.clearTimeout() JavaScript 1.0

cancel deferred execution

Synopsis

```
window.clearTimeout(timeoutId)
```

Arguments

timeoutId
A value returned by setTimeout() that identifies the timeout to be canceled.

Description

clearTimeout() cancels the execution of code that has been deferred with the setTimeout() method. The *timeoutId* argument is a value returned by the call to setTimeout() and identifies which (of possibly more than one) block of deferred code to cancel.

See Also

Window.setTimeout()

Window.close() JavaScript 1.0

close a browser window

Synopsis

```
window.close()
```

Description

The close() method closes the top-level browser window specified by *window*. A window can close itself by calling self.close() or simply close().

In JavaScript 1.1, only windows opened by JavaScript can be closed by JavaScript. This prevents malicious scripts from causing the user's browser to exit.

There is no meaningful way to close a frame within a window. Thus, the close() method should be invoked only for Window objects that represent top-level browser windows, not for those that represent frames.

See Also

Window.open(), the closed and opener properties of Window

Window.confirm( ) JavaScript 1.0

ask a yes-or-no question

Synopsis

```
window.confirm(question)
```

Arguments

question
: The plain text (not HTML) string to be displayed in the dialog box. It should generally express a question you want the user to answer.

Returns

`true` if the user clicks the **OK** button; `false` if the user clicks the **Cancel** button.

Description

The `confirm( )` method displays the specified *question* in a dialog box that pops up over *window*. The appearance of the dialog box is platform-dependent, but it generally contains graphics that indicate that the user is being asked a question. The dialog box contains **OK** and **Cancel** buttons that the user can use to answer the question. If the user clicks the **OK** button, `confirm( )` returns `true`. If the user clicks **Cancel**, `confirm( )` returns `false`.

The dialog box that is displayed by the `confirm( )` method is *modal*—that is, it blocks all user input to the main browser window until the user dismisses the dialog box by clicking on the **OK** or **Cancel** buttons. Since this method returns a value depending on the user's response to the dialog box, JavaScript execution pauses in the call to `confirm( )`, and subsequent statements are not executed until the user responds to the dialog box.

Usage

Note that the *question* displayed in the dialog box is a string of plain text, not formatted HTML. You can use the newline character, "\n", in your strings to break your question across multiple lines. You can also do some rudimentary formatting using spaces and can approximate horizontal rules with underscore characters, but the results depend greatly on the font used in the dialog box and thus are system-dependent.

Also, there is no way to change the labels that appear in the buttons of the dialog box (to make them read **Yes** and **No**, for example). Therefore, you should take care to phrase your question or message in such a way that **OK** and **Cancel** are suitable responses.

See Also

Window.alert( ), Window.prompt( )

Window.defaultStatus JavaScript 1.0

the default status line text

Synopsis

```
window.defaultStatus
```

Description

`defaultStatus` is a read/write string property that specifies the default text that will appear in the window's status line. Web browsers typically use the status line to display the browser's progress while loading a file and to display the destination of hypertext links that the mouse is over. While it is not displaying any of these transient messages, the status line is, by default, blank. However, you can set the `defaultStatus` property to specify a default message to be displayed when the status line is not otherwise in use, and you can read the `defaultStatus` property to determine what the default message is. The text you specify may be temporarily overwritten with other messages, such as those that are displayed when the user moves the mouse over a hypertext link, but the `defaultStatus` message is always redisplayed when the transient message is erased.

If you set `defaultStatus` for a Window object that is a frame, the message you specify is visible whenever the mouse is within that frame (regardless of whether that frame has focus). When you specify `defaultStatus` for a top-level window that contains no frames, your message is always visible when the window is visible. If you specify `defaultStatus` for a top-level window that contains frames, your message is visible only when the mouse is over the borders that separate the frames. Thus, in order to guarantee visibility of a message in a framed document, you should set `defaultStatus` for all frames in the document.

Usage

`defaultStatus` is used to display semipermanent messages in the status line. To display transient messages, use the `status` property.

See Also

Window.status

Window.focus( ) JavaScript 1.1

give keyboard focus to a top-level window

Synopsis

```
window.focus( )
```

Description

The `focus( )` method gives keyboard focus to the top-level browser window specified by the Window object. If the Window object is a frame, keyboard focus is given to the frame and to the top-level window that contains that frame.

On most platforms, a top-level window is brought forward to the top of the window stack when it is given focus.

See Also

Window.blur()

Window.forward( )

Netscape 4

go forward to next document

Synopsis

```
window.forward( )
```

Description

Calling `forward( )` makes the browser display the next document in *window*, exactly as if the user had clicked on the window's **Forward** button.

Note that for framed documents, there may be differences between the behavior of `Window.forward( )` and `History.forward( )`.

Window.handleEvent( )

Netscape 4

pass an event to the appropriate handler

Synopsis

```
window.handleEvent(event)
document.handleEvent(event)
layer.handleEvent(event)
htmlElement.handleEvent(event)
```

Arguments

event

An Event object to be handled.

Returns

Whatever value is returned by the event handler that is invoked to handle *event*.

Description

`handleEvent( )` is a method of the Window, Document, and Layer classes and of all HTML elements that support event handlers. When invoked on any object *o*, `handleEvent( )` determines the type of its *event* argument and passes that Event object to the appropriate handler of *o*.

See Also

Window.routeEvent(); Chapter 19

Window.home( )

Netscape 4

display the home page

Synopsis

```
window.home( )
```

Description

Calling `home()` makes the browser display its own configured home page, as if the user had clicked the browser's **Home** button.

Window.moveBy() JavaScript 1.2

move a window to a relative position

Synopsis

```
window.moveBy(dx, dy)
```

Arguments

dx The number of pixels to move the window to the right.

dy The number of pixels to move the window down.

Description

`moveBy()` moves the *window* to the relative position specified by *dx* and *dy*. For security reasons, browsers may restrict scripts so they cannot move a window off the screen.

Window.moveTo() JavaScript 1.2

move a window to an absolute position

Synopsis

```
window.moveTo(x, y)
```

Arguments

x The X-coordinate of the new window position.

y The Y-coordinate of the new window position.

Description

`moveTo()` moves the *window* so its upper-left corner is at the position specified by *x* and *y*. For security resasons, browsers may restrict this method so it cannot move a window offscreen.

Window.name JavaScript 1.0; read/write in JavaScript 1.1

the name of a window

Synopsis

```
window.name
```

Description

The *name* property is a string that specifies the name of *window*. This property is read-only in JavaScript 1.0 and read/write in JavaScript 1.1. The name of a top-level window is initially specified by the *name* argument of the `Window.open( )` method. The name of a frame is initially specified by the name attribute of the `<frame>` HTML tag.

The name of a top-level window or frame may be used as the value of a `target` attribute of an `<a>` or `<form>` tag. Using the `target` attribute in this way specifies that the hyperlinked document or the results of form submission should be displayed in the named window.

The initial window opened by the browser and any windows opened with the **New Web Browser** menu item initially have no name (i.e., `name == ""`), so these windows cannot be addressed with a `target` attribute from a separate top-level window. In JavaScript 1.1, you can set the name attribute to remedy this situation.

See Also

Form.target, Link.target

Window.navigate( ) — Internet Explorer 3

load a new URL

Synopsis

```
window.navigate(url)
```

Arguments

url

A string that specifies the URL to be loaded and displayed.

Description

The `Window.navigate( )` method of Internet Explorer loads the specified *url* into the specified *window* ("navigates to" the *url*).

`navigate( )` is not supported by Netscape. The same function can be accomplished both in Netscape and IE by assigning the desired *url* to the `location` property of the desired *window*.

See Also

Location, the `location` property of the Window object

Window.onblur — JavaScript 1.1

the handler invoked when the window loses keyboard focus

Synopsis

```
<body onblur="handler" ... >
<frameset onblur="handler" ... >
window.onblur
```

Description

The `onblur` property of a Window specifies an event handler function that is invoked when the window loses keyboard focus.

The initial value of this property is a function that contains the semicolon-separated JavaScript statements specified by the `onblur` attribute of the `<body>` or `<frameset>` tags.

In the Netscape 4 event model, the `onblur` handler function is passed an Event object as an argument. In the IE event model, no argument is passed, but the applicable Event object is available as the `event` property of the Window object that contains the *`element`*.

Usage

If your web page has animation, you can use the `onblur()` event handler to stop the animation when the window doesn't have the input focus. In theory, if the window doesn't have the focus, the user probably can't see it or isn't paying attention to it.

See Also

Window.blur(), Window.focus(), Window.onfocus; Chapter 19; Event, EventListener, and EventTarget in the DOM reference section

Window.onerror

JavaScript 1.1; buggy in Netscape 6/6.1

the handler invoked when a JavaScript error occurs

Synopsis

You register an `onerror` event handler like this:

```
window.onerror=handler-func
```

The browser invokes the handler like this:

```
window.onerror(message, url, line)
```

Arguments

`message`
: A string that specifies the error message for the error that occurred.

`url`
: A string that specifies the URL of the document in which the error occurred.

`line`
: A number that specifies the line number at which the error occurred.

Returns

`true` if the handler has handled the error and JavaScript should take no further action; `false` if JavaScript should post the default error message dialog box for this error.

Description

The `onerror` property of the Window object specifies an error handler function that is invoked when a JavaScript error occurs in code executing in that window. By default, JavaScript displays an error dialog box when an error occurs. You can customize error handling by providing your own `onerror` event handler.

You define an `onerror` event handler for a window by setting the `onerror` property of a Window object to an appropriate function. Note that unlike other event handlers in JavaScript, the `onerror` handler cannot be defined in an HTML tag.

When the onerror handler is invoked, it is passed three arguments: a string specifying the error message, a string specifying the URL of the document in which the error occurred, and a number that specifies the line number at which the error occurred. An error handling function may do anything it wants with these arguments: it may display its own error dialog box or log the error in some way, for example. When the error handling function is done, it should return true if it has completely handled the error and wants JavaScript to take no further action or false if it has merely noted or logged the error in some fashion and still wants JavaScript to display the error message in its default dialog box.

Note that while this event handler returns true to tell the browser to take no further action, most Form and form element event handlers return false to prevent the browser from performing some action, such as submitting a form. This inconsistency can be confusing.

You can turn off error handling entirely for a window by setting the onerror property of the window to a function that returns true and does nothing else. You can restore the default error-handling behavior (the dialog box) by setting onerror to a function that returns false and does nothing else.

Bugs

This event handler is correctly triggered by errors in Netscape 6 and Netscape 6.1, but the values passed as the message, URL, and line number arguments are incorrect, so although you can use it to detect the occurrence of an error, you cannot use it to obtain any useful information about the error.

Window.onfocus — JavaScript 1.1

the handler invoked when a window is given focus

Synopsis

```
<body onfocus="handler" ... >
<frameset onfocus="handler" ... >
window.onfocus
```

Description

The onfocus property of a Window specifies an event handler function that is invoked when the window is given keyboard focus.

The initial value of this property is a function that contains the semicolon-separated JavaScript statements specified by the onfocus attribute of the <body> or <frameset> tags.

In the Netscape 4 event model, the onfocus handler function is passed an Event object as an argument. In the IE event model, no argument is passed, but the applicable Event object is available as the event property of the Window object that contains the *element*.

Usage

If your web page has animation, you can use the onfocus event handler to start the animation and the onblur handler to stop it, so it runs only when the user is paying attention to the window.

See Also

Window.blur(), Window.focus(), Window.onblur; Chapter 19; Event, EventListener, and EventTarget in the DOM reference section

Window.onload JavaScript 1.0

the handler invoked when a document finishes loading

Synopsis

```
<body onload="handler" ... >
<frameset onload="handler" ... >
window.onload
```

Description

The onload property of a Window specifies an event handler function that is invoked when a document or frameset is completely loaded into its window or frame.

The initial value of this property is a function that contains the semicolon-separated JavaScript statements specified by the onload attribute of the <body> or <frameset> tags.

When the onload event handler is invoked, you can be certain that the document has fully loaded, and therefore that all scripts within the document have executed, all functions within scripts are defined, and all forms and other document elements have been parsed and are available through the Document object.

Usage

If any of your document's event handlers depend on the document being fully loaded, you should check that it is loaded before executing those handlers. If the network connection were to stall out after a button appeared in the document but before the parts of the document that the button relied on were loaded, the user would get unintended behavior or an error message after clicking the button. One good way to verify that the document is loaded is to use the onload handler to set a variable—loaded, for example—to true and to check the value of this variable before doing anything that depends on the complete document being loaded.

See Also

Window.onunload; Chapter 19; Event, EventListener, and EventTarget in the DOM reference section

Window.onmove Netscape 4; not supported on Netscape 4 Unix platforms

the handler invoked when a window is moved

Synopsis

```
<body onmove="handler" ... >
<frameset onmove="handler" ... >
window.onmove
```

Description

The onmove property of the Window object specifies an event handler function that is invoked when the user moves a top-level window to a new position on the screen.

The initial value of this property is a function that contains the JavaScript statements specified by the onmove attribute of the HTML `<body>` or `<frameset>` tag that defined the window. When an event handler function is defined by an HTML attribute, it is executed in the scope of *element* rather than in the scope of the containing window.

The onmove handler function is passed an Event object as an argument. The properties of this object contain information about the new position of the window.

Window.onresize JavaScript 1.2

the handler invoked when a window is resized

Synopsis

```
<body onresize="handler" ... >
<frameset onresize="handler" ... >
window.onresize
```

Description

The `onresize` property of the Window object specifies an event handler function that is invoked when the user changes the size of the window or frame.

The initial value of this property is a function that contains the JavaScript statements specified by the `onresize` attribute of the HTML `<body>` or `<frameset>` tag that defined the window. When an event handler function is defined by an HTML attribute, it is executed in the scope of *element* rather than in the scope of the containing window.

In the Netscape 4 event model, the `onresize` handler function is passed an Event object as an argument. In the IE event model, no argument is passed, but the applicable Event object is available as the event property of the Window object that contains the *element*.

In Netscape, the new size of the window is available from the `width` and `height` properties of the Event object.

Window.onunload JavaScript 1.0

the handler invoked when the browser leaves a page

Synopsis

```
<body onunload="handler" ... >
<frameset onunload="handler" ... >
window.onunload
```

Description

The `onunload` property of a Window specifies an event handler function that is invoked when the browser "unloads" a document or frameset in preparation for loading a new one.

The initial value of this property is a function that contains the semicolon-separated JavaScript statements specified by the onunload attribute of the <body> or <frameset> tags. The onunload event handler provides the opportunity to perform any necessary cleanup of the browser state before a new document is loaded.

When the browser leaves a site using frames, the onunload handler of the frameset is invoked before the onunload handler for each of the frames. This is the reverse of the order in which the onload event handler is invoked.

The onunload( ) handler is invoked when the user has instructed the browser to leave the current page and move somewhere else. Therefore, it is usually inappropriate to delay the loading of the desired new page by popping up dialog boxes (with Window.confirm( ) or Window.prompt( ), for example) from an onunload event handler.

See Also

Window.onload; Chapter 19; Event, EventListener, and EventTarget in the DOM reference section

Window.open( )

JavaScript 1.0; enhanced in JavaScript 1.1

open a new browser window or locate a named window

Synopsis

```
window.open(url, name, features, replace)
```

Arguments

url
: An optional string that specifies the URL to be displayed in the new window. If this argument is omitted, or if the empty string is specified, the new window does not display a document.

name
: An optional string of alphanumeric and underscore characters that specifies a name for the new window. This name can be used as the value of the target attribute of <a> and <form> HTML tags. If this argument names a window that already exists, the open( ) method does not create a new window, but simply returns a reference to the named window. In this case, the *features* argument is ignored.

features
: A string that specifies which features of a standard browser window are to appear in the new window. The format of this string is specified in the "Window Features" section. This argument is optional; if it is not specified, the new window has all the standard features.

replace
: An optional boolean argument that specifies whether the URL loaded into the new page should create a new entry in the window's browsing history or replace the current entry in the browsing history. If this argument is true, no new history entry is created. This argument was added in JavaScript 1.1. Note that it doesn't make much sense to use this argument for newly created windows; it is intended for use when changing the contents of an existing window.

Returns

A reference to a Window object, which may be a newly created or an already existing one, depending on the *name* argument.

Description

The `open( )` method looks up an existing window or opens a new browser window. If the *name* argument specifies the name of an existing window, a reference to that window is returned. The returned window displays the URL specified by *url*, but the *features* argument is ignored. This is the only way in JavaScript to obtain a reference to a window which is known only by name.

If the *name* argument is not specified, or if no window with that name already exists, the `open( )` method creates a new browser window. The created window displays the URL specified by *url* and has the name specified by *name* and the size and controls specified by *features* (the format of this argument is described in the next section). If *url* is the empty string, `open( )` opens a blank window.

The *name* argument specifies a name for the new window. This name may contain only alphanumeric characters and the underscore character. It may be used as the value of the `target` attribute of an `<a>` or `<form>` tag in HTML to force documents to be displayed in the window.

In JavaScript 1.1, when you use `Window.open( )` to load a new document into a named window, you can pass the *replace* argument to specify whether the new document has its own entry in the window's browsing history or whether it replaces the history entry of the current document. If *replace* is `true`, the new document replaces the old. If this argument is `false` or is not specified, the new document has its own entry in the Window's browsing history. This argument provides functionality much like that of the `Location.replace( )` method.

Don't confuse `Window.open( )` with `Document.open( )`—the two methods perform very different functions. For clarity in your code, you may want to use `Window.open( )` instead of `open( )`. In event handlers defined as HTML attributes, `open( )` is usually interpreted as `Document.open( )`, so in this case, you must use `Window.open( )`.

Window Features

The *features* argument is a comma-separated list of features that will appear in the window. If this optional argument is empty or not specified, all features are present in the window. On the other hand, if *features* specifies any one feature, any features that do not appear in the list do not appear in the window. The string should not contain any spaces or other whitespace. Each element in the list has the format:

```
feature[=value]
```

For most features, the *value* is `yes` or `no`. For these features, the equals sign and the *value* may be omitted—if the feature appears, `yes` is assumed, and if it doesn't, `no` is assumed. For the `width` and `height` features, *value* is required and must specify a size in pixels.

The available features and their meanings are:

`channelmode`
: Specifies whether the window should appear in channel mode. IE 4 only.

`dependent`
: If set to "no", specifies that the new window should not be a dependent child of the current window. Netscape 4 only.

`directories`
: Directory buttons, such as "What's New" and "What's Cool". Netscape only.

`fullscreen`
: Specifies whether the window should appear in full-screen mode. IE 4 only.

`height`
: Specifies the height, in pixels, of the window's document display area.

`innerHeight`
: Specifies the height, in pixels, of the window's document display area. Netscape 4 only.

`innerWidth`
: Specifies the width, in pixels, of the window's document display area. Netscape 4 only.

`left`
: The X-coordinate, in pixels, of the window. IE 4 only. In Netscape, use `screenX`.

`location`
: The input field for entering URLs directly into the browser.

`menubar`
: The menu bar.

`outerHeight`
: Specifies the total height, in pixels, of the window. Netscape 4 only.

`innerWidth`
: Specifies the total width, in pixels, of the window. Netscape 4 only.

`resizable`
: If this feature is not present or is set to `no`, the window does not have resize handles around its border. (Depending on the platform, the user may still have ways to resize the window.) Note that a common bug is to misspell this feature as "resizeable," with an extra "e."

`screenX`
: The X-coordinate, in pixels, of the window. Netscape 4 only. Use `left` in IE 4.

`screenY`
: The Y-coordinate, in pixels, of the window. Netscape 4 only. Use `top` in IE 4.

`scrollbars`
: Enables horizontal and vertical scrollbars when they are necessary.

`status`
: The status line.

`toolbar`
: The browser toolbar, with **Back** and **Forward** buttons, etc.

`top`
: The Y-coordinate, in pixels, of the window. IE 4 only. Use `screenY` in Netscape.

`width`
: Specifies the width, in pixels, of the window's document display area.

See Also

Location.replace( ), Window.close( ), the `closed` and `opener` properties of Window

Window.print( ) — Netscape 4, Internet Explorer 5

print the document

Synopsis

window.print( )

Description

Calling `print( )` prints the current document, exactly as if the user had clicked the browser's **Print** button.

Window.prompt( ) — JavaScript 1.0

get string input in a dialog box

Synopsis

window.prompt(*message*, *default*)

Arguments

message
: The plain-text (not HTML) string to be displayed in the dialog box. It should ask the user to enter the information you want.

default
: A string that is displayed as the default input in the dialog box. Pass the empty string ("") to make `prompt( )` display an empty input box.

Returns

The string entered by the user, the empty string if the user did not enter a string, or `null` if the user clicked **Cancel**.

Description

The `prompt( )` method displays the specified *message* in a dialog box that also contains a text input field and **OK**, **Clear**, and **Cancel** buttons. Platform-dependent graphics in the dialog box help indicate to the user that her input is desired.

If the user clicks the **Cancel** button, `prompt( )` returns `null`. If the user clicks the **Clear** button, `prompt( )` erases any current text in the input field. If the user clicks the **OK** button, `prompt( )` returns the value currently displayed in the input field.

The dialog box that is displayed by the `prompt()` method is *modal*—that is, it blocks all user input to the main browser window until the user dismisses the dialog box by clicking on the **OK** or **Cancel** buttons. Since this method returns a value depending on the user's response to the dialog box, JavaScript execution pauses in the call to `prompt()`, and subsequent statements are not executed until the user responds to the dialog box.

See Also

Window.alert(), Window.confirm()

Window.releaseEvents( )

Netscape 4

stop capturing events

Synopsis

```
window.releaseEvents(eventmask)
document.releaseEvents(eventmask)
layer.releaseEvents(eventmask)
```

Arguments

eventmask
: An integer that specifies the type of events that the window, document, or layer should stop capturing. This value should be one of the static event type constants defined by the Event class, or it should be a group of event type constants combined with the bitwise-OR (|) or addition operator.

Description

The `releaseEvents()` method of the Window, Document, and Layer objects performs the opposite action of the `captureEvents()` method of those classes. In the Netscape 4 event model, `releaseEvents()` specifies that the *window*, *document*, or *layer* should no longer capture events of the types specified by *eventmask*. See the "Event.TYPE" reference page for a list of the constants that can be used in the *eventmask* argument.

See Also

Event, Window.captureEvents(), Window.handleEvent(), Window.routeEvent(); Chapter 19; EventTarget.removeEventListener() in the DOM reference section

Window.resizeBy( )

JavaScript 1.2

resize a window by a relative amount

Synopsis

```
window.resizeBy(dw, dh)
```

Arguments

dw The number of pixels by which to increase the width of the window.

dh The number of pixels by which to increase the height of the window.

Description

`resizeBy( )` resizes *`window`* by the relative amounts specified by *`dh`* and *`dw`*. For security reasons, the browser may restrict this method so it makes either the width or height of the window less than 100 pixels.

Window.resizeTo( ) JavaScript 1.2

resize a window

Synopsis

```
window.resizeTo(width, height)
```

Arguments

`width`
The desired width for the window.

`height`
The desired height for the window.

Description

`resizeTo( )` resizes *`window`* so it is *`width`* pixels wide and *`height`* pixels high. For security reasons, the browser may restrict this method so that neither *`width`* nor *`height`* is smaller than 100 pixels.

Window.routeEvent( ) Netscape 4

pass a captured event to the next handler

Synopsis

```
window.routeEvent(event)
document.routeEvent(event)
layer.routeEvent(event)
```

Arguments

`event`
The captured Event object to be routed to the next event handler.

Returns

Whatever value was returned by the handler to which the *`event`* was routed.

Description

`routeEvent( )` is a method of the Window, Document, and Layer classes, and it behaves the same for all three. When a captured Event object, *`event`*, is passed to an event handler of *`window`*, *`document`*, or *`layer`*, that handler may choose to pass the event on to the next interested event handler, if any. If the window, document, or layer contains some other window (frame), document, or layer that has also used `captureEvents( )` to register interest in events of that type, the event is routed to the appropriate handler on that window, document, or layer object.

On the other hand, if there is no containing window, document, or layer object that has expressed interest in the event, `routeEvent()` passes the *event* object to the appropriate event handler of the object on which the event originated. The combination of `captureEvents()` and `routeEvent()` forms the basis of the "trickle-down" event model of Netscape 4.

See Also

Window.captureEvents(), Window.handleEvent(), Window.releaseEvents(); Chapter 19

Window.scroll()

JavaScript 1.1; deprecated in JavaScript 1.2

scroll a document in a window

Synopsis

```
window.scroll(x, y)
```

Arguments

x The X-coordinate to scroll to.

y The Y-coordinate to scroll to.

Description

The `scroll()` method moves the window's document within the window so the specified *x*- and *y*-coordinates of the document appear in the upper-left corner of the window.

The X-coordinate increases to the right, and the Y-coordinate increases down the page. Thus, `scroll(0,0)` always places the top-left corner of the document in the top-left corner of the window.

In JavaScript 1.2, the `scrollTo()` and `scrollBy()` methods are preferred over `scroll()`.

Window.scrollBy()

JavaScript 1.2

scroll the document by a relative amount

Synopsis

```
window.scrollBy(dx, dy)
```

Arguments

dx The number of pixels by which to scroll the document to the right.

dy The number of pixels by which to scroll the document down.

Description

`scrollBy()` scrolls the document displayed in window by the relative amounts specified by *dx* and *dy*.

Window.scrollTo( ) JavaScript 1.2

scroll the document

Synopsis

```
window.scrollTo(x, y)
```

Arguments

x The document X-coordinate that is to appear at the left edge of the window's document display area.

y The document Y-coordinate that is to appear at the top of the window's document display area.

Description

`scrollTo( )` scrolls the document displayed within *window* so the point in the document specified by the *x*- and *y*-coordinates is displayed in the upper-left corner, if possible.

`scrollTo( )` is preferred over the JavaScript 1.1 `Window.scroll( )` method, which does the same thing but has an inadequately descriptive name.

Window.setInterval( ) JavaScript 1.2; IE 4 supports only one of the two forms

periodically execute specified code

Synopsis

```
window.setInterval(code, interval)
window.setInterval(func, interval, args...)
```

Arguments

code
: A string of JavaScript code to be periodically executed. If this string contains multiple statements, they must be separated from each other by semicolons.

func
: A JavaScript function to be periodically executed. This form of the method is not available in IE 4.

interval
: An integer that specifies the interval, in milliseconds, between invocations of *code* or *func*.

args...
: Any number of arbitrary values to be passed as arguments to each invocation of *func*.

Returns

A value that can be passed to `Window.clearInterval( )` to cancel the periodic execution of *code* or *func*.

Description

`setInterval()` repeatedly executes the JavaScript statements specified in the string *code*, at intervals of *interval* milliseconds.

In Netscape 4, but not IE 4, a function may be passed as the first argument instead of a string. In this form of `setInterval()`, the specified function, *func*, is repeatedly invoked, at intervals of *interval* milliseconds. Any additional argument values, *args*, passed to `setInterval()` are passed as arguments to each invocation of `func()`.

In both forms, the `setInterval()` method returns a value that can later be passed to `Window.clearInterval()` to stop *code* or *func* from being repeatedly executed.

`setInterval()` is related to `setTimeout()`. Use `setTimeout()` when you want to defer the execution of code but do not want it to be repeatedly executed.

See Also

Window.clearInterval(), Window.setTimeout()

Window.setTimeout() JavaScript 1.0

defer execution of code

Synopsis

window.setTimeout(*code, delay*)

Arguments

code
: A string that contains the JavaScript code to be executed after the *delay* has elapsed.

delay
: The amount of time, in milliseconds, before the JavaScript statements in the string *code* should be executed.

Returns

An opaque value ("timeout id") that can be passed to the `clearTimeout()` method to cancel the execution of *code*.

Description

The `setTimeout()` method defers the execution of the JavaScript statements in the string *code* for *delay* milliseconds. Once the specified number of milliseconds has elapsed, the statements in *code* are executed normally. Note that they are executed only once. To execute code repeatedly, *code* must itself contain a call to `setTimeout()` to register itself to be executed again. In JavaScript 1.2, you can use `Window.setInterval()` to register code that is executed at periodic intervals.

The statements in the string *code* are executed in the context of *window*; i.e., *window* is the current window for those statements. If more than one statement appears in *code*, the statements must be separated by semicolons.

See Also

Window.clearTimeout(), Window.setInterval()

Window.status JavaScript 1.0

specify a transient status-line message

Synopsis

window.status

Description

`status` is a read/write string property that specifies a transient message to appear in the window's status line. The message generally appears only for a limited amount of time—until it is overwritten by another message or until the user moves the mouse to some other area of the window, for example. When a message specified with `status` is erased, the status line returns to its default blank state or to the default message specified by the `defaultStatus` property.

Although only top-level windows have status lines, you can also set the `status` property of frames. Doing so displays the specified message in the top-level window's status line. Transient messages set by frames are visible regardless of which frame currently has focus or which frame the mouse is currently in. This behavior differs from that of the `defaultStatus` property.

Usage

`status` is used to display transient messages in the status line. To display semipermanent messages, use the `defaultStatus` property.

In general, setting the `status` property is useful only from event handlers and in code fragments deferred with the `Window.setTimeout()` method. If you set `status` directly from a script, the message is not visible to the user. It is not displayed right away, and when it is displayed, it is likely to be immediately overwritten by a browser message such as "Document: done".

If you want to set the `status` property in the `onmouseover` event handler of a hypertext link, you must return `true` from that event handler because when the mouse goes over a link, the default action is to display the URL of that link, thereby overwriting any status message set by the event handler. By returning `true` from the event handler, you cancel this default action and leave your own `status` message displayed (until the mouse moves off the link).

See Also

Window.defaultStatus

Window.stop( )

Netscape 4

stop loading the document

Synopsis

```
window.stop( )
```

Description

Calling `stop( )` stops the browser from loading the current document, exactly as if the user had clicked the browser's **Stop** button.

PART V

W3C DOM Reference

This part of the book is a complete reference to all of the objects, properties, functions, methods, and event handlers in the JavaScript implementation of the W3C DOM. The first few pages of this part explain how to use this reference material.

W3C DOM Reference

This part of the book is a reference section that documents the interfaces, methods, and properties defined by the W3C Level 1 and Level 2 DOM standards. Intermediate and advanced programmers who are writing for the newest generation of standards-compliant web browsers will use this reference section, in conjunction with the core and client-side JavaScript references in Parts III and IV. The introduction and sample reference page explain how to use and get the most out of this reference section. There are significant differences between this reference section and the other two, and you should read this introduction carefully so you can fully understand the reference information it contains.

Like the core and client-side references, this reference section is arranged alphabetically. The reference pages for the methods and properties of DOM interfaces are alphabetized by their full names, which include the names of the interfaces that define them. For example, if you want to read about the `appendChild()` method of the Node interface, you would look under "Node.appendChild," not just "appendChild."

To save space in this enlarged fourth edition of the book, properties in this reference section do not have reference pages of their own (all interfaces and methods do have their own reference pages, however). Instead, each property is completely documented in the reference page for the interface that defines it. For example, you can read about the `tagName` property of the Element interface in the "Element" reference page.

Sometimes you may find that you don't know the name of the interface that defines the method or property you want to look up, or you may not be sure which of the three reference sections to look up a class or interface in. Part VI of this book is a special index designed to help with these situations. Look up the name of a class, interface, method, or property, and it will tell you which reference section to look in and which class to look under in that section. For example, if you look up "Document," it will tell you that both the client-side and DOM reference sections have entries under that name. And if you look up the name "firstChild," it will tell you that `firstChild` is a property of Node, which you can read about in this DOM reference section.

Once you've found the reference page you're looking for, you shouldn't have much difficulty finding the information you need. Because the DOM standard is intended to work with languages other than JavaScript, however, it was written with typed languages (such as Java and C++) in mind. Although JavaScript is an untyped language, the property and method type information defined by the standard is still quite useful and is included in the reference pages in this section. This means that method and property synopses in this section use a syntax that is more like Java than like JavaScript. What follows is a sample reference page titled "Sample Entry" that demonstrates the structure of each reference page and explains how to interpret the information presented in each section. Even if you are already well familiar with the third edition of this book, take the time to read this page before diving into the DOM reference section.

Sample Entry

Availability

how to read DOM reference pages

Inherits from

Title and Short Description

Every reference entry begins with a four-part title block like that above. The entries are alphabetized by title. The short description, shown below the title, gives you a quick summary of the item documented in the entry; it can help you quickly decide if you're interested in reading the rest of the page.

Availability

The availability information is shown in the upper-right corner of the title block. This information tells you what level and what module of the DOM standard defines the interface or method. Since properties do not have their own reference pages, they do not have availability information. If the availability of a property is different from the availability of the interface that defines it, this fact is noted in the description of the property.

Inherits from

DOM interfaces can inherit properties and methods from other interfaces. If a DOM interface inherits from another interface, the inheritance hierarchy is shown in the lower-right corner of the title block. For example, the "Inherits from" information for the HTMLElement interface looks like this:

Node → Element → HTMLElement

This indicates that HTMLElement inherits from the Element interface, which in turn inherits from the Node interface. When you see this section, you may also want to look up the other listed interfaces.

Subinterfaces

This section contains the opposite of the "Inherits from" information: it lists any interfaces that inherit from this one. For example, the "Subinterfaces" section of the reference page for the Element interface specifies that HTMLElement is a subinterface of Element and inherits Element's methods and properties.

Also Implements

The modular structure of the DOM standard means that some interfaces have been broken into multiple separate interfaces, so that implementations have to implement only the interfaces that are part of the modules they support. It is common for an object that implements one interface (such as Document) to also implement several other simple interfaces (such as DocumentCSS, DocumentEvent, and DocumentViews) that provide functionality specific to other modules. When an interface has minor interfaces that are intended to be implemented along with it, those minor interfaces are listed in this section.

Constants

Some DOM interfaces define a set of constants that serve as the values for a property or as the arguments to a method of that interface. The Node interface, for example, defines important constants to serve as the set of legal values for the `nodeType` property of all Document nodes. When an interface defines constants, they are listed and documented in this section. The listings include the type, the name, and the value (in that order) of each constant. See the "DOM Types" section for a discussion of the syntax used in these listings. Note that constants are static properties of the interface itself, not of instances of that interface.

Properties

If the reference page documents an interface, this section lists and documents the properties defined by that interface. Each entry in the list specifies the name and type of the property and may also include other keywords that provide additional information about the property. Note that in this Java-style syntax, the name of the property comes last, and all the information that precedes the name provides type and other information about the property. For example, the HTMLTableElement and HTMLTableCellElement interfaces define properties that include the following:

`HTMLTableCaptionElement caption`
: The `caption` property. It refers to an object of type HTMLTableCaptionElement.

`readonly HTMLCollection rows`
: The `rows` property. It refers to an HTMLCollection object and is read-only: you can query the value of the property, but you cannot set it.

`deprecated String align`
: The `align` property. It is a string, but it is deprecated and its use is discouraged.

`readonly long cellIndex`
: The `cellIndex` property. It is a long integer value (see the "DOM Types" section) and is read-only.

Methods

If the reference page documents an interface, this section lists the names of the interface's methods and provides a short description of each. Full documentation for each method is found in a separate reference page.

Synopsis

If the reference page documents a method, this section presents the method signature or synopsis. This section uses a Java-style syntax to specify (in order):

- The type of the method return value, or `void` if the method does not return anything.
- The name of the method.
- The type and name (in that order) of each argument of the method. These are presented as a comma-separated list of argument types and names within parentheses. If the method does not take any arguments, you simply see the parentheses: `()`.
- The types of exceptions, if any, that the method can throw.

For example, the "Synopsis" section of the `Node.insertBefore()` method looks like this:

```
Node insertBefore(Node newChild,
                  Node refChild)
    throws DOMException;
```

You can glean the following information from this synopsis: the name of the method is "insertBefore"; it returns a Node object; the first argument is a Node object and specifies the "newChild" (presumably the one to be inserted); the second argument is also a Node object and specifies the "refChild" (presumably the node before which the other is inserted); and the method may, in some circumstances, throw an exception of type DOMException.

The subsections that follow the synopsis provide additional information about the arguments, return value, and exceptions of the method. See also the "DOM Types" section for more information about the Java-style syntax used here to specify the types of method arguments.

Arguments

If a method has arguments, the "Synopsis" section is followed by an "Arguments" subsection that lists the names of the arguments and describes each one. Note that argument names are listed in *italics*, to indicate that they are not to be typed literally but instead represent some other value or JavaScript expression. To continue with the previous example, the "Arguments" section of `Node.insertBefore()` looks like this:

newChild
: The node to be inserted into the tree. If it is a DocumentFragment, its children are inserted instead.

refChild
: The child of this node before which *newChild* is to be inserted. If this argument is `null`, *newChild* is inserted as the last child of this node.

Returns

The "Synopsis" section specifies the data type of the method's return value, and the "Returns" subsection provides additional information. If the method has no return value (i.e., if it is listed in the "Synopsis" section as returning `void`), this section is omitted.

Throws

This section explains the kinds of exceptions the method can throw and under what circumstances it throws them.

DOM Types

DOM reference pages use a Java-style syntax for specifying the types of constants, properties, method return values, and method arguments. This section provides more information about that syntax. Note that the reference pages themselves do not have "DOM Types" sections!

The general syntax is:

```
modifiers type name
```

The name of the constant, property, method, or method argument always comes last and is preceded by type and other information. The modifiers used in this reference section (note that these are not actually legal Java modifiers) are:

`readonly`
: Specifies that a property value can be queried but cannot be set.

`deprecated`
: Specifies that a property is deprecated and its use should be avoided.

`unsigned`
: Specifies that a numeric constant, property, return value, or method argument is unsigned; i.e., it may be zero or positive, but may not be negative.

The types of DOM constants, properties, method return values, and method arguments do not always correspond directly to the types supported by JavaScript. For example, some properties have a type of `short` which specifies a 16-bit integer. Although JavaScript only has a single numeric type, this reference section uses the DOM type simply because it provides more information about what range of numbers are legal. The DOM types you will encounter in this reference section are:

`String`
: A core JavaScript String object.

`Date`
: A core JavaScript Date object (this is not commonly used).

`boolean`
: A boolean value: `true` or `false`.

`short`
: A short (16-bit) integer. This type may have the `unsigned` modifier applied to it.

`long`
: A long (64-bit) integer. This type may have the `unsigned` modifier applied to it.

`float`
: A floating-point number. This type may not have the `unsigned` modifier applied to it.

`void`
: This type is used for method return values only; it indicates that the method does not return any value.

Any other type
: Any other types you see in this reference section are names of other DOM interfaces (for example, Document, DOMImplementation, Element, HTMLTableElement, and Node).

Description

Most reference pages contain a "Description" section, which is the basic description of the interface or method that is being documented. This is the heart of the reference page. If you are learning about an interface or method for the first time, you may want to skip directly to this section and then go back and look at previous sections such as "Synopsis," "Properties," and "Methods." If you are already familiar with an interface or method, you probably won't need to read this section and instead will just want to quickly look up some specific bit of information (such as the name of a property or the type of an argument from the "Properties" or "Arguments" sections).

In some pages, this section is no more than a short paragraph. In others, it may occupy a page or more. For some simple methods, the "Arguments," "Returns," and "Throws" sections document the method sufficiently by themselves, so the "Description" section is omitted.

Example

Reference pages for some commonly used interfaces and methods include an example in this section to illustrate typical usage of the interface or method. Most pages do not contain examples, however—you'll find those in first half of this book.

See Also

Most reference pages conclude with cross-references to related reference pages that may be of interest. Most of these cross-references are to other reference pages in this DOM reference section. Some are to individual property descriptions contained within an interface reference page, however, and others are to related reference pages in the client-side reference section or to chapters in the first two parts of the book.

Reference pages that document interfaces (but not those that document methods) may have additional paragraphs at the end of the "See Also" section. These are cross-references that show how the interface is used. A "Type of" paragraph lists properties whose values are objects that implement the interface. A "Passed to" paragraph lists methods that take an argument that implements the interface. A "Returned by" paragraph lists methods that return an object that implements the interface. These cross-references show how you can obtain an object of this interface and what you can do with it once you have obtained it.

AbstractView — DOM Level 2 Views

a window displaying a document

Also Implements

ViewCSS

If the DOM implementation supports the CSS module, any object that implements the AbstractView interface also implements the ViewCSS interface. For convenience, the method defined by the ViewCSS interface is listed under "Methods."

Properties

`readonly Document document`

The Document object that is displayed by this View object. This Document object also implements the DocumentView interface.

Methods

`getComputedStyle( )` *[DOM Level 2 CSS]*
: This ViewCSS method returns a read-only CSSStyleDeclaration that represents the computed style information for a specific document element.

Description

In the DOM, a *view* is an object that displays a document in some way. The Window object of client-side JavaScript is such a view. This AbstractView interface is a very preliminary step toward standardizing some of the properties and methods of the Window object. It simply specifies that all View objects have a property named `document` that refers to the document they display. In addition, if an implementation supports CSS style sheets, all View objects also implement the ViewCSS interface and define a `getComputedStyle( )` method for determining how an element is actually rendered in the view.

The `document` property gives every view a reference to the document it displays. The reverse is true also: every document has a reference to the view that displays it. If a DOM implementation supports the View module, the object that implements the Document interface also implements the DocumentView interface. This DocumentView interface defines a `defaultView` property that refers to the window in which the document is displayed.

This interface has the word "Abstract" in its name to emphasize the fact that it is merely the beginning of a standardized window interface. In order to be useful, future levels of the DOM standard will have to introduce a new interface that extends AbstractView and adds other properties or methods.

See Also

Document.defaultView

Type of: Document.defaultView

AbstractView.getComputedStyle( ) — DOM Level 2 CSS

retrieve the CSS styles used to render an element

Synopsis

```
CSSStyleDeclaration getComputedStyle(Element elt,
                                     String pseudoElt);
```

Arguments

`elt`
: The document element whose style information is desired.

`pseudoElt`
: The CSS pseudoelement, or `null` if there is none.

Returns

A read-only CSSStyleDeclaration object (which typically also implements the CSS2-Properties interface) that specifies the style information used to render the specified element in this view. Any length values queried from this object are always absolute or pixel values, not relative or percentage values.

Description

An element in a document may obtain style information from an inline `style` attribute and from any number of style sheets in the style-sheet "cascade." Before the element can actually be displayed in a view, its style must be "computed" by extracting style information from the appropriate parts of the cascade.

This method allows access to those computed styles. By contrast, the `style` property of an element gives you access only to the inline styles of an element and tells you nothing about style-sheet attributes that apply to the element. Note that this method also provides a way to determine the actual pixel coordinates at which an element is rendered in this view.

`getComputedStyle()` is actually defined by the ViewCSS interface. In any DOM implementation that supports the View and CSS modules, any object that implements AbstractView always implements ViewCSS also. So, for simplicity, this method has been listed with AbstractView.

In Internet Explorer, similar functionality is available through the nonstandard `currentStyle` property of each HTMLElement object.

See Also

CSS2Properties, CSSStyleDeclaration, HTMLElement.style

Attr

DOM Level 1 Core

an attribute of a document element

Node → Attr

Properties

`readonly String name`
: The name of the attribute.

`readonly Element ownerElement` *[DOM Level 2]*
: The Element object that contains this attribute, or `null` if the Attr object is not currently associated with any Element.

`readonly boolean specified`
: `true` if the attribute was explicitly specified in the document source or set by a script. `false` if the attribute was not explicitly specified but a default value is specified in the document's DTD.

`String value`
: The value of the attribute. When reading this property, the attribute value is returned as a string. When you set this property to a string, it automatically creates a Text node that contains the same text and makes that Text node the sole child of the Attr object.

Description

An Attr object represents an attribute of an Element node. Attr objects are associated with Element nodes but are not directly part of the document tree (and have a `null parentNode` property). You can obtain an Attr object through the `attributes` property of the Node interface or by calling the `getAttributeNode()` method of the Element interface.

Attr objects are nodes, and the value of an Attr is represented by the child nodes of the Attr node. In HTML documents, this is simply a single Text node. In XML documents, however, Attr nodes may have both Text and EntityReference children. The `value` property provides a shortcut for reading and writing the value of an attribute as a String.

In most cases, the easiest way to work with element attributes is with the `getAttribute()` and `setAttribute()` methods of the Element interface. These methods use strings for attribute names and values and avoid the use of Attr nodes altogether.

See Also

Element

Passed to: Element.removeAttributeNode(), Element.setAttributeNode(), Element.setAttributeNodeNS()

Returned by: Document.createAttribute(), Document.createAttributeNS(), Element.getAttributeNode(), Element.getAttributeNodeNS(), Element.removeAttributeNode(), Element.setAttributeNode(), Element.setAttributeNodeNS()

CDATASection — DOM Level 1 XML

a CDATA section in an XML document — Node → CharacterData → Text → CDATASection

Description

This infrequently used interface represents a CDATA section in an XML document. Programmers working with HTML documents never encounter nodes of this type and do not need to use this interface.

CDATASection is a subinterface of Text and does not define any properties or methods of its own. The textual content of the CDATA section is available through the `nodeValue` property inherited from Node or through the `data` property inherited from CharacterData. Although CDATASection nodes can often be treated in the same way as Text nodes, note that the `Node.normalize()` method does not merge adjacent CDATA sections.

See Also

CharacterData, Text

Returned by: Document.createCDATASection()

CharacterData — DOM Level 1 Core

common functionality for Text and Comment nodes — Node → CharacterData

Subinterfaces

Comment, Text

Properties

`String data`

The text contained by this node.

`readonly unsigned long length`

The number of characters contained by this node.

W3C DOM Reference

Methods

`appendData( )`
: Appends the specified string to the text contained by this node.

`deleteData( )`
: Deletes text from this node, starting with the character at the specified offset and continuing for the specified number of characters.

`insertData( )`
: Inserts the specified string into the text of this node at the specified character offset.

`replaceData( )`
: Replaces the characters starting at the specified character offset and continuing for the specified number of characters with the specified string.

`substringData( )`
: Returns a copy of the text starting at the specified character offset and continuing for the specified number of characters.

Description

CharacterData is the superinterface for Text and Comment nodes. Documents never contain CharacterData nodes; they contain only Text and Comment nodes. Since both of these node types have similar functionality, however, that functionality has been defined here so that both Text and Comment can inherit it.

See Also

Comment, Text

CharacterData.appendData( ) — DOM Level 1 Core

append a string to a Text or Comment node

Synopsis

```
void appendData(String arg)
    throws DOMException;
```

Arguments

arg
: The string to be appended to the Text or Comment node.

Throws

This method throws a DOMException with a code of `NO_MODIFICATION_ALLOWED_ERR` if called on a node that is read-only.

Description

This method appends the string *arg* to the end of the data property for this node.

CharacterData.deleteData( )

DOM Level 1 Core

delete characters from a Text or Comment node

Synopsis

```
void deleteData(unsigned long offset,
                unsigned long count)
    throws DOMException;
```

Arguments

offset
    The position of the first character to be deleted.

count
    The number of characters to be deleted.

Throws

This method may throw a DOMException with one of the following code values:

INDEX_SIZE_ERR
    The *offset* or *count* argument is negative, or *offset* is greater than the length of the Text or Comment node.

NO_MODIFICATION_ALLOWED_ERR
    The node is read-only and may not be modified.

Description

This method deletes characters from this Text or Comment node, starting with the character at the position *offset* and continuing for *count* characters. If *offset* plus *count* is greater than the number of characters in the Text or Comment node, all characters from *offset* to the end of the string are deleted.

CharacterData.insertData( )

DOM Level 1 Core

insert a string into a Text or Comment node

Synopsis

```
void insertData(unsigned long offset,
                String arg)
    throws DOMException;
```

Arguments

offset
    The character position within the Text or Comment node at which the string is to be inserted.

arg
    The string to insert.

Throws

This method may throw a DOMException with one of the following code values in the following circumstances:

`INDEX_SIZE_ERR`
: *offset* is negative or greater than the length of the Text or Comment node.

`NO_MODIFICATION_ALLOWED_ERR`
: The node is read-only and may not be modified.

Description

This method inserts the specified string *arg* into the text of a Text or Comment node at the specified position *offset*.

CharacterData.replaceData( ) DOM Level 1 Core

replace characters of a Text or Comment node with a string

Synopsis

```
void replaceData(unsigned long offset,
                 unsigned long count,
                 String arg)
   throws DOMException;
```

Arguments

offset
: The character position within the Text or Comment node at which the replacement is to begin.

count
: The number of characters to be replaced.

arg
: The string that replaces the characters specified by *offset* and *count*.

Throws

This method may throw a DOMException with one of the following code values in the following circumstances:

`INDEX_SIZE_ERR`
: *offset* is negative or greater than the length of the Text or Comment node, or *count* is negative.

`NO_MODIFICATION_ALLOWED_ERR`
: The node is read-only and may not be modified.

Description

This method replaces *count* characters starting at position *offset* with the contents of the string *arg*. If the sum of *offset* and *count* is greater than the length of the Text or Comment node, all characters from *offset* on are replaced.

CharacterData.substringData( )

DOM Level 1 Core

extract a substring from a Text or Comment node

Synopsis

```
String substringData(unsigned long offset,
                     unsigned long count)
    throws DOMException;
```

Arguments

offset
: The position of the first character to be returned.

count
: The number of characters in the substring to be returned.

Returns

A string that consists of *count* characters of the Text or Comment node starting with the character at position *offset*.

Throws

This method may throw a DOMException with one of the following code values:

`INDEX_SIZE_ERR`
: *offset* is negative or greater than the length of the Text or Comment node, or *count* is negative.

`DOMSTRING_SIZE_ERR`
: The specified range of text is too long to fit into a string in the browser's JavaScript implementation.

Description

This method extracts the substring that starts at position *offset* and continues for *count* characters from the text of a Text or Comment node. This method is useful only when the amount of text contained by the node is larger than the maximum number of characters that can fit in a string in a browser's JavaScript implementation. In this case, a JavaScript program cannot use the `data` property of the Text or Comment node directly and must instead work with shorter substrings of the node's text. This situation is unlikely to arise in practice.

Comment

DOM Level 1 Core

an HTML or XML comment

Node → CharacterData → Comment

Description

A Comment node represents a comment in an HTML or XML document. The content of the comment (i.e., the text between `<!--` and `-->`) is available through the `data` property inherited from the CharacterData interface or through the `nodeValue` property inherited from the Node interface. This content may be manipulated using the various methods inherited from CharacterData.

See Also

CharacterData

Returned by: Document.createComment()

Counter

DOM Level 2 CSS

a CSS counter( ) or counters( ) specification

Properties

`readonly String identifier`
: The name of the counter.

`readonly String listStyle`
: The list style for the counter.

`readonly String separator`
: The separator string for nested counters.

Description

This interface represents a CSS `counter()` or `counters()` value. Consult a CSS reference for more information.

See Also

Returned by: CSSPrimitiveValue.getCounterValue()

CSS2Properties

DOM Level 2 CSS2

convenience properties for all CSS2 attributes

Properties

This interface defines a large number of properties: one property for each CSS attribute defined by the CSS2 specification. The property names correspond closely to the CSS attribute names, with minor changes required to avoid syntax errors in JavaScript. Multiword attributes that contain hyphens, such as "font-family," are written without hyphens in JavaScript, and each word after the first is capitalized: `fontFamily`. Also, the "float" attribute conflicts with the reserved word `float`, so it translates to the property `cssFloat`.

The complete set of properties is listed in the following table. Since the properties correspond directly to CSS attributes, no individual documentation is given for each property. See a CSS reference, such as *Cascading Style Sheets: The Definitive Guide*, by Eric A. Meyer (O'Reilly), for the meaning and legal values of each. All of the properties are strings. Setting any of these properties may throw the same exceptions, for the same reasons as a call to `CSSStyleDeclaration.setProperty()`.

azimuth	background	backgroundAttachment	backgroundColor
backgroundImage	backgroundPosition	backgroundRepeat	border

```
borderBottom          borderBottomColor    borderBottomStyle     borderBottomWidth
borderCollapse        borderColor          borderLeft            borderLeftColor
borderLeftStyle       borderLeftWidth      borderRight           borderRightColor
borderRightStyle      borderRightWidth     borderSpacing         borderStyle
borderTop             borderTopColor       borderTopStyle        borderTopWidth
borderWidth           bottom               captionSide           clear
clip                  color                content               counterIncrement
counterReset          cssFloat             cue                   cueAfter
cueBefore             cursor               direction             display
elevation             emptyCells           font                  fontFamily
fontSize              fontSizeAdjust       fontStretch           fontStyle
fontVariant           fontWeight           height                left
letterSpacing         lineHeight           listStyle             listStyleImage
listStylePosition     listStyleType        margin                marginBottom
marginLeft            marginRight          marginTop             markerOffset
marks                 maxHeight            maxWidth              minHeight
minWidth              orphans              outline               outlineColor
outlineStyle          outlineWidth         overflow              padding
paddingBottom         paddingLeft          paddingRight          paddingTop
page                  pageBreakAfter       pageBreakBefore       pageBreakInside
pause                 pauseAfter           pauseBefore           pitch
pitchRange            playDuring           position              quotes
richness              right                size                  speak
speakHeader           speakNumeral         speakPunctuation      speechRate
stress                tableLayout          textAlign             textDecoration
textIndent            textShadow           textTransform         top
unicodeBidi           verticalAlign        visibility            voiceFamily
volume                whiteSpace           widows                width
wordSpacing           zIndex
```

Description

This interface defines one property for each CSS attribute defined by the CSS2 specification. If the DOM implementation supports this interface (which is part of the "CSS2" feature), all CSSStyleDeclaration objects also implement CSS2Properties. Reading one of the properties defined by this interface is equivalent to calling `getPropertyValue()` for the corresponding CSS attribute, and setting the value of one of these properties is equivalent to calling `setProperty()` for the corresponding attribute. The properties defined by CSS2Properties include properties that correspond to CSS shortcut attributes, and CSS2Properties handles these shortcut properties correctly.

See Also

CSSStyleDeclaration

CSSCharsetRule

DOM Level 2 CSS

an @charset rule in a CSS style sheet

CSSRule → CSSCharsetRule

Properties

`String encoding`

The character encoding specified by the `@charset` rule. If you set this property to an illegal value, a DOMException with a code of `SYNTAX_ERR` is thrown. If the rule or style sheet is read-only, an attempt to set this property throws a DOMException with a code of `NO_MODIFICATION_ALLOWED_ERR`.

Description

This interface represents an `@charset` rule in a CSS style sheet. Consult a CSS reference for details.

CSSFontFaceRule

DOM Level 2 CSS

an @font-face rule in a CSS style sheet

CSSRule → CSSFontFaceRule

Properties

`readonly CSSStyleDeclaration style`

The set of styles for this rule.

Description

This interface represents an `@font-face` rule in a CSS style sheet. Consult a CSS reference for details.

CSSImportRule

DOM Level 2 CSS

an @import rule in a CSS style sheet

CSSRule → CSSImportRule

Properties

`readonly String href`

The URL of the imported style sheet. The value of this property does not include the "url()" delimiter around the URL value.

`readonly MediaList media`

A list of media types to which the imported style sheet applies.

`readonly CSSStyleSheet styleSheet`

The CSSStyleSheet object that represents the imported style sheet, or `null` if the style sheet has not yet been loaded or if the style sheet was not loaded because, for example, the media type did not apply.

Description

This interface represents an `@import` rule in a CSS style sheet. The `styleSheet` property represents the imported style sheet.

CSSMediaRule

DOM Level 2 CSS

an @media rule in a CSS style sheet

CSSRule → CSSMediaRule

Properties

`readonly CSSRuleList cssRules`

An array (technically, a CSSRuleList) of all the rules nested within this `@media` rule block.

`readonly MediaList media`

The list of media types to which the nested rules apply.

Methods

`deleteRule( )`

Deletes the nested rule at the specified position.

`insertRule( )`

Inserts a new rule at the specified position within this `@media` rule block.

Description

This interface represents an `@media` rule, and all of its nested rules, in a CSS style sheet. It defines methods that allow you to insert and delete nested rules. Consult a CSS reference for details.

CSSMediaRule.deleteRule( )

DOM Level 2 CSS

delete a rule in an @media block

Synopsis

```
void deleteRule(unsigned long index)
    throws DOMException;
```

Arguments

index

The position within the `@media` rule block of the rule to be deleted.

Throws

This method throws a DOMException with one of the following `code` values in the following circumstances:

`INDEX_SIZE_ERR`

index is negative or is greater than or equal to the number of rules in `cssRules`.

`NO_MODIFICATION_ALLOWED_ERR`

The rule is read-only.

Description

This method deletes the rule at the specified position in the `cssRules` array.

CSSMediaRule.insertRule( )

DOM Level 2 CSS

insert a new rule into an @media block

Synopsis

```
unsigned long insertRule(String rule,
                         unsigned long index)
    throws DOMException;
```

Arguments

rule
The complete, parseable CSS string representation of the rule to be added.

index
The position at which the new rule is to be inserted into the `cssRules` array, or the `cssRules.length` to append the new rule at the end of the array.

Returns

The value of the *index* argument.

Throws

This method throws a DOMException with one of the following code values in the following circumstances:

`HIERARCHY_REQUEST_ERR`
CSS syntax does not allow the specified *rule* at the specified position.

`INDEX_SIZE_ERR`
index is negative or greater than `cssRules.length`.

`NO_MODIFICATION_ALLOWED_ERR`
This `@media` rule and its `cssRules` array are read-only.

`SYNTAX_ERR`
The specified *rule* contains a syntax error.

Description

This method inserts the specified *rule* into the `cssRules` array at the specified *index*.

CSSPageRule

DOM Level 2 CSS

an @page rule in a CSS style sheet

CSSRule → CSSPageRule

Properties

`String selectorText`
The page selector text for this rule. Setting this property to an illegal value throws a DOMException with a code of `SYNTAX_ERR`. Setting this property when the rule is read-only throws a DOMException with a code of `NO_MODIFICATION_ALLOWED_ERR`.

`readonly CSSStyleDeclaration style`
The set of styles for this rule.

Description

This interface represents an @page rule in a CSS style sheet, which is typically used to specify the page layout for printing. Consult a CSS reference for details.

CSSPrimitiveValue

DOM Level 2 CSS

a single CSS style value

CSSValue → CSSPrimitiveValue

Constants

The following constants are the legal values for the primitiveType property. They specify the type of the value and, for numeric values, the units in which the value is represented.

unsigned short CSS_UNKNOWN = 0
: The value is not recognized, and the implementation does not know how to parse it. The textual representation of the value is available through the cssText property.

unsigned short CSS_NUMBER = 1
: A unitless number. Query with getFloatValue( ).

unsigned short CSS_PERCENTAGE = 2
: A percentage. Query with getFloatValue( ).

unsigned short CSS_EMS = 3
: A relative length measured in ems (the height of the current font). Query with getFloatValue( ).

unsigned short CSS_EXS = 4
: A relative length measured in exs (the "x-height" of the current font). Query with getFloatValue( ).

unsigned short CSS_PX = 5
: A length measured in pixels. Query with getFloatValue( ). Pixel lengths are relative measurements, in the sense that their size depends on the display resolution, and they cannot be converted to inches, millimeters, points, or other absolute lengths. However, pixels are also one of the most commonly used units, and they are treated as absolute values for the purposes of AbstractView.getComputedStyle( ), for example.

unsigned short CSS_CM = 6
: An absolute length measured in centimeters. Query with getFloatValue( ).

unsigned short CSS_MM = 7
: An absolute length measured in millimeters. Query with getFloatValue( ).

unsigned short CSS_IN = 8
: An absolute length measured in inches. Query with getFloatValue( ).

unsigned short CSS_PT = 9
: An absolute length measured in points (1/72 of an inch). Query with getFloatValue( ).

unsigned short CSS_PC = 10
: An absolute length measured in picas (12 points). Query with getFloatValue( ).

unsigned short CSS_DEG = 11
: An angle measured in degrees. Query with getFloatValue( ).

unsigned short CSS_RAD = 12
: An angle measured in radians. Query with getFloatValue( ).

`unsigned short CSS_GRAD = 13`
: An angle measured in grads. Query with `getFloatValue()`.

`unsigned short CSS_MS = 14`
: A time measured in milliseconds. Query with `getFloatValue()`.

`unsigned short CSS_S = 15`
: A time measured in seconds. Query with `getFloatValue()`.

`unsigned short CSS_HZ = 16`
: A frequency measured in hertz. Query with `getFloatValue()`.

`unsigned short CSS_KHZ = 17`
: A frequency measured in kilohertz. Query with `getFloatValue()`.

`unsigned short CSS_DIMENSION = 18`
: A unitless dimension. Query with `getFloatValue()`.

`unsigned short CSS_STRING = 19`
: A string. Query with `getStringValue()`.

`unsigned short CSS_URI = 20`
: A URI. Query with `getStringValue()`.

`unsigned short CSS_IDENT = 21`
: An identifier. Query with `getStringValue()`.

`unsigned short CSS_ATTR = 22`
: An attribute function. Query with `getStringValue()`.

`unsigned short CSS_COUNTER = 23`
: A counter. Query with `getCounterValue()`.

`unsigned short CSS_RECT = 24`
: A rectangle. Query with `getRectValue()`.

`unsigned short CSS_RGBCOLOR = 25`
: A color. Query with `getRGBColorValue()`.

Properties

`readonly unsigned short primitiveType`
: The type of this value. This property holds one of the constants defined in the previous section.

Methods

`getCounterValue()`
: For values of type `CSS_COUNTER`, returns the Counter object that represents the value.

`getFloatValue()`
: Returns a numeric value, converting it, if necessary, to the specified units.

`getRectValue()`
: For values of type `CSS_RECT`, returns the Rect object that represents the value.

`getRGBColorValue()`
: For values of type `CSS_RGBCOLOR`, returns the RGBColor object that represents the value.

`getStringValue( )`
: Returns the value as a string.

`setFloatValue( )`
: Sets a numeric value to the specified number of the specified units.

`setStringValue( )`
: Sets a string value to the specified string of the specified type.

Description

This subinterface of CSSValue represents a single CSS value. Contrast it with the CSSValue-List interface, which represents a list of CSS values. The word "primitive" in the name of this interface is misleading; this interface can represent some complex types of CSS values, such as counters, rectangles, and colors.

The `primitiveType` property holds one of the previously defined constants and specifies the type of the value. The various methods defined by this interface allow you to query values of various types and also to set numeric and string values.

See Also

Counter, CSSValue, CSSValueList, Rect, RGBColor

Type of: RGBColor.blue, RGBColor.green, RGBColor.red, Rect.bottom, Rect.left, Rect.right, Rect.top

CSSPrimitiveValue.getCounterValue( ) — DOM Level 2 CSS

return a Counter value

Synopsis

```
Counter getCounterValue( )
    throws DOMException;
```

Returns

The Counter object that represents the value of this CSSPrimitiveValue.

Throws

This method throws a DOMException with a code of `INVALID_ACCESS_ERR` if the `primitiveType` property is not `CSS_COUNTER`.

Description

This method returns a Counter object that represents a CSS counter. There is no corresponding `setCounterValue( )`, but you can modify the value by setting the properties of the returned Counter object.

CSSPrimitiveValue.getFloatValue( ) — DOM Level 2 CSS

get a numeric value, possibly converting units

Synopsis

```
float getFloatValue(unsigned short unitType)
    throws DOMException;
```

Arguments

unitType
: One of the CSSPrimitiveValue type constants that specifies the desired units for the returned value.

Returns

The floating-point numeric value of this CSSPrimitiveValue, expressed in the specified units.

Throws

This method throws a DOMException with a code of `INVALID_ACCESS_ERR` if this CSSPrimitiveValue holds a non-numeric value, or if the value cannot be converted to the requested type of units. (See the next section for more about unit conversion.)

Description

For CSSPrimitiveValue objects that hold numeric values, this method converts those values to the specified units and returns the converted values.

Only certain types of unit conversions are allowed. Lengths may be converted to lengths, angles to angles, times to times, and frequencies to frequencies. Obviously, however, a length measured in millimeters cannot be converted to a frequency measured in kilohertz. Also, not all lengths can be converted. Relative lengths (lengths measured in ems, exs, or pixels) can be converted to other relative lengths but cannot be converted to absolute lengths. Similarly, absolute lengths cannot be converted to relative lengths. Finally, percentage values cannot be converted to any other unit type, except for color percentage values, which express a percentage of 255 and can be converted to the `CSS_NUMBER` type.

CSSPrimitiveValue.getRectValue( ) — DOM Level 2 CSS

return a Rect value

Synopsis

```
Rect getRectValue( )
    throws DOMException;
```

Returns

The Rect object that represents the value of this CSSPrimitiveValue.

Throws

This method throws a DOMException with a code of `INVALID_ACCESS_ERR` if the `primitiveType` property is not `CSS_RECT`.

Description

This method returns a Rect object that represents a CSS rectangle. There is no corresponding `setRectValue( )` method, but you can modify the value by setting the properties of the returned Rect object.

CSSPrimitiveValue.getRGBColorValue( ) — DOM Level 2 CSS

get the RGBColor value

Synopsis

```
RGBColor getRGBColorValue( )
    throws DOMException;
```

Returns

The RGBColor object that represents the value of this CSSPrimitiveValue.

Throws

This method throws a DOMException with a code of `INVALID_ACCESS_ERR` if the `primitiveType` property is not `CSS_RGBCOLOR`.

Description

This method returns an RGBColor object that represents a color. There is no corresponding `setRGBColorValue( )` method, but you can modify the value by setting the properties of the returned RGBColor object.

CSSPrimitiveValue.getStringValue( ) — DOM Level 2 CSS

query a CSS string value

Synopsis

```
String getStringValue( )
    throws DOMException;
```

Returns

The string value of this CSSPrimitiveValue.

Throws

This method throws a DOMException with a code of `INVALID_ACCESS_ERR` if the `primitiveType` property is not `CSS_STRING`, `CSS_URI`, `CSS_IDENT`, or `CSS_ATTR`.

CSSPrimitiveValue.setFloatValue( )

DOM Level 2 CSS

set the numeric value

Synopsis

```
void setFloatValue(unsigned short unitType,
                   float floatValue)
    throws DOMException;
```

Arguments

unitType
: One of the CSSPrimitiveValue constants that specifies the numeric type units for this value.

floatValue
: The new value (measured in *unitType* units).

Throws

This method throws a DOMException with a code of `NO_MODIFICATION_ALLOWED_ERR` if the CSS attribute with which this value is associated is read-only. It throws a DOMException with a code of `INVALID_ACCESS_ERR` if that CSS attribute does not allow numeric values or does not allow values with the specified *unitType*.

Description

This method specifies the unit type and numeric value for this CSSPrimitiveValue.

CSSPrimitiveValue.setStringValue( )

DOM Level 2 CSS

set the string value

Synopsis

```
void setStringValue(unsigned short stringType,
                    String stringValue)
    throws DOMException;
```

Arguments

stringType
: The type of the string being set. This must be one of the CSSPrimitiveValue constants `CSS_STRING`, `CSS_URI`, `CSS_IDENT`, or `CSS_ATTR`.

stringValue
: The new string value to be set.

Throws

This method throws a DOMException with a code of `NO_MODIFICATION_ALLOWED_ERR` if the CSS attribute with which this value is associated is read-only. It throws a DOMException with a code of `INVALID_ACCESS_ERR` if that CSS attribute does not allow string values or does not allow values with the specified *stringType*.

Description

This method sets the string value and string type for this CSSPrimitiveValue.

CSSRule

DOM Level 2 CSS

a rule in a CSS style sheet

Subinterfaces

CSSCharsetRule, CSSFontFaceRule, CSSImportRule, CSSMediaRule, CSSPageRule, CSS-StyleRule, CSSUnknownRule

Constants

These constants represent the various types of rules that may appear in a CSS style sheet. They are the legal values of the type property, and they specify which of the above subinterfaces this object implements.

```
unsigned short UNKNOWN_RULE = 0;     // CSSUnknownRule
unsigned short STYLE_RULE = 1;       // CSSStyleRule
unsigned short CHARSET_RULE = 2;     // CSSCharsetRule
unsigned short IMPORT_RULE = 3;      // CSSImportRule
unsigned short MEDIA_RULE = 4;       // CSSMediaRule
unsigned short FONT_FACE_RULE = 5;   // CSSFontFaceRule
unsigned short PAGE_RULE = 6;        // CSSPageRule
```

Properties

`String cssText`

The textual representation of the rule. If you set this property, it may throw a DOMException with one of the following code values for one of the following reasons:

`HIERARCHY_REQUEST_ERR`

The specified rule is not legal at this location in the style sheet.

`INVALID_MODIFICATION_ERR`

The new value of the property is a rule of a different type than the original value.

`NO_MODIFICATION_ALLOWED_ERR`

The rule or the style sheet that contains it is read-only.

`SYNTAX_ERR`

The specified string is not legal CSS syntax.

`readonly CSSRule parentRule`

The containing rule of this rule, or `null` if this rule does not have a parent. An example of a CSS rule with a parent is a style rule within an `@media` rule.

`readonly CSSStyleSheet parentStyleSheet`

The CSSStyleSheet object that contains this rule.

`readonly unsigned short type`

The type of CSS rule this object represents. The legal values for this property are the previously listed constants. This CSSRule interface is never implemented directly, and the value of this property specifies which more specific subinterface is implemented by this object.

W3C DOM Reference

Description

This interface defines properties that are common to all types of rules in CSS style sheets. No object directly implements this interface; instead, they implement one of the more specific subinterfaces listed earlier. The most important subinterface is probably CSSStyleRule, which describes a CSS rule that defines a document style.

See Also

CSSStyleRule

Type of: CSSRule.parentRule, CSSStyleDeclaration.parentRule, CSSStyleSheet.ownerRule

Returned by: CSSRuleList.item( )

CSSRuleList — DOM Level 2 CSS

an array of CSSRule objects

Properties

`readonly unsigned long length`
  The number of CSSRule objects in this CSSRuleList array.

Methods

`item( )`
  Returns the CSSRule object at the specified position. Instead of explicitly calling this method, JavaScript allows you to simply treat the CSSRuleList object as an array and to index it using standard square-bracket array notation. If the specified index is too large, this method returns `null`.

Description

This interface defines a read-only ordered list (i.e., an array) of CSSRule objects. The `length` property specifies the number of rules in the list, and the `item( )` method allows you to retrieve the rule at a specified position. In JavaScript, CSSRuleList objects behave like JavaScript arrays, and you can query an element from the list using square-bracket array notation instead of calling the `item( )` method. (Note, however, that you cannot assign new nodes into a CSSRuleList using square brackets.)

See Also

Type of: CSSMediaRule.cssRules, CSSStyleSheet.cssRules

CSSRuleList.item( ) — DOM Level 2 CSS

get the CSSRule at the specified position

Synopsis

```
CSSRule item(unsigned long index);
```

Arguments

index

The position of the rule to retrieve.

Returns

The CSSRule object at the specified position, or `null` if *index* is not a valid position.

CSSStyleDeclaration — DOM Level 2 CSS

a set of CSS style attributes and their values

Also Implements

If the implementation supports the "CSS2" feature in addition to the "CSS" feature (as most web browsers do), all objects that implement this interface also implement the CSS2Properties interface. CSS2Properties provides commonly used shortcut properties for setting and querying the values of CSS attributes. See "CSS2Properties" for details.

Properties

`String cssText`

The textual representation of the style attributes and their values. This property consists of the complete text of the style rule, minus the element selector and the curly braces that surround the attributes and values. Setting this property to an illegal value throws a DOMException with a code of `SYNTAX_ERR`. Setting it for a read-only style sheet or rule throws a DOMException with a code of `NO_MODIFICATION_ALLOWED_ERR`.

`readonly unsigned long length`

The number of style attributes in this style declaration.

`readonly CSSRule parentRule`

The CSSRule object that contains this CSSStyleDeclaration, or `null` if this style declaration is not part of a CSS rule (such as for CSSStyleDeclaration objects that represent inline HTML style attributes).

Methods

`getPropertyCSSValue()`

Returns a CSSValue object that represents the value of the named CSS attribute, or `null` if that attribute is not explicitly set in this style declaration block or if the named style is a "shortcut" attribute.

`getPropertyPriority()`

Returns the string "important" if the named CSS attribute is explicitly set in this declaration block and has the `!important` priority qualifier specified. If the attribute is not specified, or has no priority, returns the empty string.

`getPropertyValue()`

Returns the value of the named CSS attribute as a string. Returns the empty string if the attribute is not specified in this declaration block.

`item( )`
: Returns the name of the CSS attribute at the specified position in this style declaration block. In JavaScript, the CSSStyleDeclaration object can be treated as an array and indexed using square brackets instead. See also the `length` property.

`removeProperty( )`
: Deletes a named CSS attribute from this declaration block.

`setProperty( )`
: Sets a named CSS attribute to the specified string value and priority for this declaration block.

Description

This attribute represents a CSS *style declaration block*: a set of CSS attributes and their values, separated from each other by semicolons. The style declaration block is the portion of a style rule within curly braces in a CSS style sheet. The value of the HTML `style` attribute also constitutes a style declaration block.

The `item( )` method and the `length` property allow you to loop through the names of all CSS attributes specified in this declaration block. In JavaScript, you can also simply treat the CSSStyleDeclaration object as an array and index it using square-bracket notation instead of calling the `item( )` method explicitly. Once you have the names of the CSS attributes specified in this declaration, you can use other methods of this interface to query the values of those attributes. `getPropertyValue( )` returns the value as a string, and `getPropertyCSSValue( )` returns the attribute value as a CSSValue object. (Note that the DOM API refers to CSS style attributes as "properties." I use the term "attributes" here to avoid confusing them with JavaScript object properties.)

In most web browsers, every object that implements CSSStyleDeclaration also implements the CSS2Properties interface, which defines an object property for each CSS attribute defined by the CSS2 specification. You can read and write the values of these convenience properties instead of calling `getPropertyValue( )` and `setProperty( )`.

See Also

CSS2Properties

Type of: CSSFontFaceRule.style, CSSPageRule.style, CSSStyleRule.style, HTMLElement.style

Returned by: Document.getOverrideStyle( ), AbstractView.getComputedStyle( )

CSSStyleDeclaration.getPropertyCSSValue( ) — DOM Level 2 CSS

return a CSS attribute value as an object

Synopsis

```
CSSValue getPropertyCSSValue(String propertyName);
```

Arguments

propertyName
    The name of the desired CSS attribute.

Returns

A CSSValue object that represents the value of the named attribute if it is explicitly specified in this style declaration, or `null` if the named attribute is not specified. This method also returns `null` if *propertyName* specifies a CSS shorthand attribute, since shorthand attributes specify more than one value and cannot be represented with CSSValue objects.

CSSStyleDeclaration.getPropertyPriority( ) — DOM Level 2 CSS

get the priority of a CSS attribute

Synopsis

```
String getPropertyPriority(String propertyName);
```

Arguments

propertyName
    The name of the CSS attribute.

Returns

The string "important" if the named CSS attribute is explicitly specified in this declaration block and has the `!important` priority modifier. Returns the empty string otherwise.

CSSStyleDeclaration.getPropertyValue( ) — DOM Level 2 CSS

get the value of a CSS attribute as a string

Synopsis

```
String getPropertyValue(String propertyName);
```

Arguments

propertyName
    The name of the CSS attribute whose value is desired.

Returns

The string value of the named CSS attribute, or the empty string if that attribute is not explicitly set in this declaration block.

Description

This method returns the value of the named CSS attribute as a string. Unlike `getPropertyCSSValue( )`, this method works with shortcut attributes as well as regular attributes. See also the various convenience properties of the CSS2Properties interface.

CSSStyleDeclaration.item( ) DOM Level 2 CSS

get the CSS attribute name at the specified position

Synopsis

```
String item(unsigned long index);
```

Arguments

index
The position of the desired CSS attribute name.

Returns

The name of the CSS attribute at *index*, or the empty string if *index* is negative or greater than or equal to the `length` property.

Description

The CSSStyleDeclaration interface represents a collection of CSS style attributes and their values. This method allows you to query the name of the CSS attribute by position and, in conjunction with the `length` property, allows you to iterate through the set of CSS attributes specified in this style declaration. Note that the order of CSS attributes as returned by this method does not necessarily correspond to the order in which they appear in the document or style sheet source.

As an alternative to this `item( )` method, JavaScript allows you to simply treat a CSSStyle-Declaration object as an array of CSS attribute names and use standard square-bracket array syntax to obtain the attribute name at a specified position.

CSSStyleDeclaration.removeProperty( ) DOM Level 2 CSS

delete a CSS attribute specification

Synopsis

```
String removeProperty(String propertyName)
    throws DOMException;
```

Arguments

propertyName
The name of the CSS attribute to be deleted.

Returns

The value of the named CSS attribute as a string, or the empty string if the named attribute is not explicitly specified in this style declaration.

Throws

If this style declaration is read-only, this method throws a DOMException with a code of `NO_MODIFICATION_ALLOWED_ERR`.

Description

This method deletes a named attribute from this style declaration block and returns the value of the attribute.

CSSStyleDeclaration.setProperty( )

DOM Level 2 CSS

set a CSS style attribute

Synopsis

```
void setProperty(String propertyName,
                 String value,
                 String priority)
    throws DOMException;
```

Arguments

propertyName
: The name of the CSS attribute to set.

value
: The new value of the attribute, as a string.

priority
: The new priority of the attribute. This argument should be "important" if the attribute specification is `!important`; otherwise, it should be the empty string.

Throws

This method throws a DOMException with a code of `SYNTAX_ERR` if the specified *value* argument is malformed. It throws a DOMException with a code of `NO_MODIFICATION_ALLOWED_ERR` if the style declaration or the attribute being set is read-only.

Description

This method adds the named CSS attribute with its value and priority to this style declaration, or, if the declaration already contains a value for the named attribute, it simply sets the value and priority for that existing attribute.

Using `setProperty()` to add a new CSS attribute to a style declaration may insert the new attribute at any position and may, in fact, totally shuffle the order of all existing attributes. Therefore, you should not use `setProperty()` while you are iterating through the set of attribute names with the `item()` method.

CSSStyleRule

DOM Level 2 CSS

a style rule in a CSS style sheet

CSSRule → CSSStyleRule

Properties

`String selectorText`
: The selector text that specifies the document elements this style rule applies to. Setting this property raises a DOMException with a code of `NO_MODIFICATION_ALLOWED_ERR` if

W3C DOM Reference

the rule is read-only, or a code of `SYNTAX_ERR` if the new value does not follow CSS syntax rules.

`readonly CSSStyleDeclaration style`
: The style values that should be applied to elements specified by `selectorText`.

Description

This interface represents a style rule in a CSS style sheet. Style rules are the most common and important kinds of rules in style sheets: they specify style information that is to be applied to a specific set of document elements. `selectorText` is the string representation of the element selector for this rule, and `style` is a CSSStyleDeclaration object that represents the set of style names and values to apply to the selected elements.

See Also

CSSStyleDeclaration

CSSStyleSheet

DOM Level 2 CSS

a CSS style sheet

StyleSheet → CSSStyleSheet

Properties

`readonly CSSRuleList cssRules`
: An array (technically, a CSSRuleList) of the CSSRule objects that comprise the style sheet. This includes all at-rules in addition to the actual style rules.

`readonly CSSRule ownerRule`
: If this style sheet was imported by an `@import` rule in another style sheet, this property holds the CSSImportRule object that represents that `@import` rule. Otherwise, it is `null`. When this property is non-`null`, the inherited `ownerNode` property is `null`.

Methods

`deleteRule()`
: Deletes the rule at the specified position.

`insertRule()`
: Inserts a new rule at the specified position.

Description

This interface represents a CSS style sheet. The `cssRules` property lists the rules contained in the style sheet, and the `insertRule()` and `deleteRule()` methods allow you to add and delete rules from that list.

See Also

StyleSheet

Type of: CSSImportRule.styleSheet, CSSRule.parentStyleSheet

Returned by: DOMImplementation.createCSSStyleSheet()

CSSStyleSheet.deleteRule( )

DOM Level 2 CSS

delete a rule from a style sheet

Synopsis

```
void deleteRule(unsigned long index)
    throws DOMException;
```

Arguments

index
: The index within the cssRules array of the rule to be deleted.

Throws

This method throws a DOMException with a code of INDEX_SIZE_ERR if *index* is negative or greater than or equal to cssRules.length. It throws a DOMException with a code of NO_MODIFICATION_ALLOWED_ERR if this style sheet is read-only.

Description

This method deletes the rule at the specified *index* from the cssRules array.

CSSStyleSheet.insertRule( )

DOM Level 2 CSS

insert a rule into a style sheet

Synopsis

```
unsigned long insertRule(String rule,
                         unsigned long index)
    throws DOMException;
```

Arguments

rule
: The complete, parseable text representation of the rule to be added to the style sheet. For style rules, this includes both the element selector and the style information.

index
: The position in the cssRules array at which the rule is to be inserted or appended.

Returns

The value of the *index* argument.

Throws

This method throws a DOMException with one of the following code values in the following circumstances:

HIERARCHY_REQUEST_ERR
: CSS syntax does not allow the specified rule at the specified location.

INDEX_SIZE_ERR
: *index* is negative or greater then cssRules.length.

`NO_MODIFICATION_ALLOWED_ERR`
The style sheet is read-only.

`SYNTAX_ERR`
The specified *rule* text contains a syntax error.

Description

This method inserts (or appends) a new CSS *rule* at the specified *index* of the `cssRules` array of this style sheet.

CSSUnknownRule

DOM Level 2 CSS

an unrecognized rule in a CSS style sheet

CSSRule → CSSUnknownRule

Description

This interface represents a rule in a CSS style sheet that the browser did not recognize and could not parse (typically because it is defined by a version of the CSS standard that the browser does not support). Note that this interface does not define any properties or methods of its own. The text of the unrecognized rule is available through the inherited `cssText` property.

CSSValue

DOM Level 2 CSS

the value of a CSS style attribute

Subinterfaces

CSSPrimitiveValue, CSSValueList

Constants

The following constants specify the valid values for the `cssValueType` property:

`unsigned short CSS_INHERIT = 0`
This constant represents the special value "inherit", which means that the actual value of the CSS style attribute is inherited. The `cssText` property is "inherit" in this case.

`unsigned short CSS_PRIMITIVE_VALUE = 1`
The value is a primitive value. This CSSValue object also implements the more specific CSSPrimitiveValue subinterface.

`unsigned short CSS_VALUE_LIST = 2`
The value is a compound value consisting of a list of values. This CSSValue object also implements the more specific CSSValueList subinterface and behaves as an array of CSSValue objects.

`unsigned short CSS_CUSTOM = 3`
This constant is defined to allow extensions to the CSS object model. It specifies that this CSSValue represents a value of some type that is not defined by the CSS or DOM standards. If you are working with an implementation that supports such extensions, the CSSValue object may also implement some other interface (such as the SVGColor interface defined by the Scalable Vector Graphics standard) that you can use.

Properties

`String cssText`

The textual representation of the value. Setting this property may throw a DOMException. A code of `SYNTAX_ERR` indicates that the new value does not follow legal CSS syntax. A code of `INVALID_MODIFICATION_ERR` specifies that you tried to set a value of a different type than the original value. A code of `NO_MODIFICATION_ALLOWED_ERR` indicates that the value is read-only.

`readonly unsigned short cssValueType`

The kind of value this object represents. The four legal values of this property are defined by the previously listed constants.

Description

This interface represents the value of a CSS attribute. The `cssText` property gives the value in textual form. If the `cssValueType` property is `CSSValue.CSS_PRIMITIVE_VALUE`, this CSSValue object also implements the more specific CSSPrimitiveValue interface. If `cssValueType` is `CSSValue.CSS_VALUE_LIST`, this CSSValue represents a list of values and also implements the CSSValueList interface.

See Also

CSSPrimitiveValue, CSSValueList

Returned by: CSSStyleDeclaration.getPropertyCSSValue( ), CSSValueList.item( )

CSSValueList

DOM Level 2 CSS

a CSSValue that holds an array of CSSValue objects

CSSValue → CSSValueList

Properties

`readonly unsigned long length`

The number of CSSValue objects in this array.

Methods

`item( )`

Returns the CSSValue object at the specified position in the array, or `null` if the specified position is negative or if it is greater than or equal to `length`.

Description

This interface represents an array of CSSValue objects and is itself a type of CSSValue. The `item( )` method can be used to retrieve the CSSValue object at a specified position, but in JavaScript, it is easier to simply index the array using standard square-bracket notation.

The order of CSSValue objects in a CSSValueList array is the order in which they appear in the CSS style declaration. Some CSS attributes whose value is a CSSValueList may also have the value none. This special value translates into a CSSValueList object with a `length` of 0.

CSSValueList.item( ) DOM Level 2 CSS

get the CSSValue at the specified position

Synopsis

```
CSSValue item(unsigned long index);
```

Arguments

index
: The position of the desired CSSValue.

Returns

The CSSValue object at the specified position in this CSSValueList, or `null` if *`index`* is negative or is greater than or equal to `length`.

Document DOM Level 1 Core

an HTML or XML document Node → Document

Subinterfaces

HTMLDocument

Also Implements

DocumentCSS
: If the implementation supports the CSS module, the object that implements this Document interface also implements the DocumentCSS interface and its `getOverrideStyle( )` method.

DocumentEvent
: If the implementation supports the Events module, the object that implements this Document interface also implements the DocumentEvent interface and its `createEvent( )` method.

DocumentRange
: If the implementation supports the Range module, the object that implements this Document interface also implements the DocumentRange interface and its `createRange( )` method.

DocumentStyle
: If the implementation supports the StyleSheets module, the object that implements this Document interface also implements the DocumentStyle interface and its `styleSheets` property.

DocumentTraversal
: If the implementation supports the Traversal module, the object that implements this Document interface also implements the DocumentTraversal interface and its `createNodeIterator( )` and `createTreeWalker( )` methods.

DocumentView
: If the implementation supports the Views module, the object that implements this Document interface also implements the DocumentView interface and its `defaultView` property.

Because these interfaces define commonly implemented additions to the Document interface, their properties and methods are listed and documented here, as if they were directly part of the Document interface.

Properties

`readonly AbstractView defaultView` *[DOM Level 2 Views]*
: The default view of this document. In a web-browser environment, this property specifies the Window object (which implements the AbstractView interface) in which the document is displayed.

  Note that this property is technically part of the DocumentView interface; it is defined by the Document object only in implementations that support the Views module.

`readonly DocumentType doctype`
: For XML documents with a `<!DOCTYPE>` declaration, specifies a DocumentType node that represents the document's DTD. For HTML documents and for XML documents with no `<!DOCTYPE>`, this property is `null`. Note that the property is read-only, and the node to which it refers is also read-only.

`readonly Element documentElement`
: A reference to the root element of the document. For HTML documents, this property is always the Element object representing the `<html>` tag. This root element is also available through the `childNodes[]` array inherited from Node.

`readonly DOMImplementation implementation`
: The DOMImplementation object that represents the implementation that created this document.

`readonly StyleSheetList styleSheets` *[DOM Level 2 StyleSheets]*
: A collection of objects representing all style sheets embedded in or linked into a document. In HTML documents, this includes style sheets defined with `<link>` and `<style>` tags.

  Note that this property is technically part of the DocumentStyle interface; it is defined by the Document object only in implementations that support the StyleSheets module.

Methods

`createAttribute()`
: Creates a new Attr node with the specified name.

`createAttributeNS()` *[DOM Level 2]*
: Creates a new Attr node with the specified name and namespace.

`createCDATASection()`
: Creates a new CDATASection node containing the specified text.

`createComment()`
: Creates a new Comment node containing the specified string.

`createDocumentFragment()`
: Creates a new, empty DocumentFragment node.

`createElement()`
: Creates a new Element node with the specified tag name.

`createElementNS()` *[DOM Level 2]*
: Creates a new Element node with the specified tag name and namespace.

`createEntityReference()`
Creates a new EntityReference node that refers to an entity with the specified name. If the DocumentType object for this document defines an Entity with that name, the newly created EntityReference node is given the same read-only children that the Entity node has.

`createEvent()` *[DOM Level 2 Events]*
Creates a new synthetic Event object of the named type. Technically, this method is defined by the DocumentEvent interface; it is implemented by the Document object only in implementations that support the Events module.

`createNodeIterator()` *[DOM Level 2 Traversal]*
Creates a NodeIterator object. This method is technically part of the DocumentTraversal interface; it is implemented by the Document object only in implementations that support the Traversal module.

`createProcessingInstruction()`
Creates a new ProcessingInstruction node with the specified target and data string.

`createRange()` *[DOM Level 2 Range]*
Creates a new Range object. This method is technically part of the DocumentRange interface; it is implemented by the Document object only in implementations that support the Range module.

`createTextNode()`
Creates a new Text node to represent the specified text.

`createTreeWalker()` *[DOM Level 2 Traversal]*
Creates a TreeWalker object. This method is technically part of the DocumentTraversal interface; it is implemented by the Document object only in implementations that support the Traversal module.

`getElementById()` *[DOM Level 2]*
Returns a descendant Element of this document that has the specified value for its `id` attribute, or `null` if no such Element exists in the document.

`getElementsByTagName()`
Returns an array (technically a NodeList) of all Element nodes in this document that have the specified tag name. The Element nodes appear in the returned array in the order in which they appear in the document source.

`getElementsByTagNameNS()` *[DOM Level 2]*
Returns an array of all Element nodes that have the specified tag name and namespace.

`getOverrideStyle()` *[DOM Level 2 CSS]*
Gets the CSS override style information for the specified Element (and an optional named pseudoelement). This method is technically part of the DocumentCSS interface; it is implemented by the Document object only in implementations that support the CSS module.

`importNode()` *[DOM Level 2]*
Makes a copy of a node from some other document that is suitable for insertion into this document.

Description

The Document interface is the root node of a document tree. A Document node may have multiple children, but only one of those children may be an Element node: it is the root element of the document. The root element is most easily accessed through the `documentElement` property. The `doctype` and `implementation` properties provide access to the DocumentType object (if any) and the DOMImplementation object for this document.

Most of the methods defined by the Document interface are "factory methods" that are used to create various types of nodes that can be inserted into this document. The notable exceptions are `getElementById( )` and `getElementsByTagName( )`, which are quite useful for finding a specific Element or a set of related Element nodes within the document tree.

Contrast this Document object to the Document object documented in the client-side reference section of this book. The Level 0 properties and methods of that client-side Document object are formally defined by the DOM standard in the HTMLDocument interface. See "HTMLDocument" in this reference section for the DOM equivalent of the traditional client-side JavaScript Document object.

The Document interface is defined by the Core module of the DOM Level 2 specification. A number of the other modules define "add-on" interfaces that are intended to be implemented by the same object that implements the Document interface. For example, if an implementation supports the CSS module, the object that implements this interface also implements the DocumentCSS interface. In JavaScript, the properties and methods of these add-on interfaces can be used as if they were defined by Document, and for that reason, those methods and properties are listed here. See the earlier "Also Implements" section for a full list of the add-on interfaces for Document.

See Also

HTMLDocument

Type of: AbstractView.document, HTMLFrameElement.contentDocument, HTMLIFrameElement.contentDocument, HTMLObjectElement.contentDocument, Node.ownerDocument

Returned by: DOMImplementation.createDocument( )

Document.createAttribute( ) — DOM Level 1 Core

create a new Attr node

Synopsis

```
Attr createAttribute(String name)
    throws DOMException;
```

Arguments

name

The name for the newly created attribute.

Returns

A newly created Attr node with its `nodeName` property set to *name*.

Throws

This method throws a DOMException with a code of `INVALID_CHARACTER_ERR` if *name* contains an illegal character.

See Also

Attr, Element.setAttribute(), Element.setAttributeNode()

Document.createAttributeNS() DOM Level 2 Core

create an Attr with a name and namespace

Synopsis

```
Attr createAttributeNS(String namespaceURI,
                       String qualifiedName)
    throws DOMException;
```

Arguments

namespaceURI
: The unique identifier of the namespace for the Attr, or `null` for no namespace.

qualifiedName
: The qualified name of the attribute, which should include a namespace prefix, a colon, and a local name.

Returns

A newly created Attr node with the specified name and namespace.

Throws

This method may throw a DOMException with one of the following `code` values in the following circumstances:

`INVALID_CHARACTER_ERR`
: *qualifiedName* contains an illegal character.

`NAMESPACE_ERR`
: *qualifiedName* is malformed, or there is a mismatch between *qualifiedName* and *namespaceURI*.

`NOT_SUPPORTED_ERR`
: The implementation does not support XML documents and therefore does not implement this method.

Description

`createAttributeNS()` is just like `createAttribute()` except that the created Attr node has a name and namespace instead of just a name. This method is useful only with XML documents that use namespaces.

Document.createCDATASection() DOM Level 1 Core

create a new CDATASection node

Synopsis

```
CDATASection createCDATASection(String data)
    throws DOMException;
```

Arguments

data

The text of the CDATASection to create.

Returns

A newly created CDATASection node, with the specified *data* as its contents.

Throws

If the document is an HTML document, this method throws a DOMException with a code of `NOT_SUPPORTED_ERR` because HTML documents do not allow CDATASection nodes.

Document.createComment( ) — DOM Level 1 Core

create a new Comment node

Synopsis

```
Comment createComment(String data);
```

Arguments

data

The text of the Comment node to create.

Returns

A newly created Comment node, with the specified *data* as its text.

Document.createDocumentFragment( ) — DOM Level 1 Core

create a new, empty DocumentFragment node

Synopsis

```
DocumentFragment createDocumentFragment( );
```

Returns

A newly created DocumentFragment node with no children.

Document.createElement( ) — DOM Level 1 Core

create a new Element node

Synopsis

```
Element createElement(String tagName)
    throws DOMException;
```

Arguments

tagName

The tag name of the Element to be created. Since HTML tags are case-insensitive, you may use any capitalization for HTML tag names. XML tag names are case-sensitive.

Returns

A newly created Element node with the specified tag name.

Throws

This method throws a DOMException with a code of `INVALID_CHARACTER_ERR` if *tagName* contains an illegal character.

Document.createElementNS( ) DOM Level 2 Core

create a new Element node using a namespace

Synopsis

```
Element createElementNS(String namespaceURI,
                        String qualifiedName)
    throws DOMException;
```

Arguments

namespaceURI
: The unique identifier for the namespace of the new Element, or `null` for no namespace.

qualifiedName
: The qualified name of the new Element. This should include a namespace prefix, a colon, and a local name.

Returns

A newly created Element node, with the specified tag name and namespace.

Throws

This method may throw a DOMException with one of the following `code` values in the following circumstances:

`INVALID_CHARACTER_ERR`
: *qualifiedName* contains an illegal character.

`NAMESPACE_ERR`
: *qualifiedName* is malformed, or there is a mismatch between *qualifiedName* and *namespaceURI*.

`NOT_SUPPORTED_ERR`
: The implementation does not support XML documents and therefore does not implement this method.

Description

`createElementNS( )` is just like `createElement( )` except that the created Element node has a name and namespace instead of just a name. This method is useful only with XML documents that use namespaces.

Document.createEntityReference( )

DOM Level 1 Core

create a new EntityReference node

Synopsis

```
EntityReference createEntityReference(String name)
    throws DOMException;
```

Arguments

name

The name of the referenced entity.

Returns

A new EntityReference node that references an entity with the specified name.

Throws

This method may throw a DOMException with one of the following code values:

`INVALID_CHARACTER_ERR`

The specified entity name contains an illegal character.

`NOT_SUPPORTED_ERR`

This is an HTML document and does not support entity references.

Description

This method creates and returns an EntityReference node that refers to an entity with the specified name. Note that it always throws an exception if this is an HTML document, because HTML does not allow entity references. If this document has a DocumentType node, and if that DocumentType defines an Entity object with the specified name, the returned EntityReference has the same children as the referenced Entity node.

Document.createEvent( )

DOM Level 2 Events

create an Event object

Synopsis

```
Event createEvent(String eventType)
    throws DOMException;
```

Arguments

eventType

The name of the event module for which an Event object is desired. See the "Description" section for a list of valid event types.

Returns

A newly created Event object of the specified type.

Throws

This method throws a DOMException with a code of `NOT_SUPPORTED_ERR` if the implementation does not support events of the requested type.

Description

This method creates a new event type of the type specified by the *eventType* argument. Note that the value of this argument should not be the (singular) name of the event interface to be created, but instead should be the (plural) name of the DOM module that defines that interface. The following table shows the legal values for *eventType* and the event interface each value creates.

eventType argument	Event interface	Initialization method
HTMLEvents	Event	`initEvent( )`
MouseEvents	MouseEvent	`initMouseEvent( )`
UIEvents	UIEvent	`initUIEvent( )`
MutationEvents	MutationEvent	`initMutationEvent( )`

After creating an Event object with this method, you must initialize the object with the initialization method shown in the table. See the appropriate Event interface reference page for details about the initialization method.

This method is actually defined not by the Document interface but by the DocumentEvent interface. If an implementation supports the Events module, the Document object always implements the DocumentEvent interface and supports this method.

See Also

Event, MouseEvent, MutationEvent, UIEvent

Document.createNodeIterator( ) DOM Level 2 Traversal

create a NodeIterator for this document

Synopsis

```
NodeIterator createNodeIterator(Node root,
                                unsigned long whatToShow,
                                NodeFilter filter,
                                boolean entityReferenceExpansion)
    throws DOMException;
```

Arguments

root
: The root of the subtree over which the NodeIterator is to iterate.

whatToShow
: A bitmask of one or more NodeFilter flags that specify which types of nodes should be returned by this NodeIterator.

filter
: An optional node filter function for the NodeIterator, or `null` for no node filter.

entityReferenceExpansion
 true if the NodeIterator should expand entity references in XML documents, or false otherwise.

Returns

A newly created NodeIterator object.

Throws

This method throws a DOMException with a code of NOT_SUPPORTED_ERR if the *root* argument is null.

Description

This method creates and returns a new NodeIterator object to iterate over the subtree rooted at the *root* node, using the specified filters.

This method is not actually part of the Document interface but is instead defined by the DocumentTraversal interface. If an implementation supports the Traversal module, the Document object always implements DocumentTraversal and defines this method.

See Also

Document.createTreeWalker(), NodeFilter, NodeIterator

Document.createProcessingInstruction() DOM Level 1 Core

create a ProcessingInstruction node

Synopsis

```
ProcessingInstruction createProcessingInstruction(String target,
                                                   String data)
    throws DOMException;
```

Arguments

target
 The target of the processing instruction.

data
 The content text of the processing instruction.

Returns

A newly created ProcessingInstruction node.

Throws

This method may throw a DOMException with one of the following code values in the following circumstances:

INVALID_CHARACTER_ERR
 The specified *target* contains an illegal character.

NOT_SUPPORTED_ERR
 This is an HTML document and does not support processing instructions.

Document.createRange( ) — DOM Level 2 Range

create a Range object

Synopsis

```
Range createRange( );
```

Returns

A newly created Range object with both boundary points set to the beginning of the document.

Description

This method creates a Range object that can be used to represent a region of this document or of a DocumentFragment associated with this document.

Note that this method is actually defined not by the Document interface but by the DocumentRange interface. If an implementation supports the Range module, the Document object always implements DocumentRange and defines this method.

Document.createTextNode( ) — DOM Level 1 Core

create a new Text node

Synopsis

```
Text createTextNode(String data);
```

Arguments

data
: The content of the Text node.

Returns

A newly created Text node that represents the specified *data* string.

Document.createTreeWalker( ) — DOM Level 2 Traversal

create a TreeWalker for this document

Synopsis

```
TreeWalker createTreeWalker(Node root,
                            unsigned long whatToShow,
                            NodeFilter filter,
                            boolean entityReferenceExpansion)
    throws DOMException;
```

Arguments

root
: The root of the subtree over which this TreeWalker is to walk.

whatToShow
A bitmask of one or more NodeFilter flags that specify which types of nodes should be returned by this TreeWalker.

filter
An optional node filter function for the TreeWalker, or `null` for no node filter.

entityReferenceExpansion
`true` if the TreeWalker should expand entity references in XML documents, or `false` otherwise.

Returns

A newly created TreeWalker object.

Throws

This method throws a DOMException with a code of `NOT_SUPPORTED_ERR` if the *root* argument is `null`.

Description

This method creates and returns a new TreeWalker object to traverse the subtree rooted at the *root* node, using the specified filters.

This method is not actually part of the Document interface but is instead defined by the DocumentTraversal interface. If an implementation supports the Traversal module, the Document object always implements DocumentTraversal and defines this method.

See Also

Document.createNodeIterator(), NodeFilter, TreeWalker

Document.getElementById() DOM Level 2 Core; in DOM Level 1, defined by HTMLDocument

find an element with the specified unique ID

Synopsis

```
Element getElementById(String elementId);
```

Arguments

elementId
The value of the `id` attribute of the desired element.

Returns

The Element node that represents the document element with the specified `id` attribute, or `null` if no such element is found.

Description

This method searches the document for an Element node with an `id` attribute whose value is *elementId*, and returns that Element. If no such Element is found, it returns `null`. The value of the id attribute is intended to be unique within a document, and if this method finds more than one Element with the specified *elementId*, it may return one at random or it may return null.

In HTML documents, this method always searches for attributes named id. In XML documents, however, it searches for any attribute whose *type* is id, regardless of what the attribute name is. If XML attribute types are not known (because, for example, the XML parser could not locate the document's DTD), this method always returns null.

This is an important and commonly used method since it provides a simple way to obtain the Element object that represents a specific document element. Note that it provides functionality similar to the nonstandard document.all[] array defined by Internet Explorer 4 and later. Finally, note that the name of this method ends with "Id", not with "ID"; be careful not to misspell it.

See Also

Document.getElementsByTagName(), Element.getElementsByTagName(), HTMLDocument.getElementsByName()

Document.getElementsByTagName( ) DOM Level 1 Core

return all Element nodes with the specified name

Synopsis

```
Node[] getElementsByTagName(String tagname);
```

Arguments

tagname

The tag name of the Element nodes to be returned, or the wildcard string "*" to return all Element nodes in the document regardless of tag name. For HTML documents, tag names are compared in a case-insensitive fashion.

Returns

A read-only array (technically, a NodeList) of all Element nodes in the document tree with the specified tag name. The returned Element nodes are in the same order in which they appear in the document source.

Description

This method returns a NodeList (which you can treat as a read-only array) that contains all Element nodes from the document that have the specified tag name, in the order in which they appear in the document source. The NodeList is "live"; i.e., its contents are automatically updated as necessary if elements with the specified tag name are added to or removed from the document.

HTML documents are case-insensitive, and you can specify *tagname* using any capitalization; it matches all tags with the same name in the document, regardless of how those tags are capitalized in the document source. XML documents, on the other hand, are case-sensitive, and *tagname* matches only tags with the same name and exactly the same capitalization in the document source.

Note that the Element interface defines a method by the same name that searches only a subtree of the document. Also, the HTMLDocument interface defines `getElementsByName( )`, which searches for elements based on the value of their `name` attributes rather than their tag names.

Example

You can find and iterate through all `<h1>` tags in a document with code like the following:

```
var headings = document.getElementsByTagName("h1");
for(var i = 0; i < headings.length; i++) {  // Loop through the returned tags
    var h = headings[i];
    // Now do something with the <h1> element in the h variable
}
```

See Also

Document.getElementById(), Element.getElementsByTagName(), HTMLDocument.getElementsByName()

Document.getElementsByTagNameNS( ) — DOM Level 2 Core

return all Element nodes with a specified name and namespace

Synopsis

```
Node[] getElementsByTagNameNS(String namespaceURI,
                              String localName);
```

Arguments

namespaceURI
: The unique identifier of the namespace of the desired elements, or "*" to match all namespaces.

localName
: The local name of the desired elements, or "*" to match any local name.

Returns

A read-only array (technically, a NodeList) of all Element nodes in the document tree that have the specified namespace and local name.

Description

This method works just like `getElementsByTagName( )` except that it searches for elements by namespace and name. It is useful only with XML documents that use namespaces.

Document.getOverrideStyle( ) — DOM Level 2 CSS

get the override style for a specified element

Synopsis

```
CSSStyleDeclaration getOverrideStyle(Element elt,
                                     String pseudoElt);
```

Arguments

elt

The element for which the override style is desired.

pseudoElt

The pseudoelement of `elt`, or `null` if there is none.

Returns

A CSSStyleDeclaration object that represents the override style information for the specified element and pseudoelement. The returned object typically also implements the more commonly used CSS2Properties interfaces.

Description

This method returns a CSSStyleDeclaration object (which typically also implements CSS2Properties) for a specified element and optional pseudoelement. You may make use of this returned object to make changes to the displayed style of the specified element without disturbing the inline style of that element and without modifying the style sheets of the document. Conceptually, the returned value represents a style declaration within an "override" style sheet that takes precedence over all other style sheets and inline styles (except for `!important` declarations in the user style sheet).

Note that this method is defined not by the Document interface but by the DocumentCSS interface. If an implementation supports the CSS module, the Document object always implements DocumentCSS and defines this method.

See Also

CSSStyleDeclaration, CSS2Properties, AbstractView.getComputedStyle( ), HTMLElement.style

Document.importNode( ) — DOM Level 2 Core

copy a node from another document for use in this document

Synopsis

```
Node importNode(Node importedNode,
                boolean deep)
    throws DOMException;
```

Arguments

importedNode

The node to be imported.

deep

If `true`, recursively copy all descendants of *importedNode* as well.

Returns

A copy of *importedNode* (and possibly all of its descendants) with its `ownerDocument` set to this document.

Throws

This method throws a DOMException with a code of `NOT_SUPPORTED_ERR` if *`importedNode`* is a Document or DocumentType node, since those types of nodes cannot be imported.

Description

This method is passed a node defined in another document and returns a copy of the node that is suitable for insertion into this document. If *deep* is `true`, all descendants of the node are also copied. The original node and its descendants are not modified in any way. The returned copy has its `ownerDocument` property set to this document but has a `parentNode` of `null` since it has not yet been inserted into the document. EventListener functions registered on the original node or tree are not copied.

When an Element node is imported, only the attributes that are explicitly specified in the source document are imported with it. When an Attr node is imported, its `specified` property is automatically set to `true`.

See Also

Node.cloneNode()

DocumentCSS

see Document

DocumentEvent

see Document

DocumentFragment

DOM Level 1 Core

adjacent nodes and their subtrees

Node → DocumentFragment

Description

The DocumentFragment interface represents a portion—or fragment—of a document. More specifically, it represents one or more adjacent Document nodes and all of the descendants of each. DocumentFragment nodes are never part of a document tree, and the inherited `parentNode` property is always `null`. DocumentFragment nodes exhibit a special behavior that makes them quite useful, however: when a request is made to insert a DocumentFragment into a document tree, it is not the DocumentFragment node itself that is inserted but each of the children of the DocumentFragment instead. This makes DocumentFragment useful as a temporary placeholder for nodes that you wish to insert, all at once, into a document. DocumentFragment is also particularly useful for implementing document cut, copy, and paste operations, particularly when combined with the Range interface.

You can create a new, empty DocumentFragment with `Document.createDocumentFragment()`, or you can use `Range.extractContents()` or `Range.cloneContents()` to obtain a DocumentFragment that contains a fragment of an existing document.

See Also

Range

Returned by: Document.createDocumentFragment(), Range.cloneContents(), Range.extractContents()

DocumentRange

see Document

DocumentStyle

see Document

DocumentTraversal

see Document

DocumentType

DOM Level 1 XML

the DTD of an XML document

Node → DocumentType

Properties

`readonly NamedNodeMap entities`
: This NamedNodeMap is a list of Entity objects declared in the DTD and allows Entity objects to be queried by name. Note that XML parameter entities are not included. This NamedNodeMap is immutable—its contents may not be altered.

`readonly String internalSubset` *[DOM Level 2]*
: The internal subset of the DTD (i.e., the portion of the DTD that appears in the document itself rather than in an external file). The delimiting square brackets of the internal subset are not part of the returned value. If there is no internal subset, this property is `null`.

`readonly String name`
: The name of the document type. This is the identifier that immediately follows `<!DOCTYPE>` at the start of an XML document, and it is the same as the tag name of the document's root element.

`readonly NamedNodeMap notations`
: A NamedNodeMap that contains Notation objects representing all notations declared in the DTD. It also allows Notation objects to be looked up by notation name. This NamedNodeMap is immutable—its contents may not be altered.

`readonly String publicId` *[DOM Level 2]*
: The public identifier of the external subset of the DTD, or `null` if none was specified.

`readonly String systemId` *[DOM Level 2]*
: The system identifier of the external subset of the DTD, or `null` if none was specified.

Description

This infrequently used interface represents the DTD of an XML document. Programmers working exclusively with HTML documents never need to use this interface.

Because a DTD is not part of a document's content, DocumentType nodes never appear in the document tree. If an XML document has a DTD, the DocumentType node for that DTD is available through the doctype property of the Document node.

DocumentType nodes are immutable and may not be modified in any way.

See Also

Document, Entity, Notation

Type of: Document.doctype

Passed to: DOMImplementation.createDocument()

Returned by: DOMImplementation.createDocumentType()

DocumentView

see Document

DOMException

DOM Level 1 Core

signals exceptions or errors for core DOM objects

Constants

The following constants define the legal values for the code property of a DOMException object. Note that these constants are static properties of DOMException, not properties of individual exception objects.

`unsigned short INDEX_SIZE_ERR = 1`
: Indicates an out-of-bounds error for an array or string index.

`unsigned short DOMSTRING_SIZE_ERR = 2`
: Indicates that a requested text is too big to fit into a string in the current JavaScript implementation.

`unsigned short HIERARCHY_REQUEST_ERR = 3`
: Indicates that an attempt was made to place a node somewhere illegal in the document tree hierarchy.

`unsigned short WRONG_DOCUMENT_ERR = 4`
: Indicates an attempt to use a node with a document that is different from the document that created the node.

`unsigned short INVALID_CHARACTER_ERR = 5`
: Indicates that an illegal character is used (in an element name, for example).

`unsigned short NO_DATA_ALLOWED_ERR = 6`
: Not currently used.

`unsigned short NO_MODIFICATION_ALLOWED_ERR = 7`
: Indicates that an attempt was made to modify a node that is read-only and does not allow modifications. Entity, EntityReference, and Notation nodes, and all of their descendants, are read-only.

`unsigned short NOT_FOUND_ERR = 8`
: Indicates that a node was not found where it was expected.

`unsigned short NOT_SUPPORTED_ERR = 9`
: Indicates that a method or property is not supported in the current DOM implementation.

`unsigned short INUSE_ATTRIBUTE_ERR = 10`
: Indicates that an attempt was made to associate an Attr with an Element when that Attr node was already associated with a different Element node.

`unsigned short INVALID_STATE_ERR = 11` *[DOM Level 2]*
: Indicates an attempt to use an object that is not yet, or is no longer, in a state that allows such use.

`unsigned short SYNTAX_ERR = 12` *[DOM Level 2]*
: Indicates that a specified string contains a syntax error. Commonly used with CSS property specifications.

`unsigned short INVALID_MODIFICATION_ERR = 13` *[DOM Level 2]*
: Indicates an attempt to modify the type of a CSSRule or CSSValue object.

`unsigned short NAMESPACE_ERR = 14` *[DOM Level 2]*
: Indicates an error involving element or attribute namespaces.

`unsigned short INVALID_ACCESS_ERR = 15` *[DOM Level 2]*
: Indicates an attempt to access an object in a way that is not supported by the implementation.

Properties

`unsigned short code`
: An error code that provides some detail about what caused the exception. The legal values (and their meanings) for this property are defined by the constants just listed.

Description

A DOMException object is thrown when a DOM method or property is used incorrectly or in an inappropriate context. The value of the `code` property indicates the general type of exception that occurred. Note that a DOMException may be thrown when reading or writing a property of an object as well as when calling a method of an object.

The descriptions of object properties and methods in this reference include a list of exception types they may throw. Note, however, that certain commonly thrown exceptions are omitted from these lists. A DOMException with a code of `NO_MODIFICATION_ALLOWED_ERR` is thrown any time an attempt is made to modify a read-only node, such as an Entity node or one of its descendants. Thus, most methods and read/write properties of the Node interface (and of its subinterfaces) may throw this exception. Because read-only nodes appear only in XML documents and not in HTML documents, and because it applies so universally to the methods and writable properties of Node objects, the `NO_MODIFICATION_ALLOWED_ERR` exception is omitted from the descriptions of those methods and properties.

Similarly, many DOM methods and properties that return strings may throw a DOMException with a code of `DOMSTRING_SIZE_ERR`, which indicates that the text to be returned is too long to be represented as a string value in the underlying JavaScript implementation. Although this type of exception may theoretically be thrown by many properties and methods, it is very rare in practice and is omitted from the descriptions of those methods and properties.

Note that not all exceptions in the DOM are signaled with a DOMException. Exceptions having to do with events and event handling cause an EventException object to be thrown, and exceptions involving the DOM Range module cause a RangeException to be thrown.

See Also

EventException, RangeException

DOMImplementation — DOM Level 1 Core

methods independent of any particular document

Also Implements

DOMImplementationCSS, HTMLDOMImplementation

If a DOM implementation supports the HTML and CSS modules, the DOMImplementation object also implements the DOMImplementationCSS and HTMLDOMImplementation interfaces. For convenience, the methods of these trivial interfaces are listed here along with the core DOMImplementation methods.

Methods

`createCSSStyleSheet()` *[DOM Level 2 CSS]*

This DOMImplementationCSS method creates a new CSSStyleSheet object.

`createDocument()` *[DOM Level 2]*

Creates a new Document object with a root element (the `documentElement` property of the returned Document object) of the specified type.

`createDocumentType()` *[DOM Level 2]*

Creates a new DocumentType node.

`createHTMLDocument()` *[DOM Level 2 HTML]*

This HTMLDOMImplementation method creates a new HTMLDocument object and populates it with `<html>`, `<head>`, `<title>`, and `<body>` elements.

`hasFeature()`

Checks whether the current implementation supports a specified version of a named feature.

Description

The DOMImplementation interface and its HTMLDOMImplementation and DOMImplementationCSS subinterfaces are placeholders for methods that are not specific to any particular Document object but rather are "global" to an implementation of the DOM. You can obtain a reference to the DOMImplementation object through the `implementation` property of any Document object.

See Also

Type of: Document.implementation

DOMImplementation.createCSSStyleSheet( ) DOM Level 2 CSS

create a CSSStyleSheet object

Synopsis

```
CSSStyleSheet createCSSStyleSheet(String title,
                                  String media)
    throws DOMException;
```

Arguments

title
The title of the style sheet.

media
A comma-separated list of media types to which the style sheet should apply.

Returns

A CSSStyleSheet object.

Throws

A DOMException with a code of SYNTAX_ERR if the *media* argument is malformed.

Description

This method creates a new CSSStyleSheet object. Note, however, that as of Level 2, the DOM standard does not yet define any way to associate a newly created CSSStyleSheet object with a document.

createCSSStyleSheet( ) is defined not by the DOMImplementation interface but by its DOMImplementationCSS subinterface. If an implementation supports the "CSS" feature, its DOMImplementation object implements this method.

DOMImplementation.createDocument( ) DOM Level 2 Core

create a new Document and the specified root element

Synopsis

```
Document createDocument(String namespaceURI,
                        String qualifiedName,
                        DocumentType doctype)
    throws DOMException;
```

Arguments

namespaceURI
The unique identifier of the namespace of the root element to be created for the document, or null for no namespace.

qualifiedName
The name of the root element to be created for this document. If *namespaceURI* is not `null`, this name should include a namespace prefix and a colon.

doctype
The DocumentType object for the newly created Document, or `null` if none is desired.

Returns

A Document object with its `documentElement` property set to a root Element node of the specified type.

Throws

This method may throw a DOMException with the following `code` values in the following circumstances:

`INVALID_CHARACTER_ERR`
qualifiedName contains an illegal character.

`NAMESPACE_ERR`
qualifiedName is malformed, or there is a mismatch between *qualifiedName* and *namespaceURI*.

`NOT_SUPPORTED_ERR`
The current implementation does not support XML documents and has not implemented this method.

`WRONG_DOCUMENT_ERR`
doctype is already in use for another document or was created by a different DOMImplementation object.

Description

This method creates a new Document object and the specified root `documentElement` object for that document. If the *doctype* argument is non-`null`, the `ownerDocument` property of this DocumentType object is set to the newly created document.

This method is used to create XML documents and may not be supported by HTML-only implementations. Use `createHTMLDocument( )` to create a new HTML document.

See Also

createDocumentType( ), createHTMLDocument( )

DOMImplementation.createDocumentType( ) — DOM Level 2 Core

create a DocumentType node

Synopsis

```
DocumentType createDocumentType(String qualifiedName,
                                String publicId,
                                String systemId)
    throws DOMException;
```

Arguments

qualifiedName
: The name of the document type. If you are using XML namespaces, this may be a qualified name that specifies a namespace prefix and a local name separated by a colon.

publicId
: The public identifier of the document type, or `null`.

systemId
: The system identifier of the document type, or `null`. This argument typically specifies the local filename of a DTD file.

Returns

A new `DocumentType` object with an `ownerDocument` property of `null`.

Throws

This method may throw a DOMException with one of the following `code` values:

`INVALID_CHARACTER_ERR`
: *qualifiedName* contains an illegal character.

`NAMESPACE_ERR`
: *qualifiedName* is malformed.

`NOT_SUPPORTED_ERR`
: The current implementation does not support XML documents and has not implemented this method.

Description

This method creates a new DocumentType node. This method specifies only an external subset of the document type. As of Level 2, the DOM standard does not provide any way for specifying an internal subset, and the returned DocumentType does not define any Entity or Notation nodes. This method is useful only with XML documents and may not be supported by HTML-only implementations.

DOMImplementation.createHTMLDocument( ) — DOM Level 2 HTML

create a skeletal HTML document

Synopsis

```
HTMLDocument createHTMLDocument(String title);
```

Arguments

title
: The title of the document. This text is used as the content of the `<title>` element of the newly created document.

Returns

The new HTMLDocument object.

Description

This method creates a new HTMLDocument object with a skeletal document tree that includes the specified title. The `documentElement` property of the returned object is an `<html>` element, and this root element has `<head>` and `<body>` tags as its children. The `<head>` element in turn has a `<title>` child, which has the specified *`title`* string as its child.

`createHTMLDocument( )` is defined not by the DOMImplementation interface but by its HTMLDOMImplementation subinterface. If an implementation supports the "HTML" feature, its DOMImplementation object implements this method.

See Also

DOMImplementation.createDocument( )

DOMImplementation.hasFeature( )

DOM Level 1 Core

determine whether the implementation supports a feature

Synopsis

```
boolean hasFeature(String feature,
                   String version);
```

Arguments

`feature`
: The name of the feature for which support is being tested. The set of valid feature names for the DOM Level 2 standard is listed in the upcoming table. Feature names are case-insensitive.

`version`
: The feature version number for which support is being tested, or `null` or the empty string `""` if support for any version of the feature is sufficient. In the Level 2 DOM specification, supported version numbers are 1.0 and 2.0.

Returns

`true` if the implementation completely supports the specified version of the specified feature, or `false` otherwise. If no version number is specified, the method returns `true` if the implementation completely supports any version of the specified feature.

Description

The W3C DOM standard is modular, and implementations are not required to implement all modules or features of the standard. This method is used to test whether a DOM implementation supports a named module of the DOM specification. The availability information for each entry in this DOM reference includes the name of the module. Note that although Internet Explorer 5 and 5.5 include partial support for the DOM Level 1 specification, this important method is not supported before IE 6.

The complete set of module names that may be used as the *feature* argument are shown in the following table.

Feature	Description
Core	Node, Element, Document, Text, and the other fundamental interfaces required by all DOM implementations are implemented. All conforming implementations must support this module.
HTML	HTMLElement, HTMLDocument, and the other HTML-specific interfaces are implemented.
XML	Entity, EntityReference, ProcessingInstruction, Notation, and the other node types that are useful only with XML documents are implemented.
StyleSheets	Simple interfaces describing generic style sheets are implemented.
CSS	Interfaces that are specific to CSS style sheets are implemented.
CSS2	The CSS2Properties interface is implemented.
Events	The basic event-handling interfaces are implemented.
UIEvents	The interfaces for user-interface events are implemented.
MouseEvents	The interfaces for mouse events are implemented.
HTMLEvents	The interfaces for HTML events are implemented.
MutationEvents	The interfaces for document mutation events are implemented.
Range	The interfaces for manipulating ranges of a document are implemented.
Traversal	The interfaces for advanced document traversal are implemented.
Views	The interfaces for document views are implemented.

Example

You might use this method in code like the following:

```
// Check whether the browser supports the DOM Level 2 Traversal API
if (document.implementation &&
    document.implementation.hasFeature &&
    document.implementation.hasFeature("Traversal", "2.0")) {
  // If so, use it here...
}
else {
  // If not, traverse the document some other way
}
```

See Also

Node.isSupported()

DOMImplementationCSS

see DOMImplementation

Element

DOM Level 1 Core

an HTML or XML element

Node → Element

Subinterfaces

HTMLElement

Properties

`readonly String tagName`

The tag name of the element. This is the string "P" for an HTML `<p>` element, for example. For HTML documents, the tag name is returned in uppercase, regardless of its capitalization in the document source. XML documents are case-sensitive, and the tag name is returned exactly as it is written in the document source. This property has the same value as the `nodeName` property of the Node interface.

Methods

`getAttribute()`

Returns the value of a named attribute as a string.

`getAttributeNS()` *[DOM Level 2]*

Returns the string value of an attribute specified by local name and namespace URI. Useful only with XML documents that use namespaces.

`getAttributeNode()`

Returns the value of a named attribute as an Attr node.

`getAttributeNodeNS()` *[DOM Level 2]*

Returns the Attr value of an attribute specified by local name and namespace URI. Useful only with XML documents that use namespaces.

`getElementsByTagName()`

Returns an array (technically, a NodeList) of all descendant Element nodes of this element that have the specified tag name, in the order in which they appear in the document.

`getElementsByTagNameNS()` *[DOM Level 2]*

Like `getElementsByTagName()`, except that the element tag name is specified by local name and namespace URI. Useful only with XML documents that use namespaces.

`hasAttribute()` *[DOM Level 2]*

Returns `true` if this element has an attribute with the specified name, or `false` otherwise. Note that this method returns `true` if the named attribute is explicitly specified in the document source or if the document's DTD specifies a default value for the named attribute.

`hasAttributeNS()` *[DOM Level 2]*

Like `hasAttribute()`, except that the attribute is specified by a combination of local name and namespace URI. This method is useful only with XML documents that use namespaces.

`removeAttribute()`

Deletes the named attribute from this element. Note, however, that this method deletes only attributes that are explicitly specified in the document source for this element. If the DTD specifies a default value for this attribute, that default becomes the new value of the attribute.

`removeAttributeNS()` *[DOM Level 2]*

Like `removeAttribute()`, except that the attribute to be removed is specified by a combination of local name and namespace URI. Useful only for XML documents that use namespaces.

`removeAttributeNode()`
: Removes the specified Attr node from the list of attributes for this element. Note that this works only to remove attributes that are explicitly specified in the document source for this attribute. If the DTD specifies a default value for the removed attribute, a new Attr node is created to represent the default value of the attribute.

`setAttribute()`
: Sets the named attribute to the specified string value. If an attribute with that name does not already exist, a new attribute is added to the element.

`setAttributeNS()` *[DOM Level 2]*
: Like `setAttribute()`, except that the attribute to be set is specified by the combination of a local name and a namespace URI. Useful only with XML documents that use namespaces.

`setAttributeNode()`
: Adds the specified Attr node to the list of attributes for this element. If an attribute with the same name already exists, its value is replaced.

`setAttributeNodeNS()` *[DOM Level 2]*
: Like `setAttributeNode()`, but this method is suitable for use with nodes returned by `Document.createAttributeNS()`. Useful only with XML documents that use namespaces.

Description

The Element interface represents HTML or XML elements or tags. The `tagName` property specifies the name of the element. The `getElementsByTagName()` method provides a powerful way to locate element descendants of a given element that have a specified tag name. The various other methods of this interface provide access to the attributes of the element. If you give an element a unique identifier using the `id` attribute in your document source, you can then easily locate the Element node that represents that document element with the useful `Document.getElementById()` method. To create a new Element node for insertion into a document, use `Document.createElement()`.

In HTML documents (and many XML documents) all attributes have simple string values, and you can use the simple methods `getAttribute()` and `setAttribute()` for any attribute manipulation you need to do.

If you are working with XML documents that may contain entity references as part of attribute values, you will have to work with Attr objects and their subtree of nodes. You can get and set the Attr object for an attribute with `getAttributeNode()` and `setAttributeNode()`, or you can iterate through the Attr nodes in the `attributes[]` array of the Node interface. If you are working with an XML document that uses XML namespaces, you'll need to use the various methods whose names end with "NS".

In the DOM Level 1 specification, the `normalize()` method was part of the Element interface. In the Level 2 specification, `normalize()` is instead part of the Node interface. All Element nodes inherit this method and can still use it.

See Also

HTMLElement, Node

Type of: Attr.ownerElement, Document.documentElement

Passed to: Document.getOverrideStyle( ), AbstractView.getComputedStyle( )

Returned by: Document.createElement( ), Document.createElementNS( ), Document.getElementById( )

Element.getAttribute( )

DOM Level 1 Core

return the string value of a named attribute

Synopsis

```
String getAttribute(String name);
```

Arguments

name

The name of the attribute whose value is to be returned.

Returns

The string value of the named attribute. If the attribute does not have a value specified in the document and does not have a default value specified by the document type, the return value is the empty string ("").

Description

`getAttribute( )` returns the value of a named attribute of an element. In HTML documents, attribute values are always strings, and this method returns the complete attribute value. Note that the objects that represent HTML elements also implement the HTMLElement interface and one of its tag-specific subinterfaces. Therefore, all standard attributes of standard HTML tags are also available directly as properties of the Element object.

In XML documents, attribute values are not available directly as element properties and must be looked up by calling a method. For many XML documents, `getAttribute( )` is a suitable method for doing this. Note, however that in XML attributes may contain entity references, and in order to obtain complete details about such attributes, you must use `getAttributeNode( )` to obtain the Attr node whose subtree represents the complete attribute value. The Attr nodes for an element are also available in an `attributes[]` array inherited from the Node interface. For XML documents that use namespaces, you may need to use `getAttributeNS( )` or `getAttributeNodeNS( )`.

Example

The following code illustrates two different ways of obtaining an attribute value for an HTML `<img>` element:

```
// Get all images in the document
var images = document.body.getElementsByTagName("IMG");
// Get the SRC attribute of the first one
var src0 = images[0].getAttribute("SRC");
// Get the SRC attribute of the second simply by reading the property
var src1 = images[1].src;
```

W3C DOM Reference

See Also

Element.getAttributeNode( ), Node.attributes

Element.getAttributeNode( )

DOM Level 1 Core

return the Attr node for the named attribute

Synopsis

```
Attr getAttributeNode(String name);
```

Arguments

name

The name of the desired attribute.

Returns

An Attr node whose descendants represent the value of the named attribute, or `null` if this element has no such attribute.

Description

`getAttributeNode( )` returns an Attr node that represents the value of a named attribute. Note that this Attr node can also be obtained through the `attributes` property inherited from the Node interface.

The attribute value is represented by the descendants of the Attr nodes. In HTML documents, an Attr node has a single Text node child, and it is always easier to query an attribute value by calling `getAttribute( )`, which returns the value as a string. `getAttributeNode( )` is necessary only when you are working with XML documents that contain entity references in their attribute values.

See Also

Element.getAttribute( ), Element.getAttributeNodeNS( ), Node.attributes

Element.getAttributeNodeNS( )

DOM Level 2 Core

return the Attr node for an attribute with a namespace

Synopsis

```
Attr getAttributeNodeNS(String namespaceURI,
                        String localName);
```

Arguments

namespaceURI

The URI that uniquely identifies the namespace of this attribute, or `null` for no namespace.

localName

The identifier that specifies the name of the attribute within its namespace.

Returns

The Attr node whose descendants represent the value of the specified attribute, or `null` if this element has no such attribute.

Description

This method works like `getAttributeNode( )`, except that the attribute is specified by the combination of a namespace URI and a local name defined within that namespace. This method is useful only with XML documents that use namespaces.

See Also

Element.getAttributeNode( ), Element.getAttributeNS( )

Element.getAttributeNS( ) — DOM Level 2 Core

get the value of an attribute that uses namespaces

Synopsis

```
String getAttributeNS(String namespaceURI,
                      String localName);
```

Arguments

namespaceURI
: The URI that uniquely identifies the namespace of this attribute, or `null` for no namespace.

localName
: The identifier that specifies the name of the attribute within its namespace.

Returns

The string value of the named attribute. If the attribute is not explicitly specified in the document and does not have a default value specified by the document type, this method returns the empty string.

Description

This method works just like the `getAttribute( )` method, except that the attribute is specified by a combination of namespace URI and local name within that namespace. This method is useful only with XML documents that use namespaces.

See Also

Element.getAttribute( ), Element.getAttributeNodeNS( )

Element.getElementsByTagName( ) — DOM Level 1 Core

find descendant elements with a specified tag name

Synopsis

```
Node[] getElementsByTagName(String name);
```

Arguments

name
The tag name of the desired elements, or the value "*" to specify that all descendant elements should be returned, regardless of their tag names.

Returns

An array (technically, a NodeList) of Element objects that are descendants of this element and have the specified tag name.

Description

This method traverses all descendants of this element and returns an array (really a NodeList object) of Element nodes representing all document elements with the specified tag name. The elements in the returned array appear in the same order in which they appear in the source document.

Note that the Document interface also has a `getElementsByTagName( )` method that works just like this one but that traverses the entire document, rather than just the descendants of a single element. Do not confuse this method with `HTMLDocument.getElementsByName( )`, which searches for elements based on the value of their `name` attributes rather than by their tag names.

Example

You can find all `<div>` tags in a document with code like the following:

```
var divisions = document.body.getElementsByTagName("div");
```

And you can find all `<p>` tags within the a `<div>` tag with code like this:

```
var paragraphs = divisions[0].getElementsByTagname("p");
```

See Also

Document.getElementById(), Document.getElementsByTagName(), HTMLDocument.getElementsByName()

Element.getElementsByTagNameNS( ) DOM Level 2 Core

return descendant elements with the specified name and namespace

Synopsis

```
Node[] getElementsByTagNameNS(String namespaceURI,
                              String localName);
```

Arguments

namespaceURI
The URI that uniquely identifies the namespace of the element.

localName
The identifier that specifies the name of the element within its namespace.

Returns

An array (technically, a NodeList) of Element objects that are descendants of this element and have the specified name and namespace.

Description

This method works like `getElementsByTagName()`, except that the tag name of the desired elements is specified as a combination of a namespace URI and a local name defined within that namespace. This method is useful only with XML documents that use namespaces.

See Also

Document.getElementsByTagNameNS(), Element.getElementsByTagName()

Element.hasAttribute()

DOM Level 2 Core

determine whether this element has a specified attribute

Synopsis

```
boolean hasAttribute(String name);
```

Arguments

name

The name of the desired attribute.

Returns

`true` if this element has a specified or default value for the named attribute, and `false` otherwise.

Description

This method determines whether an element has an attribute with the specified name, but does not return the value of that attribute. Note that `hasAttribute()` returns `true` if the named attribute is explicitly specified in the document and also if the named attribute has a default value specified by the document type.

See Also

Attr.specified, Element.getAttribute(), Element.setAttribute()

Element.hasAttributeNS()

DOM Level 2 Core

determine whether this element has a specified attribute

Synopsis

```
boolean hasAttributeNS(String namespaceURI,
                       String localName);
```

Arguments

namespaceURI
: The unique namespace identifier for the attribute, or `null` for no namespace.

localName
: The name of the attribute within the specified namespace.

Returns

`true` if this element has an explicitly specified value or a default value for the specified attribute; `false` otherwise.

Description

This method works like `hasAttribute( )`, except that the attribute to be checked for is specified by namespace and name. This method is useful only with XML documents that use namespaces.

See Also

Element.getAttributeNS( ), Element.setAttributeNS( )

Element.removeAttribute( ) — DOM Level 1 Core

delete a named attribute of an element

Synopsis

```
void removeAttribute(String name);
```

Arguments

name
: The name of the attribute to be deleted.

Throws

This method may throw a DOMException with a `code` of `NO_MODIFICATION_ALLOWED_ERR` if this element is read-only and does not allow its attributes to be removed.

Description

`removeAttribute( )` deletes a named attribute from this element. If the named attribute has a default value specified by the document type, subsequent calls to `getAttribute( )` will return that default value. Attempts to remove nonexistent attributes or attributes that are not specified but have a default value are silently ignored.

See Also

Element.getAttribute( ), Element.setAttribute( ), Node.attributes

Element.removeAttributeNode( )

DOM Level 1 Core

remove an Attr node from an element

Synopsis

```
Attr removeAttributeNode(Attr oldAttr)
    throws DOMException;
```

Arguments

oldAttr
: The Attr node to be removed from the element.

Returns

The Attr node that was removed.

Throws

This method may throw a DOMException with the following code values:

`NO_MODIFICATION_ALLOWED_ERR`
: This element is read-only and does not allow attributes to be removed.

`NOT_FOUND_ERR`
: *oldAttr* is not an attribute of this element.

Description

This method removes (and returns) an Attr node from the set of attributes of an element. If the removed attribute has a default value specified by the DTD, a new Attr is added representing this default value. If is often simpler to use `removeAttribute( )` instead of this method.

See Also

Attr, Element.removeAttribute( )

Element.removeAttributeNS( )

DOM Level 2 Core

delete an attribute specified by name and namespace

Synopsis

```
void removeAttributeNS(String namespaceURI,
                       String localName);
```

Arguments

namespaceURI
: The unique identifier of the namespace of the attribute, or `null` for no namespace.

localName
: The name of the attribute within the specified namespace.

Throws

This method may throw a DOMException with a code of `NO_MODIFICATION_ALLOWED_ERR` if this element is read-only and does not allow its attributes to be removed.

Description

`removeAttributeNS( )` works just like `removeAttribute( )`, except that the attribute to be removed is specified by name and namespace instead of simply by name. This method is useful only with XML documents that use namespaces.

See Also

Element.getAttributeNS( ), Element.removeAttribute( ), Element.setAttributeNS( )

Element.setAttribute( ) — DOM Level 1 Core

create or change an attribute of an element

Synopsis

```
void setAttribute(String name,
                  String value)
    throws DOMException;
```

Arguments

name
: The name of the attribute that is to be created or modified.

value
: The string value of the attribute.

Throws

This method may throw a DOMException with the following `code` values:

`INVALID_CHARACTER_ERR`
: The *name* argument contains a character that is not allowed in HTML or XML attribute names.

`NO_MODIFICATION_ALLOWED_ERR`
: This element is read-only and does not allow modifications to its attributes.

Description

This method sets the specified attribute to the specified value. If no attribute by that name already exists, a new one is created. Note that Element objects that represent the tags of an HTML document also implement the HTMLElement interface and (usually) one of its tag-specific subinterfaces. As a shortcut, these interfaces define properties that correspond to the standard HTML attributes for each tag, and it is usually easier to set an HTML attribute simply by setting the appropriate property.

The *value* argument is a plain string. If you are working with an XML document and need to include an entity reference in an attribute value, use `setAttributeNode( )`.

Example

```
// Set the TARGET attribute of all links in a document
var links = document.body.getElementsByTagName("A");
for(var i = 0; i < links.length; i++) {
    links[i].setAttribute("TARGET", "newwindow");
}
```

See Also

Element.getAttribute(), Element.removeAttribute(), Element.setAttributeNode()

Element.setAttributeNode() DOM Level 1 Core

add a new Attr node to an Element

Synopsis

```
Attr setAttributeNode(Attr newAttr)
    throws DOMException;
```

Arguments

newAttr
: The Attr node that represents the attribute to be added or whose value is to be modified.

Returns

The Attr node that was replaced by *newAttr*, or `null` if no attribute was replaced.

Throws

This method may throw a DOMException with a code of the following values:

`INUSE_ATTRIBUTE_ERR`
: *newAttr* is already a member of the attribute set of some other Element node.

`NO_MODIFICATION_ALLOWED_ERR`
: The Element node is read-only and does not allow modifications to its attributes.

`WRONG_DOCUMENT_ERR`
: *newAttr* has a different `ownerDocument` property than the Element on which it is being set.

Description

This method adds a new Attr node to the set of attributes of an Element node. If an attribute with the same name already exists for the Element, *newAttr* replaces that attribute, and the replaced Attr node is returned. If no such attribute already exists, this method defines a new attribute for the Element.

It is usually easier to use `setAttribute()` instead of `setAttributeNode()`. However, you should use `setAttributeNode()` when you need to define an attribute whose value contains an entity reference for an XML document.

See Also

Attr, Element.setAttribute()

Element.setAttributeNodeNS( ) DOM Level 2 Core

add a namespace Attr node to an Element

Synopsis

```
Attr setAttributeNodeNS(Attr newAttr)
    throws DOMException;
```

Arguments

newAttr
The Attr node that represents the attribute to be added or whose value is to be modified.

Returns

The Attr node that was replaced by *newAttr*, or `null` if no attribute was replaced.

Throws

This method throws exceptions for the same reasons as `setAttributeNode( )`. It may also throw a DOMException with a code of `NOT_SUPPORTED_ERR` to signal that the method is not implemented because the current implementation does not support XML documents and namespaces.

Description

This method works just like `setAttributeNode( )`, except that it is designed for use with Attr nodes that represent attributes specified by namespace and name.

This method is useful only with XML documents that use namespaces. It may be unimplemented (i.e., throw a `NOT_SUPPORTED_ERR`) on browsers that do not support XML documents.

See Also

Attr, Element.setAttributeNS(), Element.setAttributeNode()

Element.setAttributeNS( ) DOM Level 2 Core

create or change an attribute with a namespace

Synopsis

```
void setAttributeNS(String namespaceURI,
                    String qualifiedName,
                    String value)
    throws DOMException;
```

Arguments

namespaceURI
The URI that uniquely identifies the namespace of the attribute to be set or created, or `null` for no namespace.

qualifiedName
: The name of the attribute, specified as a namespace prefix followed by a colon and a name within the namespace.

value
: The new value of the attribute.

Throws

This method may throw a DOMException with the following `code` values:

`INVALID_CHARACTER_ERR`
: The *qualifiedName* argument contains a character that is not allowed in HTML or XML attribute names.

`NAMESPACE_ERR`
: *qualifiedName* is malformed, or there is a mismatch between the namespace prefix of *qualifiedName* and the *namespaceURI* argument.

`NO_MODIFICATION_ALLOWED_ERR`
: This element is read-only and does not allow modifications to its attributes.

`NOT_SUPPORTED_ERR`
: The DOM implementation does not support XML documents.

Description

This method is like `setAttribute()`, except that the attribute to be created or set is specified by a namespace URI and a qualified name that consists of a namespace prefix, a colon, and a local name within the namespace. In addition to letting you change the value of an attribute, this method allows you to change the namespace prefix of an attribute.

This method is useful only with XML documents that use namespaces. It may be unimplemented (i.e., throw a `NOT_SUPPORTED_ERR`) on browsers that do not support XML documents.

See Also

Element.setAttribute(), Element.setAttributeNode()

ElementCSSInlineStyle

see HTMLElement

Entity

DOM Level 1 XML

an entity in an XML DTD

Node → Entity

Properties

`readonly String notationName`
: The notation name (for unparsed entities), or `null` if there is none (for parsed entities). See the `notations` property of DocumentType for a way to look up a Notation node by name.

`readonly String publicId`
: The public identifier for this entity, or `null` if none was specified.

W3C DOM Reference

`readonly String systemId`
The system identifier for this entity, or `null` if none was specified.

Description

This infrequently used interface represents an entity in an XML document type definition (DTD). It is never used with HTML documents.

The name of the entity is specified by the `nodeName` property inherited from the Node interface. The entity content is represented by the child nodes of the Entity node. Note that Entity nodes and their children are not part of the document tree (and the `parentNode` property of an Entity is always `null`). Instead, a document may contain one or more references to an entity; see "EntityReference" for more information.

Entities are defined in the DTD of a document, either as part of an external DTD file or as part of an "internal subset" that defines local entities specific to the current document. The DocumentType interface has an `entities` property that allows Entity nodes to be looked up by name. This is the only way to obtain a reference to an Entity node; because they are part of the document type, Entity nodes never appear as part of the document itself.

Entity nodes and all of their descendants are read-only and cannot be edited or modified in any way.

See Also

DocumentType, EntityReference, Notation

EntityReference

DOM Level 1 XML

a reference to an entity defined in an XML DTD

Node → EntityReference

Description

This infrequently used interface represents a reference from an XML document to an entity defined in the document's DTD. Character entities and predefined entities such as `<` are always expanded in XML and HTML documents, and EntityReference nodes never appear in HTML documents, so programmers working exclusively with HTML documents never need to use this interface. Note also that some XML parsers expand all entity references. Documents created by such parsers do not contain EntityReference nodes.

This interface defines no properties or methods of its own. The inherited `nodeName` property specifies the name of the referenced entity. The `entities` property of the DocumentType interface provides a way to look up the Entity object with that name. Note, however, that the DocumentType may not contain an Entity node with the specified name (because, for example, nonvalidating XML parsers are not required to parse the "external subset" of the DTD). In this case, the EntityReference has no children. On the other hand, if the DocumentType does contain an Entity node with the specified name, the child nodes of the EntityReference are copies of the child nodes of the Entity node and represent the content of the entity. Like Entity nodes, EntityReference nodes and their descendants are read-only and cannot be edited or modified.

See Also

DocumentType

Returned by: Document.createEntityReference()

Event

DOM Level 2 Events

information about an event

Subinterfaces

MutationEvent, UIEvent

Constants

These constants are the legal values of the `eventPhase` property; they represent the current phase of event propagation for this event:

`unsigned short CAPTURING_PHASE = 1`
: The event is in its capturing phase.

`unsigned short AT_TARGET = 2`
: The event is being handled by its target node.

`unsigned short BUBBLING_PHASE = 3`
: The event is bubbling.

Properties

`readonly boolean bubbles`
: `true` if the event is of a type that bubbles (unless `stopPropagation()` is called); `false` otherwise.

`readonly boolean cancelable`
: `true` if the default action associated with the event can be canceled with `preventDefault()`; `false` otherwise.

`readonly EventTarget currentTarget`
: The Document node that is currently handling this event. During capturing and bubbling, this is different from `target`. Note that all nodes implement the EventTarget interface, and the `currentTarget` property may refer to any node; it is not restricted to Element nodes.

`readonly unsigned short eventPhase`
: The current phase of event propagation. The three previous constants define the legal values for this property.

`readonly EventTarget target`
: The target node for this event; i.e., the node that generated the event. Note that this may be any node; it is not restricted to Element nodes.

`readonly Date timeStamp`
: The date and time at which the event occurred (or, technically, at which the Event object was created). Implementations are not required to provide valid time data in

this field, and if they do not, the `getTime( )` method of this Date object should return 0. See the Date object in the core reference section of this book.

`readonly String type`
: The name of the event that this Event object represents. This is the name under which the event handler was registered, or the name of the event handler property with the leading "on" removed. For example, "click", "load", or "submit". See Table 19-3 in Chapter 19 for a complete list of event types defined by the DOM standard.

Methods

`initEvent( )`
: Initializes the properties of a newly created Event object.

`preventDefault( )`
: Tells the web browser not to perform the default action associated with this event, if there is one. If the event is not of a type that is cancelable, this method has no effect.

`stopPropagation( )`
: Stops the event from propagating any further through the capturing, target, or bubbling phases of event propagation. After this method is called, any other event handlers for the same event on the same node will be called, but the event will not be dispatched to any other nodes.

Description

This interface represents an event that occurred on some node of the document and contains details about the event. Various subinterfaces of Event define additional properties that provide details pertinent to specific types of events.

Many event types use a more specific subinterface of Event to describe the event that has occurred. However, the event types defined by the HTMLEvents module use the Event interface directly. These event types are: "abort", "blur", "change", "error", "focus", "load", "reset", "resize", "scroll", "select", "submit", and "unload".

See Also

EventListener, EventTarget, MouseEvent, UIEvent; Chapter 19

Passed to: EventTarget.dispatchEvent()

Returned by: Document.createEvent()

Event.initEvent( ) DOM Level 2 Events

initialize the properties of a new Event

Synopsis

```
void initEvent(String eventTypeArg,
               boolean canBubbleArg,
               boolean cancelableArg);
```

Arguments

eventTypeArg
: The type of event. This may be one of the predefined event types, such as "load" or "submit", or it may be a custom type of your own choosing. Names that begin with "DOM" are reserved, however.

canBubbleArg
: Whether the event will bubble.

cancelableArg
: Whether the event may be canceled with `preventDefault( )`.

Description

This method initializes the `type`, `bubbles`, and `cancelable` properties of a synthetic Event object created by `Document.createEvent( )`. This method may be called on newly created Event objects only before they have been dispatched with the `EventTarget.dispatchEvent( )` method.

Event.preventDefault( ) DOM Level 2 Events

cancel default action of an event

Synopsis

```
void preventDefault( );
```

Description

This method tells the web browser not to perform the default action (if any) associated with this event. For example, if the `type` property is "submit", any event handler called during any phase of event propagation can prevent the form submission by calling this method. Note that if the `cancelable` property of an Event object is `false`, either there is no default action or there is a default action that cannot be prevented. In either case, calling this method has no effect.

Event.stopPropagation( ) DOM Level 2 Events

do not dispatch an event any further

Synopsis

```
void stopPropagation( );
```

Description

This method stops the propagation of an event and prevents it from being dispatched to any other Document nodes. It may be called during any phase of event propagation. Note that this method does not prevent other event handlers on the same Document node from being called, but it does prevent the event from being dispatched to any other nodes.

EventException

DOM Level 2 Events

signals an event-specific exception or error

Constants

The following constant defines the one legal value for the `code` property of an EventException object. Note that this constant is a static property of EventException, not a property of individual exception objects.

`unsigned short UNSPECIFIED_EVENT_TYPE_ERR = 0`

An Event object has a `type` property that is uninitialized, or is `null` or the empty string.

Properties

`unsigned short code`

An error code that provides some detail about what caused the exception. In the Level 2 DOM there is only one possible value for this field, defined by the constant above.

Description

An EventException is thrown by certain event-related methods to signal a problem of some sort. (In the DOM Level 2 specification, an exception of this type is thrown only by `EventTarget.dispatchEvent()`).

EventListener

DOM Level 2 Events

an event handler function

Methods

`handleEvent()`

In languages such as Java that do not allow functions to be passed as arguments to other functions, you define an event listener by defining a class that implements this interface and includes an implementation for this `handleEvent()` method. When an event occurs, the system calls this method and passes in an Event object that describes the event.

In JavaScript, however, you define an event handler simply by writing a function that accepts an Event object as its argument. The name of the function does not matter, and the function itself is used in place of an EventListener object. See the "Example" section.

Description

This interface defines the structure of an event listener or event handler. In languages such as Java, an event listener is an object that defines a method named `handleEvent()` that takes an Event object as its sole argument. In JavaScript, however, any function that expects a single Event argument, or a function that expects no argument, can serve as an event listener.

Example

```
// This function is an event listener for a "submit" event
function submitHandler(e) {
```

```
    // Call a form-validation function defined elsewhere
    if (!validate(e.target))
        e.preventDefault( );  // If validation fails, don't submit form
}

// We might register the event listener above like this
document.forms[0].addEventListener("submit", submitHandler, false);
```

See Also

Event, EventTarget; Chapter 19

Passed to: EventTarget.addEventListener( ), EventTarget.removeEventListener( )

EventTarget — DOM Level 2 Events

event listener registration methods

Methods

`addEventListener( )`
: Adds an event listener to the set of event listeners for this node.

`dispatchEvent( )`
: Dispatches a synthetic event to this node.

`removeEventListener( )`
: Removes an event listener from the set of listeners of this Document node.

Description

In DOM implementations that support events (i.e., those that support the "Events" feature), all nodes in the document tree implement this interface and maintain a set or list of event listener functions for each node. The `addEventListener( )` and `removeEventListener( )` methods allow listener functions to be added and removed from this set.

See Also

Event, EventListener; Chapter 19

Type of: Event.currentTarget, Event.target, MouseEvent.relatedTarget

Passed to: MouseEvent.initMouseEvent( )

EventTarget.addEventListener( ) — DOM Level 2 Events

register an event handler

Synopsis

```
void addEventListener(String type,
                      EventListener listener,
                      boolean useCapture);
```

Arguments

type
: The type of event for which the event listener is to be invoked. For example, "load", "click", or "mousedown".

listener
: The event listener function that will be invoked when an event of the specified type is dispatched to this Document node.

useCapture
: If `true`, the specified *listener* is to be invoked only during the capturing phase of event propagation. The more common value of `false` means that the *listener* will not be invoked during the capturing phase but instead will be invoked when this node is the actual event target or when the event bubbles up to this node from its original target.

Description

This method adds the specified event listener function to the set of listeners registered on this node to handle events of the specified *type*. If *useCapture* is `true`, the listener is registered as a capturing event listener. If *useCapture* is `false`, it is registered as a normal event listener.

`addEventListener( )` may be called multiple times to register multiple event handlers for the same type of event on the same node. Note, however, that the DOM makes no guarantees about the order in which multiple event handlers will be invoked.

If the same event listener function is registered twice on the same node with the same *type* and *useCapture* arguments, the second registration is simply ignored. If a new event listener is registered on this node while an event is being handled at this node, the new event listener is not invoked for that event.

When a Document node is duplicated with `Node.cloneNode( )` or `Document.importNode( )`, the event listeners registered for the original node are not copied.

See Also

Event, EventListener; Chapter 19

EventTarget.dispatchEvent( ) DOM Level 2 Events

dispatch a synthetic event to this node

Synopsis

```
boolean dispatchEvent(Event evt)
    throws EventException;
```

Arguments

evt
: The Event object to be dispatched.

Returns

`false` if the `preventDefault()` method of *evt* was called at any time during the propagation of the event, or `true` otherwise.

Throws

This method throws an `EventException` with its `code` property set to `EventException.UNSPECIFIED_EVENT_TYPE_ERR` if the Event object *evt* was not initialized or if its `type` property was `null` or the empty string.

Description

This method dispatches a synthetic event created with `Document.createEvent()` and initialized with the initialization method defined by the Event interface or one of its subinterfaces. The node on which this method is called becomes the target of the event, but the event first propagates down the document tree during the capturing phase, and then, if the `bubbles` property of the event is `true`, it bubbles up the document tree after being handled at the event target itself.

See Also

Document.createEvent(), Event.initEvent(), MouseEvent.initMouseEvent()

EventTarget.removeEventListener() DOM Level 2 Events

delete an event listener

Synopsis

```
void removeEventListener(String type,
                         EventListener listener,
                         boolean useCapture);
```

Arguments

type
: The type of event for which the event listener is to be deleted.

listener
: The event listener function that is to be removed.

useCapture
: `true` if a capturing event listener is to be removed; `false` if a normal event listener is to be removed.

Description

This method removes the specified event listener function. The *type* and *useCapture* arguments must be the same as they were in the corresponding call to `addEventListener()`. If no event listener is found that matches the specified arguments, this method does nothing.

Once an event listener function has been removed by this method, it will no longer be invoked for the specified *type* of event on this node. This is true even if the event listener is removed by another event listener registered for the same type of event on the same node.

W3C DOM Reference

HTMLAnchorElement

DOM Level 1 HTML

a hyperlink or anchor in an HTML document

Node → Element → HTMLElement → HTMLAnchorElement

Properties

This interface defines the properties in the following table, which correspond to the HTML attributes of the <a> tag.

Property	Attribute	Description
`String accessKey`	`accesskey`	Keyboard shortcut
`String charset`	`charset`	Encoding of the destination document
`String coords`	`coords`	Used inside `<map>` elements
`String href`	`href`	URL of the hyperlink
`String hreflang`	`hreflang`	Language of the linked document
`String name`	`name`	Name of the anchor
`String rel`	`rel`	Link type
`String rev`	`rev`	Reverse link type
`String shape`	`shape`	Used inside `<map>` elements
`long tabIndex`	`tabindex`	Link's position in tabbing order
`String target`	`target`	Name of the frame or window in which the destination document is to be displayed
`String type`	`type`	Content type of the destination document

Methods

`blur()`
: Takes keyboard focus away from the link.

`focus()`
: Scrolls the document so the anchor or link is visible and gives keyboard focus to the link.

Description

This interface represents an <a> tag in an HTML document. `href`, `name`, and `target` are the key properties, representing the most commonly used attributes of the tag.

HTMLAnchorElement objects can be obtained from the `links` and `anchors` HTMLCollection properties of the HTMLDocument interface.

Example

```
// Get the destination URL of first the hyperlink in the document
var url = document.links[0].href;
// Scroll the document so the anchor named "_bottom_" is visible
document.anchors['_bottom_'].focus();
```

See Also

Link and Anchor objects in the client-side reference section

HTMLAnchorElement.blur( )

DOM Level 1 HTML

take keyboard focus away from a hyperlink

Synopsis

```
void blur();
```

Description

For web browsers that allow hyperlinks to have the keyboard focus, this method takes keyboard focus away from a hyperlink.

HTMLAnchorElement.focus( )

DOM Level 1 HTML

make a link or anchor visible and give it keyboard focus

Synopsis

```
void focus();
```

Description

This method scrolls the document so the specified anchor or hyperlink is visible. If the element is a hyperlink and the browser allows hyperlinks to have keyboard focus, this method also gives keyboard focus to the element.

HTMLBodyElement

DOM Level 1 HTML

the <body> of an HTML document

Node → Element → HTMLElement → HTMLBodyElement

Properties

`deprecated String aLink`
: The value of the `alink` attribute. Specifies the color of "active" links; that is, the color of a link when the mouse has been pressed over it but has not yet been released.

`deprecated String background`
: The value of the `background` attribute. Specifies the URL of an image to use as a background texture for the document.

`deprecated String bgColor`
: The value of the `bgcolor` attribute. Specifies the background color of the document.

`deprecated String link`
: The value of the `link` attribute. Specifies the normal color of unvisited hyperlinks.

`deprecated String text`
: The value of the `text` attribute. Specifies the foreground color (the color of text) for the document.

`deprecated String vLink`
: The value of the `vlink` attribute. Specifies the normal color of "visited" hyperlinks that have already been followed.

Description

The HTMLBodyElement interface represents the `<body>` tag of a document. All HTML documents have a `<body>` tag, even if it does not explicitly appear in the document source. You can obtain the HTMLBodyElement of a document through the `body` property of the HTMLDocument interface.

The properties of this object specify default colors and images for the document. Although these properties represent the values of `<body>` attributes, the Level 0 DOM made these same values accessible through properties (with different names) of the Document object. See the Document object in the client-side reference section of this book for details.

Although these color and image properties belong more appropriately to the HTML-BodyElement interface than they do to the Document object, note that they are all deprecated because the HTML 4 standard deprecates the `<body>` attributes that they represent. The preferred way to specify colors and images for a document is using CSS styles.

Example

```
document.body.text = "#ff0000";          // Display text in bright red
document.fgColor = "#ff0000";            // Same thing using old DOM Level 0 API
document.body.style.color = "#ff0000";   // Same thing using CSS styles
```

See Also

Document object in the client-side reference section

HTMLCollection — DOM Level 1 HTML

array of HTML elements accessible by position or name

Properties

`readonly unsigned long length`
: The number of elements in the collection.

Methods

`item()`
: Returns the element at the specified position in the collection. You can also simply specify the position within array brackets instead of calling this method explicitly.

`namedItem()`
: Returns the element from the collection that has the specified value for its `id` or `name` attribute, or `null` if there is no such element. You may also place the element name within array brackets instead of calling this method explicitly.

Description

An HTMLCollection is a collection of HTML elements with methods that allow you to retrieve the elements by their position in the document or by their `id` or `name` attribute. In JavaScript, HTMLCollection objects behave like read-only arrays, and you may use JavaScript square-bracket notation to index an HTMLCollection by number or by name instead of calling the `item()` and `namedItem()` methods.

A number of the properties of the HTMLDocument interface (which standardizes the DOM Level 0 Document object) are HTMLCollection objects, which provide convenient access to document elements such as forms, images, and links. The HTMLCollection object also provides a convenient way to traverse the elements of an HTML form, the rows of an HTML table, the cells of a table row, and the areas of a client-side image map.

HTMLCollection objects are read-only: you cannot assign new elements to them, even when using JavaScript array notation. They are "live," meaning that if the underlying document changes, those changes are immediately visible through all HTMLCollection objects.

Example

```
var c = document.forms;           // This is an HTMLCollection of form elements
var firstform = c[0];             // It can be used like a numeric array
var lastform = c[c.length-1];     // The length property gives the number of elements
var address = c["address"];       // It can be used like an associative array
var address = c.address;          // JavaScript allows this notation, too
```

See Also

NodeList

Type of: HTMLDocument.anchors, HTMLDocument.applets, HTMLDocument.forms, HTMLDocument.images, HTMLDocument.links, HTMLFormElement.elements, HTMLMapElement.areas, HTMLSelectElement.options, HTMLTableElement.rows, HTMLTableElement.tBodies, HTMLTableRowElement.cells, HTMLTableSectionElement.rows

HTMLCollection.item() — DOM Level 1 HTML

get an element by position

Synopsis

```
Node item(unsigned long index);
```

Arguments

index

The position of the element to be returned. Elements appear in an HTMLCollection in the same order in which they appear in the document source.

Returns

The element at the specified *index*, or `null` if *index* is less than zero or greater than or equal to the `length` property.

Description

The item( ) method returns a numbered element from an HTMLCollection. In JavaScript, it is easier to treat the HTMLCollection as an array and to index it using array notation.

Example

```
var c = document.images;  // This is an HTMLCollection
var img0 = c.item(0);     // You can use the item( ) method this way
var img1 = c[1];          // But this notation is easier and more common
```

See Also

NodeList.item( )

HTMLCollection.namedItem( ) DOM Level 1 HTML

get an element by name

Synopsis

```
Node namedItem(String name);
```

Arguments

name
    The name of the element to be returned.

Returns

An element with the specified *name*, or null if no elements in the HTMLCollection have that name.

Description

This method finds and returns an element from the HTMLCollection that has the specified name. If any element has an id attribute whose value is the specified name, that element is returned. If no such element is found, an element whose name attribute has the specified value is returned. If no such element exists, namedItem( ) returns null.

Note that any HTML element may be given an id attribute, but only certain HTML elements—such as forms, form elements, images, and anchors—may have a name attribute.

In JavaScript, it is easier to treat the HTMLCollection as an associative array and to specify *name* between square brackets using array notation.

Example

```
var forms = document.forms;                  // An HTMLCollection of forms
var address = forms.namedItem("address");  // Finds <form name="address">
var payment = forms["payment"]  // Simpler syntax: finds <form name="payment">
var login = forms.login;         // Also works: finds <form name="login">
```

HTMLDocument

DOM Level 1 HTML

the root of an HTML document tree

Node → Document → HTMLDocument

Properties

readonly HTMLCollection anchors

An array (HTMLCollection) of all anchors in the document. For compatibility with The Level 0 DOM, this array contains only <a> elements that have a name attribute specified; it does not include anchors created with an id attribute.

readonly HTMLCollection applets

An array (HTMLCollection) of all applets in a document. These include applets defined with an <object> tag and all <applet> tags.

HTMLElement body

A convenience property that refers to the HTMLBodyElement that represents the <body> tag of this document. For documents that define framesets, this property refers to the outermost <frameset> tag.

String cookie

Allows cookies to be queried and set for this document. See "Document.cookie" in the client-side reference section.

readonly String domain

The domain name of the server from which the document was loaded, or null if there is none. Contrast with the read/write Document.domain property in the client-side reference section.

readonly HTMLCollection forms

An array (HTMLCollection) of all HTMLFormElement objects in the document.

readonly HTMLCollection images

An array (HTMLCollection) of all <img> tags in the document. Note that for compatibility with the Level 0 DOM, images defined with an <object> tag are not included in this collection.

readonly HTMLCollection links

An array (HTMLCollection) of all hyperlinks in the document. These include all <a> tags that have an href attribute, and all <area> tags.

readonly String referrer

The URL of the document that linked to this document, or null if this document was not accessed through a hyperlink.

String title

The contents of the <title> tag for this document.

readonly String URL

The URL of the document.

Methods

close()

Closes a document stream opened with the open() method, forcing any buffered output to be displayed.

`getElementById()`
: Returns the element with the specified `id`. In the Level 2 DOM, this method is inherited from the Document interface.

`getElementsByName()`
: Returns an array of nodes (a NodeList) of all elements in the document that have a specified value for their `name` attribute.

`open()`
: Opens a stream to which new document contents may be written. Note that this method erases any current document content.

`write()`
: Appends a string of HTML text to an open document.

`writeln()`
: Appends a string of HTML text followed by a newline character to an open document.

Description

This interface extends Document and defines HTML-specific properties and methods that provide compatibility with the DOM Level 0 Document object (see the Document object in the client-side reference section). Note that HTMLDocument does not have all the properties of the Level 0 Document object. The properties that specify document colors and background images have been renamed and moved to the HTMLBodyElement.

Finally, note that in the Level 1 DOM, HTMLDocument defines a method named `getElementById()`. In the Level 2 DOM, this method has been moved to the Document interface, and it is now inherited by HTMLDocument rather than defined by it. See the "Document.getElementById()" entry in this reference section for details.

See Also

Document.getElementById(), HTMLBodyElement; Document object in the client-side reference section

Returned by: HTMLDOMImplementation.createHTMLDocument()

HTMLDocument.close() — DOM Level 1 HTML

close an open document and display it

Synopsis

```
void close();
```

Description

This method closes a document stream that was opened with the `open()` method and forces any buffered output to be displayed. See the "Document.close()" entry in the client-side reference section for full details.

See Also

HTMLDocument.open(); Document.close() in the client-side reference section

HTMLDocument.getElementById( )

see Document.getElementById( )

HTMLDocument.getElementsByName( )

DOM Level 1 HTML

find elements with the specified name attribute

Synopsis

```
Node[] getElementsByName(String elementName);
```

Arguments

elementName
The desired value for the name attribute.

Returns

An array (really a NodeList) of elements that have a name attribute of the specified value. If no such elements are found, the returned NodeList is empty and has a length of 0.

Description

This method searches an HTML document tree for Element nodes that have a name attribute of the specified value and returns a NodeList (which you can treat as an array) containing all matching elements. If there are no matching elements, a NodeList with length 0 is returned.

Do not confuse this method with the Document.getElementById( ) method, which finds a single Element based on the unique value of an id attribute, or with the Document.getElementsByTagName( ) method, which returns a NodeList of elements with the specified tag name.

See Also

Document.getElementById(), Document.getElementsByTagName()

HTMLDocument.open( )

DOM Level 1 HTML

begin a new document, erasing the current one

Synopsis

```
void open( );
```

Description

This method erases the current HTML document and begins a new one, which may be written to with the write( ) and writeln( ) methods. After calling open( ) to begin a new document and write( ) to specify document content, you must always remember to call close( ) to end the document and force its content to be displayed.

This method should not be called by a script or event handler that is part of the document being overwritten, since the script or handler will itself be overwritten.

See "Document.open()" in the client-side reference section, but note that this standardized version of that method can be used only to create new HTML documents and does not accept the optional *mimetype* argument that the Level 0 version does.

Example

```
var w = window.open("");          // Open a new window
var d = w.document;               // Get its HTMLDocument object
d.open();                         // Open the document for writing
d.write("<h1>Hello world</h1>");  // Output some HTML to the document
d.close();                        // End the document and display it
```

See Also

HTMLDocument.close(), HTMLDocument.write(); Document.open() in the client-side reference section

HTMLDocument.write( ) DOM Level 1 HTML

append HTML text to an open document

Synopsis

`void write(String text);`

Arguments

text
The HTML text to be appended to the document.

Description

This method appends the specified HTML text to the document, which must have been opened with the `open()` method and must not yet have been closed with `close()`.

See "Document.write()" in the client-side reference section for complete details, but note that this standardized version of that Level 0 method accepts only a single string argument, not an arbitrary number of arguments.

See Also

HTMLDocument.open(); Document.write() in the client-side reference section

HTMLDocument.writeln( ) DOM Level 1 HTML

append HTML text and a newline to an open document

Synopsis

`void writeln(String text);`

Arguments

text
The HTML text to be appended to the document.

Description

This method is like `HTMLDocument.write()`, except that it follows the appended text with a newline character, which can be useful when writing the content of a <pre> tag, for example.

See Also

Document.writeln() in the client-side reference section

HTMLDOMImplementation

see DOMImplementation

HTMLElement

DOM Level 1 HTML

the base interface for all HTML elements

Node → Element → HTMLElement

Also Implements

ElementCSSInlineStyle

If the implementation supports CSS style sheets, all objects that implement this interface also implement the ElementCSSInlineStyle interface. Because CSS support is quite common in web browsers, the `style` property defined by that interface is included here for convenience.

Subinterfaces

HTMLAnchorElement	HTMLAppletElement	HTMLAreaElement
HTMLBRElement	HTMLBaseElement	HTMLBaseFontElement
HTMLBodyElement	HTMLButtonElement	HTMLDListElement
HTMLDirectoryElement	HTMLDivElement	HTMLFieldSetElement
HTMLFontElement	HTMLFormElement	HTMLFrameElement
HTMLFrameSetElement	HTMLHRElement	HTMLHeadElement
HTMLHeadingElement	HTMLHtmlElement	HTMLIFrameElement
HTMLImageElement	HTMLInputElement	HTMLIsIndexElement
HTMLLIElement	HTMLLabelElement	HTMLLegendElement
HTMLLinkElement	HTMLMapElement	HTMLMenuElement
HTMLMetaElement	HTMLModElement	HTMLOListElement
HTMLObjectElement	HTMLOptGroupElement	HTMLOptionElement
HTMLParagraphElement	HTMLParamElement	HTMLPreElement
HTMLQuoteElement	HTMLScriptElement	HTMLSelectElement
HTMLStyleElement	HTMLTableCaptionElement	HTMLTableCellElement
HTMLTableColElement	HTMLTableElement	HTMLTableRowElement
HTMLTableSectionElement	HTMLTextAreaElement	HTMLTitleElement
HTMLUListElement		

Properties

`readonly CSS2Properties style`

The value of the `style` attribute that specifies inline CSS styles for this element. This property is not actually defined directly by the HTMLElement interface; instead, it is defined by the ElementCSSInlineStyle interface. If a browser supports CSS style sheets, all of its HTMLElement objects implement ElementCSSInlineStyle and define this `style` property. The value of this property is an object that implements the CSSStyle-Declaration interface and the (more commonly used) CSS2Properties interface.

`String className`
: The value of the `class` attribute of the element, which specifies the name of a CSS class. Note that this property is not named "class" because that name is a reserved word in JavaScript.

`String dir`
: The value of the `dir` attribute of the element, which specifies the text direction for the document.

`String id`
: The value of the `id` attribute. No two elements within the same document should have the same value for `id`.

`String lang`
: The value of the `lang` attribute, which specifies the language code for the document.

`String title`
: The value of the `title` attribute, which specifies descriptive text suitable for display in a "tooltip" for the element.

Description

This interface defines properties that represent the attributes shared by all HTML elements. All HTML elements implement this interface, and most implement a tag-specific subinterface that defines properties for each of that tag's attributes. In addition to the properties listed here, see the "HTMLElement" reference page in the client-side reference section for a list of DOM Level 0 event handler properties that are supported by all HTML elements in a document.

Some HTML tags do not allow any attributes other than the universal attributes allowed on all HTML tags and represented by the properties of HTMLElement. These tags do not have their own tag-specific subinterface, and elements of this type in the document tree are represented by an HTMLElement object. The tags without a tag-specific interface of their own are the following:

`<abbr>`	`<acronym>`	`<address>`	`<b>`
`<bdo>`	`<big>`	`<center>`	`<cite>`
`<code>`	`<dd>`	`<dfn>`	`<dt>`
`<em>`	`<i>`	`<kbd>`	`<noframes>`
`<noscript>`	`<s>`	`<samp>`	`<small>`
`<span>`	`<strike>`	`<strong>`	`<sub>`
`<sup>`	`<tt>`	`<u>`	`<var>`

As you can see from the earlier "Subinterfaces" section, there are many HTML tags that *do* have tag-specific subinterfaces. Typically, a tag named *T* has a tag-specific interface named HTML*T*Element. For example, the `<head>` tag is represented by the HTMLHead-Element interface. In a few cases, two or more related tags share a single interface, as in the case of the <h1> through <h6> tags, which are all represented by the HTMLHeadingElement interface.

Most of these tag-specific interfaces do nothing more than define a JavaScript property for each attribute of the HTML tag. The JavaScript properties have the same names as the attributes and use lowercase (e.g., `id`) or, when the attribute name consists of multiple words, mixed-case (e.g., `className`). When an HTML attribute name is a reserved word in Java or JavaScript, the property name is changed slightly. For example, the `class` attribute of all HTML tags becomes the `className` property of the HTMLElement interface because `class` is a reserved word. Similarly, the `for` attribute of <label> and <script> tags becomes the `htmlFor` property of the HTMLLabelElement and HTMLScriptElement interfaces because `for` is a reserved word. The meanings of those properties that correspond directly to HTML attributes are defined by the HTML specification, and documenting each one is beyond the scope of this book.

The following table lists all the HTML tags that have a corresponding subinterface of HTMLElement. For each tag, the table lists the interface name and the names of the properties and methods it defines. All properties are read/write strings unless otherwise specified. For properties that are not read/write strings, the property type is specified in square brackets before the property name. Because these interfaces and their properties map so directly to HTML elements and attributes, most interfaces do not have reference pages of their own in this book, and you should consult an HTML reference for details. The exceptions are interfaces that define methods and interfaces that represent certain particularly important tags, such as the <body> tag. These interfaces are marked with a * in the table, and you can look them up in this reference section for further details.

HTML tag	DOM interface, properties, and methods
all tags	**HTMLElement***: `id`, `title`, `lang`, `dir`, `className`
<a>	**HTMLAnchorElement***: `accessKey`, `charset`, `coords`, `href`, `hreflang`, `name`, `rel`, `rev`, `shape`, `[long] tabIndex`, `target`, `type`, `blur()`, `focus()`
<applet>	**HTMLAppletElement**†: `align`†, `alt`†, `archive`†, `code`†, `codeBase`†, `height`†, `hspace`†, `name`†, `object`†, `vspace`†, `width`†
<area>	**HTMLAreaElement**: `accessKey`, `alt`, `coords`, `href`, `[boolean] noHref`, `shape`, `[long] tabIndex`, `target`
<base>	**HTMLBaseElement**: `href`, `target`
<basefont>	**HTMLBaseFontElement**†: `color`†, `face`†, `size`†
<blockquote>, <q>	**HTMLQuoteElement**: `cite`
<body>	**HTMLBodyElement***: `aLink`†, `background`†, `bgColor`†, `link`†, `text`†, `vLink`†
 	HTMLBRElement: `clear`†
<button>	**HTMLButtonElement**: `[readonly HTMLFormElement] form`, `accessKey`, `[boolean] disabled`, `name`, `[long] tabIndex`, `[readonly] type`, `value`
<caption>	**HTMLTableCaptionElement***: `align`†
<col>, <colgroup>	**HTMLTableColElement***: `align`, `ch`, `chOff`, `[long] span`, `vAlign`, `width`
<del>, <ins>	**HTMLModElement**: `cite`, `dateTime`

HTML tag	DOM interface, properties, and methods
<dir>	**HTMLDirectoryElement**†: [boolean] compact†
<div>	**HTMLDivElement**: align†
<dl>	**HTMLDListElement**: [boolean] compact†
<fieldset>	**HTMLFieldSetElement**: [readonly HTMLFormElement] form
<font>	**HTMLFontElement**†: color†, face†, size†
<form>	**HTMLFormElement***: [readonly HTMLCollection] elements, [readonly long] length, name, acceptCharset, action, enctype, method, target, submit( ), reset( )
<frame>	**HTMLFrameElement**: frameBorder, longDesc, marginHeight, marginWidth, name, [boolean] noResize, scrolling, src, [readonly Document] contentDocument‡
<frameset>	**HTMLFrameSetElement**: cols, rows
<h1>, <h2>, <h3>, <h4>, <h5>, <h6>	**HTMLHeadingElement**: align†
<head>	**HTMLHeadElement**: profile
<hr>	**HTMLHRElement**: align†, [boolean] noShade†, size†, width†
<html>	**HTMLHtmlElement**: version†
<iframe>	**HTMLIFrameElement**: align†, frameBorder, height, longDesc, marginHeight, marginWidth, name, scrolling, src, width, [readonly Document] contentDocument‡
<img>	**HTMLImageElement**: align†, alt, [long] border†, [long] height, [long] hspace†, [boolean] isMap, longDesc, **name**, src, useMap, [long] vspace†, [long] width
<input>	**HTMLInputElement***: defaultValue, [boolean] defaultChecked, [readonly HTMLFormElement] form, accept, accessKey, align†, alt, [boolean] checked, [boolean] disabled, [long] maxLength, name, [boolean] readOnly, size, src, [long] tabIndex, type, useMap, value, blur( ), focus( ), select( ), click( )
<ins>	See <del>
<isindex>	**HTMLIsIndexElement**†: [readonly HTMLFormElement] form, prompt†
<label>	**HTMLLabelElement**: [readonly HTMLFormElement] form, accessKey, htmlFor
<legend>	**HTMLLegendElement**: [readonly HTMLFormElement] form, accessKey, align†
<li>	**HTMLLIElement**: type†, [long] value†
<link>	**HTMLLinkElement**: [boolean] disabled, charset, href, hreflang, media, rel, rev, target, type
<map>	**HTMLMapElement**: [readonly HTMLCollection of HTMLAreaElement] areas, name
<menu>	**HTMLMenuElement**†: [boolean] compact†
<meta>	**HTMLMetaElement**: content, httpEquiv, name, scheme
<object>	**HTMLObjectElement**: code, align†, archive, border†, codeBase, codeType, data, [boolean] declare, height, hspace†, name, standby, [long] tabIndex, type, useMap, vspace†, width, [readonly Document] contentDocument‡
<ol>	**HTMLOListElement**: [boolean] compact†, [long] start†, type†

HTML tag	DOM interface, properties, and methods
<optgroup>	**HTMLOptGroupElement**: [boolean] disabled, label
<option>	**HTMLOptionElement***: [readonly HTMLFormElement] form, [boolean] defaultSelected, [readonly] text, [readonly long] index, [boolean] disabled, label, [boolean] selected, value
<p>	**HTMLParagraphElement**: align†
<param>	**HTMLParamElement**: name, type, value, valueType
<pre>	**HTMLPreElement**: [long] width†
<q>	See <blockquote>
<script>	**HTMLScriptElement**: text, htmlFor, event, charset, [boolean] defer, src, type
<select>	**HTMLSelectElement***: [readonly] type, [long] selectedIndex, value, [readonly long] length, [readonly HTMLFormElement] form, [readonly HTMLCollection of HTMLOptionElement] options, [boolean] disabled, [boolean] multiple, name, [long] size, [long] tabIndex, add( ), remove( ), blur( ), focus( )
<style>	**HTMLStyleElement**: [boolean] disabled, media, type
<table>	**HTMLTableElement***: [HTMLTableCaptionElement] caption, [HTMLTableSectionElement] tHead, [HTMLTableSectionElement] tFoot, [readonly HTMLCollection of HTMLTableRowElement] rows, [readonly HTMLCollection of HTMLTableSectionElement] tBodies, align†, bgColor†, border, cellPadding, cellSpacing, frame, rules, summary, width, createTHead( ), deleteTHead( ), createTFoot( ), deleteTFoot( ), createCaption( ), deleteCaption( ), insertRow( ), deleteRow( )
<tbody>, <tfoot>, <thead>	**HTMLTableSectionElement***: align, ch, chOff, vAlign, [readonly HTMLCollection of HTMLTableRowElement] rows, insertRow( ), deleteRow( )
<td>, <th>	**HTMLTableCellElement***: [readonly long] cellIndex, abbr, align, axis, bgColor†, ch, chOff, [long] colSpan, headers, height†, [boolean] noWrap†, [long] rowSpan, scope, vAlign, width†
<textarea>	**HTMLTextAreaElement***: defaultValue, [readonly HTMLFormElement] form, accessKey, [long] cols, [boolean] disabled, name, [boolean] readOnly, [long] rows, [long] tabIndex, [readonly] type, value, blur( ), focus( ), select( )
<tfoot>	See <tbody>
<th>	See <td>
<thead>	See <tbody>
<title>	**HTMLTitleElement**: text
<tr>	**HTMLTableRowElement***: [readonly long] rowIndex, [readonly long] sectionRowIndex, [readonly HTMLCollection of HTMLTableCellElement] cells, align, bgColor†, ch, chOff, vAlign, insertCell( ), deleteCell( )
<ul>	**HTMLUListElement**: [boolean] compact†, type†

* Indicates interfaces documented in this book.
† Indicates deprecated elements and attributes.
‡ Indicates attributes added in HTML DOM Level 2 working draft.

W3C DOM Reference

See Also

HTMLElement in the client-side reference section

Type of: HTMLDocument.body

Passed to: HTMLSelectElement.add()

Returned by: HTMLTableElement.createCaption(), HTMLTableElement.createTFoot(), HTMLTableElement.createTHead(), HTMLTableElement.insertRow(), HTMLTableRowElement.insertCell(), HTMLTableSectionElement.insertRow()

HTMLFormElement

DOM Level 1 HTML

a <form> in an HTML document

Node → Element → HTMLElement → HTMLFormElement

Properties

`readonly HTMLCollection elements`

An array (HTMLCollection) of all elements in the form.

`readonly long length`

The number of form elements in the form. This is the same value as `elements.length`.

In addition to the properties above, HTMLFormElement also defines the properties in the following table, which correspond directly to HTML attributes.

Property	Attribute	Description
`String acceptCharset`	`acceptcharset`	Character sets the server can accept
`String action`	`action`	URL of the form handler
`String enctype`	`enctype`	Encoding of the form
`String method`	`method`	HTTP method used for form submission
`String name`	`name`	Name of the form
`String target`	`target`	Frame or window name for form submission results

Methods

`reset()`

Resets all form elements to their default values.

`submit()`

Submits the form.

Description

This interface represents a `<form>` element in an HTML document. The `elements` property is an HTMLCollection that provides convenient access to all elements of the form. The `submit()` and `reset()` methods allow a form to be submitted or reset under program control.

See the Form object in the client-side reference section for more details.

See Also

Form object in the client-side reference section

Type of: HTMLButtonElement.form, HTMLFieldSetElement.form, HTMLInputElement.form, HTMLIsIndexElement.form, HTMLLabelElement.form, HTMLLegendElement.form, HTMLObjectElement.form, HTMLOptionElement.form, HTMLSelectElement.form, HTMLTextAreaElement.form

HTMLFormElement.reset( ) — DOM Level 1 HTML

reset the elements of a form to their default values

Synopsis

```
void reset( );
```

Description

This method resets each of the elements of a form to its default value. The results of calling this method are like the results of a user clicking on a **Reset** button, except that the `onreset` event handler of the form is not invoked.

See Also

Form.reset( ) in the client-side reference section

HTMLFormElement.submit( ) — DOM Level 1 HTML

submit a form

Synopsis

```
void submit( );
```

Description

This method submits the values of the form elements to the form handler specified by the form's `action` property. It submits a form in the same way that a user's clicking on a **Submit** button does, except that the `onsubmit` event handler of the form is not triggered.

See Also

Form.submit( ) in the client-side reference section

HTMLInputElement — DOM Level 1 HTML

an input element in an HTML form — Node → Element → HTMLElement → HTMLInputElement

Properties

`String accept`
: A comma-separated list of MIME types that specify the types of files that may be uploaded when this is a FileUpload element. Mirrors the `accept` attribute.

`String accessKey`
: The keyboard shortcut (which must be a single character) that a browser may use to transfer keyboard focus to this input element. Mirrors the `accesskey` attribute.

`deprecated String align`
: The vertical alignment of this element with respect to the surrounding text, or the left or right float for the element. Mirrors the `align` attribute.

`String alt`
: Alternate text to be displayed by browsers that cannot render this input element. Particularly useful when `type` is `image`. Mirrors the `alt` attribute.

`boolean checked`
: For Radio and Checkbox input elements, specifies whether the element is "checked" or not. Setting this property changes the visual appearance of the input element. Mirrors the `checked` attribute.

`boolean defaultChecked`
: For Radio and Checkbox elements, holds the initial value of the `checked` attribute as it appears in the document source. When the form is reset, the `checked` property is restored to the value of this property. Changing the value of this property changes the value of the `checked` property and the current checked state of the element.

`String defaultValue`
: For Text, Password, and FileUpload elements, holds the initial value displayed by the element. When the form is reset, the element is restored to this value. Changing the value of this property also changes the `value` property and the currently displayed value.

`boolean disabled`
: If `true`, the input element is disabled and is unavailable for user input. Mirrors the `disabled` attribute.

`readonly HTMLFormElement form`
: The HTMLFormElement object representing the `<form>` element that contains this input element, or `null` if the input element is not within a form.

`long maxLength`
: For Text or Password elements, specifies the maximum number of characters that the user will be allowed to enter. Note that this is not the same as the `size` property. Mirrors the `maxlength` attribute.

`String name`
: The name of the input element, as specified by the `name` attribute.

`boolean readOnly`
: If `true`, and this is a Text or Password element, the user is not allowed to enter text into the element. Mirrors the `readonly` attribute.

`String size`
: For Text and Password elements, specifies the width of the element in characters. Mirrors the `size` attribute. See also `maxLength`.

`String src`
: For input elements with a `type` of `image`, specifies the URL of the image to be displayed. Mirrors the `src` attribute.

`long tabIndex`
: The position of this input element in the tabbing order. Mirrors the `tabindex` attribute.

`String type`
: The type of the input element. The various types and their meanings are listed in the table in the "Description" section. Mirrors the type attribute.

`String useMap`
: For elements with a type of `image`, specifies the name of a `<map>` element that provides a client-side image map for the element.

`String value`
: The value that is passed to the server-side script when the form is submitted. For Text, Password, and FileUpload elements, this property is the text contained by the input element. For Button, Submit, and Reset elements, this is the text that appears in the button. For security reasons, the `value` property of FileUpload elements may be read-only. Similarly, the value returned by this property for Password elements may not contain the user's actual input.

Methods

`blur()`
: Takes keyboard focus away from the element.

`click()`
: If this input element is a Button, a Checkbox, or a Radio, Submit, or Reset button, this method simulates a mouse-click on the element.

`focus()`
: Transfers keyboard focus to this input element.

`select()`
: If this input element is a Text, Password, or FileUpload element, this method selects the text displayed by the element. In many browsers, this means that when the user next enters a character, the selected text will be deleted and replaced with the newly typed character.

Description

This interface represents an `<input>` element that defines an HTML input element (typically in an HTML form). An HTMLInputElement can represent various types of input elements, depending on the value of its `type` property. The allowed values for this property and their meanings are shown in the following table.

Type	Input element type
`button`	Push button
`checkbox`	Checkbox element
`file`	FileUpload element
`hidden`	Hidden element
`image`	Graphical Submit button
`password`	Masked-text entry field for passwords
`radio`	Mutually exclusive Radio button

Type	Input element type
`reset`	Reset button
`text` (default value)	Single-line text entry field
`submit`	Submit button

See Chapter 15 for more information about HTML forms and form elements. Note also that each distinct type of form input element has its own reference page in the client-side reference section of this book.

See Also

HTMLFormElement, HTMLOptionElement, HTMLSelectElement, HTMLTextAreaElement; Chapter 15; the Input object in the client-side reference section, and also its subclasses (Button, Checkbox, FileUpload, Hidden, Password, Radio, Reset, Submit, and Text)

HTMLInputElement.blur( ) DOM Level 1 HTML

take keyboard focus away from this element

Synopsis

```
void blur( );
```

Description

This method takes keyboard focus away from this form element.

HTMLInputElement.click( ) DOM Level 1 HTML

simulate a mouse-click on a form element

Synopsis

```
void click( );
```

Description

This method simulates a mouse-click on a Button, Checkbox, Radio, Reset, or Submit form element. It does not trigger the `onclick` event handler for the input element.

When called on Button elements, it may (or may not) produce the visual appearance of a button-click, but it has no other effect since it does not trigger the onclick event handler for the button. For Checkbox elements, it toggles the `checked` property. It makes unchecked Radio elements become checked but leaves checked elements alone. When called on Reset and Submit elements, the `click( )` method causes the form to be reset or submitted.

HTMLInputElement.focus( )

DOM Level 1 HTML

give keyboard focus to this element

Synopsis

```
void focus();
```

Description

This method transfers keyboard focus to this element so the user can interact with it without first clicking on it.

HTMLInputElement.select( )

DOM Level 1 HTML

select the contents of a Text element

Synopsis

```
void select();
```

Description

This method selects any text displayed in Text, Password, and FileUpload elements. In most browsers, this means that the user's next keystroke will replace the current text rather than being appended to it.

HTMLOptionElement

DOM Level 1 HTML

an <option> in an HTML form

Node → Element → HTMLElement → HTMLOptionElement

Properties

`boolean defaultSelected`
: The initial value of the `selected` attribute of the `<option>` element. If the form is reset, the `selected` property is reset to the value of this property. Setting this property also sets the value of the `selected` property.

`boolean disabled`
: If `true`, this option is disabled and the user is not allowed to select it. Mirrors the `disabled` attribute.

`readonly HTMLFormElement form`
: A reference to the `<form>` element that contains this element.

`readonly long index`
: The position of this `<option>` element within the `<select>` element that contains it.

`String label`
: The text to be displayed for the option. Mirrors the `label` attribute. If this property is not specified, the plain-text content of the `<option>` element is used instead.

`boolean selected`
: The current state of this option: if `true`, the option is selected. The initial value of this property comes from the `selected` attribute.

`readonly String text`
: The plain text contained within the `<option>` element. This text appears as the label for the option.

`String value`
: The value submitted with the form if this option is selected when form submission occurs. Mirrors the `value` attribute.

Description

This interface describes an `<option>` element within a `<select>` element.

See Also

HTMLFormElement, HTMLInputElement, HTMLSelectElement; Option and Select objects in the client-side reference section; Chapter 15

HTMLSelectElement — DOM Level 1 HTML

a <select> element in an HTML form — Node → Element → HTMLElement → HTMLSelectElement

Properties

`boolean disabled`
: If `true`, the `<select>` element is disabled and the user may not interact with it. Mirrors the `disabled` attribute.

`readonly HTMLFormElement form`
: The `<form>` element that contains this one.

`readonly long length`
: The number of `<option>` elements contained by this `<select>` element. Same as `options.length`.

`boolean multiple`
: If `true`, the `<select>` element allows multiple options to be selected. Otherwise, the selections are mutually exclusive and only one may be selected at a time. Mirrors the `multiple` attribute.

`String name`
: The name of this form element. Mirrors the `name` attribute.

`readonly HTMLCollection options`
: An array (HTMLCollection) of HTMLOptionElement objects that represent the `<option>` elements contained in this `<select>` element, in the order in which they appear.

`long selectedIndex`
: The position of the selected option in the `options` array. If no options are selected, this property is –1. If multiple options are selected, this property returns the index of the first selected option.

`long size`
: The number of options to display at once. If this property is 1, the `<select>` element will typically be displayed using a drop-down menu or list. If it is greater than 1, the `<select>` is typically displayed using a fixed-size list control, with a scrollbar if necessary. Mirrors the `size` attribute.

`long tabIndex`
: The position of this element in the tabbing order. Mirrors the `tabindex` attribute.

`readonly String type`
: If `multiple` is `true`, this property is "select-multiple". Otherwise, it is "select-one".

Methods

`add( )`
: Inserts a new HTMLOptionElement into the `options` array, either by appending it at the end of the array or by inserting it before another specified option.

`blur( )`
: Takes keyboard focus away.

`focus( )`
: Transfers keyboard focus to this element.

`remove( )`
: Removes the `<option>` element at the specified position.

Description

This interface represents a `<select>` element in an HTML form. The `options` property provides convenient access to the set of `<option>` elements it contains, and the `add( )` and `remove( )` methods provide an easy way to modify the set of options.

See Also

HTMLFormElement, HTMLOptionElement; Option and Select objects in the client-side reference section; Chapter 15

HTMLSelectElement.add( ) — DOM Level 1 HTML

insert an <option> element

Synopsis

```
void add(HTMLElement element,
         HTMLElement before)
    throws DOMException;
```

Arguments

`element`
: The HTMLOptionElement to be added.

`before`
: The element of the `options` array before which the new *`element`* should be added. If this argument is `null`, *`element`* is appended at the end of the `options` array.

W3C DOM Reference

Throws

This method throws a DOMException with a code of `NOT_FOUND_ERR` if the *before* argument specifies an object that is not a member of the `options` array.

Description

This method adds a new `<option>` element to this `<select>` element. *`element`* is an HTMLOptionElement that represents the `<option>` element to be added. *before* specifies the HTMLOptionElement before which *`element`* is to be added. If *before* is part of an *OPTGROUP*, *`element`* is always inserted as part of that same group. If *before* is `null`, *`element`* becomes the last child of the `<select>` element.

See Also

Select object in the client-side reference section

HTMLSelectElement.blur( ) — DOM Level 1 HTML

take keyboard focus away from this element

Synopsis

```
void blur( );
```

Description

This method takes keyboard focus away from this element.

HTMLSelectElement.focus( ) — DOM Level 1 HTML

give keyboard focus to this element

Synopsis

```
void focus( );
```

Description

This method transfers keyboard focus to this `<select>` element so the user can interact with it using the keyboard instead of the mouse.

HTMLSelectElement.remove( ) — DOM Level 1 HTML

remove an <option>

Synopsis

```
void remove(long index);
```

Arguments

`index`

The position within the `options` array of the `<option>` element to be removed.

Description

This method removes the <option> element at the specified position in the `options` array. If the specified *index* is less than zero or greater than or equal to the number of options, the `remove()` method ignores it and does nothing.

See Also

Select object in the client-side reference section

HTMLTableCaptionElement

DOM Level 1 HTML

a <caption> in an HTML table — Node → Element → HTMLElement → HTMLTableCaptionElement

Properties

`deprecated String align`
: The horizontal alignment of the caption with respect to the table. The value of the `align` attribute. Deprecated in favor of CSS styles.

Description

A <caption> element in an HTML table.

See Also

Type of: HTMLTableElement.caption

HTMLTableCellElement

DOM Level 1 HTML

a <td> or <th> cell in an HTML table — Node → Element → HTMLElement → HTMLTableCellElement

Properties

`readonly long cellIndex`
: The position of this cell within its row.

In addition to the `cellIndex` property, this interface defines the properties in the following table, which correspond directly to the HTML attributes of the <td> and <th> elements.

Property	Attribute	Description
`String abbr`	`abbr`	See HTML specification
`String align`	`align`	Horizontal alignment of cell
`String axis`	`axis`	See HTML specification
`deprecated String bgColor`	`bgcolor`	Background color of cell
`String ch`	`char`	Alignment character
`String chOff`	`choff`	Alignment character offset
`long colSpan`	`colspan`	Columns spanned by cell
`String headers`	`headers`	`id` values for headers for this cell
`deprecated String height`	`height`	Cell height in pixels

Property	Attribute	Description
deprecated boolean noWrap	nowrap	Don't word-wrap cell
long rowSpan	rowspan	Rows spanned by cell
String scope	scope	Scope of this header cell
String vAlign	valign	Vertical alignment of cell
deprecated String width	width	Cell width in pixels

Description

This interface represents <td> and <th> elements in HTML tables.

HTMLTableColElement

DOM Level 1 HTML

a <col> or <colgroup> in an HTML table

Node → Element → HTMLElement → HTMLTableColElement

Properties

This interface defines the properties in the following table, each of which corresponds to an HTML attribute of a <col> or <colgroup> element.

Property	Attribute	Description
String align	align	Default horizontal alignment
String ch	char	Default alignment character
String chOff	choff	Default alignment offset
long span	span	Number of columns represented by this element
String vAlign	valign	Default vertical alignment
String width	width	Width of the column(s)

Description

This interface represents a <col> or <colgroup> element in an HTML table.

HTMLTableElement

DOM Level 1 HTML

a <table> in an HTML document

Node → Element → HTMLElement → HTMLTableElement

Properties

`HTMLTableCaptionElement caption`

A reference to the <caption> element for the table, or `null` if there is none.

`readonly HTMLCollection rows`

An array (HTMLCollection) of HTMLTableRowElement objects that represent all the rows in the table. This includes all rows defined within <thead>, <tfoot>, and <tbody> tags.

`readonly HTMLCollection tBodies`

An array (HTMLCollection) of HTMLTableSectionElement objects that represent all the <tbody> sections in this table.

`HTMLTableSectionElement tFoot`
: The <tfoot> element of the table, or null if there is none.

`HTMLTableSectionElement tHead`
: The <thead> element of the table, or null if there is none.

In addition to the properties just listed, this interface defines the properties in the following table to represent the HTML attributes of the <table> element.

Property	Attribute	Description
deprecated String align	align	Horizontal alignment of table in document
deprecated String bgColor	bgcolor	Table background color
String border	border	Width of border around table
String cellPadding	cellpadding	Space between cell contents and border
String cellSpacing	cellspacing	Space between cell borders
String frame	frame	Which table borders to draw
String rules	rules	Where to draw lines within the table
String summary	summary	Summary description of table
String width	width	Table width

Methods

`createCaption()`
: Returns the existing <caption> for the table, or creates (and inserts) a new one if none already exists.

`createTFoot()`
: Returns the existing <tfoot> element for the table, or creates (and inserts) a new one if none already exists.

`createTHead()`
: Returns the existing <thead> element for the table, or creates (and inserts) a new one if none already exists.

`deleteCaption()`
: Deletes the <caption> element from the table, if it has one.

`deleteRow()`
: Deletes the row at the specified position in the table.

`deleteTFoot()`
: Deletes the <tfoot> element from the table, if it has one.

`deleteTHead()`
: Deletes the <thead> element from the table, if one exists.

`insertRow()`
: Inserts a new, empty <tr> element into the table at the specified position.

Description

This interface represents an HTML <table> element and defines a number of convenience properties and methods for querying and modifying various sections of the table. These methods and properties make it easier to work with tables, but they could also be duplicated with core DOM methods.

See Also

HTMLTableCaptionElement, HTMLTableCellElement, HTMLTableColElement, HTMLTableRowElement, HTMLTableSectionElement

HTMLTableElement.createCaption( )

DOM Level 1 HTML

get or create a <caption>

Synopsis

```
HTMLElement createCaption( );
```

Returns

An HTMLTableCaptionElement object representing the `<caption>` element for this table. If the table already has a caption, this method simply returns it. If the table does not have an existing `<caption>`, this method creates a new (empty) one and inserts it into the table before returning it.

HTMLTableElement.createTFoot( )

DOM Level 1 HTML

get or create a <tfoot>

Synopsis

```
HTMLElement createTFoot( );
```

Returns

An HTMLTableSectionElement representing the `<tfoot>` element for this table. If the table already has a footer, this method simply returns it. If the table does not have an existing footer, this method creates a new (empty) `<tfoot>` element and inserts it into the table before returning it.

HTMLTableElement.createTHead( )

DOM Level 1 HTML

get or create a <thead>

Synopsis

```
HTMLElement createTHead( );
```

Returns

An HTMLTableSectionElement representing the `<thead>` element for this table. If the table already has a header, this method simply returns it. If the table does not have an existing header, this method creates a new (empty) `<thead>` element and inserts it into the table before returning it.

HTMLTableElement.deleteCaption( )

DOM Level 1 HTML

delete the <caption> of a table

Synopsis

```
void deleteCaption();
```

Description

If this table has a `<caption>` element, this method removes it from the document tree. Otherwise, it does nothing.

HTMLTableElement.deleteRow( )

DOM Level 1 HTML

delete a row of a table

Synopsis

```
void deleteRow(long index)
    throws DOMException;
```

Arguments

index

Specifies the position within the table of the row to be deleted.

Throws

This method throws a DOMException with a code of `INDEX_SIZE_ERR` if *index* is less than zero or is greater than or equal to the number of rows in the table.

Description

This method deletes the row at the specified position from the table. Rows are numbered in the order in which they appear in the document source. Rows in `<thead>` and `<tfoot>` sections are numbered along with all other rows in the table.

See Also

HTMLTableSectionElement.deleteRow()

HTMLTableElement.deleteTFoot( )

DOM Level 1 HTML

delete the <tfoot> of a table

Synopsis

```
void deleteTFoot();
```

Description

If this table has a `<tfoot>` element, this method removes it from the document tree. If the table has no footer, this method does nothing.

HTMLTableElement.deleteTHead() DOM Level 1 HTML

delete the <thead> of a table

Synopsis

```
void deleteTHead();
```

Description

If this table has a <thead> element, this method deletes it; otherwise, it does nothing.

HTMLTableElement.insertRow() DOM Level 1 HTML

add a new, empty row to the table

Synopsis

```
HTMLElement insertRow(long index)
    throws DOMException;
```

Arguments

index

The position at which the new row is to be inserted.

Returns

An HTMLTableRowElement that represents the newly inserted row.

Throws

This method throws a DOMException with a code of `INDEX_SIZE_ERR` if *index* is less than zero or greater than the number of rows in the table.

Description

This method creates a new HTMLTableRowElement representing a <tr> tag and inserts it into the table at the specified position.

The new row is inserted in the same section and immediately before the existing row at the position specified by *index*. If *index* is equal to the number of rows in the table, the new row is appended to the last section of the table. If the table is initially empty, the new row is inserted into a new <tbody> section that is itself inserted into the table.

You can use the convenience method `HTMLTableRowElement.insertCell()` to add content to the newly created row.

See Also

HTMLTableSectionElement.insertRow()

HTMLTableRowElement

DOM Level 1 HTML

a <tr> element in an HTML table

Node → Element → HTMLElement → HTMLTableRowElement

Properties

`readonly HTMLCollection cells`
: An array (HTMLCollection) of HTMLTableCellElement objects representing the cells in this row.

`readonly long rowIndex`
: The position of this row in the table.

`readonly long sectionRowIndex`
: The position of this row within its section (i.e., within its `<thead>`, `<tbody>`, or `<tfoot>` element).

In addition to the properties just listed, this interface also defines the properties in the following table, which correspond to the HTML attributes of the `<tr>` element.

Property	Attribute	Description
`String align`	`align`	Default horizontal alignment of cells in this row
`deprecated String bgColor`	`bgcolor`	Background color of this row
`String ch`	`char`	Alignment character for cells in this row
`String chOff`	`choff`	Alignment character offset for cells in this row
`String vAlign`	`valign`	Default vertical alignment for cells in this row

Methods

`deleteCell()`
: Deletes the specified cell from this row.

`insertCell()`
: Inserts an empty `<td>` element into this row at the specified position.

Description

This interface represents a row in an HTML table.

HTMLTableRowElement.deleteCell( )

DOM Level 1 HTML

delete a cell in a table row

Synopsis

```
void deleteCell(long index)
    throws DOMException;
```

Arguments

index
: The position in the row of the cell to delete.

Throws

This method throws a DOMException with a code of `INDEX_SIZE_ERR` if *index* is less than zero or is greater than or equal to the number of cells in the row.

Description

This method deletes the cell at the specified position in the table row.

HTMLTableRowElement.insertCell( ) DOM Level 1 HTML

insert a new, empty <td> element into a table row

Synopsis

```
HTMLElement insertCell(long index)
    throws DOMException;
```

Arguments

index
: The position at which the new cell is to be inserted.

Returns

An HTMLTableCellElement object that represents the newly created and inserted `<td>` element.

Throws

This method throws a DOMException with a code of `INDEX_SIZE_ERR` if *index* is less than zero or is greater than the number of cells in the row.

Description

This method creates a new `<td>` element and inserts it into the row at the specified position. The new cell is inserted immediately before the cell that is currently at the position specified by *index*. If *index* is equal to the number of cells in the row, the new cell is appended at the end of the row.

Note that this convenience method inserts `<td>` data cells only. If you need to add a header cell into a row, you must create and insert the `<th>` element using `Document.createElement( )` and `Node.insertBefore( )` or related methods.

HTMLTableSectionElement DOM Level 1 HTML

a header, footer, or body section of a table Node → Element → HTMLElement → HTMLTableSectionElement

Properties

`readonly HTMLCollection rows`
: An array (HTMLCollection) of HTMLTableRowElement objects representing the rows in this section of the table.

In addition to the rows property, this interface defines the properties in the following table, which represent the attributes of the underlying HTML element.

Property	Attribute	Description
String align	align	Default horizontal alignment of cells in this section of the table
String ch	char	Default alignment character for cells in this section
String chOff	choff	Default alignment offset for cells in this section
String vAlign	valign	Default vertical alignment for cells in this section

Methods

`deleteRow( )`
: Deletes the numbered row from this section.

`insertRow( )`
: Inserts an empty row into this section at the specified position.

Description

This interface represents a <tbody>, <thead>, or <tfoot> section of an HTML table.

See Also

Type of: HTMLTableElement.tFoot, HTMLTableElement.tHead

HTMLTableSectionElement.deleteRow( ) — DOM Level 1 HTML

delete a row within a table section

Synopsis

```
void deleteRow(long index)
    throws DOMException;
```

Arguments

index
: The position of the row within this section.

Throws

This method throws a DOMException with a code of INDEX_SIZE_ERR if *index* is less than zero or is greater than or equal to the number of rows in this section.

Description

This method deletes the row at the specified position within this section. Note that for this method *index* specifies a row's position within its section, not within the entire table.

See Also

HTMLTableElement.deleteRow( )

HTMLTableSectionElement.insertRow( )

DOM Level 1 HTML

insert a new, empty row into this table section

Synopsis

```
HTMLElement insertRow(long index)
    throws DOMException;
```

Arguments

index
The position within the section at which the new row is to be inserted.

Returns

An HTMLTableRowElement that represents the newly created and inserted `<tr>` element.

Throws

This method throws a DOMException with a code of `INDEX_SIZE_ERR` if *index* is less than zero or is greater than the number of rows in this section.

Description

This method creates a new `<tr>` element and inserts it into this table section at the specified position. If *index* equals the number of rows currently in the section, the new row is appended at the end of the section. Otherwise, the new row is inserted immediately before the row that is currently at the position specified by *index*. Note that for this method, *index* specifies a row position within a single table section, not within the entire table.

See Also

HTMLTableElement.insertRow()

HTMLTextAreaElement

DOM Level 1 HTML

a <textarea> element in an HTML form

Node → Element → HTMLElement → HTMLTextAreaElement

Properties

`String accessKey`
A keyboard shortcut (a single character) that the web browser can use to transfer keyboard focus to this element. Mirrors the `accesskey` attribute.

`long cols`
The width of this element in character columns. Mirrors the `cols` attribute.

`String defaultValue`
The initial content of the text area. When the form is reset, the text area is restored to this value. Setting this property changes the displayed text in the text area.

`boolean disabled`
If `true`, this element is disabled and the user cannot interact with it. Mirrors the `disabled` attribute.

`readonly HTMLFormElement form`
: The HTMLFormElement that represents the <form> element containing this text area, or `null` if this element is not inside a form.

`String name`
: The name of this <textarea> element, as specified by the `name` attribute.

`boolean readOnly`
: If `true`, this element is read-only and the user cannot edit any of the displayed text. Mirrors the `readonly` attribute.

`long rows`
: The height of the text area in text rows. Mirrors the `rows` attribute.

`long tabIndex`
: The position of this element in the tabbing order. Mirrors the `tabindex` attribute.

`readonly String type`
: The type of this element, for compatibility with HTMLInputElement objects. This property always has the value "textarea".

`String value`
: The text currently displayed in the text area.

Methods

`blur( )`	Takes keyboard focus away from this element.
`focus( )`	Transfers keyboard focus to this element.
`select( )`	Selects the entire contents of the text area.

Description

This interface represents a <textarea> element that creates a multiline text-input field in an HTML form. The initial contents of the text area are specified between the <textarea> and </textarea> tags. The user may edit this value and query and set the text with the `value` property (or by modifying the Text node child of this element).

See Also

HTMLFormElement, HTMLInputElement; Textarea in the client-side reference section; Chapter 15

HTMLTextAreaElement.blur( ) — DOM Level 1 HTML

take keyboard focus away from this element

Synopsis

```
void blur( );
```

Description

This method takes keyboard focus away from this element.

HTMLTextAreaElement.focus( ) DOM Level 1 HTML

give keyboard focus to this element

Synopsis

```
void focus();
```

Description

This method transfers keyboard focus to this element so the user can edit the displayed text without having to first click on the text area.

HTMLTextAreaElement.select( ) DOM Level 1 HTML

select the text in this element

Synopsis

```
void select();
```

Description

This method selects all the text displayed by this `<textarea>` element. In most browsers, this means that the text is highlighted and that new text entered by the user will replace the highlighted text instead of being appended to it.

LinkStyle DOM Level 2 StyleSheets

a style sheet associated with a node

Properties

`readonly StyleSheet sheet`
: The StyleSheet object associated with this node.

Description

In DOM implementations that support the StyleSheets module, this interface is implemented by any Document node that links to a style sheet or defines an inline style sheet. The `sheet` property then provides a way to obtain the StyleSheet object associated with the node.

In HTML documents, the `<style>` and `<link>` elements implement this interface. Those elements are represented by the HTMLStyleElement and HTMLLinkElement interfaces, which do not have their own entries in this reference. See "HTMLElement" for more information about those interfaces.

In XML documents, style sheets are included with a processing instruction. See "ProcessingInstruction" for more information.

See Also

HTMLElement, ProcessingInstruction

MediaList

DOM Level 2 StyleSheets

a style sheet's list of media types

Properties

`readonly unsigned long length`

The length of the array; the number of media types in the list.

`String mediaText`

A comma-separated text representation of the complete media list. Setting this property may throw a DOMException with a code of `SYNTAX_ERR` if the new value contains a syntax err, or a code of `NO_MODIFICATION_ALLOWED_EXCEPTION` if the media list is read-only.

Methods

`appendMedium()`

Adds a new media type to the end of the list.

`deleteMedium()`

Removes the specified media type from the list.

`item()`

Returns the media type at the specified position in the list, or `null` if the index is invalid. In JavaScript, you can also treat the MediaList object as an array and index it using normal square-bracket array notation instead of calling this method.

Description

This interface represents a list or array of media types for a style sheet. `length` specifies the number of elements in the list, and `item()` allows a specific media type to be retrieved by position. `appendMedium()` and `deleteMedium()` allow entries to be appended to and deleted from the list. JavaScript allows a MediaList object to be treated as an array, and you can use square-bracket notation instead of calling `item()`.

The HTML 4 standard defines the following media types (they are case-sensitive, and must be written in lowercase letters): `screen`, `tty`, `tv`, `projection`, `handheld`, `print`, `braile`, `aural`, and `all`. The `screen` type is most relevant to documents being displayed in web browsers on desktop or laptop computers. The `print` type is used for styles intended for printed documents.

See Also

Type of: StyleSheet.media

MediaList.appendMedium( )

DOM Level 2 StyleSheets

add a new media type to the list

Synopsis

```
void appendMedium(String newMedium)
    throws DOMException;
```

Arguments

newMedium

The name of the new media type to append. See the "MediaList" reference page for the set of valid media type names.

Throws

This method may throw a DOMException with a code of `NO_MODIFICATION_ALLOWED_ERR` if the media list is read-only, or `INVALID_CHARACTER_ERR` if the specified *newMedium* argument contains illegal characters.

Description

This method appends the specified *newMedium* to the end of the MediaList. If the MediaList already contains the specified media type, it is first removed from its current position and then appended at the end of the list.

MediaList.deleteMedium( )

DOM Level 2 StyleSheets

remove a media type from the list

Synopsis

```
void deleteMedium(String oldMedium)
    throws DOMException;
```

Arguments

oldMedium

The name of the media type to remove from the list. See the "MediaList" reference page for the set of valid media type names.

Throws

This method throws a DOMException with a code of `NOT_FOUND_ERR` if the list does not contain the specified *oldMedium* media type, or `NO_MODIFICATION_ALLOWED_ERR` if the media list is read-only.

Description

This method deletes the specified media type from this MediaList, or throws an exception if the list does not contain the specified type.

MediaList.item( )

DOM Level 2 StyleSheets

index an array of media types

Synopsis

```
String item(unsigned long index);
```

Arguments

index

The position of the desired media type within the array.

Returns

The media type (a string) at the specified position within the MediaList, or `null` if *index* is negative or is greater than or equal to `length`. Note that in JavaScript, it is usually simpler to treat a MediaList object as an array and index it using square-bracket array notation instead of calling this method.

MouseEvent

DOM Level 2 Events

details about a mouse event

Event → UIEvent → MouseEvent

Properties

`readonly boolean altKey`

Whether the **Alt** key was held down when the event occurred. Defined for all types of mouse events.

`readonly unsigned short button`

Which mouse button changed state during a mousedown, mouseup, or click event. A value of 0 indicates the left button, a value of 2 indicates the right button, and a value of 1 indicates the middle mouse button. Note that this property is defined when a button changes state; it is not used to report whether a button is held down during a mousemove event, for example. Also, this property is not a bitmap: it cannot tell you if more than one button is held down.

Netscape 6.0 and 6.01 use the values 1, 2, and 3 instead of 0, 1, and 2. This is fixed in Netscape 6.1.

`readonly long clientX, clientY`

Numbers that specify the X and Y coordinates of the mouse pointer relative to the "client area," or browser window. Note that these coordinates do not take document scrolling into account; if an event occurs at the very top of the window, `clientY` is 0 regardless of how far down the document has been scrolled. These properties are defined for all types of mouse events.

`readonly boolean ctrlKey`

Whether the **Ctrl** key was held down when the event occurred. Defined for all types of mouse events.

`readonly boolean metaKey`
: Whether the **Meta** key was held down when the event occurred. Defined for all types of mouse events.

`readonly EventTarget relatedTarget`
: Refers to a node that is related to the `target` node of the event. For mouseover events, it is the node the mouse left when it moved over the target. For mouseout events, it is the node the mouse entered when leaving the target. `relatedTarget` is undefined for other types of mouse events.

`readonly long screenX, screenY`
: Numbers that specify the X and Y coordinates of the mouse pointer relative to the upper-left corner of the user's monitor. These properties are defined for all types of mouse events.

`readonly boolean shiftKey`
: Whether the **Shift** key was held down when the event occurred. Defined for all types of mouse events.

Methods

`initMouseEvent( )`
: Initializes the properties of a newly created MouseEvent object.

Description

This interface defines the type of Event object that is passed to events of types click, mousedown, mousemove, mouseout, mouseover, and mouseup. Note that in addition to the properties listed here, this interface also inherits the properties of the UIEvent and Event interfaces.

See Also

Event, UIEvent; Chapter 19

MouseEvent.initMouseEvent( ) — DOM Level 2 Events

initialize the properties of a MouseEvent object

Synopsis

```
void initMouseEvent(String typeArg,
                    boolean canBubbleArg,
                    boolean cancelableArg,
                    AbstractView viewArg,
                    long detailArg,
                    long screenXArg,
                    long screenYArg,
                    long clientXArg,
                    long clientYArg,
                    boolean ctrlKeyArg,
                    boolean altKeyArg,
                    boolean shiftKeyArg,
```

```
boolean metaKeyArg,
unsigned short buttonArg,
EventTarget relatedTargetArg);
```

Arguments

The many arguments to this method specify the initial values of the properties of this MouseEvent object, including the properties inherited from the Event and UIEvent interfaces. The name of each argument clearly indicates the property for which it specifies the value, so they are not listed individually here.

Description

This method initializes the various properties of a newly created MouseEvent object. It may be called only on a MouseEvent object created with `Document.createEvent()` and only before that MouseEvent is passed to `EventTarget.dispatchEvent()`.

MutationEvent

DOM Level 2 Events

details about a document change

Event → MutationEvent

Constants

The following constants represent the set of possible values for the `attrChange` property:

`unsigned short MODIFICATION = 1`
: An Attr node was modified.

`unsigned short ADDITION = 2`
: An Attr node was added.

`unsigned short REMOVAL = 3`
: An Attr node was removed.

Properties

`readonly unsigned short attrChange`
: How the attribute was changed, for DOMAttrModified events. The three possible values are defined in the "Constants" section.

`readonly String attrName`
: The name of the attribute that was changed for DOMAttrModified events.

`readonly String newValue`
: The new value of the Attr node for DOMAttrModified events, or the new text value of a Text, Comment, CDATASection, or ProcessingInstruction node for DOMCharacterDataModified events.

`readonly String prevValue`
: The previous value of an Attr node for DOMAttrModified events, or the previous value of a Text, Comment, CDATASection, or ProcessingInstruction node for DOMCharacterDataModified events.

`readonly Node relatedNode`
: The relevant Attr node for DOMAttrModified events, or the parent of the node that was inserted or removed for DOMNodeInserted and DOMNodeRemoved events.

Methods

`initMutationEvent( )`
: Initializes the properties of a newly created MutationEvent object.

Description

This interface defines the type of Event object that is passed to events of types listed here (note that none of these event types are cancelable with `Event.preventDefault( )`):

DOMAttrModified
: Generated when an attribute of a document element is added, removed, or changed. The target of the event is the element that contains the attribute, and the event bubbles up from there.

DOMCharacterDataModified
: Generated when the character data of a Text, Comment, CDATASection, or Processing-Instruction node changes. The event target is the node that changed, and the event bubbles up from there.

DOMNodeInserted
: Generated after a node is added as a child of another node. The target of the event is the node that was inserted, and the event bubbles up the tree from there. The `relatedNode` property specifies the new parent of the inserted node. This event is not generated for any descendants of the inserted node.

DOMNodeInsertedIntoDocument
: Generated after a node is inserted into the document tree, as well as for nodes that are inserted directly into the tree and nodes that are indirectly inserted when an ancestor is inserted. The target of this event is the node that is inserted. Because events of this type may be targeted at every node in a subtree, they do not bubble.

DOMNodeRemoved
: Generated immediately before a node is removed from its parent. The target of the event is the node being removed, and the event bubbles up the document tree from there. The `relatedNode` property holds the parent node from which the node is being removed.

DOMNodeRemovedFromDocument
: Generated immediately before a node is removed from the document tree. Separate events are generated for the node that is directly removed and for each of its descendant nodes. The target of the event is the node that is about to be removed. Events of this type do not bubble.

DOMSubtreeModified
: Generated as a kind of summary event when a call to a DOM method causes multiple mutation events to be fired. The target of this event is the most deeply nested common ancestor of all changes that occurred in the document, and it bubbles up the document tree from that point. If you are not interested in the details of the changes but merely want to be notified which portions of the document have changed, you may prefer to register listeners for this type of event.

MutationEvent.initMutationEvent( )

DOM Level 2 Events

initialize the properties of a new MutationEvent

Synopsis

```
void initMutationEvent(String typeArg,
                       boolean canBubbleArg,
                       boolean cancelableArg,
                       Node relatedNodeArg,
                       String prevValueArg,
                       String newValueArg,
                       String attrNameArg,
                       unsigned short attrChangeArg);
```

Arguments

The various arguments to this method specify the initial values of the properties of this MutationEvent object, including the properties inherited from the Event interface. The name of each argument clearly indicates the property for which it specifies the value, so the arguments are not listed individually here.

Description

This method initializes the various properties of a newly created MutationEvent object. It may be called only on a MutationEvent object created with `Document.createEvent( )` and only before that MouseEvent is passed to `EventTarget.dispatchEvent( )`.

NamedNodeMap

DOM Level 1 Core

a collection of nodes indexed by name or position

Properties

`readonly unsigned long length`
: The number of nodes in the array.

Methods

`getNamedItem( )`
: Looks up a named node.

`getNamedItemNS( )` *[DOM Level 2]*
: Looks up a node specified by namespace and name.

`item( )`
: Obtains the node at a specified position within the NamedNodeMap. In JavaScript, you can also do this by using the node position as an array index.

`removeNamedItem( )`
: Deletes a named node from the NamedNodeMap.

`removeNamedItemNS( )` *[DOM Level 2]*
  Deletes a node specified by name and namespace from the NamedNodeMap.

`setNamedItem( )`
  Adds a new node to (or replaces an existing node in) the NamedNodeMap. The `nodeName` property of the Node object is used as the name of the node.

`setNamedItemNS( )` *[DOM Level 2]*
  Adds a new node to (or replaces an existing node in) the NamedNodeMap. The `namespaceURI` and `localName` properties of the Node object are used as the node name.

Description

The NamedNodeMap interface defines a collection of nodes that may be looked up by their `nodeName` property or, for nodes that use namespaces, by their `namespaceURI` or `localName` properties.

The most notable use of the NamedNodeMap interface is the `attributes` property of the Node interface: a collection of Attr nodes that may be looked up by attribute name. Many of the methods of NamedNodeMap are similar to the methods of Element for manipulating attributes. Element attributes are usually most easily manipulated through the methods of the Element interface, and the NamedNodeMap interface is not commonly used.

NamedNodeMap objects are "live," which means that they immediately reflect any changes to the document tree. For example, if you obtain a NamedNodeMap that represents the attributes of an element and then add a new attribute to that element, the new attribute is available through the NamedNodeMap.

See Also

NodeList

Type of: DocumentType.entities, DocumentType.notations, Node.attributes

NamedNodeMap.getNamedItem( ) DOM Level 1 Core

look up a node by name

Synopsis

```
Node getNamedItem(String name);
```

Arguments

name
  The value of the `nodeName` property of the node to look up.

Returns

The named node, or `null` if no node with that name was found.

NamedNodeMap.getNamedItemNS( )

DOM Level 2 Core

look up a node by name and namespace

Synopsis

```
Node getNamedItemNS(String namespaceURI,
                    String localName);
```

Arguments

namespaceURI
: The namespaceURI property of the desired node, or null for no namespace.

localName
: The localName property of the local node.

Returns

The element of the NamedNodeMap that has the specified namespaceURI and localName properties, or null if there is no such node.

Description

getNamedItemNS( ) looks up an element of a NamedNodeMap by namespace and local name. It is useful only with XML documents that use namespaces.

NamedNodeMap.item( )

DOM Level 1 Core

return an element of a NamedNodeMap by position

Synopsis

```
Node item(unsigned long index);
```

Arguments

index
: The position or index of the desired node.

Returns

The node at the specified position, or null if *index* is less than zero or greater than or equal to the length of the NamedNodeMap.

Description

This method returns a numbered element of a NamedNodeMap. In JavaScript, NamedNodeMap objects behave like read-only arrays, and you can use the node position as an array index within square brackets instead of calling this method.

Although the NamedNodeMap interface allows you to iterate through its nodes by position, it does not represent an ordered collection of nodes. Any changes made to the

NamedNodeMap (such as by `removeNamedItem( )` or `setNamedItem( )`) may result in a complete reordering of the elements. Thus, you must not modify a NamedNodeMap while you are iterating through its elements.

See Also

NodeList

NamedNodeMap.removeNamedItem( ) — DOM Level 1 Core

delete a node specified by name

Synopsis

```
Node removeNamedItem(String name)
    throws DOMException;
```

Arguments

name

The `nodeName` property of the node to be deleted.

Returns

The node that was removed.

Throws

This method throws a DOMException with a code of `NO_MODIFICATION_ALLOWED_ERR` if the NamedNodeMap is read-only and does not allow deletions, or a code of `NOT_FOUND_ERR` if no node with the specified *name* exists in the NamedNodeMap.

Description

Deletes a named node from a NamedNodeMap. Note that if the NamedNodeMap represents the set of attributes for an Element, removing the Attr node for an attribute that was explicitly set in the document may cause the removed Attr to be automatically replaced by a new Attr node representing the default value (if any exists) of the attribute.

See Also

Element.removeAttribute( )

NamedNodeMap.removeNamedItemNS( ) — DOM Level 2 Core

delete a node specified by namespace and name

Synopsis

```
Node removeNamedItemNS(String namespaceURI,
                       String localName)
    throws DOMException;
```

Arguments

namespaceURI
: The namespaceURI property of the node to be removed, or null for no namespace.

localName
: The localName property of the node to be removed.

Returns

The node that was removed.

Throws

This method throws exceptions for the same reason as removeNamedItem( ).

Description

This method works just like removeNamedItem( ), except that the node to be removed is specified by namespace and local name rather than just by name. This method is typically useful only with XML documents that use namespaces.

NamedNodeMap.setNamedItem( )

DOM Level 1 Core

add a node to or replace a node in a NamedNodeMap

Synopsis

```
Node setNamedItem(Node arg)
    throws DOMException;
```

Arguments

arg
: The node to be added to the NamedNodeMap.

Returns

The node that was replaced, or null if no node was replaced.

Throws

This method may throw a DOMException with one of the following code values:

HIERARCHY_REQUEST_ERR
: *arg* is a node of a type that is not suitable for this NamedNodeMap (e.g., is not an Attr node).

INUSE_ATTRIBUTE_ERR
: *arg* is an Attr node that is already associated with an element.

NO_MODIFICATION_ALLOWED_ERR
: The NamedNodeMap is read-only.

WRONG_DOCUMENT_ERR
: *arg* has a different ownerDocument than the document from which the NamedNodeMap was created.

Description

`setNamedItem()` adds the specified node to a NamedNodeMap and allows it to be looked up using the value of the node's `nodeName` property. If the NamedNodeMap already contains a node with that name, that node is replaced and becomes the return value of the method.

See Also

Element.setAttribute()

NamedNodeMap.setNamedItemNS()

DOM Level 2 Core

add a node to a NamedNodeMap using namespaces

Synopsis

```
Node setNamedItemNS(Node arg)
    throws DOMException;
```

Arguments

arg

The node to be added to the NamedNodeMap.

Returns

The node that was replaced, or `null` if no node was replaced.

Throws

This method throws exceptions for the same reasons as `setNamedItem()`. It may also throw a DOMException with a code of `NOT_SUPPORTED_ERR` if it is called in an implementation that does not support XML documents or XML namespaces.

Description

This method works like `setNamedItem()`, except that the node added to the NamedNodeMap can later be looked up by its `namespaceURI` and `localName` properties instead of by its `nodeName` property. This method is useful only with XML documents that use namespaces. Note that this method may be unsupported (i.e., may throw an exception) in implementations that do not support XML documents.

Node

DOM Level 1 Core

a node in a document tree

Subinterfaces

Attr, CharacterData, Document, DocumentFragment, DocumentType, Element, Entity, EntityReference, Notation, ProcessingInstruction

Also Implements

EventTarget

If the DOM implementation supports the Events module, every node in the document tree also implements the EventTarget interface and may have event listeners registered on it. The methods defined by the EventTarget interface are not included here; see the "EventTarget" and "EventListener" reference pages for details.

Constants

All Node objects implement one of the subinterfaces listed above. Every Node object has a nodeType property that specifies which of the subinterfaces it implements. These constants are the legal values for that property; their names are self-explanatory. Note that these are static properties of the Node( ) constructor function; they are not properties of individual Node objects. Also note that they are not supported by Internet Explorer 4, 5, or 6.

```
Node.ELEMENT_NODE = 1;                  // Element
Node.ATTRIBUTE_NODE = 2;                // Attr
Node.TEXT_NODE = 3;                     // Text
Node.CDATA_SECTION_NODE = 4;            // CDATASection
Node.ENTITY_REFERENCE_NODE = 5;         // EntityReference
Node.ENTITY_NODE = 6;                   // Entity
Node.PROCESSING_INSTRUCTION_NODE = 7;  // ProcessingInstruction
Node.COMMENT_NODE = 8;                  // Comment
Node.DOCUMENT_NODE = 9;                 // Document
Node.DOCUMENT_TYPE_NODE = 10;           // DocumentType
Node.DOCUMENT_FRAGMENT_NODE = 11;       // DocumentFragment
Node.NOTATION_NODE = 12;                // Notation
```

Properties

readonly NamedNodeMap attributes

If this node is an element, specifies the attributes of that element. attributes is a NamedNodeMap object that allows attributes to be queried by name or by number and returns them in the form of Attr objects. In practice, it is almost always easier to use the getAttribute( ) method of the Element interface to obtain an attribute value as a string. Note that the returned NamedNodeMap object is "live": any changes to the attributes of this element are immediately visible through it.

readonly Node[] childNodes

Contains the child nodes of the current node. This property should never be null: for nodes with no children, childNodes is an array with length zero. This property is technically a NodeList object, but it behaves just like an array of Node objects. Note that the returned NodeList object is "live": any changes to this element's list of children are immediately visible through the NodeList.

readonly Node firstChild

The first child of this node, or null if the node has no children.

readonly Node lastChild

The last child of this node, or null if the node has no children.

`readonly String localName` *[DOM Level 2]*
In XML documents that use namespaces, specifies the local part of the element or attribute name. This property is never used with HTML documents. See also the `namespaceURI` and `prefix` properties.

`readonly String namespaceURI` *[DOM Level 2]*
In XML documents that use namespaces, specifies the URI of the namespace of an Element or Attribute node. This property is never used with HTML documents. See also the `localName` and `prefix` properties.

`readonly Node nextSibling`
The sibling node that immediately follows this one in the `childNodes[]` array of the `parentNode`, or `null` if there is no such node.

`readonly String nodeName`
The name of the node. For Element nodes, specifies the tag name of the element, which can also be retrieved with the `tagName` property of the Element interface. For other types of nodes, the value depends on the node type. See the upcoming table in the "Descriptions" section for details.

`readonly unsigned short nodeType`
The type of the node; i.e., which subinterface the node implements. The legal values are defined by the previously listed constants. Since those constants are not supported by Internet Explorer, however, you may prefer to use hardcoded values instead of the constants. In HTML documents, the common values for this property are 1 for Element nodes, 3 for Text nodes, 8 for Comment nodes, and 9 for the single top-level Document node.

`String nodeValue`
The value of a node. For Text nodes, holds the text content. For other node types, the value depends on the `nodeType`, as shown in the upcoming table.

`readonly Document ownerDocument`
The Document object of which this node is a part. For Document nodes, this property is `null`.

`readonly Node parentNode`
The parent node (or container node) of this node, or `null` if there is no parent. Note that Document and Attr nodes never have parent nodes. Also, nodes that have been removed from the document or are newly created and have not yet been inserted into the document tree have a `parentNode` of `null`.

`String prefix` *[DOM Level 2]*
For XML documents that use namespaces, specifies the namespace prefix of an Element or Attribute node. This property is never used with HTML documents. See also the `localName` and `namespaceURL` properties. Setting this property can cause an exception if the new value contains illegal characters, is malformed, or does not match the `namespaceURI` property.

`readonly Node previousSibling`
The sibling node that immediately precedes this one in the `childNodes[]` array of the `parentNode`, or `null` if there is no such node.

Methods

appendChild( )

Adds a node to the document tree by appending it to the childNodes[] array of this node. If the node is already in the document tree, it is removed and then reinserted at its new position.

cloneNode( )

Makes a copy of this node, or of the node and all its descendants.

hasAttributes( ) *[DOM Level 2]*

Returns true if this node is an Element and has any attributes.

hasChildNodes( )

Returns true if this node has any children.

insertBefore( )

Inserts a node into the document tree immediately before the specified child of this node. If the node being inserted is already in the tree, it is removed and reinserted at its new location.

isSupported( ) *[DOM Level 2]*

Returns true if the specified version number of a named feature is supported by this node.

normalize( )

"Normalizes" all Text node descendants of this node by deleting empty Text nodes and merging adjacent Text nodes.

removeChild( )

Removes (and returns) the specified child node from the document tree.

replaceChild( )

Removes (and returns) the specified child node from the document tree, replacing it with another node.

Description

All objects in a document tree (including the Document object itself) implement the Node interface, which provides the fundamental properties and methods for traversing and manipulating the tree. The parentNode property and childNodes[] array allow you to move up and down the document tree. You can enumerate the children of a given node by looping through the elements of childNodes[] or by using the firstChild and nextSibling properties (or the lastChild and previousSibling properties, to loop backward). The appendChild( ), insertBefore( ), removeChild( ), and replaceChild( ) methods allow you to modify the document tree by altering the children of a node.

Every object in a document tree implements both the Node interface and a more specialized interface, such as Element or Text. The nodeType property specifies which subinterface a node implements. You can use this property to test the type of a node before using properties or methods of the more specialized interface. For example:

```
var n;   // Holds the node we're working with
if (n.nodeType == 1) {        // Or compare to the constant Node.ELEMENT_NODE
    var tagname = n.tagName;  // If the node is an Element, this is the tag name
}
```

The nodeName and nodeValue properties specify additional information about a node, but their value depends on nodeType, as shown in the following table. Note that subinterfaces typically define specialized properties (such as the tagName property of Element nodes and the data property of Text nodes) for obtaining this information.

nodeType	nodeName	nodeValue
ELEMENT_NODE	The element's tag name	null
ATTRIBUTE_NODE	The attribute name	The attribute value
TEXT_NODE	#text	The text of the node
CDATA_SECTION_NODE	#cdata-section	The text of the node
ENTITY_REFERENCE_NODE	The name of the referenced entity	null
ENTITY_NODE	The entity name	null
PROCESSING_INSTRUCTION_NODE	The target of the PI	The remainder of the PI
COMMENT_NODE	#comment	The text of the comment
DOCUMENT_NODE	#document	null
DOCUMENT_TYPE_NODE	The document type name	null
DOCUMENT_FRAGMENT_NODE	#document-fragment	null
NOTATION_NODE	The notation name	null

See Also

Document, Element, Text; Chapter 17

Node.appendChild( ) DOM Level 1 Core

insert a node as the last child of this node

Synopsis

```
Node appendChild(Node newChild)
    throws DOMException;
```

Arguments

newChild

The node to be inserted into the document. If the node is a DocumentFragment, it is not directly inserted, but each of its children are.

Returns

The node that was added.

Throws

This method may throw a DOMException with one of the following code values in the following circumstances:

`HIERARCHY_REQUEST_ERR`
: The node does not allow children, or it does not allow children of the specified type, or *newChild* is an ancestor of this node (or is this node itself).

`WRONG_DOCUMENT_ERR`
: The `ownerDocument` property of *newChild* is not the same as the `ownerDocument` property of this node.

`NO_MODIFICATION_ALLOWED_ERR`
: This node is read-only and does not allow children to be appended, or the node being appended is already part of the document tree and its parent is read-only and does not allow children to be removed.

Description

This method adds the node *newChild* to the document, inserting it as the last child of this node. If *newChild* is already in the document tree, it is removed from the tree and then reinserted at its new location. If *newChild* is a DocumentFragment node, it is not inserted itself; instead, all its children are appended, in order, to the end of this node's `childNodes[]` array. Note that a node from (or created by) one document cannot be inserted into a different document. That is, the `ownerDocument` property of *newChild* must be the same as the `ownerDocument` property of this node.

Example

The following function inserts a new paragraph at the end of the document:

```
function appendMessage(message) {
    var pElement = document.createElement("P");
    var messageNode = document.createTextNode(message);
    pElement.appendChild(messageNode);    // Add text to paragraph
    document.body.appendChild(pElement);  // Add paragraph to document body
}
```

See Also

Node.insertBefore( ), Node.removeChild( ), Node.replaceChild( )

Node.cloneNode( ) — DOM Level 1 Core

duplicate a node and, optionally, all of its descendants

Synopsis

```
Node cloneNode(boolean deep);
```

Arguments

deep
: If this argument is `true`, `cloneNode( )` recursively clones all descendants of this node. Otherwise, it clones only this node.

Returns

A copy of this node.

Description

The `cloneNode( )` method makes and returns a copy of the node on which it is called. If passed the argument `true`, it recursively clones all descendants of the node as well. Otherwise, it clones only the node and none of its children. The returned node is not part of the document tree, and its `parentNode` property is `null`. When an Element node is cloned, all of its attributes are also cloned. Note, however, that EventListener functions registered on a node are not cloned.

Node.hasAttributes( )

DOM Level 2 Core

determine whether a node has attributes

Synopsis

```
boolean hasAttributes( );
```

Returns

`true` if this node has one or more attributes; `false` if it has none. Note that only Element nodes can have attributes.

See Also

Element.getAttribute( ), Element.hasAttribute( ), Node.attributes

Node.hasChildNodes( )

DOM Level 1 Core

determine whether a node has children

Synopsis

```
boolean hasChildNodes( );
```

Returns

`true` if this node has one or more children; `false` if it has none.

See Also

Node.childNodes

Node.insertBefore( )

DOM Level 1 Core

insert a node into the document tree before the specified node

Synopsis

```
Node insertBefore(Node newChild,
                  Node refChild)
    throws DOMException;
```

Arguments

newChild
: The node to be inserted into the tree. If it is a DocumentFragment, its children are inserted instead.

refChild
: The child of this node before which *newChild* is to be inserted. If this argument is `null`, *newChild* is inserted as the last child of this node.

Returns

The node that was inserted.

Throws

This method may throw a DOMException with the following `code` values:

`HIERARCHY_REQUEST_ERR`
: This node does not support children, or it does not allow children of the specified type, or *newChild* is an ancestor of this node (or is this node itself).

`WRONG_DOCUMENT_ERR`
: The `ownerDocument` property of *newChild* and this node are different.

`NO_MODIFICATION_ALLOWED_ERR`
: This node is read-only and does not allow insertions or the parent of *newChild* is read-only and does not allow deletions.

`NOT_FOUND_ERR`
: *refChild* is not a child of this node.

Description

This method inserts the node *newChild* into the document tree as a child of this node. The new node is positioned within this node's `childNodes[]` array so that it comes immediately before the *refChild* node. If *refChild* is `null`, *newChild* is inserted at the end of `childNodes[]`, just as with the `appendChild( )` method. Note that it is illegal to call this method with a *refChild* that is not a child of this node.

If *newChild* is already in the document tree, it is removed from the tree and then reinserted at its new position. If *newChild* is a DocumentFragment node, it is not inserted itself; instead, each of its children is inserted, in order, at the specified location.

Example

The following function inserts a new paragraph at the beginning of a document:

```
function insertMessage(message) {
    var paragraph = document.createElement("p");  // Create a <p> Element
    var text = document.createTextNode(message);  // Create a Text node
    paragraph.appendChild(text);                  // Add text to the paragraph
    // Now insert the paragraph before the first child of the body
    document.body.insertBefore(paragraph, document.body.firstChild)
}
```

See Also

Node.appendChild( ), Node.removeChild( ), Node.replaceChild( )

Node.isSupported( )

DOM Level 2 Core

determine if a node supports a feature

Synopsis

```
boolean isSupported(String feature,
                    String version);
```

Arguments

feature
: The name of the feature to test.

version
: The version number of the feature to test, or the empty string to test for support of any version of the feature.

Returns

`true` if the node supports the specified version of the specified feature, and `false` if it does not.

Description

The W3C DOM standard is modular, and implementations are not required to implement all modules or features of the standard. This method tests whether the implementation of this node supports the specified version of the named feature. See the "DOMImplementation.hasFeature()" reference page for a list of values for the *feature* and *version* arguments.

See Also

DOMImplementation.hasFeature()

Node.normalize( )

DOM Level 1 Core

merge adjacent Text nodes and remove empty ones

Synopsis

```
void normalize( );
```

Description

This method traverses all descendants of this node and "normalizes" the document by removing any empty Text nodes and merging all adjacent Text nodes into a single node. This can sometimes be useful to simplify the tree structure after node insertions or deletions.

See Also

Text

Node.removeChild()

DOM Level 1 Core

remove (and return) the specified child of this node

Synopsis

```
Node removeChild(Node oldChild)
    throws DOMException;
```

Arguments

oldChild
: The child node to remove.

Returns

The node that was removed.

Throws

This method may throw a DOMException with the following code values in the following circumstances:

`NO_MODIFICATION_ALLOWED_ERR`
: This node is read-only and does not allow children to be removed.

`NOT_FOUND_ERR`
: *oldChild* is not a child of this node.

Description

This method removes the specified child from the `childNodes[]` array of this node. It is an error to call this method with a node that is not a child. `removeChild()` returns the *oldChild* node after removing it. *oldChild* continues to be a valid node and may be reinserted into the document later.

Example

You can delete the last child of the document body with this code:

```
document.body.removeChild(document.body.lastChild);
```

See Also

Node.appendChild(), Node.insertBefore(), Node.replaceChild()

Node.replaceChild()

DOM Level 1 Core

replace a child node with a new node

Synopsis

```
Node replaceChild(Node newChild,
                  Node oldChild)
    throws DOMException;
```

Arguments

newChild
: The replacement node.

oldChild
: The node to be replaced.

Returns

The node that was removed from the document and replaced.

Throws

This method may throw a DOMException with the following `code` values:

`HIERARCHY_REQUEST_ERR`
: This node does not allow children, or does not allow children of the specified type, or *newChild* is an ancestor of this node (or is this node itself).

`WRONG_DOCUMENT_ERR`
: *newChild* and this node have different values for `ownerDocument`.

`NO_MODIFICATION_ALLOWED_ERR`
: This node is read-only and does not allow replacement, or *newChild* is the child of a node that does not allow removals.

`NOT_FOUND_ERR`
: *oldChild* is not a child of this node.

Description

This method replaces one node of the document tree with another. *oldChild* is the node to be replaced, and must be a child of this node. *newChild* is the node that takes its place in the `childNodes[]` array of this node.

If *newChild* is already part of the document, it is first removed from the document before being reinserted at its new position. If *newChild* is a DocumentFragment, it is not inserted itself; instead each of its children is inserted, in order, at the position formerly occupied by *oldChild*.

Example

The following code replaces a node `n` with a `<b>` element and then inserts the replaced node into the `<b>` element, which reparents the node and makes it appear in bold:

```
// Get the first child node of the first paragraph in the document
var n = document.getElementsByTagName("p")[0].firstChild;
var b = document.createElement("b");  // Create a <b> element
n.parentNode.replaceChild(b, n);      // Replace the node with <b>
b.appendChild(n);                     // Reinsert the node as a child of <b>
```

See Also

Node.appendChild(), Node.insertBefore(), Node.removeChild()

NodeFilter

DOM Level 2 Traversal

a function to filter the nodes of a document tree

Constants

The following three constants are the legal return values for node filter functions. Note that they are static properties of the object named NodeFilter, not properties of individual node filter functions:

`short FILTER_ACCEPT = 1`
: Accept this node. A NodeIterator or TreeWalker will return this node as part of its document traversal.

`short FILTER_REJECT = 2`
: Reject this node. A NodeIterator or TreeWalker will behave as if this node does not exist. Furthermore, this return value tells a TreeWalker to ignore all children of this node.

`short FILTER_SKIP = 3`
: Skip this node. A NodeIterator or TreeWalker will not return this node, but it will recursively consider its children as part of document traversal.

The following constants are bit flags that can be set in the *whatToShow* argument to the `createNodeIterator()` and `createTreeWalker()` methods of the Document object. Each constant corresponds to one of the types of Document nodes (see the "Node" reference page for a list of node types) and specifies that a NodeIterator or TreeWalker should consider nodes of that type during its traversal of the document. Multiple constants can be combined using the logical OR operator `|`. `SHOW_ALL` is a special value with all bits set: it indicates that all nodes should be considered, regardless of their type.

```
unsigned long SHOW_ALL = 0xFFFFFFFF;
unsigned long SHOW_ELEMENT = 0x00000001;
unsigned long SHOW_ATTRIBUTE = 0x00000002;
unsigned long SHOW_TEXT = 0x00000004;
unsigned long SHOW_CDATA_SECTION = 0x00000008;
unsigned long SHOW_ENTITY_REFERENCE = 0x00000010;
unsigned long SHOW_ENTITY = 0x00000020;
unsigned long SHOW_PROCESSING_INSTRUCTION = 0x00000040;
unsigned long SHOW_COMMENT = 0x00000080;
unsigned long SHOW_DOCUMENT = 0x00000100;
unsigned long SHOW_DOCUMENT_TYPE = 0x00000200;
unsigned long SHOW_DOCUMENT_FRAGMENT = 0x00000400;
unsigned long SHOW_NOTATION = 0x00000800;
```

Methods

`acceptNode()`
: In languages such as Java that do not allow functions to be passed as arguments, you define a node filter by defining a class that implements this interface and includes an implementation for this function. The function is passed a node and must return one of the constants `FILTER_ACCEPT`, `FILTER_REJECT`, or `FILTER_SKIP`. In JavaScript, however,

you create a node filter simply by defining a function (with any name) that accepts a node argument and returns one of the three filter constants. See the following sections for details and an example.

Description

A node filter is an object that can examine a Document node and tell a NodeIterator or TreeWalker whether to include the node in its document traversal. In JavaScript, a node filter is simply a function that takes a single node argument and returns one of the three `FILTER_` constants defined earlier. There is no NodeFilter interface; there is simply an object named NodeFilter that has properties that define those constants. To use a node filter, you pass it to the `createNodeIterator()` or `createTreeWalker()` method of the Document object. Your node filter function will then be called to evaluate nodes when you use the resulting NodeIterator or TreeWalker object to traverse the document.

Node filter functions should ideally be written so that they do not themselves alter the document tree and do not throw any exceptions. Also, node filters are not allowed to base their filtering decisions on the history of past invocations of those filters.

Example

You might define and use a node filter function as follows:

```
// Define a node filter that filters out everything but <h1> and <h2> elements
var myfilter = function(n) {  // Filter node n
    if ((n.nodeName == "H1") || (n.nodeName == "H2"))
        return NodeFilter.FILTER_ACCEPT;
    else
        return NodeFilter.FILTER_SKIP;
}

// Now create a NodeIterator that uses the filter
var ni = document.createNodeIterator(document.body,  // Traverse the document body
                                     NodeFilter.SHOW_ELEMENT,  // Elements only
                                     myfilter,  // Filter by tag name
                                     false);  // No entity expansion
```

See Also

NodeIterator, TreeWalker

Type of: NodeIterator.filter, TreeWalker.filter

Passed to: Document.createNodeIterator(), Document.createTreeWalker()

NodeIterator **DOM Level 2 Traversal**

iterate through a filtered sequence of Document nodes

Properties

`readonly boolean expandEntityReferences`

Whether this NodeIterator traverses the children of EntityReference nodes (in XML documents). The value is specified as an argument to `Document.createNodeIterator()` when the NodeIterator is first created.

readonly NodeFilter filter
: The node filter function that was specified for this NodeIterator in the call to `Document.createNodeIterator()`.

readonly Node root
: The root node at which the NodeIterator begins iterating. The value of this property is specified in the call to `Document.createNodeIterator()`.

readonly unsigned long whatToShow
: A set of bit flags (see "NodeFilter" for a list of valid flags) that specifies what types of Document nodes this NodeIterator will consider. If a bit is not set in this property, the corresponding node type will always be ignored by this NodeIterator. Note that the value of this property is specified in the call to `Document.createNodeIterator()`.

Methods

detach()
: "Detaches" this NodeIterator from its document so that the implementation no longer needs to modify the NodeIterator when the document is modified. Call this method when you are done using a NodeIterator. After `detach()` has been called, any calls to other NodeIterator methods will cause exceptions.

nextNode()
: Returns the next node in the filtered sequence of nodes represented by this NodeIterator, or `null` if the NodeIterator has already returned the last node.

previousNode()
: Returns the previous node in the filtered sequence of nodes represented by this NodeIterator, or `null` if there is no previous node.

Description

A NodeIterator represents the sequence of Document nodes that results from traversing a document subtree in document source order and filtering the nodes using a two-stage process. Create a NodeIterator object with `Document.createNodeIterator()`. Use the `nextNode()` and `previousNode()` methods to iterate forward and backward through the sequence of nodes. Call `detach()` when you are done with a NodeIterator, unless you are sure that the NodeIterator will be garbage collected before the document is modified. Note that the properties of this interface are all read-only copies of the arguments passed to `Document.createNodeIterator()`.

To be returned by the `nextNode()` or `previousNode()` methods, a node must pass two filtration steps. First, the node type must be one of the types specified by the `whatToShow` property. See "NodeFilter" for a list of constants that can be combined to specify the *`whatToShow`* argument to `Document.createNodeIterator()`. Next, if the `filter` property is not `null`, each node that passes the `whatToShow` test is passed to the filter function specified by the `filter` property. If this function returns `NodeFilter.FILTER_ACCEPT`, the node is returned. If it returns `NodeFilter.FILTER_REJECT` or `NodeFilter.FILTER_SKIP`, the NodeIterator skips the node. Note that when a node is rejected by either of these filtration steps, it is only the node itself that is rejected; the children of the node are not automatically rejected and are subject to the same filtration steps.

NodeIterator objects remain valid even if the document tree they are traversing is modified. The `nextNode()` and `previousNode()` methods return nodes based on the current

W3C DOM Reference

state of the document, not the state of the document that existed when the NodeIterator was created.

See Also

NodeFilter, TreeWalker; Chapter 17

Returned by: Document.createNodeIterator( )

NodeIterator.detach( )

DOM Level 2 Traversal

free a NodeIterator object

Synopsis

```
void detach( );
```

Description

DOM implementations keep track of all NodeIterator objects created for a document, because they may need to modify the state of the NodeIterator when certain Document nodes are deleted. When you are certain that a NodeIterator isn't needed anymore, call `detach( )` to tell the implementation that it no longer needs to keep track of it. Note, however, that once you call this method any subsequent call to `nextNode( )` or `previousNode( )` will throw an exception.

Calling `detach( )` is not required, but doing so may improve performance when the document is being modified and the NodeIterator object is not immediately garbage collected.

NodeIterator.nextNode( )

DOM Level 2 Traversal

iterate to the next node

Synopsis

```
Node nextNode( )
    throws DOMException;
```

Returns

The next node in the sequence of nodes represented by this NodeIterator, or `null` if the last node has already been returned.

Throws

If this method is called after a call to `detach( )`, it throws a DOMException with a code of `INVALID_STATE_ERR`.

Description

This method iterates forward through the sequence of nodes represented by this NodeIterator. If this is the first time it is called for a NodeIterator, it returns the first node in the sequence. Otherwise, it returns the node that follows the one that was previously returned.

Example

```
// Create a NodeIterator to represent all elements in the document body
var ni = document.createNodeIterator(document.body, NodeFilter.SHOW_ELEMENT,
                                     null, false);
// Loop forward through all nodes in the iterator
for(var e = ni.nextNode( ); e != null; e = ni.nextNode( )) {
    // Do something with element e
}
```

NodeIterator.previousNode( ) DOM Level 2 Traversal

iterate to the previous node

Synopsis

```
Node previousNode( )
    throws DOMException;
```

Returns

The previous node in the sequence of nodes represented by this NodeIterator, or `null` if there is no previous node.

Throws

If this method is called after a call to `detach( )`, it throws a DOMException with a code of `INVALID_STATE_ERR`.

Description

This method iterates backward through the sequence of nodes represented by this NodeIterator. It returns the node before the one that was most recently returned by `previousNode( )` or `nextNode( )`. If there is no such node in the sequence, it returns `null`.

NodeList DOM Level 1 Core

a read-only array of nodes

Properties

`readonly unsigned long length`
: The number of nodes in the array.

Methods

`item( )`
: Returns the specified element of the array.

Description

The NodeList interface defines a read-only ordered list (i.e., an array) of Node objects. The `length` property specifies how many nodes are in the list, and the `item( )` method allows you to obtain the node at a specified position in the list. The elements of a NodeList are always valid Node objects: NodeLists never contain `null` elements.

In JavaScript, NodeList objects behave like JavaScript arrays, and you can query an element from the list using square-bracket array notation instead of calling the `item()` method. However, you cannot assign new nodes to a NodeList using square brackets. Since it is always easier to think of a NodeList object as a read-only JavaScript array, this book uses the notation `Node[]` (i.e., a Node array) instead of NodeList. See "Element.getElementsByTagName()," for example, which is listed as returning a `Node[]` instead of a NodeList object. Similarly, the `childNodes` property of the Node object is technically a NodeList object, but the "Node" reference page defines it as a `Node[]`, and the property itself is usually referred to as "the `childNodes[]` array."

Note that NodeList objects are "live": they are not static, but immediately reflect changes to the document tree. For example, if you have a NodeList that represents the children of a specific node and you then delete one of those children, the child will be removed from your NodeList. Be careful when you are looping through the elements of a NodeList if the body of your loop makes changes to the document tree (such as deleting nodes) that may affect the contents of the NodeList!

See Also

NamedNodeMap

Type of: Node.childNodes

Returned by: Document.getElementsByTagName(), Document.getElementsByTagNameNS(), Element.getElementsByTagName(), Element.getElementsByTagNameNS(), HTMLDocument.getElementsByName()

NodeList.item( ) — DOM Level 1 Core

get an element of a NodeList

Synopsis

```
Node item(unsigned long index);
```

Arguments

`index`

The position (or index) of the desired node in the NodeList. The index of the first node in the NodeList is 0, and the index of the last Node is `length`–1.

Returns

The node at the specified position in the NodeList, or `null` if *`index`* is less than zero or greater than or equal to the length of the NodeList.

Description

This method returns the specified element of a NodeList. In JavaScript, you can use the square-bracket array notation instead of calling `item()`.

Notation

DOM Level 1 XML

a notation in an XML DTD

Node → Notation

Properties

`readonly String publicId`
: The public identifier of the notation, or `null` if none is specified.

`readonly String systemId`
: The system identifier of the notation, or `null` if none is specified.

Description

This infrequently used interface represents a notation declaration in the document type definition (DTD) of an XML document. In XML, notations are used to specify the format of an unparsed entity or to formally declare a processing instruction target.

The name of the notation is specified by the inherited `nodeName` property. Because notations appear in the DTD and not the document itself, Notation nodes are never part of the document tree, and the `parentNode` property is always null. The `notations` property of the DocumentType interface provides a way to look up Notation objects by notation name.

Notation objects are read-only and cannot be modified in any way.

See Also

DocumentType

ProcessingInstruction

DOM Level 1 XML

a processing instruction in an XML document

Node → ProcessingInstruction

Properties

`String data`
: The content of the processing instruction (i.e., the first non-space character after the target up to but not including the closing ?>).

`readonly String target`
: The target of the processing instruction. This is the first identifier that follows the opening <?; it specifies the "processor" for which the processing instruction is intended.

Description

This infrequently used interface represents a processing instruction (or PI) in an XML document. Programmers working with HTML documents will never encounter a ProcessingInstruction node.

See Also

Returned by: Document.createProcessingInstruction()

Range

DOM Level 2 Range

represents a contiguous range of a document

Constants

These constants specify how the boundary points of two Range objects are to be compared. They are the legal values for the *how* argument to the `compareBoundaryPoints()` method. See the "Range.compareBoundaryPoints()" reference page.

`unsigned short START_TO_START = 0`
: Compare the start of the specified range to the start of this range.

`unsigned short START_TO_END = 1`
: Compare the start of the specified range to the end of this range.

`unsigned short END_TO_END = 2`
: Compare the end of the specified range to the end of this range.

`unsigned short END_TO_START = 3`
: Compare the end of the specified range to the start of this range.

Properties

The Range interface defines the following properties. Note that all of these properties are read-only. You cannot change the start or end points of a range by setting properties; you must call `setEnd()` or `setStart()` instead. Note also that after you call the `detach()` method of a Range object, any subsequent attempt to read any of these properties throws a DOMException with a code of `INVALID_STATE_ERR`.

`readonly boolean collapsed`
: `true` if the start and the end of the range are at the same point in the document—that is, if the range is empty or "collapsed."

`readonly Node commonAncestorContainer`
: The most deeply nested Document node that contains (i.e., is an ancestor of) both the start and end points of the range.

`readonly Node endContainer`
: The Document node that contains the end point of the range.

`readonly long endOffset`
: The end point position within `endContainer`.

`readonly Node startContainer`
: The Document node that contains the starting point of the range.

`readonly long startOffset`
: The position of the range's starting point within `startContainer`.

Methods

The Range interface defines the following methods. Note that if you call `detach()` on a range, any subsequent calls of any methods on that range throw a DOMException with a code of `INVALID_STATE_ERR`. Because this exception is ubiquitous within this interface, it is not listed in the reference pages for the individual Range methods.

`cloneContents( )`
: Returns a new DocumentFragment object that contains a copy of the region of the document represented by this range.

`cloneRange( )`
: Creates a new Range object that represents the same region of the document as this one.

`collapse( )`
: Collapses this range so that one boundary point is the same as the other.

`compareBoundaryPoints( )`
: Compares a boundary point of the specified range to a boundary point of this range, and returns –1, 0, or 1, depending on their order. Which points to compare is specified by the first argument, which must be one of the previously defined constants.

`deleteContents( )`
: Deletes the region of the document represented by this range.

`detach( )`
: Tells the implementation that this range will no longer be used and that it can stop keeping track of it. If you call this method for a range, subsequent method calls or property lookups on that range throw a DOMException with a code of `INVALID_STATE_ERR`.

`extractContents( )`
: Deletes the region of the document represented by this range, but returns the contents of that region as a DocumentFragment object. This method is like a combination of `cloneContents( )` and `deleteContents( )`.

`insertNode( )`
: Inserts the specified node into the document at the start point of the range.

`selectNode( )`
: Sets the boundary points of this range so that it contains the specified node and all of its descendants.

`selectNodeContents( )`
: Sets the boundary points of this range so that it contains all the descendants of the specified node but not the node itself.

`setEnd( )`
: Sets the end point of this range to the specified node and offset.

`setEndAfter( )`
: Sets the end point of this range to immediately after the specified node.

`setEndBefore( )`
: Sets the end point of this range to immediately before the specified node.

`setStart( )`
: Sets the start position of this range to the specified offset within the specified node.

`setStartAfter( )`
: Sets the start position of this range to immediately after the specified node.

`setStartBefore( )`
: Sets the start position of this range to immediately before the specified node.

`surroundContents()`
: Inserts the specified node into the document at the start position of the range and then reparents all the nodes within the range so that they become descendants of the newly inserted node.

`toString()`
: Returns the plain-text content of the document region described by this range.

Description

A Range object represents a contiguous range or region of a document, such as the region that the user might select with a mouse drag in a web browser window. If an implementation supports the Range module, the Document object defines a `createRange()` method that you can call to create a new Range object. (Be careful, however: Internet Explorer defines an incompatible `Document.createRange()` method that returns an object similar to, but not compatible with, the Range interface.) The Range interface defines a number of methods for specifying a "selected" region of a document and several more methods for implementing cut and paste–type operations on the selected region.

A range has two boundary points: a start point and an end point. Each boundary point is specified by a combination of a node and an offset within that node. The node is typically an Element, Document, or Text node. For Element and Document nodes, the offset refers to the children of that node. An offset of 0 specifies a boundary point before the first child of the node. An offset of 1 specifies a boundary point after the first child and before the second child. If the boundary node is a Text node, however, the offset specifies a position between two characters of that text.

The properties of the Range interface provide a way to obtain boundary nodes and offsets of a range. The methods of the interface provide a number of ways to set the boundaries of a range. Note that the boundaries of a range may be set to nodes within a Document or a DocumentFragment.

Once the boundary points of a range are defined, you can use `deleteContents()`, `extractContents()`, `cloneContents()`, and `insertNode()` to implement cut-, copy-, and paste-style operations.

When a document is altered by insertion or deletion, all Range objects that represent portions of that document are altered, if necessary, so that their boundary points remain valid and they represent (as closely as possible) the same document content.

For further details, read the reference pages for each of the Range methods and see the discussion of the Range API in Chapter 17.

See Also

Document.createRange(), DocumentFragment; Chapter 17

Passed to: Range.compareBoundaryPoints()

Returned by: Document.createRange(), Range.cloneRange()

Range.cloneContents()

DOM Level 2 Range

copy range contents into a DocumentFragment

Synopsis

```
DocumentFragment cloneContents()
    throws DOMException;
```

Returns

A DocumentFragment object that contains a copy of the document content within this range.

Throws

If this range includes a DocumentType node, this method throws a DOMException with a code of `HIERARCHY_REQUEST_ERR`.

Description

This method duplicates the contents of this range and returns the results in a DocumentFragment object.

See Also

DocumentFragment, Range.deleteContents(), Range.extractContents()

Range.cloneRange()

DOM Level 2 Range

make a copy of this range

Synopsis

```
Range cloneRange();
```

Returns

A new Range object that has the same boundary points as this range.

See Also

Document.createRange()

Range.collapse()

DOM Level 2 Range

make one boundary point equal to the other

Synopsis

```
void collapse(boolean toStart)
    throws DOMException;
```

Arguments

toStart

If this argument is true, the method sets the end point of the range to the same value as the starting point. Otherwise, it sets the starting point to the same value as the end point.

Description

This method sets one boundary point of the range to be the same as the other point. The point to be modified is specified by the *toStart* argument. After this method returns, the range is said to be "collapsed": it represents a single point within a document and has no content. When a range is collapsed like this, its collapsed property is true.

Range.compareBoundaryPoints( ) — DOM Level 2 Range

compare positions of two ranges

Synopsis

```
short compareBoundaryPoints(unsigned short how,
                            Range sourceRange)
    throws DOMException;
```

Arguments

how

Specifies how to perform the comparison (i.e., which boundary points to compare). Legal values are the constants defined by the Range interface.

sourceRange

The range that is to be compared to this range.

Returns

–1 if the specified boundary point of this range is before the specified boundary point of sourceRange, 0 if the two specified boundary points are the same, or 1 if the specified boundary point of this range is after the specified boundary point of sourceRange.

Throws

If sourceRange represents a range of a different document than this range does, this method throws a DOMException with a code of WRONG_DOCUMENT_ERR.

Description

This method compares a boundary point of this range to a boundary point of the specified sourceRange and returns a value that specifies their relative order in the document source. The *how* argument specifies which boundary points of each range are to be compared. The legal values for this argument, and their meanings, are as follows:

Range.START_TO_START

Compare the start points of the two Range nodes.

Range.END_TO_END

Compare the end points of the two Range nodes.

`Range.START_TO_END`
: Compare the start point of *sourceRange* to the end point of this range.

`Range.END_TO_START`
: Compare the end point of *sourceRange* to the start point of this range.

The return value of this method is a number that specifies the relative position of this range to the specified *sourceRange*. Therefore, you might expect the range constants for the *how* argument to specify the boundary point for this range first and the boundary point for `sourceRange` second. Counterintuitively, however, the `Range.START_TO_END` constant specifies a comparison of the *end* point of this range with the *start* point of the specified *sourceRange*. Similarly, the `Range.END_TO_START` constant specifies a comparison of the *start* point of this range with the *end* point of the specified range.

Range.deleteContents( ) DOM Level 2 Range

delete a region of the document

Synopsis

```
void deleteContents( )
    throws DOMException;
```

Throws

If any portion of the document that is represented by this range is read-only, this method throws a DOMException with a code of `NO_MODIFICATION_ALLOWED_ERR`.

Description

This method deletes all document content represented by this range. When this method returns, the range is collapsed with both boundary points at the same position. Note that the deletion may result in adjacent Text nodes that can be merged with a call to `Node.normalize( )`.

See "cloneContents( )" for a way to copy document content and "extractContents( )" for a way to copy and delete document content in a single operation.

See Also

Node.normalize( ), Range.cloneContents( ), Range.extractContents( )

Range.detach( ) DOM Level 2 Range

free a Range object

Synopsis

```
void detach( )
    throws DOMException;
```

Throws

Like all Range methods, `detach( )` throws a DOMException with a code of `INVALID_STATE_ERR` if it is called on a Range object that has already been detached.

Description

DOM implementations keep track of all Range objects created for a document, because they may need to change the range boundary points when the document is modified. When you are certain that a Range object isn't needed any more, call the `detach( )` method to tell the implementation that it no longer needs to keep track of that range. Note that once this method has been called for a Range object, any use of that Range will throw an exception. Calling `detach( )` is not required but may improve performance in some circumstances when the document is being modified and a Range object is not subject to immediate garbage collection.

Range.extractContents( ) — DOM Level 2 Range

delete document content and return it in a DocumentFragment

Synopsis

```
DocumentFragment extractContents( )
    throws DOMException;
```

Returns

A DocumentFragment node that contains the contents of this range.

Throws

This method throws a DOMException with a code of `NO_MODIFICATION_ALLOWED_ERR` if any part of the document content to be extracted is read-only, or a code of `HIERARCHY_REQUEST_ERR` if the range contains a DocumentType node.

Description

This method deletes the specified range of a document and returns a DocumentFragment node that contains the deleted content (or a copy of the deleted content). When this method returns, the range is collapsed, and the document may contain adjacent Text nodes (which can be merged with `Node.normalize( )`).

See Also

DocumentFragment, Range.cloneContents( ), Range.deleteContents( )

Range.insertNode( ) — DOM Level 2 Range

insert a node at the start of a range

Synopsis

```
void insertNode(Node newNode)
    throws RangeException,
           DOMException;
```

Arguments

newNode

The node to be inserted into the document.

Throws

This method throws a RangeException with a code of `INVALID_NODE_TYPE_ERR` if newNode is an Attr, Document, Entity, or Notation node.

This method also throws a DOMException with one of the following code values under the following conditions:

`HIERARCHY_REQUEST_ERR`
: The node that contains the start of the range does not allow children, or it does not allow children of the specified type, or *newNode* is an ancestor of that node.

`NO_MODIFICATION_ALLOWED_ERR`
: The node that contains the start of the range, or any of its ancestors, is read-only.

`WRONG_DOCUMENT_ERR`
: newNode is part of a different document than the range is.

Description

This method inserts the specified node (and all its descendants) into the document at the start position of this range. When this method returns, this range includes the newly inserted node. If *newNode* is already part of the document, it is removed from its current position and then reinserted at the start of the range. If *newNode* is a DocumentFragment node, it is not inserted itself, but all of its children are inserted, in order, at the start of the range.

If the node that contains the start of the range is a Text node, it is split into two adjacent nodes before the insertion takes place. If *newNode* is a Text node, it is not merged with any adjacent Text nodes after it is inserted. To merge adjacent nodes, call `Node.normalize( )`.

See Also

DocumentFragment, Node.normalize()

W3C DOM Reference

Range.selectNode( ) — DOM Level 2 Range

set range boundaries to a node

Synopsis

```
void selectNode(Node refNode)
    throws RangeException,
           DOMException;
```

Arguments

refNode
: The node to be "selected" (i.e., the node that is to become the content of this range).

Throws

A RangeException with a code of `INVALID_NODE_TYPE_ERR` if *refNode* is an Attr, Document, DocumentFragment, Entity, or Notation node, or if any ancestor of *refNode* is a DocumentType, Entity, or Notation node.

A DOMException with a code of `WRONG_DOCUMENT_ERR` if *refNode* is part of a different document than the one through which this range was created.

Description

This method sets the contents of this range to the specified *refNode*. That is, it "selects" the node and its descendants.

See Also

Range.selectNodeContents( )

Range.selectNodeContents( ) DOM Level 2 Range

set range boundaries to the children of a node

Synopsis

```
void selectNodeContents(Node refNode)
    throws RangeException,
           DOMException;
```

Arguments

refNode
: The node whose children are to become the contents of this range.

Throws

A RangeException with a code of `INVALID_NODE_TYPE_ERR` if *refNode* or one of its ancestors is a DocumentType, Entity, or Notation node.

A DOMException with a code of `WRONG_DOCUMENT_ERR` if *refNode* is part of a different document than the one through which this range was created.

Description

This method sets the boundary points of this range so that the range contains the children of *refNode*.

See Also

Range.selectNode( )

Range.setEnd( ) DOM Level 2 Range

set the end point of a range

Synopsis

```
void setEnd(Node refNode,
            long offset)
    throws RangeException,
           DOMException;
```

Arguments

refNode
: The node that contains the new end point.

offset
: The position of the end point within *refNode*.

Throws

A RangeException with a code of INVALID_NODE_TYPE_ERR if *refNode* or one of its ancestors is a DocumentType, Entity, or Notation node.

A DOMException with a code of WRONG_DOCUMENT_ERR if *refNode* is part of a different document than the one through which this range was created, or a code of INDEX_SIZE_ERR if *offset* is negative or is greater than the number of children or characters in *refNode*.

Description

This method sets the end point of a range by specifying the values of the endContainer and endOffset properties.

Range.setEndAfter( ) DOM Level 2 Range

end a range after a specified node

Synopsis

```
void setEndAfter(Node refNode)
    throws RangeException,
           DOMException;
```

Arguments

refNode
: The node after which the end point of the range is to be set.

Throws

A RangeException with a code of INVALID_NODE_TYPE_ERR if *refNode* is a Document, DocumentFragment, Attr, Entity, or Notation node, or if the root container of *refNode* is not a Document, DocumentFragment, or Attr node.

A DOMException with a code of WRONG_DOCUMENT_ERR if *refNode* is part of a different document than the one through which this range was created.

Description

This method sets the end point of this range to fall immediately after the specified *refNode*.

Range.setEndBefore( ) DOM Level 2 Range

end a range before the specified node

Synopsis

```
void setEndBefore(Node refNode)
    throws RangeException,
           DOMException;
```

Arguments

refNode
The node before which the end point of the range is to be set.

Throws

This method throws the same exceptions in the same circumstances as `Range.setEndAfter( )`. See that method for details.

Description

This method sets the end point of this range to fall immediately before the specified *refNode*.

Range.setStart( ) DOM Level 2 Range

set the start point of a range

Synopsis

```
void setStart(Node refNode,
              long offset)
    throws RangeException,
           DOMException;
```

Arguments

refNode
The node that contains the new start point.

offset
The position of the new start point within *refNode*.

Throws

This method throws the same exceptions, for the same reasons, as `Range.setEnd( )`. See that method for details.

Description

This method sets the start point of this range by specifying the values of the `startContainer` and `startOffset` properties.

Range.setStartAfter( ) DOM Level 2 Range

start a range after the specified node

Synopsis

```
void setStartAfter(Node refNode)
    throws RangeException,
           DOMException;
```

Arguments

refNode
: The node after which the start point of the range is to be set.

Throws

This method throws the same exceptions in the same circumstances as `Range.setEndAfter( )`. See that method for details.

Description

This method sets the starting point of this range to be immediately after the specified *refNode*.

Range.setStartBefore( )

DOM Level 2 Range

start a range before the specified node

Synopsis

```
void setStartBefore(Node refNode)
    throws RangeException,
           DOMException;
```

Arguments

refNode
: The node before which the start point of the range is to be set.

Throws

This method throws the same exceptions in the same circumstances as `Range.setEndAfter( )`. See that method for details.

Description

This method sets the starting point of this range to be immediately before the specified *refNode*.

Range.surroundContents( )

DOM Level 2 Range

surround range contents with the specified node

Synopsis

```
void surroundContents(Node newParent)
    throws RangeException,
           DOMException;
```

Arguments

newParent
: The node that is to become the new parent of the contents of this range.

Throws

This method throws a DOMException or RangeException with one of the following code values in the following circumstances:

`DOMException.HIERARCHY_REQUEST_ERR`
: The container node of the start of the range does not allow children or does not allow children of the type of *newParent*, or *newParent* is an ancestor of that container node.

`DOMException.NO_MODIFICATION_ALLOWED_ERR`
: An ancestor of a boundary point of the range is read-only and does not allow insertions.

`DOMException.WRONG_DOCUMENT_ERR`
: *newParent* and this range were created using different Document objects.

`RangeException.BAD_BOUNDARYPOINTS_ERR`
: The range partially selects a node (other than a Text node), so the region of the document it represents cannot be surrounded.

`RangeException.INVALID_NODE_TYPE_ERR`
: *newParent* is a Document, DocumentFragment, DocumentType, Attr, Entity, or Notation node.

Description

This method reparents the contents of this range to *newParent* and then inserts *newParent* into the document at the start position of the range. It is useful to place a region of document content within a `<b>` or `<span>` element, for example.

If *newParent* is already part of the document, it is first removed from the document and any children it has are discarded. When this method returns, this range begins immediately before `newParent` and ends immediately after it.

Range.toString( ) — DOM Level 2 Range

get range contents as a plain-text string

Synopsis

```
String toString();
```

Returns

The contents of this range as a string of plain text without any markup.

RangeException — DOM Level 2 Range

signals a range-specific exception

Constants

The following constants define the legal values for the `code` property of a RangeException object. Note that these constants are static properties of RangeException, not properties of individual exception objects.

`unsigned short BAD_BOUNDARYPOINTS_ERR = 1`
The boundary points of a range are not legal for the requested operation.

`unsigned short INVALID_NODE_TYPE_ERR = 2`
An attempt was made to set the container node of a range boundary point to an invalid node or a node with an invalid ancestor.

Properties

`unsigned short code`
An error code that provides some detail about what caused the exception. The legal values (and their meanings) for this property are defined by the constants just listed.

Description

A RangeException is thrown by certain methods of the Range interface to signal a problem of some sort. Note that most exceptions thrown by Range methods are DOMException objects. A RangeException is generated only when none of the existing DOMException error constants is appropriate to describe the exception.

Rect — DOM Level 2 CSS

a CSS rect( ) value

Properties

`readonly CSSPrimitiveValue bottom`
The bottom of the rectangle.

`readonly CSSPrimitiveValue left`
The left side of the rectangle.

`readonly CSSPrimitiveValue right`
The right side of the rectangle.

`readonly CSSPrimitiveValue top`
The top of the rectangle.

Description

This interface represents a CSS `rect(top right bottom left)` value, as used with the CSS `clip` attribute, for example. Consult a CSS reference for details.

See Also

Returned by: CSSPrimitiveValue.getRectValue( )

RGBColor — DOM Level 2 CSS

a CSS color value

Properties

`readonly CSSPrimitiveValue blue`
The blue component of the color.

`readonly CSSPrimitiveValue green`
The green component of the color.

`readonly CSSPrimitiveValue red`
The red component of the color.

Description

This interface represents a color specified in the RGB color space. The properties are CSSPrimitiveValue objects that specify the values of the red, green, and blue components of the color. Each CSSPrimitiveValue holds a number in the range 0–255 or a percentage in the range 0–100%.

See Also

Returned by: CSSPrimitiveValue.getRGBColorValue()

StyleSheet

DOM Level 2 StyleSheets

a style sheet of any type

Subinterfaces

CSSStyleSheet

Properties

`boolean disabled`
If `true`, the style sheet is disabled and is not applied to the document. If `false`, the style sheet is enabled and is applied to the document (unless the `media` property specifies that the style sheet should not be applied to documents of this type).

`readonly String href`
The URL of a style sheet that is linked into the document, or `null` for inline style sheets.

`readonly MediaList media`
A list of media types for which this style sheet should be applied. If no media information is supplied for the style sheet, this property is a valid MediaList object that has a `length` of 0.

`readonly Node ownerNode`
The Document node that links the style sheet into the document, or the node that contains an inline style sheet. In HTML documents, this property refers to a `<link>` or `<style>` element. For style sheets that are included within other style sheets rather than directly in the document, this property is `null`.

`readonly StyleSheet parentStyleSheet`
The style sheet that included this one, or `null` if this style sheet was included directly in the document. See also "CSSStyleSheet.ownerRule."

`readonly String title`
The title of the style sheet, if one is specified. A title may be specified by the `title` attribute of a `<style>` or `<link>` tag that is the `ownerNode` of this style sheet.

`readonly String type`
The type of this style sheet, as a MIME type. CSS style sheets have a type of "text/css".

Description

This interface represents a style sheet that is associated with this document. If this is a CSS style sheet, the object that implements this StyleSheet interface also implements the CSSStyleSheet subinterface and defines properties and methods that allow you to examine and set the CSS rules that comprise the style sheet. See "CSSStyleSheet" for details.

If a DOM implementation supports style sheets, you can obtain a complete list of the style sheets associated with a document through the `Document.styleSheets` property. Furthermore, the HTML `<style>` and `<link>` elements and XML style-sheet ProcessingInstruction nodes implement the `LinkStyle` interface and provide a reference to the StyleSheet through a property named `sheet`.

See Also

CSSStyleSheet, Document.styleSheets, LinkStyle

Type of: LinkStyle.sheet, StyleSheet.parentStyleSheet

Returned by: StyleSheetList.item( )

StyleSheetList — DOM Level 2 StyleSheets

an array of style sheets

Properties

`readonly unsigned long length`

The number of StyleSheet objects in the array.

Methods

`item( )`

Returns the StyleSheet object at the specified position in the array, or `null` if the specified position is negative or is greater than or equal to `length`.

Description

This interface defines an array of StyleSheet objects. `length` specifies the number of style sheets in the array, and `item( )` provides a way to retrieve the style sheet at a given position. In JavaScript, you can treat a StyleSheetList object as a read-only array, and you can index it using ordinary square-bracket array notation instead of calling the `item( )` method.

See Also

Type of: DocumentStyle.styleSheets

StyleSheetList.item( ) — DOM Level 2 StyleSheets

index an array of style sheets

Synopsis

```
StyleSheet item(unsigned long index);
```

Arguments

index
: The position of the desired style sheet within the array.

Returns

The StyleSheet object at the specified position within the array, or `null` if *index* is negative or is greater than or equal to `length`. Note that in JavaScript, it is usually simpler to treat a StyleSheetList object as an array and index it using square-bracket array notation instead of calling this method.

Text — DOM Level 1 Core

a run of text in an HTML or XML document — Node → CharacterData → Text

Subinterfaces

CDATASection

Methods

`splitText()`
: Splits this Text node into two at the specified character position and returns the new Text node.

Description

A Text node represents a run of plain text in an HTML or XML document. Plain text appears within HTML and XML elements and attributes, and Text nodes typically appear as children of Element and Attr nodes. Text nodes inherit from CharacterData, and the textual content of a Text node is available through the `data` property inherited from CharacterData or through the `nodeValue` property inherited from Node. Text nodes may be manipulated using any of the methods inherited from CharacterData or with the `splitText()` method defined by the Text interface itself. Text nodes never have children.

See "Node.normalize()" for a way to remove empty Text nodes and merge adjacent Text nodes from a subtree of a document.

See Also

CharacterData, Node.normalize()

Returned by: Document.createTextNode(), Text.splitText()

Text.splitText() — DOM Level 1 Core

split a Text node in two

Synopsis

```
Text splitText(unsigned long offset)
    throws DOMException;
```

Arguments

offset
: The character position at which to split the Text node.

Returns

The Text node that was split from this node.

Throws

This method may throw a DOMException with one of the following `code` values:

`INDEX_SIZE_ERR`
: *offset* is negative or greater than the length of the Text or Comment node.

`NO_MODIFICATION_ALLOWED_ERR`
: The node is read-only and may not be modified.

Description

This method splits a Text node in two at the specified *offset*. The original Text node is modified so that it contains all text content up to, but not including, the character at position *offset*. A new Text node is created to contain all the characters from (and including) the position *offset* to the end of the string. This new Text node is the return value of the method. Additionally, if the original Text node has a `parentNode`, the new node is inserted into this parent node immediately after the original node.

The CDATASection interface inherits from Text, and this `splitText()` method can also be used with CDATASection nodes, in which case the newly created node is a CDATASection rather than a Text node.

See Also

Node.normalize()

TreeWalker — DOM Level 2 Traversal

traverse a filtered document subtree

Properties

`Node currentNode`
: The current position of this TreeWalker and the node relative to which all of the TreeWalker traversal methods operate. This is the node most recently returned by one of those traversal methods or, if none of those methods have been called yet, it is the same as the `root` property.

: Note that this is a read/write property, and you can set it to any valid Document node—even one that is not a descendant of the original `root` node or one that would be rejected by the filters used by this TreeWalker. If you change the value of this property, the traversal methods operate relative to the new node you specify. Attempting to set this property to `null` throws a DOMException with a `code` of `NOT_SUPPORTED_ERR`.

`readonly boolean expandEntityReferences`
: This read-only property specifies whether this TreeWalker object expands entity references it encounters while traversing XML documents. The value of this property is set by the call to `Document.createTreeWalker()`.

`readonly NodeFilter filter`
: The node filter function, if any, that was specified for this TreeWalker in the call to `Document.createTreeWalker()`. If no node filter is in use, this property is `null`.

`readonly Node root`
: This read-only property specifies the `root` node at which the TreeWalker begins traversal. It is the initial value of the `currentNode` property and is specified in the call to `Document.createTreeWalker()`.

`readonly unsigned long whatToShow`
: This read-only property is a set of bit flags (see "NodeFilter" for a list of valid flags) that specifies the types of Document nodes this TreeWalker will consider. If a bit is not set in this property, the corresponding node type will always be ignored by this TreeWalker. Note that the value of this property is specified in the call to `Document.createTreeWalker()`.

Methods

`firstChild()`
: Returns the first child of the current node that is not filtered out, or `null`.

`lastChild()`
: Returns the last child of the current node that is not filtered out, or `null`.

`nextNode()`
: Returns the next node (in document source order) that is not filtered out, or `null`.

`nextSibling()`
: Returns the next sibling of the current node that is not filtered out, or `null`.

`parentNode()`
: Returns the parent or nearest ancestor of the current node that is not filtered out, or `null`.

`previousNode()`
: Returns the previous node (in document source order) that is not filtered out, or `null`.

`previousSibling()`
: Returns the nearest previous sibling of the current node that is not filtered out, or `null`.

Description

A TreeWalker filters a specified document subtree and defines methods that allow programs to traverse the filtered tree (which may have a significantly different structure than the original document tree). Create a TreeWalker object with the `createTreeWalker()` method of the Document object. Once a TreeWalker is created, you can use its `firstChild()` and `nextSibling()` methods to traverse the filtered subtree it represents in the same way that you might use the `firstChild` and `nextSibling` properties of the Node interface to traverse an unfiltered document tree.

A TreeWalker applies the same two filtration steps that a NodeIterator does. The various traversal methods defined by TreeWalker will return only nodes that pass both filters. First, the node type must be one of the types specified by the `whatToShow` property. See "NodeFilter" for a list of constants that can be combined to specify the *whatToShow* argument to `Document.createTreeWalker()`. Second, if the `filter` property is not `null`, each node that passes the `whatToShow` test is passed to the filter function specified by the `filter` property. If this function returns `NodeFilter.FILTER_ACCEPT`, the node is returned. If it returns `NodeFilter.FILTER_REJECT`, the node and all of its descendants are skipped by the TreeWalker (this differs from NodeIterator filtration, in which descendants are never automatically rejected). If the node filter function returns `NodeFilter.FILTER_SKIP`, the TreeWalker ignores the node but does consider its descendants.

Unlike NodeIterators, TreeWalkers are not modified when the underlying document is modified. The current node of a TreeWalker remains unchanged, even if that node is removed from the document. (And, in this case, the TreeWalker can be used to traverse the tree of deleted nodes, if any, that surround that current node.)

Example

```
// A NodeFilter that rejects <font> tags and any element with a
// class="sidebar" attribute and any descendants of such an element
var filter = function(n) {
    if (n.nodeName == "FONT") return NodeFilter.FILTER_SKIP;
    if (n.nodeType == Node.ELEMENT_NODE && n.className == "sidebar")
        return NodeFilter.FILTER_REJECT;
    return NodeFilter.FILTER_ACCEPT;
}

// Create a TreeWalker using the filter above
var tw = document.createTreeWalker(document.body,  // Walk HTML document body
                                   // Consider all nodes except comments
                                   ~NodeFilter.SHOW_COMMENT,
                                   filter,  // Use filter above
                                   false);  // Don't expand entity references

// Here's a recursive function that traverses a document using a TreeWalker
function traverse(tw) {
    // Remember the current node
    var currentNode = tw.currentNode;

    // Loop through the children of the current node of the TreeWalker
    for(var c = tw.firstChild(); c != null; c = tw.nextSibling()) {
        process(c);     // Do something to process the child
        traverse(tw);  // And recursively process its children
    }

    // Put the TreeWalker back in the state we found it in
    tw.currentNode = currentNode;
}
```

See Also

NodeFilter, NodeIterator; Chapter 17

Returned by: Document.createTreeWalker()

W3C DOM Reference

TreeWalker.firstChild( )

DOM Level 2 Traversal

return the first child that is not filtered out

Synopsis

```
Node firstChild();
```

Returns

The first child of the current node that is not filtered out, or `null` if there is no such child.

Description

This method sets `currentNode` to the first child of the current node that is not filtered out and returns that child. If there is no such child, it leaves `currentNode` unchanged and returns `null`.

TreeWalker.lastChild( )

DOM Level 2 Traversal

return the last child that is not filtered out

Synopsis

```
Node lastChild();
```

Returns

The last child of the current node that is not filtered out, or `null` if there is no such child.

Description

This method sets `currentNode` to the last child of the current node that is not filtered out and returns that child. If there is no such child, it leaves `currentNode` unchanged and returns `null`.

TreeWalker.nextNode( )

DOM Level 2 Traversal

return the next node that is not filtered out

Synopsis

```
Node nextNode();
```

Returns

The node that follows the current node in the document source and is not filtered out, or `null` if there is none.

Description

This method sets `currentNode` to the next node (in document source order) that is not filtered out and returns that node. If there is no such node, or if the search for the next node takes the TreeWalker outside of the root subtree, currentNode remains unchanged and the method returns null.

Note that this method "flattens" the document tree structure and returns nodes in the order in which they appear in the document source. Calling nextNode( ) may cause the current node to move down, sideways, or up the document tree. This type of flattening traversal can also be performed with NodeIterator.nextNode( ).

TreeWalker.nextSibling( ) — DOM Level 2 Traversal

return the next sibling that is not filtered out

Synopsis

```
Node nextSibling( );
```

Returns

The next sibling of the current node that is not filtered out, or null if there is no such sibling.

Description

This method sets currentNode to the next sibling of the current node that is not filtered out and returns that sibling. If there is no such sibling, it leaves currentNode unchanged and returns null.

TreeWalker.parentNode( ) — DOM Level 2 Traversal

return the nearest ancestor that is not filtered out

Synopsis

```
Node parentNode( );
```

Returns

The nearest ancestor of the current node that is not filtered out, or null if there is no such ancestor.

Description

This method sets currentNode to the nearest ancestor of the current node that is not filtered out and returns that ancestor. If there is no such ancestor, it leaves currentNode unchanged and returns null.

TreeWalker.previousNode( ) — DOM Level 2 Traversal

return the previous node that is not filtered out

Synopsis

```
Node previousNode( );
```

Returns

The nearest node that precedes the current node in the document source and is not filtered out, or `null` if there is none.

Description

This method sets `currentNode` to the previous node (in document source order) that is not filtered out and returns that node. If there is no such node, or if the search for the previous node takes the TreeWalker outside of the `root` subtree, `currentNode` remains unchanged and the method returns `null`.

Note that this method "flattens" the document tree structure and returns nodes in the order in which they appear in the document source. Calling `previousNode( )` may cause the current node to move down, sideways, or up the document tree. This type of flattening traversal can also be performed with `NodeIterator.previousNode( )`.

TreeWalker.previousSibling( ) — DOM Level 2 Traversal

return the previous sibling that is not filtered out

Synopsis

```
Node previousSibling( );
```

Returns

The previous sibling of the current node that is not filtered out, or `null` if there is no such sibling.

Description

This method sets `currentNode` to the closest previous sibling of the current node that is not filtered out and returns that sibling. If there is no such sibling, it leaves `currentNode` unchanged and returns `null`.

UIEvent — DOM Level 2 Events

details about user interface events — Event → UIEvent

Subinterfaces

MouseEvent

Properties

`readonly long detail`

A numeric detail about the event. For click, mousedown, and mouseup events (see "MouseEvent"), this field is the click count: 1 for a single-click, 2 for a double-click, 3 for a triple-click, and so on. For DOMActivate events, this field is 1 for a normal activation or 2 for a "hyperactivation," such as a double-click or **Shift-Enter** combination.

`readonly AbstractView view`

The window (the "view") in which the event was generated.

Methods

`initUIEvent()`
: Initializes the properties of a newly created UIEvent object, including the properties inherited from the Event interface.

Description

The UIEvent interface is a subinterface of Event and defines the type of Event object passed to events of type DOMFocusIn, DOMFocusOut, and DOMActivate. These event types are not commonly used in web browsers, and what is more important about the UIEvent interface is that it is the parent interface of MouseEvent.

See Also

Event, MouseEvent; Chapter 19

UIEvent.initUIEvent( ) — DOM Level 2 Events

initialize the properties of a UIEvent object

Synopsis

```
void initUIEvent(String typeArg,
                 boolean canBubbleArg,
                 boolean cancelableArg,
                 AbstractView viewArg,
                  long detailArg);
```

Arguments

typeArg
: The event type.

canBubbleArg
: Whether the event will bubble.

cancelableArg
: Whether the event may be canceled with `preventDefault()`.

viewArg
: The window in which the event occurred.

detailArg
: The `detail` property for the event.

Description

This method initializes the `view` and `detail` properties of this UIEvent and also the `type`, `bubbles`, and `cancelable` properties inherited from the Event interface. This method may be called only on newly created UIEvent objects, before they have been passed to `EventTarget.dispatchEvent()`.

ViewCSS

see AbstractView

PART VI

Class, Property, Method, and Event Handler Index

This part of the book is an index to all of the classes, properties, methods, and event handlers in JavaScript. You can use this index to help you find the reference material for these items.

Class, Property, Method, and Event Handler Index

You can use the following index when you want to look up something in one of the reference sections but don't know where to look. For example, if you want to look up a class or interface but don't know which reference section documents it, you can look up the name of the class or interface here: the index will tell you the reference section in which you'll find it. The notation "[Core]" means the core JavaScript reference section, "[Client]" means the client-side reference section, and "[DOM]" means the DOM reference section.

If you want to look up a method, property, or event handler but don't know what class defines it, you can look up the method, property, or handler name in this index. It will tell you which class or classes (in which reference sections) to look under.

A

B

C

D

E

F

G

H

I

J

K

L

M

N

O

P

Q

R

S

T

Index

Symbols

We'd like to hear your suggestions for improving our indexes. Send email to *index@oreilly.com*.

Numbers

A

B

C

D

E

F

G

H

I

J

K

L

N

O

P

Q

R

S

T

U

V

W

X

Y

Z

About the Author

David Flanagan is a computer programmer who spends most of his time writing about JavaScript and Java. His other books with O'Reilly include *JavaScript Pocket Reference*, *Java in a Nutshell*, *Java Foundation Classes in a Nutshell*, and *Java Examples in a Nutshell*. David has a degree in computer science and engineering from the Massachusetts Institute of Technology. He lives with his wife and son in the U.S. Pacific Northwest between the cities of Seattle, Washington and Vancouver, British Columbia.

Colophon

Our look is the result of reader comments, our own experimentation, and feedback from distribution channels. Distinctive covers complement our distinctive approach to technical topics, breathing personality and life into potentially dry subjects.

The animal on the cover of *JavaScript: The Definitive Guide, Fourth Edition* is a Javan rhinoceros. All five species of rhinoceros are distinguished by their large size, thick armor-like skin, three-toed feet, and single or double snout horn. The Javan rhinoceros, along with the Sumatran rhinoceros, is one of two forest-dwelling species. The Javan rhinoceros is similar in appearance to the Indian rhinoceros, but smaller and with certain distinguishing characteristics (primarily skin texture).

Rhinoceroses are often depicted standing up to their snouts in water or mud. In fact, they can frequently be found just like that. When not resting in a river, rhinos will dig deep pits in which to wallow. Both of these resting places provide a couple of advantages. First, they give the animal relief from the tropical heat and protection from blood-sucking flies. (The mud that the wallow leaves on the skin of the rhinoceros provides some protection from flies, also.) Second, mud wallows and river water help support the considerable weight of these huge animals, thereby relieving the strain on their legs and backs.

Folklore has long held that the horn of the rhinoceros possesses magical and aphrodisiacal powers and that humans who gain possession of the horns will gain those powers, also. This is one of the reasons why rhinos are a prime target of poachers. All species of rhinoceros are in danger, and the Javan rhino population is the most precarious. Fewer than 100 of these animals are still living. At one time Javan rhinos could be found throughout southeastern Asia, but they are now believed to exist only in Indonesia and Vietnam.

Rachel Wheeler was the production editor for *JavaScript: The Definitive Guide, Fourth Edition*, and Leanne Soylemez and Jane Ellin were the copyeditors. Rachel Wheeler, Sheryl Avruch, and Matt Hutchinson were the proofreaders. Mary Brady, Claire Cloutier, Tatiana Apandi Diaz, and Ann Schirmer provided quality control. Maureen Dempsey, Derek Di Matteo, Darren Kelly, Edie Shapiro, and Sarah Sherman provided production assistance. Ellen Troutman-Zaig wrote the index.

Edie Freedman designed the cover of this book. The cover image is a 19th-century engraving from the Dover Pictorial Archive. Emma Colby produced the cover layout with QuarkXPress 4.1 using Adobe's ITC Garamond font.

David Futato designed the interior layout. Neil Walls converted the files from XML to FrameMaker 5.5.6. The text font is Linotype Birka; the heading font is Adobe Myriad Condensed; and the code font is LucasFont's TheSans Mono Condensed. The illustrations that appeared in earlier editions of this book were created in Macromedia Freehand 5.0 by Chris Reilley. For this fourth edition, Robert Romano created and updated figures using Macromedia Freehand 9 and Adobe Photoshop 6. This colophon was written by Clairemarie Fisher O'Leary.

Whenever possible, our books use a durable and flexible lay-flat binding. If the page count exceeds this binding's limit, perfect binding is used.